D1534847

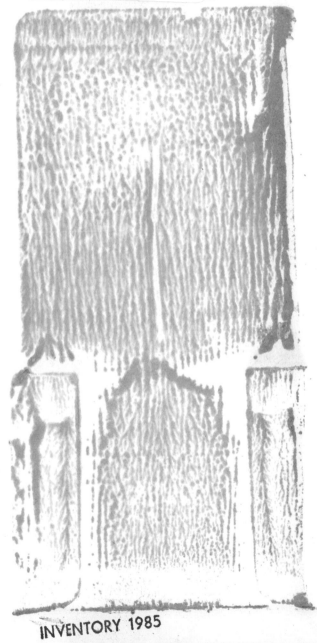

INVENTORY 1985

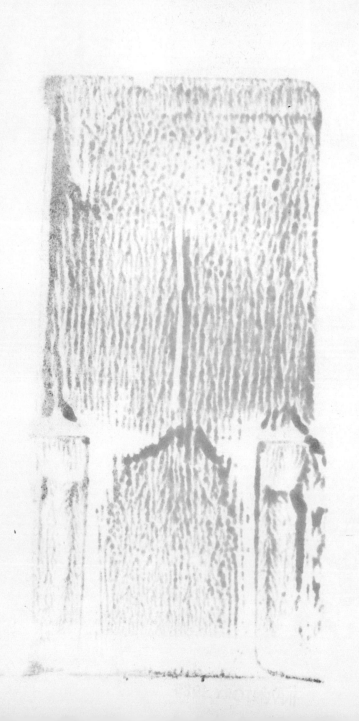

GLADSTONE AND THE IRISH NATION

WILLIAM EWART GLADSTONE

GLADSTONE
AND THE
IRISH NATION

by

J. L. HAMMOND

ARCHON BOOKS
1964

First published by
Longmans Green & Co. Ltd. in 1938

Second edition published in the
United States by Archon Books,
The Shoe String Press Inc.,
Hamden, Connecticut

First edition   1938
Second edition 1964

Printed in Great Britain

PREFACE

The great length of this book demands an apology and an explanation.

Mr. Gladstone's great Irish effort, which began in 1868 when he carried his first Resolutions on the Irish Church in the House of Commons and ended in 1893 when his second Home Rule Bill was destroyed by the House of Lords, was an uphill battle against two of the deepest instincts in British politics; one the belief that the English social system was suitable to Ireland; the other that Ireland could remain what she was when the Union had been made, a country governed by England through the agency of the Protestant ascendancy, without danger to the Empire or unhappiness to herself. Those were the fixed ideas of most politicians down to 1868. We may perhaps describe Mr. Gladstone's career by saying that he used the democratic forces created by the second and third Reform Bills to break down the prejudices that had governed England's treatment of Ireland during two-thirds of the nineteenth century.

To describe his difficulties, the nature and extent of his success, the sources of his belief and his strength, it was necessary then to give a survey of earlier social history, an account of his education, temperament and individual views, and an interpretation of the special character of his sympathy with democracy. These are all complicated topics and no writer could do them justice in a short or summary sketch.

The large politics of the subject therefore required a full book. But there were special reasons why detailed treatment of the kind that readers are apt to find irksome was essential.

Mr. Gladstone's difficulties as a pioneer in Irish reform were closely concerned with his personal relationships; with his management or mismanagement of his Cabinets. The prejudices he had to overcome were hard set in many Liberal minds. It was not enough to give a general view of those relationships, for the judgment formed by the reader of his wisdom will often depend on his treatment of particular issues in the day to day life of a Government. It was therefore necessary to discuss his relations with other politicians in detail and, as this detail concerned other reputations besides his own, it was the writer's duty to set out documents bearing on questions which though they may seem small to-day, had great influence on events.

When Lord Morley wrote his great biography, Hartington and Chamberlain, Gladstone's principal opponents in his last struggle, and Harcourt, his principal opponent in the early 'eighties, were all alive. To-day the reader can learn of their part in these controversies from Mr. Bernard Holland's *Life of the Duke of Devonshire*, Mr. Garvin's great work on Chamberlain, and Mr. Gardiner's masterly biography of Harcourt. Lord Morley's reminiscences have also been made available partly in his book of Recollections and partly in Mr. Hirst's interesting volumes on his early life and letters. Of the other biographies that have appeared since Lord Morley wrote, one stands out as specially important for the light it throws on the history of the Irish question. This is Sir Arthur Hardinge's *Life of Lord Carnarvon*, Viceroy in 1885. This book tells the story of the treatment of the Irish problem by Lord Salisbury's first Government from the inside. As the events made intelligible by this book had a decisive influence on the course of politics, every writer on Mr. Gladstone's career must draw largely on its revelations. Lord Carnarvon died in 1890, but the biography was not published till 1925.

In another respect conditions have changed. When Lord Morley wrote he had to treat as confidential the negotiations carried on between Gladstone and Parnell through the agency of Captain and Mrs. O'Shea. On these it is no longer necessary to keep silence for the silence was broken by Mrs. O'Shea who published her own account of these transactions. Those transactions are described in

these pages in great detail with abundant documents, for they
have clearly a great importance for the student of Gladstone's Irish policy. Of the documents that are now made
public, three things may perhaps be said here. They show
(1) that as early as the 'seventies Gladstone's chief colleagues
were aware that his mind was moving to Home Rule ;
(2) that the suspicion that his actions in the autumn and
winter of 1885 were ruled or influenced by the desire for
office was absolutely without basis ; and (3) that Parnell went
to surprising lengths in 1882 and 1883 in the hope of obtaining large Irish reform without violence. In this sense these
documents help the reader to do justice to Parnell as well as
to Gladstone.

It may be hoped perhaps that in this way the book may
serve a purpose of wider importance. A great deal must
turn for both peoples on the spirit in which the Irish and the
British look back on this long struggle. If Gladstone's
efforts were well understood, if it were known in Ireland
with what single-minded devotion he pursued the great
purpose of her freedom, if there were no shadow of suspicion
on his motives and methods, he would be remembered only
with gratitude. Mr. Tilney Bassett tells us in his book on
the Gladstone Papers that it was the custom till lately in
Italy to teach the children in the schools that Gladstone
was one of the benefactors of their nation. Yet what sacrifices of comfort, of popularity, of power did he make for
Italy in comparison with the sacrifices he made for Ireland?
The more his career is examined, the higher will his reputation stand, for the clearer will it be that his great struggle
for Ireland's freedom was unmixed with any personal
ambitions of his own.

Nor must it be forgotten that the policy that Gladstone
urged on the British people and brought within sight of
success ran counter to the fixed ideas of the statesmen of the
day of all countries. Few men dreaded centralization more
than de Tocqueville. Yet de Tocqueville said, "A people
which, in the presence of the great military monarchies of
Europe, would proceed to break up its sovereignty would
seem to me to forswear, by this single fact, its power and

perhaps its existence and its name." This was what, in the eyes of many of his contemporaries, Gladstone was asking the British Empire to do. It is argued in these pages that he was right in thinking that Irish Home Rule was a British interest as well as an Irish interest. But to do justice both to his own courage and to the perplexities of the British people it is necessary to keep in mind the strength of the great body of fear against which he brought the nobler spirit of his faith in moral forces, and the reconciling power of freedom. On the day of Judgment the British people may be glad to remember that in 1886 nearly half the nation and in 1892 more than half the nation was ready to follow this old man's summons to a splendid adventure.

The struggle described in these pages was distinguished from all other political conflicts by the atmosphere of passion that surrounded it. Any writer who discusses it in any aspect must try to reproduce that atmosphere without himself coming under its influence. That may be impossible for anybody whose sympathies are engaged. If any of Mr. Gladstone's opponents are treated unfairly in these pages, the offence is not wilful or deliberate. Nobody can follow the struggle, or the several incidents that embittered it, without realizing both how complex were the problems politicians had to face, and how deep and disturbing were the emotions they excited. It has been necessary, in order to do justice to Mr. Gladstone's achievement, and to the character of his task, to give prominence to the violence displayed on this question by statesmen whose reputation rests on other qualities displayed in their treatment of other questions. Lord Salisbury's caustic and wounding wit, so often noticed in these pages, gave a special complexion to his opposition to Home Rule. But nobody who works on Mr. Gladstone's papers can fail to see that Mr. Gladstone held him in high honour, and admired and trusted his wisdom and strength as Foreign Minister. To-day, as it happens, the most powerful champion of Mr. Gladstone's ideas of public law is the son of his great Conservative adversary.

I am indebted to His Majesty the King for gracious permission to publish a number of important Cabinet documents. Lord Gladstone of Hawarden allowed me to make the fullest use of the Gladstone Papers. Lady Gladstone, the widow of Viscount Gladstone, the Herbert Gladstone of these pages, was kind enough to put her husband's papers at my disposal and they were of great value. Such a book as this could not be written without the use of letters and papers from Mr. Gladstone's most important colleagues and friends, Cardinal Manning, Lord Granville, Lord Hartington, Lord Spencer, the Duke of Argyll, Lord Rosebery, Lord Selborne, Lord Morley, Mr. Forster, Mr. Bright, Mr. Chamberlain, Sir William Harcourt, Sir George Trevelyan, Lord Thring, Sir Robert Hamilton and others. I am most grateful to their representatives for leave to publish their letters.

I am under special obligations to Lord Crewe who has most kindly read a good part of my book and helped me generously with advice and criticisms. It was a piece of great good fortune that I was able to consult the wisdom and experience of a statesman who had been actively concerned in the government of Ireland and in two Home Rule Bills; as Viceroy in 1892 and as a leading member of Mr. Asquith's Cabinet in 1912. Neither he nor any other of the friends who have helped me has any responsibility for any statement or conclusion presented in these pages. I have benefited largely from conversations with others who had direct knowledge of the struggle of those years: with Lord Balfour, who as Mr. Gerald Balfour played so important a part in constructive politics in Ireland, Lord Howard of Penrith who was Private Secretary to his brother-in-law, Lord Carnarvon, when Viceroy in 1885, Mr. Henry Harrison, the last survivor of Parnell's supporters in the grim struggle of Committee Room Fifteen, Lady Bryce, and with two of Mr. Gladstone's private secretaries, the late Sir George Murray and Sir George Leveson Gower.

Of Mr. Tilney Bassett's assistance I can only say that without it the book could not have been written: my debt to his unique knowledge of the Gladstone Papers and his judgment in the use of them is beyond description. Miss

PREFACE

Edith Stopford did me the great service of mastering a great mass of correspondence on the Irish land question and she gave me most valuable guidance and advice on that difficult subject. My wife, besides helping me in other ways, did me a similar service in the investigation and the description of the incidents of the Kilmainham Treaty and Mr. Gladstone's relations with Parnell through Captain and Mrs. O'Shea. Miss Girdlestone gave me great help in the management and ordering of the great mass of documents that have passed through my hands. Many friends have given me advice and criticism ; I must mention in particular Mr. E. G. Collieu, Mr. David Davies, Dr. G. P. Gooch, Mr. H. M. F. Hammond, Mr. F. W. Hirst, Dr. H. D. Henderson, Mr. Desmond MacCarthy, Mr. R. J. G. Mayor, Mrs. Vaughan Nash, and Dr. Arnold Toynbee.

I am indebted to Messrs. George Allen and Unwin who have kindly allowed me to make use in this book of a chapter I contributed to the volume *Essays in honour of Gilbert Murray*, as well as to the editors of that volume; I have also to thank Lady Gwendolen Cecil, Lord Carnarvon, Sir Humphrey Milford, Messrs. Macmillan, Cassells, Constable, Hodder and Stoughton and John Murray for leave to make extracts from books that they published. A number of books have been published since Morley's Life appeared by relatives or friends of Mr. Gladstone which throw light on this subject. Chief among them, of course is, *After Thirty Years* published in 1928 by Viscount Gladstone; this book is the leading authority on several of the incidents of this struggle. In 1932 Sir Charles Mallett published a Memoir *Herbert Gladstone*. Other books throwing light on the Gladstone family and atmosphere are the Diaries of Lady Frederick Cavendish, Mrs. Gladstone's niece, and Mrs. Drew's book *Catherine Gladstone*. Lord Kilbracken's *Reminiscences*, and a memoir by Sir Edward Hamilton, gave the impressions of two of Mr. Gladstone's most trusted private secretaries.

Two important collections of *Gladstone Letters* have been published. Mr. Lathbury edited a number of Gladstone's *Letters on Religion* and Mr. Tilney Bassett a number of his letters to his wife. Mrs. Drew published a volume of *Letters*

PREFACE

written to her by Lord Acton and another volume of Acton's correspondence was edited by Messrs. Figgis and Laurence. Mr. Tilney Bassett has published a little book on the Gladstone papers and Mr. Ivor Thomas a memoir of Lord Gladstone of Hawarden.

Mr. Gladstone's career in particular aspects has recently been made the subject of important books by distinguished writers of special authority : Mr. Guedalla has described his relations with the Queen and with Palmerston; Mr. Hirst his brilliant achievements as financier; and Dr. Seton Watson his Eastern policy. Dr. Paul Knaplund has published two careful studies, one of Mr. Gladstone's Foreign Policy, the other of his Imperial Policy, and Mr. Francis Hyde of his work at the Board of Trade. Mr. Garratt and Dr. Eyck have given illuminating but more general surveys. Mr. Francis Birrell wrote a brilliant little biography and Mr. Somervell has published a study of Gladstone and Disraeli that gave pleasure to the admirers of both. Parnell has also been made the subject lately of important studies, by Mr. St. John Ervine, Miss Joan Haslip and Mr. Henry Harrison. Miss Haslip brings out the effect of his private anxieties on his health and strength and Mr. Harrison has revealed the secret history of his love affair. To all of these books I am indebted. Mr. Harrison's book is all important for the Divorce case; and it is the basis of my chapter on the subject. I have also profited by his reminiscences of the crisis.

Letters given or mentioned in these pages for which no authority is named are taken from the Gladstone Papers.

Hemel Hempsted.
July, 1938.

TO
L.B.H.

CONTENTS

CONTENTS

LIST OF ILLUSTRATIONS

NEW INTRODUCTION BY

M. R. D. FOOT
St Catherine's College, Oxford

NEW INTRODUCTION

In the graveyard of the remote village in County Mayo where Michael Davitt was born, a Celtic cross to his memory bears the words ' Blessed is he that hungers and thirsts after justice, for he shall receive it.' Davitt had scant justice from the British in his lifetime. The modern Irish republic, that stems in large part from his work, ignores him : the hall in the National Museum in Dublin devoted to the struggle for liberation from the British crown revealed, when recently visited, no relic, no photograph, no mention of his name. Officially, he has become an unperson. Yet he received justice, from the pen of another lover of justice, in the pages that follow, which show him as Parnell's equal—even in some respects his superior—during many critical years of the contest for Ireland's freedom.

Lawrence Hammond thought this kind of historical just dealing the main task of his life. He was a man it was a joy to know, a man of extraordinary charm ; someone said of him that, ' although constantly a leader in vehement political controversies, he never made a personal enemy or lost a friend.' [1] He was also a man of outstanding integrity. In a series of celebrated studies, he and his wife Barbara exposed the working conditions of town and country labourers in the early stages of industrial capitalism. Later research has indicated that these influential books painted too dark a picture of the whole mass of experience, of misery and happiness mixed, that in fact made up English working-class life between the middle of the eighteenth and the middle of the nineteenth century ; and a very recent publication attacks the Hammonds' methods of handling evidence.[2] But such afterthoughts do not make the injustices unearthed

[1] Quoted by Gilbert Murray, writing on him in the *Dictionary of National Biography, 1941–1950*, 352.
[2] E. P. Thompson *The Making of the English Working Class* (1963).

by the Hammonds any more just ; they only revise the perspective we view them in.

Gladstone's work and Ireland's problems long preoccupied Hammond. Born in 1872, he grew up among the great Home Rule controversies of the eighties and nineties ; as editor of the *Speaker*—an ancestor of the *New Statesman*—from 1899 to 1907 he lived in the world of current Liberal politics immediately after Gladstone's death. In 1920 the *Manchester Guardian*, for which he had reported the Paris peace conference, sent him to Ireland at the depth of the Troubles. His was one of the influential voices that at last persuaded the British to give the Irish back their independence, and he never forgot these Irish experiences. With his steady concern for justice, he determined one day to set straight the record of recent Irish history. The book that follows was his magnum opus, the crowning achievement of his life of authorship ; his longest book, the last one he finished, and in the view of those well qualified to judge by far his best ; yet also the least known.

It was unlucky in its moment of birth a quarter of a century ago. The original edition, published by Messrs Longmans, was with reviewers in September and appeared in October 1938 ; the Munich agreement was dated 29 September. Ironically, for the couple of years that stocks of it were available, of all his books it sold the worst : only a few hundred copies. Poor sales can partly be accounted for by the book's complication, great length, and consequent high price. Besides, few people wanted to read about Gladstone in those two years of turmoil and disruption, 1939 and 1940, that followed when politicians turned their backs on mutual trust, good faith, the concert of the powers, all the principles of Gladstonian foreign policy. Early in 1941 all the remaining publishers' stocks were destroyed by enemy action, and the plates the book had been printed from suffered the same fate in another fire on the same night.

Getting it back into print was difficult for several reasons. Trouble and expense were only two of them. The copyright was not Hammond's own. It belonged to the Gladstone trustees, who had covered some of Hammond's expenses in preparing the book, and had offered the publishers help with the high cost of getting it into print at all ; in return for the copyright, they had provided Hammond with a special facility of which more in a moment. Hammond, the soul of conscientiousness, no doubt felt under such obligations to them that he could not well press them to republish work for which he and not they would get credit ; and so things stood when Hammond died in 1949. His widow and others made various attempts to resuscitate the book, none of them successful till now. She died in 1962.

It would have been desirable from a scholar's point of view to correct the text, for it fell in places below both Longmans' and Hammond's standards of accuracy. Apart from misprints and slips, there are a number of points on which communications made to the author after the book appeared, or the results of later research by other historians, indicate changes are needed. Moreover detailed references could now be given for Hammond's hundreds of extracts from the Gladstone Papers, which were still unnumbered when he originally worked on them. In the end, accidentally, there has turned out to be no chance for this sort of revision in detail ; the book is here, warts and all, for a new generation to survey. Pedants will lament the uncorrected slips, the lack of British Museum Additional MSS numbers, and some missing amplifications. But the book's great merits far outweigh its defects.

For this remains the most formidable and incisive piece of original research yet published on the history of England or Ireland in the second half of the nineteenth century. Hammond's contemporary Wickham Steed once said, ' There are no facts in Ireland, only passions more or less historical.' Yet Hammond, with his wife's and Edith Stopford's help, established over the indefatigable years many facts of importance, facts in economic and in political history: ranging from the development of land legislation, through the significance of tribal feuds near the Connemara coast and the precise reasons for Lord Frederick Cavendish's fatal appointment to Dublin, to the channels Parnell used for setting his views before British ministers.

Yet a much broader claim than mere industry can be sustained for the author of this book. He would have been the last man to compare himself with Thomas Hobbes, the greatest English political theorist ; but something Trevor-Roper once wrote of *Leviathan* has some application to *Gladstone and the Irish Nation* : ' The function of genius is not to give new answers, but to pose new questions, which time and mediocrity can resolve.' [1] Genius, that overworked word, is hardly claimed for Hammond ; but he did perform in this book one of the hardest and the most rewarding of historians' tasks. He took a tale, once part of the current stock of political dispute, later erected into a commonplace of history books ; examined it ; proved it to be baseless ; and laid out his proof in clear, nervous, readable prose. The tale—still too widely credited, because of this book's limited circulation—was that Gladstone was only converted to Home Rule when the general election at the end of 1885 appeared to offer him a further chance of office if he took Home Rule up, and allied his party with the newly arrived Parnellites who had won over four-fifths of the Irish seats. Hammond was able to show, through his grasp of the Gladstone Papers, how far this legend diverged from the truth : both because Gladstone had long looked favourably on policies that would give the Irish a much larger say in running their own affairs, and because at the time his principal object—however maladroitly pursued—was to get his Conservative opponents to remain in power and put through Home Rule themselves.

To impose a convincing new interpretation on long familiar, hackneyed material was a valuable enough achievement, but Hammond did more. He did with Gladstone what Gladstone did with Homer [2] ; meditated long on his work, and secured new and original insights into what it

---

[1] *New Statesman and Nation*, 28 July 1945, 61.
[2] See page 54 below.

meant. Just as scholars can smile at some—not all [1]—of the details of Gladstone's Homeric studies, earnest young students of the nineteenth century can pick holes in the details of Hammond's work ; in both cases, knocking chips off the façade leaves the strength and proportion of the intellectual structure unaffected in its grandeur. The extraordinary stature of that quite extraordinary old man comes out in this book with a force that even Morley missed. Moreover Hammond applied to the events of Gladstone's story the fund of classical learning he had acquired himself at Oxford, and thus added a dimension to it that Gladstone would have appreciated. Hence the occasional reflexions on ancient history or society [2] ; hence also the even, rhythmical flow of the prose ; hence above all the philosophical tone. Though Hammond was an agnostic—what today would be called a humanist—and Gladstone was a high Anglican, Hammond held as strongly as Gladstone did that political leaders need to pursue moral policies. Gladstone's sense of moral mission in his political life was matched on Hammond's part by an equal earnestness, even more free of priggery. Hammond's intellect and insight enabled him to move with ease among the problems that responsible men have to face ; hence his grasp of what was really at issue between the English and the Irish nations, and the clarity of his picture of how moral problems are met or evaded in politics. Hence too the pathos as he unfolded the dark tale of misunderstanding, mistrust, cross purposes, and confusion that led Gladstone's essentially noble Irish policy to founder.

It has not lately been fashionable to lay much emphasis on individuals in recent British history. Writers have

[1] Gilbert Murray, in a letter to Hammond in 1938, warned him not to underestimate the surviving value of much of Gladstone's Homeric scholarship (J. L. Hammond papers, not yet numbered, Bodleian Library).

[2] ' When I went up to St John's ', he said once, ' I had been learning Greek for ten years ; when my wife went to Lady Margaret Hall she did not even know the Greek alphabet. They gave her a first in Mods and in Greats, and me a second in both.' The university made amends to him in 1933, when he and his wife were made honorary doctors of letters at the same ceremony.

preferred to attempt qualitative analysis, by looking into constitutional structure or class or religious interests; or quantitative analysis, by inspecting voting or party membership figures ; or local analysis, by considering the affairs of various provincial centres, such as Leeds and Birmingham whose rivalry twisted the course of Anglo-Irish history in December 1885. In the week of John F. Kennedy's assassination, it seems hardly necessary to point out that the fate of modern democracies can still to a noticeable extent be determined by individuals. In the days Hammond wrote about, individual statesmen may not have been as all-important as *Times* leaders, *Punch* cartoonists, and the man on the Clapham omnibus thought. But a political battle fought by Lord Salisbury and Lord Hartington, by Michael Davitt and Charles Stewart Parnell, by Joseph Chamberlain and by Gladstone was a battle of giants indeed ; and these Homeric figures have found a prose Homer in J. L. Hammond.

The book was not widely reviewed when it appeared, but the notices it did get—outside Ulster, where traditions of long standing inhibited sympathy for Gladstone—were markedly friendly. A few specific comments on details are annexed.[1] The only complaint made at all often was that Hammond had been rather too hard on Hartington. Violet Markham, for example, wrote to him to say that while she was no doubt prejudiced, as Paxton's grand-daughter, in favour of the Cavendishes, people in Derbyshire found them shy and neighbourly rather than haughty ; besides, ' a man who said the proudest day of his life was when his pig took first prize at Skipton Fair isn't somehow the figure as I found it in your book.' Arthur Ponsonby on the other hand was glad that this overrated character had been cut down to size ; adding, ' I have a curious letter from him asking my father to send *a loaded revolver* which he had left in his bedroom in Balmoral, just as you or I might write for a toothbrush we had left behind.' [2]

---

[1] Pages xxxiii–v.
[2] 18 January, 20 February 1939 ; J. L. Hammond Papers, Bodleian Library.

Lord Charnwood, more seriously, admired the book since it brought out Gladstone's character as ' one of the few *very* great men, because he taught his countrymen to think nobly, a lesson which they have never since entirely or for long forgotten,—and did more, for (not less than Lincoln, and far more than any other man except perhaps Mazzini) he impressed a stamp of nobility upon the idea of democracy itself.' [1] Hammond's principal achievement in these pages was indeed to set up for all to see Gladstone's character as a leader of men, and as an example to follow.

The book may have received a great indirect compliment in the major reversal of British imperial policy executed in 1947, when India and Pakistan were released from forced dependence on the British crown. Attlee the Prime Minister responsible for this change never heard the Gladstonian example cited, at the time, as the model for relations between the retiring mother country and these other nations emerging, or re-emerging, into independence. But, consciously or no, his great act of liberating statesmanship followed the Gladstonian model, as Hammond had set it out nine years before ; and Harold Laski at least, among the Labour Party's intellectuals, had studied Hammond's book with enthusiasm. Gladstone indeed had prescribed ' Govern them upon a principle of freedom ' as the way to deal with dependent territories overseas as far back as 1855, in a speech that presaged much later Commonwealth theory. [2]

What in *Gladstone and the Irish Nation* might be held to need revision in the light of new work ?

A few important additions have been made since 1938 to the primary sources available in print, including the diary of one of Gladstone's colleagues and his full correspondence with another. Kimberley's diary covers only five years in time and 44 pages in space, but its shrewd common-sensical comments—unknown to Hammond—are useful. [3]

[1] *Ibid.*, undated [1939].

[2] Paul Knaplund *Gladstone and Britain's Imperial Policy* (1927), 225.

[3] Ethel Drus ed Lord Kimberley *Journal of Events during the Gladstone Ministry 1868–1874*, Camden Miscellany xxi (Camden third series, xc, 1958).

Miss Ramm's publication in four volumes of practically the whole exchange of letters between Gladstone and Granville represents a more formidable undertaking.[1] Here, fully yet unobtrusively annotated, the correspondence between two intimate political friends can be read consecutively over many years, leaving the reader with a far sounder understanding of how the business of government was managed then than before he began. At dozens of points in Hammond's narrative, especially in the early eighties, his account of what was passing can be checked and amplified [2] by reference to these letters exchanged between the Liberal leaders of the two Houses of Parliament. All the ones Hammond quotes can be seen in extenso ; and the characters of the writers emerge clear-cut.

On the Unionist side, we now have a long retrospective account of the Home Rule disruption by Joseph Chamberlain, mainly dictated in 1891.[3] By that date he was too sharply separated from Gladstone to give the leader he had formerly revered any credit for large-mindedness or even for straight dealing ; present bitterness no doubt affected judgements on the recent past. What he says of his dealings with O'Shea in the eighties fully justifies Hammond's strictures on that inconstant intermediary ; about the ruinous divorce Chamberlain reveals nothing.

There are also some useful extracts from statutes, speeches, and correspondence printed in the second volume of Costin and Watson.[4]

Hammond's book has of course much influenced other historians, but his conclusions are not universally accepted. For instance, the latest treatment of the Act of Union of 1800

---

[1] Agatha Ramm ed *The Political Correspondence of Mr Gladstone and Lord Granville* ; 1868–1876, 2 v (Camden third series, lxxxi–ii, 1952), and 1876–1886, 2 v (1962).

[2] For a particularly striking amplification of one of Hammond's main points, the earliness of Gladstone's leanings towards Home Rule, see page xxxiii below, erratum to page 160.

[3] C. H. D. Howard ed Joseph Chamberlain *A Political Memoir 1880–1892* (1953).

[4] W. C. Costin and J. Steven Watson *The Law and Working of the Constitution*, 2 v (1952).

is less stern to Pitt than Hammond shows himself below.[1]
Hammond, who was a reasonable man as well as an
ardent Foxite, would have been ready to admit the
cogency of Steven Watson's argument. In the same authoritative series, the Oxford History of England, Woodward's
Irish chapter bears evident marks of Hammond's thought.[2]
And Ensor's volume, *England 1870–1914*, was seen in draft
by Hammond, who was deep in the present book while
Ensor was writing ; Ensor gladly accepted substantial
amendments from him, particularly to his version of the
Home Rule crisis of 1886.[3]

Four biographies are of some value as aids to a reassess-
ment of Gladstone and Ireland. The slightest of them,
begun by Hammond himself about a year before he died,
was a short sketch of Gladstone, handed over half-completed
to the present writer and finished in close accordance with
Hammond's opinions.[4] Mrs Battiscombe's *Mrs Gladstone :
The Portrait of a Marriage* (1956) is of double interest for the
Irish story. It shows, with clarity and affection, the sort of
woman Gladstone chose as his companion for sixty years ;
and it explains how his womenfolk, headed by his wife and
her niece Lady Frederick Cavendish, combined together to
keep him chained to the oar of Irish reform long after he
desired to rest. Sir Philip Magnus's *Gladstone* (1954) is the
latest full length biography of him. It has the great advantage over previous lives that its author had the run of all
the family correspondence at Hawarden. Many hitherto
unknown incidents, ranging from the picturesque to the
absurd, decorate the book as a result. Otherwise, it relies
on previous books, not least on Hammond's, and on its
author's own reflexions, which are not wholly sympathetic
in tone. By contrast, R. R. James's *Rosebery* (1963) is
written with full respect for its subject. James's passages on
Ireland are comparatively few, and Rosebery emerges as

---

[1] J. Steven Watson *Reign of George III* (1960), 387–405.
[2] Sir E. L. Woodward *The Age of Reform*, 2 ed (1962), 328–64.
[3] R. C. K. Ensor—J. L. Hammond correspondence 1935, Hammond
papers, Bodleian.
[4] *Gladstone and Liberalism* (1952, 2 ed 1964).

even less of a Home Ruler than in Hammond's treatment of him ; but the book deserves mention for its portrait of Gladstone as a failing titan, seen through the eyes of a close though critical friend.

On English politics in general, H. J. Hanham's *Elections and party management : Politics in the time of Disraeli and Gladstone* (1959), an analysis of party and electoral machinery between the Reform Acts of 1867 and 1884, goes into much valuable background detail of a kind Hammond had no opportunity to examine. Henry Pelling's study of *The Origins of the Labour Party* (1954) has some useful observations on the impact of the Irish example on English and Scottish labour ; a subject covered from the other side of the Irish Sea by T. W. Moody in an article on ' Michael Davitt and the British Labour Movement 1882–1906 '.[1] C. H. D. Howard extends knowledge of the 1885 election by a study of the press.[2]

There are several articles in *Irish Historical Studies* which supplement Hammond or fill out lacunae in his book ; among them David Thornley on ' The Irish home rule party and parliamentary obstruction, 1874–87 ' (xii. 38, 1960) ; C. H. D. Howard on the ' Central Board ' scheme of 1884–5 (viii. 324, 1953) ; and Henry Harrison, ' Parnell's Vindication ' (v. 231, 1947), on the co-operation between Chamberlain, O'Shea, and Buckle the editor of *The Times* while the Special Commission was sitting. Under Harrison's inspiration, *The Times* withdrew in the fourth volume of its autobiography various anti-Parnellite and anti-Gladstonian allegations made—probably by Buckle—in the third.[3]

Irish parliamentary politics have also been the subject of three books of importance, two of them by F. S. L. Lyons— *The Irish Parliamentary Party 1890–1910* (1951), a study of what happened after Parnell had been removed from the leadership, and *The Fall of Parnell* (1960), dealing with the

[1] *Transactions of the Royal Historical Society*, 5 series, iii. 53 (1953).
[2] ' The Parnell Manifesto and the Schools Question ', *English Historical Review* lxii. 42 (1947).
[3] *History of ' The Times '* iv. 1145–8 (1952), retracting much of *ibid.* iii. 43–89 (1947).

last year of his life. The other, Conor Cruise O'Brien's *Parnell and his Party 1880–90* (1957), is the only book published since 1938 that matches Hammond's own for range, depth, and scholarly intensity in its dealings with Hammond's subject, which it views from the Irish side with admirable force ; its conclusions parallel Hammond's rather than contest them.

Something also needs to be said about Hammond's sources. The last sentence of his preface reads : ' Letters given or mentioned in these pages for which no authority is named are taken from the Gladstone Papers.' Nothing further could be said in 1938, for Tilney Bassett was still then engaged in the enormous task of assembling the quarter of a million or so documents the Prime Minister had left behind him into the 750 volumes of British Museum Additional MSS they fill today. Hammond worked at his elbow, and they went through many of the Irish papers together ; but more years passed before Bassett's work was done and the Museum authorities' official MS numbers were allotted. This collection of papers now has the unique distinction of a volume to itself in the Museum's printed catalogue.[1] In this indispensable scholar's tool each MS volume is listed and described ; 350 pages of index follow. (This index carefully lists from and to whom letters and memoranda went, but does not try to index what they contained.)

The collection's content may be worth outlining. Over 500 volumes of it consist of letters ; most of them to Gladstone, though twenty-five large ledgers (Add MSS 44527–51) contain his secretaries' copies of over 20,000 of the letters he wrote while in office. Among the rest, there are nearly eighty volumes of official papers, and thirteen more of the notes he made during cabinet meetings. Most of these last highly important documents are currently being prepared for the press ; but till quite recently access to them was restricted. Hammond saw them ; but with that fierce anxiety not to be under any sort of obligation to government,

---

[1] *British Museum Catalogue of Additions to the Manuscripts. The Gladstone Papers, Additional MSS 44086–44835* (1953).

which led him twice to refuse a knighthood,[1] he did not
embark on the cumbrous business of getting the Cabinet
secretariat's leave to publish extracts from them.

The Museum's collection of Gladstone Papers, vast and
still partly unexplored as it is, deals only with politics and
literature. One part of Gladstone's political papers, his
correspondence with the Queen, lies outside it ; though in
the Museum on permanent loan, and visible with the
Gladstone family's consent. Hammond used this correspondence little, as Guedalla's *The Queen and Mr Gladstone* and the
Ponsonby papers covered his needs. Nor did he explore
Herbert or Mary Gladstone's papers, of which the Museum
now holds some 200 volumes ; nor E. W. Hamilton's chatty
and revealing diary, soon to be published. The large body
of Gladstone family papers still at Hawarden, now amply
covered by Magnus, Hammond also left alone ; for he had
a still more revealing source to draw upon, the special
facility the Gladstone trustees extended to him alone.

The innermost written records of Gladstone's life are in
his diary, which remains inaccessible, though it is being
prepared for publication in full. Thirty years after his death,
his family deposited it at Lambeth ; believing that quota-
tions from it out of context might lead to regrettable mis-
conceptions, and that in the custody of the Archbishops of
Canterbury it would be safe. By then Herbert Gladstone had
dictated a bowdlerised version of it, that is, one that omitted
two of the points of principal interest in it : Gladstone's reflexions on his own sinfulness, and everything that bore—as a
great deal did—on his lifelong struggle to get prostitutes to give
up their trade. Hammond was allowed to read this trun-
cated though absorbing document, on the condition which
he strictly kept that he did not quote it among his sources
nor tell his friends he had seen it. Henry Gladstone (Lord
Gladstone of Hawarden), the Prime Minister's last surviving
son, who took a keen interest in the preparation of this book
but did not live to read it, no doubt imposed this condition
to protect the Trustees against other requests for a sight

[1] Private information

of the same document ; the secret was for many years
well kept. From Hammond's reading of the abbreviated
diary much of the richness of this book derives, for it enabled
him to get behind the political front presented in the contemporary biographies of Gladstone and to understand more
about the forces that moved him.

A note of the principal errata is annexed.

M. R. D. F.

St Catherine's College, Oxford
28 November 1963

ANNEX : ERRATA

Page	line	change	
4	11	*for*	1828 *read* 1829
5	20 & n		Powicke pointed out [1] that Hammond had been led into error here by Toynbee ; English cultural influence in the eighth century was stronger than Irish.
12	24	*for*	1828 *read* 1829
52 69 159	15–16 31 36 6		In fact Gladstone visited Ireland twice ; but the second journey amounted to no more than stepping ashore for a few hours from a passing steamer in the summer recess of 1880. The passages referred to are all therefore slightly inaccurate.
63	1	*for*	1850 *read* 1851
	3	*for*	same *read* previous
	13	*for*	1856 *read* 1857
64	6	*for*	1877 *read* 1876
89	5	*for*	nearly *read* over
	6–7	*for*	February 1867 *read* June 1866
160	12		This could not have been written had Hammond seen Gladstone to Granville, 20 November 1877 (Ramm i. 57–9), which included the following passage : ' Had the Home Rulers a real leader whom they were disposed to follow I cannot think it would be difficult to arrange a *modus vivendi* with them. As to any thing more than that I am not

[1] F. M. Powicke to J. L. Hammond, 18 April 1943, Hammond Papers, Bodleian.

Page line   change

160   12   sanguine, even if I suppose my own opinions about Local Government to be those of the party, which they are not, for I go much farther than the ' average ' Liberal. On this subject however my lips have been closed except as to a general declaration '.

180   29   *for*   1876 *read* 1875

231   10   *for*   11,000 *read* 11,000,000

281   15   *for*   Richard Grosvenor *read* Granville

297   4   *for*   June 1 *read* June 2

397   3   from end *for* father *read* brother

436   24   Whenever Alfred (Viscount) Milner's diary is published, a good deal more will be known about the origins both of the Home Rule and of the Liberal Unionist parliamentary organizations ; Milner at the time was Goschen's private secretary, an unsuccessful Liberal candidate at the election, and the principal organizer behind the scenes of the Liberal Unionist lobby.

497   21   *for*   his first *read* Gladstone's second

498   12   Hubert Henderson protested [1] at a merely municipal view of Chamberlain in the mid-eighties ; his approach to political questions already in Henderson's view bore strong marks of his later imperialism.

522   last of footnote *for* 32 *read* 22

524   2   Sir George Leveson-Gower suggested [2] Jowett's name should be omitted : ' He supported Dizzy's Eastern policy in the seventies. His only Liberalism was ecclesiastical and theological.'

613   last but one   *add after* ' Bill ' '—or against it '.

[1] Henderson to Hammond 13 April 1939, Hammond Papers, Bodleian.

[2] Leveson-Gower to Hammond, 27 December 1938, *ibid.*

Page   line   change

649   1–2   Henderson contested [1] the view that the
                  divorce case was fatal to Home Rule, which
                  had lost its last chance five years earlier when
                  Salisbury refused to take it up. Hammond
                  can hardly have failed to consider Hender-
                  son's view, and reject it, when planning his
                  book ; but the second opinion is worth record.

670   11   Leveson-Gower noted [2] that Granville, his
                  uncle, was by this time very deaf, and ' would
                  therefore have been most unlikely to hear a
                  remark in the Cabinet, unless loudly and
                  pointedly directed to himself. Further I am
                  sure that, had he heard, he would have
                  certainly mentioned it to me, and I should
                  have as certainly remembered his doing so.'

695   4   *for*   eighty-five *read* eighty-four
      5   *for*   eighty-nine *read* eighty-eight

711   30   *for*   second Government *read* first Government

[1] Henderson to Hammond 13 April 1939, Hammond Papers,
Bodleian.
[2] Leveson-Gower to Hammond, 27 December 1938, *ibid.*

CHAPTER I

PITT'S LEGACY

Gladstone, brooding over the tragedy of Khartoum, reflected that the greatest mistakes in politics were often the most excusable. He instanced, besides his Government's fatal choice of Gordon for the Sudan, Pitt's quarrel with revolutionary France. The destruction of the Irish Parliament in 1800 falls for many minds into the same category. England had passed through a terrible danger. The Irish rebellion of 1798 had followed on the French attempt to invade Ireland in 1796, an attempt that had been defeated by the storms of the sea. Fortune might not always be so benevolent and England, it might be argued, might find herself one day attacked by a French Army, using as its base an Ireland more hostile to England than to England's enemies. Was not the Union the surest way of averting this danger?

Lecky, after the most dispassionate discussion, concluded that Pitt was wrong, that England had for the time complete security in the temper of the Irish Parliament, and that both countries stood to gain by delay.[1] But Pitt was the prisoner of his fears. What if the Irish Parliament, obeying the advice of Liberals like Fox in England and Grattan in Ireland, should admit Catholics? Pitt was afraid both of the Presbyterian Radicals of the North and the Catholic peasants. So long as those discontented elements were divided by religion, England was secure. But concessions might remove that quarrel and lead to a combination against English power. In fear of such combination he had used to the full the power of intrigue and management that had been left to English Ministers by the settlement of 1782, giving the Irish Parliament legislative independence. The

[1] *Ireland in the eighteenth century*, v. 418.

extinction of the Irish Parliament seemed to him to offer an escape from an anxiety that had long haunted his mind, and made him hostile to liberal plans to which, under other conditions, he would have given sympathy and help.

When England made her Union with Scotland in 1707 the bulk of the people of Scotland were Presbyterians, and the Act of Union recognized the religion of the people of Scotland as Scotland's religion. When England made her Union with Ireland in 1800, the bulk of the people of Ireland were Catholics and the Act of Union recognized as Ireland's religion not the religion of the people of Ireland but the religion of her conquerors. Pitt still held, as he had held in 1784, that the " Protestant ascendancy was the bond between England and Ireland," and one of the main objects of the Union was to preserve the Church Establishment.[1] Parnell once said that law is to the English what religion is to the Irish. Pitt believed that this perverse arrangement, under which the religion that had the fewest adherents in Ireland was to be for ever her State religion, was the keystone of the Union.[2] It is not surprising that a man who so under-estimated the vitality of religion and so over-estimated the power of law left his successors a task beyond their strength. Such a calculation makes Agricola's belief, seventeen centuries earlier, that he could conquer and hold Ireland with a single legion and a few irregulars,[3] look sober and cautious.

This case for the Union might seem more English than Irish, but Pitt told the House of Commons that its benefits would be more Irish than English.[4] His speeches on the Union are the best proof of his sincerity, for they reveal as nothing else could, the artificial light by which he judged the vast problem that he was putting into the hands of his successors.

Mill attributed the English reputation for hypocrisy to the confidence that the English people have in their own

[1] Rosebery, *Pitt*, 200.
[2] In 1774 North's Government with great courage legalized the Catholic religion, in what had formerly been French Canada by the Quebec Act.
[3] Tacitus, *Agricola* XXIV.
[4] House of Commons, April 21, 1800.

institutions and their own ideas. Of this habit of mind
there is no better example than Pitt. He believed that the
English had discovered the secret of order and good government, which was to combine in one society the enterprise
and wealth of a capitalist class with the experience and spirit
of an aristocracy. The Irish possessed an aristocracy, and
the Church which was now anchored on the Act of Union
was a symbol and organ of its power. But they were sadly
deficient in enterprise and wealth. The Union would bring
capital to Ireland, and the English statesman who brought
her this gift would be like Prometheus bringing fire from
heaven to aid man in his first struggles with nature. He
had sought to bestow this boon on the Irish people by a
commercial treaty in 1785, but that effort had been defeated
by faction in England fomenting distrust in Ireland. The
Union would remove such obstacles and give Ireland prosperity as well as order.

Lord Acton said of Pitt that though the strongest of
Ministers, he was among the weakest of legislators. His
strength and his weakness alike came from his implicit
confidence in the methods he employed, and the ideas by
which he was guided. His cold arrogance gave him the
mastery over the mind of his age and the will of the House
of Commons, making him a strong and efficient Minister
able to disentangle the dangerous disorder left by the
American War and the careless and corrupt administration
of Lord North. But in legislation he was misled by this very
quality. An all-important truth, so well understood by
Fox who declared " that we ought not to presume to
legislate for a nation with whose feelings and affections, wants
and interests, opinions and prejudices we have no sympathy," was beyond his grasp. English ideas were better
than Irish, and therefore Englishmen would make better
laws for Ireland than any the Irish could make for themselves. A man who legislates in this spirit may easily do
what Pitt did, and answer what looked like a simple question
in such a way as to compel his successors to answer not one
question but a hundred. England was to spend a century
trying to find the answers.

Pitt's conduct after he carried the Union illustrates the easy confidence with which he had acted. He admitted that there were two grievances that demanded a remedy, the grievances of the Catholics who were ineligible for Parliament, and the grievances of the poorest peasants who paid tithes to an alien Church. When the Union was discussed in Ireland, the Catholics were led to expect that it would be followed by reforms removing these hardships. Pitt, after making one effort to overcome the King's hostility to the first reform, abandoned both the first and the second.[1] The first reform was carried in 1828 by Wellington, who disapproved of it, but held that the agitation it had excited in Ireland would lead to a serious civil war if the concession were withheld any longer. The second was carried in 1838, after the passing of ten Coercion Acts and the frequent use of military force to suppress disturbances when tithe was collected. Ireland was thus taught at the outset of her career under the Union by Pitt himself that she could only gain justice by violence. That is a dangerous lesson to teach any people, and Irish history has shown how consistently a nation will act on it when once that lesson has been mastered.[2]

Nobody, unless it was Fox, could rival Pitt in the art of clothing his policy in Virgilian hexameters. The lines he used when commending the Union to the House of Commons served his purpose well.

Non ego nec Teucris Italos parere jubebo
Nec mihi regna peto; paribus se legibus ambae
Invictae gentes aeterna in foedera mittant.

To those who follow the history of the next hundred years

[1] Canning advised Pitt to drop the Union rather than carry it without this concession.

[2] A great admirer and himself the author of an important Irish Act has written of Pitt's conduct about Irish tithe: " It was a grievance that came home to mind and pocket. It was a hardship of long standing, known to all, denied by none. Grattan had framed a scheme for relief; the Duke of Rutland had years before appealed to Pitt to take it up; Lord Loughborough had drafted a Bill. Pitt could have readily passed a measure settling the question without difficulty or opposition. He never once tried or lifted a finger to remedy this great and admitted grievance and it is impossible to suggest a real justification for the neglect." Ashbourne, *Pitt: Some Chapters of his Life and Times*, p. 305.

these lines have a mocking ring. But Pitt knew what he meant by them. He believed that equal laws meant giving to Ireland England's land system, England's experience and initiative as a capitalist society, and, so far as this could be done, England's reasonable and discreet religion. All the problems that had taxed political philosophers of other ages were to be resolved by the wealth of the Barings and the wisdom of the Cavendishes. Make Ireland like England and all this would follow.

It is not surprising that in the strain which this task threw on the Empire Ireland spread as much confusion in the politics of England as England spread in the life of Ireland. For Ireland was not a blank surface on which England could put what pattern she liked. She had a proud history in art, letters, religion and the gentle education of mankind. When Charles Martel was saving Western Europe from the Arab at the Battle of Tours, the light that Europe was receiving from the British Isles shone not from England but from Ireland.[1] And if in the eighth century Irish civilization was a greater power in the world than English, in the eighteenth the ghost of that civilization was a greater power in Ireland than the institutions imposed by English conquest. The task Pitt gave to England was that of maintaining an alien Church, an alien land system and an alien view of property and justice, against native custom, and popular will, and against a tradition that had been strong enough to absorb generation after generation of immigrant blood.

Thus the two countries were involved in a bitter and perpetual struggle. On one side Coercion Acts were so frequent that it was suggested from time to time that it would be simpler to pass a permanent Act and keep it ready for use, much as the Spartans saved themselves trouble by

[1] " The period of Irish cultural superiority over the Continent and over Britain may be conventially dated from the foundation of the monastic university of Clonmacnois in Ireland in A.D. 548 to the foundation of the Irish monastery of St. James at Ratisbon, circa A.D. 1090. Throughout those five and a half centuries, it was the Irish who imparted culture and the English and Continentals who received it." Toynbee, *Study of History*, II. 329. In later centuries Irish soldiers were about as well-known in all the countries of Europe as the missionaries of earlier ages.

declaring war formally on the Helots every year.[1] Evictions were so ruthless that great parts of Ireland looked in normal times like a society ravaged by storm and revolution. On the other side Government after Government fell in England on Irish issues: Minister after Minister was diverted from the plan of his career: parties were broken up and their programmes thrown into confusion: Parliament was compelled to spend months finding means to defeat an unprecedented skill in the use of its forms for the obstruction of its business : of the passions that swept politics in the 'eighties, Salisbury told the Queen that they had torn England in two and that she scarcely counted in the diplomatic balance of Europe. Even a greater shock was to be given to the power and traditions of Parliament before the two countries parted, for the Parliament of the nation which had invented and perfected its system found its authority challenged, on the eve of a European War by a rival government with an army of its own. Pitt hoped that England would give to the Irish people in the place of its tribal quarrels her own Olympian serenity. The tables had been turned. Ireland brought into English politics passions more disturbing to the English peace than the turbulence of her new cities, of which Pitt spoke in such dread when he passed his Treason and Sedition Bill, and built new barracks to keep soldiers and citizens apart.

The Irish regarded themselves in all this tragical history as the victims of the rapacity of England. That legend has pursued the reputation of the English people to all the distant places where Irishmen have been scattered by famine, misery, and wrong. But this view of the relations of the two countries is incomplete and misleading. There were times when England acted from passion and struck brutal blows in temper. But England did not lay waste the homes of Irish peasants, as Verres plundered Sicily or Brutus Cyprus, in the cruelty of avarice. Her cruelty was the steady and unconscious cruelty of egotism and arrogance. She gave Ireland, as she believed, the best she had to give. The

---

[1] Herbert Paul, writing at the beginning of this century, counted eighty-seven Acts. *Modern History of England*, Vol. I, p. 131.

calamity was that there was no nation in Europe whose best, as it happened, was so bad for the Irish peasant. When Pitt observed that if Ireland did not accept the Union she might fall into the Jacobin fire, he thought there was no more to be said. Sixty years later the most acute English student of this problem remarked that the true remedy for the agrarian problem that had baffled every British statesman was to give the Irish peasant what Hoche would have given him in 1798. The French Revolution looked to Pitt like confusion and plunder: the British Constitution like order and justice. After a century of violent experiments with British ideas, peasant Ireland has found peace in the system France established on her own soil and would have established in Ireland if the winds had blessed her plans. By that time the struggle for the land had grown into a wider struggle, and the fate of the Act of Union itself had become involved in the fate of that alien social system, to which Pitt had looked with such confidence for the rescue of the Irish people from its difficulties.

In this sad and angry history Gladstone's career is a more interesting study and a more important force than that of any man of his age. The last care of his life, Ireland was almost the first, for one of his earliest letters as an Eton schoolboy was a defence of Catholic emancipation. His Irish record in its mistakes and its wisdom, its illusions and its insight, reflects better than anything else the chief qualities of a temperament, conservative and fearless, conventional and independent. It was by gradual stages that the truth which guided his later policy stole upon a mind taught by Peel, and through Peel, by Pitt. But when his slow and obstinate judgment had been convinced, he shrank from no duty and from no sacrifice demanded by his new and disturbing knowledge. For no man in Europe was moved and guided by so stern a passion for redressing the wrongs that his country had inflicted and regaining her good name in the world's esteem.

CHAPTER II

" It is always a most difficult task which a people assumes when it attempts to govern, either in the way of incorporation or as a dependency, another people very unlike itself. But whoever reflects on the constitution of society in these two countries, with any sufficient knowledge of the states of society which exist elsewhere, will be driven, however unwillingly, to the conclusion that there is probably no other nation of the civilized world, which, if the task of governing Ireland had happened to devolve on it, would not have shown itself more capable of that work than England has hitherto done. The reasons are these: First there is no other nation which is so conceited of its own institutions, and of all its modes of public action, as England is ; secondly there is no other civilized nation which is so far apart from Ireland in the character of its history, or so unlike it in the whole constitution of its social economy; and none therefore, which, if it applies to Ireland the modes of thinking and maxims of government which have grown up within itself, is so certain to go wrong."

J. S. MILL, England and Ireland, 1868.

To understand the history of Ireland in the half century that followed the Union it is a help to glance at the history of England. For the Union brought the Irish people under the class that governed the English; if the rule of that class was harsh and short-sighted in Ireland, it was harsh and short-sighted in England; if the Irish people had reasons for discontent, so had the English; if Ireland had her Whiteboys and her Rockites, the English had their Luddites and Captain Swing; the Governments that threw Coercion Act after Coercion Act to Ireland and sent troops to crush the peasants, passed the Combination Laws, praised the violence of Peterloo, and gave England the Six Acts as a remedy for unemployment and distress. The Reform Bill did not put an end to the disturbances that marked the painful rise of the new industrial order. It was followed by the Owenite Trade Unions, the Tolpuddle sentences, the Chartist movement, the march on Newport, and the Special Commissions. Between 1800 and 1848 disorder and strife are almost as much a part of English as of Irish history.

After 1850 Irish and English history diverge. Disorder disappears in England and grows in Ireland. Why does one melt away while the other gathers force and volume? When this question is answered, the complicated Irish question becomes simpler and less difficult to understand.

In the view of the English governing class, as in that of Pitt, the safeguards of civilization were to be found in the effective defence of two sets of rights: the rights of property and the rights of capital. A people that gave unqualified respect to these claims need trouble little about arranging its social life. The attempt to base the government of a society in revolution on this narrow principle produced the cruelties and hardships that made the 'thirties and 'forties so terrible a chapter in English history. The long hours of the factory, the savage farce of life in mine and furnace, the untempered misery of women and children, the bleak and desolate towns of this age without parks or libraries or theatres, the degrading atmosphere of a society in which human life seemed to have lost all sense of noble purpose, these were the effects of this unimaginative view of politics, and the cause of the discontent that filled the murmuring cities of the Industrial Revolution. Such is the history of half a century in England, and during that half century English history resembles Irish.

By 1850 England was beginning to climb out of this pit. The worst features of the new industrial life had been softened; the Ten Hours Act had given the workman for the first time a share in leisure and the amenities of civilization; Public Health Acts had made some way against apathy and selfishness; the towns were laying out parks and building libraries; schools were spreading. All this improvement was aided and hastened by the increase in trade and prosperity that followed the Repeal of the Corn Laws and the Railways. In 1867 the workman was enfranchised, and his

influence was seen at once in legislation giving more freedom
to the trade unions, making education universal, increasing
the amenities of town life, and checking further the arbitrary
power of the employer.   Gradually and slowly the nation
was learning to use its new resources of wealth and knowledge, not, as it used them at first, merely for the enrichment
of a class but for the civilization of a society.

Before leaving England for Ireland one more detail must
be noted. This is a mobile world. The village labourer
who cannot bear his tyranny any longer can escape to the
canals, the railways, or the industries of the town. And the
man of enterprise and courage, quicker or steadier than his
fellows or better able to distinguish between means and ends
in life, has before him the hope of a career and perhaps a
fortune.

The struggles of half a century against the absolute claims
of property and capital had thus gained for the rights of
man and the rights of society their first recognition in
English politics. The central figure in this English struggle
is the workman. When we turn to the corresponding
struggle in Ireland, the central figure is not the workman
but the peasant. The use to which England had put her
power over Ireland in the early days of industrial development had destroyed Irish industry, and made Ireland,
outside Ulster, a country of agriculture. Hence the struggle
for the rights of self-respect, for some footing in the State,
for some regard for human dignity in social life, which
makes up the history of both countries in the first half of the
nineteenth century, is in England a workman's, in Ireland
a peasant's, struggle.

The land system, beneath whose crushing weight the
peasant carried on this struggle, was the result of a series of
confiscations by which the land had passed into the ownership of immigrant conquerors and settlers.   Until late in the
eighteenth century the attempt to keep power and property
in Protestant hands was carried to such lengths that Catholics
were forbidden to purchase land or take it on lease for more
than thirty years. The landlords, unlike the landlords in
England, left their land alone, making no improvements and

investing no capital. At the time of the Union a third of them were absentees who let out their land to middlemen who sublet to peasants.

The competition for farms was so keen that the landlord or middleman could get what rent he liked. Thus on every estate there was a mass of small farmers. At the bottom of the scale were the cottiers, labourers who cultivated a small plot of land, paying their rent in labour. In a country where the alternative to work on the land was destitution, a man in this position could be forced to accept whatever conditions the middleman imposed. During the French war, when corn growing prospered in Ireland as in England, immense profit could be made out of the necessities of this class and their passion for the land. For the cottier growing his crop of potatoes cleaned the ground for the landlord's crop of corn. Consequently the war led to a great increase in the number of the cottiers and the subdivision of farms and tenancies. The war thus increased tenancies of all classes, and sometimes there would be four or five sets of middlemen between the man who owned the soil and the man who tilled it. The Act of Union was followed by a new increase in the number of life tenancies, because a life tenant was treated as a 40s. freeholder and had the parliamentary vote. The landlord liked to have these freeholders on his estate, for he assumed that they would always vote at his bidding and swell his importance.

It would be difficult to imagine any society making any tolerable kind of life out of conditions so adverse to energy, integrity, or social peace. The tenant, whether a considerable tenant, or a small tenant, or even a cottier, has to put up the buildings on his holding and make all the improvements. The competition for farms is so eager that a landlord can rack-rent as much as he likes. The man who puts up the buildings has no security against eviction, and if he is evicted he loses every penny he has spent on his farm and all the fruits of his labour in improving it. The small tenants, having no alternative livelihood, subdivide and subdivide until estates are covered with masses of destitute families. In Ireland as in England population is growing fast; between

1800 and 1841 it rose from 5,000,000 to 8,175,000. Thus a country where everything depends on making agriculture an efficient industry has a land system under which the men working on the soil have no incentive to energy or providence. Of the mass of poor cottiers Sir Walter Scott wrote that their cottages would scarce serve for pigsties in Scotland. " Almost alone among mankind," wrote Mill, " the Irish cottier is in this condition that he can scarcely be better off or worse off by any act of his own."

So long as the war lasted with its large profits, even so perverse a system as this could maintain itself. The adversity that followed peace with the fall of prices brought a crisis. Many of the middlemen disappeared, and the landlords found their estates on their hands. Like the English landlords they had lived luxuriously in the day of prosperity, and they felt acutely the loss of income. They held that the right method to retrieve their fortunes was to convert arable to pasture, and to consolidate their estates by getting rid of their small tenants. They turned the great mass of their tenants into tenants at will or yearly tenants. They got rid also of their forty-shilling freeholders. These tenants had revolted during the O'Connell agitation and voted against their landlords. They were disfranchised when Catholic Emancipation was conceded in 1828, and the landlords had no longer any reason for keeping them on their estates. In two years from the passing of the Act they shrank from 191,000 to 14,200.[1]

To a few far-sighted observers it was clear that the way to give vigour to agriculture and stability to Irish society was, not to throw the reins to the landlord, but to give to the people working on the soil the means and the motive to work hard and well. Ireland was a country in which agriculture was carried on by peasants who, by competing against each other for the only source of livelihood, enabled the landlord or his middleman to ask what rent he liked. In England the landlord found capital for agriculture. In a country where the landlord was a mere rent-receiver, the landlord's function, as it is understood in England, had to be

---

[1] J. E. Pomfret, *The Struggle for Land in Ireland*, p. 15.

discharged by the peasant, or by the State, or by the two in co-operation. This truth was urged on the Government by foreign observers like the Frenchman Gustave de Beaumont, by an English radical Poulett Scrope, by the most distinguished thinker on politics, John Stuart Mill, by the Irish Poor Law Commission of which the chairman was Archbishop Whateley, and in a modified form by the Devon Commission appointed by Peel in 1845.

Unhappily the English Government took a very different view of the problem. When the landlords began getting rid of their peasants they found these Governments more landlord than the landlords. For it was the fashionable view of the time that the peasant was an obsolete figure and an economic embarrassment. It was his destiny, as his contribution to the process of civilization, to become a day labourer. England had in this respect been the great pioneer. The right policy then was, not to try to make the peasant efficient, but to abolish him. The magic word was clearance. The landlord who did nothing for the land was to be helped to get rid of the peasants on whose efforts agriculture depended. Mill said in the 'forties that you could count on your fingers the landlords who had made improvements. Lord Cowper made the same statement in the House of Lords in the 'eighties.[1] Yet, so implicit and uncritical was the confidence of the governing class in its own narrow view and its own narrow experience, that its only solution for agrarian distress and stagnation was to throw still more power to a class that had shown itself quite unfitted to use it. To understand this perversity we must remember that McCulloch was predicting at this time that France would become the pauper warren of Europe, because she had a large peasant owning class instead of the labourer who worked on the English farms.

Lord Middleton, in the interesting book he wrote to redistribute the blame for Irish misgovernment between England and Ireland, reminded Irish critics of English policy that the peasant was no better off in most of Europe at this time than in Ireland.[2] But the Irish critic might

---

[1] Ap. 22 and May 2, 1887.   [2] *Ireland, Dupe or Heroine*, p. 40.

point to examples of two revolutions that put this story in a different light: the French and the Danish. England got rid of her own peasants, as Arnold Toynbee and Sir William Ashley showed, because when the old medieval customs and tenures were resolved government was in the hands of the landlord class. In countries where the landlords did not control the government, the fate of the peasant was very different. France and Denmark are interesting cases because their agrarian revolutions took place just before the chapter of Irish history that is now under discussion. By three stages the French Revolution released the peasant from all his services and obligations and made him his own master. France was in the hands of the Jacobins. Denmark was in the hands of a king who was independent of the landlords, and who wished to protect the peasant as a good and useful force in society. Consequently, when these medieval relations were brought to an end, the peasant was given security of tenure, and the cottagers were given plots of land. From this revolution there emerged in time the most successful agricultural community in Europe. If then the Irish peasant had come under France, he would have been established on the soil, and the landlords would have received little compensation: if under Denmark, the landlords would have received compensation, but the peasant would have been enfranchised and made secure. Unhappily the Government that had his fate in its hands had neither the Jacobin view of France nor the large conservative view of Denmark. It was a Government that believed that a society that kept its peasants was losing its place in the march of man.

The history of the years following the Peace of 1815 is therefore the history of a war waged upon the Irish peasant. Though the landlord was a despot there were two checks on his power. One was the common law. A landlord wishing to eject a tenant had to go to a superior court, and this involved expense and delay. When the potato crop failed in 1816 great numbers of peasants could not pay their rent. The landlords asked the Government for legislation to cheapen and simplify eviction, and the Government complied, passing Acts in 1816 and 1818. The landlord was enabled to bring an action in a county court and to get his tenant out in two months at a cost of £2. He was also enabled to distrain his tenant's growing crop, to keep it till it was ripe, and then sell it when harvested. The Irish law was thus made much harsher than the English, and the Government gave the Irish landlords, who were mere rent receivers, power that was not possessed by the English landlords, who put capital, and sometimes brains and initiative, into the development of their estates.

The second check on the landlords' power was the danger of widespread popular resistance. This force used in Yorkshire in the 'thirties had compelled a Government to modify the severities of the new Poor Law. Used in the Chartist movement, it had brought Parliament, as Lord John Russell admitted, to consider the social abuses of the new industrial life. The Irish did not need any instruction in this method of resisting oppression. On the contrary their emigrants were often leaders in English agitation, and men like Doherty, Bronterre O'Brien and Fergus O'Connor played an important part in the trade unions and other rebel movements on English soil. The Irish had learnt these arts in a bitter and savage school. The peasants, faced with hostile landlords and a hostile Government, formed or revived secret societies and averted or avenged eviction by outrage. Their societies were called Whiteboys, Rockites, Threshers, or Blackfeet, and they sought to set up a rival terror to the terror that the landlord had within his power.

" But for the salutary dread of the Whiteboy Association," wrote Poulett Scrope in 1834, " ejectment would desolate Ireland and decimate her population, casting forth thousands of families like noxious weeds rooted out of the soil on which they have hitherto grown, perhaps too luxuriantly, and fling them away to perish in roadside ditches. Yes, the Whiteboy system is the only check on the ejectment system ; and weighing one against the other, horror against horror, and crime against crime, is perhaps the lesser evil of the two."[1]

[1] Quoted Pomfret, *The Struggle for Land in Ireland*, p. 25.

These societies directing their blows at landlord, agent, or the peasant who took a farm from which another had been evicted, were some check on the policy of clearance. The Government answered with Insurrection Acts, Arms Acts, Peace Preservation Acts, and the suspension of Habeas Corpus. These Acts were used and military force employed to collect tithe, an exaction that Pitt had admitted to be a scandal at the time of the Union. During the first half century after the Union there were only five years when Ireland was under the ordinary law.

The confidence of the ruling class in its plan of giving a free hand to the landlord was shown in an extreme case in its treatment of an alternative policy presented by the Royal Commission, appointed in 1835 to consider the question of introducing the Poor Law into Ireland. This Commission was appointed by Melbourne and it included among its members Whateley the Protestant, and Murray the Catholic, Archbishop of Dublin. This Commission sat for three years. It reported against introducing workhouses and set out a large scheme of agrarian development. It proposed that a Board should be created charged with the duty of improving waste and unreclaimed land, with authority to construct main drains and roads at the expense of the property benefited; that a general drainage Act should be passed for land already in cultivation; that the cottiers' cabins should be replaced by better houses, and cottiers given allotments on the waste; that agricultural model schools should be established, and that tenants for life should be given greater freedom. Thus the Commissioners proposed a constructive solution for the problem of the under-employed population and the under-cultivated land.[1] But, whilst they objected to the workhouse system, they wished to establish Poor Law Commissioners and to introduce poor rates in order to make provision for the sick, the infirm, and the aged. They were in favour also of encouraging, aiding, and supervising, overseas emigration. In fact their report anticipated a good deal that is to be found in the

[1] It is interesting to note that Nassau Senior, the economist, was in favour of the scheme for waste lands.

Report of the English Poor Law Commission of 1907, and some of the public work connected with the names of the Balfour brothers, Horace Plunkett, and Augustine Birrell. The response of the Government to this report shows better than anything else how absolute was its faith in its own ideas. The scheme was rejected without consideration, and George Nicholls, of the English Poor Law Commission, was sent on a flying visit to Ireland. " Your attention need not be very specially given," wrote Lord John Russell, " to the plans for the general improvement of Ireland contained in the report of the commissioners of inquiry."[1] Nicholls reported in favour of the workhouse system, with the refusal of all relief outside the workhouse and the division of the poor rate between owner and occupier. The Government accepted his view and passed an Act in 1838 in accordance with this plan.

This episode brings out most clearly the fundamental cause of the English failure in Ireland. Among the official papers that were published by the Government was a letter from Sir George Cornewall Lewis to the Chancellor of the Exchequer discussing this report. Lewis rejects as wrong in principle any attempt to rescue Irish agriculture, and the community dependent upon it, by constructive effort.

" A Government can only, as it seems to me, attempt to accelerate the improvement of the soil by *indirect* means. In this as in most other cases connected with the *material* part of civilization, its functions are simply negative; it can do no more than remove obstacles to amelioration and suffer a society to proceed unchecked in its natural career of advancement."[2]

This view of politics led to disastrous consequences in England, but in England private enterprise was active and wealth and industry were increasing, whereas in Ireland these forces were negligible. A formula for which England paid with confusion, and wasted energy, Ireland paid with stagnation, famine, and death.

Not less instructive is Lewis' argument for the workhouse.

[1] Quoted from *Vice-Regal Commission on Irish Poor Law*, 1906, p. 4, by O'Brien, *Economic History of Ireland from the Union to the Famine*, p. 182.

[2] *P.P.*, 1837, LI, p. 282.

C

It contains an admirable description of the state of agrarian society.

" Now the main purpose of a Poor Law for Ireland is (by offering to the poor man a sure maintenance in case of absolute need) to loosen his hold upon the land and thus to relieve the landlord from the incubus which now presses upon him. No greater mistake can be committed than to suppose that the present tenure of landed property in Ireland is beneficial to the landlords. In this instance, as in many others, the evils of a selfish and oppressive policy have recoiled upon the authors. By letting their estates to middlemen, by encouraging the sub-division of land, and the multiplication of the people, by originating or conniving at the oppression of their tenantry and by perverting the administration of justice the landlords have raised a spirit which they are now unable to lay.

" The Irish landlord and tenant may be said, in general, to live in a constant state of *mutual fear*. The tenant fears lest he should be unable to pay his rent, and that, consequently, his goods should be distrained, or he himself ejected; the landlord fears lest, if he enforces his rights or attempts any improvement which may infringe the Whiteboy rules, his person or property should be attacked or his new tenant murdered."

This excellent description leads to an astonishing conclusion.

" In the present condition of Ireland I can conceive no other means except a strongly guarded poor law, of restoring to the landowners the power of doing what they will with their own, a power which however liable to abuse is essential to the advancement of agriculture, and the improvement of the soil and to the consequence of these, an amelioration of the state both of the tenants and the labourers."[1]

This was written in 1837. The agitation over Factory Reform was then active in England. The millowners had already had their power curbed by a series of Factory Acts; their mills were inspected by Government officials; their workpeople had rights, guarded and limited it is true, as trade unionists. Within ten years they were to be compelled to submit to a reduction of working hours that affected adults as well as children. In all these ways they were

[1] *P.P.*, 1837, LI, p. 261.

denied the power of doing what they liked with their own. Their critics had said many harsh things of them but nobody had ever accused them of blacker sins than those that Lewis ascribed in this passage to Irish landlords. Yet Lewis could think of no other way of rescuing Ireland from misery and misgovernment than this plan of giving full power to the men who had originated or connived at the oppression of their tenants and perverted the administration of justice. Is it surprising that England, giving Ireland her best brains, brought her to the great Famine of 1846 and 1847?

That calamity supplied the remedy for which Lewis was looking. This is not the place to describe its terrible course or the efforts made by Governments to check its ravages. Necessity compelled statesmen to surrender some fixed ideas, but men acting against their convictions are apt to produce compromises that are ineffective. For our purpose the important fact to note is that in this instance, Providence, helped by man's previous efforts, had effected just that clearance of the peasant population that Lewis and his enlightened contemporaries desired. Over 700,000 people died of hunger,[1] nearly two million emigrated, the population of Ireland which had risen between 1800 and 1841 from five millions to over eight, fell between 1841 and 1851 to six millions and a half. In 1841 there were 698,549 holdings under 15 acres and 127,967 over 15 acres; in 1851 the figures were 317,665 and 290,401. Thus more than half the holdings under 15 acres had disappeared, and with them 70 per cent. of the cabins.

The English rulers were now able to put into practice their own ideas of what should be done with Ireland. The cottiers had gone. The landlords had been hard hit; a third of them were ruined and estates were heavily mortgaged. In 1849 the Government passed the Encumbered Estates Act facilitating the sale of estates, in order to substitute for insolvent landlords men with capital and enterprise. Land quickly changed hands. By 1857 the new Court had transferred a third of the soil of Ireland.

---

[1] *Fact and Figures about Ireland*, p. 6, by Grimshaw (formerly Irish Registrar General).

Of the 80,000 purchasers 90 per cent. were Irish. These new
landlords were just the men that the English economists
had been looking for; they meant to make money out of
their property. They began to press hardly on their
tenants and the Government passed new laws in 1851 and
1860 to increase their power of eviction.

If the English economists and legislators were right, Ireland's problem should have been solved. The new landlords,
who had bought land cheap, had ample power to do what
they liked with their own. The clearance had been much
greater than anything that could have been expected from
building a thousand workhouses. The famine had broken
the spirit of the peasants, and emigration had removed the
more active and enterprising of the youth of the country.
Every weapon that could be devised for shaking the tenants'
hold on the land, and for giving the landlords full power,
had been supplied. We see the results in the history of the
next ten years. Between 1849 and 1860 37,300 families,
numbering about 200,000 persons were evicted.[1]

" In one Union," said Sir Robert Peel,[2] " at a time of famine,
within one year, 15,000 persons have been driven from their
homes. . . . I do not think the records of any country, civilised or
barbarous, ever presented such scenes of horror." " All the
better land is turned into pasture; and on what remains of the
soil, the remnant of the peasants are allowed to huddle together.
In a few months whole counties such as Meath or Tipperary, are
depopulated and changed into prairies like those of America.—
The latifundia extend farther than the eye can reach. In ten
years 252,000 peasant homes are destroyed and a million and a
half of the Irish people cross to America."[3]

This was clearance with a vengeance. Mill writing in
1868, observes that there was no improvement in the
condition of the poorest peasants in spite of the immense
reduction in their numbers.

Let us now turn back to our English parallel. By 1870,
as we have seen, the workman had gained for himself from

---

[1] Dubois, *Contemporary Ireland*, 222.

[2] Quoted in Duffy, *Young Ireland*, p. 239. Peel was Irish Secretary.

[3] Clearances, as we have said, took the best of the land in order to turn it into
grazing and left the rest to the peasantry. Dubois, *op. cit.*, p. 236.

Parliament a number of concessions. Factory Acts and Mines Acts, Truck Acts and Trade Unions, gave him certain rights against his employer. He had also the Parliamentary vote. To understand the position of the Irish peasant we must imagine the workman obliged to work at what hours his employer wished, for what terms he liked to offer, without protection of any kind from the law, and without a vote. We must suppose that between 1850 and 1870 his position had grown worse and not better. Industrial warfare has sometimes been embittered in England by evictions, as in the strike of the miners of Durham and Northumberland in 1830. But in Ireland eviction was part of the normal life of society. In October, 1835, Lord Duncannon wrote to Lord John Russell that a landlord in Carlow had turned off his property sixty-three families, all of them good tenants who had paid their rent, on the ground that they had voted for Catholic candidates.[1] In the 'seventies Lord Leitrim used to give notice to all his tenants every April in order to make eviction easy.[2]

We can perhaps best appreciate the effect of sixty years of English rule by comparing the argument Lord Clare used for the Union in the House of Lords with a statement by Kimberley in the 'sixties.

" What then was the situation of Ireland at the Revolution and what is it this day? The whole power and property of the country has been conferred by successive monarchs of England upon an English colony composed of three sets of English adventurers who poured into the country at the end of three successive rebellions. Confiscation is their common title and from their first settlement they have been hemmed in on every side by the old inhabitants of the island, brooding over their discontents in sullen indignation. . . . What then, was the security of the English settlers for their physical existence at the Revolution? And what is the security of their descendants at this day? The powerful and commanding protection of Great Britain. If by any fatality it fails, you are at the mercy of the old inhabitants of the island."[3]

[1] Spencer Walpole, *Life of Lord John Russell*, I, 274.
[2] Pomfret, *op. cit.*, p. 22, quoting *Report of Poor Law Commissioners*, 1870, 15.
[3] Ashbourne, *Pitt : Some Chapters of his Life and Times*, p. 295.

Sixty years later a British Viceroy showed how this protection was given.

" The landed proprietors," said Kimberley in the House of Lords in 1864," are supported by the force of the United Kingdom in a position, which, I am convinced if Ireland stood alone, they could not possibly maintain, and this country is strictly responsible for seeing that its military force is not applied in perpetuity to save the landlords from measures which they have neglected to provide and which otherwise might be forced upon them."[1]

During sixty years England had been tempering the power of the employed and of the industrial system to the poor; in the same time the power of the landlord in Ireland was maintained in its most rigorous forms by the aid of England. In 1870 the condition of the English workers is better, that of the Irish peasant worse, than in 1800.

To complete the contrast one last feature of Irish economy must be noted. One part of Ireland escaped the unqualified tyranny that cast these shadows over the life of the peasant. Over most of the Province of Ulster there obtained a customary tenure, known as Tenant Right or the Ulster custom, under which the tenant had certain rights, the right to continued occupancy at a fair rent, and the right to sell his improvements if he left the farm. The three chief principles embodied in this custom were known as the three Fs: Fair Rent, Fixity of Tenure, and Free Sale. These customs went back to the plantation of Ulster by James the First and they are probably to be explained by the difference between the Protestant farmers who were planted there and the native Irish who had to take whatever their alien conquerors imposed. Thus to understand the position of the Irish peasant we must imagine the workmen of Lancashire, Cheshire, and other industrial districts, entirely at the mercy of their employers with one enclave, say the West Riding of Yorkshire, where they were protected by custom as strong as law. Can anybody suppose that, under those conditions, England would have been a nation easy to govern?

---

[1] Pomfret, *op. cit.*, p. 69.

CHAPTER III

In 1868 Disraeli told the House of Commons that more
than one fourth of the Irish people were paupers, and paupers
in a helpless condition. In 1870 Gladstone told the House
of Commons that the Irish labourers were as badly off as
they had been under the Penal Laws of the eighteenth
century. Such was the plight of Ireland seventy years after
the Act of Union, during which time Pitt's remedies for
Irish poverty and Irish discord had been applied by statesmen and seconded by calamity. England was now to hear
a great deal about the three Fs—Fair Rent, Fixity of Tenure,
and Free Sale—which described the Ulster custom. The
government and history of Ireland in the past seventy years
might also be summed up in three Fs—Feudal Rights, Free
Trade, and Famine. They had produced the Irish society
whose evils and injustices a great Englishman tried seriously
to understand and remove, when neglect and improper
treatment had made them, not merely a danger to Ireland,
but a danger to the British Empire.

English social history during this period is, as we have
noted, the result of a revolt against the principles of government that had dominated the mind of the ruling class:
principles that could be summed up in the phrase, the
Rights of Property. In that revolt different forces were
combined: philanthropists like Shaftesbury, thinkers like
Chadwick and Kay, working class discontent expressing
itself in moderate bodies like the Ten Hours Committees and
rebel movements like Chartism. In the history of the Irish
problem we find similar forces, and they had a considerable
effect in educating opinion. They were, however, powerless against certain fixed obstacles, and by 1868, when Glad-

stone opened the second chapter of this history, they had
produced scarcely any results.

The statesman who occupies in this struggle the place
Shaftesbury holds in the other is John Bright, whose speeches
on Ireland are among the noblest of his career. As early as
1847 he denounced English oppression of the Irish peasant
with as much earnestness as Shaftesbury had shown in
denouncing the wrongs of the women and children in factory
and mine. With great courage, supported only by John
Stuart Mill, he urged the House of Commons in 1867 to
look beyond the anger and the fear excited by the early
Fenian outbreak and to ask themselves whether it was not
true, as was stated in the Petition he presented, that Fenianism was the child of injustice. The counterpart of Chadwick
is Thomas Drummond, who was under-secretary at Dublin
Castle for five years during Melbourne's Government, 1835-
1840. His fearless behaviour to the powerful Orange
faction, his wise and resolute action, in checking intimidation
and the irregular discipline of the landlords by organizing a
police force and appointing stipendiary magistrates, removed
some dark scandals from the government of Ireland. His
famous warning to the Irish landlords, that property has
duties as well as rights, was the sharpest comment that
could be made on the spirit in which most English Governments treated Irish problems. His moral power was shown
in an even more striking manner. For the first and the only
time in Irish history, an Irish peasant organization was
formed to bring agrarian offenders to justice. All the difficulties that obstructed the administration of justice disappeared; witnesses came forward to give evidence and
juries convicted. This happened in Tipperary, hitherto a
lawless county. Drummond's death at the age of forty-
three was one of those fatalities that seemed to pursue the
Irish people.[1] Mill, because almost alone among his con-

---

[1] Three other men all of whose lives were valuable to Ireland for one reason
or another died before they were fifty: Parnell, Arnold Toynbee, Frederick
Cavendish.

To appreciate Drummond's achievement the reader should turn to De
Beaumont's description of an Irish Court of Justice. De Beaumont, *L'Irlande
Sociale, politique et religieuse*, p. 327.

temporaries he was interested in the social life of Europe, understood the Irish problem as nobody else understood it, and his writings on this subject have a fire and a passion not always found in his pages. Ireland had thus the help of a great orator, a noble civil servant, and a profound and earnest thinker.

Moreover, just as the English reformers in Parliament had the support of a constitutional movement in the Ten Hours Committees, as well as the sometimes embarrassing support of a rebel movement in Chartism, so in Ireland the cause of agrarian reform, urged by men of revolutionary temper like Lalor and Stephens, was preached for a time by a strong body of moderate opinion. After the collapse of Young Ireland a Tenants Right League was formed in 1850, representing a powerful combination of forces. For under the pressure of the famine some of the Ulster landlords violated the Ulster custom, and in consequence Ulster joined hands with certain societies which had been formed in the rest of Ireland to help the peasants on whom had fallen either the blow or the threat of eviction. The first of these societies adopted as its motto Drummond's phrase about the duties of property.

Out of all this discontent and alarm there grew a movement for four objects: the determination of a fair rent by valuation, security from disturbance so long as this rent was paid, the right of the tenant to sell his interest, and a provision of relief for arrears of rent that had accumulated with the famine. This movement arising out of a circular signed by John Gray, the proprietor of the *Freeman's Journal*, who was an Anglican, by Samuel Greer, an Ulster Presbyterian, and by Frederick Lucas, a Catholic and proprietor of the *Tablet*, was so successful that at the General Election it sent fifty-two members to Parliament, pledged to independence and to the League programme. This party was helped by the recent change in the franchise. Ireland under the Reform Act of 1832 had roughly 98,000 voters; by 1850 the figure had fallen to 61,000; by the Irish Voters Act of 1850 the number was raised to 165,000. Of these 135,000 were voters in the counties.

There is again another resemblance between the social reform movements in the two countries. In the Irish, as in the English case, Governments took great trouble to inquire into the facts. Inquiries were incessant. Committees and Commissions were always investigating Irish problems. Melbourne had set up the Irish Poor Law Commission which outlined the large comprehensive scheme already mentioned. Peel set up the Devon Commission which made admirable proposals in 1845. In 1850 a Committee of the House of Commons, examining the condition of certain disturbed districts, urged the Government to redress the wrongs of the peasants, and to secure them in the right to their own improvements.

How was it then that all these efforts produced no result, and that, when Gladstone rose on a winter's day in 1870 to open a new chapter in this history, there was not a single Act on the Statute Book for the protection of the Irish tenant, though the laws had been amended time after time in favour of the landlord, and no less than forty-two Coercion Acts had been passed in forty years?

There are two large considerations that supply the answer. In one of the rare instances where the Roman Empire had to meet rebellion, a Roman general made a speech into which Tacitus put tersely the advantages Gaul received from Roman rule. His last touch was interesting and piquant. He said that Gaul got the full benefit of the rule of a good Emperor, and, when Rome had a bad one, Gaul escaped the evils of his rule which fell on those at home.[1] If we turn this saying round we get an excellent description of English rule in Ireland between the Act of Union and the passing of the Reform Bill of 1867. For there was nothing in English politics or institutions to hinder a bad Government, and everything to hinder a good one when treating Irish problems. The Irish landlords were all powerful in England, partly because many of them were English landlords, and partly because, as the *Times* put it when criticizing

---

[1] Tacitus, *Hist.*, IV, LXXIV. Speech of Cerealis to the Treviri and the Lingones.

" Et laudatorum principum usus ex aequo, quamvis procul agentibus; saevi proximis ingruunt."

a very moderate Bill introduced by a Conservative Minister in 1852, " The same interests exist on both sides of the Channel, and those who are prepared to invade the landlords property in the one country will speedily be called upon for a similar violation of principle in the other."

So powerful an interest could be defeated by a rival powerful interest with great popular backing, as was shown in the Repeal of the Corn Laws. It could be brought under some degree of control when a problem became acute that affected the English people at home, as was shown when dirt and neglect were spreading cholera and disease through the English towns. It is significant that the *Times*, which denounced the gentlest handling of landlords' rights in Ireland, had supported Free Trade and Public Health when those questions were English, affecting English welfare, and agitated in English constituencies. In the case of the issue between landlord and peasant in Ireland there was no such pressure. Minister or thinker had to push his case with little help.

Moreover feudal property was more concerned for its rights than its rents, its prestige than its interests. It was an outrage to abolish the Corn Laws; it was a greater outrage to say that the landlord's power should be qualified by law. This was a direct challenge to property at its most sensitive point; a challenge to the principles for which, above all others, the House of Lords was on guard. What chance had such a challenge with no great English body of feeling behind it? The House of Lords, which had had to surrender rotten boroughs and the Corn Laws to English popular force, had a simple task in defending these threatened rights against Ministers who could appeal only to reason. Polybius, when a hostage in Italy, asked Cato to bring his case before the Senate, but Cato advised him strongly to avoid coming under the notice of that body. Odysseus, he reminded Polybius, when once he had escaped from the den of the Cyclops, took care not to re-enter it. The House of Lords was Ireland's Cyclops' den. Gladstone said afterwards that if it had allowed Peel to pass his Bill, carrying out some of the recommendations of the Devon Commission in 1845, the land question would have been solved. Disraeli took the same view of the Bills brought in by the Irish Attorney-General of the Conservative Government of 1852, which were ultimately destroyed by that ruthless Cyclops.

There was another obstacle to success. An acute observer has remarked that it was the great misfortune of Ireland in the eighteenth century that she had two masters: England and the English garrison in Ireland.

" From a political point of view the régime thus imposed on the country was the worst that could possibly be imagined; namely a combination of the government peculiar to a colony or dependency with that of a ruling class which, though all powerful in Ireland, was not itself independent. Had England governed Ireland directly, mere self-interest would have made it protect the weak against the strong. Had it, on the other hand, handed over all power to the ruling caste, self-interest would have induced that caste to promote efficient government. But, as it was, Ireland was controlled by ' the garrison ' and ' the garrison ' was controlled by England, with the result that all sense of responsibility, all zeal for the common interest disappeared."[1]

Fox had made use of this metaphor in a famous speech: " The Protestant ascendency has been compared to a garrison in Ireland. It is not in our power to add to the strength of that garrison, but I would convert the besiegers themselves into the garrison." Fox and his friends wanted the English Government to encourage the Irish Parliament to admit the Catholics and to befriend the movement in Ireland for breaking down the great divisions that separated the mass of the people from a small privileged minority. Pitt's policy was the opposite, and, as Lecky showed, he obstructed and defeated that movement.[2] In the Union he professed to have found a method of escape from this principle of discord, but the Union, as he devised it, left this ascendency established. Consequently any English Government that wanted to settle an Irish problem in a

---

[1] Dubois, p. 35.

[2] " One fact . . . is as certain as anything in Irish history—that if the Catholic question was not settled in 1795, rather than in 1829, it is the English Government, and the English Government alone, that was responsible for the delay." Lecky, *History of Ireland*, Vol. III, p. 287.

large spirit had to face the hostility of this privileged ruling class.

During most of the century this class had a liberum veto on Irish policy. When Melbourne, who was unusual among English statesmen of this time in being better in Ireland than in England, partly, as his critics would say, because he depended on O'Connell, was Prime Minister, there was a pitched battle between this interest and Drummond, the great reforming secretary. Ireland had an excellent Viceroy in Mulgrave, better known as Normanby, an excellent Chief Secretary in Morpeth, and Lord John Russell, though he made the fatal mistake of rejecting the plans of the Irish Commission on the Poor Laws, was wholehearted in his sympathy with Drummond's views and temper. For a few years there was a new spirit in the administration of Ireland. But the strength of the garrison was shown in the successful pressure it put on Peel and Lyndhurst, and the years when Ireland was best governed were those in which the Government was most embarrassed by resistance in Parliament.[1] A comparison between the difficulties the Melbourne Government met in struggling to give Ireland municipal institutions and a constabulary not under Orange control, with those that had to be overcome in setting up municipal institutions in England and an efficient police force, shows how badly England was handicapped in treating Irish problems by the conditions inherited at the Union.

Under those conditions England in governing Ireland obeyed, as a rule, the bad influences in Irish life, and disregarded the good. The privileged minority were allowed to obstruct and delay the redress of the grievances of tithe, and the abolition of the Protestant monopoly of the Corporations. On the other hand, it happened more than once that good advice given by Irishmen was rejected, because it did not happen to suit the political and economic prejudices of the English governing class. This happened,

[1] Lord John Russell remembering Peel's conduct on these occasions said bitterly in 1845 " Peel and the good government of Ireland seem to me a contradiction in terms." Gladstone afterwards confessed his own part in supporting Peel. *Aspects of the Irish Question*, p. 268.

as we have seen, in the case of the proposals of the Irish Commission on the Poor Laws for a constructive scheme of land settlement and housing. In 1834 a Commission on Railways pointed out that conditions in Ireland differed from those in England, and that in Ireland it would be better to set up State railways than to trust to private enterprise. Resolutions urging this course were twice adopted in the House of Commons but no action was taken.

The behaviour of successive Governments over agricultural education was still more remarkable. In Ireland the need for such education was grasped as early as 1826, when a committee of Ulster landlords set up an agricultural school at Templemoyle in County Londonderry. In 1833 the National Board started giving agricultural education in its Training College, and took a farm for this purpose at Glasnevin near Dublin. Templemoyle, transferred to the National Board after the Famine, was used to produce skilled farmers; Glasnevin to produce teachers qualified to give elementary education in agricultural science in the schools. In 1844 the Board started the practice of appointing a travelling instructor, and in 1850, with the concurrence of the Poor Law Board, they encouraged agricultural education in the workhouse schools. These ideas had received strong support from the Devon Commission, and two Lord Lieutenants, Clarendon in 1847, and Spencer in 1872, were warmly in favour of this development. But there was strong opposition from England, from the Treasury with its narrow ideas and the Liverpool Financial Reform Association, which held that public money was being used for improper purposes. Under this influence English Ministers were hostile, and in 1860 Cardwell, as Irish Secretary, went so far as to persuade the Poor Law Board to drop its agricultural teaching.

It would be unjust to describe the English rulers of Ireland during this disastrous period as deliberately malevolent. Several of them took trouble and risk in the effort to provide remedies for Irish distress. This was true of Melbourne's efforts for Municipal Reform and the removal of the grievances of the tithe payer, and of Peel's decision to increase the grant to Maynooth. Gladstone said afterwards that the Whigs had suffered greatly as a party from their efforts to help Ireland. Lord John Russell wanted to control ejectments in 1848, but he was overruled by Palmerston and Grey. Behind this long record of failure there were qualities of will and conscience that under other conditions would have produced reform and improvement. But the conditions were such that Ireland got as a rule the worst out of statesmen who elsewhere served the cause of progress with tolerable success. Peel himself was convinced by the Devon Commission that the case of the Irish tenants was good and urgent. Indeed he told Napier, as Napier told the House of Commons years afterwards, that he believed that nothing stood between Ireland and contentment except this grievance. That was too sanguine a view, but it shows that Peel was in earnest when he proposed to legislate on the subject. Unhappily he was defeated in his effort to provide the remedy that he thought so pressing, and Ireland had reason to remember him rather for his bad actions than his good intentions: his behaviour in putting O'Connell on his trial before a packed Protestant jury: his rejection of Drummond's ideas for railway expansion. All Lord John Russell's sympathy brought Ireland less benefit than the mischief he caused by his Ecclesiastical Titles Bill, for that blunder re-awakened religious strife in Ireland, and helped to break up the Tenants League. Palmerston's long rule in English politics, disastrous as it was in some respects, was fortunate for Italian freedom: but Ireland knew him for a phrase by which the truth was made to stand upon its head: the phrase tenant right is landlord wrong. In England Cardwell was the friend of efficiency, in Ireland of ignorance.

As with men, so with measures. The effect of the Repeal of the Corn Laws in England was to stimulate our export trade, and thus to increase the prosperity of the new industrial towns. It was not till the 'seventies that agriculture suffered the injury which many had feared, for agricultural prices did not fall until the disastrous improvement of land and sea transport brought the wheat districts of the Middle and Western States within reach of Europe. So far as the price of food went the first effect of Repeal was not to reduce it but to prevent the rise that would have come with the general rise in prices. The Irish poor living on potatoes received no benefit from a measure that kept the price of wheat from rising, and, as an agricultural country, Ireland suffered whatever injury Repeal was ultimately to cause to her chief industry.[1]

The most striking illustration of this truth that England during these years was treating her own problems with her right hand and Irish problems with her left, is to be found in the record of the statesman, who had in some respects the clearest and boldest mind of his time, Disraeli. Even Mill himself, prophet of noble and lonely truth, was not more outspoken than the Disraeli of 1844.

" I want to see a public man come forward and say what the Irish question is. One says that it is a physical question; another a spiritual. Now it is the absence of the aristocracy; now the absence of railways. It is the Pope one day and potatoes the next. A dense population inhabit an island where there is an established church which is not their church; and a territorial aristocracy, the richest of whom live in a distant capital. Thus they have a starving population, an alien Church, and in addition the weakest executive in the world.

" Well, what then would gentlemen say if they were reading of a country in that position? They would say at once, ' The remedy is revolution '. But the Irish could not have a revolution and why? Because Ireland is connected with another and a more powerful country. Then what is the consequence? The connection with England became the cause of the present state of Ireland. If the connection with England prevented a revolution and a revolution was the only remedy, England logically is in the odious position of being the cause of all the misery of Ireland. What then is the duty of an English Minister ? To effect by his policy all those changes which a revolution would effect by force. That is the Irish question in its integrity."[2]

<hr>

[1] Fay, *The Corn Laws and Social England*, p. 118. The quinquennial average of wheat prices was £2 14s. 9d. for 1841-1845, and £2 16s. 0d. for 1851-1855. Tooke and Newmarch estimated that but for Repeal, the price in 1848 would have been 73s. instead of 56s. 10d.

[2] Disraeli, House of Commons, February 16, 1844.

Twenty years later, when reminded of this striking outburst, Disraeli tried to soften its effect, and he was no doubt uncomfortable over the contrast between his rhetoric and his actions. That contrast must strike all dispassionate students of Disraeli's career. It is apparent in his English politics, for the author of *Sybil* scarcely lifted a finger during the struggles for Factory Reform and Public Health in the 'forties. But if the contrast is apparent in his English politics, it is very much more important in his Irish. He made an effort, it is true, when Chancellor of the Exchequer in Derby's Government in 1852, to redress the tenants' grievances, and the Bills introduced by that Government, though they conceded much less than was needed or, according to Sir John Young, than the best landlords were ready to accept, were the best introduced by any Government before 1870. But the language he used in 1844 would have led his hearers to expect that he would exert his influence strongly and persistently in favour of these reforms. In fact he hardly ever spoke about them; he let Derby spoil his Bills in 1852, and he never afterwards made any considerable effort to educate his countrymen on these Irish problems, or to help those who sought to solve them. In some cases he fomented the suspicions of property, calling even the modest proposals of Sir John Young in 1855 communistic, and treating Irish misery as an argument rather for coercion than for reform.

What is the explanation? It is to be found in his character and his circumstances. The secret of his insight into problems that his age misunderstood lay in his detachment. A Jew, with the quick mind and imagination of his race, he had a great advantage as a critic of politics and customs over public men who had all been brought up in the same tradition, within the same circle of ideas and experience.[1] The author of *Sybil* was studying the society in which he lived, as he might have studied some interesting society on the continent of Europe. Truths that escaped men blinded by routine and habit caught his attention and passed

---

[1] The mutual attraction of Disraeli and Bright was in this respect something like the friendship between Bonar Law and Lloyd George.

through his vivid and stimulating mind into literature. But the secret of his strength as a critic was the secret of his weakness as a man of action. Though he saw further than most men of his age, and was in this sense more effective than the governing class, he had less of the instinct for management and was in this sense less. It was a calamity for England that a man of his genius and intellectual independence was so little in office, and in judging Peel's conduct in breaking up his party in 1845 this unhappy consequence must be taken into account. But it is difficult to imagine a man of energy like Gladstone or Chamberlain, however serious the obstacles in his way, making the speech Disraeli made in 1844, and then taking so little interest in the problem he had painted with such vivid truth.

Of the tragedy of Disraeli's career we get a powerful impression in the interview Hyndman described in his book of reminiscences. Hyndman, his head full of ardent ideas about reform, called on the old lion at the end of his life, and he tells us how Disraeli received him, of the melancholy warning he gave him against confidence, and the sad tone in which he spoke of his own failure to make his ideas effective in Conservative policy. " It is a very difficult country to move, Mr. Hyndman, and one in which there is more disappointment than success."

A study of the short history of the Derby Government of 1852 brings his difficulties clearly into view. In that Government, one of the weakest in capacity that held office in the nineteenth century, there were three men who wanted to reform the Irish land system. They were Disraeli himself, Chancellor of the Exchequer, Sir John Napier, the Irish Attorney General, and the Chief Secretary, Lord Naas, better known in history as the Lord Mayo who made a great mark as Viceroy in India, before he fell to the knife of a convict when visiting a prison in the Andaman Islands. These three men were sincerely anxious to carry reform, and the Bills introduced by Napier were better than any offered to the House of Commons until Gladstone began to legislate. Disraeli put himself in touch with Shee, Lucas, and Gavan Duffy, the leaders of the Tenant Right League, who incidentally held the balance in the House of Commons, hoping to find some means of co-operating with them. He so far satisfied them that they decided to support the Budget against the Whig attack. But their plans were defeated. Lord Roden, the leader of the Orange Party, to whom news of these negotiations came from an official engaged in them, heckled and frightened the Government, and Derby and his colleagues threw Disraeli over.

The discovery that he, a man with ideas, was at the mercy of men without them, doubtless gave Disraeli a stronger relish for the Reform Bill which he carried by such brilliant tactics in 1867. It helps also to explain his generous behaviour in trying to persuade Gladstone in 1858 to rejoin the Conservatives.

Of the Peelites who had been adrift since the fall of the Aberdeen Government in 1855, Gladstone more often than not had been in agreement with Disraeli on important questions. He had voted with him in the crucial divisions on the China War, and on the Conspiracy to Murder Bill introduced by Palmerston after Orsini's attempt on the life of the Emperor Napoleon. It was clear that, apart from the Italian question, he and Disraeli had more in common than he and Palmerston. The Conservatives were very hopeful of bringing him back, and Derby spoke of him as a " half regained Eurydice." If Disraeli had been thinking only of his career, he had strong motives for discouraging overtures to a man who was bound to be his most formidable rival for the leadership of the party. If, on the other hand, he was sincerely anxious to push reform against the sullen weight of property in his party, he might well desire to enlist this powerful force, thinking that however mysterious the curve on which it seemed to move, it would be found on his side when it came to a clear issue between public claims and class interest. It is significant that, faced with this choice, he wrote to his rival, pleading for his co-operation with such urgency as to justify the description he gave to Bishop Wilberforce, to whom he said that he had gone down on his knees to Gladstone.

What would have happened if Gladstone, who answered

stiffly, had accepted his magnanimous advances nobody can say. Disraeli's overture was rejected and he was left to fight his own battles with his party. So far as Ireland was concerned the result was disastrous. There could not be a greater contrast than that between his Irish and his British record when Prime Minister between 1874 and 1880. His Home Secretary was Cross, a man of conscience, industry, and determination. With the enfranchised town worker behind him Disraeli could give effect to ideas that he had put before the world in *Sybil* thirty years earlier, and his Government is gratefully remembered for some admirable and much needed legislation on labour, health, and housing. His Irish record was very different. He put an ineffective Act on the Statute Book, creating an examining University in Ireland, but he left all her social problems untouched. It is significant that in 1879, twenty-five years after his striking description of Irish needs, he committed Ireland to the care of James Lowther, an easy-going cynic, whose remedy for Irish distress was still the remedy that had been fashionable before the famine, clearance, and depopulation.

CHAPTER IV

THE EFFECT OF THE CRUELTY AND LAWLESSNESS OF IRELAND ON THE ENGLISH TEMPER

A severe critic of the English treatment of Ireland, Gustave de Beaumont, writing in 1839, gave a terrible picture of the Irish peasant. " Violent and vindictive, the Irishman displays the most ferocious cruelty in his acts of vengeance. . . . The punishments he invents in his savage fury cannot be contemplated without horror." To understand the cruelty of the agrarian war in Ireland it is necessary to consider its causes; to understand the failure of England in Ireland it is necessary to take into account its effects. For in a sense it may be said that the virtues of the English combined with their vices to disable them from finding the remedies for Irish suffering and injustice. They contrasted the orderly and restrained character of English political and social conflict with the murders and mutilations that made the struggle of the Irish peasant so grim and savage.

De Beaumont said of this cruelty that it was due mainly to Irish history. Unhappily few people knew less of that history than the English. The English, having even in the worst of the problems of the industrial revolution no other cause for conflict than a division of class and of interests, were little able to enter into the difficulties of a people divided bitterly by race, religion, and history. Nobody saw this more clearly than de Beaumont. He pointed out that it often happens that conquerors, after the first convulsions of conquest are over, endeavour to efface its cruel memories. " Ireland presents exactly the opposite case of conquerors who, instead of arresting the violent outrages of conquest, lend all their efforts to perpetuate them."

The student of this painful subject will note that though

during the agrarian war the English knew as a rule only of
the cruelties of the peasants, history sees in this respect no
difference between peasant and ruler, between rebel and
police.   The year 'ninety-eight, so terrible in its crimes, so
fatal in its memories, was not less savage on one side than the
other.   The peasants were capable of any cruelty, but so
were the yeomanry.   " Within these twelve months," said
the great Abercromby of the troops he was given to command
in Ireland, " every crime, every cruelty that could be committed by Cossacks or Calmucks, has been transacted here."[1]
" These men," said Cornwallis, the Viceroy, " have served
their country, but they now take the lead in rapine and
murder."   Pitt, it will be remembered, when listening with
Wilberforce to a debate in the House of Lords, was so
indignant when he heard Lord Clare describe and defend
what the magistrates and the militia had done in Ireland
that he walked out in disgust.[2]   In the tithe war, a war in
which the peasants' grievances had been admitted by Pitt
in 1800 and regarded at that time by Lansdowne as the
chief social evil in Ireland, the Anglican clergy were as
ruthless as any of their victims.[3]   Yet many of these clergy
must have been in the position of Mr. Armstrong in Trollope's novel *The Kellys and the O'Kellys*, whose congregation
consisted of his own family and three policemen.   And
throughout the agrarian war it is difficult to say whether
the moonlighter was more merciless than the evicting landlord.   In 1861 the *Times*, no indulgent judge of the Irish
peasant, wrote of the evictions on the Derryveagh estates, a
blow struck by a landowner against the Ribbon movement:

---

[1] Lecky, *History of Ireland*, IV, 208.   Another uncompromising Unionist,
Goldwin Smith, who was unable to accept even the milder projects of agrarian
reform, said of these outrages, " The loyalist faction in Ireland must take its
place in history beside Robespierre, Couthon, and Carrier."   *Irish History and
Irish Character*, p. 170.
[2] R. Coupland, *Wilberforce*, p. 268.
[3] " The war of the parson against the peasant is raging in Ireland.   The
minister of the gospel of peace with his own hands loads the pistols of his bailiffs
and marches them on tithe gathering expeditions.   It was not to be expected
that the winter would pass over without bloodshed in the quarrel between
Catholic pauper and Protestant divine; nor has it.   The intelligence from
Ireland this week is such that no other country, civilized or savage, could
furnish." *Spectator*, January 16, 1836.

" To invoke the aid of the sheriff and the presence of the resident magistrate to turn out some fifty families, numbering 244 souls, many of them children, who did not know their right hand from their left, and none of them, so far as appears, legally or morally convicted of guilty complicity, by way of checking Ribandism, is equally repugnant to English feelings and to English common sense."[1]

A few months later the *Times*, commenting on the evictions on the estates of two Irish peers, observed " Terrorism is not to be met by terrorism, for terrorism itself is the parent of crime, and a fellowship in undeserved suffering, except in rare cases, prepares men's minds for another kind of fellowship of which Ireland has seen too much."[2] Monsell, himself an Irish landlord and a moderate Liberal, said of the action of Adair at Derryveagh in throwing " 240 persons on the bleak hill side to starve " that if it had taken place in Rome or Naples, or Syria, " it would have been denounced as an atrocity demonstrative of the bad state of the Government which permitted it."[3]

Cruelty then belonged to Irish manners and to Irish history, and it was not peculiar to any Irish class. But to understand the cruelty of the Irish peasant we must remember that he believed that he was cruel in a just cause.

" In the moral feelings of the Irish people the right to hold the land goes, as it did in the beginning, with the right to till it. . . . Even the Whiteboy and the Rockite, in their outrages against the landlord, fought for, not against, the sacredness of what was property in their eyes, for it is not the right of the rent receiver but the right of the cultivator, with which the idea of property is connected in the Irish popular mind. These facts being notorious and the feelings engendered by them being in part at least perfectly reasonable in the eye of every civilized people in the world except England, it is a characteristic specimen of the practical sense by which England is supposed to be distinguished that she should persist to this hour in forcing upon a people with such feelings and such antecedents, her own idea of absolute property in the land."[4]

[1] April 24, 1861.
[2] June 26, 1861.
[3] *House of Commons*, April 19, 1861.
[4] J. S. Mill, *England and Ireland*, 1868.

Thirty years earlier Cornewall Lewis, in a penetrating study of the Irish disturbances, said that a deliberate system of crime will spread far when there is a real grievance to justify it.

" An ordinary murderer earns execration, but a Whiteboy who carries into effect the wishes of his own order, who executes a law of opinion, has nothing to fear but the power of the magistrates, for he knows that the sharper the pain he inflicts, the louder and more general will be the approbation of his fellows."

Ireland was thus in a state of civil war, and civil war is more brutal than any other kind of war.   Cornewall Lewis said in 1836 that the apparently wanton cruelty of the peasants betokened a mind thoroughly reckless about the infliction of pain.[1]   Mr. Yeats has observed of the scene in Synge's *Playboy of the Western World*, where the peasants listen to the youth describing how he had killed his father, " The countryman thinks the more terrible the crime the greater must the provocation have been."[2] That is a true and illuminating comment on the whole history of agrarian crime in Ireland.

There is one significant and interesting proof of the truth of this view that the Irish peasant was ruthless because he believed that he was averting or avenging crime.   Everybody remembers the description given by Thucydides of the demoralizing results of the plague in Athens, when man's life seemed to depend so entirely on outside chance that he became reckless and wicked.   The Famine had just the contrary result on Ireland.   It was marked by a great diminution of agrarian outrage.   The peasant, that is, was less violent when starving to death just because distress on such a portentous scale seemed due to something other than the immediate injustice of his rulers.   Could stronger proof be needed of the moral passion behind the agrarian movements that produced the crimes which spread such horror in England?   For there was no parallel in English politics to

[1] *Causes of Disturbances in Ireland*, p. 301.

For a picture of the later moonlighting in Ireland see George Moore's *Parnell and his Ireland*.

[2] *Dramatis Personae*, p. 187.

the intensity of this sense of wrong, a sense far more direct and concrete than any consciousness of injustice in the Chartist movements. The English workman found himself in a cold world in which his comfort was overlooked and his self respect wounded. But he had not seen, what men like Davitt had seen, women and children flung out upon the mountains, whose right to live in their cottages on their own land seemed to every Irish peasant as sacred as any right in history.

Lecky has remarked that conquering peoples are more given to callous cruelty, and oppressed and suffering peoples to vindictive cruelty. It is easy to see why there should be more vindictive cruelty in Ireland than in England, for though there were gross inequalities of justice in England, England was very far indeed from being a society in which private revenge had to take the place of a penal system. In Ireland an oppressive landlord was punished by the peasant or not punished at all. In such an atmosphere the punishment invented by private revenge is apt to be more terrible than the punishment inflicted elsewhere by public tribunals.

England then had less room for vindictive cruelty than Ireland. And if England was less vindictive, there was also a reason why she was less callous. The overgrowth of her town life has been by general admission a great disaster, both in the vices it has fostered and the virtues it has destroyed. But if England had too much town life, Ireland has had too little. For town life, no less than country life, serves a purpose in the education of man. The etymology of the word pagan is significant. It was first used to mark the contrast between the Christian towns with their gentler manners of the third, fourth and fifth centuries and the country districts where pagan cults survived.[1] It is in the country that men learn to like beauty and peace and a life lived at Nature's slow and quiet pace, but the stir and the excitement of common life in the city are a force for good as well as a force for evil. We may say that Nature taught the Greek to make the Parthenon, but it was in his common

---

[1] Ferdinand de Lot in *L'Histoire du Moyen Age*, p. 334.

life, after he had built the temples and theatres of Athens,

> that high her pensive towers
> might hallow their throng'd cities and, transfeaturing
> Nature's wild landscape to the sovranty of Mind,
> comfort his mortality with immortal grace[1]

that he learned to respect the humanity of Euripides.
Wordsworth found the same law in the Middle Ages.

> Around those Churches, gathered Towns
> Safe from the feudal Castle's haughty frowns ;
> Peaceful abodes, where Justice might uphold
> Her scales with even hand, and culture mould
> The heart to pity.

We can see the process of education in town life in the
immense difference between the English towns at the
beginning and the middle of the nineteenth century.   As
late as 1784, in the fury of the General Election of that year,
Fox's opponents at Dover relieved their feelings by burning a
fox alive.[2]   Bull baiting was abolished in 1835 after a
struggle in which Sheridan, a humane townsman, was on
one side and William Windham, a humane country
gentleman, on the other.   Lord Hobhouse, who was born
in 1819 and died in 1904, used to say that the change that
struck him most when he looked back over his life was the
improvement in the treatment of animals in London.   When
he was a boy the hunting of dogs and cats in the streets was
a common spectacle.   To-day there is a wide difference
between town and country sensibility.   The kindly country
squire who takes his children cub or hare hunting as a matter
of course cannot understand the sensitive townsman for whom
such enjoyments, to use a phrase of Burke's, dishonour the
name of a gentleman.   Dr. Gilbert Murray and Lord
Halifax are both highly civilized men, but pleasures which
one of them holds in the moral aversion in which they were

---

[1] *Testament of Beauty*, I, 628.

[2] Horace Walpole, who was a humanitarian (his was one of the first voices
raised against the use of chimney boys), wrote about this " savage meanness",
" I detest a country inhabited by such stupid barbarians." *Horace Walpole's
England*, p. 336.   Letter, April 11, 1784.

held by St. Thomas More, the other pursues and enjoys with the ardour of William Rufus.[1]

We can see the same difference in Ireland. *The Playboy of the Western World* opens with a scene in which the girl in the shebeen, describing the violent young man she admires, asks " Where now will you meet the like of Daneen Sullivan knocked the eye from a peeler, or Marcus Quin, God rest him, got six months for maiming ewes, and he a great warrant to tell stories of holy Ireland till he'd have the old women shedding down tears about their feet. Where will you find the like of them, I'm saying? " The great outcry against the play when it was put on the stage in Dublin was partly the shock given to the town mind by the crude ferocity of this raw peasant life: " maiming ewes " for a political grudge was to the townsmen of this age like the burning of a fox at Dover a century earlier. Some of Synge's critics complained that such a passage did harm because it confirmed the English in their view that the Irish were cruel. Yeats answered that Ireland had suffered because Irishmen had examined every impression of Irish life to see what was its effect on the political claims of Ireland. Synge was the rushing up of the buried fire, " an explosion of all that had been denied or refused, a furious impartiality in indifferent turbulent sorrow." He was like Burns saying what the people did not want to have said.[2] If the play had only been seen by peasants there would have been no such outcry. Davitt, who had the strongest dislike of the mutilation of animals in the agrarian war, had lived as boy and young man in a town. The dislike of the Irish peasant was thus partly the result of ignorance and prejudice, but it was partly the horror felt by a people with these higher standards of humanity towards the cruelty practised in an implacable agrarian war.

Davitt, moving among English workmen, knew that the ordinary Englishman was horrified by the Irish outrages.

---

[1] If Arrian the friend of Hadrian, who wrote on hunting as well as on the wars of Alexander, is typical of his age, there was more sensibility among hunters in the second century than there is among harriers and beaglers in the twentieth century.

[2] *Dramatis Personae*, pp. 135–138.

Parnell, on the other hand, never thought the indignation
sincere. He looked on the English as an insensitive people
who affected in this instance an emotion useful to their
political designs. In his early days in the House of Commons he had led a crusade against flogging in the army.
Chamberlain had supported him, but he found it a hard
battle. Harcourt and Hartington opposed him. In the
end he won his case after one of his followers had compelled
the Minister of War to produce a " cat " in the Library so
that members could examine this instrument of torture.[1]
And as a politician he saw around him an exploiting world,
with little conscience or remorse about the cruelties it
inflicted. Imperialism was not troubled in fashionable
circles with much discomfort of mind about its victims.
Parnell knew what shadows were thrown over the splendid
wealth that England drew from the distant tropics; how
many a proud Englishman was like the Florentine brothers
in Keats' *Isabella*, for whom men and women had suffered
from " stinging whip " " in torched mines and noisy
factories," for whom the Ceylon diver " went naked to the
hungry shark," for whom " did seethe

> A thousand men in troubles wide and dark;
> Half ignorant, they turned an easy wheel
> That set sharp racks at work, to pinch and peel."

  Parnell could not understand why the Irish outrages
shocked men and women who apparently did not care what
happened in the mines and plantations that gave them
wealth and a great figure in the world. He would perhaps
have agreed with the pessimist who said that men are always
beasts of prey, murdering each other. The only difference
science has made is that whereas they used to murder their
fellows for a bit of raw fish, the fish to-day is cooked.[2] For
the great polished societies that were spreading their empires
over the defenceless wealth of Africa the fish was cooked,
but there were ruder societies in which the fish was still raw,
and this evicting and moon-lighting Ireland was one of them.
Parnell, a hard man himself, hardened in this atmosphere of

[1] Joan Haslip, *Parnell*, p. 92.
[2] Faguet, *Politicians and Moralists of the Nineteenth Century*, p. 258.

war, did not understand the kind of impression the second sort of society made upon the first. The crimes behind the successes of the Rhodesian empire makers were known to few but the crimes of the Irish agrarian war were known in every village in England.

The causes of Irish cruelty are plain enough to anybody who studies Irish history. The effects on the English temper are not difficult to understand, for the public opinion of one country on the condition or character of another is rarely based on the understanding of the past. Unhappily for the prospects of reconciliation between the two countries the neglect of Irish grievances due to this misunderstanding turned Ireland more and more against England. If England thought Ireland a footpad, Ireland thought England a monster. The state of mind of Ireland was described by O'Connor Morris, *Times* correspondent in Ireland in 1870, an Irishman who, though he supported the Land Act of 1870, was a strong and active opponent of Gladstone's later legislation. In 1870 he gave a picture of Irish discontent. He explained that nearly three-quarters of the soil of Ireland was held by 573,000 persons, of whom three-quarters were a mere peasantry,

" disabled from the very nature of the case from making a perfectly free contract, and bound to the soil as the source of existence.". . ."An effort of the imagination is required to comprehend the sentiment of the peasant who knows that the whole force of law may be used to destroy his rights iniquitously and work his ruin; he will be discontented in proportion to the weakness of the checks that he can successfully oppose; he can never enjoy complete security, and social disturbance inevitably follows. Yet the State still maintains this vicious system; the power—nay the armed force of government—is employed to vindicate that which is sometimes an exhibition of extreme wrong; and the authority of the Crown is invoked to support what may be acts of mere spoliation."[1]

It is often surprising to a student of history to see how much the statesmen of an age may misread or neglect the problems of their time without any sensational disaster.

[1] *The Land Question of Ireland*, by W. O'Connor Morris.

The fate that rules the world seems sometimes too indulgent to expect very much of human nature. Unhappily there is one invariable exception. In the relations of England and Ireland fate has shown no mercy to blind or dilatory politics. Englishmen, looking at the agrarian history described in these chapters, believed first that the true remedy of Irish distress was clearance and depopulation, secondly that this remedy had been applied by nature at the Famine, with results that were as beneficent in their effect as they were painful in their incidence. The application of these ideas had a consequence of which only a few Englishmen had fleeting presentiments. It created Fenian Ireland, and Fenian America. To these events Lecky attributed " the savage hatred of England that animates great bodies of Irishmen on either side of the Atlantic."

Lavaleye, in his study of the Irish agrarian problem, pointed out that the agrarian war was made on landlord, or agent, or peasant who broke the peasants law, whether English or Irish, Catholic or Protestant. The first victim of the Land League was a Catholic priest. If English statesmen had known how to remedy the grievances that had brought this rival peasant law, peasant discipline, and peasant crime into power, Ireland might never have passed to the second stage of widespread racial hatred. It was the neglect or mishandling of this mass of misery that made English government intolerable to an agrarian unpolitical population. Some Irishmen hated England from their knowledge of distant history, history so ancient as to be mixed here and there with legend. The peasants hated her from their knowledge of more recent history, history of which they and their children were the victims.

This hostility found by chance an immediate outlet. For the great flight from death by hunger in Ireland, which made such an impression on the world, was followed by the American Civil War, and when that war ended thousands of Irish soldiers were let loose, ready to turn their arms and their passions against the people under whose callous rule Irishmen had had to choose between death or exile. Thus everything conspired to make the war of peasant upon the landlord a war of Ireland against England. Fenianism was able to call the New World to redress the balance of the Old, with results that embarrassed English politics at home and abroad for half a century. During the Great War, as we know from the letters of our Ambassador in the United States, victory or defeat for the Allies seemed at times to turn on the consequences of the great English failure in the 'thirties, 'forties, 'fifties, and 'sixties of last century.

Down to the Famine the problem of Irish order was confined to Ireland. In 1866 the Fenians of New York invaded Canada; a Fenian schooner scuttled a British schooner; in 1867 the war was brought to London by an explosion at Clerkenwell Prison, the first of a series of similar outrages. Yet all this violence was not as important as the steady pressure of the Fenian vote on American politics. England, finding Ireland a domestic anxiety, had turned her into an international danger.

And the England that so acted was at the height of her self confidence; never had her statesmen been so sure, with wealth increasing before their eyes as never before in history, that they had mastered all the secrets of good government and progress.

" I entertain a prejudice," said one of the most distinguished spokesmen of this dominant school, " derived from Scotland and adopted by Adam Smith, that a man is at liberty to do what he likes with his own, and that having land, it is not unreasonable that he should be free to let his land to a person of full age upon the terms on which they shall mutually agree. That I believe to be reason and good political economy."

So spoke Robert Lowe in March 1868. A statesman who could offer this reflection as wisdom's last word, on the problem described in these chapters, can only be compared to Lauderdale who, half a century earlier, resisting a mild Factory Bill, had argued that an employer was the best judge of the different degrees of strength of his workmen, and the most likely to avoid overworking them, the people he described as workmen being children of nine and ten.

To the average Englishman the stages through which

Ireland had changed from a public nuisance to a public danger all marked the ferocity and perversity of the Irish character. Abroad a different view was taken. Mazzini and Metternich alike, bitterly as they hated each other's views, were touched by the spectacle of the great Irish exodus.

" They come and tell us," said Mazzini, " that it is a well ordered state of society in which, for lack of a few potatoes, thousands and even millions are reduced to starvation." " Ireland," said Metternich, " is passing forth. It is wending its way to the North American States . . . to ask for an empty space of ground."[1] To the optimism of men like Lowe Lavaleye put a startling view, " Suppose l'Irlande perdue au milieu de l'Océan, mais occupée comme le Norvege, par des paysans propriétaires; je réponds que l'île serait plus riche, plus heureuse qu'aujourdhui."

Between an England so confident in her ignorance and misunderstanding and an Ireland so deep in passion and misery perpetual conflict was inevitable. Peace could only be made when England found a leader who could see Ireland, not as England but as Europe saw her. No man started with a mind more British in its economic setting than the great pupil of Peel who kept the House of Commons under his spell for five hours when he expounded the first of his famous Budgets in 1853. We have now to discover what other influences guided and formed the politics of the man whose first gift to Ireland was the income tax, and to see how the lessons that Gladstone, the British economist, learned from Gladstone, the European scholar, made him the prophet and the champion of her freedom.

[1] Berkeley, *Italy in the making*, p. 164.

CHAPTER V

If we put aside Cobden, whose large outlook and persuasive genius England lost by his early death in 1865, there were only two men in English politics who combined with power over men's minds the quality that was most needed for the solution of the Irish problem. To change the English temper towards Ireland, to shake fundamental views of property and economics, to overcome all the prejudices that estrange men divided by race, religion, and history, to interest Parliament in duties to which it was indifferent, this was a task in which no man could hope to succeed if his mind never moved outside the English orbit. The first qualification then that this task demanded was detachment from the English atmosphere.

Disraeli, as we have seen, possessed this quality, but he lacked others that were essential. He was fighting an uphill battle within his party when first he tried his hand on Ireland. By the time he had power in his grasp old age was stealing upon him; his first enthusiasms had faded; he had thrown himself into new plans which cost less effort and brought greater glory. The man who had called for revolution in the 'forties blamed Gladstone's first Land Bill in 1870, which to-day is only criticized as too gentle in its treatment, as giving to confiscation the sanction of law.

The other public man who had this quality was Gladstone. For if Disraeli stood out among the men of his age by a special experience and outlook, Gladstone too lived in a world of his own. He was, like Disraeli, an enigma to his age. He had affinities with Peel, with Graham, with Aberdeen, with Shaftesbury, with Cobden, and with Bright, but as soon as you name any one of them, differences not less striking than those affinities leap into the mind. To understand his course in Irish politics it is necessary to have a clear impression of his character and his ruling ideas.

There are some statesmen of whom you may say that the clue to their conduct is to be found, not in their speeches on politics, but in the use they make of their leisure. This is emphatically true of Gladstone. It would be possible to explain Disraeli's career, though not of course to do it justice, without a study of his novels. Gladstone, on the other hand, is unintelligible without a study of his mind as it revealed itself on paper. As a speaker he was often obscure and mystifying. " What a marvellous talent is this," said Cobden, after listening to the speech in which he explained in 1845 why he had resigned from Peel's Government on the Maynooth Grant, " here have I been sitting listening with pleasure for an hour to his explanation, and yet I know no more why he left the Government than before he began."[1] His style in writing was often difficult, but a mere glance at his published works will show where his main interests were to be found. In politics a man cannot always choose his tasks, but his diversions are his own. Their character, their influence, and, above all, the spirit in which they are pursued, reveal the man who is often half hidden beneath the surface he presents to the House of Commons. This does not mean, of course, that a man like Gladstone is one thing in private and another in public. Far from it. It means that the Gladstone of the House of Commons and the Gladstone on the public platform, whatever the task or excitement of the moment, must be viewed and examined in the light thrown on his character by the subjects he studies in his library, and the purpose to which he puts them.

The first thing that must strike anybody who looks at Gladstone's writings, or reads his private letters and his diaries, is that he is as much interested in religion as in politics. A clergyman's life had been his first choice. " I am willing to persuade myself," he wrote to his brother in 1830, " that in spite of other longings which I often feel, my heart is prepared to yield other hopes and other desires for this—of

[1] Morley, *Life of Gladstone*, Vol. I, p. 278.

being permitted to be the humblest of those who may be commissioned to set before the eyes of man, still great even in his ruins, the magnificence and the glory of Christian truth. Especially as I feel that my temperament is so excitable, that I should fear giving up my mind to other subjects which have ever proved sufficiently alluring to me, and which I fear would make my life a fever of unsatisfied longings and expectations."[1]

After he had entered politics he regarded himself as first of all the servant of the Church. In 1845 he wrote to his wife:

" . . . I have a growing belief, that I shall never be enabled to do much good for the Church in Parliament (if at all!) except after having seemed first a traitor to it and being reviled as such. I mean that it is now for the highest interest of the Church to give gold for freedom—but there are so many who will not allow the gold to be touched even though they value freedom and so many more who will have the Church to keep all the gold that it may be the price and the pledge of her slavery. Ireland, Ireland! that cloud in the west, that coming storm, the minister of God's retribution upon cruel and inveterate and but half-atoned injustice! Ireland forces upon us these great social and great religious questions—God grant that we may have courage—to look them in the face and to work through them. Were they over—were the path of the Church clear before her as a body able to take her trial before God and the world upon the performance of her work as His organ for the recovery of our country—how joyfully would I retire from the barren exhausting strife of merely political contention. I do not think that you would be very sorrowful? As to ambition in its ordinary sense, we are spared the chief part of its temptations."[2]

In 1874, when he retired from the leadership of the Liberal party, he wrote to his wife: " I am convinced that the welfare of mankind does not now depend on the State or the world of politics; the real battle is being fought in the world of thought. . . ."[3] In 1878 he published seven volumes in which he had put together articles that he had written in the last thirty-six years. Of these volumes three

[1] Morley, *op. cit.*, Vol. I, p. 83.
[2] Baden, October 12, 1845. See A. Tilney Bassett, *Gladstone to his Wife*, p. 64.
[3] A. Tilney Bassett, *op. cit.*, p. 202.

and a half are devoted entirely and directly to religion.

Moreover in writing on religion he defended this, or attacked that, without any regard to his interests or convenience as a politician, or to the interests or convenience of the party of which he was the leader. His religious controversies injured him as a politician, but it is clear that he never gave a thought to their consequences to his career. His passionate attacks on the Vatican Decrees in 1874 are a good illustration. In 1869 he had disestablished the Irish Church, and excited the bitter hostility of the great body of churchmen both in Ireland and in England who were not wise enough to appreciate the effects of that measure, but he threw away the support that this brought him from Irish Catholics by an outburst from which his best friends sought to dissuade him. In 1877 when he paid his first and only visit to Ireland, the *Times* could describe him as one of the most unpopular of English statesmen. " The author of the abortive University Bill, the antagonist of Vaticanism was better remembered in Ireland than the Minister who framed and introduced the Irish Church and Irish Land Bills."[1]

Gladstone then put religion first among his interests. But what did he mean by religion? It is here that we come to his fundamental and guiding principle in politics. He was essentially European where most of his countrymen were English; catholic where they were insular. He regarded himself as engaged in a conflict between violence and justice, between wrong and right, between truth and error, not on the stage of the life of England but on the larger stage of the life of Europe. He would have said with St. Augustine, " remota itaque justitia quid sunt regna nisi magna latrocinia," but he would not have given the words St. Augustine's meaning. For St. Augustine meant that all civil States are founded on wrongdoing, and all power in the world based on injustice, and he quoted, in support of his view, the apt

[1]November 13, 1877. Gladstone wrote to his wife on February 17, 1875, " Cardinal Cullen has, I think in a Christian spirit, brought me into his Lenten Pastoral and desires his people to pray for me—that I may become sensible of the wrong I have done the Pope and the Church." Tilney Bassett, *op. cit.*, p. 212.

retort of the pirate who told Alexander the Great that he was called a pirate, because he robbed with a small ship, whereas Alexander was called an emperor, because he robbed with a great fleet. St. Augustine had in mind that contrast between civil kingdoms and the kingdom of God which, as we shall see, had so saddening a significance to Newman. Gladstone, on the other hand, believed that civil States could be taught to obey the law of God, and he dramatized politics as a perpetual struggle between violence and justice for the allegiance of men's minds and wills.

To that conflict he gave his ardour as a writer, his industry as a scholar, his power as an orator and leader of men. Let anybody, who doubts whether this was the driving force in his life of energy and passion, note how rarely it happened that he was neither working in politics, nor writing in his study, for a cause that touched one or other of the issues that this conflict raised in his active and excited mind. This is the spirit that dominates and guides all his voluminous writings on religion and culture. A man with his sense of duty and purpose could never have devoted all the time and energy that he spent on Homer and Hellenism, unless he had regarded them as indissolubly connected with his ideas of truth and religion. In 1858 he published three large volumes on Homer. The reader who examines the diary of his life given in Morley's volumes will note that there are no less than eighteen years after 1858 in which it is recorded that he published either a book or an article on Homer or some Greek topic.[1] The only other subject to which he devoted as much time was Christianity, either in its conflicts with science, or its internal debates and divisions. To understand Gladstone the politician, Gladstone the man with the European sense, or, as we might now call it, the

---

[1] Gladstone was sensitive about the complaint that was sometimes heard that he neglected his duties for Homer. Writing to Delane, Editor of *The Times* on February 4, 1874, about a complimentary article that had touched on his work on Homer he said " My translation of the Shield of Achilles was executed, I think in 1866 and 1867 and some time before the formation of the Government. Slight as the result may appear or be, it cost me a good deal of labour and I have given no such labour during the last five years to anything except the public service." On another occasion he wrote a similar letter to R. H. Hutton.

League of Nations sense, we must study his treatment of these subjects and their influence on his mind.

Gladstone's work on Homer does not receive much serious attention from scholars. This is not surprising. For scholars are interested in his work as scholarship, and viewed in that light his studies are dismissed as eccentric, extravagant, full of the strangest fancies and illusions. But Mr. Herbert Paul in his brilliant biography, after noting some of his fantasies and showing how grotesque they look to the scientific student of language and mythology, added with truth that the work none the less remains " a marvellous example of deep and even sublime meditation upon all that is suggested by the greatest epic poems of the world." It is those meditations that give the clue to his European sense. If we are considering Gladstone as a Homeric scholar, we are chiefly concerned to know whether he understood the Homeric poems; if we are considering him as a man holding passionately views that distinguish him from others, we are chiefly concerned to know how he understood them. For if these books are examined, not as contributions to Homeric scholarship, but as revelations of his outlook on history, they help to explain how, why, and where, he differed not only from men who opposed him in politics, but from men who supported him.

In the noble speech that he made on Gladstone's death Lord Salisbury said that politics hardly provided a parallel to the example he had set of a great Christian man. Nobody who studies his books on Homer will doubt that he has a place of his own as a Christian scholar. There is so much complexity in his character, such casuistry in the use he made of his mind, that it is dangerous to attempt to describe him simply in any aspect, but we may perhaps give a just impression of that special place if we say that he was a Christian as earnest as the Evangelicals whose fold he had quitted, who put the Greeks where they put the Jews, and Homer where they put the Old Testament. For he held that God had used the Jews to teach man how man should treat God, and the Greeks to teach man how man should treat man. The Mosaic books were intended to present a picture of human society in one master relation, not a picture of human society " drawn at large." That was the function of the Greeks, and of Homer in particular. To the Jews was delivered spiritual truth; imaginative culture, the education of the intellectual soul, the development of civilized politics, these were the province of the Greeks.

" It was the Greek mind transferred, without doubt, in some part through Italy, but yet only transferred, and still Greek both in origin and in much of its essence, in which was shaped and tempered the original mould of the modern European civilization. I speak now of civilization as a thing distinct from religion, but destined to combine and coalesce with it. The power derived from this source was to stand in subordinate conjunction with the Gospel, and to contribute its own share towards the training of mankind."[1]

Christianity after the Advent had

" marched for fifteen hundred years at the head of human civilization. . . . Its learning has been the learning of the world, its art the art of the world, its genius the genius of the world. . . . Before the Advent, it was quite otherwise. The treasure of Divine Revelation was then hidden in a napkin; it was given to a people who were almost forbidden to impart it ; at least, of whom it was simply required, that they should preserve it without variation. They had no world-wide vocation committed to them; they lay ensconced in a country which was narrow and obscure; obscure not only with reference to the surpassing splendour of Greece and Rome, but in comparison with Assyria, or Persia, or Egypt. They have not supplied the Christian ages with laws and institutions, arts and sciences, with the chief models of greatness in genius or in character.[2] The Providence

---

[1] W. E. Gladstone, *Homer and the Homeric Age*, Vol. I, p. 5.

[2] There was a special and dramatic significance in this choice. " An un-honoured undistinguished race, simply elected to be the receivers of the Divine Word, and having remained its always stiffnecked and almost reluctant guardians, may best have suited the aim of Almighty Wisdom; because the medium, through which the most precious gifts were conveyed, was pale and colourless, instead of being one flushed with the splendours of Empire, Intellect and Fame." Vol. II, p 533. The Emperor Julian drew from this a very different moral. He said that if the Christians were right, God had left mankind in gross ignorance for millions of years except for a paltry race inhabiting part of Palestine. If he was the God of all, why had he so treated the rest of mankind? What reason had they for gratitude? Labriolle, *La réaction païenne*, p. 391.

of God committed this work to others; and to Homer seems to have been intrusted the first, which was perhaps, all things considered, also the most remarkable stage of it."[1]

It is easy to see what importance classical civilization held, on this view of history, in Gladstone's Christianity. But this does not exhaust its services to Christendom. For Gladstone thought not only that the Greeks had left mankind lessons, not to be learnt from the Bible, which it could use after Christianity had brought its full light into the world. He held also that Christianity itself, in its early history, had been saved by the influence of the Greek tradition from some dangerous and blighting errors. For of the early ascetics, like Tertullian, who, as Gibbon said, " showed no more indulgence to a tragedy of Euripides than to a combat of gladiators," Gladstone wrote that, if Greek civilization had not come to the rescue, this school " would have placed the kingdom of grace in permanent and hopeless discord with the kingdoms of nature, reason, truth and beauty, kingdoms established by the same Almighty Hand." Gladstone discussed this aspect of early Christianity in the remarkable Address he gave at Edinburgh University in 1865 on the " Place of Ancient Greece in the Providential Order." Christianity meant for Gladstone not merely the truth to be found in the pages of the Bible, but a whole tradition of art and letters and politics, chiefly Greek and Roman in achievement and experiment, illuminated and guided by the Christian revelation, and itself contributing to its power.

Thus Gladstone wrote this vast book with a religious purpose. When he was a boy, Homer was read at school, but not much studied at the Universities. Gladstone was passionately anxious to persuade Oxford that Homer should be studied " for his theology, history, ethics, politics, for his never-ending lessons upon manners, arts and society. . . . He is second to none of the poets of Greece as the poet of boys; but he is far advanced before them all, even before Æschylus and Aristophanes, as the poet of men."[2] Society,

---

[1] *op. cit.*, Vol. II, p. 529 f.
[2] *op. cit.*, Vol. I, p. 20.

he said, rested on four words γάμος, ὅρκος, θέμις, θεός and in
these volumes he travels over " the great map of humanity
that Homer unfolds to our gaze," tracing the fortunes and
adventures of ideas and institutions in which those four words
find form and colour, expression and life. Nowhere, perhaps,
in literature, so daring and wilful is his ingenuity, so passionate
his ardour, so superb his rhetoric, have the sublime and the
ridiculous been thrown together on such a splendid stage.

Modern scholarship has of course destroyed the foundations
on which Gladstone built some of the most cherished of his
fantasies, but the reader who is watching the development of
his political mind will be struck by the affinities between the
spirit of his reflections on the morals of Homeric society with
the spirit of Murray's *Rise of the Greek Epic*. Like everybody
else he finds in Homer a strange blend of evil and good,
brutality and gentleness, the savage and the civilized. Of
these discrepancies in Homer's Heaven he gives an explanation that seemed less remarkable to his age than it would to
ours, for he held that Olympus with its habits and morals
and ceremonies represented a survival of " the truth brought
by our first parents from Paradise " overlaid and corrupted
by depraved human fables, partly imported, partly invented,
by the Greeks. Here his Christian interpretation puts him
in direct contrast to the modern view in which Olympus
becomes less, instead of more, disreputable when the Greeks
begin to think more about its distinguished inhabitants.[1]
The discrepancies on earth, on the other hand, he explained
not by the sins of the Greeks but by their virtue. For
Homeric society was a vigorous civilization in its early
youth, very close in time and space to a savage world.

" The Homeric gentleman, with his civilization, stood, in respect
to barbarism, like him who voyages by sea,

> ' digitis a morte remotus
> quattuor aut septem ';

[1] He found in this Heaven traces of the doctrine of the Trinity and of the
tradition that the seed of the woman was to crush the serpent's head. He was
distressed that the institution of the Sabbath had faded out altogether, but he
pointed out that it is quickly forgotten by Christians who settle in heathen lands
or those whose energies are absorbed in a ceaseless conflict with the yet untamed
powers of nature.

only the thickness of the plank is between him and the wilderness which he has left: and if passion makes a breach, the mood of the wild beast reappears."[1]

It is this part of the work that concerns us in examining Gladstone's outlook. None of Gladstone's speculations about Homer, about his date, about his geography, about his gods, or even about his Greeks, affect the significance or the value of his description and discussion of this society.

Burke said that Homer gave the Trojans the virtues that make a man loved, and the Greeks those that make a man admired. Gladstone admitted that " the amiable affections, with the sense of humanity, if not the principles of honour and justice, are exhibited in the detail of the *Iliad* as prevailing among the Trojans, little less than among the Greeks."[2] But he finds that the Greeks

" had laid more firmly than their adversaries those great corner stones of human society, which are named in their language, θέμις, ὅρκος, and γάμος.   In the polity of Troy we find more scope for impulse, less for deliberation and persuasion; more weight given to those elements of authority which do not depend on our free will and intelligence, less to those which do; less of organisation and of diversity, less firmness and tenacity of tissue, in the structure of the community."[3]

This is why the Greeks were chosen by Providence to give the first lessons in politics to Europe.

Looking for those lessons, Gladstone is just as ardent and as resourceful as the Christians of another school who shut themselves up with the Book of Daniel or the Book of Revelation to find some special light on the problems of their own day. It is here that we find the Gladstone with the League of Nations mind, concerned, before everything else, for the great corner stones of human society. Few will read these pages unmoved as they find him marking in

---

[1] Vol. II, p. 451. " Neither the Greeks nor the Trojans appear to have been ferocious in the treatment of enemies. The extreme point to which they go is that of giving no quarter; but they never, even in the exasperation of battle, inflict torture with their weapons. The immolation of twelve Trojan youths over the dead Patroclus is doubtless cruel; but it falls far short of what the passions of war have produced in other times and countries. With the manner of inflicting death, passion never has to do." Vol. II, p. 450.

[2] *ibid.*, Vol. III, p. 193.   [3] *ibid.*, Vol. III, p. 247.

Homeric custom " the germ of a law of Nations," in
Homeric debate the beginning of Parliamentary government,
in Homeric praise of the orator the sign of a society in
which the renown of wisdom could rival the renown to be
won in war, discovering with true Gladstonian art and
skill the large part that public spirit plays in the wrath of
Achilles, explaining why piracy, which resembled the forays
of border warfare between England and Scotland, was
looked on with indulgence, dwelling on the significance of
aidôs, " too comprehensive and too delicate for our rendering
by a single term in the English, perhaps in any modern,
tongue," describing " the touching contrast between the
chastity of Helen's mind and the unlawful conditions in
which she lived," or showing how far the women of Homer
excelled the women of the Old Testament in dignity and the
respect they compelled in a rough age. " She is
importuned," he says of Penelope among the angry suitors,
" but she is not insulted. She feels horror and aversion
but she has no cause for fear. Such, in the morning of
Greek life, was the reverence that hedged a woman, as she
sat alone and undefended in the midst of powerful and
abandoned men."

Nobody can look upon this work as an intellectual
exercise, the diversion of a man of affairs who is interested in
scholarship or science. It should rather be compared with
the work of a hermit in his cell.[1] It is as serious, as absorbing,
as passionate a task, as the work of St. Jerome on the
Scriptures or that of St. Augustine on *De Civitate Dei*. The
reader will find here the whole of Gladstone; the eloquence
of which the spell still lives for those who turn to such
passages as the closing sentences of the first speech on the
Home Rule Bill; the mastery of detail that never slipped
over the complexities of the Budget, or the impenetrable

[1] On March 30, 1875, Gladstone wrote in his diary that his prospective
work would not be Parliamentary. " My tie will be slight to an assembly with
whose tendencies I am little in harmony at the present time; nor can I flatter
myself that what is called the public out-of-doors is more sympathetic. But
there is much to be done with the pen, all bearing much on high and sacred
things, for even Homeric study, as I view it, is in this very sense of high importance, and what lies beyond this is concerned directly with the great subject of
Belief."

riddles of the Irish Land system; the delight in pursuing bypaths in discussion that entertained the House of Commons and embarrassed the Whips; the ingenuity, the refinements, some will say the casuistry, that could find a defence for the most equivocal of his actions and the most palpable of the errors of his colleagues.   Of this stupendous effort we may say, as of his speeches on the Bulgarian atrocities, or his speeches on his Irish policy

> Potuit quae plurima virtus
> Esse, fuit:

for there had gone into this task, as into those, all the strength of his Christian passion.

There were better scholars than Gladstone among his contemporaries.   There were men whose feeling for religion was as deep and passionate as his own.   But he stood apart in sharing the religious feeling of Wilberforce and Shaftesbury and bringing within its glowing heat the culture of Greece and Rome.   Many a scholar has been moved as he was by the tender passages in Homer, Andromache with her child, Argos dying as he catches the footfall of his long lost master, by the delicate beauty of the meeting of Odysseus and Nausicaa, or the deep pathos of the speech of Achilles to Priam, but few scholars read those passages as he read them with the sense that these scenes were the handiwork of God himself, painting the soft light of a Christian dawn.[1]

In some respects there is a close resemblance between Shaftesbury and Gladstone.   Though one was Evangelical and the other High Church, they used the same language about the government of the world and the relations of man and God.   But there was this important difference between them.   Shaftesbury's Christianity, like that of most of his contemporaries, was based on the Bible.[2]   A mind fed on

---

[1] See e.g., his incisive and lively attack on Milton's *Paradise Regained* in his *Place of Ancient Greece in the Providential Order*.

[2] The difference is illustrated by their views of Seeley's *Ecce Homo*. Shaftesbury spoke of it at a public meeting as "the most pestilential book ever vomited forth from the jaws of Hell."   Gladstone welcomed it as " a strong constructive book on the Christian system " and described it as " this noble book."   Letter to Macmillan, December 25, 1865, Lathbury, *Gladstone's Correspondence on Church and Religion* 2, 88.

the Bible is not thereby drawn to Europe, or the European tradition or to European history, with any special or significant sympathy.[1] On the contrary. The Dopper Boer, the ardent Orangeman, find no reason in their study of the Old Testament for thinking that they have common interests with Christians whose Christianity is the thing they dislike most about them. Even in cultivated minds the Bible is in this sense often an insulating influence, and Gladstone observed with justice in his essay on Italy and her Church that " in matters of religion poets might still with truth sing of the penitus toto divisos orbe Britannos." Gladstone's Christianity, on the other hand, was based not on the Bible alone or chiefly but on Homer, Aristotle, Augustine, Dante, and Butler. Of these the two to whom he devoted most study and time were Homer and Dante. A man whose Christianity draws its breath in such an atmosphere lives in the heart and mind of Europe.

Gladstone was brought up as an Evangelical, and he kept certain Evangelical qualities to the end of his life. Whether this large interest in the history of civilization was a cause or an effect of his escape from Evangelicalism, whether, that is, looking on history in this light be renounced its narrow spirit, or whether as he reflected on Christianity in a larger setting as a catholic European culture, he read Homer with a new understanding, is not clear. But it is clear that his Christian interpretation of classical culture, and his catholic interpretation of Christian truth, were closely connected. To understand the connection between his Hellenism and his Christianity it is useful to glance at the description given by Morley of the attitude of Mill to the Oxford movement. For Mill, widely as he differed from Gladstone in many respects, resembled him in his admiration for Hellenism, and his view of its place in the history of civilization.

" He used to tell us," says Morley, " that the Oxford theologians had done for England something like what Guizot, Villemain, Michelet, Cousin had done a little earlier for France; they had opened, broadened, deepened the issues and meanings of European history; they had reminded us that history is

[1] See Fisher, *History of Europe*, II, 640.

European; that it is quite unintelligible if treated as merely local."[1]

The impulse to a wider view of Christianity than that in which he had been bred was first stirred in Gladstone's mind by a visit to Rome in 1830, when his imagination was seized, as he put it, by the idea of the Church as " a sublime construction, based throughout upon historical fact uplifting the idea of the community in which we live." This impression was strengthened by his friendship first with Manning and Hope, and then with Acton and Döllinger.

The way in which the Oxford Movement influenced him is specially significant. He described it in later life when giving an account of his movement from Evangelicalism to " a Catholic position."

" I do not mean here to touch upon the varied stages of this long journey, and I shall only at present say that the Oxford Tracts had little to do with it; nothing at all to do with it, I should be inclined to say, except in so far as it was partly, and very considerably, due to them that Catholicism, so to speak, was in the air, and was exercising an influence on the religious frame of men without their knowing it; just as I have very long suspected, perhaps I ought to say believed, that Seneca, Aurelius, and Epictetus were largely influenced in the tone of their works by Christianity in the air, to which they probably would have denied, and did not indeed know, that they were in any way indebted."[2]

It is clear from this that Gladstone, like Mill, was attracted to the Oxford Movement by his European sense. His feeling for unity was displayed in one of the last acts of his life, a letter to Pope Leo XIII in 1896.

Thus Gladstone was both European and religious in a sense in which those terms could not be applied to any of his contemporaries. Almost all the important acts of his career are prompted by this sense for moral law in the public life of Europe, and this feeling for its history. In 1840 he called down the strong displeasure of the House of Commons by the violence with which he attacked our policy and proceedings in China, and the reckless outbursts into which his

---

[1] Morley, op. cit., I, 163.
[2] Lathbury, *Gladstone's Correspondence on Church and Religion*, Vol. I, p. 265.

indignation tempted him. In 1850 he published his famous Letters about the Naples Prisons, appealing to the conscience of conservative Europe. In the same year he had his great encounter with Palmerston over Don Pacifico, whose wrongs at the hands of a Greek mob inspired Palmerston to speak " from the dusk of one day to the dawn of the next " on the modern meaning of *Civis Romanus sum.* In 1854 he supported the Crimean War on the ground that Russia had taken into her own hands a question that should be settled not by a single Power but by Europe. In 1855 he opposed the further prosecution of the war on the ground that it had changed its character, and become a selfish enterprise in which the welfare of Europe was forgotten. In 1856 he opposed Palmerston's China War. In 1857 he attacked the English view that the project of the Suez Canal should be obstructed, because it threatened British interests. His decision to join the Liberal party, as Mr. Guedalla observed, sprang from his sympathy with Palmerston and Russell as friends of Italian unity, and his opposition to the Austrophil policy of Derby and Disraeli. During that long struggle he earned the gratitude and lasting friendship of the Italian people. He offered a characteristic solution for the Pope's difficulties, proposing that he should give up the Temporal Power and that he should be sheltered in regard to his external position by a European guarantee.[1] In 1870 he

---

[1] See his elaborate plan for making the Pope suzerain in the Papal States with the King of Italy as ruler, and a European Act to which all the signatories of the Treaty of Vienna should be parties along with the Italian Kingdom. "Any breach of the stipulations by the King of Italy should be a *casus belli* for any of these Powers." This long memorandum dated March 27, 1863, is given in Lathbury's *Gladstone's Correspondence on Church and Religion*, II, 391. On June 22 of that year he wrote to Döllinger. "In the autumn of 1859, I think the British Cabinet would have been very glad to use any influence it possessed for the purpose of securing to the Pope the Suzerainty of all his States, with competent revenue, and European Guarantees for his independence and with the King of Italy exercising, as his permanent and hereditary Vicegerent, the ordinary functions of government. But it is now, I apprehend, too late for such a measure." Lathbury Vol. II, p. 34. On September 18, 1870 (the month that the Italian troops entered Rome) he wrote to Manning that he had always been in favour of this plan. Of his attitude to this question he could say with justice what few other English supporters of the Italian claims could have said, " It is with no Protestant, no Anglican eye, that I look upon the present condition of Italy." Letter to Manning, October 15, 1864, Lathbury II, 35.

protected Belgium in the Franco-German War, and he wished to mobilize the neutral Powers against the annexation of Alsace-Lorraine. Throughout the long and difficult struggle over the Alabama Incident he held his Government together, through one crisis after another, and brought England to accept an unpopular award. In 1877 he left his studies to resist Disraeli's Eastern policy, and he fought the election of 1880 on his conception of a foreign policy based on respect for public law.

Thus he judged every question with the mind of a man to whom Europe was a family of nations, a family in which England had her place, and her share of duty and of pride. For he saw the moral relations of peoples more vividly than any of his contemporaries in England or in Europe. Consequently, when his view of the claims of public law demanded a sacrifice of national pride or national interest, he acted as if something that existed only in his imagination could be made a moral force in the world by the power of a noble example. Thus the words Alabama[1] and Majuba,[2] which cost him thousands of votes at the time, and, so far as the second was concerned, a great deal in reputation then and afterwards, represented not only what was best in his

[1] " Although I may think the sentence was harsh in its extent, and unjust in its basis, I regard the fine imposed on this country as dust in the balance compared with the moral value of the example set when these two great nations of England and America—which are among the most fiery and the most jealous in the world with regard to anything that touches national honour—went in peace and concord before a judicial tribunal rather than resort to the arbitrament of the sword." Gladstone, House of Commons, June 15, 1880. See Morley, Vol. II, p. 393.

[2] One observer noted at the time the significance of Majuba. Sir Charles Gavan Duffy, one of the leaders of Young Ireland in 1848, who had returned after an honourable career in Australian politics, published in 1882 a pamphlet in support of the Irish Land Bill of 1881. In that pamphlet he made the following reference to Majuba.

" No fact in European affairs in my day impressed me more than one that is quite recent. A handful of Dutch farmers sorely wounded the pride and spirit of the English people by successfully resisting their arms. It would have been easy to have stirred the British nation into a murderous and exterminating rage against them. But a Minister who felt that they were fighting for justice, that they had been robbed of their country, and had a right to regain it, with a magnanimity nearly without parallel in history, stopped in the midst of war to proffer them all they demanded. If he will do as much for Ireland, it will place a wreath on his brow that will never fade."

mind and character, but what was his deepest instinct, the sense of duty to Europe.

The early chapters of this book have tried to describe the Irish problem that had baffled English statesmen between the Union and the reforms of Gladstone's first Government. The true remedies had been refused, partly by the sense of property, partly by the obstinate self-confidence of the economist, partly by the sheer weight of apathy and ignorance. There was little sympathy between English and Irish either in the House of Commons or elsewhere. The relations of the peoples were made more difficult by misunderstandings that went far back into history and were kept alive by the discords of religion. To all these misunderstandings had been added new elements of strife. In the Italian struggle, when the English were ardent for Garibaldi and Italian freedom, Irish volunteers, inspired by their religious sympathies, but remembering also the Pope's noble efforts in 1846 for the victims of the Irish famine, were defending his unpopular claims. Nearer home Irishmen, after making the United States the enemy of England, were plotting against her peace in her own capital and her crowded cities.

Anybody who studies English domestic history in the first half of the nineteenth century can see how stupendous were the difficulties that beset the public men who were trying to reconstruct our social life after the first shock of the Industrial Revolution. If such had been the difficulties in England, how much greater were they in Ireland, where, in addition to the obstacles offered to reform by fear or apathy, there were the obstacles offered by all these bitter memories?

Reform was hopeless except in the hands of a man so powerful and resolute that he could move and hold the imagination of the English people and force new and strange views upon them. Nobody else could enlist the public sense of justice on behalf of a race alien in manners, in temper, in religion, and in history, Nobody else could create the new spirit that was needed for the first step in a great moral revolution. The two public men who had been the first to

F

grasp the character of the Irish problem, Mill and Bright, were guided by a sure instinct when they looked to Gladstone, with his commanding gifts, for this task, for even such gifts as his were less important than the large spaces under which his mind was moving.

CHAPTER VI

GLADSTONE'S IRISH RECORD BEFORE 1868 AND HIS CONVERSION

A study of Gladstone's temperament makes it clear that he was the Englishman best able and most likely to make a serious effort to reconcile England and Ireland.[1] Yet anybody who listened to the debates in the House of Commons in the 'fifties and early 'sixties would have been surprised to be told that this was to be the main task of the last twenty years of his life. The Irish members knew him best as the Chancellor of the Exchequer who had imposed on Ireland in 1853 the Income Tax that Peel had withheld ten years earlier. His speeches on Irish social conditions showed no special discernment and followed the accepted opinion of the day.

" If it be true," he said on June 12, 1863, " that Irish landlords reside less on their estates than the landlords of Scotland or Yorkshire or Devonshire, that may be a circumstance to be much regretted but I do not believe there is any way in which this House can address itself to so serious an evil. I know of no way in which the House can address itself to correct that evil except by endeavouring to do everything in its power to improve the social and economical condition of Ireland, and give its people equal rights and advantages with the rest of the kingdom in regard to the security, confidence and freedom of their enjoyment and disposal of their property."

Two years later, discussing an Irish motion about distress in Ireland, he made a speech that was sharply criticized in

---

[1] It is to the credit of Meredith Townsend, one of the acutest minds of the day, that as early as 1864 he foretold Gladstone's Irish future. In a character sketch in the *Spectator*, October 29, 1864, he wrote, " he perhaps alone among statesmen would have the art and the energy to try as a deliberate plan to effect the final conciliation of Ireland." Morley, II, 177.

the Commons by Lord Salisbury, then Lord Robert Cecil, as containing " principles that were too harsh and restrictive." Lord Robert Cecil argued that in dealing with Ireland you had to remember that England had destroyed her industries, and that the Penal Laws had crippled her agriculture by preventing the granting of leases to Catholics. It was necessary to " preserve with the most sacred respect the rights of the landlords" but it was impossible to apply to a country with so different a history the rigid practice suitable to England.   Anybody who heard that debate might well think that the first great effort for agrarian reform would come, not from Gladstone, but from Robert Cecil. Yet five years later Gladstone struck the first great blow in the battle that was to end with the creation of a new agrarian Ireland, much more like the Ireland that Hoche would have made than the Ireland that Pitt saved from his Jacobin grasp.

To understand Gladstone's neglect of the Irish problem during these years, it is necessary to see how he was engaged, what were the circumstances that kept him from studying it, and how his course was affected by his character.   This will explain, not only why he was inactive then, but where and how his plans miscarried later in his treatment of Irish questions.

In 1845 Gladstone travelled on the Continent and he had conversations with Guizot and others that made a profound impression on him.   For they gave him the view that statesmen and observers of other countries took of the treatment of Ireland by England, and that view haunted him to the end of his life.   He wrote about it afterwards to Guizot.

" It is very unlikely that you should remember a visit I paid you, I think at Passy in the autumn of 1845, with a message from Lord Aberdeen about international copyright.   The Maynooth Act had just been passed.   Its author, I think, meant it to be final.   I had myself regarded it as *seminal*.   And you in congratulating me upon it, as I well remember, said we should have the sympathies of Europe in the work of giving Ireland justice—a remark which evidently included more than the measure just

passed, and which I ever after saved and pondered. It helped
me on towards what has been since done."[1]

At the time he wrote to his wife the remarkable letter
quoted in the last chapter in which he referred to Ireland as
" that cloud in the West, that coming storm, the minister of
God's retribution upon cruel and inveterate and but half-
atoned injustice."

On his return home he decided to visit Ireland with Hope-
Scott and Philip Pusey, but the visit was cancelled at the last
moment. He wrote to Hope-Scott, " As Ireland is likely to
find this country and parliament so much employment for
years to come, I feel rather oppressively an obligation to try
and see it with my own eyes instead of using those of other
people, according to the limited measure of my means."
The chief object of the visit was to look at close quarters at
the institutions for religion and education of the country
and at the character of the people. Pusey in writing about
the visit referred to the agrarian war. " It will not alarm
you if I state my belief that in these agrarian outrages the
Irish peasants have been engaged in a justifiable civil war,
because the peasant ejected from his land could not longer
by any efforts of his own preserve his family from the risk of
starvation. This view is that of a very calm utilitarian,
George Lewis." Morley in telling of this project adds,
" The expedition was put off by Pusey's discovery that the
Times was despatching a correspondent to carry on agrarian
investigations. Mr. Gladstone urged that the Irish land
question was large enough for two, and so indeed it swiftly
proved, for Ireland was now on the edge of the black
abysses of the famine."[2] In 1877 on the occasion of his
only visit to Ireland, Gladstone gave rather a different
account. " A most peculiar and important circumstance of
a family nature, and one which no one could have anticipated, prevented the fulfilment of the plan and to my great
grief we were never able to set it on foot."[3]

Gladstone only once visited Ireland; Disraeli never.

[1] Gladstone to Guizot in 1872. Morley, *op. cit.*, II, p. 240.

[2] Morley, *op. cit.*, I, p. 281.

[3] *Times*, November 9, 1877.

On that fact Mr. Buckle made the only comment that there is to be made. " To those who reflect upon the prolonged contentions of the rivals over Irish policy and the dominating hold which Ireland obtained over Gladstone's later career, these facts must seem incredible, were they not true."[1] If Gladstone had visited Ireland in 1845 it is possible that his visit might have had results as important as his visit to Naples in 1850. As it was, for the next twenty years he took very little notice of Irish affairs, and then he threw himself into the Irish problem as the main task of his life. What is the explanation?

Gladstone's imagination was governed, as we have seen, by his strong European sense. Sometimes in his career this sense was absorbed in Ireland; at others it found its field for action and rhetoric elsewhere. Between 1845 and 1865 public affairs provided ample occupation for this energy and feeling, with the Crimean War, the China War, the Italian revolution, the French panics, the Cobden Treaty, the Ecclesiastical Titles Bill. Gladstone took an eager part in all these debates and in addition he went to the Ionian Islands as Commissioner in 1858. Thus the events of these years kept his European sense occupied and excited. On the Italian question, which was perhaps closest to his heart, the Irish and he were in sharp conflict.

The first thing to note then is that in the sphere where they touched his imagination the politics of those years took him away from Ireland.

During most of this time he was a Minister and a busy Minister. He was in Peel's Government in 1845, in Aberdeen's Government from 1853 to 1855, in Palmerston's Governments from 1859 to 1865, and in Russell's Government from 1865 to 1867. Now Gladstone was the type of man who becomes absorbed in his task and unable when engaged on it to give much attention to anything else. This was undoubtedly a weakness for which he paid when he was Prime Minister. He used a metaphor once that describes and reflects on his temperament. " Swimming for his

---

[1] Buckle, *Life of Disraeli*, Vol. II, p. 687.

life, a man does not see much of the country through which
the river winds, and I probably know little of these years
through which I busily work and live."[1] The office he held
in all these Governments, except the first, was that of
Chancellor of the Exchequer. There he won sensational
triumphs as orator, as financier, and as tactician. Sir
Charles Wood, later Lord Halifax, had been Chancellor of
the Exchequer for the six years of Lord John Russell's
Government and he had left the office, in Herbert Paul's
phrase, an Augean Stable.[2] Incompetent finance Ministers
had been a constant feature of Whig Governments. Whether
we consider the extraordinary improvement Gladstone made
in our finances, the help he brought to industry and commerce, the speeches he made in explaining his plans (Bulwer
Lytton said of one of them that it would remain among the
monuments of English eloquence as long as the language
lasted), the skill by which he overcame the Lords' attempt
to defeat him over the abolition of the Paper Duties, or the
address by which he got his way in a difficult Cabinet with a
hostile Prime Minister at its head, we must recognize that
Gladstone's career as Chancellor of the Exchequer revealed
the vast scope and range of his power and bestowed immense
and lasting benefits on the English people.[3] It is not surprising that he was absorbed in his office. Apart from its
importance to the welfare and interests of all classes of
Englishmen, the office in Gladstone's hands was an instrument for improving foreign relations, for he took of course an
active part in co-operating with Cobden to secure the commercial treaty with France. That treaty, in his eyes as in
Cobden's, was of value chiefly as a check to the forces that
were driving England and France dangerously near war.
To Fould, one of Napoleon's finance Ministers, Gladstone
wrote when leaving office in 1866," The statesmen of to-day

[1] Morley, *op. cit.*, II, p. 256. December, 1868.

[2] On the other hand Wood showed more discernment than Gladstone in
1853, for he strongly opposed Gladstone's extension of the income tax to Ireland.
Morley, *op. cit.*, Vol. I, p. 465.

[3] Mr. F. W. Hirst has given a full and admirable account of this side of his
career in his book *Gladstone as Financier and Economist*. See also Mr. G. T.
Garratt's most interesting discussion, *The Two Mr. Gladstones*, Chapter III.

have a new mission opened to them; the mission of substituting the concert of nations for their conflicts, and of teaching
them to grow great in common, and to give to others by
giving to themselves.   Of this beneficent work a good share
has fallen to the departments with which we have respectively
been connected."[1]   Gladstone's career at the Treasury was
thus an event of capital importance both to England and to
Europe.

All this is true, and yet it is true that in some respects
the office of Chancellor of the Exchequer was a bad school
for him; or rather that it was a school in which he stayed too
long.   He fell there into a habit of looking at every problem
with the eyes of a Chancellor of the Exchequer from which
he never broke free.[2]   Applying this Treasury mind to
Ireland in a pedantic spirit he fell easily into the view of
those who held that the Famine had solved the agrarian
problem, and that it was dangerous to begin spending
public money in a country which would soon learn to lean
on England.   During these years, and even afterwards
when he was fully alive to the importance of the Irish
problem, he was always pursuing small plans for saving
on the constabulary, or on the method of collecting revenue,
or on some other item of expenditure.   In the 'eighties
the luckless Spencer, a Viceroy living on a volcano, was
pestered by his Prime Minister with inquiries about such
details.   Thus he was absorbed in a task which drew him
into the school that was too ready to dismiss all projects for
active Irish policy as impracticable or risky.

It is difficult to-day to understand the feeling for economy,
as a sacred principle, that possessed Gladstone.   For we
live at a distance from the scandals and confusion that
Gladstone's master, Peel, found enveloping and embarrassing
the nation's finance when first he entered public life.   Sir
James Graham, another of Gladstone's heroes, published in
the last days of the old regime a pamphlet on pensions and
sinecures that had a wider and more stimulating influence

---

[1] Morley, II, p. 56.

[2] His imposition of the income tax on Ireland in 1853 he criticized in 1894 on
the ground that he did not go back to the Union, whence the difficulty sprang,
but only to the Union of the Exchequers in or about 1817.   Morley, I, p. 647.

in the struggle for reform than he had designed or desired. Cobbett, whom he would not have welcomed as an ally, used it with great effect in the economy campaign in which he liked to quote Swift's saying that " a sense of shame and a belly filled with public money were never companions for a single hour." To men like Peel and Gladstone economy was a religion, because they remembered a time when the poverty of the poor was embittered and increased by the lax ideas about public money that were held by the eighteenth-century oligarchy. In 1862 Gladstone cited Austria as an example of the mischief of prodigal expenditure: he declared that all excess in the public expenditure beyond the legitimate wants of the country was a great political and, above all, a great moral evil.

Unfortunately Gladstone's interpretation of " legitimate wants," was often so rigid and narrow as to cramp and disable his constructive judgment. He was, as he himself observed, a slow learner, and Acton has noted the curious combination of this trait with an intellect remarkable for originality and independence. The effect of the Treasury atmosphere on his mind lasted much longer than the effect of the Tory principles, with which he started on his political career, for it lasted throughout his life. One of the great advantages that the Balfour brothers, who were afterwards to make such notable contributions to the solution of the agrarian problem in Ireland, possessed over Gladstone, was that neither of them had ever been Chancellor of the Exchequer. To understand the effect of that office on Gladstone, we have only to ask ourselves what he would have made of himself as a domestic reformer if his powerful and penetrating mind had been employed, not on the problems of the Treasury, but on those of the Local Government Board. It was a great misfortune that, at a time when social reconstruction was urgently needed, the office of the Chancellor of the Exchequer enjoyed such prestige that leading men sought it naturally, as the chief prize for ascending talent, while the Departments connected with town life, housing, and labour, were treated as relatively unimportant. Both Gladstone and Disraeli suffered in consequence, though

Disraeli suffered less than Gladstone, for he never made Gladstone's fatal mistake of combining that office with the office of Prime Minister.

During twenty years then Gladstone's European imagination was actively excited by events outside Ireland, and his experience and absorption in Treasury problems encouraged him to accept the dominant view in official circles that the famine had solved Ireland's agrarian problem, or had made it possible to solve it by such measures as the Encumbered Estates Act. As Chancellor of the Exchequer, he was apt to look on the Irishmen in the House of Commons as men whose object it was to rob the Treasury. " The scene was sickening," he wrote to his wife after one debate in 1859, "and all the Irish were there most of them vying with one another in eagerness to plunder the public purse."[1] But to understand why he neglected Ireland in the 'fifties, and then threw himself into Irish problems at the end of the 'sixties, we must look a little further into his position.

Gladstone, who resembled Disraeli in his independence, resembled him also in his loneliness. His contemporaries were bewildered by his strange and unaccountable mind, and provoked by his excitable manners and his brooding moods. He had more enemies than friends in the House of Commons. " He is hated as much as, or more than, he is loved," said Dean Church; " he is fierce sometimes and wrathful and easily irritated; he wants knowledge of men and speaks rashly."[2] He was unhappy with colleagues and he was serving for most of the time under a Prime Minister whom he mistrusted as much as he mistrusted Disraeli. " For the first time," he wrote to his wife in 1857 " is her (England's) government guided by a man without convictions of duty: by a man who systematically panders to whatever is questionable or bad in the public mind."[3] His letters to his wife show that in spite of his dazzling victories in debate he was diffident about his position and that he was aware of his faults of manner and temper. " There is

---

[1] *Gladstone to his Wife*, edited by A. Tilney Bassett, p. 124.
[2] Morley, *op. cit.*, II, p. 155.
[3] Tilney Bassett, *op. cit.*, p. 114.

no man," he wrote, " however near to me with whom I am
fit to be habitually when hard worked . . . setting a tired
mind to work is like setting a man to run up and down
stairs when his limbs are weary."[1] " I am sore with conflicts about the public expenditure," he wrote to Russell in
October, 1865, " which I feel that other men would either
have escaped, or have conducted more gently and less
fretfully."[2]   Dilke's memoirs give a picture of the impression that he made on young men in the House who thought
that he came down with a crushing hand on men of independent spirit, and they illustrate the criticism that was
passed on him that he did not know the difference between
leading and driving.   Others put it that his impatience with
slow minds made him seem overbearing.   In 1865 a Conservative member, lavish of compliments to his power and
even to his temper, remarked on his unpopularity with the
rank and file of his party.[3]

Grattan gave an alarming picture of the qualifications
demanded in a party leader in the House of Commons in
the early years of the century.

" He must be affable in manner, generous in disposition, have a
ready hand, an open house and a full purse. He must have a
good cook for the English members, fine words and fair promises
for the Irish and sober calculations for the Scotch. He must
sacrifice time and temper and fortune; his private affairs, his
health and his constitution."[4]

Parties asked rather less than this of their leaders in the days
of Disraeli and of Gladstone, but Gladstone lacked the first
qualification on this list. To the ordinary man he was not
affable; he had what Cicero calls the *vultus clausus*; or as
Morley put it he " lacked ' the little civilities and hypocrisies' of political society."[5] His friend Sir Thomas
Acland wrote him a very frank letter in January 1868
about the complaints that were rife in the House of Commons. Some complained " that there is so little easy

[1] *ibid.*, p. 41.
[2] Spencer Walpole, *Life of Lord John Russell*, Vol. II, p. 422.
[3] Morley, *op. cit.*, II, p. 157.
[4] Grattan, *Life and Times*, V, p. 417.
[5] Morley, II, p. 172.

contact with the small fry, as when Palmerston sat in the
tea-room, and men were gratified by getting private speech
with their leader."

This difficulty hampered Gladstone all his life and was
closely connected with another complaint reported by
Acland; the complaint that Gladstone was too much
immersed in Homer and *Ecce Homo* and that he did not take
the trouble to read the newspapers or feel the pulse of his
followers.

" One man personally complained that when you sought his
opinion, you spent the whole interview in impressing your own
view on him, and hardly heard anything he might have to say."
. . . " Whatever your own tastes may be for literature, and however strengthening and refreshing to your own mind and heart it
may be to dig into the old springs, still the people don't understand it; they consider you their own, as a husband claims his
wife's devotion."[1]

Gladstone would have said with Cicero, " Do you think that
I could find material for my daily speeches on so manifold
a variety of subjects did I not cultivate my mind with study,
or that my mind would endure so great a strain did I not
study to provide it with relaxation?"[2]   But his interests
divided him from the great majority of the members of the
House of Commons; he was at his happiest in the society of
Acton, Döllinger, Morley, men who liked to discuss with him
subjects that would have fallen rather flat in the tea-room of
the House of Commons.

Gladstone's lack of what Morley called the little civilities
and hypocrisies of political society belonged to his strict
and Spartan idea of self respect.   He would never flatter
a man in order to get something from him.   At one time
his Government was greatly embarrassed by the humours
and chagrins of a young and brilliant member, who was
always on the look out for slights and grievances.   These
trivial crises were a continual nuisance to Ministers who had
Egypt, Ireland and South Africa, on their tired hands.   A
letter Granville wrote to Gladstone about this troublesome

[1] Morley, *op. cit.*, II, pp. 172-3.
[2] *Pro Archia Poeta*, VI, 12.

colleague is highly significant. " If you could bring yourself to say in his presence one half of the handsome things
you say about him behind his back, the position would be
much easier." That was just what Gladstone could not do.
There was indeed something almost perverse in Gladstone's
treatment of personal questions. Chamberlain, when
President of the Board of Trade, was very anxious that T. H.
Farrer (afterwards Lord Farrer) should be given the K.C.B.
on the ground, among others, that he had been such an
effective friend to Free Trade principles. But Farrer had
never had the C.B. and Gladstone held out against Chamberlain on this punctilio. In 1885 Bright sent him a request for
an honour for a friend and Gladstone gave it as little
consideration as he would have given to a suggestion from a
stranger.

Gladstone was conscious of the unfriendliness of the House
and his party, and this atmosphere affected his spirit and his
self-confidence. For he was specially subject to atmosphere,
since he was essentially an orator, a man who uses his
imagination to excite and guide the imagination of others.
To bring out his full power, a task or cause had to engage
his imagination, for he worked at a high temperature.
Gladstone resembled Burke rather than Bentham. A man
like Bentham serves his nation by addressing himself to the
task of reforming abuses, and improving institutions, in
patient detail, substituting principle for custom, order for
confusion. A man like Burke has his conscience or his
imagination excited by some special aspect of politics, some
large and generous impulse, some great and terrible wrong.
The first uses science, the second art; the first will see a
problem, the second a truth, that the other misses.

When given a definite task Gladstone of course could use
his immense faculty for mastering detail and expounding
plans with consummate success. This was the secret, not
only of his triumphs as Chancellor of the Exchequer, but also
of his power to meet and overcome all opponents in debate
on such complicated measures as his Irish Land Bills. But
he did not set out on any large reform until his imagination
had been excited, and his imagination was not excited unless

he saw some hope of exciting the imagination of others. He took naturally an imaginative view of politics, but his imagination would brood sadly and aloof until he saw the moment for making others feel what he felt. He believed himself that he had the gift for seeing when public opinion could be influenced and educated. He described this sense in a note written towards the end of his life. " It is an insight into the facts of particular eras, and their relation one to another, which generates in the mind a conviction that the materials exist for forming a public opinion and for directing it to a particular end."[1]   This is not quite the same view as that which Cicero advanced in his own defence when abandoning his resistance to the triumvirs,[2] for Gladstone would never have kept silent when something he thought wrong was advocated or practised. But he was an opportunist, as Morley says, in the sense in which that word stands for common sense. He thought, that is, that if you want to carry a reform you had better choose the moment when you are most likely to address yourself to public opinion with success.

Gladstone's despondency about Irish reform under these conditions was shown in a letter to the Warden of Glenalmond in the summer of 1865 when he said that Irish disestablishment was " remote and apparently out of all bearing on the practical politics of the day."[3]   He was himself by this time in favour of disestablishment, but he regarded his political career as drawing to its close. He was working at the question, and anxious to make his views known, even though he saw no prospect of their success in a government of which Palmerston was the head. In the spring of 1865, when a Radical member, Dillwyn, put down a motion to the effect that the present position of the Irish Church was unsatisfactory, and called for the early attention of the Government, he proposed, claiming a good deal more liberty for himself than he ever conceded to a colleague, to

[1] Morley, II, p. 241.
[2] " id enim jubet idem ille Plato, quem ego vehementer auctorem sequor, tantum contendere in re publica, quantum probare tuis civibus possis." *Ad. Fam.*, I, 9, 18.
[3] Morley, *op. cit.*, II, 239.

give his persònal views as if he were a private member. Palmerston not unnaturally asked him whether " it was possible for a member of a Government speaking from the Treasury bench so to sever himself from the Body Corporate to which he belongs as to be able to express opinions as an individual and leave himself free to act upon different opinions." Gladstone made a long speech in which he assented to the first part of the motion but held that the Government could not assent to the second. The speech made a great impression. An Irish Conservative emphasized the difference between Gladstone's view and that of Palmerston. A Radical member, Grant Duff, declared that the debate would become historical and that he saw in Gladstone's speech the beginning of the end of the great Irish difficulty.

Grant Duff's forecast was too sanguine but, so far as Gladstone and all that he could accomplish was concerned, it was accurate. As long ago as 1845, as we have seen, he had decided that disestablishment, so far from weakening a Church, might release it from burdens. This was the result of the larger conception of the place and meaning of the Christian Church in Europe which had possessed his mind since his first visit to Rome. In the early 'sixties he had decided that when the opportunity came he would act upon this view. In the later 'sixties the atmosphere became favourable for action. The death of Palmerston, in October 1865, had removed a great moral obstacle to reform. Then the movement for extending the franchise and its triumph in 1867 had brought a new force into public life; a force that Gladstone believed he could use for large and generous purposes. Lastly, though Gladstone had in many respects an uncomfortable and anxious position in the House of Commons, he had been growing steadily in popular favour, and he was now looked upon as the natural leader of democracy. Church said of him " There never was a man so genuinely admired for the qualities which deserve admiration—his earnestness, his deep popular sympathies, his unflinching courage; and there never was a man more deeply hated both for his good points and for undeniable defects and failings. But they love him much less in the House than they do out of doors."[1] Palmerston grasped the same truth from another point of view.

" Lord Palmerston," said Clarendon, " regarded him as combining all the elements calculated to produce a most dangerous character for this country. . . . Enthusiasm, passion, sympathy, simplicity—these were the qualities which moved the masses ; and Gladstone had them all. He would always be more powerful out of office than in it."[2]

Perhaps the first important indication of Gladstone's new mood of confidence, and his new grasp of the Irish problem, was given in a speech he made at Southport on December 19, 1867. That speech was significant for three reasons. The first is his treatment of Fenianism. A few days before there had been a Fenian outrage at Clerkenwell Prison in which twelve persons had been killed. Yet Gladstone chose this moment to urge the British people not to confound the cause of Fenianism with the cause of Ireland, and to remember that, if the public were excited, the excitement would find its way to the jury box and affect even the bench of justice. He referred to the Fenian invasion of Canada as a proceeding of which it would be difficult to find on record anything more inexcusable and abominably wicked. " Canada has inflicted no wrongs on Ireland; Ireland has wrongs; Canada has no power to remedy them." Thus he told the British people shocked, angry, and frightened, by Fenian violence, that Ireland had grievances and that it was the duty of the British people to remove them. When this had been done, " instead of hearing in every corner of Europe the most painful commentaries on the policy of England towards Ireland we may be able to look our fellow Europeans in the face." The second notable feature of his speech was his description of the need for considering Irish ideas in treating Irish problems.

" There are certain matters in which the very effect of a Union requires that the three should have a common opinion and a common policy. So far as that goes I would not for a moment

[1] Quoted Morley, *Life of Gladstone*, Vol. II, p. 177.
[2] H. C. T. Bell, *Palmerston*, II, p. 234.

listen to any plans whatever for separate institutions and a separate policy for England, Scotland or Ireland; but this I venture to say that in all matters except that, no man ought to be able to say that any one of these nations is governed according to the traditions, the views or the ideas of another."

Thirdly, he spoke for the first time of the need for agrarian legislation. He explained that outside Ulster there was no protection for tenants' improvements, and that Parliament would have to lay aside all its prejudices in dealing with this problem.

Gladstone had now reached a stage in the development of his views on Ireland which can perhaps be best described by a passage in a letter of Burke's.

" What I have always thought of the matter is this—that the most poor, illiterate, and uninformed people upon earth are judges of a *practical* oppression. It is a matter of feeling; and as such persons have generally felt most of it, and are not of an over-lively sensibility, they are the best judges of it. But for the *real cause*, or the *appropriate remedy*, they ought never to be called into council about the one or the other."[1]

Gladstone was now convinced that the Irish people were to be believed when they said that they suffered under a bad agrarian system, though he would have been slow to believe that the peasant victims were the best judges of the legislation that was needed.

This conviction started him on the career as Irish reformer which was to be his main task for the rest of his life. He did not see then how vast a task he was undertaking or where it would lead him. But he was certain where his duty lay. On December 1, 1868, when he received a summons from Windsor to form his first Government, he was felling a tree at Hawarden. " After a few minutes," said Evelyn Ashley who was with him, " the blows ceased, and Mr. Gladstone resting on the handle of his axe, looked up and with deep earnestness in his voice and with great intensity in his face, exclaimed, ' My mission is to pacify Ireland '."[2] It says something for the generosity of the new

[1] Letter to Sir Hercules Langrishe, M.P., January, 1792. *Works*, Vol. VI, p. 346.
[2] Morley, *op. cit.*, II, p. 252.

G

popular electorate that the man, to whom it looked with such confidence and affection, had shown by his acts and speeches that this would be the first use to which he would put the energy and driving force that the enfranchisement of the artisan had brought into English politics.   From this time began a new chapter in the relations of England and Ireland, and of Gladstone and democracy.

CHAPTER VII

GLADSTONE'S FIRST GOVERNMENT

When Shaftesbury's Life appeared in 1886 with long extracts from his diaries, Gladstone, who had been judged very severely in its pages, remarked that reading it had been an excellent discipline for him. He treated it as he often treated books he read, marking and noting passages that had a special interest for him. He also wrote a short paper on the book, saying that though he had been pained to find how badly Shaftesbury thought of him, its revelations had raised Shaftesbury higher than ever in his esteem.

It is not surprising that Gladstone found a great many reflections in these diaries that attracted his sympathy. For the two men had much in common. Each of them believed that he was serving God in public life in a special sense, and that he had been chosen as the agent or instrument of the divine purpose.[1]

" May I say to you," Shaftesbury wrote to Canon Wilberforce at the end of his life, " as a spiritual friend, that I very sincerely and conscientiously declare, that in my long career my highest consolation has been to know that I was the servant of our Lord, and my highest honour that I was believed to be such."[2]

So Gladstone wrote in his Diary about his Bulgarian campaign, on December 29, 1878.

" In the great physical and mental effort of speaking, often to large audiences, I have been as it were upheld in an unusual manner and the free effective use of voice has been given me to my

---

[1] Newman had the same view of his own case, thinking that God was saving him for some great purpose. See for illustrations, *Oxford Apostles*, by Faber, pp. 143, 321, 443.

[2] Hodder, *Life of Shaftesbury*, Vol. III, p. 500.

own astonishment. Was not all this for a purpose. . . . I am aware that language such as I have here used is often prompted by fanaticism. But not always. It is to be tried by tests. I have striven to apply them with all the sobriety I can; and with a full recollection that God sometimes sees fit to employ as His instruments for particular purposes of good those with whom notwithstanding he has yet a sore account to settle."

After his triumph in 1880 he wrote on May 10 :

" At 4.15 I went down to the House with Herbert. There was a great and fervent crowd in Palace Yard and much feeling in the House. It almost over-powered me as I thought by what deep and hidden agencies I have been brought back into the vortex of political action and contention. It has not been in my power these last six months to make notes as I could have wished, of my own thoughts and observances from time to time of the new access of strength which in some important respects has been administered to me in my old age and of the remarkable manner in which Holy Scripture has been inwardly supplied me for admonition and for comfort. Looking calmly over these secrets of experience, I do believe that the Almighty has employed me for His purposes in a manner larger or more special than before, and has strengthened me and led me on gradually, though I must not forget the admirable saying of Hooker that evil ministers of good things are like torches, a light to others, waste to themselves."

The two men also agreed in thinking that England had grossly ill-treated Ireland in the past. On December 12, 1846, Shaftesbury wrote in his diary.

" Ireland is manifestly set for our punishment, the slow but just punishment of a ruling power that thrust upon it Popery, anarchy, and unsympathetic proprietors. The nation is irreconcilable to the Saxon authority. Our late repentance, and numerous benefits, are perverted to our injury. Famine stalks through the land. We expend money for their maintenance at the rate of £127,000 a week; and the starving peasantry can save, from this effort of mercy and munificence, enough to purchase arms to a greater extent than was ever before known for the assault and overthrow of their benefactors! And yet so besotted are we, that all this is turned into an additional argument for the endowment of the Irish priesthood! . . ."

On December 29 he wrote, " Ireland is terrible, terrible, terrible. And the year 1847 will be worse than 1846. Counsel

has perished from among us. We are at our wit's end. It is a
just retribution for our sins towards that country. ' Be sure your
sin will find you out.' "[1]

In 1845 Gladstone wrote to his wife in the letter already
given in full, " Ireland, Ireland! that cloud in the west, that
coming storm, the minister of God's retribution upon cruel
and inveterate and but half-atoned injustice! "

In 1870 he wrote to Granville: " To this great country
the state of Ireland after 700 years! of our tutelage, is in my
opinion so long as it continues, an intolerable disgrace, and a
danger so absolutely transcending all others, that I call
it the only real danger of the noble Empire of the Queen."

There was however an important difference between
Gladstone and Shaftesbury. Shaftesbury could not detach
himself from the atmosphere of the English Protestant.

" Depend upon this," he said, " the difficulty lies with the sacer-
dotal and monkish orders, who, reversing the piety of Aaron,
stand between the living and the dead—the living word of God
and the dead congregation. Only allow profound security of
life and limb, with free discussion and an open Bible, and you
will cease to be perplexed in your determination how Ireland is
to be governed—Ireland
' Great, glorious, and free;
Bright flower of the earth, and first gem of the sea.' "[2]

If Shaftesbury had applied the same reasoning to
Lancashire and the West Riding he would not have gone
down to history as the most famous name in the history of
factory reform. In 1881 he wrote to Lowe expressing his
agreement with Lowe's argument that anything which
helped the transfer of land from the Irish landlord would
retard the civilization of Ireland, and he actually praised the
House of Lords for rejecting the clauses of the Relief of
Distress Act of that year which provided for compensation
for disturbance:[3] an act which is universally admitted to
have been one of the worst blunders of its career, and to have
been a principal cause of the distress and disorder of the

[1] Hodder's *Shaftesbury*, Vol. II, p. 183.
[2] Hodder, *op. cit.*, Vol. II, p. 100.
[3] Martin, *Life of Sherbrooke*, Vol. II, p. 455.

'eighties. A man might therefore combine a lively sense of
the wrongs Ireland had suffered with a dull sense of the
need for redress and reform.

Gladstone was saved from this impotent conclusion by his
European sense, by his power to see Irish history through
a larger window. But though he could see Irish history as
an Irishman saw it, he was slow to see Irish problems
through Irish eyes. He combined Irish memory of the past
with English intuitions in the present. It has been said of
Richelieu that if he had not despotism in the heart, he had
it in the brain. Most of Gladstone's contemporaries, looking
at Ireland, had England in their heart, and England in their
brain; Gladstone had Ireland in his heart, but he had in his
brain a disturbing element of England, and of Treasury
England.

Before he took office, Gladstone had made it clear that
in his view the two most pressing Irish problems were the
problem of the Church and the problem of the land system.
To these two problems he addressed himself, and before he
had been two years in office he had put on the Statute Book
two measures of capital importance. The Irish Church was
disestablished in 1869; the first great Land Act for Ireland
was passed in 1870.

The first step Gladstone took was characteristic, for it
was the result of his governing desire to make his peace with
his conscience, and to make his peace with the public. Most
men at the age of sixty are not too much burdened by the
recollection of views they expressed when they were thirty.
But Gladstone's early work on Church and State had not
passed so easily out of his mind; it still troubled his pillow.
Now, when about to put an end to the Irish Establishment,
he could not be happy until he had explained to the world
by what new light he had been brought to this idea of his
duty. So he wrote the " chapter of autobiography " which
appears in the seventh volume of his *Gleanings from Past
Years*. Before publishing it in 1868 he sent it to Granville,
who replied.

" I had conflicting feelings in beginning to read it. I have a passion for autobiography. No work, certainly none of fiction, ever interested me so much as the somewhat uneventful autobiography of Gibbon. I had naturally the greatest curiosity to learn the history of the working of your mind in the change which has taken place since the publication of your book, but I had also a feeling that the less a person in your position publishes the better, that the explanation was unnecessary, and would only lead to fresh attacks. In this state of mind, I set to work. You appeared to me happy in your motto, and introduction, excellent in your argument why you should publish.

" The description of your book gave me little pleasure for the obvious reason that I never liked or quite understood it, but when I came to your personal history, I never read anything which delighted me more—so candid, so simple, and so clear—it is perfectly unanswerable."

That chapter of autobiography is interesting and characteristic. Gladstone showed that as early as 1847 he had refused to pledge himself to the support of the Irish Church, though by that refusal he injured his chances of election at Oxford where he was a candidate for the first time. " The representation of that University was, I think, stated by Mr. Canning to be to him the most coveted prize of political life. I am not ashamed to own that I desired it with an almost passionate fondness."[1] His later action was governed by his usual rule of life. He had voted against motions for inquiry in the House of Commons because he did not think " the season for action had come," but he let his friends know that when the time came he would support disestablishment, in case they desired to nominate somebody else as a candidate for Oxford. His retrospect made it perfectly clear that the speech he made in the House of Commons in 1865, when he declared that this was the question of the future, implied no sudden breach with his past, or a sudden illumination on a question on which his mind had hitherto been dark. The article—so far as Gladstone's integrity was concerned—was, as Granville said, unanswerable.

This first chapter of the new relations between England and Ireland was a chapter of brilliant success. For the disestablishment of the Irish Church was, like the abolition

---

[1] *Gleanings of Past Years*, Vol. VII, p. 126.

of the Slave Trade, a reform that seemed almost insuperably difficult until a Minister, who combined power and zeal, undertook it, and then it was achieved with such apparent ease as to make everybody wonder why it had been looked upon with such apprehension. But a study of the circumstances explains why it was that the Irish problem, which in its history discovered, as no other problem discovered, the weakness of the parliamentary system, and came near to wrecking that system, revealed in this particular episode, not its weakness, but its strength. Indeed, we may say that, if England had ever captured again, in her treatment of Ireland, the wisdom and the good fortune that blessed this moment, half a century of disaster would have been avoided.

There are times in his career when Gladstone assumes a more splendid or a more heroic character, but there is no time in his career when he commanded, as he did on this occasion, all the elements of success. In exposition, in debate, he was at his best. His opening speech on March 1, 1869, explaining the scheme for the disestablishment of the Irish Church, received from Disraeli a compliment that he did not often deserve, for Disraeli said that, though his speech had lasted three and a half hours, there was not a word in it that could be spared. But if he excelled in debate, where he usually found himself a master, he succeeded too in those personal negotiations where he was more used to failure. He had before the Irish Church Bill was on the Statute Book as much tension and fatigue as would have worn down anybody else—Archbishop Tait described him as " still looking very ill " in September 1869—but he managed his temper admirably, and combined, as Granville put it, firmness and conciliation, with great success.

Conditions so favourable were never known again in the history of English relations with Ireland.

When Gladstone's Cabinet took office in December, 1868, the opinion of the country on this question had been given in unmistakable manner. The House of Commons which had been dissolved in November, 1868, was a Liberal House of Commons with a Conservative Government in office.

At the election of 1865, 361 Liberals had been returned to 294 Conservatives. Russell had been defeated on his Reform Bill in June 1866, and given place to Derby. Disraeli, Derby's Chancellor of the Exchequer, had brought off his great *coup* and carried his Reform Bill. For nearly two years the Conservatives, first under Derby (February 1867—February 1868), and then under Disraeli (February 1868—December 1868) had remained in office. In this Liberal House of Commons Gladstone had carried a resolution condemning the Irish Establishment, against the Government, by 330 votes to 265, and he had carried through the Commons a Bill suspending the exercise of patronage in the Irish Church. Thus the question had already been fully debated before the election, and at the election, which had given Gladstone a majority of 128, the opinion of the nation had been declared without doubt.

If the will of the nation had been declared without doubt at the election, Gladstone's Government had the further advantage that this was the first election after the passing of the second Reform Bill. There was still a good deal of nervousness about this new electorate, and the friends of the House of Lords, and the Queen, were anxious to avoid anything like a direct struggle between the Lords and the constituencies. Salisbury was influenced by this sense of danger. When the Disestablishment Bill went to the Lords in June, 1869, he declared that, where the electorate had spoken clearly, it was not the business of the House of Lords to resist the nation's will. The Queen too, little as she liked the Bill, was anxious to help towards a settlement, and from first to last she used her good offices for peace with great tact and success.

The nation then had declared for reform, and even strong champions of the Irish Church had recognized this fact, and all that followed from it. There was this further advantage, that there was no practicable alternative to the Government's policy. Some English Conservatives would have preferred to proceed by way of concurrent endowment, but for this there was no support. Dufferin sent Gladstone a series of resolutions passed by the Liberal Society of the North of Ireland in the summer of 1869, protesting against schemes of concurrent endowment on the ground, among others, that the Roman Catholics, the Presbyterians, and the Methodists, were all opposed to it. Gladstone characteristically wrote to a correspondent, saying that he regarded himself as following in the steps of Pitt and Castlereagh, with the difference that religious equality, which in their days could be promoted by concurrent endowment, demanded now the alternative method of disestablishment.

It is unnecessary to relate in detail the negotiations that ended in the passing of the Bill, or to discuss the particular degree of credit due to the different actors. The Queen took a most important part. Indeed if it is desired to illustrate the change that came over the Queen and her view of her duty, after the intoxicating years of Disraeli's flattery, no better proof could be found than the contrast between her action in 1869 and her action in 1885. If she had met the later Irish crisis in the spirit in which she acted in 1869, history might have taken a different course. On this occasion, much as she disliked disestablishment, she helped to avert the quarrel between the two Houses which she dreaded as a consequence of this conflict, and she acted with a keen sense of her responsibility to her Prime Minister. She inquired whether she could help by speaking to the Bishop of Peterborough, and she asked what exactly it would be proper for her to say to him. Gladstone replied by giving her complete freedom, on the understanding that what she said to him was said to him alone. Gladstone's own sense of his debt to her appears in the letter he wrote to Granville on July 24, " Pray combine my thanks with your own, for the powerful and valuable aid which she imparted through the Dean, always of course within the limits of the constitution." Never in her reign did she show more clearly what special purpose can be served by a sovereign who can put private feeling under the control of a sense of duty, at once guided and defined by understood principles.

Salisbury had all the Queen's reasons for dreading an unnecessary conflict, and his personal relations with Gladstone and their mutual regard made it easy for him to use his great influence in the cause of peace. Archbishop Tait and Bishop Magee, the latter of whom made the most brilliant of all the speeches against the Bill, co-operated for a settlement. Of the Irish churchmen far the most important in this crisis was Archdeacon Stopford, father of Mrs. J. R. Green, who helped Gladstone by advice and by intelligence on the Irish situation. When thanking Stopford later for a pamphlet on the University question, April 2, 1873, Gladstone wrote, " I trace in your suggestions the same decisive, accurate, vigorous, and manly mind, of the working of which I had such valuable experience at the time of the Irish Church Bill." But the most surprising event in the history of this settlement was the surrender of Cairns, who had shown not less stubbornness than ability in resisting the Government's policy. How little the Government had expected this climax we can see from a letter Gladstone wrote to Granville on June 21.

" If Salisbury is in consultation with Cairns, what hope have we that his conclusions can represent anything except the general result of the ideas and wishes of our opponents, and will not Cairns himself be the principal agent—not merely from the votes at his back but from the character of his mind compared to the others—in bringing them into shape? "

It is interesting to remember that Dean Stanley was a strong opponent of the Bill, and that the famous scholar, Thirlwall, was the only Bishop to speak in its favour.

Of the result of disestablishment Gladstone gave a perfectly true forecast in his speech in the House of Commons. He recalled the scene in *King Lear*, where Edgar persuades Gloucester that he has fallen over the cliffs of Dover:

> " Ten masts at each make not the altitude
> Which thou hast perpendicularly fell:
> Thy life's a miracle."

And yet but a little while after the old man is relieved from his delusion and finds he has not fallen at all.

If the credit for the peaceful conclusion is to be divided, there was no doubt in anybody's mind that the driving force which had made this reform inevitable, either by peaceful settlement, or by the imposition of the national will on the House of Lords, was the personal power of the Prime Minister. In describing the atmosphere in which the struggle was begun, the chronicler in the Annual Register observed that most people expected that the struggle would last for years, and involve the fate of more than one Government. When the battle was over the same writer described and discussed its unexpected character.

" Such was the conclusion of the proceedings which carried to a successful termination the Irish Church Bill of 1869—a measure certainly of very remarkable character, whether we regard its principle, its structure, or the history of its progress through Parliament. . . . It was carried through its various stages, in the face of a united and powerful opposition, mainly by the resolute will and unflinching energy of the Prime Minister, who throughout the long and arduous discussions, in which he took the leading part, displayed in full measure those qualities of acuteness, force of reasoning and thorough mastery of his subject for which he had long been conspicuous, but which were never more signally exhibited than on this occasion. Upon the whole, whatever may be thought of its merits or demerits, it can hardly be disputed that the Act for the Disestablishment of the Irish Church, introduced and carried into a law within somewhat less than five months, was the most remarkable legislative achievement of modern times."[1]

The problem of the Land to which Gladstone next turned was unfortunately more complicated. In this case the combination of the Irish heart and the English brain enabled Gladstone to pass a Bill which recognized for the first time a principle of great and revolutionary importance, but prevented him from offering an effective solution of the agrarian problem. He worked with great industry, and won general admiration by his single-handed defence of his

[1] *Annual Register*, 1869, p. 119. The *Times* in a leading article, September 25, 1871, on the Disestablishment of the Irish Church, wrote, " We may then consider that the work which three years ago appeared to many so gigantic is substantially achieved. The result must be considered creditable to all who have had a share in accomplishing it, but it must be attributed in the first instance to the wisdom and completeness with which the Act of 1869 was drawn."

measure against such formidable antagonists as Roundell Palmer (afterwards Lord Selborne) and Cairns, but the Bill resembled too much the effort of a brilliant amateur, and Gladstone admitted ten years later that it had disappointed his high hopes.

In this case he was not nearly so comfortable inside his Cabinet as he had been when the Irish Church was in the melting pot. Granville, in a letter of September 25, 1869, spoke of "those who will take a purely landlord view," naming in this category "Lowe, Argyll, Clarendon, Cardwell, and very moderately so Hartington." The most energetic letter writer in this group was Argyll, and Morley has observed of his correspondence with Gladstone, " I know no more singular reading. . . . Mr. Gladstone trying to lead his argumentative colleague over one or two of the barest rudiments of the history of Irish land, and occasionally showing in the process something of the quality of the superior pupil teacher acquiring to-day material for the lesson of to-morrow."[1] Both Argyll and Lowe were very much afraid of admitting arguments and principles that, as Gladstone put it, might one day cross the water. Gladstone laid stress on the inequality of bargaining between landlord and tenant in Ireland.

" If," said Argyll, " we are to legislate for the special protection of all who in the ' struggle for existence ' are placed at a comparative disadvantage in bargaining for the means of subsistence, I fear that this principle will carry us a long way. Even in Manufacturing Industry the Poor cannot deal on equal terms with the Capitalist, and, as regards land, the quantity of which can never be increased, its owners must always have a position of immense advantage over its occupiers, so long as they possess the full incidents and Rights which have hitherto been considered as attaching to ownership."

He was gradually won over to consent to a larger plan, because, as he put it, " you had to recognize that everything in Ireland was in a mess." But to the end he regarded this legislation as provisional, a process in the transition to the English system.

[1] *Life of Gladstone*, II, p. 290.

Gladstone thus had a powerful party in the Cabinet against him and he had little help outside. For this he was himself a good deal to blame. He had neglected the important duty of educating the public and the official mind. Almost all the great reforms in British social history have been the result of a long process of education. Marx pointed out that the English Parliament had set an example to the world by instituting inquiries, and in this way exposing mischief and abuses. This was the result of the character that Parliament had assumed in the eighteenth century of a tribunal where grievances might be examined. In the eighteenth century these inquiries often led to little result, but in the nineteenth they became very important. For a man who wanted to legislate could supply himself with valuable information and a valuable support by calling for a Committee or a Commission. By this process an able bureaucrat like Chadwick could furnish so overwhelming a case for action, that a reformer, using his documents, could overcome both the selfishness of the vested interests, and the lazy indifference of Parliament or the public. In this way a few men like Chadwick, Southwood Smith, Toynbee, Sadler, Fielden, and Shaftesbury, had achieved the great successes of the 'forties, in making factory reform effective, and in introducing a system of public health. This method should have been used in 1869. If Gladstone had set up a small and effective Committee to study the agrarian problem, while he was disestablishing the Irish Church, he would have gained two great advantages. In the first place he would have seen the problem in its true perspective and character. In the second place he would have been infinitely stronger in meeting the opposition of the vested interests, and in breaking down public apathy.

Gladstone got little help from the Irish Members. There was no effective Irish party in the House to supply enthusiasm and he shrank from using the knowledge and judgment of Irishmen like Sir John Gray who could have given him valuable advice. For he remembered how Melbourne's Government had suffered in popularity and reputation from its dependence on the support of O'Connell, a relationship that had had such excellent results in Ireland.[1] He was consequently unduly nervous of putting his Government into a similar position. His sympathies were with Ireland but certain English prejudices still clung obstinately to his conservative mind. For, although he had escaped from the English delusion that everything that was wrong in Ireland was due to Irish character, the mixed blood of Spaniard and Tartar to which Bishop Berkeley had traced its unsatisfactory qualities, or the Popish religion or native lawlessness, it was long before he escaped from the influence of the English habit of treating Ireland as a society whose good was to be pursued by English statesmen acting on their own initiative and by their own light.

Under the influence of this remarkable view Gladstone declined Bessborough's proposal that he should see Gray, though he had been warned that the attitude of the *Freeman's Journal* to his Bill would make all the difference in Ireland. As Morley put it, " It was, however, almost a point of honour in those days for British cabinets to make Irish laws out of their own heads." When Gladstone paid his tardy visit to Ireland in 1877, the *Times* remarked, " Mr. Gladstone is to be considered; even now, an adventurous explorer in Ireland. His former colleagues, his present opponents, have legislated for that strange country, admitting its peculiarities and sometimes severely censuring them, but very few of them knowing anything of Irish life." Gladstone's action at this time illustrated this peculiarity. He was dissatisfied, not unjustly, with his Irish information, and he asked Goschen to release Lambert, the efficient bureaucrat serving under him at the Poor Law Board, for special work in Ireland. " The only alternative I have," he wrote, " would be to go to Ireland myself which I would willingly do, but you can judge of the political imprudence and impropriety of such a measure which puts it out of the question."[2]

The weaknesses of the Land Bill were due to these

[1] See his speech : House of Commons, March 29, 1865.

[2] In a note from Granville to him on October 6, 1871, there is a sentence " How does the reproach strike you that not only no royalties go to Ireland but that no Minister condescends to do so? "

causes. Gladstone did not grasp the full and true character of the problem, and his efforts to solve that problem on his own lines were embarrassed by the strength of the opposition. As he had no impressive Blue Book to produce, he relied largely, in urging the case for reform, on the rise and growth of Fenianism. This was characteristic. It was his instinct always, as it had been Burke's, to consider the effect of a policy on the imagination of a society, and to consider what a statesman could learn of the problems of a society from studying its imagination. This habit came from his temperament as an orator. There were times in his career when this way of looking at politics lifted him to a plane that men moving in the hard light of common day could never have reached. It gave to his successes and failures alike an heroic quality. It was the secret of his strength.

But it has its dangers. Gladstone with rare honesty said that until Ireland shook England's complacency by the Fenian outrages nothing was done in the way of reform. This was painfully true. It was a reflection on English statesmanship and on Gladstone's statesmanship. Gladstone who, in his casuistical moods, would hardly admit the truth of a self-evident proposition, and exasperated his contemporaries by his ingenuity in splitting hairs, was ready at other times not only to admit a truth that seemed to wound his pride and the pride of his nation, but to make that truth the basis of his policy. No doubt a man who says that the disorder of a country is evidence that there is something wrong with its government speaks the truth, and salutary truth. Bentham put that truth in a remark that applies to a great deal of Irish history.

" If associations spring up in a country powerful enough to intimidate its government, with all its executive force at its back, and with all its influence too powerful to put down—if and when a great majority of the nation is seen on one side and its government on another—it is a pretty clear indication that the general discontent of the country is well founded."

But to make agitation the reason for reform is to provoke at once resistance and antagonism. Men hate to think that they are yielding to violence, and they fear that if they yield to violence to-day, they will have to yield to violence again to-morrow. When Gladstone sent her the Land Bill, the Queen, who always represented this John Bull temper, protested against what she considered his one-sided view of the causes of Irish distress.

" The Queen would therefore, have liked, when the insecurity of tenure is spoken of on one hand as a grievance to the occupier of the soil, that the lawless determination neither to pay rent nor to suffer eviction, should have been denounced on the other, as a violation of the rights of property which could not be allowed for a moment."[1]

Gladstone's own ideas at the beginning were modest enough. He told Argyll that he had learnt how mistaken had been his view of the Irish problem when he had supported Cardwell's Bill of 1866, but his correspondence with Fortescue, his Chief Secretary, shows with how gingerly a step he moved towards the remedy that he was later to press. Fortescue found (December 4, 1869) that so good a judge as Lord Monck held that a compulsory settlement of rents by a public authority was an essential reform. This was a revolutionary proposal, breaking against all the most firmly fixed of English ideas. Fortescue, when he told Gladstone of Monck's view, said that he was himself against attempting to deal directly with rent. On the other hand he thought " that something must be done to stop rack-renting " and he proposed that a tenant who considered himself oppressively rented should be able to go into court, surrender his farm, and call on the Court to compel his landlord to buy him out or leave him in occupation at a fair rent.

" The Court would say, after hearing the landlord's reply and his offer as to the rent which he will accept from the tenant, whether it is a proper case or not, in which to make an award against the landlord on surrender of the farm by the tenant—if so the Court would treat the case as one of disturbance of tenant's occupation by landlord, *not* for non-payment of rent."

This plan might well have struck anybody except Gladstone as too elaborate and complicated a method of avoiding the

---

[1] Guedalla, *The Queen and Mr. Gladstone*, Vol. I, p. 217.

H

direct dealing with rent that Fortescue deprecated, but it
was not on this ground that Gladstone demurred. " I am a
good deal staggered," he wrote in reply (December 5,
1869), " at the idea of any interference with present rents."[1]
If he had proceeded by way of careful and skilled enquiry he
would probably have been less upset by this proposal. But
his full and conscientious correspondence with Fortescue
and Spencer suggests that though by this time his knowledge
of Irish history was considerable his information about
existing conditions was inadequate. He commented rather
sharply on the quality of this information to Fortescue,
remarking that the memoranda as yet printed had not done
much to advance the consideration of the land question,
and more than once he had to complain of delays at Dublin
Castle.

Gladstone was soon convinced that a good deal more was
needed than he had at first supposed, and he showed
characteristic courage and energy in facing this truth
and acting upon it. The next few weeks were spent in the
struggle to win the consent of his reluctant colleagues to a
much larger measure. At one time it seemed doubtful
whether the Cabinet would hold together under the strain.
The principle that the tenant was entitled to compensation
for his own improvements had been accepted in several
previous Bills, and so far everybody was prepared to go.
But the view of what Granville had called the landlord party
was that this was as far as it was necessary or desirable to go,
and that Irish grievances would disappear if the law recognized that in certain cases the improvements on the farm
had been made by the tenant and not by the landlord. The
desirable object was to draw Irish practice as far as possible
into the English model by encouraging leases. Gladstone,
now enlightened by his Law Officers and his Chief Secretary, had to persuade them to accept a totally new principle,
which, as he said, would be unpalatable to several of them,
the principle of compensation for disturbance. Gradually
he gained his point, but, though he gained the consent of his
colleagues, he did not gain their conviction. Lowe wrote

---

[1] Morley, *op. cit.*, Vol. II, p. 291.

praising the force of Gladstone's arguments, but he added that he feared he was steering upon the rocks. At last on January 25, Gladstone could report in his diary that his Cabinet difficulties were over, " Thank God."

Gladstone had a hard fight in the Cabinet, for he was single-handed. Fortescue was an ineffective ally, because Fortescue by himself was a very different person from Fortescue with Sullivan, the able Law Officer at his side. The other colleague who might have been expected to help was John Bright, but he was incapacitated by two causes. In the first place he was not at all in good health, for he was on the verge of the breakdown which soon afterwards took him for a time into private life. He did not actually resign for a year, but long before his resignation he was disabled. There is a letter from Kimberley to Gladstone, on March 12, about a proposal that he, Kimberley, should go and see Bright to tell him or Mrs. Bright what the Government had decided to do about the Fenians, saying that Bright was too ill. But Bright was half-hearted in helping Gladstone against his moderates because he was full of his own plan, a scheme for Land Purchase. Granville sent Gladstone an interesting letter in the early stages of this discussion, May 26, 1869, in which he described Bright's difficult temper. In the end Bright's plan was adopted, and Gladstone later gave him handsome praise for this reform,[1] but he had to warn him at the time that his aloofness from the controversy that was raging between the reformers and the landlord party in the Cabinet was putting the whole scheme of the Bill in danger, whilst his own plan covered a small part only of the problem.

The recognition of a right to compensation for disturbance, or, as it was put sometimes, the recognition of occupation as a form of property, was in principle a remarkable step forward. Gladstone even thought he had solved the problem of rack-renting. For he believed that by this method, a kind of fiction which treated occupation as property, and thus brought the new principle into some sort of organic relation to the principle of the Bill, Ireland could

[1] See his speech in Dublin, November, 1877.

have the benefit, without the disadvantages, of rent regulation. He wrote in this sense to Manning, on February 16, 1870.

"By this post I send you 2 copies of our last print of the Irish Land Bill. I cannot yet say whether it will be finally, or only approximately accurate, but the substance of it you may take for granted. You will at once see that here as oftentimes the circuitous road is really the only one practicable, and is to be much preferred to scaling and descending precipices. It would be most objectionable to call in public authority to determine every case of proposed eviction on the merits, and would tend to draw towards the Government more than ever the hatred of the people.

"The policy of the Bill is this, to prevent the Landlord from using this terrible weapon of undue and unjust eviction by so framing the handle that it shall cut his hands with the sharp edge of pecuniary damages. The man evicted without any fault, and suffering the usual loss by it will receive whatever the custom of the country gives and where there is no custom according to a scale beginning with 7 years rent, under or up to £10 valuation, and ending with 2 years rent over £100: besides whatever he can claim for permanent buildings or reclamation of land. Wanton eviction will, as I hope, be extinguished by provisions like these. And if they extinguish wanton eviction, they will also extinguish those demands for *unjust* augmentations of rent, which are only formidable to the occupier because the power of wanton, or arbitrary eviction is behind them. I give you here, for the information of your Irish brethren, what is in truth the pith of over 8 or 10 columns of the small print of the *Times* to-day: to which you and they will not have the time to pay attention. I am confident you will think we have honourably and thoroughly redeemed our pledge.

"The reception *thus far* has been beyond my expectation good in all quarters. Please give one copy to Cardinal Archbishop Cullen."

Gladstone's view of the importance of this new principle was shared by the Conservative leaders, but whereas he welcomed it as a method of protecting the small tenant, they dreaded it as a gross interference with the power of the landlord. It is not surprising that it encountered violent hostility. Disraeli, who did not divide the House against the second reading of the Bill, attacked this clause with great asperity, on the ground that it would affect the security of all landlords and all property, without giving Ireland any advantage. Gladstone in reply said that Disraeli had attacked one of the main pillars of the Bill. For the Bill had three great provisions.

" One was the confirmation of Irish customs. Another grand provision was the assertion of the principle that improvements made by the tenant were the property of the tenant. And a third principle of the Bill, which was by far the most prominent in the lengthened statement it was my duty to inflict upon the House was that damages for eviction were to be paid to the tenant."

It was over this new principle that the battle chiefly raged, and as the fate of the Act turned largely on the section giving effect to it, its history must be told. In its original form the clause proposed to allow tenants evicted for non-payment of rent to claim compensation, if the Court held that there were special grounds. The clause passed through the House of Commons in this form but it was struck out in the Lords. Salisbury declared that the clause would give the Court the power of revising the rents of every landlord in Ireland. There was no country in the world where power was given to a Court to revise rents to which two parties had agreed. The clause negatived the rule of honesty, that what a man contracted to do he should be made to do. The Commons tried to meet the objections of the Lords by confining the clause to cases where the rent was below £15, and by defining more closely the special grounds. The Court was to be empowered to give compensation if it found that the rent was " excessive." Gladstone explained that the Government made this concession " with the greatest pain and reluctance," and emphasized once more the importance they attached to this clause. His earnestness is intelligible, for he had by this time received a memorandum through Manning, in which the Irish Catholic Bishops had expressed themselves as dissatisfied with the Bill, and Gladstone was passionately anxious that his Bill should give the small tenant

effective protection against oppression. The Lords accepted
this compromise with one change, a change that proved of
great practical importance. They changed the word
" excessive " to " exorbitant." Gladstone accepted this
change with great reluctance after a strong appeal from
Granville who was leading in the Lords.

Gladstone had achieved something like a miracle within
his Cabinet and in the House of Commons, but his Bill fell
far short of the desires of the Tenant Right Party. That
party had lately been revived and reorganized under Sir
John Gray, the proprietor of the *Freeman's Journal*. Gray
divided against the second reading, and put his case against
the Bill in a good sentence. " It is a great and solid and, I
will add, a noble and generous advance. But the interests
of the people must be considered in a full settlement. The
Irish tenants do not require a Bill of pains and penalties
against their landlords. They ask for a Bill of rights for
themselves." The same view was taken by the Dublin
Municipal Council (Dublin did not then possess a City
Council) and Gladstone replied with the impatience that is
natural in a man who is more conscious of the difficulties
he has overcome than of the desires he has left unsatisfied.
He wrote to Dublin in this spirit on March 17, 1870.

The Catholic Bishops too took a less confident view than
Gladstone of the efficacy of his plan. Manning, answering
Gladstone's letter of February 16 describing his Bill and
sending him copies of the text, had sent an encouraging
report on the temper of the Bishops.

" As the Bill only came yesterday," he wrote on February 21,
1870, " they have not yet told me their judgment upon the
scheme. But more than one expressed his sense that you had
gone far to meet the great evils under which the people suffer. . . .
Meanwhile I shall read your speech which has just come. I
have seen enough of it already to enable me to say that you have
as you said honourably redeemed your pledge; and I look as the
Irish bishops do, to you as the statesman whose name will go
down to history as the friend of Ireland."

But after studying the scheme the Bishops had some important and pertinent criticisms to offer. They gave Manning

a list of amendments that they considered necessary to make the Bill effective.

" They prefer for various reasons of their own," he wrote on March 1, " to communicate through a channel which cannot be regarded as official and they desire me to say that though they feel strongly and unanimously on the subjects mentioned in their note, they regard your measure as a great boon to Ireland and the beginning of a new and happier state. They say that as the measure now stands they fear that it cannot be regarded as a settlement of the question. . . . They fear in chief that no *money* checks will restrain evictions as the incoming tenant will repay the landlord and that no sufficient security is provided against exorbitant raising of the rent which is equivalent to eviction."

The amendments they suggested are interesting in light of the later history of the agrarian question, for they included the provisions that became law in 1881.

Gladstone regarded these suggestions as quite impracticable and no doubt it would have been impossible even for him to push them through Parliament. He wrote to Manning on March 12, 1870.

" Your letter of the 7th reached me last evening. At an early hour in the morning, we had divided on the Land Bill. The Conservative party will aim at changes in Committee, which, although probably not so intended, will effectually maim the measure and make it useless for its purpose. They may, it is likely, decide against it on the 3rd Reading, though I do not think Disraeli will do this, if he can help it. I have not a doubt that we shall be able to resist these attempts effectually. I consider that we are pledged this year in a different sense to that of last year. We must not pass a Bill less favourable to the Irish occupier, than our Bill as it now stands. On the other hand I am bound in frankness to say that the paper inclosed in your former letter proposes changes in the Bill, which neither the nation, nor the Parliament, nor the Cabinet, could adopt. We might as well propose the repeal of the Union. You cannot be fairly asked to enter into details. But take simply these 2 facts— 1. Not 1 man has ventured to argue in the House of Commons for these changes. 2. We now propose for the Irish occupier, by a permanent law, provisions which place him, in comparison with the farmers of *England* and *Scotland*, in a position of high

priviledge and immunity. You will at once see that as regards
the great Irish question, all is now at stake. . . ."

Gladstone's letters show how hard pressed he was in this
struggle, and how passionately he desired the success of his
Bill.

He wrote a long letter to Manning on April 16, lamenting
the bad influence of the Vatican Decrees of Papal Infalli-
bility on the atmosphere in which he was trying to legislate
for Ireland, making every kind of Irish reform more difficult
by its effect on the English temper.

" What I have described," he wrote, " is no matter of speculation; I know it by actual and daily touch. . . . It is to me a matter
of profound grief; especially as regards Land in Ireland. For I
feel as if the happiness of some millions of God's creatures were
immediately committed to us, so far as the things of this life (and
their influence on another) are concerned; and until it is disposed
of, it seems to engross and swallow up my whole personal
existence."

On the 21st he wrote to Argyll:

" I am engaged in an arduous correspondence with Palmer.
He has nearly been the death of the Land Bill, but I do hope he
will remit a little. I for my part will be no party to passing an
inadequate Bill. The *next* Bill will be adequate and something
more. The something more I should regret, and have striven to
avert but the return has been grievous and the excess though
grave would be the lesser evil."

It is not difficult to understand why a Bill that seemed
inadequate to the Catholic Bishops seemed to Gladstone
effective and comprehensive. For the Bill covered all the
600,000 tenant occupiers in Ireland. There were two
methods of proceeding for the relief of the occupiers and the
Act of 1870 adopted both. It altered the law between
landlord and tenant in such a way as to give tenants protection, and it provided machinery by which tenants might
be converted into owners. The changes that the Bill
made by the first method were infinitely complicated, for the
conditions were such that no simple Act would meet the case,
and the statesman who carried it suffered from what his
critics called his *nimia subtilitas* and had a natural taste for

exploring and constructing labyrinths. The best short description of the Act is given in Eversley's *Agrarian Tenures* (p. 104).

" This Act legalised the Customs of Ulster and any like custom in other parts of Ireland, and gave to tenants who held under them, the protection of the law. It then proceeded to enact for the rest of Ireland a somewhat analogous system. It reversed the presumption of law that improvements belong to the owner of the land and secured both past and present improvements to the tenants, and enabled them to claim compensation for them on the determination of their tenancies. It laid down a further scale of compensation for disturbance, ranging from seven years rent in respect of holdings valued at less than £10 a year to less amounts for larger holdings, payable beyond the value of improvements on eviction for any other cause than non-payment of rent."

This is a very short summary of the changes in the law between landlord and tenant, and one addition must be made to it. For, as we have seen in certain cases, e.g., if the rent were " exorbitant," compensation might be claimed even if eviction was due to non-payment of rent. Moreover the Act contained what were commonly known as the Bright clauses, to aid and encourage the conversion of tenants into owners. These enabled the Treasury to advance two-thirds of the purchase money on the sale of any holding to its tenant, repayable by equal annual instalments, and interest spread over thirty-five years at the rate of £5 for every £100 advanced.

But the Bishops had put their finger on the weakness of the Bill. The tenant wanted not to be compensated when he left his holding but to be secure against eviction. The Act gave him no such security. The word " exorbitant " was interpreted in the Courts in such a way as to nullify the protection offered by the Bill. Hence though a revolution had been accomplished on paper, in practice the tenants found, when the agricultural crisis put the Act to a stern test, that it was of little help to them. The Lords had destroyed its virtue.

The Bright clauses too which at the time seemed too ambitious were in fact so mild as to be useless. But these truths, though they were known before long, were not known when Gladstone went out of office. He believed then that his Act had been a great success. Spencer told Gladstone on January 27, 1874, that even the figures for the Bright clauses were not unsatisfactory, and the statistics of crime were very favourable.

These two measures were the public evidence of the sincerity and the force of Gladstone's sense of duty to the Irish people. But he was busy behind the scenes with other efforts which produced no result. He wanted, as Disraeli had wanted, to establish a Royal Residence in Ireland. In order to bring the government of Ireland into a more sympathetic relation to the Irish people, he proposed also to abolish the office of Viceroy, and to substitute for it a purely ceremonial office, for which he designed the Prince of Wales, giving Ireland at the same time as political Minister a Secretary of State. In making these proposals he had two main ideas in his head. He was very much struck by the want of public spirit in the Irish aristocracy, and he thought that if the Prince had a Court in Ireland he would encourage the Irish governing class to take more interest in her institutions and her welfare. In this way he hoped to counteract the tendency which had been so active in Ireland ever since Dublin lost her Parliament. This plan had in his view also the advantage that it would give to the Irish people that sentimental interest in their connexion with Great Britain the lack of which was one of the chief difficulties in her government. Unfortunately Gladstone's plan was related to his great desire to give the Prince of Wales serious and responsible employment. The Queen did not share that desire. On the contrary she opposed it warmly, and as she had at the same time what Gladstone called " a magnificent twist in her mind on the subject of Ireland," the proposal to give him this employment was doubly damned. Gladstone pressed his views with great vigour, and maintained them with an obstinacy that the Queen warmly resented.[1] The plan was extinguished to the

---

[1] The very important correspondence on this subject can be found in Mr. Guedalla's book, *The Queen and Mr. Gladstone*, Vol. I, Chapter 5.

regret not only of Gladstone but of his colleagues. If this plan had been adopted it is not unlikely that the great Irish constructive movement, of which Sir Horace Plunkett was the leading spirit at the end of the century, would have begun thirty years earlier, with results to Ireland and to England of infinite importance.

CHAPTER VIII

Gladstone's combination of strength of body and strength of mind looks so impressive that the effect of strain on his health has often been under-estimated. Everybody knows about him that when he was over seventy he could fell the stoutest tree in the park, or walk twenty miles in the mountains, and that when he was over eighty he could speak for three or four hours in the House of Commons, meeting and defeating every opponent in turn, whether what was wanted at the moment was subtle and winding argument, or hot and over-powering passion. It has generally been supposed that he was always well and vigorous. Yet a study of his diaries shows how often he was ill, and ill at critical moments. He was in bed when Gordon was sent to the Sudan; in bed when Gordon's request for Zobeir was refused. During the 1880 Government he spent months at Cannes, sending commands and remonstrances as embarrassing to his colleagues as those sent by Tiberius to the Senate from Capri.

Let anybody consider what he had done in the first two years of office. His Government was a strong team—perhaps the strongest team to be found in the history of Cabinets—but in its fiercest struggles he had been single-handed. So far as the internal conflict over Irish land was concerned, Gladstone would have had an easier time if that team had been as weak as it was strong. Those two Bills alone would have exhausted the strength of most men. But Gladstone had in addition the cares of a Prime Minister occupied with two great problems: the problem of the Education Bill of 1870 and the civil war it excited in the Liberal party, the problem presented by the outbreak of war between France and Germany, and its first consequences to the peace and balance of Europe. Gladstone in the autumn of 1870 was a very different man from Gladstone in the autumn of 1868.

To understand what kind of strain he was suffering we must remember that physical exhaustion was a small part of it. He had the orator's excitable temperament, and the Evangelical conscience. After a long talk with Bright about this time he remarked in his diary, " My conversation with him yesterday evening kept me awake till four. A most rare event; but my brain assumes in the evening a feminine susceptibility, and resents any unusual strain, though, strange to say, it will stand a debate in the H. of C."[1] During the last three years of his first term of office his susceptibility was specially tried.

In politics a man has often to defend decisions that he does not himself approve. That is a condition of Cabinet Government and Cabinet legislation; it is the penalty of office. In nine cases out of ten this constraint does not cause the speaker or Minister serious discomfort. But there are times and occasions when a statesman finds himself in a false position, of such a kind that a man less sensitive than Gladstone is ill at ease. Pitt gave that impression after his desertion of the Catholics, for Fox remarked that he exhibited a kind of hydrophobia whenever the Catholic question was debated. Gladstone's strong sense of the guilt of England in her relations with Ireland distressed his peace of mind whenever he was obliged to use force, or to resist any movement that was connected with her smarting sense of self respect. His colleagues soon detected and regretted or resented this perpetual undertone.

" I am all against sitting in perpetual sackcloth and ashes," wrote Argyll on November 27, 1869, " because the Irish are violent and disaffected. It is true no doubt that Ireland formerly has been ill used and ill governed, and it is true also that the diseased condition of the country is due in some measure to these old sins of England. But for the last two generations at least there has been a general disposition to deal justly with Ireland, and not only a disposition but a steady progress in legislative

[1] Morley, *Life of Gladstone*, Vol. II, p. 381.

reform." " Perhaps," answered Gladstone (November 27, 1869), " I overdid the sombre colouring of the Irish Land question or the Irish case generally, but it is very dark, and I see neither truth nor policy in optimising on it.   Indeed the people of this island neither know in any tolerable degree how bad it is in itself, nor do they feel as they ought how disgraceful it is to themselves."

This wound—if that is the right name for Gladstone's discomfort—was kept open by friends and opponents alike who reminded him of his denunciation of alien oppression on the Continent.   Butt, pleading for the Fenian prisoners, recalled his attack on the Bourbon Government in Naples. He was engaged in a controversy, amicable but of deadly seriousness, with Manning over the Papal States, Manning being an out and out supporter of the Papal claims; and Manning too made use of the Irish analogy for Gladstone's embarrassment.   Thus in addition to the physical exhaustion caused by his immense efforts in the Cabinet and in Parliament, Gladstone was subject to something much more wearing: the nervous tension that a man feels when his conscience and his reason find it hard to come to terms, or at any rate to make more than temporary and provisional accommodations.   It is easy to see in the whole history of Gladstone's attempts to govern Ireland the effect of this tension.   He cannot open his mouth without betraying his fundamental dissatisfaction with the position he occupies; when he scolds he scolds with violence; when he argues he is obviously arguing as much with his own conscience as with his opponents.

This explains what must strike every close student of his first Government, the contrast between the triumphs of its first two years and its failures after 1870.   This is specially true of Ireland.   In 1860 and 1870 Gladstone was patient, considerate, full of hope and interest in a great effort at pacification.   After 1870 he was impatient, wilful, tactless, betraying faults of judgment and temper that affected both his politics and his relations with his colleagues.   He was a sick man, with all a sick man's petulance and obstinacy.

It is unnecessary to describe here the different occasions

on which Gladstone showed want of balance. One illustration may be given, the case of his appointment to the
Rectory of Ewelme. In 1871 this living was separated from
the Chair of Divinity at Oxford, with which it had been
combined, and Oxford was compensated for this loss by a
provision that the Crown should only appoint to the Rectory
a person who was a member of Convocation of the University. When the living fell vacant, Gladstone offered it to
two men who fulfilled this condition, and they both declined.
He then offered it to a man called Harvey, excellently
qualified in all other respects, but a graduate not of Oxford
but of Cambridge. This difficulty was got over by his
incorporation as a member of Oriel. Thus, when Gladstone made him Rector of Ewelme, he was technically a
member of Convocation. Strictly speaking the letter of the
law had been observed, but so flagrant a breach of its spirit
roused violent storms in Parliament and outside.

The new Rector was not a friend of Gladstone's; he was
not even known to him; nor was he a Liberal in politics.
Gladstone's conduct was a piece of completely disinterested
injustice. It is hard to believe that any other man in his
position who had attacked, or was preparing to attack,
almost all the great interests, the landlords, the coalowners,
and the brewers, who was challenging nationalist sentiment by
a bold stand for a great principle over Alabama, who had
put a great strain on the loyalty of many of his supporters by
his treatment of the denominational schools in the Education
Act, would have thought it worth while to provoke this
violent quarrel in order to put an obscure clergyman, who
had published an edition of the works of an obscure Father,
into the particular living for which, and for which alone, he
was disqualified by a special provision. It looked, as it was,
a piece of wanton, perverse, and high handed folly, and it
showed how Gladstone's temper and judgment were giving
way. He was an overworked and overstrained man.

The effects were seen in his treatment of Irish politics.

Gladstone's Government was faced from the first with the
problem of order in Ireland. In the autumn of 1869 there
was a serious epidemic of agrarian crime. There was also

an agitation on foot for the release of the Fenian prisoners. Gladstone's Government had released forty of these prisoners early in 1869,[1] and Spencer reported good results in a letter on March 30, but the agitation grew, and before long Gladstone was urging Clarendon, his Foreign Minister, to provide him with facts about the treatment of political prisoners in other countries.   In the early part of 1870 the Government agreed to refuse the request for the release of the remaining prisoners, but in the autumn, when the agitation had subsided, Gladstone urged his colleagues to reconsider the question, arguing very reasonably that advantage should be taken of a calm spell to make concessions that it was inadvisable to make in time of storm.   It was some months before he gained their consent, and then he spoilt the concession by insisting that the released prisoners should not live in Ireland.   He may have been influenced by the conduct of O'Donovan Rossa who, after his release, had continued to play a violent part in politics, and had been returned for Tipperary, though as a felon he could not sit.   His election was a great blow to the Government, for it did not encourage the view that the Irish were as grateful as they might have been expected to be for the Irish Land Act.   But this unfortunate decision meant that so many more Irishmen with grievances were sent to the United States, where the view of Irish politics which they held was powerfully represented in a population driven from its home by famine and misgovernment.

Agrarian disturbances forced the Government to pass a Coercion Act at the time of the Land Act, and another in 1871.   This was a cruel blow to Gladstone, and he struggled hard to escape it.   A study of his correspondence with Spencer, Fortescue, and Hartington, shows how conscientiously he took his duty as Prime Minister, and with what minute and incessant care he sifted and examined the case for coercion before he accepted it.   His zeal indeed led

---

[1] On October 10, 1868, Tennyson wrote to Gladstone saying he had received a pamphlet about the treatment of Irish prisoners in Dartmoor.   " I don't much believe in the accuracy of the Irish generally but I wish you who enlightened us formerly on the Neapolitan prisons to consider whether here too there be not a grievous wrong to be righted."

him into a suggestion which illustrated that want of tact which was so serious a weakness in his political equipment, for he proposed to send Kimberley, an ex-Viceroy, to Dublin, to look into the case, a proposal that, not unnaturally, hurt Spencer's feelings and had on that account to be abandoned. Gladstone exhausted every device in order to satisfy himself that these Acts were necessary before he accepted them, and a study of the innumerable documents that passed between Dublin and Whitehall would convince the most suspicious of England's critics that at this time, at any rate, coercion was applied with the utmost reluctance.

Thus Gladstone found himself, with all his splendid work for Ireland, drifting into the position so vividly described by Lord John Russell when he summed up the English treatment of Ireland. " Your oppressions have taught the Irish to hate you, your concessions to brave you." Was this a curse from which no man could escape, however noble his aims, and however deep his sympathy with the Irish people?

Gladstone had meant from the first to follow up his Church and Land Acts by a third reform, an attempt to meet the grievances of the Catholics in respect of University education. But before he had matured his scheme he had to face a new development in Ireland. In the autumn of 1870 a Home Government Association was formed to demand a Parliament for Ireland for her domestic affairs, leaving to the Imperial Parliament the relations of the United Empire with foreign States, and all matters connected with the stability of the Empire. There was to be no interference with the prerogatives of the Crown, and no disturbance of the principles of the Constitution. As might be expected from the tone of these demands, the new body was not a popular and revolutionary organization. It combined all kinds of respectable people in its ranks, drawing support indeed from some surprising quarters. For just as some of the politicians who overthrew Wellington and helped to give victory to the cause of Reform in 1832 were Tory Diehards, who could not forgive him Catholic Emancipation, so the first Home Rulers included Orange Diehards, who could

I

not forgive England for disestablishing the Irish Church. The movement however soon found a leader in Isaac Butt, formerly a Tory, an able lawyer who had made his mark, first as an authority on the Land problem, then as an advocate defending the Fenian prisoners, and in the following year he was elected Member for Limerick.

The Home Rule movement in Ireland was at this time slight in force and unrepresentative in character. It was in no sense a great popular demand. So powerful an Irishman as Cardinal Cullen called it " the bubble of a moment."[1] No English statesman was likely to consider that it was his duty to proceed to a revolution in the relations of the two countries before he had tried to remove the grievances that inspired what force there was behind this agitation. The most eloquent and powerful argument against that revolution was put by the staunchest friend Ireland had in England, and nobody can read Mill's pamphlet, " England and Ireland," published in 1868, without seeing that a man whose chief wish was to reconcile England and Ireland might regard Home Rule at that stage as a policy of despair. Mill's view was that as Irish grievances against England were far greater than any that the American colonists had suffered, separation would be followed by as much bitterness as that which had marked the relations of Great Britain and the United States ever since the War of Independence. The two countries would arm against each other, and Ireland's geographical position would give her, in all quarrels in which England was engaged, the place Belgium held as the cockpit of the quarrels of the Continent. The true policy was not to break the Union but to make it attractive to the Irish people. There was however one important qualification in Mill's argument. Disastrous though he held separation to be, he held that it would be less disastrous than the continued misgovernment of Ireland by England.

Gladstone's position was very much that of Mill. He did not want to encourage the Home Rule movement, for he believed that the Irish problem could be solved if England

---

[1] Gladstone's letter to Granville, November 4, 1873.

could learn to look at Irish problems with Irish eyes. He was conservative enough to dread a great organic change, a great constitutional experiment, as an adventure that might have the most mischievous consequences. The short history of the Paris commune had made a great impression on English minds.

But though Gladstone was not a Home Ruler at this time, anybody who studied his speeches, or his letters to his colleagues, could see that if conditions changed he might well become one. The *Times*, in a leader in September, 1871, remarked:

" Many people might well be anxious to know what the Premier thinks of Home Rule. He has given the world several surprises and is supposed to be subject to sudden conversions. A Conservative education struggles in vain with a temperament of sentimental Liberalism which cannot bear to refuse anything which anybody sincerely and earnestly sighs for."

This last sentence describes something in Gladstone's mind, though it describes it wrongly. Gladstone had in him a capacity for refusing, which made him sometimes a very difficult and disobliging colleague. His strong and narrow convictions about expenditure and the care of public money made him an obstinate opponent of demands that were at once popular and enlightened. As Chancellor of the Exchequer there was not much of the *nimium gaudens popularibus auris* about him. But the quality that the *Times* called a temperament of sentimental Liberalism was a belief, held more passionately by him than by any of his contemporaries, that government must somehow be reconciled with justice. He believed that England could meet every reasonable Irish demand, but he made it plain to his colleagues that the demand for Home Rule must be defeated, not by force, but by generosity. It is significant that he considered Butt's return to Parliament in 1871 a great advantage.

Gladstone's own position lent itself to misunderstanding, increased by his gift for elaborate and subtle argument, but when it is examined it is perfectly clear. If a man had said to him, " Do you think it a good thing now to set up a Parliament in Dublin? " he would have answered "No." If however his questioner had gone on to say, "Do you think that if the Irish people one day demand such a Parliament, after you have made a serious effort to solve her problems and to satisfy her imagination, England should resist such a demand? " the answer would equally have been "No." Between 1871 and 1874 his utterances, public and private, caused confusion, just because his position was peculiar. He was against Home Rule as an immediate policy; he would have been glad to see the demand for Home Rule abate under the influence of good reforms; he wanted to try his plan for a Royal Residence and the regeneration of the Irish gentry; he had still his scheme of University reform in the cupboard; he was doubtful whether any workable scheme for Home Rule had yet been devised. On these grounds he did not wish to say anything to encourage the agitation. He was therefore in agreement to this extent with his colleagues. On the other hand he held with Mill that it would be better to grant Home Rule than to govern Ireland perpetually against her will. To this extent he agreed with Butt. None of his colleagues considered the question from this point of view. A man might argue that Home Rule was, on its merits, the right solution for Irish misgovernment. That was the view of a very few Englishmen, of whom the most distinguished was Dilke.[1] A man might argue that Home Rule was so serious a mischief and danger to Great Britain that it could not be conceded, even if the alternative was a permanently dissatisfied Ireland. That was the view taken, for example, by Kimberley, in a long letter that he sent to Gladstone on June 28, 1871, on the proposal to abolish the office of Lord Lieutenant and substitute the Prince of Wales as a purely ceremonial Viceroy.[2]

[1] Dilke voted with Butt in 1874.

[2] This paper concluded with a strong sentence about Home Rule. "Persuaded as I am that in no circumstances whatever should England permit the withdrawal of Ireland from its connexion with her, that we must treat the question of separation as the North did the question of breaking up the American Union I should not hesitate to meet the Home Rule agitators by a measure for a closer administrative connexion between the two countries." Gladstone approved of the rest of the paper and it was circulated in the Cabinet, but he demurred to this sentence and it was taken out.

Gladstone took neither of these views. He still believed that England could combine justice to Ireland with a single Parliament. But he did not believe that the single Parliament could be maintained, if the Irish people refused to accept it, after England had done all that she could to remedy Ireland's wrongs. It is significant that in the only speech he made against Home Rule he laid it down that England had to satisfy Europe.

It is easy to see that Gladstone, holding these views, was in a position of great delicacy. If he had made a speech expressing them, he would obviously have encouraged the agitation in Ireland, which was what he wished to avoid. On the other hand it was difficult to say anything to discourage that agitation without doing violence to his own conscience, and giving an untrue impression of his views. His speeches, his letters, and, above all, the letters of his colleagues, show these two currents guiding his tortuous and indirect mind. As such violent attacks were made afterwards on his character for consistency and honesty in his treatment of the Irish problem, it is interesting to note that Hartington, who was his Irish Secretary, said in public, when the first quarrel over Home Rule was raw and bitter, in 1886, that none of his colleagues had any reason to complain of his later views, and that Randolph Churchill, speaking in the same angry atmosphere, said that he had found, on looking into history, that Gladstone had never made a single speech against Home Rule after 1871.

The speech to which Churchill alluded was made in Aberdeen in September, 1871. It was made a few months after the disturbing episode of the Paris Commune. Two great Irish measures had just been carried; Gladstone fresh from his great struggle to make his colleagues concede to Ireland reforms that they chiefly dreaded because they feared that England and Scotland might be tempted to ask for them, was more alive, at the moment, to the special benefits that Ireland had received than to the special disadvantages she suffered. His Treasury mind was always on the watch against Irish demands on the public purse. Ireland was, for the moment, quiet, and he liked to think that she was

quiet because he had given her the Land Act. " I have
looked in vain," he said, " for the setting forth of any practical scheme of policy which the Imperial Parliament is not
equal to deal with, or which it refuses to deal with, and which
is to be brought about by Home Rule." He had thus
every motive for putting the objections to Home Rule as
strongly as he could. It is not improbable that he
put them rather more strongly than he supposed. His
colleagues were delighted with his speech. But the speech
had a curious sequel. A few weeks later Jonathan Pim, an
Irish Member, published a tract on Home Rule in which he
made some effective criticism of Gladstone's speech, treating
it as completely hostile. This tract he sent to Gladstone,
whose letter in reply would perhaps have bewildered some
of those who had admired it. He wrote on November 21,
1871 :

" I thank you for your tract on the subject of Home Rule, which
I have read with much interest. I am obliged to demur altogether to the accuracy of the view which you have presented in it
of my speech at Aberdeen, but I should be unwilling to dwell on
anything which would tend to create or exhibit differences of
opinion in a matter where I think as to all questions of principle
we are really agreed."

Thus even the single speech that Randolph Churchill could
find condemning the demand for Home Rule appeared to
its author to be in substantial agreement with the views of
this Irish Home Ruler.

Gladstone's next speech on the subject was made in the
House of Commons in May, 1872. It was made in the course
of a debate on the proposal to repeal a law, that had been
passed by Grattan's Parliament in 1793, limiting the right to
hold public meetings. Hartington said that it was desirable
to hold this weapon in reserve, arguing incidentally that some
of the new Home Rulers were connected with the old Fenian
movement. Butt demurred, declaring that many of them
were " men of high position and large property." He
believed " that the whole Irish people would make their
demand at the next election in such a form that every
Englishman would feel it necessary for the peace of the

Empire that the demand should be granted." Gladstone made a most conciliatory speech. At Aberdeen he had asked:

" Can any sensible man, can any rational man suppose that at this time of day, in this condition of the world, we are going to disintegrate the capital institutions of this country, for the purpose of making ourselves ridiculous in the eyes of all mankind, and crippling any power we possess for bestowing benefits through legislation on the country to which we belong? "

In his speech in the House of Commons he called Butt's attention to the Constitution of the United States (Butt had spoken of a federal relationship between Great Britain and Ireland) to enforce his contention that you could not have existing in a country two separate legislatures, co-ordinate in power.

"There must be somewhere, in the last resort, an appeal to that supreme authority which, in case of necessity, holds in its hand the solution of every problem that may arise. No doubt it is the virtue of a truly free country to multiply subaltern authorities, and subaltern authorities, not with powers granted in a narrow spirit of egotism, but making local government and local institutions strong to the uttermost point of the strength which they can develop, and finding in the strength of local authorities and in that development of local government the surest source of strength for the central government. That is the spirit in which the supreme authority of the Imperial authority would always be exercised."

Sir John Gray, speaking as a Home Ruler, said he was pleased to recognize in the speech of the Prime Minister the broad principles on which the advocates of Home Rule based their demand. So difficult was it for Gladstone to open his mouth on this question without either doing violence to his conscience, or encouraging a demand that he did not wish to encourage. An Irishman wrote to Hartington, contrasting the tone of the speeches of the two Ministers, and saying that Gladstone's speech had given an immense impetus to the Home Rule cry.

Gladstone's casuistical tastes found congenial employment all through his career in explaining to his friends that

they agreed when they seemed to differ. On this question
he spent his time shocking his friends and then reassuring
them. But they were not really under any delusion about
his sentiments. Hartington wrote to Spencer a few days
after the speech in the House of Commons telling him that
he had warned Gladstone that if a certain appointment were
made, the vacancy it would create would be filled by a
Home Ruler. " I am sorry to say Gladstone did not seem
so much shocked as he ought. His views on Home Rule are
much too Liberal in my opinion, and if they will only profess
to maintain the supremacy of the Imperial Parliament he
does not mind what they go in for."[1]

This fundamental difference was displayed in Gladstone's
view of the treatment of the Fenians. Writing to Spencer
in September, 1870, he complains that the Law Officers
seem to think that

" we are not to release the prisoners until Fenianism is at an end.
This, I think, indicates a wrong conception of the question.
What we have to do is to defy Fenianism, to rely on public sentiment, and to provide (as we have been doing) the practical
measures that place the public sentiment on our side, an operation which I think is retarded by any semblance of severity to
those whose offence we admit among ourselves to have been an
ultimate result of our misgovernment of the country."

Gladstone felt the strain of this uneasy equilibrium. He
smarted when Irishmen charged him with being a good
Liberal on the Continent and a bad Liberal at home. He
had to defend acts and decisions that were repugnant, such
as the decision, taken by Spencer and Hartington, to forbid
Irishmen to hold meetings in Phoenix Park, at a time when
Englishmen were allowed to use Trafalgar Square for
demonstrations of sympathy with the Commune. Moreover
he was learning how little gratitude there is in politics. It
is not surprising that after his Herculean efforts on behalf
of the Irish people he should have been a little unreasonable
in his view of his claims on their gratitude. All this combined to disturb his equanimity, to make his nerves unsteady
and irritable, and to shake his judgment. Nobody who

[1] Holland, *Life of Devonshire*, I, 96.

LORD HARTINGTON

looks at the incidents which caused such agitation at the end of his term of office—his behaviour over the Rectory of Ewelme and the promotion of Collier—can avoid the conclusion that such provoking and wilful blunders were the mark of an overworked and overstrained man.

In December, 1870, Fortescue left the Irish Office to become President of the Board of Trade. Gladstone wanted Hartington to succeed him. There was much to be said for this choice, for Gladstone had in his mind his ambitious plan for reforming the government of Ireland by making the Prince of Wales a ceremonial Viceroy, and creating an Irish Secretary of State. Obviously an aristocrat like Hartington would be an admirable person to fit into this scheme. There was, however, one fundamental difficulty. Hartington hated the prospect. He felt about banishment to Ireland as Ovid felt about banishment to the Black Sea. He had no mind to give up his amusements and his parties. On receiving this refusal Gladstone was more intent than ever on sending Hartington to Ireland, for whereas he had thought before that it would be an excellent thing for Ireland, he now thought it an excellent thing for Hartington. This son of a great Whig house needed discipline, and Gladstone felt about giving him the Irish Office as he felt about giving the Prince of Wales employment. Instead of asking himself whether a man who hated going to Ireland. was likely to take a sympathetic view of the Irish when he got there, he argued that a man who might one day lead the Liberal party must be compelled to learn the importance of public duty. So he struggled with Hartington and overcame his reluctance.

His relations with Hartington, perhaps for this reason, were not very happy, and they ended in an incident that rankled in Hartington's mind. Gladstone formed the impression in the summer of 1873, on inadequate evidence, that both Spencer and Hartington wanted to resign, and under this belief he wrote Hartington an extraordinary letter (August 12, 1873), inviting him to return to the Post Office, leaving his place in Ireland to W. E. Forster. Hartington, who had dreaded Ireland as dull exile, replied that he would not care to go back to the Post Office after " holding a much more important and interesting office," and that he would prefer to go out of the Government altogether. At the same time he wrote to Spencer:

" I am therefore so far as I know out altogether, at which I shall greatly rejoice; but I must say I am not much pleased at the manner in which it has been done. I don't know from whom Mr. Gladstone has heard that I will not stay after you, and the alacrity with which my supposed wishes are now consulted is a contrast to the pressure he put on me to stay in April. The fact is that the place is wanted for Forster, who can't stay in his present office, with Bright in office, without offending the Dissenters." [1]

Gladstone replied to Hartington by reading him another lecture on his duty, speaking of his own personal conviction about the claim " which the Crown as well as the country has upon the services of men born to great positions and properties and to hereditary rights of legislation." Granville tried to make peace and to soften the effects of Gladstone's inconsiderate behaviour. In the end both Spencer and Hartington stayed on till Gladstone made his surprise dissolution in 1874. But Gladstone was in private quite impenitent. He wrote to Granville (August 19, 1873), " Hartington has many good qualities besides his birth, but I am tempted to say he sells them rather dear." When Hartington left office he left with a sense of grievance.[2] Gladstone had treated him with a want of courtesy, and none of his plans of reform had come to anything. As his relations with Gladstone were an important element in Liberal politics for the next twelve years, these wounds to his pride were not mere passing trifles.

Hartington, though he had gone with such ill will to the Irish Office, and had believed himself that his dislike of his office would make him a bad Minister, had formed and presented some very sensible views after he had got there. He urged the importance of two reforms: the reorganization

[1] Holland, *Life of Devonshire*, I, 123.

[2] Hartington made his grievances public after the Home Rule split, stating that he had tried in vain to interest Gladstone and his colleagues in Irish local government reform. In this complaint he was fully justified.

of the railways under Government control, and the reform of Irish administration, in order to give Irishmen more control of their own arrangements. Gladstone had said in 1867 that no boon would be so great to Ireland as a measure to secure cheapness of railway transit. When he took office he was still in this frame of mind, and he complained that Bright, who was ready to make the State a stockjobber in land, shrank from a modest reform of the railways. At that time Gladstone had still some of the temper of the old President of the Board of Trade, who had shocked Palmerston, twenty years earlier, by recommending nationalization of the English railways. The case for this Irish reform was now stronger than in 1867. For a Special Commission, appointed by Disraeli, had reported in its favour; seventy-eight Peers and ninety Irish Members signed a memorial in support, and every Grand Jury and Municipal Corporation petitioned to the same effect. Hartington found himself in the position that Fortescue had occupied in the winter of 1869. He had the Cabinet against him, partly from its individualist prejudices, and partly from its preoccupation with other measures. If Gladstone had supported Hartington as he had supported Fortescue, he could have beaten down the resistance of the Cabinet, as he had done in the case of the Land Bill. Unfortunately he gave him little support. On February 10, 1873, Hartington wrote to him in real distress, because he had made a very strong speech in the previous year on the nationalization of the railways, and he found it intolerable that he should be expected to oppose a reform he had pronounced urgent. He asked to be allowed to treat it as an open question. Gladstone sent a characteristic reply postponing decision.

If the case for railway reform was strong, that for Local Government reform was even stronger. The rise of the new Home Rule party, supported by men of all classes and views, was due to impatience with the incompetent administration of Ireland under Dublin Castle and the Grand Juries. The right answer to that demand was, obviously, to improve the methods and change the spirit of that administration. Gladstone realized this, and on October 12, 1873, he wrote

to Spencer, " I entirely share Hartington's desire to have a
good and legitimate measure for the home transaction of
Irish business, such as may strip Home Rule of any show of
reason." But he neglected this question, as he neglected the
other. He allowed, that is, the fears and prejudices of his
colleagues, and the obstacles due to the state of business
to obstruct these urgent reforms.[1]

What is the explanation? There are two explanations,
and they are both connected with his fatigue and strain.
The first is that he had made up his mind that quite a
different reform was more urgent than either of those recommended by Hartington. This was of course University
reform.

Almost every Government in turn recognized that something had to be done about University Reform in Ireland.
Gladstone's predecessors had attempted such a reform, and
all his sympathies, tastes, and inclinations drew him to this
task. He worked with incessant vigour, reading, writing,
thinking, and arguing, and in the end produced a scheme for
which there was a good deal to be said on paper, but against
which there was one unanswerable argument. Nobody
wanted it. By his scheme, Trinity College Dublin, Maynooth, and the Colleges of Cork and Belfast, were to be
combined in a new University. In the hope of reconciling
the opponents of mixed education to this arrangement, not
only theology, but moral philosophy and history, were to be
excluded from the curriculum. If the conditions had been
specially favourable for the reform of the Irish Church,
University Reform was a more difficult task at this time than
it would have been earlier. For the leading Catholic
spokesman was no longer Murray, the Archbishop of
Dublin who had worked so well with Whateley, but Cullen,
a stiff and unbending adherent of the most rigid and exclusive school. When Cullen died in 1878 the *Times* remarked
that at the time of his appointment the Irish Catholic
Church was almost as free as the Gallican. " His com-

---

[1] It is only fair to point out that Disraeli, who had not given Ireland a single
great measure, behaved even worse over the railways. This, though the first
politician to press for this reform was his hero, Lord George Bentinck. See
Holland, *Life of Devonshire*, Vol. I, p. 103.

mission from the Vatican was to make it Roman." Spencer wrote to Gladstone on February 25 reporting a talk with Cullen, whom he found strongly adverse, on the ground that it perpetuated the mixed system of education to which he had always been opposed.

Manning was in favour of the Bill, and he wrote to Cullen strongly urging him to accept it. At first he was hopeful of success, but by March 7 he knew that his efforts with the Irish bishop had failed. " Non-endowment, mixed education, and godless colleges are three bitter things to them." " This," he wrote to Gladstone, " is not your fault, nor the Bill's fault, but the fault of England and Scotland and three anti-catholic centuries." Cullen condemned the Bill with great violence in a pastoral on the 9th, and its fate was settled. Gladstone's Bill, disliked by the Irish Catholics on one ground, was disliked by English Radicals on others. It was defeated on second reading, on March 11, by 287 votes to 284. Forty-three Liberals voted against the Bill. It was a bitter blow to Gladstone. Yet at the moment it showed him at his best. For of the speech he made in its defence so bitter a critic as Fawcett[1] said that it was so powerful that if the House had voted when he sat down, the Bill would have been almost unanimously carried. The Speaker, Brand, paid it a compliment on other grounds, " a magnificent speech, generous, high minded, and without a taint of bitterness, although he was sorely tried, especially by false friends." But although adversity, now as always, brought out his noblest qualities as well as his most versatile gifts as an orator, the bitterness of this disappointment helped to determine his course in politics for some years to come.

Hartington had been opposed to this unfortunate Bill from the first, and he wrote long letters to Gladstone that deserved more attention than they received. For Gladstone, who had in some ways a remarkably resilient mind, had in others a remarkably stiff mind. His sense of power, and his confidence in his weight of experience, made him at times arbitrary and self-willed, and slow to consider the

---

[1] Of Fawcett's speech against the Bill, Manning wrote to Gladstone, " Fawcett's animosity is a true honour," March 3, 1873.

suggestions and schemes of others. This was part of his strength, as it was part of his weakness. If he had not had it, he could not have forced his personality and his ideas on politics with such success. But it shut his eyes sometimes to important truths and to important problems. In this case he was mortified by the rejection of his University plan; he was consequently wanting in vigour in taking up and pushing even remedies that he approved. He was a soured man. Of his two great plans for pacifying Ireland one had been destroyed by the Queen, the other by the Catholic bishops.

But something else was happening in Gladstone's mind. He was turning for refreshment to the fatal fascination of public economy. In August, 1873, he took the office of Chancellor of the Exchequer when Lowe had to leave it in disgrace. Burke said of Chatham that a peep into the Royal Closet intoxicated him. A peep into the Treasury was equally fatal to Gladstone's judgment. He was intoxicated, but intoxicated with soda water. All his noble enthusiasms were deflated in a cold, dry, unimaginative atmosphere of severity and public thrift. In the autumn of 1873 Fortescue wrote to him recommending a man as inspector of Irish antiquities. Gladstone had strong sympathy with Irish sentiment, and an interest in Irish history that astonished Parnell who did not share it. But he could not forget that he was Chancellor of the Exchequer. In a letter that shows how wrong it is for a man to combine that office with any other, he replied (October 18, 1873) that it was his duty as Chancellor of the Exchequer to find reasons for objecting to a new post, rather than to consider the fitness of a man to fill it. The *Times* description of him as a man in whom a Conservative education struggled with a sentimental Liberalism, was misleading unless " Conservative education" was given a special meaning. He was really a man in whom a luminous European sense struggled with the spirit of a high-principled miser, a great catholic genius with a pedantic reverence for the precedents and traditions of Whitehall. He was a high-minded miser because he firmly believed, as the best men among whom he spent his youth had believed, that the misery of the poor was due chiefly to public extravagance, and the waste and misuse of the nation's resources. Send his imagination over the mountains of Europe and he had the eye of an eagle; shut him up in the Treasury cupboards and he was like a captive hawk whose eyes had been sealed.

It is this conflict that makes his career so difficult to understand and so interesting to follow. In his great moments he is the most striking figure in Europe; in his little moments he seems a man meant to spend his life on small change. Meredith was not alone in feeling that there were two Gladstones. " Gladstone divides me; half of him I respect deeply; and the other half seems not worthy of satire." In the first half of his spell as Prime Minister he had been at his best. F. D. Maurice said of him, " I admire him for his patient attention to details, and for the pains which he takes to secure himself from being absorbed in them by entering into large and general studies." In his great battle over Irish land he had shown just the combination that Maurice praised. He had taken a large historical view of the problem, and having grasped it in this spirit he had mastered the details of reform by his conscientious work upon them. He had shown at once the best qualities of Burke, and the best qualities of Peel. But in these last years, bitter with disappointment and strife within his party, the other Gladstone, the Gladstone George Meredith described as not worthy of satire, was creeping back.

Troubles came thick and fast upon him. In the summer of 1873 three of his Ministers, Lowe, Monsell, and Ayrton, were involved in an irregularity, for it was discovered that a sum of £800,000 had been applied by an official of the Post Office without the authority of Parliament to the extension of the Telegraph system. The Government escaped a vote of censure, but there was widespread dissatisfaction. Monsell, the Postmaster General, was punished with a Peerage, and Lowe had to leave the Treasury for the Home Office. Gladstone reluctantly succeeded him. This involved Gladstone in another embarrassment. A discussion arose on the question whether, in taking the office of

Chancellor of the Exchequer he had, or had not, vacated his seat at Greenwich. Jessel and Coleridge, the Law Officers, thought he had not; the Lord Chancellor, Selborne, and the Lord Advocate thought he had. Gladstone observed that the trial would take as long as the Tichborne case. The question was important as well as interesting because it was known that Gladstone's seat was not safe. In the end the dilemma was resolved by dissolution, January 24, 1874, and it was believed by many that Gladstone dissolved in order to escape from this difficulty. There is no evidence in his papers to support this view.[1]

Gladstone dissolved as Chancellor of the Exchequer, and his address showed how completely he was under the influence of this atmosphere. For in it he held out hope of repealing the income tax. Lecky has called this a shameless bribe. Dr. Clapham shows, on the contrary, that it was part of Gladstone's general scheme of finance; if it had been carried, he would have substituted for it a reconstruction and increase of the death duties. Dr. Clapham goes so far as to say that " in view of his record, failure to make it, in some season of fair weather, would have been greatly to his discredit,"[2] and his chief criticism of Gladstone is that he did not realize that the fair weather was over. It is significant that Disraeli, who was generally credited with larger views of social duty, instead of attacking this part of Gladstone's programme, merely said that repeal had always been an object of Conservative policy; his Government reduced the tax to 2d. One young Radical, whose relations with Gladstone were later to be as important as those of Hartington, made a comment on this paragraph in the address which was a more serious criticism than Lecky's. Chamberlain, fresh from his attack on the slums of Birmingham, his head full of plans for civilizing the English towns called this " the meanest public document that has ever, in like circumstances, proceeded from a statesman of the first rank."[3] For that is how the dread of taxation and the belief that men and towns, left to themselves, would find

---

[1] See the remarks in Morley, II, 472.
[2] Clapham, *Economic History of Great Britain*, II, 404.   [3] Garvin, I, 220.

their way out of barbarism, the view of the high-minded men among whom Gladstone had been brought up, looked to the new Radicals who wished to apply drastic and direct remedies to distress. To Gladstone the misery of the poor was still firmly associated with public extravagance and waste. Bribe or no bribe, the address made a poor impression on the electorate. The Liberals fell from 372 to 244; the Conservatives rose from 286 to 350. Gladstone who had affronted the two most powerful social interests in England, to do Ireland justice, was answered by the return of fifty-eight Home Rulers, and Fortescue, the minor hero of the Land Act, lost his seat in Louth, and had to find refuge in the House of Lords.

The fifty-eight Home Rulers were in one sense an ungrateful comment on Gladstone's reforms. In another sense they might be regarded as his pupils. In his election address (January 23, 1874) he had said little about reform, but he had a sentence that caught attention:

" I fear that the time has not yet come when you can anticipate a diminution in the calls for legislative labour. Permanent and solid as is the Union of the three Kingdoms, they present varieties of circumstance, of organization, and even of law. These varieties, combined with the vast development of Imperial interests, add seriously to the duties of Parliament, which, indeed, have reached a point where they seem, for the present, to defy all efforts to overtake them. I think we ought not only to admit, but to welcome, every improvement in the organization of local and subordinate authority, which, under the unquestioned control of Parliament, would tend to lighten its labours and to expedite the public business."

To one of his Irish friends who took alarm at the phrase he sent a characteristic answer on January 28.

" I thank you for your letter and good wishes. In my address I have endeavoured to state clearly the principle on which I should endeavour to deal with all questions relating to the increase of local or sectional powers in the U.K. With respect to Home Rule I have not yet heard an authoritative or binding definition of the phrase which appears to be used by different persons in different senses. Until this phrase comes to have a definite and certain

K

meaning, I have not thought myself justified in referring to it, but have indicated plainly in another form the test which I should apply to its interpretation."

Spencer also wrote to him about this passage (January 30, 1874):

" Touching ' Home Rule ' I think it right to tell you that in certain quarters a sentence of your Address has been interpreted into encouragement of ' Home Rule.'

" I send some printed Extracts which show this and Bessborough who is here tells me that Lord Meath and a very friendly and anti Home Rule Kilkenny Gentleman understood you as at all events giving a loophole to ' Home Rulers.'

" I need not say that I know that your remarks were general and equally applicable to England and Scotland as to Ireland, but Home Rulers differ so widely in their views that the most Moderate would easily accept your views as a definition of their Home Rule principles.

" I think it right that you should know this as you may wish to take an opportunity of explaining your opinion.   In the face of Hartington's Address I cannot myself think that people would be justified in thinking that you and the Gov^t winked at Home Rule.

" The more I see of the Elections the more dishonest and mischievous do I think those who adopt the cry."

Gladstone answered:

" I thank you for your letter and inclosures.   I have not seen Hartington's address, but he and I have been in correspondence and in entire accord about Home Rule.   The paragraph in my address to which you find that objection is taken by some rather weak-kneed brethren was read to and unanimously approved by the Cabinet.

Hartington's letter is not among the papers, but Gladstone's answer was as follows:

January 25. 74.

" With the whole substance of your note I agree.   I have no addition or qualification to suggest except this: it is not necessary perhaps for them to use the word Union, and they may I think safely express a desire to facilitate and extend local self-government (a) in all parts of the country (of course for them in Ireland specially) (b) under the supremacy and controul of the Imperial

Parliament. These two restrictions or specifications I think make all safe."

Eleven years later Gladstone still tried to persuade his colleagues that his views and theirs on Ireland were in accord. But by that time the chasm was so sharp that even he could not throw across it a makeshift bridge of words.

CHAPTER IX

AFTER 1874

The election of 1874 had so decisive an influence on Gladstone's later career that it is necessary to understand the mood in which it left him. He had been at the head of the first Government to be formed after the enfranchisement of the town workman. He had had as his colleagues the most capable set of men who had ever made up a Cabinet. His Government had carried reforms of the greatest importance, giving expression and effect to the temper and the energy of the democratic force that had come into public life. For the first time England had now a national system of public education, and a national system of local government. The Ballot Act had protected the workman voter; the Coal and Metalliferous Mines Acts laid the basis of all our modern mining legislation; Selborne's Supreme Court of Judicature Act had tidied up a great deal of costly confusion. The Government had struck a great blow for the principle of arbitration over the Alabama question.[1] In Ireland the Church had been disestablished and, as Gladstone believed, the sting had been taken out of an unjust and provocative land system. Such a record of courage and success might well justify the confidence the new electorate had shown in 1868 in the Liberal party and in Gladstone.

Yet the Government had been condemned unmistakably at the polls. What made it worse, the condemnation had come not merely from its opponents but from its friends. The Education Bill had irritated the Nonconformists; the

[1] How much tenacity and courage were needed to overcome the national pride of the English may be judged from Lord Salisbury's jibe that the increase in the drink bill at this time meant that Englishmen had had to drown their sense of shame. Nobody could call Salisbury a Jingo.

Government's serious attempt to meet the critics of the Contagious Diseases Acts had roused them to fury; if the employer class had been alienated by the Mines Act, and by the Factory Bill brought in by a prominent Liberal, Mundella, the workmen had been alienated by the unsatisfactory Act which the Government had passed on the status of the Trade Unions. Lastly, though Gladstone believed he had appeased Ireland, it had been decided, when he thought of paying a visit to Ireland in 1872, that the danger of a hostile demonstration made it inadvisable, and at the election Irish Liberals had been displaced by Home Rulers. Thus the adverse verdict was not merely the answer of the vested interests to the challenge of a reforming Government; it was a bitter comment by those whom the Government had thought that it was serving on the value of the blessings they had received.

Gladstone was a highly sensitive man, and he was so deeply wounded by what he thought such gross ingratitude that he decided to go out of politics.[1] It is significant that in the first hour of disappointment, signing himself " ever warmly yours, though smitten hip and thigh," he wrote to his friend Panizzi, the chief librarian of the British Museum, a letter discussing and describing, in a spirit certainly not wanting in optimism, the blessings Christianity had brought into the world.

In this mood full of distaste for politics and homesick for religion, he entered on a task in which his European sense found a large field for his gifts and taste for polemical

---

[1] The effect of the collapse of the Irish University Bill and its sequel on Bright is shown in a letter he wrote to Granville, January 25, 1875.

" He (Gladstone) was scandalously treated by a few Englishmen, Fawcett, Torrens, Bouverie, Horsman, Peel, etc., and by the whole Irish contingent who prostrated themselves before their bishops and destroyed the best Minister whom England had ever seen. For a time the work of the party is done. ' Home Rule,' hollow and false as to all good, is real enough for some mischief, and the Roman party treacherous to its friends, knows no limit to its baseness in the pursuit of objects which will remain, I hope, for ever unattainable. The party then is weakened and for a time destroyed, and I cannot see for it any immediate or early restoration." Fitzmaurice, *Life of Granville*, Vol. II, p. 143. Mrs. Gladstone thought Gladstone's decision wrong. See her uneasy and pathetic letter to Gladstone of January 12, 1875, Tilney Bassett, *Gladstone to his Wife*, p. 208.

writing. His feeling for a Catholic culture that should unite
Europe had been shocked and distressed by the decrees
adopted by the Vatican Council in July, 1870, declaring
Papal Ex-Cathedra definitions of faith and morals infallible.
This result had followed long and eager debates in which
Newman, Döllinger, Acton, Darboy, Dupanloup, Hefele,
and several of the most learned and devoted leaders of
Catholic thought had been on the losing side. Four
hundred and fifty-one bishops voted with the Pope, eighty-
one against him, and sixty-two for further enquiry. Oddly
enough the Pope's victory came at the moment when the
Franco-German War was about to relieve Rome of the
French garrison which had kept the Pope on his throne
since 1848. "Thus the last of the Pontiffs to exercise
temporal power was invested, by way of compensation for
what the war took from him, with unlimited control over the
minds of all good Catholics throughout the world."[1]

Gladstone had watched this struggle at first with alarm
and then with anguish:

" My vision only enables me to discern," he wrote to Manning,
" within the Latin communion a determined movement towards
the isolation and absolutism of the clergy, and the establishment
of an impassible chasm between the Christian religion and the
thought of man; in fact exactly what Voltaire would have
desired and Bossuet and Pascal would have wept over."

He is said to have been stirred to write on the subject by
his visit to Döllinger in September, 1874, and " the spectacle
of a man, so wise, pious, and learned under the ban of the
Church."[2] Whatever the immediate cause, it was perhaps
unlikely that once he was withdrawn from the active
leadership of politics, he would have long remained silent
on a question in which his most solemn feelings were so
deeply engaged. He had already been turning from
politics to his favourite interests. Just before the election he
wrote on " Evolution " in the *Contemporary Review*. In
February, the month in which he went out of office, the same
review published his article on " The Shield of Achilles."

[1] Paul, *History of Modern England*, Vol. III, p. 348.
[2] *Letters of Lord Acton to Mary Gladstone*, edited by Herbert Paul, p. xlv.

In April, 1874, he wrote to his wife, " I am convinced that the welfare of mankind does not now depend on the State or the world of politics, the real battle is being fought in the world of thought."[1] In May and June he wrote further articles on Homer, and in the autumn he discussed Ritualism and Ritual. It was in November that he published his first pamphlet on the Vatican Decrees in their bearing on civil allegiance: a political expostulation.

Two passages from his pamphlets give a good idea of his spirit.

" If any motive connected with religion helped to sway me, it was not one of hostility but the reverse. My hostility, at least, was the sentiment which we feel towards faults which mar the excellencies, which even destroy the hope and the promise of those whom we are fain to love. Attached to my own religious communion, the Church of my birth and my country, I have never loved it with a merely sectional or insular attachment, but have thankfully regarded it as that portion of the great redeemed Christian family in which my lot had been cast—not by but for me. . . . Therefore I will say, and I trust to the spirit of Charity to interpret me, I have always entertained a warm desire that the better elements might prevail over the worse in that great Latin communion which we call the Church of Rome; and which comprises one half or near one half of Christendom ; for the Church which gave us Thomas à Kempis, and which produced the scholarlike and statesmanlike mind of Erasmus, the varied and attractive excellencies of Colet and of More; for the Church of Pascal and Arnauld, of Nicole and Quesnal; for the Church of some now living among us, of whom none would deny that they are as humble, as tender, as self renouncing, and as self abased— in a word as Evangelical as the most ' Evangelical ' of Protestants possibly can be."

" In some of the works to which I am now offering my rejoinder a protest is raised against their discussion in the name of Peace. I will not speak of the kind of peace which the Roman Propaganda has for the last thirty years been carrying through the private homes of England. But I look out on the world; and I find that now, in great part since the Vatican Decrees, the Church of Rome through the Court of Rome and its Head the Pope, is in direct feud with Portugal, with Spain, with Germany, with

[1] Tilney Bassett, *op. cit.*, p. 201.

Switzerland, with Austria, with Russia, with Brazil, with most of South America; in short, with the far larger part of Christendom."

Gladstone was justified, however strong his language in controversy, in his contention that his fundamental desire was for unity. " I am not proud of isolation but deplore it," he had written in 1850, and one of the last acts of his life was to address a solemn appeal to Pope Leo XIII for religious union. But the very strength of this desire added vehemence to his anger when he saw a step being taken which in his judgment raised a new and terrible barrier between the Latin communion and his own. He hated the decrees because they struck a blow at the hope of the unity of Christendom " repudiating both modern thought and ancient history." He felt indeed about this revolution as he felt about Disraeli's Imperialism, that it was an attack on the unity of Europe, substituting for " Rome's old proud boast of *semper eadem* a policy of violence and change."

The pamphlets, for the first was soon followed by a rejoinder to his critics, had an immense sale, and caused great excitement all over Europe. The second brought him a note of gratitude from the statesman with whom of all others he had least sympathy, Bismarck himself. Gladstone believed that his pamphlets had had an excellent effect in Europe and at home. He told Granville that he had increased the difficulties in the way of a restoration of the Temporal Power. He wrote in his diary December 29, 1875, " I hope my polemical episode is over. It has virtually occupied more than a twelvemonth but good has been done, especially in Italy." Many doubted then and more have doubted since.[1] Acton would have dissuaded him from publishing. Newman was one of many who answered him, and his answer—too courteous to please the Pope, who had called Gladstone " a viper attacking the bark of St. Peter "—was followed by letters between the

---

[1] Lathbury thinks that they might have done some good if they had appeared in 1870 but that their effect in 1874 was unfortunate. Lathbury, *Gladstone : Correspondence on Church and Religion*, II, 47.

two in which Newman assured Gladstone, thanking him for a letter he called " forbearing and generous," that " it has been a great grief to me to have had to write against one whose career I have followed from first to last with so much (I may say) loyal interest and admiration."[1] But the pamphlets cost Gladstone the friendship of Manning. This coming disaster had thrown its shadow over their correspondence from the beginning of the discussion.

" Would to God," Gladstone had written as early as October 1869, " that the personal feelings which will, I trust, ever subsist between us, were not accompanied at least on my side by a painful apprehension of an increasing divergence, and an approach of a state of things in which what is to the mind of one the salvation of faith and church, is to the mind of the other their destruction."

In January of the following year he ended a letter in a similar tone. " Of the Council I will say nothing except to express my earnest desire that it may end well; the only thing it is in my power to say without the fear of giving you pain." Their friendship could not survive the bitter argument into which they were drawn when Gladstone took his angry pen into his hand. A few years later they met, but passed each other with a mere acknowledgment as bare acquaintances, just as Fox and Burke passed each other in the House of Lords when they met for the business of the impeachment of Hastings after Burke had repulsed Fox's affection. They were not reconciled till 1887, when Home Rule, which separated Gladstone from so many of his colleagues, brought them together again. There were only two men to whom Gladstone signed himself at this time habitually " Yours affectionately." They were Argyll and Manning. Home Rule destroyed the friendship of the first but gave him back the friendship of the second.

His pamphlets inevitably did him a great deal of harm in

[1] Newman began his answer to Gladstone (in the form of a letter to the Duke of Norfolk) with a friendly note. " Yet not a little may be said in explanation of a step which so many of his admirers and well wishers deplore. I own to a deep feeling that Catholics may in a good manner thank themselves and no one else, for having alienated from them so religious a mind." *Difficulties felt by Anglicans*, Vol. II, p. 176.

Ireland. Cullen, like Manning, had been a strong supporter of the policy of Pope Pius IX, both in his quarrels with Italy and his Vatican Decrees, and Gladstone had now stepped into a controversy in which he alienated not only the supporters of the Pope, but opponents like Newman. Cullen spoke of him more in sorrow than in anger. Cardinal Cullen, Gladstone wrote to his wife, on February 17, 1875, " has, I think in a christian spirit, brought me into his Lenten Pastoral, and desires his people to pray for me—that I may become sensible of the wrong I have done the Pope and the Church."[1] The course and collapse of the University Bills had created a certain strain in the relations between Gladstone and the Irish Bishops, and this further conflict added another. For Gladstone himself recognized that it would widen the breach between Liberals and the Irish party.[2]

The pamphlets injured Gladstone also at home. They revealed the wide gulf that separated him from the life and mind of his party. Great domestic problems were forcing themselves on public notice whilst he was giving up all his energy to this crusade. Chamberlain, full of his experience of the evils of the new town life, was nursing the hot indignation that was to explode a few years later against the lethargy of Hartington and his Whigs. He had discovered, as he put it in the *Fortnightly Review* in October, 1875, "that we have in our midst a vast population more ignorant than the barbarians whom we profess to convert, more miserable than the most wretched in other countries to whom we attempt from time to time to carry succour and relief."[3] In the Liberal party he found little interest or conscience on these matters and the man who could fire its spirit was devoting all the passion and concentration of his vehement

[1] Tilney Bassett, *op. cit.*, p. 212.
[2] Letter to Granville, December, 7, 1874.
[3] Garvin I, 220. Bridges was to put this truth later in the *Testament of Beauty*, Book IV, 357.

> See how cross-eyed the pride of our world-wide crusade
> against Nigerian slavery, while the London poor
> in their Victorian slums lodged closer and filthier
> than the outraged alien; and under liberty's name
> our Industry is worse fed and shut out from the sun.

personality to this strange and remote problem. Gladstone said of the decrees that he attacked that he looked on them as the most portentous of all events in the history of the Christian Church.[1] " An Ex-Minister," observed Chamberlain, " who devotes his leisure to a critical examination of the querulousness of an aged priest is hardly in sympathy with the robust common sense of English Liberalism."[2]

This passionate argument occupied Gladstone's energy and imagination, as he says, for twelve months. For the leadership of the party he had a growing distaste. He had written at once after the election to Granville telling him that he wished to renounce it and in January, 1875, he formally retired. His successor's place was not likely to be too pleasant, for, however difficult his colleagues had sometimes found Gladstone as Prime Minister, such discomfort was nothing to that of leading a party of which he was the most brilliant and the most irresponsible member. Still the succession was regarded as a prize, and the party was divided about the man to whom it should be given. Hartington was looked on as a Whig, and Forster as a Radical, but Forster had lost important Radical support (including that of Bright and Chamberlain) over the Education Bill and he refused to stand against Hartington. Gladstone wrote Hartington a letter so characteristic and significant that it deserves to be given.

Private   Hawarden.
                                        Feb. 2. 75.

My dear Hartington,

You will perhaps consider that I am out of court, and not in a condition to lay upon others the burden I have myself eschewed. Nor do I place my own title high: altho' one of my grounds of action has certainly been that difficulties, and grave ones, existed for me, which did not exist for others.

You may possibly recollect the opinion I gave you (close to the spot where I am now writing) at the time when you handsomely agreed to take the Irish Office. It was plain that this must come. During the fretful agitation of the last 18 or 20 days, my opinion

[1] Morley, *Gladstone*, II, 512.
[2] Garvin, I, 222.

has not for a moment varied, as to what ought to be, and what, I think, by hook or by crook, will be. I both admit, and plead, that the Leadership of the Liberals in both Houses ought to be, and cannot help being, light and negative rather than positive, in a degree unknown, at least in the H. of Commons, for the last 45 years. It approached nearly to this in 1867 after the important defeat. In 1868 it altered its character solely because the great Irish question came up in force. Let me be plain. What is good, and what is less good, in you have combined to give the public an inadequate idea of your force. You have not been a good attendant in Parliament relatively to your *political* rank. Your real and undeniable modesty has worked in the same direction as the comparatively small number of your appearances. Those who are now choosing you, and can choose no one but you, partly on negative grounds, will be perhaps surprised, certainly pleased, when they come to know by experience the quantity of available material, pith, and manhood that is in you. I am using a great freedom in writing thus. But I do not think you are one to require, or much to care for apologies in critical circumstances.

I think that as an equitable man, viewing all circumstances of the past and future, you will be disposed to admit that the public, that your country, has some unpaid claims upon you. I do not think you will be able strongly to urge that there is any other person in particular who ought to take that which is now thrust upon you. The diffidence, which is your best defence, will, nevertheless, not suffice to make a good and complete defence. While the demand upon you will be lighter, much lighter, than usual, the reasons for not declining to meet it are certainly stronger than usual.

One circumstance in this case will, I think, bring you some compensatory pleasure. Your family has for a series of years been much at the head of all families belonging to the Liberal aristocracy of England for its exertions and distinctions in the cause; and your assumption of the post will give, as well as take, honour where it is due.

Believe me yours sincerely,
W. E. GLADSTONE.

The tone and the implications of this letter throw a good deal of light on the strange history of the relations of these two men during the next ten years.

Gladstone was not thinking of politics at all when he

handed over the party to Hartington. His mind was running on another subject. In May he wrote to his wife: "I am feeling my way towards the purposes of the rest of my life. It will I dare say clear by degrees. For the general business of the country my ideas and temper are thoroughly out of harmony with the ideas and temper of the day, especially as they are represented in London."[1] A long entry in his diary a few weeks earlier shows how little sympathy there was between him and the new House of Commons.

"March 30, 1875. . . . Also I endeavoured to lay out before C. my views about the future and remaining section of my life. In outline they are indefinite, but in substance definite. The main point is this, that setting aside exceptional circumstances, which would have to provide for themselves, my prospective work is not Parliamentary. My tie will be slight to an assembly with whose tendencies I am little in harmony at the present time; nor can I flatter myself that what is called the public out-of-doors is more sympathetic. But there is much to be done with the pen, all bearing much on high and sacred things, for even Homeric study, as I view it, is in this very sense of high importance, and what lies beyond this is concerned directly with the great subject of Belief. By thought, good or evil, on these matters, the destinies of mankind are at this time affected infinitely more than by the work of any importance in Parliament. God has in some measure opened this path for me. May He complete the work."

It is interesting to speculate on what would have happened if the Eastern question had not come into politics in 1876. Gladstone always talked of himself as longing for a retreat into a life of contemplation. The year before he talked in his diary of the great business of "unwinding the coil of life." His friends doubted whether he did not mislead himself. Granville, commenting on this desire, remarked when urging Gladstone not to give up the leadership: "The question of work is serious, but with your extraordinary mental activity and fecundity, and your temperament, will you ever find yourself in a position in which you will not strain your physical strength?" Would Gladstone's temperament ever have allowed him to give up

[1] Tilney Bassett, *op. cit.*, p. 215.

the evening of his life to a spell of quiet self-absorbing meditation, away from the fierce conflicts of passion and justice
in the world? For Gladstone had this urgent driving sense
of duty, and he combined it with a nervous constitution
that made him combative, passionate, and excitable. He
knew this himself. " This *sort* of controversy," he wrote of
his conflict with Palmerston in 1864, " keeps the nerves too
highly strung, and makes me sensitive, fretful, and impatient."[1] His friends knew it well. " It is a pity," Cornewall Lewis said, " to put so much heat, so much irritability
into business; now I am as cool as a fish." In the diaries of
Lady Frederick Cavendish, the reader has a picture of the
intense feeling, the nervous tension, that Gladstone's sense
of the importance of the issues for which he was fighting
brought into his life. She saw him on the day when it
looked as if the Irish Church Bill would be shipwrecked, and
the following day when the shipwreck was averted. " July
20, 1869. Uncle W. dined. He was very unhappy dreading worse terms being imposed on the Church hereafter and
foreboding danger to the House of Lords: July 22. Matters
all arranged. Uncle W. came home absolutely overcome.
He said he wanted to go straight to church."

It is difficult to think that anything but the sealed door of
a Trappist cell would ever have kept that impatient eager
spirit out of the life of conflict in the wicked world. But to
understand Gladstone's later career, and his relations with
his colleagues, it must be remembered that though he
was in politics for another twenty years, he believed that
he was there under some constraining force; that he never
regarded himself as a party leader, but as a man who would
step aside to-morrow, kept in active life by this or that
mission. " I am certain," he wrote in his diary on December
29, 1885, " that there is one keen and deep desire to be
extricated from the life and contention in which a chain of
incidents have for the last four years detained me against
all my will." He had no large constructive scheme of
reforms on which his heart was set. He was in his own view
a man called back to public life by the Eastern crisis,

[1] Tilney Bassett, *op. cit.*, p. 164.

occupied afterwards with particular problems for which he felt a special responsibility. Among them of course Ireland took the chief place.

This is not the place to discuss his great campaign against Disraeli's Eastern policy. Three things only need be said about it here. The first is that it obviously provided a theatre for his special genius and sense of duty. The European question, which at one time had meant the Crimean War, at another the war for the freedom and unity of Italy, meant now the struggle between the rights of the Balkan peoples and the selfish aims of an Imperialist British policy. The power with which he conducted that struggle, the insight and foresight that he showed, the success with which he averted war, the splendid lessons he taught the new democracy about the principles that should guide the foreign policy of a self-respecting people, the remarkable triumph that he won for a high-minded view of duty against all the intoxicating impulses of pride and selfish passion,[1] all these gave him an ascendancy over the imagination of his countrymen which compelled the Queen, against her will, to make him Prime Minister in 1880. Dilke, a very critical commentator on Gladstone, remarked in his diary,

" The Conservatives no doubt thought that Mr. Gladstone's attitude [on the Eastern question] was mere emotional facility, a mere exhibition of spasmodic power of transient enthusiasm, an effect rather of temperament than of conviction. . . . The public, however, saw more clearly. Power over the moral fibre of other

[1] Dilke notes in his diary at this time, " On Sunday, March 10th, in coming back from the Grosvenor Gallery, I passed a great mob, who were going to howl at Mr. Gladstone—at this time the ordinary Sunday afternoon diversion of the London rough." (Gwynn and Tuckwell, *Life of Dilke*, Vol. I, p. 249.) Two other sidelights on Gladstone's position at this time in other eyes than those of the London roughs may be given. The first from his diaries.

March 10, 1878. " Went to the levy. The Princess for the first time received me dryly. The Duke of Cambridge black as thunder, did not even hold out his hand. Prince Christian could not but follow suit. This is not very hard to bear." The second from Jowett's Letters. April 3, 1878. " Gladstone is undone in general opinion, but his wonderful power of speech and a sort of clientèle among dissenters and in manufacturing towns will always make him formidable."

natures is not given to those whose own nature is wanting in this moral force. . . ."[1]

But there are two other things to be said of his superb achievement. It not unnaturally embarrassed the leader of the party in the House of Commons, and in this way so far from restoring unity it led to further discord. Gladstone describing the atmosphere in one of the debates when the Front Opposition Bench were against him, remarked " such a scene of solitary struggle I never remember." On the third of May, 1877, Dilke predicted that next week the Liberal party would cease to exist.[2] The party would be equally divided; Hartington would resign and Goschen succeed. He said that 110 Members were going to vote with Gladstone, about the same number with the Front Bench, and the rest, including most of the Irish Members would abstain. This crisis was averted by a concession on Gladstone's part at the last moment. But his energy was much more appreciated outside than inside the House of Commons, and thus he was in 1880, as in 1868, a leader forced on Parliament by the enthusiasm and confidence out of doors. We are given a good picture of the strain by Lady Frederick Cavendish, who was well placed for seeing all sides in this difficult arrangement. She was a favourite niece of Mrs. Gladstone; she was the wife of Lord Frederick Cavendish for whom Gladstone had the affection of a father; she was the sister-in-law of Hartington. In February, 1878, she describes the tension created by the differences between Gladstone and Hartington on the Eastern question, " two men so utterly unlike in disposition and mode of viewing things."

" . . . I am come round to the conviction (which Papa always held strongly) that he should either have continued to lead the party, or withdrawn from Parliament altogether, or taken a Peerage. It is immensely to the credit of both him and Cavendish that they have pulled together at all, and is due to the perfect honesty and sense of duty of both."

Hartington once explained his difficult relations with Gladstone in a single sentence. " He was a Peelite and I was a Palmerstonian."

---

[1] Gwynn and Tuckwell, *Life of Dilke*, Vol. I, p. 218.   [2] *ibid.*, Vol. I, p. 221.

The other important fact was its influence on the temper and the temperature of party politics. What were the causes of the extreme bitterness of party strife in the next ten years? One undoubtedly was the emergence of a few young men of great gifts and violent manners. During these years Chamberlain came to the front, making his mark, first by his most honourable career as Mayor of Birmingham, then by the ability and the bitterness of his speeches, lastly by his success in organizing party strength and giving to politics the doubtful blessing of the caucus. Chamberlain threw himself into two agitations: one a social agitation, the other the Eastern agitation. Chamberlain had his counterpart on the other side, in the Fourth Party, which made itself such a force in the Parliament of 1880. The resemblance between Chamberlain and Randolph Churchill was very close, and each of them made himself a power in his own party by the same gifts in debate, and the same insolence in attack.

These personal forces helped to create the extraordinary violence that marked the politics of the next few years. But was there not another cause? Gladstone tried to persuade himself that his own tempestuous eloquence had had no influence in exciting this animosity. Yet it is obvious that the greatest orator of the day could not assail the chief Minister in a series of superb speeches, treating the issues that divided them as moral issues, holding up his rival's policy to public indignation, without bringing on himself a flood of answering passion. The Queen he made an enemy for life, for she could no more forgive him his attacks on Disraeli, than he could forgive Disraeli his attacks on Peel.[1] But it was not the Queen only who could not

---

[1] The Queen wrote to Sir Henry Ponsonby, on April 8, 1880, " What the Queen is specially anxious to have impressed on Lords Hartington and Granville is, firstly, that Mr. Gladstone *she* could have nothing to do with, for she considers his whole conduct since '76 to have been one series of violent, passionate invective against and abuse of Lord Beaconsfield, and that *he caused* the Russian war and made the task of the Government of this country most difficult in times of the greatest difficulty and anxiety, and did all to try and prevent England from holding the position which, thanks to Lord Beaconsfield's firmness, had been restored to her." *Queen Victoria's Letters*, Second Series, Vol. III, p. 75.

L

forgive him. The hatred between Disraeli and Gladstone which might have died in Disraeli's grave, lived in the hearts of his followers, and Gladstone's Government was treated from the first day of its life to the last with implacable injustice. It may reasonably be held that Gladstone saved England from war at the time, that no other man could have done this, and that he could not have done it if he had not used his sternest weapons. But he made retaliation inevitable. Thus by another of those coincidences which seem to strew themselves over Irish history, English politics were complicated by special and vindictive passion at the very moment when the Irish agitation was assuming a new and more dangerous character, demanding as never before a spirit of reason and tolerance in those who had to meet its challenge.

Granville wrote the Queen a letter, April 24, 1880, in which he tactfully reminded her that Beaconsfield as well as Gladstone let himself go at times. " Lord Beaconsfield and Mr. Gladstone are men of extraordinary ability; they dislike each other more than is usual among public men. Of no other politician Lord Beaconsfield would have said in public, that his conduct was worse than those who committed the Bulgarian atrocities. He has a power of saying in two words that which drives a person of Mr. Gladstone's peculiar temperament into a great state of excitement." *Queen Victoria's Letters*, Second Series, Vol. III, p. 86.

CHAPTER X

THE NEW IRISH PARTY

In the six years during which Gladstone was a free lance, striking first at Pio Nono and then at Disraeli blows that resounded through the world, Irish politics were passing through a revolution that was as dark to him as to other Englishmen. The Home Rule movement when Cardinal Cullen called it a bubble was a respectable agitation in which men of all classes and all religions took part. Its leader was Isaac Butt who, starting as a Protectionist and a Tory, had been drawn into sympathy with national sentiment, first by his study of the land system, then by his defence of the Fenian prisoners. Butt was a man of great ability, courage, and public spirit, an able Parliamentarian, but the victim of drink and debt. In the House of Commons he was on good terms with the Liberals, with whom he was often in agreement, and, oddly enough, on intimate terms with Randolph Churchill, whose father was at that time Viceroy. Churchill was attracted to the Irish cause, and had some notion of enlisting Irish support as a political force of his own. He was himself a Tory, with Radical ideas and generous sympathies, very critical of his leaders, quite ready to strike ahead of his party, or even against it.

Thus the Home Rule party when Gladstone drove his first thunderbolts across the mountains of Europe was not a party of substance. It was not indeed an idle party. Year after year Butt introduced a Home Rule motion, or a demand for a new Land Bill, or a new University Bill, making effective speeches and impressing the House of Commons by his intellectual abilities. But there was nothing except his special interests to distinguish him from an English member, for he had a great respect for the House of Commons, and a lawyer's regard for its rules and traditions. Butt believed to the last that by orderly methods in the House of Commons, and the pressure of the Irish votes in the English towns, the English people would be brought to give Ireland a Parliament.

To other and more impatient Irishmen this seemed a foolish optimism. They felt that the Home Rule movement was languid and formal, a debating rather than a driving force, allowed, as the *Times* put it, a field day once a year on the understanding that nothing was to come of it. Mr. Yeats has described the revolution which in four years transferred the leadership of the Irish cause to these rebels, and gave a new character to the Irish problem. The Home Rule movement under Butt, he says, " lacked hereditary passion." " Parnell, finding that this lack made Butt's party powerless, called in the peasants' tenacity and violence."[1] Irish history between 1876 and 1880 is the history of this revolution, a revolution of which the incidents and results could be watched in the House of Commons, in Ireland, in the Colonies, and, not least, in the United States.

To describe this revolution in detail is outside the scope of this book, but a brief account must be given of the men who organized it, and the forces it brought into active life. The two chief agents were men as unlike each other in background, in personal history, and in character, as any two men of their time. They had indeed only two things in common. They were both born in 1846, and they were both born in Ireland.

There was nothing of the peasant about Parnell. The founder of his family was a mercer who became Mayor of Congleton in Cheshire in the reign of James the First. His grandson bought an estate in Ireland. Parnell's family thus belonged, not to the native population that had suffered in Ireland, but to the invading class that had enjoyed power and prestige. Of that class they were enlightened members. His great-grandfather, Sir John Parnell, had been Chancellor of the Exchequer in Grattan's Parliament, and had taken a

---

[1] Yeats, *Dramatis Personae*, p. 37.

leading part in the struggle that ended in the great concession of 1782, though he had opposed Flood on Parliamentary Reform, and Grattan on the Catholic question. Later he had been one of the ablest opponents of the Union. He was universally respected as a man of incorruptible integrity, high principle, and striking gifts. One of his sons was an active Radical in the House of Commons, held office under Grey and Melbourne, and took a peerage as Lord Congleton. Parnell's grandfather sat in the House of Commons. His father lived on his estate at Avondale, a good landlord and a good neighbour. There was nothing in the Parnell family history to explain Parnell's decision to call in the peasants' tenacity and violence for a life and death struggle with England.

For Parnell's anti-English spirit came not from his father but from his mother. His father had been the least active and prominent of all the Parnells in politics. But he had fortified the Radical temper of his family by marrying the daughter of a distinguished American admiral, who had won fame in fighting against the British, and had left to his children an inheritance of anti-English feeling. Parnell's mother lived to a great age, but she kept to the day of her death her political hatred of the English; her hatred, as she put it, of the English dominion. She had two wars in her blood: the war for independence and the war of 1812. Thus Parnell was, as Meredith said of Lycophron, " a rebel with his mother in his brows."

Parnell inheriting this temper, but otherwise indifferent to politics, went to Magdalene College, Cambridge, and came away full of the arrogance of the English. " These English," he said to his brother, " despise us because we are Irish. But we must stand up to them. That's the way to treat the Englishman; stand up to him." Still his Irish pride and self-consciousness seemed to sleep for some years and he was chiefly famous after leaving Cambridge as a cricketer. Then his indignation was excited by the Fenian trials; he took to politics, and in 1875 he entered the House of Commons as M.P. for Meath, determined to " stand up to the English." Of the success he ultimately obtained in that

character the most vivid impression is perhaps to be found
in a remark of Dilke, who was not an admirer of his political
intelligence. " Dealing with him was like dealing with a
Foreign Power."

The story of Parnell's rise in the House of Commons was
as dramatic and tragical as the story of his fall. It was
dramatic, because it was a duel between a man, who began
as a halting speaker and an ill-instructed politician, and a
veteran, who was not only a first-rate speaker but an expert
on the questions that he brought before the House of
Commons, in which the upstart overthrew the veteran.
With the help of Biggar, a Belfast merchant, small and
deformed in person, Parnell made obstruction such an art
that the task of protecting its dignity and its rights became
for some years the principal preoccupation of Parliament,
and the chief anxiety of English Ministers. For this kind of
career Parnell was admirably suited, in one respect, by
temperament, since he resembled Castlereagh, with whom
his ancestor had fought over the Union; despising the House
of Commons, he was indifferent to its contempt or its dislike.
So far as agrarian reform went, he was not at first or by
nature more revolutionary than Butt. Where they differed
was in the field of tactics. Butt held that the dignity of
Parliaments was the common interest of democracy all the
world over, and that the Irish party should use its forms to
make their demands in an orderly manner. Parnell
believed that the only way of making the House of Commons
attend to the needs of Ireland, which it meant to neglect,
was so to use its forms as to prevent it from attending to the
needs of England, which it was obliged to consider. The
battle was fought in the House of Commons and in the
Home Rule organizations outside. Parnell won over the
organizations to his view. The struggle was tragical, for
in its last stages Butt was a dying man and Parnell did not
spare him.[1] In the House of Commons Parnell had to

---

[1] The last chapter of Butt's life was distressing and discreditable to his
countrymen. He had impoverished himself for Ireland, and yet an effort to
relieve him by national subscription failed. He is not the only victim of the
ingratitude and suspicion that Irish history has bred in the Irish character.
Mr. Yeats remarks of the fate of Synge, " Those who accuse Synge of some

MICHAEL DAVITT

wait for the leadership till after the General Election of
1880. On Butt's death in March, 1879, the Irish Members
chose as their leader William Shaw, a Protestant merchant,
once a Nonconformist Minister, an honest and capable
man, but mortally wounded at the start by an Irish witti-
cism. For it was said of him that he was known in England
as the leader of the Home Rule Party, and in Ireland as the
Chairman of the Munster Bank.

But Parnell's rise in the House of Commons was only
part, and the less important part, of this Irish revolution.
The strength behind the new party was built up in Ireland
and America on the basis of a great mass of agrarian misery
and resentment. To understand this new party we must
turn to the second of the makers of the new Ireland.

Two years after Parnell entered the House of Commons
there stepped into the daylight from his prison cell a one-
armed man whose history had run a very different course
from that of the Wicklow squire. If, instead of belonging
to the troublesome Irish race, Michael Davitt had been a
countryman of Mazzini and Garibaldi, his career would
have fired the imagination of thousands of Englishmen as a
tragedy of poverty and patriotism. As a boy of five he had
been flung out with his parents and their children from their
cabin in the mountains of Mayo. When eleven he had lost
an arm in a Lancashire cotton mill while employed on tasks
that the law forbade to children. Struggling with the
difficulties of life in the random occupations of an industrial
town, he had been drawn into the Fenian brotherhood in
1865, and five years later had been sent to penal servitude
for fifteen years for collecting arms. In 1877 he was
released on ticket of leave. His history, his own and that
of his family, thus divided him widely from Parnell. One
other contrast must be noted. Parnell had been drawn into
politics by resentment, inspired and fed by English behaviour.
In Davitt, as everybody testified who knew him, the dominat-

base motive are the great-grandchildren of the Dublin men who accused Smith
O'Brien of being paid by the Government to fail. It is of such men as these
that Goethe thought when he said, ' The Irish always seem to me like a pack of
hounds dragging down some noble stag.' " (*Dramatis Personae*, p. 101.) Parnell was one day to suffer under the same law.

ing passion was love of Ireland. The explanation is not obscure. Davitt's patriotism embraced not only Ireland but the poor of the world, including the poor of England. If life at Cambridge had shown Parnell one side of the English character, a Lancashire cotton mill had shown Davitt another.

When Lovett went to prison in 1838 he spent his time thinking out and planning a new policy for the working-class movement. Davitt, when he went to prison in 1870, used his long hours of solitude in the same way. The Irish revolutionary forces were scattered over the world. How could they be brought together? Irish nationalist sentiment lived on the traditions and legends of tragedies, such as the Famine, the failure of 1848, the failure of the Fenian effort of 1866 to 1870. The Butt party seemed without life or fire. The more ambitious and energetic movements were divided between Physical Force elements and Moral Force elements. How could all these forces be combined? How could the impulses and emotions stirred by this awakened patriotism be made an effective force, giving direction and purpose to the mind and the spirit of the Irish people? This was the problem as Davitt saw it, and he found the answer in his experience of life and his study of history: in the Ireland he had seen with his own eyes and the Ireland he had seen with the eyes of Lalor. In Ireland there were thousands of rack-rented peasants, men living day and night under the shadow of eviction; in England, in Scotland, in the colonies, and, above all, in the United States, there were thousands of men and women who, themselves or their fathers, had been driven from their homes by the landlord power. A common injustice made them one. This potential power, as Davitt called it, had been neglected. What was wanted, if the Irish cause was to be made a living and active force, was to fling all this passion, this sense of lasting wrong, against the system whose victims looked forward in their homes with a fear that could not sleep, and backward in their exile with a hatred that could not forget. The Irish land system and English rule were aspects of each other. The man who struck at one, struck at both.

When he came out of prison, Davitt took these constructive ideas to the United States. For four months, employing great tact in order to keep himself in touch with all sections of Irish sentiment, he preached his doctrine. At a final meeting held in Boston on December 20, 1878, three resolutions were carried. The first demanded national self-government for Ireland; the second called on the Nationalist party in Ireland to keep itself independent, and to press for constructive social remedies; the third pressed for agrarian reform to save the peasants. The State was to buy up the land and sell it, or let it in perpetuity, to the tenants. When he took his programme to Ireland Davitt had a disappointment, for the Fenians rejected it. But he found support elsewhere, and he persevered. He went to his native county, Mayo, where he had a striking success. He held a meeting to protest against an increase of rents on the estate of a Catholic priest, Canon Burke. Seven thousand peasants attended his meeting, and the rents were promptly reduced by twenty-five per cent.

Six weeks later Parnell decided to throw in his lot with this movement. In spite of the condemnation of the Bishop of Tuam, he attended a great meeting at Westport where he urged eight thousand peasants to " defend their homesteads." The movement was now started. Davitt, a few weeks later, founded the National Land League of Mayo. The landlords were to sell out; if they declined, compulsion was to be used; if they persisted in rack-renting and eviction, they were to be met by peasants' combinations. The League was to publish the facts about rents and to show where the rents exceeded the Griffith valuation, a valuation made in 1852 for purposes of taxation, and to give notice of impending evictions in order to arrange for meetings of protest. The names of the men who took a farm from which a tenant had been evicted were to be published, and also the names of those who offered a higher rent than that paid by the occupier. The land crusade was thus converted from a movement for tenant right into a movement for the preservation of Ireland's peasants.

In October, 1879, the Land League was organized at

Dublin as a national institution with two objects: the reduction of rack-rents, and the promotion of the ownership of the soil by the occupiers. These objects were to be pursued by spreading organization among tenant farmers; by defending those who were threatened with eviction for refusing to pay unjust rents; by facilitating the working of the Bright clauses through the coming winter; and by obtaining such a reform in the law relating to land as would enable every tenant to become the owner of his holding by paying a fair rent for a limited number of years. Parnell was elected President, with Davitt, Brennan, and Kettle, as secretaries. Brennan was an ex-Fenian, and Kettle had been a follower of Butt. Davitt had succeeded in bringing together the most formidable force that Ireland had yet collected, by combining social discontent with political ardour. His enterprise had a most encouraging sequel. Parnell went to the United States, gained for this new movement the sympathy of men like Ward Beecher and Wendell Phillips, the great anti-slavery leader,[1] and as the grandson of Admiral Stewart, by a rare indulgence, was allowed to address Congress.[2] He had a triumphal tour. " He went everywhere, and everywhere he was received with open arms. Large towns and small vied with each other in showing honour to him and sympathy for the cause he represented. Public bodies presented addresses to him. Irish soldiers lined the streets through which he passed. Governors of States waited upon him."[3]

Parnell and Davitt were both in their very different ways men of genius and character, but their rapid success was not due only to their capacity for leadership. Nature had come to their aid. For calamity had overtaken agriculture, and with calamity the landlord's war on the peasant had broken out again. Ireland had three or four prosperous years after the election of 1874; agrarian crime had almost ceased; evictions had been fewer than ever before in the history of

---

[1] Wendell Phillips said, " I came here . . . from a keen desire to see the man that has compelled John Bull to listen." Eversley, *Gladstone and Ireland*, p. 103.

[2] This honour Parnell shared with Lafayette and Kossuth. Eversley, *op. cit.*, p. 103.

[3] Barry O'Brien, *Life of Parnell*, I, p. 204.

the century. But in 1877 agricultural prices, which to everybody's surprise had been little affected by the Repeal of the
Corn Laws, felt the first results of the building of the great
American railways, and the new competition of American
meat and grain.   At the same time Ireland passed through
a series of bad seasons.   The loss in the value of crops
for the three years following 1877 was put at £26 millions,
the equivalent of two and a half years rental for all Ireland.
In the Western counties dependent on the potato crop the
conditions were desperate, for statistics of the crop in 1879
showed a loss of seventy-five per cent.   The distress was
aggravated by the failure of crops in England, for the
economy of the Irish family depended in part on the earn-
ings by immigrant Irish labourers during the harvest months
in England.   Further confusion was caused by the collapse
of credit.   Under the Act of 1870 the small tenant had
something on which to borrow, his ambiguous tenant right.
Banks and gombeen men had flourished and spread, demanding and receiving exorbitant interest, and taking high
risks.   With adversity these creditors pressed for repayment;
tenants failed in great numbers, and where they could
satisfy their immediate creditors they were left with nothing
for the rent.

The Land Bill as it left the hands of Gladstone and
Fortescue had made some provision for a catastrophe of this
kind.   For the Courts were to be given power to consider
special circumstances in deciding whether a landlord should
be allowed to evict a tenant for non-payment of rent without
compensation.   But the House of Lords had removed this
check on eviction, by leaving it to the Court to decide not
whether there were any special circumstances to be considered, but whether the rent demanded was exorbitant.
Gladstone, it will be remembered, had objected most strongly
to this amendment, and as it proved with good reason,
for the term had been so interpreted as to make this section
worthless.   The weakened Act was a feeble anchor in the
storm.   Evictions increased rapidly; in 1877 the number of
families evicted was 463; in 1878, 980; in 1879, 1,238; in
1880, 2,110.   It was in this Ireland, with ruin and exile

once more a daily danger to every peasant home, that Parnell
and Davitt made agrarian misery the basis of a new and
powerful agitation for Home Rule.

It was unfortunate that the Irish Secretary, when these
disasters fell on Irish agriculture, was a man whose ideas
still belonged to the age of the 'forties, a survivor of the
school which had believed that England could solve her
problems by dispeopling Ireland, her neighbour, not understanding that she was peopling in the process a more dangerous Ireland in the distance. James Lowther, who had
succeeded Hicks Beach in that office, denied that there was
any connection between the Irish Land Laws and the
agrarian distress, and to a deputation that suggested a
distribution of seed potatoes to the peasants, he replied that
what Ireland needed was grass seed, the kind of answer
that might have been given by a hard-bitten economist in
the days before the Famine. But Hugh Law, famous in
the history of the Land Laws, who had been Attorney
General for Ireland in Gladstone's first Government and
was Lord Chancellor in his second, managed to insert in the
inadequate Bill that the Government introduced for relieving
Irish distress by granting loans for public works, a clause
modifying the landlords' rights of eviction, when money
had been borrowed under the Bill. This clause, though it
passed this unsympathetic House of Commons, was too much
for the House of Lords and they rejected it.

The Liberal party in the House of Commons was not more
united on Ireland than on other questions, and a study of the
opinions expressed by different members at this time shows
what difficulties were to beset Gladstone, when next he
tried to meet the Irish problem. In April, 1877, the
O'Donoghue moved in the House of Commons " that in
order to ensure to the Irish tenantry the benefits intended to
be conferred by the Act of 1870, it was essential that steps
should be taken to prevent the exaction of rents which
virtually confiscate the improvements declared by that Act
to be the property of the tenant." Hartington, opposing
the motion, said " the motion meant valued rents, or it
meant nothing at all; a principle which involved valued

rents appeared to him to conflict altogether with the freedom of contract." In January, 1880, the *Times* remarked that Bright ridiculed the idea that anyone but the landlord and the tenant can determine the fair rent of a holding, and that he stuck to his own idea of purchase though that in turn was ridiculed by Fawcett. In the course of a debate on a motion made by Shaw, on July 24, 1879, on the subject of University education, Fawcett made a direct attack on a phrase that expressed better than any other the spirit of Gladstone's Irish policy.

" It was sometimes said by Irish members that a certain section of English members wish to govern Ireland according to English ideas, but, to make a slight alteration in the words, he thought that a more unfortunate phrase than that of governing Ireland by Irish ideas had never been invented. Governing Ireland according to Irish ideas led straight to Home Rule, and Home Rule simply meant the disruption of the Empire."

But in a debate in July, 1877, on a motion introduced by O'Connor Power, one of the ablest of Parnell's small party, and seconded by Butt, calling for the pardon of the Fenian prisoners, Fawcett had supported the Irish demand, whereas Hartington, on the ground that pardon was wrong, opposed it, and Forster voted against it on the ground that the decision must not be taken out of the hands of the Government by Parliament, though he himself clearly inclined to the Irish view.

Gladstone took throughout a course of his own. In April, 1877, he voted, without speaking, against a motion by Shaw for a Committee on Home Rule. In this debate Fawcett, Hartington, and Forster, had all spoken against the motion, Forster declaring that he preferred Repeal of the Union to Home Rule, and predicting that the support for Home Rule would decline in Ireland. Gladstone spoke, but not on the question at issue. He intervened to explain that a letter he had written to support Kay, the well-known educational reformer, who was standing at Salford, had been written before, and not after, Kay had promised to vote for an inquiry into Home Rule. In the debate on Shaw's motion on University education, in which Fawcett had deprecated the government of Ireland by Irish ideas, he thus described the behaviour of his own mind on Irish questions. "The rule which I take for my own guidance is this—this is pre-eminently an Irish question—I do not wish, unless driven by some high consideration of Irish policy, to separate myself in such a matter from those who represent the general and well considered feeling of Ireland."

On the question of releasing the Fenian prisoners he made a characteristic speech. He said he could not vote for the resolution for he held that Parliament should proceed in such a matter not by resolution, but by an address to the Crown. At the same time he argued strongly for release, and Eversley says that it was this speech that led to their release in the next year. One of the prisoners thus released was Davitt. But Gladstone did not stop there. Butt, in arguing for release, had said that the offence of those who had been implicated in the Manchester attack was at most a case of constructive murder. A member resented and condemned this version of their offence. There was no need at all for Gladstone to intervene, and it is safe to say that nobody else in his position would have run the risk of appearing to palliate a crime that had shocked England. But Gladstone went on to say that it was going beyond the limits of accuracy to say that it was a deliberate and atrocious murder, and that in this case the murder of a single policeman had been expiated by three lives. Gladstone was sharply criticized for his speech, and some of his critics argued that he had no right to make it, since his own Government had left this handful of Fenians in prison. Granville, writing to Gladstone in November, 1877, said:

"With regard to the Manchester prisoners, the thing ought to be done, if possible, by a Government and not by an Opposition. If I remember right, in our Cabinet, you, Bright and I were the most inclined to leniency. I suspect if MacMahon, or the Emperor of Austria were exactly in the same position, public opinion in this country would be entirely for their giving an amnesty. . . ."

An Irish speaker, June 11, 1877, put an analogy which was likely to attract the attention of English Liberals:

"There was now on the Continent of Europe a man upon whose

head the price of thousands of pounds had been set by the Austrian Government. He had taken up arms against the Emperor of Austria, and no doubt had been the cause of death to thousands of Austrian soldiers. He was a violent politician. And yet now what was he? Prime Minister of Austria."[1]

In 1877 Gladstone paid his one and only visit to Ireland. He invited Balfour to accompany him. His letter of invitation has not survived. Balfour answered regretting that he could not leave his family in Scotland. He was there for about three weeks. He received the freedom of the City of Dublin, and he was welcomed at Maynooth in a friendly spirit, though it was hinted to him that his Vatican pamphlets were not forgotten. He stayed in the houses of Whig lords, and there is nothing in his diaries to show that he went below the surface of the society in which he found himself. He was interested in the sermons he heard in Anglican churches, and he noted that in most of the houses where he stayed there were family prayers only once a day. The *Times* said of his visit that it hoped other public men would follow his example, and that in this respect English Ministers had been strangely negligent. Gladstone and Bright, it was observed in the same article, were old men, belonging to the past, and young men should show their interest in these questions. Gladstone's references to his visit would justify that description, for they show a strange want of freshness or vigour of mind.

The truth is that he was still too much absorbed in the Eastern question to give much thought to Ireland. In the autumn he had some correspondence with Butt about the Irish University question, and he sent Butt's letter to Hartington, who replied reasonably enough that the Liberals had found out in 1873 what a difficult question it was for an English party. A letter Granville sent him on November 21, 1877, shows that Gladstone had consulted him on a larger programme.

" I can readily understand that some concessions might beneficially be made to the Irish in the matter of self-Gov[t] and shall

---

[1] The speaker referred to Andrassy, who was Foreign Minister not Prime Minister.

be very desirous to hear in what direction and how far you think it can be done.

" Butt's letter, a fair one from his point of view, shows a wish to come on his own terms to an arrangement with the liberal party, or at least with a portion of it. But what with the disjointed state of the Home rulers, and the feeling of the nonconformists and others in England and Scotland, any understanding with him now, appears to me to be dangerous, and premature.

" The difficulties about Irish University Education are great, and must be felt by you more than by most people."

Nothing more is known of the proposals to which Granville referred. In one respect Gladstone's mind moved from its earlier rigidity. In May, 1879, he made a speech which showed that he was more ready than he had been to consider the use of public money in Ireland. Shaw Lefevre, whose public spirit in this cause nothing could tire or discourage, had succeeded in persuading Parliament to appoint a Committee to consider the defects in the arrangements for land purchase. The Committee, of which he was Chairman, reported in 1878 in favour of increasing the proportion of the purchase money to be advanced by the State, and making the terms of repayment by the tenant easier, and in May, 1879, he passed a resolution demanding these changes. In the course of this debate Justin McCarthy made his maiden speech. He paid Gladstone a compliment, and passed on him a criticism, both of them just and significant.

" Burke in one of his speeches on Fox's India Bill paid a high tribute to the genius of Fox, but at the same time he gave him a warning. He praised Fox for having put to pay his ease, his security, his interest, his power, and even his darling popularity, on behalf of a people he had never seen: the people of India. He believed the Right Hon. the member for Greenwich had also risked his security, his power, his popularity, on behalf of a people he had then never seen, the people of Ireland. But Burke went to on say that Fox ought to be sure, when he entered upon his scheme of benevolence, to make full use of his time, and to give the whole length of his reins to his benevolence, and it had sometimes seemed to him that, whatever might be the reason, the Government of the Right Hon. the member for Greenwich had not given the whole length of the reins to their benevolent intentions, although they had certainly established a great principle and made a great opening for the final settlement of the Land Question, when they endeavoured to satisfy the demands of the Irish people."

Gladstone's speech showed that he combined his dread of grants in aid with a strong desire to give effective help to this Irish purpose. " Though uneasy about the prolonged and indefinite continuance of very large subventions to local bodies, even for purposes of great value and utility," he held that this claim was superior to the ordinary claims of local bodies. " These sanitary and other local demands are very fair and legitimate indeed, but after all they come simply to a question of a certain money economy." The claim before them was not simply an economical claim. " It is a moral, social, and political claim, connected with a purpose that goes right to the heart of the great Irish question."

The Government accepted the resolution, but did nothing.[1] Next year, 1880, Disraeli dissolved Parliament. At the end of six years of office he was leaving Ireland in the most desperate condition of misery and discontent. His Government had scarcely lifted a finger to reform abuses or to introduce improvements. The Liberal tradition of reform had been set aside. Yet the author of the famous phrases of 1844 asked his countrymen, in a letter to the Viceroy, to notice in this terrible picture one blot only, the rise of a separatist movement.

" Nevertheless a danger, in its ultimate results scarcely less disastrous than pestilence and famine, and which now engages your Excellency's anxious attention, distracts that country. A portion of its population is attempting to sever the Constitutional tie which unites it to Great Britain in that bond which has favoured the power and prosperity of both."

To this Gladstone replied in his election address.

" Gentlemen, those who endangered the Union with Ireland were the party that maintained there an alien Church, an unjust

[1] Effect was given to the recommendations of the Lefevre Committee in the Land Act of 1881.

M

Land Law, and franchises inferior to our own; and the true supporters of the Union are those who firmly uphold the supreme authority of Parliament, but exercise that authority to bind the three nations by the indissoluble tie of liberal and equal laws."

Hartington expressed the hope that the men of reasonable and moderate views in Ireland would be induced, by the violence of Parnell on one side, and the violence of Beaconsfield on the other, to look to the Liberal party for the satisfaction of their just demands. But in the elections of 1880 Irish politics played little part. The people of England were making their choice between two men, who stood head and shoulders above their fellows, both over seventy, and one of them very near his end, the rival artists who had fascinated the public imagination, the heroes of a struggle in which Constantinople seemed nearer than Dublin, and the snows of Afghanistan than the mists of Mayo and Connemara.

CHAPTER XI

GLADSTONE'S SECOND GOVERNMENT, 1880

THE STRUGGLE FOR ORDER AND REFORM

When Gladstone kissed hands in April, 1880, as Prime Minister for the second time, he looked like a man at the summit of his power. He had overthrown a statesman and a policy, both of them apparently popular and firmly established. He had started his campaign on the Eastern question with the support of less than half the Liberal party and of scarcely any of its leaders. Offering to the electors a solemn and elaborate argument for an overruling European sense in foreign policy, he had attacked a statesman who had given to British interests and British power all the attractions of religion and romance. With this programme, ascetic, disinterested, almost academic, he had wrested from Disraeli his command over the imagination of the English people. The Conservatives had lost over a hundred seats.[1] To understand Gladstone's achievement we may recall the event of the last election fought on a comparable issue. In 1857 Palmerston, censured in the House of Commons for the iniquity of his Chinese war, had dissolved Parliament and put the Manchester School to rout. What Gladstone had done in these years was to make himself the master of the England created by the second Reform Bill, as Palmerston had once made himself the master of the England created by the first.

Unhappily, Gladstone's strength was illusory, and to understand the disasters that overwhelmed his second Government it is necessary to glance at the causes of his weakness.

[1] At the dissolution there were 351 Conservatives, 250 Liberals, and 51 Home Rulers. After the election the figures were 243, 349, and 60.

The biographers of Christopher Columbus agree that his extraordinary courage and persistence in facing and overcoming all the obstacles that were put in the way of his stupendous adventure were largely due to his conviction that he had been called by God to this special mission. Gladstone, as it has been noted, had the same sustaining and encouraging sense. It explains what Houghton well described as the " one idea at a time faculty, which is at once his weakness and his strength." Shaftesbury felt that he was God's instrument, whether he was pressing for the Ten Hours day, or for the closing of museums on Sundays, whether he was attacking Lord Londonderry, the great mineowner, or Dr. Pusey, the great Tractarian. His whole career was clothed in this Evangelical atmosphere of a divinely inspired life. Gladstone's view of his own case was rather different. He held that God had given him, not so much a general mission in the world, as a series of particular missions all of them reflecting a common spirit and purpose based on his European outlook. He was Prime Minister in the Government that gave England an education system, and the Ballot, but he did not regard himself as acting specially for Providence in passing these measures. He thought that his special mission was to awaken and keep alive an English conscience on the outward relations of the British people. This conviction, as Houghton said, gave him his strength, for he threw into the cause to which he was devoting himself at the moment the full power of his compelling and fascinating personality. His descent on politics in this spirit was like the descent of the wild vigour of the Revolutionary armies on feudal politics in eighteenth-century Europe.

But though it was a source of strength to him as a crusader, this spirit was a source of weakness to him as a Prime Minister. For, when he threw himself into a cause, he could think of nothing else, and, though this concentration adds to a man's power when he wants to convince a nation that nothing else matters, it takes from his power when he has to use his judgment over a large field of politics. This is the difference between the task of the orator and that of the Prime

Minister. Gladstone, fresh from his triumph as an orator, stepped into the office of Prime Minister with his mind full of the problems that had absorbed him during his campaign. Ireland was, unfortunately, not one of them. Irish distress, Irish discontent, Irish grievances, these had become pressing questions. Gladstone, his mind on Bulgaria, Afghanistan, the Zulus, and the Boers, gave them little of his attention. He thought that all that was needed was some reform of his Land Act of 1870, restoring the remedies that had been forbidden by the Lords. It was unfortunate that his visit to Ireland had been badly timed, for it came before the disasters of 1879, and, as we have seen, it taught him next to nothing.[1]

This then was one weakness. In 1868 he became Prime Minister, knowing that he had on his hands a formidable Irish problem. In 1880 he became Prime Minister with a problem more serious than that of 1868, but he was blind to it.

The second weakness was only known to his intimate friends and his colleagues. Gladstone was in politics with only half his mind and will; he was like a man who, although not yet in the *crise de départ*, has given provisional orders to his coachman. Every year when he talked with himself in his diary, as his birthday came round or the closing day of the year, he described his longing to retire into a life of contemplation. His view of his own career was that he retired from active politics in 1874; that he was brought back by the emergency of the Eastern crisis, in respect of which he recognized a special responsibility as he was one of the authors of the Crimean War; that he had to take office in 1880 in order to give effect to promises he had made in that campaign; but that, as soon as this had been done, he would withdraw. In one conversation with his wife (November 21, 1881) he explained that he hoped to retire, not only from politics, but from social life. In 1875 (December 29) he had written in his diary:

[1] In December, 1880, Gladstone wrote to Granville and Childers that Cowper was unequal to his difficult task as Viceroy, and that he (Gladstone) would have got a man of more experience for that office if he had known what his Government would have to encounter in Ireland.

" In the great business of unwinding the coil of life I have made some progress by resigning the Leadership, selling my house (needful for pecuniary reasons) and declining public occasions, but more has yet to be done. To minimise my presence in London is alike needful for my work and for the great business of solemn recollection and retention."

In 1879 (December 28th) he wrote:

" Three things I would ask of God over and above all the bounty which surrounds me. This first, that I may escape into retirement, this second, that I may speedily be enabled to divest myself of everything resembling wealth. And the third—If I may— that when God calls me He may call me speedily."

" A strong man in me," he wrote in 1883 (December 31), " wrestles for retirement, the strong One stands at the gate of exit and forbids, I hope only for a time. There is a bar to the continuance of my political life fixed, as I hope, with the life of the present parliament, and there is a hope that it may not last as long. But for this I do not know how my poor flesh and blood, or my poor soul and spirit, could face the prolongation of cares and burdens so much beyond my strength at any age and at this age so cruelly exclusive of the great work of penitential recollection and lifting of the heart which has lingered so long."

His contemporaries, and students of his career, find it difficult to bring the Gladstone, longing to withdraw from politics and society, into harmony with the Gladstone whom they knew and admired, or hated, in the active warfare of the House of Commons. For, as Sir Edward Hamilton has said of him, " in spite of his pacific nature, he was eminently contentious, even militant in debate. He was like Mr. Fox, who when asked why he disputed so vehemently about some trifle, replied ' I must do it; I cannot live without discussion '."[1] " As to your own desire to retire altogether from public life," Argyll wrote to him on February 4, 1880, " I find it very difficult to conceive you existing and yet not contending more or less in politics. No doubt you have many other pursuits but the bent and habit of a mind during a whole life is not easily thrown off."

Whether Gladstone deceived himself or not, the disabling effect of this conviction or illusion was very clear. When

[1] *Memoir*, p. 8.

Gladstone took office in 1868, in 1886, and in 1892, he had a definite constructive purpose in mind: an immense task calling for all his energy and will-power. In 1880 he took office, thinking of himself as little more than a caretaker winding up two or three difficult questions before retiring. In 1881, by a stupendous effort, he carried the most revolutionary measure that passed through Parliament in the nineteenth century. It was a superb achievement, illustrating the courage, the will-power, and the debating ascendancy of the only man who could have forced it through the House of Commons. But it was a Bill that Gladstone never expected to propose when he took office in April, 1880. He had no idea then that so sweeping a measure would be needed. And, after he had passed it, he was convinced that other Irish reforms would be needed, but he did not think of himself as the statesman who should undertake them; he regarded them as reforms that would be undertaken by his successors, while he himself was meditating in his distant cell. In consequence, he never gave his mind to the detailed study of these problems. As we shall see, he was travelling very definitely towards the great plan that he produced in 1886. In 1884 he said at a private dinner, that he had a sneaking liking for Parnell, then regarded as an untouchable, and that Home Rule would be a matter for serious consideration within ten years.[1]   But he was not working at the problem of Irish government, for he thought that task would fall to others.

So little did Gladstone grasp the character of his task that he took himself the office of Chancellor of the Exchequer. From the birth of the new Government, down to December, 1882, amid all the storms that shook its reputation and threatened its life, he kept that office in his own hands. His action would be difficult to reconcile with common prudence, even if there had been nothing but his health to be taken into account. He was seventy-one years of age, head of a Government which had no right to expect an easy and untroubled life. He soon discovered that, by a secret under-

---

[1] West, *Diaries*, Vol. II, p. 140. It is interesting to note that one of the guests at this party was Buckle, editor of the *Times*.

standing made by his predecessors, England was tied to France for the defence of common financial interests in Egypt, and he knew that the policy against which he had thundered at the elections, and before, had left other embarrassing legacies behind it. He took the Chancellorship, and by August he was so seriously ill that bulletins were published every few hours, an illness he himself attributed to his hard work at the Budget. Morley remarks that his first Budget justified his decision to take that office; his speech delighted the House, as his Budget speeches always did, gave new heart to his friends and brought dismay to his opponents, who found that, though their own Governments had long been pressed by the farmers to get rid of the Malt Duty, it was Gladstone who found a way of doing this. It is surely a curious perspective in which the abolition of the Malt Duty is considered an achievement that was worth the health of a Prime Minister whose vigilance and initiative were pressingly demanded by the care of British interests in Europe, Africa, and Asia, all of them critical, as well as by the needs of Ireland, every day becoming more difficult. But, apart from this consideration, there was every reason why Gladstone should not have been Chancellor of the Exchequer. It is not a coincidence that of the Conservatives who were to make their mark by constructive legislation in Ireland, Gibson, the Balfour brothers, Wyndham, not one had ever held that dangerous office. Gladstone was gravely embarrassed in the next two years because he had taken on his shoulders an old Man of the Seas.[1]

The weakness due to the state of Gladstone's mind was accentuated by the character of his Cabinet. When it was

---

[1] Gladstone was haunted by the thought of waste in Ireland. This fear returned continually to his mind, often at times when most urgent problems were demanding his undivided attention. On May 8 he wrote to Forster ;

"Ireland has been illegitimately paid for unjust inequalities by an unjust preference in much lavish public expenditure. . . . I am afraid you may find in the secretary's office a bad tradition. I do not recollect ever, during nearly ten years for which I have been Finance Minister, to have received from a secretary for Ireland (tho' some of them have been Treasury men) a single suggestion for the reduction of any expense whatever." A mind less shut up in its fixed Treasury notions would surely have perceived the significance of this fact.

being formed the *Times* remarked that if Hartington, an acknowledged Whig, had been Prime Minister, he would have been compelled to give the Radicals a real share in the Government; that Gladstone, with more haste than accuracy, was called a revolutionary, and that he would be obliged to reassure the Whigs. This Gladstone did, when making up his Cabinet, with a thoroughness that alarmed the *Times* itself. " It is a practical question to be tested by future experience whether the moderating influences thus accumulated within the Cabinet may not prove too strong for Mr. Gladstone himself to control."[1] When it is remembered that one of Gladstone's colleagues was Argyll, these apprehensions were natural enough. For Argyll had written to Gladstone at the time of the fight in the Lords over the 1870 Bill (January 23, 1870):

" Pray let me remind you of one thing which weighs much upon my mind. We must contemplate a severe fight—possibly one in which the House of Peers may differ seriously with the House of Commons. It ought to be a matter of conscience with every member of that House to ask it to agree to nothing which he can't defend from his heart as just and in the public interest."

If such a claim were allowed no Cabinet legislation of importance would ever be possible, for every such measure must contain provisions distasteful to some members of the Cabinet. The Education Act of 1870 included in its Cowper Temple clause a principle as obnoxious to the Prime Minister as to any strict sectarian in the country. In 1880 one of the best speeches in support of the Compensation for Disturbance Bill was made by Hartington, who was himself strongly opposed to it. When he sat down Shaw Lefevre congratulated him on his effective argument for the Bill. " I hope," he grimly replied, " it persuaded others. It did not persuade me."[2]

Gladstone's mistake in giving so Whig a complexion to his Government was partly the result of his ignorance of the new electorate, and partly the result of his keen desire to keep the historical Whig families in the Liberal party as long

[1] April 27, 1880.
[2] Eversley, *Gladstone and Ireland*, p. 117.

as possible. His view on this point was best expressed in a
letter he wrote some years later to Lord Edmond Fitzmaurice, when Fitzmaurice, after some hesitation, decided
in favour of Home Rule. Gladstone, deploring the effect
of the Liberal Unionist secession, said that John Stuart
Mill had called the old Liberal party a " Broad Church."
" Liberal Unionism has strongly tended to make us a narrow
Church and to break up the old and invaluable habit of
Liberal England which looked to a Liberal aristocracy and a
Liberal leisured class as the natural and therefore the best
leaders of the Liberal movement." Gladstone had two
scales when judging men for public life; one scale for the
Whig, another for the Radical. His Cabinet in 1880
revealed the results of his bias.

This would have mattered less if Gladstone had been able
to co-operate with the Radical leader in his Cabinet; if he
could ever have established with Chamberlain in 1880 the
relations he had established with Bright in 1870, or the
more intimate relations he was afterwards to establish with
Morley. But in his mind Chamberlain was an unknown
and an uneasy quantity. The caucus was partly the secret,
partly the symbol, of his power in the country, and this new
democratic force was as little congenial to Gladstone as to
his Whig colleagues. Chamberlain soon got into hot
water with his colleagues. Apart from his provocations to the
Queen, he had a habit of independent speech which provoked their sense of what was proper and respectful to the
Cabinet in a new Minister, and he and Dilke used their
Press friendships to push their own ideas against the
opposition of their colleagues. In these ways Chamberlain
came under suspicion as a man whose methods were uncon-
ventional, if not unscrupulous.[1] Gladstone never trusted
him, and this want of confidence was a fatal weakness. For
there were only two men in the Government who had any
commanding and constructive gifts to bring to the service

---

[1] Though the two most important disclosures ever made to the Press were
made in the days of select Aristocratic Cabinets; the disclosure to the *Times*
in 1845 about the Corn Laws and that of 1854 about the decision of the Aberdeen
Cabinet to send an ultimatum to Russia. See *Life of Aberdeen* by Lady F.
Balfour, II, 198.

of the Irish problem, and those two men never learnt to work together.

Nothing in Gladstone's career and character is more interesting than the character of his personal relationships. He said himself that all public men were unintelligible, and that there was only one man of all those with whom he had worked whom he understood, and that man was Aberdeen. He was himself an island, and he supposed that all men were islands. There was however one bridge by which he could cross to other minds: the bridge of ancient culture. By this bridge he became in his old age the friend of Morley, agnostic though he was, as he became the friend of Catholics like Acton and Döllinger. But there was no such bridge between him and the two men who were ultimately to wreck the main purpose of his life: the aristocrat Hartington, and the Radical Chamberlain.

One other fact must be noted about Gladstone's position. The House of Commons in 1880 was not his as the House of Commons had been his in 1870. It had important rebel elements. The *Times*, suspecting that Gladstone's sympathies would draw him to the Irish, warned him at the outset that the House of Commons would not follow him. On March 31 it read him a lecture, warning him against anything like the Lichfield House compact of 1835.

" A House of Commons once elected is apt to become a very independent body during its early years, and even if there be a nominal Liberal majority in the new House it will include a large number of men who would withdraw their support from any Government which showed a disposition to stultify our foreign policy abroad or to yield to Irish dictation and obstruction at home."[1]

Brand, the Speaker, soon made up his mind that the Liberal party were not only strong but determined to have their own way in spite of Mr. Gladstone. " He has a difficult team to drive."[2] It is significant that on the first important Irish division in the new Parliament the Government majority fell to seventy-eight.

[1] March 31, 1880.
[2] Morley, *op. cit.*, Vol. III, p. 2.

With a party behind him that could not be counted on for effective action Gladstone had to face an Opposition ready for anything in the way of resistance. Nobody can study the history of the 1880-1885 Parliament without being struck by the ferocity of its party spirit. The ordinary reader of its debates notes, as he follows disaster after disaster to the British name and to British fortunes, that this savage strife is never hushed for a moment. He will find, if he studies the private papers of statesmen that they were seriously preoccupied with this problem, fearing that it was becoming a danger to Parliamentary government. Hartington, not a man easily disturbed, was gravely concerned, and Gladstone discussed it in a characteristic letter. Gladstone persuaded himself that his own personality had nothing to do with this growth of bitterness, but others, remembering the thunder that had swept his predecessor aside, were less certain that he was right. In the place of honour on the front Opposition bench sat Sir Stafford Northcote, who was gentleness itself, but he led, in name rather than in fact, a body of men who saw in his composure an additional reason for indulging their own taste for violence. For the men who sat round him, and still more the men who sat in their rebel corner, remembered what they had suffered in the storm, and were in no mood to think of anything but revenge. The gladiators of the Fourth party found in brutality to Gladstone a weapon with which to beat their own leader.

The Government was faced, as soon as it found itself in office, with the most difficult of all problems, the problem of governing a society in which violence and justice were on one side, and law and power on the other. To understand the significance of the movement organized by Parnell and Davitt, we must place it in the same category as the revolts led by Wat Tyler in 1381, and by Robert Kett in 1549, and the greater peasants risings in France in the fourteenth and in Germany in the fifteenth and sixteenth centuries. In all these cases, as in the Irish, economic and social forces were threatening whatever of right and liberty the weaker classes held in a society under which men were grouped in an elaborate and complicated social relationship. In all these cases the demands of the rebels were just and reasonable. In 1381 the peasants wanted to have all servile dues commuted; in 1549 Kett led a revolt against inclosures, and reiterated the demand for the extinction of peasant bondage. In the Jacquerie the French peasants, like the English, were rebelling against the harsher conditions forced on them by their landlords after the Black Death, and in the German revolts the peasants were rebelling against the pressure of their lords who, anxious to compete with the new rich of the merchant class, as the English landlords in the sixteenth century competed with the new rich of industry and banking, exacted their feudal dues with a new severity. In all these cases the serf cultivators of the old manorial system were in revolt against an oppression which had become intolerable, either because its burden was increased, or because the victims had become more sensitive.

These revolts had been put down with savage cruelty, but the cause for which the peasants suffered ultimately succeeded, though of course after very long delay, both in France and in South Germany. At the French Revolution the peasant found himself the full master and owner of the plot he had once tilled as a serf, his obligations, servile and other, removed with a stroke of the pen. In South Germany serfdom persisted until the nineteenth century, but its conditions had been softened by Governments that put other interests before those of the landlords, and when the mediaeval village was dissolved the men who had been serfs became owners on easy terms. In England history had taken a different course. There the servile forms of villeinage had disappeared, much earlier than anywhere else, but the descendant of the villein found himself, when the old manorial system was taken to pieces, not a peasant but a labourer.

Ireland had never been under the manorial system but the economy of her agrarian life was not much less complicated, and the small tenant was, in many respects, in the same position as the villein. For he wanted to keep his land, he had moral claims based partly on custom, partly on his own improvements, and the conditions on which

he held his land put him at the mercy of his landlord.

Down to 1870 it had been generally agreed among educated Englishmen (with some striking exceptions, as we
have seen) that the right model for Ireland was to be found
in the English solution, under which the peasant became a
labourer. This had been the key to the British policy of
aiding the evicting landlord. Gladstone's Act of 1870 was
the first step in a new policy of protecting the tenant and
restraining the landlord but it had failed of its main purpose.
But though it had failed the old policy was doomed, thwarted
by the resistance of the peasants who had upset all the predic-
tions of the economists and survived the hard blows of the
law. For the Irish peasant was a tenacious and persistent
fellow; he clung to his plot, often preferring hunger and cold
in his own cabin to comfortable exile. He was also a perpetual nuisance, giving his landlord no peace, and full of his
grievances. Some, like Argyll, said of his grievances that
those he fostered most were imaginary, for he thought that
his family had a right to land that had only belonged to it in
legend and myth. Keats said once that imaginary grievances
put a man on the cross whereas real ones stirred him to exer-
tion. We may say of the Irish peasant, as of the Irish people in
general, that if they suffered under the first kind of grievance
they had enough of the second kind to keep them active: an
unpleasant combination for a ruling Empire.

Parnell and Davitt, organizing and mobilizing these
strong and obstinate qualities, defeated the English attempt
to force the Irish system into the pattern of the English.
They convinced the English that an Ireland of peasant
owners might be less difficult to govern than an Ireland
where the Wat Tylers and Robert Ketts found all this
inflammable material and the natural leaders of society
seemed to be more respected in the House of Lords than on
their own estates. Hence the battle on which Parnell and
Davitt entered in the 'seventies ended with an Ireland more
like Denmark than England. In Denmark where the
political conditions were just the converse of those in England, the Crown being all powerful in the one case as the

landlords were in the other, the Danish peasant while kept in bondage was defended in the eighteenth century from the landlord, who wanted to substitute more profitable methods of farming for the old peasant tillage, and in the nineteenth he became a peasant owner on favourable terms. If we may throw a complicated chapter of history into a rough phrase, we may say that he was given first security of tenure and then ownership. This is what happened to the Irish peasant, but whereas in Denmark it was a revolution made comparatively easy by the political conditions, in Ireland the political conditions were as unfavourable as they could be. This will be understood when those conditions are described.

The negligence of Disraeli's Government had left Ireland in great distress and disorder. As we have seen, the statistics of eviction in the late 'seventies had gone steadily up, from 463 in 1877 to 980 in 1878, and 1,238 in 1879. In the first six months of 1880 the figure stood at 1,241. Of these 129 were reinstated as tenants, and 494 readmitted as caretakers without any rights in the land. No less than 100,000 tenant farmers were in arrears with their rent and liable to eviction. This immense body of suffering and anxiety could be relieved directly and quickly by drastic remedies such as those that a despotic Government could apply. And those remedies were urged on the public mind by Parnell with his compact following in the new House of Commons: he had thirty-two adherents, twenty-six of the new Irish members being supporters of his rival Shaw. The Land League meeting in Dublin, in April, 1880, had drawn up two schemes of reform, one an emergency scheme, the other a permanent scheme. The temporary plan provided for the suspension of rent for two years in the case of tenancies valued at £10 or under, and in the case of tenancies over that figure a suspension of all rent in excess of the Poor Law valuation. The permanent scheme was Land Purchase. The whole price—twenty years purchase of the Poor Law valuation—was to be lent to the tenant through a loan, to be raised by the Government, repayable by the tenant in thirty-five annuities of five per cent. while a Commission of Land Administration for Ireland was to arrange for the transfer of the soil from owner to occupier. This Commission was to be authorized to acquire any estate at twenty years purchase of the Poor Law valuation, and to let the holdings on it to the tenants at a rent equivalent to three and a half per cent. of the purchase price. Davitt refused to give his name to the scheme, thinking twenty years purchase too high a price, a view that he held the more strongly because he foresaw a further fall in agricultural prices.

The case for the Irish Land League's emergency plan was overwhelming. It was a plan for a moratorium based on exceptional distress. Its principle, as Shaw Lefevre pointed out in the House of Commons, had been recognized in Roman Law and in the codes of almost every country in Europe except England. As a check to disturbing forces, it was essential as a measure of order. But it was even more important in another aspect. If Ireland was to become a country of peasant agriculture, it was as necessary to stop eviction of this kind and in this temper, as it had been necessary to protect the peasant in Denmark and France before he was emancipated. The change to peasant agriculture was taken everywhere in two stages. One stage was to give the peasant security of tenure or a recognized status. The second to make him an owner. Ireland was now in this first stage, not because England had deliberately thought out a policy of the kind, but because English statesmen were being driven to this solution. For this reason it was essential to prevent the eviction of the victims of the distress of the time. Lord George Hamilton made a great impression at the time by an analysis of the evictions in Donegal, which showed that the actual evictions were far fewer than those that figured in the statistics, because many of the evicted were readmitted as tenants at will or caretakers. If the only case for a moratorium was that eviction was throwing great numbers of families out of their homes, the fact that the figures gave too black a picture of this process was relevant. But that was, on any statesmanlike view of the problem, only part of the case. A tenant evicted and then readmitted as a caretaker or tenant at will lost his status as a tenant under the Land Act of 1870: he lost, that is, his security of tenure. He lost in fact what the Danish peasant had kept in the eighteenth century. All then that a landlord had to do in order to extinguish customary and legal rights was to evict his tenant and take him back as a caretaker.

Gladstone now took the step he should have taken in 1869. When the new Parliament met, the Chief Secretary, Forster, replying to the complaints of Irish members that the Government were neglecting Ireland, announced the appointment of a Commission on the Land question, with Bessborough, a most public spirited Irish landlord, as Chairman. Parnell urged that in the interval some temporary measure should be passed to stop evictions. The Government did not respond, and O'Connor Power, one of the ablest of Parnell's followers at that time though they quarrelled later, introduced a Bill proposing to undo the bad work of the Lords on the 1870 Bill, and to provide that compensation should be given in all cases of eviction, even in the case of non-payment of rent. Parnell had originally meant to introduce a more direct and drastic Bill suspending evictions altogether for two years, but Shaw Lefevre whom he consulted recommended this more moderate course. The Government then decided to introduce a Bill themselves. They had already a Bill before Parliament increasing loans to landlords under the late Government's Distress scheme, and at first they proposed to extend that Bill. Ultimately they decided on a separate measure.

The measure was a temporary measure to terminate at the end of 1881. A tenant evicted for non-payment of rent could claim compensation for disturbance, if he could prove that he was unable to pay his rent because of the two last bad harvests; that he was willing to continue his tenancy on just terms; and that the landlord had refused such terms. This Compensation for Disturbance Bill fell far short of the Irish demand. It applied only to

N

part of Ireland, and to tenancies rented at £30 a year or under. As the debates proceeded Forster tried to buy off opposition by amendments that would have weakened the Bill seriously; one limiting it to tenancies under £15, the other excluding cases where the landlord was willing to let the tenant sell his interest in his holding. The opposition of Parnell compelled the Government to withdraw the first, and to make the second much less dangerous. But though the Bill was judged by the Irish party too feeble to meet the needs of the time, it was much too strong for the landlord interest. One Minister, Lansdowne, a great land owner in Ireland, resigned in order to attack it. In the Commons twenty Liberals voted against it, and fifty abstained. The Lords threw it out by 282 votes to 51.

The treatment of this Bill by the Opposition shows how gigantic was the task of a Government that sought to make a reasonable reform in an atmosphere where landed property was regarded as more sacred than anything else. Beaconsfield, who must by this time have forgotten that he had ever written *Sybil*, took this view in its most extreme form. He said that this was a reconnaisance against property; that it brought insecurity into all kinds of transactions; and that " it delegated to a public officer the extraordinary power of fixing the rents of the country." Randolph Churchill called it a first step in a social war: an attempt to raise the masses against the classes. Lansdowne attacked the Bill because it singled out a particular section of the community, and a special contract into which that section had entered, and it announced with all the solemnity of an Act of Parliament that the Legislature was going to revise the terms of one of the parties to it, so that if that party failed to fulfil its obligations, the legislature would shield it from the consequences which in every civilized society result from a breach of contract.

The case for the Bill was well put by two men of whom both had been at first, and one was still, opposed to it. Argyll quoted the case of a property in Galway where eighty-nine tenants paid an aggregate rent of £1,370, and where the attempt to enforce notices of eviction had been met with great resistance. " You have in this case a population of five hundred at the mercy of the landowner who under the existing law can be evicted without one shilling to carry them to America."

"In some parts of Ireland," said Hartington, " the impoverished circumstances of the tenants have placed in the hands of the landlords a weapon which the Government never contemplated, and which enables the landlords to clear the estate of hundreds of tenants whom, in ordinary circumstances, they would not have been able to remove except by heavy pecuniary fine. I ask whether that is not a weapon calculated to enable landlords absolutely to defeat the main purposes of the (1870) Act."

Gladstone summed up the case for the Bill in a sentence: " In the failure of the crops caused by the year 1879, the act of God has replaced the Irish occupier in the condition in which he stood before the Land Act of 1870."

Argyll's assent to the Bill had been gained by Gladstone after long correspondence in which one sentence of Gladstone's gave as complete an answer to the House of Lords as could be wanted. " . . . in a state of things which requires the legislative interference of Parliament to keep the people from starvation (which has just and only just been effected) it is impossible to apply without qualification of any kind the ordinary rules of property." Gladstone was asking Parliament to accept a principle which had been applied to industry nearly half a century earlier, and the House of Lords, led by Beaconsfield, were demanding its rejection on the ground that the rights of the landowner should be treated as sacrosanct. The landowners in Denmark and Bavaria had made similar demands, but as they did not control the government of Denmark or Bavaria their demands were disregarded and the peasants had escaped. Unhappily for Ireland, and for her embarrassed ruler, the landlords had in the English Parliament the power they lacked elsewhere. Because of this predominant landlord atmosphere it was regarded as much more wicked for the agricultural poor than for the industrial poor to defend themselves, alike in England and Ireland.[1]

In Ireland the only methods that could be used for protecting the small tenant, the man who had been protected in Denmark, France and Bavaria, by Crown or Church, were the methods used by the Land League, the method of organizing resistance to payment of rent. " Mr. Parnell," the *Times* complained in December, 1879, " sticks to his text with the persistence of a man of one idea. The tenants are exhorted not to pay a penny of rent unless the landlord makes a fair abatement." The methods of the Land League were accompanied by outrages and cruelties that Davitt tried hard and courageously to stop, but to understand the temper of the English ruling class it must be remembered that the attempt to organize the peasants was in their eyes a crime in itself, quite apart from violence. England was entering on a war in which all the instincts of self preservation leagued ignorant men and women, used to a hard life, victims and pupils of cruelty, against the law of the land and the rule of property. That their case was just was proved afterwards by the sweeping reductions of rent awarded by the Land Courts. The free hand to evict, held so sacred by the Lords, was as intolerable and as obnoxious to good government as the severe exactions that the landlords would have forced on the peasants of Denmark if the Crown had been their servant.

Forster, the new Irish Secretary, had a strong claim on Irish confidence. He had taken this office, though his past might well entitle him to look for a Secretaryship of State, for in 1876 he had been regarded as a likely successor to Gladstone. He and his father had done splendid work in Ireland in the relief of distress at the time of the Famine. This experience made him quicker than Gladstone to see that drastic remedies were needed for this agrarian problem. When the House of Lords threw out his Compensation for

---

[1] In 1872, when Joseph Arch, the mildest and most respectable of Trade Union leaders, was trying to create among the agricultural labourers Trade Unions, such as were to be found in almost every industry, the landowners regarded his movement as criminal. The Bishop of Gloucester, whom Disraeli soon afterwards proposed to make Archbishop of Canterbury, told the farmers to put the trade union speakers in the horse pond.

Disturbance Bill, he replied in a tone not heard again from a Minister speaking in his place in the House of Commons until Gladstone spoke for the last time, twelve years later, warning the House of Lords that such abuse of their power must lead to its loss. Ireland was led by capable and devoted men who were organizing the peasants for an attack on the landlord system and on British rule. Forster was a firm believer in British rule, but he saw that the landlord system was not only unjust, but indefensible, and that the forces against it, drawing their strength as they did from the strongest sentiments and attachments in human nature, must sooner or later put an end to it. He wanted to reform the Land Law and to curb the landlords' power, but the House of Lords would not let him check what was, at once, an abuse in itself, and an incentive to agitation. In consequence the agitation grew, until it tempted him into the fatal alternative of coercion. In destroying his Bill the House of Lords destroyed his career.

CHAPTER XII

The chief Ministers in Gladstone's Government were aware in the summer of 1880 that they had on their hands in Ireland a very difficult and urgent problem. Their different proposals are interesting, not only for the light they throw on their problem, but also because they illustrate the differences of temperament and view within the Cabinet. It will be seen that almost every measure that was tried in the next twenty years for the solution of the Irish question was foreshadowed in these months, and that the men themselves discovered in this emergency the same qualities that they displayed in their later careers.

The most confident and energetic mind in this Cabinet was the youngest. Chamberlain was then, as always, a man of action. He proposed that the Government should take up the challenge of the Lords at once, call an autumn session, and pass again their Compensation for Disturbance Bill. At the same time he submitted a memorandum proposing a large scheme of public works, including improved communications, drainage and reclamation of lands, and aid to industrial enterprises.[1] This was the sort of programme for which he had been prepared and educated by his experience as reforming Mayor, a school as different as possible from that in which men like Granville, Argyll, and Hartington had learnt their leisurely politics. This document was circulated to the Cabinet on August 18. Nothing was done, though Forster himself liked the plan. Gladstone was at the time expiating the folly of his misspent energy on the Budget on a sick bed, but we know enough of his Treasury mind to know that he would have examined such a plan in a critical spirit.

[1] Garvin, *Life of Joseph Chamberlain*, Vol. I, p. 323.

A more revolutionary scheme than Chamberlain's was put before the Cabinet by its leader. As early as 1872 Gladstone's mind had turned to the problem of Irish government and he was now drawn again to this subject both by the state of Ireland and by the state of the House of Commons. All the arguments that had made him anxious in his first Government to put Irish administration on a new and more Irish basis had been strengthened by the success of Parnell and Davitt and the spirit and methods of the Land League. Even Cardinal Cullen, had he been alive, could hardly have called this new nationalist movement, as he had called its predecessor, a bubble, and sentiment and policy alike prompted Gladstone to treat it with respect. All these arguments were now reinforced by the change in Irish tactics in the House of Commons which had followed the fall of Butt and the rise of Parnell. For Gladstone saw the danger that deliberate obstruction must bring to Parliamentary government, and he was anxious to meet this danger by constructive change. These two motives inspired him to prepare a paper recommending Grand Committees for England, Scotland and Ireland: a reform that he thought should lead up to a general reform of Irish government.[1]

" But I must add that, besides the defeat of obstruction, and the improvement of our attitude for dealing with arrear, I conceive that devolution may supply the means of partially meeting and satisfying, at least so far as it is legitimate, another call. I refer to the call for what is styled (*in bonam partem*) 'Local Government' and (*in malam*) ' Home Rule.' "

But he was soon to find, as the *Times* had warned him, that the moderating influences he had accumulated in his Cabinet were too strong even for him to control. In nothing did his Government show its Whig character more clearly than in its rejection of this scheme. The Whig noblemen who sat round his table looked on government as the intelligent and economical administration of a world that was happy under their rule, and needed little in the way of change or reform. As they were in the House of Lords they were not aware at first hand of the grave problem

[1] Gladstone's scheme is given in an Appendix to this Chapter.

the House of Commons had to face. They were in deadly fear of Chamberlain, with his crude courage, his dislike of their class, his special knowledge of questions in which they had never interested themselves, his methods of pressure through his newspaper friends, and his command of forces that they thought irresponsible and revolutionary. They were afraid of Gladstone's impulsive and passionate crusades, and, knowing that none of them could meet him in debate or in controversy, they thought it safer to resist him at the outset. Instinct and prudence alike indisposed them to reform. " Mr. Gladstone proposed the creation of Grand Committees for England, Ireland and Scotland," wrote Chamberlain in his memorandum of the events of November 15. " He was warmly supported by Bright and myself, but the Cabinet were against him."[1] Anybody who looks ahead over the history of the next four years must conclude that in rejecting this scheme in November the Cabinet did almost as much public mischief as the House of Lords had done in July.

Gladstone, always ahead of his party where Irish government was concerned, was, as he himself said to Argyll, one of the most conservative in his Cabinet when first the Land Bill was in preparation. This great task now divided the attention of Ministers with the task of keeping order. The agrarian problem was not one problem but two. There was the problem of defining and defending the rights of the tenant: there was the problem of providing for the conversion of tenants into owners. The plans of the Land League were concerned with both problems: any Government Bill had to treat both. For even if it had been decided to introduce a complete scheme of land purchase, that scheme could not have been put into execution at once and some measure would have been necessary to prevent eviction; to settle what were the rights of the occupier and what rents he should pay. Until this was decided there was no basis for a general scheme of land purchase. Parnell had found indeed a simple basis. He proposed to use Griffiths' valuation. This was a valuation carried out under an Act of 1852 for the purpose

[1] Garvin, *op. cit.*, Vol. I, p. 328.

of local and public assessment. An official Commissioner, whom the Cabinet instructed at this time to prepare a paper on this valuation, reported that the net annual value had been taken in that valuation as the fair letting value from year to year on the basis of existing agricultural prices[1] based on the rents paid on estates where " large landed proprietors wished to have their tenants comfortable and independent." Since that time cereals had increased from 20 to 36 per cent. and the produce of grass lands from 50 to 83. It was calculated that the rateable value of Ireland had increased by 33 per cent. O'Connor Morris urged that Ireland should be revalued, and that is what happened roughly under the Land Courts. It was evident that, as Ireland was in 1880, there could be no large immediate scheme of purchase and that, whatever was done about purchase, a great deal had to be done about the other part of the problem.

It is not surprising therefore that the main struggles were concerned with the three Fs, and not with Purchase. So far as Cabinet papers show, the discussion of purchase was carried on only by Bright, Childers, Forster, and Gladstone.

Bright was still sanguine about his schemes. The Land Purchase clauses of the Act of 1870 had not had much effect. Under those clauses two-thirds of the price were lent by the State, repayable by instalments and interest, at 5 per cent. yearly for thirty-five years. As the tenant had to supply one-third of the purchase price it is not surprising to find that only 702 tenants bought under this Act, the amount of the purchase money being about £700,000.[2] Bright wanted to make these clauses more effective, and he proposed to set up four Commissions to sit at Dublin, Belfast, Limerick, and Cork, to negotiate the sales. Compulsion, he thought, might be applied in the case of lands held by Corporations, and waste lands capable of cultivation in the hands of owners unable or unwilling to improve them. His original plan had clearly had in view the more prosperous tenants. He now looked beyond them. The Connaught Commission,

[1] Paper, November, 1880 by J. Ball Greene, Commissioner of Valuation.
[2] Report of Cowper Commission, 1887.

he held, might be given special duties in respect of waste lands, and might be empowered to let small farms at almost nominal rents to small occupiers.

Childers, whose mind turned towards Irish self-government, wished to expand Bright's plan by forming County Boards who were to be the authorities for carrying out these schemes. He proposed to buy up in this way about a fifth of the wild and agricultural land for resale, taking compulsory powers if necessary. The burden and responsibility would be thrown on the County Boards, but the Imperial Government would help with the aid of the credit of the Imperial Government.

Forster liked these plans, but he doubted whether the County Boards would be strong enough at first for this purpose, though he looked forward to their establishment. " Improved county government is a pressing necessity, but not so pressing as the increase of occupying owners. And even if we make good county boards it will be some time before we could trust them to act fairly between landlord and tenant. But may we not provide in the purchase Bill for the possible future employment of county Boards? " Gladstone had written against this last sentence, " I hope so."

The plans for extending purchase under existing conditions awakened little enthusiasm in Gladstone for reasons that can well be appreciated by those who have studied the effects of his Treasury training on a character attached to carefulness and thrift. But he was not against land purchase under all conditions. Indeed the history of Land Purchase in Ireland illustrates the fundamental difference between his view and the Conservative view. He wanted Ireland to have self-government, but until she had self-government he was very reluctant to lavish public money, the benefit of which he believed would go to the landlord class. Here most Radicals were in agreement with him. The Conservatives were against self-government for Ireland but they were ready for public expenditure, even in the form that Gladstone dreaded, of putting public money into landlord pockets. Gladstone's view is well summed up in a letter he wrote to Forster on December 15, 1880:

My dear Forster,

I wish to correct an answer I gave you yesterday on a matter of some importance: or rather to enlarge it. You asked me whether I thought wider scope could be given to what we called the Bright clauses; and I replied no. I had in view the difficulties of state purchases, state-landlordism, State creditorship against small holders: and the mode in which every body would conspire against the State in carrying on this new undertaking. But I should give quite a different reply if we can combine this good with another good, namely the establishment of local self government in the Irish counties. The matter would then have in it a healthy principle of life and the impulse of public opinion would measure its operations: all the difficulties and dangers would be got rid of, or at any rate reduced to a minimum. To prevent jobbing there might be some restraining function given to the State. But the main function of the State would then be advancing money, on principles to which we are accustomed more or less: and with such great objects in view I should not be at all inclined to stint this kind of action. Of course the same plan might be applied to the conversion of tenancies into feu-duty proprietorships, and perhaps rather extensively.

Yours sincerely,
W. E. GLADSTONE.

On the other side of the problem Gladstone was a slow and gradual convert to a large and revolutionary measure. To understand his reluctance to accept the three Fs we must remember that the system they represented was regarded by everybody as a system that might be justified by necessity but was condemned by common sense. When at last the *Times* came round to this policy, it took the view that, Irish circumstances and Irish history being what they were, this arrangement was inevitable, but that in bringing it into force England was definitely putting Ireland on the footing of an imperfectly civilized society. No man in his senses would voluntarily set up dual ownership any more than he would go back to the old system of common fields and cultivation in strips. Enterprise, initiative, responsibility, all the capital virtues that made good farmers and good citizens were threatened by this revolution. Gladstone shared this view. He was very anxious that the Government should not be carried away by the influences of the hour into making a settlement that would not stand a calmer judgment.

" I feel the necessity of casting our minds forward into the future. . . . We must try to proceed as we shall wish that we had proceeded first when the current of Irish sentiment is met, in the open daylight of discussion, by the countercurrents of English and Scotch opinion, and secondly when, by the lapse of time, and restoration of public tranquillity, this matter shall be viewed in calm retrospect, say three or five or fifty years hence."

So he wrote on December 9 to Forster.   Even three months later, when he had accepted the three Fs, he had not quite thrown away the hope, as he put it to Forster on March 5, 1881, that they might " leave the way open for an eventual return to free contract as far as possible."

At first he wished to meet the new demand simply by adapting and invigorating his old Act.   He gave the Cabinet a paper in which he considered where and how the Act had succeeded and where and how it had failed.

" It does not seem difficult to mark the causes of failure; the want of power to assign; the extreme severity of the forfeiture of all claims for disturbance upon non payment of rent; the want of adequate provision against unreasonable and frequent changes in rent.   Why should we not give the power to assign; allow the allegations of reasonable causes against the forfeiture of the claims for disturbance; and restrain undue charges in rent by a mode the same in principle as that which we made use of in the Land Act to restrain capricious eviction? "

Gladstone's indirect and ingenious mind reveals itself in this complicated proposal for giving the tenant security, but Forster made short work of it.   He said that the tenant had a right of continuous occupation at a rent not exorbitant, a right " from his history and especially from the fact that he had as a rule given the land what facilities for cultivation it possesses," and that this right must be recognized explicitly by law.

Gladstone did not give way at once but he was overborne by the arguments and still more by the facts.   Writing long afterwards (in the *Nineteenth Century*, in September, 1888) he gave Forster full credit for his greater insight into this question.

" I for one felt deeply the formidable nature of the proposals which the state of Ireland absolutely required; and in justice to Forster I record the fact that he preceded me in their adoption and that he personally contributed to the formation of the strong resolutions by which we were enabled, and by which alone we could have been enabled, to confront the Land League."

The scope and strength of the proposed Bill were discussed through the late autumn and the winter months. From his letters to the Duke of Leinster and to Granville we learn that, as late as December the first, Gladstone was still hoping for something a good deal less than the three Fs. A letter to Bright on December 5 shows that he was beginning to face the larger issue.

" The question will come very seriously before us whether we shall, acting upon the principle of the Land Act, limit the exercise of proprietary rights for the safety of the country or whether we shall set out upon a new principle, convert the landlord virtually into an incumbrancer or rent charger and give over in the main to present occupiers the proprietary character."

It is possible that a stage in his advance to his later plan is represented by a curious draft Bill by Thring[1] dated December; a Bill that Thring described as " creating a species of medieval fief, in which rent is payable to the landlord by the tenant but no other service is required except that he should abstain from doing any act injurious to the landlord." This Bill is interesting for it looks like a plan for treating the Government's two problems in a single measure; for giving the tenant security and at the same time protecting order by a method less drastic and obnoxious than suspension of Habeas Corpus. The Land Commissioners were to fix rents

---

[1] The office of parliamentary counsel to the Treasury in its modern form was created by Lowe in 1869. The new official had to draft all Government Bills. (For duties and history of the office see Holdsworth *History of English Law*, vol. XI, 382.) Sir Henry Thring, afterwards Lord Thring, (1818-1907) was appointed to this office when it was created and held it till 1886. His support of Gladstone's Home Rule policy after his retirement was of great value because of his high reputation and important experience.

on the application of either party, and the tenant was to be secure against eviction so long as he complied with the conditions attached to the tenancy by the Bill. Thus the tenant had the advantage of compulsory arbitration. But he was himself to make a contribution to that principle. For any attempt to use force or threats in order to prevent or impede any tenant or landlord from carrying out any lawful contract was defined as an " agrarian crime " punishable with imprisonment for three months. For six months after the passing of the Bill the Lord Lieutenant was to have the power of arresting on suspicion. There is no correspondence on this scheme, and nothing to show whether it was discussed or why it was dropped. On January 29 Thring received instructions from the Cabinet to draft a Bill on new lines. Gladstone, who had by this time read everything he could find on the subject, and had been greatly impressed by Barry O'Brien's historical study, was now collecting his energies for the larger task from which he had shrunk.

These minutes and letters show how men's minds were moving on the agrarian question this autumn. The deciding event was the report of the Bessborough Commission, which was published on January 4, 1881, though its main recommendations were made known to Ministers in December. Four members of the Commission gave their support to the three Fs: Bessborough himself, the most highly respected of Irish landlords, Baron Dowse, a highly respected Judge of the Irish High Court, the O'Connor Don, and William Shaw, the leader of the moderate Home Rulers. The fifth Commissioner, Cavanagh, a Conservative landlord, produced a report of his own, but it was critical rather than hostile in tone. This powerful argument for reform was reinforced in the same month by the recommendations of six members of the Richmond Commission on Agriculture. This Commission, appointed by the Disraeli Government to consider the general subject of agricultural depression, published at this time a report on Ireland. All its members were agreed that the Act of 1870 had been a failure, and a minority of six which included

Carlingford who, as Fortescue, was the chief author of that Act, recommended the policy of the three Fs.

The report of the Bessborough Commission played, in the history of the Irish agrarian problem, the part played by the Factory Commissions in the history of Factory reform. To appreciate its effect in educating public opinion it is only necessary to turn to the *Times*. In 1879 the *Times* had sneered at Parnell as a man with one idea: the idea of checking the landlord's power over the rent. When O'Connor Power introduced his moderate plan for arresting evictions and rack-renting, in the summer of 1880, the *Times* had dismissed his Bill with the remark that it would be more honest to call it a bill for abolishing rent. In January, 1881, its tone was very different. " How far it may be possible to go in the direction of the Commissioners' conclusions is another matter; but it is quite certain that some means will be devised to put a check on the most serious grievance of the Irish tenantry; the raising of rents."

These Reports brought hope and daylight to the reformers, but other events were bringing embarrassment and concern. For all these deliberations were taking place under a dark shadow. While the Compensation Bill was under discussion, there was some decline in Irish violence. From April to July inclusive the monthly average of Land League meetings was fourteen, and of agrarian outrages eighty-two; in the previous six months the corresponding averages had been thirty and a hundred and eighteen. The rejection of the Compensation Bill had an immediate effect on the temper and vigour of the agitation. " If the Government had the people of England behind them," said Parnell, " the Lords dare not do this. Well, we will stiffen the back of Government, then we shall see what the Lords will do." There was the prospect of a winter of distress and bloodshed in Ireland, and fierce speeches were made by League leaders, notably Dillon. The Conservatives began to press for coercion; Forster, admitting that it might be necessary, hinted that a Coercion Bill might include a provision preventing evictions. Gladstone was away ill at the moment, and Hartington, leading the House in his absence, would give no pledge on this point. The proposal was condemned by the *Times*, and the Irish members, despairing of Parliament, returned to Ireland when the session closed on September 7, 1880, to spread revolt.

It was soon plain that the House of Lords had given a powerful stimulus to the spirit of the Land League. Its income rose to £1,000 a week, nine-tenths of it coming from America (an American Land League had been started in the summer of 1880), the rest from Great Britain's Irish centres and from Ireland. Paid organizers were appointed for the first time. The monthly average of League meetings during the last five months of 1880 rose to ninety-one. The membership gradually increased to hundreds of thousands. Active resistance to rack-renting and evictions spread from Galway, Mayo and Sligo, to Donegal, Cavan, Leitrim, Roscommon, Kerry, and West Cork. Land Courts were established by the League to settle agrarian disputes. In the ordinary courts it became almost impossible to obtain evidence or to secure convictions in agrarian cases. The leaders made provocative speeches, but usually kept within the law. They poured scorn on the Government's foreshadowed Bill, and Parnell advised the tenants to have no confidence in the Bessborough Commission. But he had more in view than mere obstruction. " Depend upon it," he said, " that the measure of the Land Bill next session will be the measure of your activity this winter. It will be the measure of your determination not to pay unjust rents; it will be the measure of your determination to keep a firm grip of your homesteads." His larger object was not forgotten. " I would not have taken off my coat and gone to this work, if I had not known that we were laying the foundation in this movement for the regeneration of our legislative independence."

Agrarian crime increased, though denounced by Davitt and, to a lesser extent, by Parnell; of the 2,590 outrages in 1880, 1,696 were committed in the last quarter. But the most disturbing event was the adoption of a new agrarian weapon. On September 17, at Ennis, Parnell recommended a device (spasmodically used in the old tithe wars, and occasionally under the Land League) for the social ostracism of the unpopular person, usually a land grabber, or perhaps a landlord or his agent. By "isolating him from his kind as if he were a leper of old" public opinion was to assert itself. Public opinion responded effectively by the "isolating" of Captain Boycott, who was forced to enlist fifty Orangemen, guarded by troops, to harvest his crops; and the "isolating" of Captain Bence Jones, for long unable either to sell his cattle in Ireland or to ship them to England. The new weapon was a manifest success. It was, Parnell declared, the only answer to the rejection of the Compensation for Disturbance Bill. The general result of boycott and outrage combined was to put such terror into the landlords that evictions were checked. Out of 2,110 evictions in 1880, only 198 occurred in the last quarter.

Thus the effect of the action of the House of Lords can be described very simply. The Government said that it was essential if they were to give Ireland peace that they should be allowed by Parliament to enforce a moratorium, to check the process of eviction until they had time to reform the law. The House of Lords refused them that power. The moratorium was in consequence enforced not by British law but by Irish violence. All the misfortunes of the following years can be attributed to this governing fact, for the Government were compelled to address themselves to two problems at once, the problem of enforcing respect for bad law, and the problem of turning bad law into good. Forster at one time played with the idea that the Government might announce that it would not introduce a Land Bill unless Ireland was quiet, but Gladstone on November 7 answered that a Government could not "withhold from the country a measure required by its wants on account of crimes committed by a limited portion of the population."

As Irish violence grew, Forster who, as we have seen, was sincerely anxious for a good Land Bill, became more and more absorbed in the growing problem of Irish disorder. As soon as he began to speak of coercion, he found, as all Irish Secretaries found, that if Dublin Castle was a strong

o

influence on one side, Gladstone's hostility was a strong influence on the other.

"With regard to the suspension of the Habeas Corpus Act," Gladstone wrote to Forster on October 25, "I look to it with feelings not only of aversion on general grounds, but of doubt and much misgiving as to the likelihood of its proving efficacious in the particular case. The crimes which at present threaten to give a case for interference, grow out of certain incitements made by speech. What we want is to enforce silence, abstention from guilty speech. I do not see how this is to be done by *Habeas Corpus if* it cannot be done by prosecution. Legal prosecutions can be multiplied if necessary far more easily than apprehensions necessarily arbitrary under a suspension of the Habeas Corpus Act."

Throughout the autumn there was friction in the Cabinet on this question. Gladstone wrote several letters putting a strong case against suspension and showing how difficult it would be to defend it. He was anxious that the law should be tested before any proposal was made to suspend it, and in September it was decided to prosecute Parnell, Dillon, Biggar, Sullivan, Sexton, Egan, and Brennan, as well as seven subordinate officials of the League, for conspiring against the Crown in preventing the payment of rents and the taking of farms from which the tenants had been evicted, for resisting the process of ejectment, and creating ill will among Her Majesty's subjects. Selborne encouraged the Government to believe that this prosecution might succeed, but he reckoned without Irish juries. This method was accepted by Chamberlain as the alternative to the suspension of Habeas Corpus.

"I do not half like the Irish prosecutions," he wrote to Dilke on October 27, 1880, "but I fear there is no alternative, except, indeed, the suspension of the Habeas Corpus, which I should like still less. Parnell is doing his best to make Irish legislation unpopular with English Radicals. The workmen here do not like to see the law set at defiance, and a dissolution on the ' Justice for Ireland ' cry would under present circumstances be a hazardous operation."[1]

---

[1] Gwynn and Tuckwell, *Life of Dilke*, Vol. I, p. 345.

The battle over Habeas Corpus was only postponed, and not postponed for long. On November 9, Cowper, the Viceroy, sent a memorandum to the Cabinet urging strongly that Habeas Corpus should be suspended, and stating that landlords, landlords' agents, resident magistrates, and officials, were all pressing for such a measure. Cowper's argument was a little lacking in coherence, as Gladstone saw, and it showed that his nerves were suffering under the strain.

" Nobody dares to evict," he wrote (though, as Gladstone observed in the margin, many landlords were in fact evicting) " and tenants of evicted farms, even those who have been in possession for more than a year, are daily giving them up. . . . We cannot say yet for certain how far the autumn rents will be paid, but it appears already that in many places tenants have refused to pay more than Government valuation. Landlords will not agree to this. They will evict, and then a great increase of outrages may be expected. . . . The sudden imprisonment of some of those who are known to instigate and to commit these crimes would strike general terror in a way that nothing else would, for no man would know how far he was suspected or whether his turn might not come next. . . . This would no doubt be a very high-handed proceeding. . . . If we are to have such a hateful thing as a Coercion Bill, let it be effective."

Forster, in a Minute circulated on the 16th, pressed for an immediate summons to Parliament in order to carry out Cowper's policy, arguing, with a confidence that was afterwards remembered against him, " that the actual perpetrators were old Fenians, and old Ribbonmen, and mauvais sujets who would slink into their holes if a few were arrested." Forster threatened to resign if Parliament were not summoned. On the other hand, Chamberlain threatened to resign if Forster got his way. He wrote to Gladstone on November 16, 1880, to say that Forster's proposal seemed to him so wrong in principle and so bad in policy, that he could not conscientiously give to it even a silent support.

" If it be adopted by the Cabinet, I shall have no alternative but to retire from the Government, though I shall take this course with the greatest pain, at being compelled to separate myself from colleagues whom I so highly esteem, and above all from a leader whom I have been proud to follow, and in whose genius and love of justice and freedom I have the most implicit confidence."

A few days later (November 18) Chamberlain sent a memorandum containing some excellent criticism of Forster's view.

" It is really impossible to suppose that the arrest of thirty subordinate agents, as proposed by Mr. Forster, would immediately stop threatening letters and the assaults on life and property which are rife all over the country. It would be like firing with a rifle at a swarm of gnats. The tenants of Ireland are universally in a state of excitement under which anyone of them, in face of provocation, may take the law into his own hands. The remedy must be one which affects all—not the arrest of individuals when a whole nation has more or less escaped from the ordinary respect of the law. The condition has been brought about by an unjust law—or by a law which under the exceptional circumstances of the country has practically worked injustice, and the only remedy is the alteration of the law."

A letter from General Gordon, which appeared in the *Times* a few days later (December 3, 1880), confirmed his conclusion. Gordon wrote to say that the condition of many of the people in the West of Ireland was worse than that of the Bulgarians, Chinese, Indians, or Anatolians.

" No half-measured Acts which left the landlord with any say to the tenantry of these portions of Ireland will be of any use. They would be rendered—as past Land Acts have been—quite abortive, for the landlords will insert clauses to do away with their force. Any half measures will only place the Government face to face with the people of Ireland as the champions of the landlord interest "

Gordon urged the Government to buy up the rights of the landlords over the whole or the greater part of eleven counties at a cost of eighty millions, and to manage them as a Crown estate.

" For the rest of Ireland I would pass an Act allowing free sale of leases, fair rents, and a Government valuation. In conclusion I must say, from all accounts and from my own observation, that the state of our fellow countrymen in the parts I have named is worse than that of any people in the world, let alone Europe. I believe that these people are made as we are, that they are patient beyond belief, loyal, but, at the same time, broken spirited and desperate, living on the verge of starvation in places in which we would not keep our cattle."

This was the population which, in the judgment of the House of Lords, was to be left to the mercies of rack-renting landlords, in the name of the rights of property and the sanctity of contracts.

Gladstone found an ingenious argument for averting an immediate Coercion Bill. He pointed out in a Minute on November 18, 1880, that the case for such a Bill could not be argued without reference to the Land Leaguers, and that such references would be improper when the Land Leaguers were on their trial. This killed the demand for an immediate summons to Parliament. But the most Gladstone could get was a reprieve. Irish violence grew, and the Radicals were reluctantly brought round to Forster's policy because they believed that without coercion they could not get a good Land Bill. The case for the compromise seemed the more plausible because, if Irishmen were making it more and more difficult to resist coercion, events were making it more and more difficult to resist the demand for a drastic agrarian Bill. Forster was in favour of both. The Cabinet decided for both.

One thing alone could have saved the Government reforms from the consequences of this decision to put the Irish people under hatches. Chamberlain pressed, but in vain, that the suspension of Habeas Corpus should be accompanied by the suspension of the landlords' power to evict. The Cabinet presumably believed it hopeless to send such a proposal to the Lords. So the year ended in gloom. Gladstone was under no illusions about the outlook for the New Year. In November, writing to the Speaker of his objections to suspending Habeas Corpus, he had given among other objections the danger that it would seriously damage the prospects of the Land Bill. On the last night of the year he had as guests at his house at dinner,

Granville, Morley, and Frederick Cavendish who was almost as close to him as a son. Morley described the evening in a letter to Chamberlain.

" Gladstone was as interesting as usual; talked about Dante, Innocent the Third, house property in London, the true theory of the Church, the enormity and monstrous absurdity of our keeping Ascension Island, etc., etc., etc. Then after dinner he took me into a corner and revealed his Coercion (scheme) much as a man might say (in confidence) that he found himself under the painful necessity of slaying his mother. It was downright piteous—his wrung features, his strained gesture, all the other signs of mental perturbation in an intense nature."[1]

Yet even Gladstone could not forsee the full extent of the calamity that was to fall upon him. He might suspect, as he talked that evening of the future, that the dark forces of Ireland's history were throwing across his plans the shadow of failure. He did not know that they were throwing across his friendships the shadow of death.

APPENDIX

GLADSTONE'S SCHEME FOR GRAND COMMITTEES

[With Mr. Gladstone's notes made on 23: Aug: /81 for The Speaker and Sir T. E. May.]

Printed for the use of the Cabinet. November 12, 1880.

CONFIDENTIAL.

OBSTRUCTION AND DEVOLUTION.

Obstruction.

THE question of obstruction in the proceedings of the House of Commons has grown to such a magnitude that it seems to require the consideration of the Government during the present recess.

2. We have subjects more or less in prospect, some of which may present increased inducements to this practice. On these it seems likely that obstruction may present a further aggravation of character.

3. Even without taking obstruction into account, while legislation has fallen into great arrear, the labours of Parliament have become unduly and almost intolerably severe.

---

[1] Garvin, *op. cit.*, Vol. I, p. 332.

4. It is the extreme pressure of business which is the secret of the strength of the obstructor proper, and which makes it pay him so well to pursue his vocation at all costs. Were the time at the disposal of the House equal to the calls upon it, it would be, in respect to him, a fund virtually unlimited, and it would no longer be so well worth his while to draw upon it.

5. The work of encountering him by repression is extremely difficult, and, as matters now stand, of doubtful issue. In the case of the Irish obstructor, this repression might answer his purpose by supplying him with a new national grievance; and as his extremest resistance would probably be popular with his constituents, the House might find that it had more than a merely personal conflict to handle.

6. It will also be admitted that any serious changes in the rules of the House of Commons, if repressive of the liberty of debate, would be grave public evils, even should we be able to avert, by their means, evils greater still.

7. It is worth while to inquire whether there may not be a way, different from that of repression, but in case of need auxiliary and preparatory to it, by which we may neutralize or reduce within more moderate bounds both the scandalous evil of obstruction and the heavy inconvenience of prolonged and manifold legislative arrear.

Devolution.

8. This way of proceeding I shall call devolution. By devolving upon other bodies a portion of its overwhelming tasks, the House of Commons may at once economize its time, reduce its arrears, and bring down to a minimum the inducement to obstruct; for obstruction will then be only the infliction of suffering, whereas now it is the frustration of purpose, the defeat of duty.

9. At the same time, whatever repression can do for us will still remain, not less than before, at our command.

10. Of this devolution, part may be to subordinate and separate authorities. On this portion of the subject I do not now touch. But part may also be to subformations out of the body of the House itself; on something like the same principle, though not in the same form, as that on which the French Chamber divides work among its Bureaux. I shall here rudely sketch some portion at least of what I think may hopefully be undertaken in this direction.

Local Government.

11. But I must add that, besides the defeat of obstruction, and the improvement of our attitude for dealing with arrear, I conceive that devolution may supply the means of partially meeting and satisfying, at least so far as it is legitimate, another call. I refer to the call for what is styled (*in bonam partem*) " Local Government," and (*in malam*) " Home Rule."

12. One word must be added to these introductory sentences. During a Parliamentary recess, since Mr. Brand became Speaker, and when we were last in office, there was a small meeting in Palace Yard, at which Sir T. Erskine May attended. He then gave a general opinion in favour of the devolution of a portion of the duties of the House to Grand Committees. The suggestion was generally approved. It evidently meant something beyond, and distinct from, what is intended in a mere extension of the practice of referring Bills to Select Committees. But the idea was not at the time pursued into much detail. It forms, I need hardly say, the ground-work of the suggestions here appended.

13. They might be extended, in scope as well as in particulars, beyond the present sketch; but this will perhaps suffice at least for raising a very important and rather many-sided question.

W.E.G.

October 23, 1880.

PROPOSITIONS

Grand Committees.

I. That Grand Committees of the House, heretofore appointed for particular classes of subjects, be, now and hereafter, [also] appointed for particular portions of the three Kingdoms, united under Her Majesty by Statutes of the Realm.

Composition.

II. That every such Grand Committee do consist of—

1. The representatives of all constituencies within the limits of that part of the country or of the United Kingdom for which the Committee may have been appointed to act, including Universities.
2. The members who may hold, or may within [ten] years have held, offices under the Crown, the duties whereof were specially related to any portion of the country within the said limits.

3. Such other members holding office under the Crown as the House may think fit to name not exceeding [six.]

4. All such members as shall think proper to attend and shall enrol their names accordingly on the list of the Committee within [three] days after the appointment of the same.

Provided that the numbers appointed under (4) shall not exceed the number appointed under 1.

Chairman.

III. The Grand Committee shall appoint its own Chairman, to hold office during the pleasure of the House, except in cases in which the House shall deem it proper to appoint the Chairman.

The Chairman shall be invested with the same powers as those which do or may belong to the Chairman of Committees in the whole House.

Procedure.

IV. Grand Committees may, if they think proper, sit during the sitting of the House; and the rules of procedure shall be the same as in the House and in the Committee of the whole House respectively, except as shall be otherwise specially provided. When the Grand Committee is engaged in considering a Bill not in detail but at large, the rule shall prevail that each member may only speak once.

Powers.

V. Grand Committees may proceed:—

(a) By inquiries through Select Committees, which they may appoint from among their own members under the title of Sub-Committees, and which shall have the powers and functions of Select Committees of the House.

(b) By Report or Resolution offered to the House.

(c) Upon Bills, or parts of Bills, in the manner hereinafter set out.

But no Grand Committee shall have any initiative power, or shall proceed except by permission under the vote of the House.

VI. Grand Committees may deal :—

(a) In Bills, or otherwise, with the subjects set out from time to time in a schedule for that purpose by the authority of the House.

(b) With the subjects which may from time to time be referred to them by vote of the House upon special motion.

VII. Any Grand Committee shall have the power of dealing with any Bill referred to it by debate and vote upon the whole measure, as well as, and both before and after considering it in detail.

In dealing with Resolutions and Reports the procedure shall be the same as in the House.

Subjects excluded.

VIII. The House will not entertain any motion for or towards the reference to a Grand Committee of any matter or Bill, or part of a Bill, relating to—
See the rule for assemblies in Canada.

   1. The Crown.
   2. The Established Churches of England or of Scotland.
   3. The Constitution of Parliament, unless as to measures operating within its own local limits.
   4. Foreign Relations.
   5. Navigation and Trade over Sea, and between the three Kingdoms.
   6. The Colonies and Dependencies of the Crown.
   7. The Posts and Telegraphs.
   8. The Ecclesiastical Law.
   9. The Trial of Elections.
  10. Peace and War.
  11. The Naval, Military, and Revenue Establishments.
  12. Coinage, Bills of Exchange, and Promissory Notes.
  13. The Public Debt and Property.
  14. The Census and Statistics.
  15. Beacons, Buoys, Lighthouses, and Quarantine.
  16. Savings Banks.
  17. Naturalization and Aliens.
  18. Patents and Copyright.
  19. Bills or other matters extending to any district beyond the local limits.

Subjects conditionally excluded.

IX. This House will not entertain any motion, except on the proposal of the Ministers of the Crown, for referring to any Grand Committee any matter or Bill touching—
   (*a*) Public Income.
   (*b*) Public Charge.
   (*c*) Local Income.
   (*d*) Local Charge.
   (*e*) Currency and banking.

Nor will the House deal with any Bill, or part of a Bill, or Report, or Resolution on the said subjects from the Grand Committees, except by recommendation from the Crown.

Relative procedure in the House.

X. With regard to Bills—
(*a*) On the subjects scheduled for Grand Committees, or
(*b*) Proposed to be referred to them,
the procedure in the House shall be as follows:—
(A.) As to Bills on the scheduled subjects—

1. The question shall be put for the reference of the Bill to the Grand Committee immediately after the question shall have been carried for the first reading of the same.
2. If the same shall be carried, the Bill shall thereupon pass to the Grand Committee, and the vote for the reference shall stand instead of a vote for the second reading.
3. After the Report of the Bill, unless the House shall think fit to recommit it to the Grand Committee [or to a Committee of the whole House], the question shall be put for the third reading.
4. No question, except the recommittal of the Bill, can be moved upon the reception of the Report.

(B.) Procedure upon Bills not scheduled, but not excluded from reference to a Grand Committee—

1. Upon notice given, a motion may be made, not more than three days nor less than one day, except by leave of the House, after the first reading of a Bill (being such as aforesaid), that the Bill be referred to a Grand Committee.
2. If the question shall be carried, the vote for the reference shall stand instead of a vote for the second reading, and the further procedure on the Bill shall be the same as in class (A).
3. If the question be lost, it cannot be renewed, except by leave of the House, and then only before the second reading.

Parts of Bills.

XI. Parts of Bills, being such as aforesaid, may be referred to a Grand Committee in the manner as now to a Select Committee, and subject to the usual order of business in the House.

XII. No Grand Committee shall have power to proceed upon any Bill or part of a Bill except for purposes within its own proper local limits.

XIII. The procedure on a Bill in the Grand Committee shall be as follows:—

    (1) The Bill shall be read a second time.

    (2) It shall be committed. [Instructions are to be moved only in the House.]

    (3) It may be recommitted.

    (4) With Report in each case to the Grand Committee sitting as a House.

    (5) And finally report to the House.

XIV. When Private Bills are referred to Grand Committees after the first reading, they shall be treated in the Grand Committees according to the rules of the House for Private Bills. But any Sub-Committee which may be appointed by the Grand Committee on a contested Bill may be appointed to sit, at the expense of parties, in such place, within the limits of their jurisdiction, as may be most convenient and economical, and shall not be precluded from sitting during an adjournment or, by authority of Parliament, during the recess of Parliament.

[An Act contemplated for simplifying the procedure of the two Houses on Private Bills, and uniting the Committees.]

Schedule of Subjects.

[I leave it for consideration whether there shall be a Table of subjects in a Schedule, or whether it will suffice to proceed by the exclusion of certain subjects, leaving all other subjects open.]

CHAPTER XIII

COERCION AND REFORM, 1881

The more Gladstone's career is studied the more significance will the student attach to the disparity between his power in the country and his power in the House of Commons, and between his power in the House of Commons and his power in the Cabinet. In 1880, though he had neglected, because he had misunderstood, the new Irish problem, and though he was handicapped by his burdens as Chancellor of the Exchequer, he drew up and submitted to the Cabinet, as we have seen, a plan for meeting the Irish problem by constructive political reform. His plan for setting up Grand Committees urged with the authority of all his experience and wisdom, was rejected by colleagues of whom hardly any had given serious thought to the Irish problem. It is clear that this was an issue in which he ought not to have accepted defeat. Defeat involved him in the alternative plan of coercion tempered by agrarian reform, as it seemed to some, or of agrarian reform tempered by coercion, as it seemed to others. It may be that from that moment the task set to Gladstone was impossible; for the House of Lords would not let him satisfy the minimum demands of the Land League, and the Land League would not let him satisfy the minimum demands of the House of Lords. In that case, when he accepted defeat at the hands of his Cabinet, a defeat due to the natural conservatism of its members and their dread of being taken by Gladstone further than they were ready to go, he let all his hopes of a satisfactory Irish policy slip through his fingers.

Whether this is true or not, the history of 1881 must be understood, as the history of his attempt to push through Parliament a policy of Irish reform under conditions so

desperate that no other statesman could have attempted it.
Under immense difficulties he succeeded in putting in the
Statute Book an Act of Parliament that outraged all the
ideas of his age, ideas in which he had himself been brought
up, and laid the foundation of Ireland's peasant society.
It must count among the greatest exploits in parliamentary
history, as a display of courage, of mastery of complicated
facts, and of personal ascendancy in debate, an immense
achievement in itself and its consequences, but not a solution
of the problem that faced his Government. That problem
remained and it baffled all Gladstone's good will and
energy down to the time of his defeat in 1885.

If Gladstone's plan of constructive political reform had
been accepted, it would have averted or at least modified the
struggle between England and the new Irish party into
which the House of Commons was drawn. For that plan
provided for the reform of parliamentary procedure and
method as part of a plan for meeting Irish wishes and needs.
To appreciate its importance we must remember that the
Irish difficulty in its influences on the temper of politicians
was a double difficulty. There was the difficulty of keeping
order in Ireland but there was also the difficulty of keeping
order in the House of Commons. The first difficulty
would have put a great strain on the relations of England
and Ireland but it was greatly aggravated by the strain
that was caused by the second. John Bright, to name one
important Englishman only, never forgave the Irish Nationalists for their treatment of the House of Commons. Yet
if a measure to which the Irish party was resolved on the
ground both of interest and duty to offer the utmost resistance was brought into the House of Commons, under the
arrangements in force in 1881, that resistance was bound to
take the form of throwing the business of the House into
disorder. The Government found itself driven to reform
procedure under conditions that made it inevitable that the
Irish party should obstruct that reform. We may say
indeed that the rejected Gladstone plan of Grand Committees
would have enabled the Government to reform procedure
with the help and sympathy of the Irish party. The defeat

of that plan threw the Government back on a policy which was bound to provoke its violent resistance.

The need for reform of procedure had become urgent. Before 1882 there was no rule under which parliamentary debate could be brought to a conclusion by compulsion on a minority. That fact is itself significant. It is significant both of the history of Parliament and of the temper of the party system. If Parliament had been chiefly important by tradition as a legislating body, its arrangements would have been reformed much earlier into a system necessary for the efficient despatch of business. But Parliament in the eighteenth century was chiefly important as a place where grievances could be presented and discussed. Parliament was a check on the Crown; it was the guardian of rights and liberties that were liable to be invaded by power. Methods and procedure suitable to such a body had been left unreformed long after Parliament had changed its character.

There was another reason for the indulgent forms of the House. Until this time the warfare of Parliament had been governed by what we may call the Wellington tradition; the over-ruling belief that opposition must be conducted on certain understood principles. An Opposition in Wellington's view should accept a measure it thought bad, rather than run the risk of revolution or serious public disorder in resisting it. That governing consideration had decided the conduct of Wellington himself over Catholic Emancipation and the Repeal of the Corn Laws. How important a part this tradition played in parliamentary government was made clear when a powerful Opposition discarded it just before the Great War, and parliamentary government was thrown at once into hopeless confusion.

As early as 1868 Parliament had changed its character in the first of these respects, for, under pressure of the wide franchise and other influences, the spirit of constructive reform was active and enterprising. In the late 'seventies it had changed its character in the second. For there was now within the House of Commons a body of men who put their own demands above the convenience, or the dignity, or the safety, of parliamentary institutions. Their ingenuity, their eloquence, their resolution, their passion, their indifference to the favour of the English parties or the opinion of the English people, all made them consummate masters of the art of obstructing and defeating the will of the House of Commons. A Parliament, elected to undo the work of Disraeli in Europe, and Asia, and Africa, found itself compelled within a few months of its birth to discover some method for enforcing its authority on twenty or thirty of its own members. Thus, at a time when it was urgently important to gain the sympathies of Ireland for a great agrarian reform, politics assumed this unfortunate appearance of a struggle between English dignity and Irish mischief, and between English law and Irish violence. Out of this struggle the House of Commons gained an important and necessary reform, but the conditions under which it was gained were so bad that for the time the evil far outweighed the good.

The defeat of Gladstone's plan had put an end to the hope of reforming procedure by consent. It was fatal also because it threw the Government back on to a policy of combining coercion and agrarian reform.

Bright and Chamberlain had consented to the combination of coercion with reform partly because both of them had been irritated by Irish lawlessness. Chamberlain had come to think it was alienating radical sympathy in England. He had created a kind of Frankenstein's monster in the caucus, for he was too apt to ask himself whether a particular measure would please or displease it. At this time he was beginning to shake his head over Irish disorder, fearing that he might be forced to fight not on those radical reforms in which he knew he would have the weight of the caucus behind him, but on the defence of Irish lawlessness on which he thought the workman would desert him.[1] He made no

[1] The *Annual Register* noted that in the provincial press Newcastle, Manchester, Bradford and South Wales were against coercion, and Birmingham, Liverpool, Leeds, the South West and Scotland in favour. Thomas Burt, the Miners' M.P., voted in every division against coercion, but Henry Broadhurst just elected said he would support coercion, though he did not like it, and that he resented the comparison made by some Irishmen between the Land League and the English trade unions.

speeches on any Irish subject in the House in 1881. Bright spoke in support of the first Coercion Bill, January 27, 1881, and observed that he had never voted before for a Coercion Bill, but that looking back he saw that every one of those Bills had been needed at the time and that the mistake was that they were not combined with reform. Both he and Chamberlain were now reconciled to coercion because it was combined with redress of grievances and because they believed that without it they could not get a good Land Bill. They were confirmed in this view by the speeches of the Front Opposition Bench, in which the Government were warned that the Opposition would not consider a Land Bill until order had been restored.

Unfortunately, when you turned from the House of Commons to Ireland, you found a flaw in this reasoning. For if conditions in England made it impossible to get a good Agrarian Bill without coercion, conditions in Ireland made it impossible to get the benefits of an Agrarian Bill in the atmosphere that was created by coercion.

Ministers were slow to grasp this truth because in the House of Commons Parnell was the leader, not of a majority of the Irish members, but of a minority. Most Englishmen thought it a misfortune that he was as strong as he was, but the real misfortune was that he was not stronger. Gladstone's dislike of a Coercion Bill, great as it was, would have been much greater if he had been in conflict with the mass of the Irish members, for he had held from the first that an English Government could not declare war on the Irish people. But Parnell's strength in Ireland was not reflected in his strength in the House of Commons. The figures in the division lists on the Coercion Bills make this clear. The *Annual Register* analysed the first division on Parnell's amendment to the Address and showed that 51 Irish members, representing 110,219 electors supported Parnell; 29 representing 55,474 electors abstained, and 22, representing 65,845, voted with the Government. The dangers of coercion were masked by these figures.[1]

---

[1] On the second reading of the Person and Property Bill—the first Coercion Bill (February, 1881), the opponents numbered fifty-six, of whom seven were

For Parnell who had at his back at Westminster only thirty or forty votes, had at his back in Ireland the Land League and a great popular movement. Gladstone and his friends still clung to the illusion that the landlords counted in Ireland as a moral power; that they had qualities of leadership of which a Government could make use. They did not realize that the Land League was something more than the creation or the instrument of agitators. It had served the interests, defended the weakness, and warmed the memories, of a class of which Parnell said with truth that it lacked the education, and the means, to protect itself; and that class was the largest class in Ireland. In Parliament, and in London society, the landlords had so much power that Governments were in no danger of overlooking it. Ministers could easily forget that that power was much greater in England than in Ireland, and that to make a good agrarian policy it was even more necessary to consider the men who controlled the Land League than to consider the men who controlled the House of Lords.

It was evident as soon as Parliament met on January 7, 1881, that Ireland would occupy most of the time of the House of Commons. For the Queen's Speech announced in addition to Coercive Legislation a Land Bill, and a Bill " for the establishment of County Government in Ireland, founded upon representative principles, and framed with the double aim of confirming popular control over expenditure, and of supplying a yet more serious want by extending the formation of habits of local self government." Forster gave notice that he would introduce two Bills, one a Bill for the better protection of persons and property in Ireland; the other, a Bill to amend the law relating to the carrying and possession of arms. Parnell moved an amendment to the Address affirming the conviction that " the peace and tranquillity of Ireland could not be promoted by suspending any of the constitutional rights of the Irish people." Parnell's

British Radicals; on the third reading forty-six, of whom five were British Radicals ; on the second reading of the Peace Preservation Bill—the second Coercion Bill (March, 1881) the opponents numbered thirty-seven, and on the third, twenty-eight. It has been said that Balfour's Coercion Bill of 1887 was the first Coercion Bill that was opposed by a majority of the Irish members.

speech on this occasion was one of his best, cold and careful in analysis, excellent in tact and temper; so hostile a critic as Gibson paid compliments to its force. If the issue had not already been decided in the Cabinet, the proceedings at this stage might well have taught Ministers the wisdom of holding their hands on coercion, for Parnell was supported by Shaw, who argued that no Coercion Bill could take effect against the force behind the agrarian agitation. Shaw's evident dislike of the Land League gave all the greater significance to his support of the amendment and also to the emphasis he laid on the active part Davitt was taking in restraining crime. But the Government were now deep in their unhappy plan, and they were drawn swiftly and inexorably into a fatal quarrel.

For the Bill that Forster introduced was so severe that the Irish party would have failed in its duty to Ireland if it had not resisted it with all its resources. The description given by Dicey justifies Morley's summary account of it as a Bill that enabled the Viceroy to lock up anybody he pleased and to detain him as long as he pleased while the Act was in force.[1] The Bill was fought at its first introduction with such skill and persistence by Parnell's party that Gladstone decided (January 31) on a continuous sitting in order to force the Bill through its first stage. But Irish endurance defeated him. The Speaker then intervened. After the House had sat for twenty-four hours on end, he sent for Gladstone on February 1, and told him that he would be ready to put the question on his own authority on two conditions; the first that the debate should be carried on until the following morning (" my object in this delay being to mark distinctly to the outside world the extreme gravity of the situation, and the necessity of the step which I was about

[1] " Under the Act of 1881, 44 Vict., c. 4, the Irish executive obtained the absolute power of arbitrary and preventive arrest, and could without breach of law detain in prison any person arrested on suspicion for the whole period for which the Act continued in force. . . . The Government could, in the case of certain crimes, abolish the right to trial by jury, could arrest strangers found out of doors at night under suspicious circumstances, could seize any newspaper inciting to treason or violence, and could prohibit any public meeting which the Lord Lieutenant believed to be dangerous to the public peace or safety." Dicey, *Law of Constitution*, p. 243.

to take ")[1] the second that Gladstone should reconsider the regulation of business, either by giving more authority to the House or by conferring authority on the Speaker. Gladstone agreed and the Speaker carried out his coup. A few days later Gladstone, after discussions with the Speaker and the leaders of the Opposition, introduced and carried resolutions giving the Speaker power to restrict discussion when urgency was voted by a majority of three to one.[2]

No two months in his life were more hateful to Gladstone than the months of February and March in which he was fighting the new Irish party. There was not a man in the House to whose temperament coercion was more distasteful; there was certainly not a Minister whose misgivings about the effect of this Irish war on the prospects of his Irish reforms were deeper. These months tried and tested all his qualities as a leader, and if he answered the test with conspicuous success, the reason was that he was defending something that he valued above everything else, the liberty and efficiency of the House of Commons. The diaries of Lady Frederick Cavendish give a striking picture of his resilience. The speech he made on February 3, in moving the resolution to give the Speaker control of debate when the House should vote by a majority of three to one that the business was urgent, won universal admiration. It was made under most difficult conditions. For to the indignation excited by Forster's violent Bill there had been added further cause of quarrel. The House had been informed that day that Davitt had been sent back to prison, and the Irish party had been exasperated by a harsh blunder little to Gladstone's liking. (Gladstone wrote to Harcourt urging him to give Davitt as much comfort in prison as was possible.) Thirty-six members were suspended after passionate scenes lasting some hours during which Gladstone as Leader of the House was, as *Punch* described him, " up

[1] Morley, *Life of Gladstone*, Vol. III, p. 52.
[2] Next year procedure was reformed and the principle of closure was adopted. (It has since of course been made much more drastic.) It is safe to say that without this reform no Home Rule Bill could have been carried through the House of Commons.

and down between his seat and the table like a hen on a hot gridiron." Yet when at last after this exhausting experience he rose to speak he made a speech of which Frederick Cavendish said that it could not have been improved if he had had a fortnight to prepare it and his own moment to deliver it.

The proposal he was making then was painful to him as an old parliamentarian who clung to the early traditions of the House of Commons[1] (Chamberlain as a business man was much more ready for the closure), but it was not nearly so painful to him as the defence of the Coercion Bill.   When a man is engaged in defending a policy which he has accepted with great reluctance from his Cabinet, his temper generally suffers.   Yet, as we study the debate, it is impossible not to note that though Gladstone was engaged in a frontal attack on the Parnellite party he never lost altogether its regard or its sympathy.   When controversy is fierce, the disappointing friend is more harshly treated than the recognized antagonist.   In the debates of this Parliament Bright and Gladstone suffered under this law; in the debates of the next, Chamberlain.   If the demeanour of these three man is studied, Gladstone appears a more magnanimous man than the others under this kind of provocation.   Bright soon lost all perspective, and his old Irish sympathies, so creditable to his past, were extinguished by what seemed to him the base ingratitude of the Irish party.[2]

[1] He wrote to the Speaker on January 20, 1881, " Difficulty lies, I fear, at the root of the case.   I can see no method of proceeding which will be effectual without placing the minority—I mean the regular minority of the House—at the mercy of the Speaker, to which, if it stood alone, they might readily consent —and also to some extent at the mercy of the Government."

In January, 1881, Dilke sent Gladstone an article in *La République Française* which he thought was written by Clemenceau, calling obstruction " des obstacles de pur formalisme qui en tout autre pays ne subsisteraient pas pendant 48 heures."

[2] In a letter from Gladstone to Granville written as early as June 15, 1869, there is a sentence that has a special interest in this regard.   " In a report of a conversation with Summer in the *New York Times* of May 31, which I have just seen, the great Senator is made apologetically to condemn Mr. John Bright in these words, ' With all the grandeur of his character, there is a very large residuum of John Bull in him—with Cobden there was not enough of this to hurt.' "   Gladstone always held that Cobden would have been on his side in 1886.

In the fierce controversy over Home Rule, when the Irishmen were so mistaken as to add to Chamberlain's considerable resources of bitter feeling by savage invective, Chamberlain so far lost his self control as to taunt them with their poverty. Gladstone never, when passions were raging at their worst, lapsed from his high standard of debating dignity.

The effect is seen in the conduct of the Irishmen toward him. On one occasion they withdrew an amendment merely on the strength of an assurance from him that the Act would not affect the right of public meeting. One of the leading Irish members spoke with the highest admiration of one of his speeches in these passionate debates, while regretting that it was made in a bad cause. The explanation is to be found in a quality of Gladstone's oratory that was noted by Mr. G. K. Chesterton as common to him and Newman:

" He had the same knack in discussion which Gladstone had, the air of not being in any way in a hurry. Young men who read Gladstone's speeches in printed books just after his career had closed in unpopularity often could not see wherein lay the overwhelming witchcraft which made vast audiences rise like one man and vast combinations follow the orator to defeat. The oratorial style seemed to them wordy and winding, full of endless parentheses and needless distinctions. The truth is, I imagine, that it was precisely the air of leisure and large-mindedness, this scrupulosity about exceptions, this allowance for misunderstandings, that gave to the final assertion its sudden fire."[1]

Bright's method, so different, so direct in its use of language, so crisp and terse in its telling simplicity, with not a word too much nor a word ill chosen, was in this sense less effective. The Irish members found it less easy to forgive him than to forgive Gladstone.

Yet in these debates even Gladstone once behaved as if there was one law for the Irish members and another for the English. In March, 1881, Healy replying to a speech by Harcourt said that Harcourt had uttered " a deliberate

[1] *The Speaker*, September 24, 1904.

untruth." He was called to order and withdrew the expression. A little later he said that a statement of Harcourt's was " distinctly untrue." He was again called to order and again withdrew the expression. A little later he said that Harcourt spoke with " his usual disingenuousness " and for this he was suspended. Let us now turn to a speech made by Gladstone on January 28, in which he quoted Parnell's recommendation of boycotting:

" You must shun him at the fair and market place and even in the house of worship by leaving him severely alone, by sending him to a moral Coventry, by isolating him from the rest of his kind as if he were the leper of old; you must show him your detestation of the crime he has committed, and you may depend upon it that if the counties of Ireland carried out this doctrine, no man, however full of avarice, how lost to shame, will transgress your unwritten code."

"What was the crime this leper had committed? It was the crime of taking a farm from which a man had been evicted." At this point Parnell interrupted to say that his words had been " unjustly evicted." Gladstone refused to accept this statement, relying on the newspaper reports. Yet if Parnell had been an English member, there is little doubt that his disclaimer would have been accepted and the argument resumed on that basis. Thus Healy was not allowed to call Harcourt disingenuous, but Gladstone thought himself entitled to treat Parnell as a liar.

By the end of March Parliament had obtained power to defend itself against disorder and the Viceroy power to lock up any Irishman on suspicion. The House of Commons now turned to agrarian reform. If the Coercion Bill was worse, the new Land Bill, introduced by Gladstone on April 7, was better than the Irish party had expected. Goschen indeed called it a Coercion Bill for landlords. For although there were qualifications and exceptions that seriously affected the success of the Bill, the three Fs, Free sale, Fixity of Tenure, and Fair Rents, were the basis of the new Bill. The extent and boldness of the Bill were a surprise to all parties and, as we know from the internal records, Gladstone himself had been a late convert to the Bill that he had now to steer through the House of Commons. Argyll[1] left the Cabinet and Hartington stayed with reluctance. " Argyll told me on Monday," Hartington wrote to Gladstone on April 6, 1881, " that he could not remain. I could not say anything against his decision for his objections to the Bill have always been stronger than mine and I find it a hard morsel to swallow." Hartington added that he hoped he " would not be asked to take part in its defence more than could be helped."

The conduct of the Land Bill of 1881 was perhaps the greatest achievement in Gladstone's career, unless we put before it his conduct of the two Home Rule Bills. He had to defend a most complicated Bill, not only against Conservatives, but against a formidable body of Whigs within his own party. Salisbury was so blind to the fundamental problem in Ireland that he persisted in regarding the Bill as a " violent innovation promoted by temporary passion." Gladstone had one important source of strength, and that source showed clearly how mistaken was Salisbury's judgment. On May 19 the House of Commons divided on the Opposition amendment, " That this House, while willing to consider any just measure founded upon sound principles that will benefit tenants of land in Ireland, is of opinion that the leading provisions of the Land Law (Ireland) Bill are in the main economically unsound, unjust and impolitic." The amendment was rejected by 352 votes to 176. The Irish vote was a significant comment on Salisbury's view. Fifty-six Irish members voted for the second reading, made up of 26 Home Rulers, 15 Liberals and 13 Conservatives. Eight voted against, 1 Liberal and 7 Conservatives. Forty abstained, 36 Parnellites and 4 Conservatives (one of them Castlereagh). Thus a majority of the Irish Conservatives supported the Bill. The explanation is simple. The

---

[1] There are two interesting little notes from Granville about Argyll's resignation (April, 1881). In one he says, " The Chancellor (Selborne) is all right. He thinks the Bill economically wrong but politically defensible. He will have a talk with Argyll but he doubts its success." In the later one he says, " Discussion with him (Argyll) is hopeless now. He has a passion for it and nothing else to do."

demand for the Bill in Ulster made it dangerous for any Ulster member to vote against it.[1]

Gladstone's letter to Argyll accepting his resignation on April 11, 1881, showed in what kind of spirit he had accepted his new task, a task so far exceeding in scope and daring anything he had contemplated when he became Prime Minister.

" As I can never take office again, our official parting is, I fear, final. . . . The completion of the land legislation for Ireland now lies before me as the chief remaining demand upon me. Every remnant of energy that I possess, and the whole determination of the Government, will be addressed to its prompt settlement."

Gladstone had spent two exhausting months on coercion, and just before he introduced the Land Bill he had brought in his Budget as Chancellor of the Exchequer. He was now about half-way through the most arduous session that Parliament had ever known. Yet he met this new call with as much energy and courage as if he had come fresh to his task. The Land Bill took up fifty-eight sittings. By Whitsuntide only four lines had been accepted, and from that time it was found necessary to give the whole time of Parliament to the Bill. The Bill exposed an immense surface to attack, and its critics included the ablest lawyers in the House of Commons. Moreover, for those struggles in detail which are of such importance in a Bill like this, Gladstone had a source of weakness as important as the source of strength that he owed to the Ulster sentiment. For though there was this useful Ulster pressure on Irish Conservatives in support of the general principle of the Bill, there was no pressure in England to help Gladstone in defending this or that provision against an amendment. For here the struggle was soon lost in technical complexities which the English electorate could not be expected to master. Salisbury took advantage of this when pressing for the Lord's amendments against the Government.

[1] Lord Derby writing in the *Nineteenth Century* predicted that the Act would have little effect on rents but that it would have the effect of keeping Ulster outside the Nationalist movement. The land grievance he argued had been a bond for discontent between Ulster and the rest of Ireland, and in this sense a danger to the Union.

Gladstone's exertions in the second year of his Government recall his most vigorous efforts in the early days of his first, and they undoubtedly told heavily on him later. If he had left most of the debating to his colleagues he might well have been worn out by his duties as Prime Minister taking decisions from day to day, distracted by the temper of the House, the violence of the conflict, and the bitter passions of a racial warfare, so distressing to his temperament, between British and Irish members. But throughout he was the leading protagonist and, in the case of the Irish Land Bill, he conducted a difficult and complicated debate almost singlehanded. Hartington speaking at the Guildhall on August 6, 1881, said that the history of the last seven months was the record of the energy and resolution, the knowledge and the resource of one man. In the House of Commons, whose sessions were of unprecedented length and heat, he commanded more respect than affection. Hated by the landlords for his treatment of property, by the Tories for his remembered Midlothian thunder, mistrusted by Irishmen and Radicals for his support of coercion, by moderate Liberals for his nationalist sympathies, separated by temperament from the only colleague whose heart was in reform, Gladstone, now seventy-two years old, guiding and managing angry and troublesome debate, dominated the House of Commons by sheer power of mind and will.

" The Ministry themselves," wrote *The Times* on July 22, 1881, " have disappeared behind one central figure and it is only at Trinity House Banquets and the like that we are reminded that the Cabinet includes other Statesmen besides Mr. Gladstone. It is true that the Prime Minister has been ably seconded by Mr. Forster and Mr. Law, but the Land Bill for good or evil will bear the mark of his personality and his alone."

A more important witness than the best informed of editors has left on record an account of Gladstone's predominant share in the dialectical struggle for the Bill.

" I was one of a Committee," says Lord Eversley, " consisting of Sir Farrer Herschell (the Solicitor General), Mr. Hugh Law, the Irish Attorney General, and Sir Henry Thring, the draftsman of the Bill, who were asked by Mr. Gladstone to advise as to the

amendments proposed to the Bill.   We met every morning during the passage of the Bill through Committee, examined the
amendments which were likely to be discussed during the sitting
and reported them to Mr. Gladstone.   But I am bound to say we
were of very little use to him.   We found that he knew more of
the subject than all of us put together.   He was never for a
moment at a loss how to meet his many opponents.   He did the
work almost alone through thirty-three sittings of the Committee,
five days of the Report stage, and four more devoted to consideration of the Lords' Amendments."[1]

There are few reforms of which the full importance has
been so much obscured by criticism of its faults.   The Act
had few friends.[2]   The Parnellites were quite right in criticizing the Act for its omissions; the Tories were quite right
in their contention that it destroyed the power of the landlord
class.   Both were quite right in prophesying a great deal of
costly and troublesome litigation.   Gladstone in writing to
thank Thring, the draftsman, for his great services on
the Bill, remarked genially that the Act would cost some
headaches to Irish judges, lawyers, and, last but not least,
Commissioners.   Gambetta talking to Dilke, laughed at a
measure which had resulted in thousands of lawsuits.   Amid
all these complaints it was often forgotten that the Act had
given the Irish tenant fair rent and fixity of tenure by the
establishment of a judicial tribunal which could fix rents for
fifteen years on the application of landlord or tenant.   The
tenant who paid the judicial rent could not be evicted.   Of
a Bill which gave Ireland that reform Gladstone was justified
in saying that it was probably the most important measure
introduced into the House of Commons since the passing of
the Reform Bill.   It handled the claims of property more
sternly than the Ten Hours Act had handled the claims of
capital, and gave the Irish peasant rights not yet gained by
the English workman.

How far the deficiencies of the Bill were due to Gladstone,

---

[1] *Gladstone and Ireland*, p. 155.

[2] Some notes on the Act, for which I am indebted to Miss Edith Stopford, are
given in an Appendix to this chapter, together with other papers including a
memorandum on Fair Rent prepared for the Cabinet by Sir Henry Thring,
Parliamentary draftsman.

how far to inexorable conditions, is a question on which argument is possible. Certainly Gladstone's metaphysical mind, his love of indirect and subtle methods, his elaborate and labyrinthine taste in argument and debate, were all reflected in the structure of the Bill and his defence of its scheme. A man who finds it easy to carry in his head as many facts and footnotes as would fill a blue book, as many hypotheses and qualifications as would fill a theological treatise, is tempted to think complexity a good thing in itself. Sir Edward Hamilton said that Gladstone could distinguish between two propositions which the plain man would regard as identical. It may be argued that, compli-cated as was the state of Irish law and Irish society, the immense revolution that this Act accomplished could have been brought about by simpler methods. That is not an easy question to answer. At least it is not unjust to suspect that a man so skilled in handling ambiguities was less afraid than he should have been of setting riddles to the court and giving headaches to the judges.[1]

There is another obvious criticism to be made on Glad-stone's preparation of the Bill. The help of two men could have made it a much better Act. One was Parnell, who had the satisfaction, in the next seven or eight years, of seeing most of the important amendments he suggested incor-porated in the Bill either by Gladstone himself or by Salisbury (the latter after stout protestations the other way). It was ridiculous that Gladstone, devising a great agrarian scheme, should have consulted Carlingford, Shaw Lefevre, Thring, and Law, and never consulted Parnell. They were all expert students in one or other department of the question, but he was expert in a field where they had no experience. Gladstone's treatment of Parnell illustrated one of his capital weaknesses. He was independent but conventional. He was independent in the sense that once his mind had been convinced on a question, he paid no regard to overwhelming opinion or to r gid fashion. His superb speeches on the

---

[1] There were 100,000 formal appeals and over 40,000 actual rehearings. The cost of having a fair rent fixed was £3 or £4, that of an appeal £10. Early appeals were chiefly on law; later appeals on valuations. The landlords spent large sums for very small results. Pomfret, *op. cit.*, 198.

Bradlaugh question are a good illustration of this side of his character. But in his relations to the Irish party he had not yet escaped from the atmosphere in which he had been bred. In that atmosphere Parnell was a man out for mischief. Gladstone always believed that the Whigs had suffered seriously in public estimation and political capacity because they had worked for a time hand in hand with O'Connell. Looking for an Irish Policy, he would consult Treasury experts, Irish landlords, English politicians, lawyers on both sides of the Irish sea, and he would read books and blue books without end, but he neglected the men who saw this question in a light in which none of his other advisers saw it, in the light of their experience as leaders of the peasants. This was a capital error, as anybody can see who studies the proposals made by the Parnellite party for improving the Bill.

Parnell, it is true, cannot be exonerated from blame for Gladstone's mistake. Archbishop Croke criticized him for abstaining from the division on the second reading, on the ground that he thereby weakened his influence in Committee. Gladstone made up his mind unfortunately that Parnell wanted to defeat his Bill without appearing to defeat it, and the abstention of his party made Gladstone extremely suspicious of his motives when proposing amendments. He wrote to the Speaker on June 7, " Parnell is looking for every opportunity to impede business for the sake of impeding the Land Bill without appearing to impede the Land Bill." Parnell was in fact well aware that the Bill was a great advance and he had no such designs as Gladstone attributed to him, but his conduct gave ground for this suspicion. The consequences did not end with the passing of the Bill. This suspicion poisoned Gladstone's mind for the next twelve months.

Gladstone's respect for Parnell's practical capacity was probably not increased by an overture that Parnell made through O'Shea in June, 1881. The suggestion is given in O'Shea's language, and it is difficult to be sure in this case, as in others where O'Shea was concerned, how far the intermediary was accurate.

O'Shea proposed that the Government should make a

large grant to the landlords to induce them to come to a settlement with their tenants out of court. The tenants had been agitating for a general reduction of rents to the level of the Griffith Poor Law valuation; this would reduce some of the landlords to beggary. But was it not possible to fix a rent that would satisfy the tenants and induce the landlords to accept it by giving them help ? He calculated the rents on the poor law valuation at ten millions and existing rents at fifteen. If a figure half way between the two was taken, and three fifths of the land came under this arrangement, it would cost the Government fifteen to twenty millions to provide compensation for the landlords, putting that compensation at ten to twelve times the amount of the reduction made in the rent. " The inducement of receiving a sum of ready money with which to pay off liabilities etc., would thus be given the landlord to meet the tenant half way, and avoid the risk, expence and uncertainty of the court."

Gladstone referred the plan to his colleagues. Forster replied, " It is not easy to give an opinion on so startling a proposal at five minutes' notice, but looking at it from the point of view of the Irish executive, one thing is certain. No rent would be paid from the moment such a proposal was accepted by the Government until it became law—and I think this also is certain—the Land League would so gain in prestige as really to govern Ireland. The League would have told the farmers to combine not to pay more rent than they please and the League would have so succeded in their effort as to make the English taxpayer secure to the farmers their demand. If this is done, in future the farmers will pay little heed to the Land Court—they will rely on the League getting for them whatever they demand."

Spencer replied that he agreed with Carlingford and Kimberley in being against this bargain. " Griffith's Valuation is no basis for adjusting rents and I do not like the idea of purchasing at the Public expence low rents for Irish Tenants and Ready Money for Irish Landlords."

Gladstone himself was hardly likely to take to the proposal to spend public money on a plan which promised so little for the future.

He wrote to O'Shea on June 14th declining it.

Private   14 June, 1881.

Dear Mr. O'Shea,

I have not failed to submit to my colleagues the letter and proposal which you have done me the honour to bring before me, and which was of too much importance for me to enter upon except in concert with them.

We feel indebted to you for the earnest and just desire you feel to promote a prompt settlement of the Land question in Ireland, and for the zeal with which you have undertaken a difficult operation, in that view.   But we do not see our way to any form of action on the basis you propose, without raising difficulties, which might prove to be greater than any of those which we have at present to encounter.   Some of these have reference to passing any proposal of this kind through Parliament; some to its effect upon those who may think themselves, or may be, over-rented in England or Scotland.   I need not enter on the grave character of the financial drain, which would be added to the liabilities, possibly very large, already entailed by the measure upon the Treasury.   For there are yet more serious considerations, which we cannot undertake to face, connected with the moral and political effect sure as we think to be produced in Ireland by such a plan, particularly as regards the Land League and the new place (as I may say) which would be given to it, as the evident director of governmental action, in the estimation of the people. Glad as we should be to extend to all parties in Ireland that favourable temper with which the Bill has [been] so largely received, we must be careful not to forfeit or compromise the position which it actually holds; and must trust for its successful progress to the good sense of those who desire more, or desire less, and to the general convictions of the people of the three Kingdoms on which we think we can rely.

Believe me, faithfully yours,

W. E. GLADSTONE.

The other adviser who could have helped Gladstone was Chamberlain, who knew nothing of Irish conditions first hand, but had an experience as a reformer which would have been of great use.   Gladstone and Chamberlain were mutually complementary, for Chamberlain lacked the large European sense which lighted Gladstone's mind to the truth about Irish government, and Chamberlain had the sense for action and experiment in social politics in which Gladstone was wanting.   Chamberlain being less afraid of bureaucracy would have seen the advantage of giving more initiative to the Land Commissioners and thereby reducing the litigation caused by the Act.

Gladstone is open to serious criticism on these grounds, but two things have to be said on the other side about his conduct of the Bill.   He once said of Argyll that he was a bad learner and that he had learnt less from thirty years of public life than many men would have learnt who were inferior to him in ability.   Gladstone when he began to learn, learnt quickly.   He started on this reform anxious to make it a small reform and to link it to his earlier Act. But he soon discovered that everything turned on fair rent, and that a rent court was essential.   This meant, as the *Times* said on July 18, 1881, " a retrogression from the political and economical doctrines which it has been the pride of the Liberal party during the last half century to enforce."[1]   Lord Grey said that the reasons put forward by Gladstone to restrict freedom of contract in Ireland were those advanced by the Revolutionary Government of France in favour of the law of maximum.   Churchill said that when a Radical Government was in power the faith of Parliament counted for nothing.   Salisbury was not less emphatic in condemning this loose view of the sanctity of contract.   The Bill, he said, gave to the tenant the right to sell that which he had never bought and to tear up contracts by which he was bound.   Gladstone was thus casting aside principles to which Liberals in the name of enterprise, and Conservatives in the name of property, had attached a religious importance.   That revolution was his achievement, and everything else followed.

The second reflexion that must be made is this.   The Government was not its own master.   Gladstone's Act left in the cold the leaseholders, who numbered about 150,000, and tenants in arrears with their rent, probably over 130,000. These were very serious omissions.   Parnell criticized the Bill

[1] The *Times* had a leader as late as January 26, 1880, in which it stated that Bright ridiculed the notion that anyone but the landlord and tenant could determine the fair rent of a holding.

on this account, and he also pointed out that the direction in the Bill about the principle on which fair rents were to be awarded by the Land Commission was unsatisfactory. The Government tried to meet these objections, and the blame for their failure is not wholly or chiefly theirs. They inserted a clause providing that on the termination of a lease the tenant was to be entitled to rank as a tenant under the Act, and to have the benefit of a judicial rent and fixity of tenure. But this clause was rejected by the House of Lords. (In 1887 Salisbury's Government had to concede this.) The Government accepted from Parnell a proposal that a tenant should not be evicted for non-payment of rent in the interval between the application to the Courts and the fixing of a judicial rent. His proposal was that a sale under writ might be stayed for six months for this purpose. The Lords threw this out. The Government tried to compromise by reducing the period to three months. This also the Lords threw out. In August the Government had to decide whether to hold out against the Lords on these points, with the possible loss of the Bill, and they decided for compromise. The Government did not neglect altogether Parnell's warning about the tenants in arrears, but the clause they introduced for their protection contained a fatal flaw. The assent of the landlord was required, and the clause with this impediment did not work. Lastly the Government did all that could be done at this stage to get over the fair rent difficulty by accepting an amendment from Healy which stipulated that rent should not be charged on the tenant's improvements.[1] But this good intention was foiled by the

---

[1] Gladstone had a great deal of discussion with his colleagues on the meaning of a fair rent and his letters show that Healy's amendment was in accord with his ideas. Thus he wrote to Law on May 28, " I really incline to think that if the House is not disposed to leave the discovery of fair rent simpliciter to the court, the best rule or indication we can give is that it is the rent which (apart from tenants' improvements) would be obtained in a market where the supply and demand are ordinarily equal." The *Times* on May 17 thus summarized Gladstone's statements on the subject, " The fair rent which Mr. Gladstone appears to have in mind is one merely excluding by the decision of the court the right of the landlord to eat up the tenant's goodwill, even the value of his improvements, by turning into rack rent the famine price of land." In one letter to Forster on June 6 Gladstone introduced a new principle suggesting that a fair rent should leave to the tenant a fair living or trading profit.

Q

Judges who destroyed the value of the concession by their decisions. In 1897 Parliament had to interfere.

Gladstone's responsibility for the omissions and mistakes of the Act can only be estimated justly when a distinction has been drawn between those that he accepted of his own free will and those that he accepted under compulsion. Did he carry as large a measure as Parliament would have allowed? The Irish bishops sent him a series of resolutions on the Bill, and in this case, as in 1870, their advice was excellent. Gladstone when acknowledging them said that, though he welcomed their help, he could not make changes that would give the Bill a new character. Eversley, who criticized the Bill, and blamed Gladstone for not paying more attention to the Irish members, thinks that Gladstone got as much out of Parliament as could be got.

So far as Gladstone himself was concerned, his chief weakness both in constructing the Bill and in defending it was his illusion that there was little rack renting. If he had realized the scale of the operations that were to follow, he might have avoided some of the litigation, as Eversley points out, by adopting the procedure that his next Government adopted in legislating on similar lines for the Scottish crofters. There the Crofting Commission was instructed to take the initiative, to make local investigations, and determine what rents should be payable in future by different districts.

The Act of 1870 had checked the process which, by treating Ireland as if she were an English county, had brought her agriculture and her people to ruin. The Act of 1881 was a turning point in her history. It had an immediate effect in stimulating among the landlord class and the Conservative party a serious demand for a policy of land purchase. In the debates excellent speeches were made in support of this policy by W. H. Smith and others, and in the following year a House of Lords Committee reported in favour of a purchase scheme, of which the *Times* remarked that it was kind to landlord and to tenant, but that less care was shown for the British taxpayer. Gladstone's Act stimulated this demand, and it created the conditions under which land purchase on a large scale became possible. For a peasant owning society could not be established on Irish soil until rents had been reduced. Under the reductions made by this Act the landlords suffered a loss of £1,551,339 on first term rents (£7,487,607 to £5,936,268) and of £491,571 on second term rents (£2,522,730 to £2,031,159). First term rents were fixed for 379,388 farms, covering 11,000,000 acres. In 219,314 cases they were fixed by judicial proceedings, in 159,994 cases by agreement supervised by the courts, and in forty cases by arbitration.[1] Of this great reform it can be said that however faulty its machinery, its principle was essential to Irish progress. No movement like the Plunkett movement of the 'nineties was possible so long as tenants could not enjoy or safeguard their own improvements, or protect themselves from landlords who exploited the famine price of land. Judged, as it must be judged, as pioneer legislation, the Act has qualities of courage and of imagination that stamp it as one of the great achievements of the century.

When Gladstone started out on this revolution, he was like the early mariners who kept close to the shore, and made their way from island to island. He was anxious never to lose touch with the Act of 1870, wishing to keep it in sight both for direction and reassurance. Then he found that he was making no progress, and at last he left the land behind him and steered boldly for the open sea. He was no longer like some Greek or Phoenician pirate creeping round the islands of the Aegean, but like Columbus himself, for he had lost his landmarks, and the Act of 1870 faded into an almost forgotten horizon. After three months strenuous navigation he came into harbour in a new Continent. Columbus, landing in the Bahamas, believed that he had found not a new world in the West, but another route to the old world in the East. Gladstone was under a similar illusion, for the revolution he had made was much vaster and more important than he knew.

---

[1] See the interesting statistics in Pomfret, *op. cit.*, pp. 199-202.

APPENDIX I

NOTES ON THE ACT OF 1881.

By EDITH STOPFORD

Although the Act dealt with a variety of subjects connected with Irish land, its most important provisions were those reforming the existing system of tenure. The Three F's were conceded. Fair Rent and Fixity of Tenure were secured by the establishment of a Judicial Tribunal which, on the application of landlord or tenant, fixed rents for a " Judicial " period of fifteen years, at the end of which time they became subject to revision by the Tribunal.[1] Although the holder of a " Judicial " tenancy was not allowed to sublet or subdivide his holding without his landlord's consent, to cause dilapidation or to oppose his landlord's right of entry for certain specified purposes, he could not be evicted except on failure to pay the judicial rent, or for infringement of the statutory conditions of his tenure. Free Sale was legalized, subject to the landlord's right of pre-emption and of veto on the incoming tenant.[2] The judicial tribunal under the Act might be either the County Court or a specially constituted Irish Land Commission, having the powers of a Court of Justice.[3]

[1] Section 8 of the Act.

An alternative method was the fixing of rent by agreement between landlord and tenant, and its registration with the court, when it became a judicial rent for 15 years, being then subject to revision. In all 40 per cent. of the first term rents and 35 per cent. of the second term rents were thus fixed. (See Pomfret, *The Struggle for Land in Ireland*, 1880–1923, p. 197.)

[2] Section I of the Act.

The value of Tenant Right probably rose after the Act, though perhaps not so much as the landlords declared. It had always been considerable where the Ulster Custom existed, and it had probably been surreptitiously in vogue on many other estates before the 1881 Act. The Report of the Lords' Select Committee on the Land Law (Ireland) Act, issued on April 28, 1882 (para. 22), states:—" The interest of the tenant in Ulster, as is well known, sells for prices varying from 10 to 30 years' purchase and upwards. But the Committee have had evidence before them that in other parts of Ireland, where tenant right has not been recognised previous to the Act of 1881, the tenants has, since that Act, sold for prices varying from 7 to 17 years' purchase and upwards." This was a chief grievance among the landlord class, who declared that, although tenant right fetched high prices, they could not get their rents.

[3] In practice the Land Commission became the principal land court, the County Court functioning comparatively seldom. The Land Commission consisted of three Commissioners (increased under the Ashbourne Act of 1885 to five)—a Chairman, with the rank of a Judge of the Supreme Court, and two lay Commissioners. The judgments of the Land Commission were final as to fact, but appeals were allowed on points of law to the Court of Appeal.

Though contracting out of the Act was only allowed in the case of tenancies valued at £150 and over, many classes of Ireland's 482,230 occupiers of over an acre were excluded from the benefits of the measure.[1] The two most important were the leaseholders, numbering about 150,000;[2] and the tenants in arrears with rent, probably over 130,000.[3] There was, it is true, an attempt to protect those among the latter who were rated at £30 or under p.a. by an Arrears clause.[4] This, on the joint application of landlord and tenant, permitted the wiping out of arrears on payment by the tenant of one year's rent and the advance by the Land Commission of a sum not exceeding one year's rent or half the antecedent arrears. Since, however, this depended on the consent of the landlord (who had to collect this charge—a prior one to rent), and since Government's loan had to be repaid by the tenant, it proved practically valueless. Other less numerous excluded tenants were:—" Future " tenants;[5] tenants who had lost their judicial rights; tenants of demesne lands and town parks; of holdings neither pastoral nor agricultural; of grazing farms let at £50 and over; and of farms on which the " English " Custom prevailed. The only protection afforded to all these, and also to such evicted tenants as did not apply to the Court for the fixing of Fair Rent, was the 1870 Act, of which the schedule of compensation for disturbance was now increased.[6] There was, too, an interesting attempt under the Act to establish the long-contested right of the tenant to the value of his improvements, a clause known as the " Healy Clause," because it was suggested by Timothy Healy, prohibiting the Court, in fixing a fair rent, from making it payable in respect of a tenant's improvements.[7] The judgment in the Court of Appeal in the case of Adams v. Dunseath in February, 1882, however, nullified this clause by declaring that a tenant's enjoyment of his improvements was sufficient compensation to him for having made them; and thenceforward, until the 1896 Land

[1] See Sections 22 and 58.

[2] This was the number of leaseholders who in 1887 had fair rents fixed on their admission to the benefits of the 1881 Act.

[3] The number of tenants in arrears with rent whose claims were allowed under the 1882 Arrears Act was 129,952.

[4] See Section 59. (See also Wemyss Reid, *Life of Gladstone*, p. 332.)

[5] " Future " Tenants were holders of tenancies created after 1/1/83. (See Section 57.) This provision shows the hope of the framers of the Act that a return to Free Contract might be ultimately possible.

[6] See Section 6.

[7] See Section 8 (9).

Act, the 1870 Act (when applicable) alone protected the tenant in this matter.[1]

The Land Purchase clauses of the 1881 Act,[2] inserted at Bright's instigation and based on the Bessborough Commission's recommendations, did not contemplate any universal extension of the principle.[3] There was a slight improvement on the 1870 Act in that three-quarters of the purchase price, in place of two-thirds, were advancable by the State through the Land Commission. But there was no change in the repayments, which remained at thirty-five annuities of 5 per cent. Chiefly owing to the tenant's difficulty in raising the remaining quarter (usually only obtainable at usurious interest), these provisions had little success, only 731 tenants in all purchasing under them. The debates on these clauses were remarkable for the first sign of a demand for a wide extension of Land Purchase from several notable Conservatives, such as Lords Salisbury and Lansdowne and Mr. W. H. Smith,[4] who feared the effects on the landlords of the tenure clauses, and began to visualize a peasant proprietary as a stablizing and Conservative element in Ireland.

The Act contained other pioneer legislation, later to be greatly developed, especially in the Congested Districts. Section 26 gave the Land Commission power to buy estates and resell them to tenants in certain circumstances. Section 31 authorized the advance of loans to companies for the reclamation of waste lands, and to tenants for the improvement of their holdings. By Section 32 the Land Commission, with Treasury sanction, was authorized to make loans amounting to £200,000 for emigration. Section 19 permitted the Land Commissioners to make the award of a

---

[1] In 1893, at the instance of Morley, a Committee of inquiry into the working of the 1881 Act, and especially into the judicial interpretation of the Healy Clause, reported in favour of its amendment. Action was not however taken till 1896.

[2] See Sections 24–36.

[3] Bright's Memorandum on the Land Act for the Cabinet showed the results which he anticipated that the Land Purchase clauses would achieve: " In ten years, at the speed I am sanguine to hope for, land to the value of fifty millions sterling will have changed hands; in twenty years more than one fourth part of all the land of Ireland may have changed hands." (See the Gladstone papers.)

[4] Lord Salisbury, after an attack on the Fair Rent clauses as class legislation, " Inflicting this great wrong on Irish landlords," urged strongly the development of Land Purchase. (See *Hansard*, Vol. 264, column 267, of 1/8/81.)

Lord Lansdowne took much the same line. (See *Hansard*, Vol. 264, column 267, of 1/8/81.)

Mr. W. H. Smith offered constructive and friendly suggestions for the extension of Land Purchase. (See *Hansard*, Vol. 263, column 1,383, of 30/7/81.)

judicial rent conditional on the tenant building cottages for his labourers, while the Board of Works was authorized to make loans on favourable terms for their erection.

The Act possessed certain grave defects, notably in its exclusion of large classes of tenants and in its lack of elasticity for altering judicial rents in case of a fall in agricultural prices; and needed considerable amendment. It did not end the competition for land, for bargaining for farms was to some extent replaced by bargaining for tenant right. It was, nevertheless, a measure of fundamental importance. Affecting ultimately over 11,000 acres, or 65 per cent. of the available land of Ireland, it destroyed for ever the doctrine of Free Contract in Irish land tenure and the absolute power of the landlord, thus revolutionizing the whole agrarian situation in Ireland.

The Parnellites objected strongly to the grant for emigration, arguing that the depopulation of Ireland had gone far enough. On the other hand they wished to strengthen the constructive part of the Act proposing to give the Land Commissioners powers of buying land and adding it to holdings in the Congested Districts. Their other amendments proposed to shorten the statutory period, to give the Land Commissioners power to deal with arrears, to include leaseholders and the tenants of town park holdings, and to date the judicial rent from the date on which the application for reduction was made.

The first three Commissioners were: Sergeant O'Hagan, Judicial Commissioner, a prominent Irish lawyer and a Catholic who had in his youth been a member of the Young Ireland party; Mr. Edward Litton, an Ulster Liberal M.P. who had taken an active part in discussing the Land question and Mr. John E. Vernon, a well-known landowner and agent. The number of sub-commissioners rose eventually to over sixty. The Commissioners were given a good character for general impartiality by the Fry Commission in 1898, which reported that the settlement of fair rents had been made with diversity of opinion and practice, sometimes with carelessness, and sometimes with that bias towards one side or the other which exists in many honest minds; but that the administration of justice had not been poisoned by any systematic endeavour on the part of the Commissioners or assistant Commissioners to benefit either side at the expense of the other (p. 26 of Report).

APPENDIX II

MEMORANDUM PREPARED FOR MINISTERS ON "FAIR RENT"

XCVIII. (2)

25th May, 1881

[May 23, 1881]

MEMORANDUM ON FAIR RENT

With Note containing definitions of " Fair Rent " Mr. Butt, Mr. Litton, and Sir Stafford Northcote.

The object of this memorandum is to show that the factors which go to make up a fair rent are themselves so indefinite and so capable of being combined in a variety of proportions that any approach to accuracy in the definition of a fair rent cannot be expected.

A *full* rent (the term " full " being designedly used for the purpose of avoiding the idea of abstract equity associated with " fair rent," or want of abstract equity associated with " rack rent ") may *in England* be described to be such rent as a tenant possessed of adequate capital and of average cultivating skill might reasonably be expected to pay for a farm, on the understanding that so paying he would be able to maintain himself and his family, and make a fair profit.

The tenants profits depend principally on,

(1) The inherent productiveness of the soil.

This is a matter to be decided by an expert in the quality of soils.

(2) The skill of the cultivator.

One man will by skill make a farm pay well where another will be ruined. Average skill only can be obtained, to be ascertained by observation of neighbouring farms. The adequacy of the capital must also in a great measure be measured by the customary expenditure of neighbouring farms.

(3) The cost of production.

    This depends on facilities for procuring manures, wages, etc.

(4) The value of the produce.

    This depends on proximity of markets, average prices, and so forth.

In England a tenant considers that he ought to make 10 per cent. profit on his capital, including as profit the expense of maintaining himself and his own remuneration.

Practically, of course, the above factors are never formally ascertained, but are arrived at by a general survey and a consideration of the condition and rents of adjoining farms.

In England a tenant " may be reasonably expected " to pay a " full rent " as above defined. " A full rent," therefore, is in England " a fair rent," or as it is often termed " rack rent,"— " rack rent " having no bad signification in England, but being identical in meaning with " full rent." " A competition or exorbitant rent " is in England something beyond " a full rent " as above defined. Such a rent is disapproved by the best surveyors, and when an estate is put up to tender, they scarcely ever take the highest tender. They consider it very bad policy to accept an offer of rent above what they consider to be a full rent, as a tenant who offers a rent above the full rent gets into difficulties and cultivates badly.

In estimating land for railways in England, a tenant from year to year holding at a full rent is considered to have no saleable value. The reason is, that in England the supply of farms is equal to the demand, and an outgoing tenant can obtain at any time a farm at a full rent. To produce a saleable value in a tenancy from year to year in England, there must be a difference between the actual rent and the full rent, and the extent of that difference, coupled with the probable duration of tenure, would be the measure of the saleable value, if such existed.

In Ireland the conditions, so far as they relate to demand for holdings, are the reverse of the conditions existing in England. A tenant can often be found for a holding; however exorbitant, or, in other words, however much above even a full rent the rent of such holding may be. Again, contrary to the practice in England, a tenant from year to year has always been considered to have a quasi saleable value in his tenancy, and is, as I am informed, entitled to receive compensation for his interest in the case of land being taken by a railroad to the extent of from three to five years purchase of the rent. Further, the Act of 1870, by giving compensation for disturbance, has affixed in certain cases a definite value to a tenancy, and the present Bill strengthens the Act of 1870 by increasing the scale of compensation, and giving to every tenant a power to sell.

The best illustration of the difference between English and Irish ideas on the subject of yearly tenancies will be furnished by an example. Lord Monck has for thirty years at least let a holding for 16s. an acre. The tenant in spite of Lord Monck's prohibiting subletting has sublet a portion of it for 24s. Now, suppose the Bill to pass and the tenant to apply to the court for a judicial rent. It is clear that 16s. is a low rent, 24s. is an exorbitant rent. I am told about 20s. would be full rent. Lord Monck thinks that about 18s. would probably be a fair rent, inasmuch as 20s. would be higher than the average of rents in the neighbourhood.

The result would seem to be that rents in Ireland may be divided into four classes: (1) competition or exorbitant rents; (2) full rents; (3) fair rents in the Irish sense; (4) low rents. No. 1 are rents considerably above full rents. No. 4 are rents considerably below full rents. No. 3, or fair rents, are rents of a district which are neither too high nor too low, according to the custom of the district.

In effect then the definition of " fair rent " in Ireland would seem to be " such a rent as a good landlord would reasonably expect a good tenant to pay, on the understanding that so paying the tenant would be able to maintain himself and his family, and make a fair profit." The difference in the factors of an English fair rent and an Irish fair rent seems to be this, that in Ireland in certain cases a customary deduction must be made from a full rent (or fair English rent) for the purpose of obtaining an Irish fair rent.

The object of the Bill then would seem to be so to qualify fair rent as to prevent the court raising low rents to full rents in cases where they ought only to be raised to fair rents.

It seems that the proper qualification of fair rent as compared with full rent cannot be obtained as in the Bill by reference to saleable valuable, for as the saleable value is inversely as the actual rent, it will make the deduction greater in the case of low rents than in the case of exorbitant rents.

Again, the direction in the Bill " that the court in fixing such rent shall have regard to the tenant's interest in the holding " has been understood, in my opinion incorrectly, to mean that the court must in *all* cases make *some deduction* in respect of the tenant's interest, whereas in the case of a low rent it is clear that the tenant's interest has been more than sufficiently regarded by the lowness of the rent, and the rent ought to be raised at once.

The conclusion to be drawn from the foregoing observations would seem to be that the definition of fair rent cannot be made precise, and that it would probably be better to say merely that " fair rent means such a rent as in the opinion of the court after hearing the parties and considering all the circumstances of the case, holding, and district, a solvent tenant might reasonably be expected to pay one year with another, after deducting from the amount of rent so found any addition thereto which may in the opinion of the court be due to improvements made by the tenant or his predecessors in title." In working out such a definition, the proper course would seem to be for the court to find a full rent, and then before raising or lowering any rent, to have regard to the average rents of well-managed estates in the district, and in particular to rents which had remained unchanged for a great number of years.

The obligation on the court to have regard to the average rents of the district would seem sufficiently expressed by the expression in the definition " considering all the circumstances of the district," while any specific reference to saleable value or otherwise appears liable to be misunderstood.

The following examples may be given of the difference between " full rent " in the English sense of the word, and " fair rent " in the Irish sense of the word, and the mode in which the principle should be applied. Suppose 100 tenants hold land worth at a full rent 1,000£., but they have only paid for thirty-one years 750£.; therefore the full rent for the district is 25 per cent. above a fair rent. A. holds at an exorbitant rent of 12£. land only worth 10£. at a full rent; the court would decide that he should pay 7£. 10s. B. holds at a low rent of 5£. land worth 10£. at a full rent; the court would decide that he also should pay 7£. 10s.

Before ending these observations it may be well to say something upon goodwill. The goodwill of a business depends on its stability, and stability involves two elements: first, the business must have attained such a fixed character as not to be liable to sudden fluctuations; and, secondly, it must be a business which does not depend on the individual superintendence or individual ability of a particular person.

For example, a grocer in the borough has a business and sells it, all he expects to get is the value of his lease, his book-debts, and the value of his stock, subject to a discount of about 30 per cent. for loss on realization. In other words, the grocer thinks himself lucky if he gets out of his shop without loss and without gain, and the goodwill, properly speaking, is worth nothing.

On the other hand, the goodwill of a business, such as Fortnum and Mason's, is worth a very large sum indeed.

The difference is this, in the first case the business depends entirely on the industry of a particular man who has not remained long enough in it to give it stability, and when he retires the business may perish with him, while in the case of Fortnum and Mason, the business has been brought by the skill, capital, and superintendence of past owners to such a state of stability or perfection that if at the present moment it were conducted by a competent superintendent or agents, little loss would be realized however many the sleeping partners may be.

To take an extreme case as illustrative of the sale of goodwill; an auctioneer's business yielding 8,000£ a year gross receipts, say 4,000£ a year net profits, would not sell for more than 1,500£, because it depends almost entirely on the skill of the auctioneer.

Again, a solicitor's business as a general rule sells for only about three years' purchase.

The business of a farmer has in England no goodwill attached to it in the mercantile sense, as it depends entirely on the skill and industry of the farmer himself, the benefits of which cannot be transmitted to a successor.

In Ireland the greed for land gives a mercantile value to almost any holding, corresponding with the value its goodwill gives a business in England.

HENRY THRING.

May 23, 1881.

NOTE

Authorities for Information in Paper

The information on which this paper is founded is derived from Lord Monck, Mr. Caird, Mr. Clutton (surveyor of the Office of Woods), and Mr. Watson (solicitor to the Post Office).

Definition of " Fair Rent " by Mr. Butt

" In fixing the rent to be specified in the declaration of tenancy the chairman shall proceed in manner following, that is to say, the rent to be fixed shall be that which a solvent and responsible tenant could afford to pay, fairly and without collusion, for the premises after deducting from such rent the addition to the letting value of the premises by any improvements made by the tenant or his predecessors in title in respect of which the tenant on quitting his farm would be entitled to compensation under the provisions of the Land Act."

(See Land Tenure (Ireland) Bill. Ordered to be printed June 18, 1878. Bill 50, clause 44.)

Definition of " Fair Rent " by Mr. Litton

" In ascertaining what shall be the fair rent of a holding, the judge shall proceed in manner following, and shall observe the following principles:—The rent to be deemed the fair rent shall be that which a solvent and responsible tenant could at the time of the inquiry afford to pay fairly and without collusion for the premises, after deducting from such rent, First:—The addition to the letting value of the premises referable to any unexhausted and suitable improvements made by the tenant or his predecessors in title, and after deducting, Secondly:—Any increase of letting value referable to the expenditure of labour or capital of the tenant, whether the same be capable of being specified in detail or not. And the judge shall further take into consideration any variation in the average price of agricultural produce or stock which shall have taken place since the holding was last in the possession of the landlord or his predecessors in title if evidence of the same be offered."

(See Fixity of Tenure (Ireland) Bill. Ordered to be printed May 24, 1880. Bill 144, sess. 2, clause 7.)

Definition of " Fair Rent " by Sir Stafford Northcote

" The fair rent of any holding shall be such a rent as in the opinion of the court, after hearing the parties and considering all the circumstances of the case, holding, and locality, a solvent and responsible tenant could afford to pay, fairly and without collusion, for the holding after deducting from such rent the addition to the letting value of the holding by any improvements made by the tenant or his predecessors in title in respect of which the tenant on quitting his holding would be entitled to compensation under the provisions of the Landlord and Tenant (Ireland) Act, 1870.

" It appears to me that there is little difference between any of the above definitions and the definition intended by the Government."

APPENDIX III

Land Law (Ireland) Act, 1881 [44 *and* 45 *Vict.*]

Definition of fair rent in Bill as introduced.

7. (1). The tenant of any present tenancy to which this Act applies may from time to time during the continuance of such tenancy, apply to the court to fix what is the fair rent to be paid.

(2). Such application may also be made by the landlord and tenant jointly.

(3). A fair rent means such a rent as in the opinion of the court, after hearing the parties and considering all the circumstances of the case, holding, and district, a solvent tenant would undertake to pay one year with another: Provided that the court, in fixing such a rent, shall have regard to the tenant's interest in the holding, and the tenant's interest shall be estimated with reference to the following considerations; that is to say:

(*a*) in the case of any holding subject to the Ulster tenant right custom or to any usage corresponding therewith with reference to the said custom or usage;

(*b*) in cases where there is no evidence of any such custom or usage with reference to the scale of compensation for disturbance by this Act provided (except so far as any circumstances of the case shown in evidence may justify a variation therefrom), and to the right (if any) to compensation for improvements effected by the tenant or his predecessors in title.

Definition of fair rent in Act.

8. (1). The Tenant of any present tenancy to which this Act applies, or such tenant and the landlord jointly, or the landlord, after having demanded from such tenant an increase of rent which the tenant has declined to accept, or after the parties have otherwise failed to come to an agreement, may from time to time during the continuance of such tenancy apply to the court to fix the fair rent to be paid by such tenant to the landlord for the holding, and thereupon the court, after hearing the parties, and having regard to the interest of the landlord and tenant respec-

tively and considering all the circumstances of the case, holding, and district, may determine what is such fair rent.

8. (9) No rent shall be allowed or made payable in any proceedings under this Act in respect of improvements made by the tenant or his predecessors in title, and for which, in the opinion of the court, the tenant or his predecessors in title shall not have been paid or otherwise compensated by the landlord or his predecessors in title.

CHAPTER XIV

THE STRUGGLE OVER THE LAND ACT IN IRELAND, 1881

The display of power of mind and strength of character makes a great impression on an assembly even if its temper from day to day is inflamed and embittered by violent passions. " As week after week and month after month passed by," said the *Annual Register*, " the spectacle of Mr. Gladstone, almost single-handed, defending each line of every clause of his Bll, filled friends and opponents alike with admiration of his vast and versatile genius." Gladstone, so sensitive to criticism and ill will, was not unconscious of this admiration or ungrateful for it. On the night of July 29, 1881, when his Bill had passed its third reading in the House of Commons, he wrote in his diary, " The Members of Parliament and the whole world have behaved to me on the occasion of this Bill with extravagant generosity. God grant modesty to me, and His blessing to the measure." If he had foreseen the future he would perhaps have changed the form of his prayer. Of modesty he had as much as any man can combine with a sense of power. What he lacked and what he needed in the next few months was patience; the patience of Cornewall Lewis who had said of himself, in contrast to Gladstone, that in the excitement of controversy, he was as cool as a fish.

Patience was needed before everything else, for the fortunes of Gladstone's Irish policy at this moment turned largely on temper. The Parnell party had two grievances against the Government; the first that the Government had passed an Act which deprived Irishmen of the fundamental guarantees of liberty that Englishmen possessed.[1] This

[1] On August 1, Parnell was suspended for the rest of the session for persisting in demanding a day to discuss the administration of the Act.

was a real and burning grievance, and it is not surprising that a party smarting under it was ready to think its second grievance to be greater than it was. The second grievance was that in its agrarian legislation the Government had not consulted this party, though it was obviously entitled, both by its expert knowledge and its representative character, to be treated with respect and consideration when this Bill was taking shape. With these grievances in their minds Irishmen might well regard the Government as hostile, both from its unfriendly Act, and from the speeches of some of its members. Harcourt they called the Red Indian of debate, and Bright, formerly so courageous a friend, made a speech on May 6, 1881, about the Irish labourer which not unnaturally exasperated the Irishmen. Parnell had suggested that the Land Commission should do something for the labourers, giving them cottages and allotments, and Bright in the course of the debate said that Parnell's proposal would bring back all the evils of the old cottier congestion, and that the trouble with the Irish labourer was that he was lazy, and that the Catholic Church had given him too many holidays. This harsh tone came as a shock to Irish members, some of whom contrasted it with the conciliatory speech made on the same subject by Forster.

The Irish temper then was naturally suspicious and resentful. Gladstone, on the other hand, saw the history of the session in rather a different light. He had spent four strenuous months forcing through Parliament a Bill which treated with rough violence principles that were held sacred not only by the Conservative party but by an important section of his own followers.[1] That Bill might seem inadequate to Parnell, but if anything was certain it was that no man less powerful, less courageous or less determined than

[1] Argyll wrote to him on April 13, 1881, " I regard it as a most unfortunate thing that you have had, or at least now intend, to throw all your personality into this Irish Land question. . . . You think you have the Cabinet with you. I wish you had heard the talk of some of them the day you went off to the Queen and left us ' mice ' without the ' cat.' Even in your presence Kimberley declared that after this Bill passed, he could not conceive any landlord spending a shilling on improvement. . . . The Cabinet has submitted to what they think Political necessity—one main ingredient in which has been your authority in proposing *anything*."

R

Gladstone could have made it into an Act of Parliament. Chamberlain, ready if anyone for bold action, declared in a speech at Birmingham in June that the Bill was the maximum that any British Parliament would grant.[1]   Moreover, though Parnell might reasonably feel that he had been slighted by the failure of the Government to consult him, Gladstone might think that he had gone some way to meet him when the Bill was in Committee.   Several of his suggestions had been taken.   His suggestion that something should be done for the cottages of the labourers was adopted, and two clauses were added to the Bill for this purpose.   On the vital question of arrears, and of the lease-holders, Gladstone had also taken account of his views, but the House of Lords had destroyed these provisions in the Bill.   In the effort to safeguard the tenants' interest he had accepted and kept in the Act an amendment from Healy. Gladstone not unnaturally thought he had earned some gratitude and perhaps some confidence, but the Irishmen gave him neither, falsely suspecting that he had abandoned the Parnellite amendments not from necessity but from secret choice.

This was a bad atmosphere in which to launch the Land Act.   It was made worse by the state of mind to which the strain of the last twelve months had reduced the Irish Secretary.   No office used up a man's nerves and patience so fast, for Dublin Castle was a little island surrounded by suspicion and hatred.   To her rulers Ireland presented both the disadvantages that come from Crown Colony government, and those that come from the free play of popular institutions.   For Ireland was equipped for criticism and not for construction, and for criticism she had unrivalled gifts; with her sharp and cruel tongue, her unbridled press, her gift for sparkling ridicule and deadly invective, her quick impulses never steadied by the use of power.   Trevelyan said when he held that office that no man could stand the

---

[1] To understand the atmosphere in which he was acting we have only to note that Salisbury, now the Conservative leader and the ablest man in the party, speaking at Newcastle this year, attributed all the trouble in Ireland to Gladstone's departure from the policy pursued by both English parties down to the death of Palmerston.

strain for more than a year. Forster was worn out. He had gone to Ireland with high hopes and noble courage, and misfortune and disappointment had crushed him. " I can never do now what I might have done in Ireland," he had said in June, 1881. He was even thinking of resignation. " It is seriously to be thought of whether, after the Land Bill is passed, I ought not to get out of it all."[1] If he had acted on this presentiment the disasters of the autumn might have been avoided.

In this atmosphere, a speech made by Parnell had a fatal effect on the minds of Forster and Gladstone. At a Convention of the Land League held in Dublin on September 14, 1881, Parnell recommended that a number of test cases should be taken into the Land Courts to test the working of the Act and its value to the small tenants. This was a sensible proposal, and Healy and others have protested, probably with justice, that there was no sinister motive behind it. Parnell considered that tenants who were going to bind themselves for fifteen years had better ascertain first of all what kind of rents the Courts were going to fix. Gray, speaking in the House of Commons five months later, pointed out that Parnell anticipated a further fall in agricultural prices with the increased pressure of American competition, and that on this ground he thought the tenants should act with caution.[2] In this forecast Parnell was of course proved right. Unhappily Parnell was speaking with an eye on the United States, for the funds that English parties could raise for their needs were subscribed secretly by private persons, but Parnell had to depend on the open support of poor Irishmen on both sides of the Atlantic. His embarrassment at this moment was an illustration of a standing difficulty. His American supporters, nursing all the bitterness of exiles, were much less ready than his supporters at home for compromise. The advice he gave to Irish tenants wore a less innocent look when he described it to the President of the Land League of America. " The Executive of the League," he wired, " is empowered to select test cases, in order

[1] Wemyss Reid, *Life of Forster*, Vol. II, p. 324.
[2] House of Commons, February 13, 1882.

that surrounding districts may realize, by the result of cases decided, the hollowness of the Act." It is not perhaps surprising that Gladstone and Forster rushed to the conclusion that this was a deliberate plan for defeating the Act, and that Parnell was out for mischief and nothing else.

This was a disastrous misunderstanding. Gladstone's Irish policy depended on the success of the Land Act; on its success both as an agrarian reform and as a political influence. He thought that it was the remedy for great social and economic mischief and the alternative to coercion. Crime had increased steadily. The figures for the first quarter of 1881 were 769; for the second 991; for the third 1060. The Land League had now 200,000 members and Parnell's sister Anna had founded a Ladies' Land League whose violence was later to prove an embarrassment to her brother. By March, 1881, more than a thousand untried suspects were in prison. Coercion had thus failed to reduce crime. On the other hand, it had increased the number of evictions. The figures had gone up from 198 in the last quarter of 1880 to 350 in the first quarter of 1881, 1,065 in the second, and 1,282 in the third. Crime and eviction seemed to follow a rhythm which quickened its pace under the stimulus of coercion. Yet to Cowper and Forster the only remedy seemed to be more coercion.

Of the atmosphere of Dublin Castle we have an excellent impression in a memorandum from Cowper, the Viceroy, sent to Gladstone in June. Cowper discussed the advantages and disadvantages of pronouncing the Land League an illegal association. To make it illegal would weaken it by depriving it of the support of the priests who would not belong to a secret association, but it might increase outrage because the central body was a restraining influence. It might be easier to attack the League through its meetings, for speakers were fortunately becoming less cautious. He concluded with a sweeping sentence, " It is hardly too much to say that in the present state of the country everybody who takes a leading part in the Land League does by the very fact of so doing incite to outrage and there is *now* hardly anybody whose detention policy would demand that I would not personally be willing to arrest." This was the man into whose hands the power of arbitrary arrest and detention had been given, yet one of the two men who were taking the leading part in the Land League, Davitt, was well known to be denouncing outrage at this very time.

Harcourt said of coercion that it was like caviare; it was unpleasant at first, but you acquired a taste for it. The truth of that sally is seen in the history of one Government after another. But there was one distinguished exception. The more Gladstone saw of coercion the less he liked it. To understand his conduct now and later it is important to grasp his view of the Irish problem at this time. He believed that in any normal society the lawbreaking elements are absorbed in the general blood stream, and that it is only when a society is sick that these elements need special and drastic treatment. Ireland had been a sick society because England who had ruled her had either neglected or misunderstood her problems. His Land Bill was the remedy for her sickness. If it was allowed to operate, Ireland would become in this respect a normal society. This did not mean that the Land Bill would itself solve all her problems. He had in mind further reforms of local government, reforms as he showed in his memorandum that would recognize her national needs and national moods, and not merely her right to a more modern system of local administration. But for the moment everything turned on the Land Act.

In his study of the Irish question one fact impressed him painfully. In other societies the spirit of self respect and self defence inspired the ordinary citizen with a sense of duty which made him a support of the law. In Ireland this was not the case. An interesting letter from Forster to Ripon on July 17, 1881, shows what a strong impression he as well as Gladstone had formed of the weakness in this regard of the Irish character. " The greatest of all Irish evils is the cowardice or at best the non-action of the moderate men; and indeed this is the best if not the sole argument for Home Rule. Sensible, moderate Irishmen let things alone and let them get from bad to worse, because they know that at a certain point we English must step in and prevent utter anarchy."[1] This was a weakness in Irish society to which Gladstone continually reverted, and he hoped that by removing the grievances and abuses of the Irish land system he was correcting injustices which had helped to produce this state of mind. Forster and Cowper still had confidence in coercion. He had none. As early as June he had written to Lorne that the Land Bill constituted nearly " the whole of our substantial resources for confronting and beating the Land League." On October 31, 1881, he wrote to Forster:

" . . . if Ireland is still divided between Orangemen and law-haters, then our task is hopeless, but our belief and contention always is that a more intelligent and less impassioned body had gradually come to exist in Ireland. It is on that body and its precepts and examples that our hopes depend, for if we are at war with a nation we cannot win."

In this temper he was so far from consenting to increase coercion that he was pressing through the summer for the release of suspects; one of them, Father Sheehy, took an inconvenient way of illustrating the bad consequences of coercion by leaving prison a much more violent man than he had entered it. As nobody could have expected to keep the turbulent Canon in prison for the rest of his life, his conduct on release might be interpreted as an argument for Gladstone's general case against coercion. But it was not the kind of argument that Gladstone would have chosen.

In Gladstone's view then, the Land Act was the first step towards making Ireland a normal and healthy society, and Parnell was resisting it for that very reason. On September 1, Gladstone wrote to Cowper urging the release of Father Sheehy as likely " to counteract Parnell's desperate game." The next day he wrote to Portarlington describing Parnell as a " speculator in public confusion." On September 8, he wrote to Forster arguing for release, " To reduce the following of Parnell by drawing away from him all well-intentioned men seems to me the key of Irish politics for the moment." His belief that Parnell had really little force behind him was

[1] Wemyss Reid, *Life of Forster*, Vol. II, p. 330.

encouraged by the bye-election at Tyrone on September 7, when the Liberal received 3,168 votes; the Conservative 3,084; and Parnell's candidate (a Unitarian Minister, afterwards well-known in England, named Harold Rylett) only 907. On September 18, 1881, Gladstone wrote to Halifax, " Parnell seems too a proper object for a just and strong description. He has not above a dozen Irish members with him and even these he rules with a rod of iron." On September 21, he wrote to the same correspondent, " It is a grave point for me to consider whether I should at Leeds describe him by his acts (though not motives) as what he is, an enemy of the Empire." Gladstone's illusion about Parnell's following was strengthened by a speech of Dillon's which he interpreted as dissenting from Parnell's policy as irresponsible. Dillon was often to embarrass English statesmen by his violence; it is unfortunate that one of the few speeches in which he seemed less violent than his colleagues had this bad result.

Gladstone, as we have seen, underrated Parnell's importance as a political leader. On the other hand, he was very much afraid of his power for mischief. He had arranged to make a series of speeches at Leeds in October and for some weeks beforehand he discussed the situation anxiously with his colleagues. On September 20, Forster wrote to him:

" I send Friday's and Saturday's *Freeman*, as I think you ought to read Parnell's speeches before you speak at Leeds. He means all the mischief possible; and the Land League under his advice will take what they call test cases into court; that is cases in which they know the Commissioners must decide against them and then they will say to the farmers, ' Trust to us and outrages and pay no attention to the " Land Act " '." Bright wrote to him on October 4, " I have felt a strong inclination to say what I have thought of Mr. Parnell—the question is whether to attack him from your eminent position will make him appear to be a greater figure than he really is. He is open to a tremendous assault on the ground of his lying statements and of the immoral sentiments he is spreading among the Irish people. . . . His main object is a break up of the United Kingdom, for he hates us and England even more than he loves Ireland."

Gladstone made up his mind to attack Parnell, but his first intention was to combine with the attack some sympathetic passages about Irish reform.   Granville to whom he spoke of his intention was uneasy:

" I shall be quite delighted at your going any length about Fair Trade," he wrote on September 15, 1881.   " On reflection I am not so sure about Home Rule.   Would it not be better to reserve any announcement till you can explain the plan?   It will of course not conciliate Parnell and Co.   On the other hand, at all our bye-elections it will be represented as truckling to them.   I am not sure whether you mean that Ireland and Scotland are to have more local government but that England is not."

Gladstone replied on September 16:

" With respect to Parnellism, I should not propose to do more than a severe and strong denunciation of it by severing *him* altogether from the Irish people and the mass of the Irish members and by saying that Home Rule has for one of its aims Local Government to which I should affix no limit except the supremacy of the Imperial Parliament and the rights of all parts of the country to claim whatever might be conceded to Ireland.   This is only a repetition of what I have often said before, and I have nothing to add or enlarge.   But I have the fear that when the occasion for action comes, which will not be in my time, many liberals may perhaps hang back and may cause further trouble."

In considering this passage it is important to remember that at this time Gladstone looked on his retirement as imminent. A few weeks later he wrote to Sir Arthur Gordon in this sense, and at this time he believed that the reforms of another session, with the establishment of the new parliamentary rules, would exhaust the claims of public duty upon his private life.

As Gladstone had afterwards to answer some energetic criticism from former colleagues on the contrast between his treatment of Parnell at this time and his treatment of him later, it is important to understand precisely the grounds on which he was now attacking him.   One sentence in a letter to Forster on the eve of his speech at Leeds puts the truth excellently.   " I mean to treat Parnell as an irrecocileable, and to take for my prospective basis this—that no force or fear of force shall, so far as the Government can decide the question, prevent the people of Ireland from having the full benefit of the Land Act." It was in this spirit that he spoke at Leeds on October 7, 1881. " He desires to arrest the operation of the Land Act, to stand as Moses stood between the living and the dead; to stand there, not as Moses stood, to arrest but to extend the plague." He contrived to do justice to his Irish sympathies while denouncing Parnell's conduct by a great panegric on O'Connell, but this was quite overshadowed by the threat with which the speech ended. " If it shall appear that there is still to be fought in Ireland a final conflict in Ireland between law on one side and sheer lawlessness on the other, if the law purged from defect and from any taint of injustice is still to be repelled and refused, and the first conditions of political society to remain unfulfilled, then I say, gentlemen, without hesitation, the resources of civilization are not yet exhausted."[1] Lady Frederick Cavendish who was on the platform wrote in her diary, " I could see, sitting near him, how deeply he felt the awful responsibility of the moment, for what he had to do was to warn Parnell and Co., that the long patience of the Government had all but reached its term."[2] Parnell retorted with a speech of defiance at Wexford:

" It is a good sign that this masquerading knight errant, this pretending champion of the rights of every other nation except those of the Irish nation, should be obliged to throw off the mask to-day and stand revealed as the man who, by his own utterances, is prepared to carry fire and sword into your homesteads unless

---

[1] Lord Acton wrote from Munich about this speech " The Irish speech (Leeds) on Friday and the economic speech on Saturday made the strongest impression on me, The treatment of Home Rule as an idea conceivably reasonable which was repeated at Guildhall, delighted me. I felt less sure of the distinction between that as a colourable scheme, and the Land League (as now working) as one altogether revolutionary and evil," *Acton's Correspondence* (Figgis and Laurence) I, 176. Acton's letter is interesting because nobody else noticed anything but the violence of the threat in the speech and also because it shows that he took a truer view than Forster and Gladstone of the Land League. For the impression made by the speech on a German in the audience, himself brought up in the sceptical Bismarckian atmosphere, see Eyck, *Gladstone*, p. 231.

[2] See her diary, Vol. II, p. 293.

you humbly abase yourselves before him and before the landlords of the country."

On October 12 the Cabinet met and after five hours decided to arrest Parnell. The League replied by a desperate gesture calling on the tenants to pay no agrarian rents until the Government had restored the constitutional rights of the people. Parnell and Dillon both condemned this folly. " A strike against rent," said Dillon, " cannot be carried out without the help of the priests and the priests cannot support so barefaced a repudiation of debt. Rome would not allow them." The Government proclaimed the League and tenants flocked into the Land Courts. Gladstone's only resource against the Land League had succeeded where coercion had failed.

Gladstone's view that disorder and disorder alone could now defeat his plan for saving Ireland from the consequences of England's past misgovernment led him to take another step in December. Dillon had underrated the zeal of some of the priests. Gladstone sent Newman a number of extracts from violent speeches and sermons delivered by Catholic priests and asked him to consider whether he should write to Rome about them. He recalled how Peel's Cabinet in 1844 had appealed to the Pope, Gregory XVI, to discourage the O'Connell agitation, and he explained that he would be loth to make such a request himself. What he wanted was that the Pope should know of these lawless speeches and consider whether they should not be discountenanced.

" My wish is as regards Ireland, in this hour of her peril and her hope, to leave nothing undone by which to give heart and strength to the hope and to abate the peril. But my wish as regards the Pope is that he should have the means of bringing those, for whom he is responsible, to fulfil the elementary duties of citizenship. I say of citizenship; of Christianity, of Priesthood, it is not for me to speak."

The Church had not been silent on the general question of disorder. In January, 1881, Pope Leo XIII had sent a letter to the Archbishop of Dublin distinguishing between a lawful movement for the remedy of grievances and the adoption of unlawful means to that end, and exhorting the Irish people to avoid all illicit agitation and all revolutionary schemes. The Irish Bishops had replied next month denouncing agrarian crimes, but adding " we cannot forget the ages of oppression and misery which have driven our people to despair of justice and equity." In September the Bishops adopted resolutions thanking Gladstone's Government for the Land Act, and calling on the clergy to guard their flocks against secret agencies and intimidations.[1] On the other hand, Lord Braye wrote to Gladstone on July 20 to protest against a speech by Manning.

The exchange of invective at Leeds and Wexford seemed to resolve politics into a duel between two men, both of them headstrong, both of them determined, and both of them fatally and wrongly convinced that he understood the other. A few weeks later the only other member of the Cabinet on whose conscience the misgovernment of Ireland was a burden, spoke not less sternly than Gladstone.

" We found," said Chamberlain at Liverpool, on October 25, 1881, " that the Government was being ousted from its place in order to make way for the leaders of the Land League whose dictates were subverting the law of the land. When it is said that it is contrary to Liberal principles to suspend the safeguards of liberty, I say that liberty is a mere phantom unless every man is free to pursue his inclinations, to consult his interest within and under the protection of the law; and when the Land League undertook in every case to supersede private judgment and to impose its dictates by force and terrorism and intimidation then it became a tyranny as obnoxious to Liberals and Liberalism as any other form of despotism."

This speech of Chamberlain's was notable for two reasons. It was criticized by Conservatives at the time and for long afterwards for a passage that seemed to them to condone earlier lawlessness and it contained a striking declaration on the Union. " I say to Ireland what the Liberals or the Republicans of the North said to the Southern States of America—the Union must be preserved. You cannot and shall not destroy it."

With Parnell in prison and the Land Courts as busy as

[1] The *Times*, January 7, February 15 and September 29, 1881.

they could be, Gladstone thought he could turn his mind to the questions that Ireland had so rudely pushed on one side. On November 4, 1881, he wrote a very long letter to Dodson, President of the Local Government Board, discussing some of the problems of local government and local taxation at home on the assumption that a large reform of both would be the first business of the next session. When Parliament met on February 7, 1882, proposals were given a prominent place in the Queen's Speech for the establishment of local government in the English and Welsh counties, for the reform of the Corporation of London and the extension of municipal government to the whole of the Metropolis. As late as March 11, 1882, Gladstone wrote to Dodson, who had been at work with a Cabinet Committee on his Bill, hoping that the Bill would be introduced before Easter. But he was soon disillusioned. On April 8 he had to write to Granville defining a very different plan, '(a) Necessary finance and procedure till Whitsuntide, (b) To refer to Grand or Standing Committees some important Bills that are not matters of policy, (c) To throw over for the year local Government in England and London Government, (d) To take serious Irish legislation for the pièce de résistance in June and July." A few days later he wrote, " our large English Bills are virtually gone overboard for the year." What would he have thought if he had known that they had gone overboard not for one year but for six, and that Ireland, which had devoured the first two years of his life as Prime Minister of this Government, was to allow him only one large measure, the enfranchisement of the village labourer, in the three years that were left to him? And that measure, as it happened, was chiefly contested and chiefly important because of the Irish consequences. For the result was the compact body of eighty-five Parnellites who demanded Home Rule in the next Parliament.

When Parliament met in February, 1882, Gladstone was under fire from all sides. His Government had locked up more than a thousand Irishmen without trial, among them a leading figure of the House of Commons, a critic whose cold power in debate had often been used to mortify

Ministers and embarrass their plans. In all parts of the House men found something high-handed in the conduct of a Government which had obtained an Act of Parliament on the plea that when armed with it they could give peace to Ireland by putting a few village ruffians under lock and key, and had then used it to shut up a formidable opponent. At the same time Ireland, which was to have been disciplined by the Coercion Act and pacified by the Land Act, was in greater disorder than ever. Parnell had been asked when he was arrested who would take his place, and he had replied, " Captain Moonlight." Captain Moonlight was now Ireland's Master. Conservative critics pointed to Irish anarchy, arguing in some cases that coercion had been too mild in character or too late in time, in others that it had been ill devised and ill executed. Irishmen, on the other side, described the arbitrary rule of Dublin Castle and the hard lot of some of the suspects, in a series of telling speeches in the course of which they reminded Gladstone more than once of his old fire over the Naples prisons.

Gladstone had thus to answer attacks from all sides, in a House at once angry and apprehensive. The landlords were upset by incidents in Ireland which threw some doubt and discredit on the administration of the Land Act, and by the speech Chamberlain had made in Liverpool in October. Lord George Hamilton called on Gladstone to disown him. " Let him get up and say that the speech which the President of the Board of Trade had made at Liverpool was one that he utterly disapproved and that any man who said it was justifiable to use a criminal organisation for parliamentary purposes was not worthy of being an English Minister." Chamberlain at Gladstone's request spoke in the debate defending his Liverpool speech with great skill.[1] Gladstone made it clear that he hated what he had had to do. The difference between his view and that of some of his colleagues at this time was evident in his comments on coercion. After describing the state of Ireland he went on:

[1] Gladstone wrote to him, on February 10, 1882, " I daresay you are aware that various references have been made in debating the address to public declarations of yours. These you will I am sure be able to meet without difficulty."

" What were the means we had in our hand to meet it with? We had the Coercion Act. . . . Does anybody suppose—I am afraid there are some who still suppose—that in the Coercion Act there is latent some remedial process, but we at least are not under that dismal superstition. We have always declared that the Act had no legitimate purpose except for a moment to clear the ground, to leave a space in which you might found—with a prospect of their free operation—your remedial measures. . . . At that time we well knew there were in Ireland but two living powers. One of them was the Land League; the other the Land Act. A desperate conflict, it was obvious, must occur between them. The question was which was to be the victor."[1]

The proceedings of Parliament were important for two reasons. Gladstone made two striking speeches on February 9 and February 16, on Home Rule, the first on an amendment to the Address moved by an Irish Home Ruler, who was not a Parnellite. Most of his speech was addressed to the difficulties of dividing Irish from Imperial questions and of devising a scheme by which Ireland could have what she wanted without the destruction of Imperial unity. In this speech he said, " I will not undertake to say to what decision this House might arrive, provided a plan were before it, under which the local affairs of Ireland could be, by some clear and definite line, separated from the Imperial affairs of Ireland." This speech in which the demand for Home Rule was treated as a serious question, made at a time when the relations between the Government and the Parnellites were very bitter, brought an immediate response from the Nationalists. Sexton thanked him warmly and said he had never more admired Gladstone's intellectual power and its sudden and masterly exercise. The *Times* received the speech with consternation, contrasting Gladstone's attitude with that of all other statesmen and warning Sexton that though Gladstone was a " statesman of almost unequalled authority," he could not change at a word " the settled convictions of the great body of Englishmen."[2]

---

[1] House of Commons, February 27, 1883.

[2] Lord Acton was delighted. " I have long wished for that declaration about self government, but I am persuaded that there has been as much statesmanship in the choice of the time as of the terms." *Acton's Correspondence*, edited by Figgis and Laurence, Vol. I, p. 176.

Next week Gladstone was attacked for this speech by Lowther who had been Disraeli's Irish Secretary in the last years of his Government. Gladstone in his reply used words of great significance. " This is a subject on which I have very clear and distinct opinions—opinions which I have never scrupled to declare. They are not shared by many gentlemen probably in this House." After this beginning he went on to describe his opinions, speaking of them as " of a speculative character." By that he meant of course that as he was expecting soon to retire.

" It is highly unlikely that I shall ever be called upon to take any practical part in any matter relating to these opinions; but I have the very strongest opinions upon matters in the nature of local government. I have the strongest objections to the tendency which I see constantly prevail to the centralization of government, not for Ireland merely but for England. . . . I believe that local institutions—the institutions of secondary authorities—are a great source of strength, and that in principle the only necessary limit to these powers is the adequate and certain provision for the supremacy of the central authority."

He went on to dissent from the view now expressed by Plunkett that Irish control of Irish affairs " must be necessarily a step towards separation," and to explain that the right way to meet the demand was to ask those who made it for their plan. " What are the provisions you propose to make for the supremacy of Parliament? " He added that he would not concede to Ireland anything that he would refuse to Scotland. He then reviewed his earlier speeches to show that he had spoken before in this sense. Next day the *Times* was more distressed than ever.

" Home Rule means a separate legislature for Ireland with the power of making laws, levying taxes, and choosing local administrators but precluded from interfering in any other than purely Irish affairs. This is the question with which Mr. Gladstone is confronted and it is to this that he gives what is for him a distinct answer."

The article then describes that answer:

" In the Prime Minister's opinion the demand that purely Irish affairs shall be under purely Irish control is not so dangerous that it ought to be refused consideration. Mr. Gladstone does not say that he would be inclined to concede the demand but he contends that the proper way of meeting it is to ask those who put it forward to state what provision they propose to make for securing the supremacy of the Imperial Parliament. We most emphatically dissent from this view which has never before been advanced in the House of Commons by a responsible Minister. It abandons the strongest part of the case—almost the whole case—against Home Rule."

The Queen not unnaturally took fright and wrote an agitated note. Gladstone replied on February 13 with a letter that was not altogether likely to soothe her fears. For he remarked that when he was a young man the self-government now practised in Canada had been regarded as a thing fatal to the unity of the Empire. Granville, to whom he submitted the letter, was doubtful about using this method of reassuring the Queen, observing that Canada was as nearly independent as she could be. This perhaps explains why, though Gladstone kept the passage in the letter, he told the Queen that he was far from implying that the degree of independence enjoyed by Canada could be safely conferred on Ireland. He added, at Granville's instance, that he would not give anything to Ireland that could not be safely given to Scotland. The danger that he feared was the danger that would arise " should a decisive majority of the representatives of Ireland unitedly demand on behalf of their country the adoption of some scheme of Home Rule, which Parliament should be compelled to refuse. To prevent the formation of such an Irish majority is, in Mr. Gladstone's view, a great object of Imperial policy." He went on to claim credit for having broken up the Irish majority in the existing House of Commons. " Mr. Gladstone can for himself only follow the course which will, as he believes, prevent its consolidation upon any basis dangerous to the Empire or the Throne. But his opinions must so soon cease to be taken into account that even this slight effort to explain them may be hardly worth Your Majesty's perusal."[1] These two speeches and his letter

---

[1] Guedalla, *The Queen and Mr. Gladstone*, Vol. II, pp. 177–178.

to the Queen show exactly the state of his mind. He was afraid of schemes of Home Rule that meant separation; he was ready to consider any scheme that took Imperial needs into account; he did not think that any considered and deliberate national demand could be resisted, and he was certain that before the time came for an active policy he would himself be back with Homer and Dante, deep in that life of contemplation which Bacon distinguished from the life of a selfish spectator because, like the life of learning in a monastery, " it was not finished in itself without casting beams upon society."

The other important event was the action of the House of Lords in setting up a Committee to inquire into the working of the Land Act. The Government resented this proceeding, and Gladstone not unnaturally remarked that it was not fair to the Act to unsettle men's minds when the Act was only a few months old. Mistakes were, of course, inevitable in the case of such experimental and pioneer legislation, in a country where there was so little in the way of a skilled civil service, and the House of Lords could make out a case if that case depended on blunders and indiscretions. But their action was chiefly important, not for its success in finding fault, but for its recommendation of an alternative policy. For the Committee produced a scheme of land purchase. The scheme was a landlord's scheme. It was criticised on that ground by the *Times*. And no doubt the new enthusiasm of the landlords for land purchase was stimulated by a sense of their own interests. On the other hand, it would be unjust to see in these schemes nothing but self interest. The leading Conservatives had begun to think of land purchase as a remedy for Irish agrarian discontent, believing that peasant owners would be a stable and steadying force in Irish politics and society. Northcote had spoken before in this sense; Salisbury had regretted, when the Land Act was debated in the Lords, that more had not been made of this part of the Bill; W. H. Smith had made an excellent speech in the Commons. Experience of the working of the Land Act had sharpened their desire for this solution, and Smith, with Gladstone's consent, got

s

into touch with officials, Treasury and Irish, in order to prepare a scheme.

This movement on the Conservative side had an important influence on Government policy. Gladstone on his side set to work on the subject and by the beginning of April Lord Frederick Cavendish and Welby, the Secretary to the Treasury, had drawn up a scheme for land purchase. Gladstone saw in this a reason and opportunity for developing local government on larger lines, and he drafted a Bill for creating provincial councils. On April 13, 1882, he wrote to Granville about this scheme:

" To make the responsibility of the purchasing tenant real, we must have bodies of real weight in Ireland with which to deal and throw upon them the working of the clauses. The Irish are too strong to be governed by agency which has to them a purely English character, and which has its seats in Downing Street and in Dublin Castle. I am much inclined to believe that the safest course in these arduous circumstances is a bold one, namely calling into existence, as the best form of local government for Ireland, four provincial bodies according to the idea of Lord Russell, which might at once be charged with the management of this question, and which might in a future year take over all the functions of County government."

With this in his mind he prepared a Bill " to constitute Provincial Councils for the Management of certain classes of local affairs." These bodies to be elected by the voters for Poor Law Guardians were to take over the duties of the Commissioners of National Education, and all the powers of the Land Commission, in respect of the purchase of estates for resale, and of advances to tenants for the purchase of their holdings.[1]

An observer behind the scenes might well have thought at this moment that at last the tide had turned. Instead of the bitter recriminations of party, he noted that Conservative and Liberal leaders alike were busy on schemes of land purchase, and that the Government were considering a bold constructive reform for which they might hope, in these conditions, for Conservative support. For the first time

[1] See Appendix to this chapter.

since any English statesman had ventured on these difficult and perilous enterprises it looked as if the two great parties might help each other instead of spending their strength in sterile conflict. Of the two reforms they had in mind one was close to Parnell's heart, and of the other he would have said, as he said of the scheme for Grand Committees that it would make for Home Rule and should be accepted.[1] Thus there was every hope that these reforms with all this British support behind them would have the support too of the great rebel chafing in his cage. For a few weeks a man might be forgiven for thinking of Ireland without despair.

APPENDIX

Printed for the use of the Cabinet.   April 7, 1882.

STRICTLY CONFIDENTIAL

PROVINCIAL COUNCILS

HEADS OF A BILL

to

Constitute Provincial Councils for the Management of certain Classes of Local Affairs.

Constitution of Provincial Councils.

1. For the purposes of this Act there shall be established four Provincial Councils. Each of such Councils shall be called the Provincial Council of the Province to which it belongs, and shall consist of such number of Representatives for each County in the Province as are set opposite to the name of such County in the schedule to this Act. Each Provincial Council shall be a Body Corporate with power to acquire and hold lands for the purposes of this Act.

Powers of the Councils.

2. There shall be transferred to the Provincial Council of each Province all the powers and duties connected with National Education in such Province of the Commissioners of National Education.

[1] Barry O'Brien, *Parnell*, 291.

All moneys provided by Parliament after the commencement of this Act for the purpose of National Education; or for the purpose of contributing towards the salaries of medical officers of workhouses and dispensaries, and sanitary officers acting in execution of the Public Health Act, or for the purpose of contributing towards the cost of District Lunatic Asylums, or for Reformatory and Industrial Schools, shall be apportioned by Parliament between the Provinces in the proportions in which the moneys provided for the same purposes were expended in the Provinces respectively on the average of the three years ending March 31, 1882.

The amount appropriated by Parliament in each year after the commencement of this Act for each of the Provinces for the several purposes aforesaid shall be applied by the Provincial Council of the Province for the purpose for which it is provided, in such manner as the Council thinks most expedient.

No greater sum shall be voted by Parliament in any year after the commencement of this Act for any of the purposes aforesaid than the sum voted for the same purpose for the year ending March 31, 1882.

Commutation of annual grant into a capital sum.[1]

3. The Provincial Council of any Province may from time to time apply to the Treasury to commute any part of the sum annually provided by Parliament for the several purposes aforesaid into a capital sum of the same value as such part. And the Treasury, if satisfied that such capital sum can be duly invested by the Council under the provisions of this Act, may cause such value to be estimated; and for the purpose of such estimate the said sum annually provided by Parliament shall be deemed to be an annual sum charged by statute upon the Consolidated Fund. The Treasury may pay the amount of such estimated value to the Provincial Council; and upon such capital sum being paid, the sum to be provided by Parliament in each year subsequent to such commutation, for such purpose, shall be reduced by the amount commuted into such capital sum.[2]

Application of capital sums.

4. The Provincial Council may invest any capital sum provided under this Act in the purchase of lands for the purpose of

---

[1] or any part thereof [*in margin* in Mr. Gladstone's writing].

[2] Why not charge upon this directly as a fund? [*In margin*; not in Mr. Gladstone's writing].

re-selling the same to the tenants in occupation thereof; or in making advances to tenants for the purpose of enabling them to purchase their holdings, and may make temporary investments in Government securities.[1]

All the powers of the Land Commission under the Land Law (Ireland) Act, 1881, with reference to the purchase of estate for resale, and with reference to making advances to tenants for the purchase of their holdings, shall be vested in the Provincial Council.

Application of proceeds of investments.

5. The accounts of the Provincial Council shall be kept in the prescribed form, and shall distinguish between sums received by the Council for interest on principal moneys and sums received in repayment of principal moneys due to the Council. The sums received for interest shall be expended by the Council from time to time for the same purpose as was provided for by the annual grant commuted under this Act into the principal sum for which such interest is paid. The sums received in repayment of principal moneys shall be reinvested from time to time under this Act.[2]

Provision of funds.

6. For the purpose of enabling the Treasury to supply funds to the Provincial Councils for the execution of this Act, the following provisions shall take effect:—

[The financial part must be settled at the Treasury.][3]

SUPPLEMENTAL PROVISIONS.

Election of Provincial Council.

7. Each Provincial Council shall consist of so many Representatives for each County in the Province as are set opposite the name of the County in the schedule to this Act. The persons qualified to vote at an election of Members to represent the County shall be [the persons who are qualified to vote at an election of Guardians under the Acts for the Relief of the Poor; and at such election each such person shall have so many votes in

[1] Under the conditions of Bright Clauses 1881 or as they may be hereafter amended [*in margin* in Mr. Gladstone's writing].

[2] Or employed to reduce the capital ? [*in margin* in Mr. Gladstone's writing].

[3] Invest Councils with alternative power to charge lands in Province [*in margin* in Mr. Gladstone's writing].

respect of each vacancy then to be filled up as he would have at an election for a Guardian.]

The election shall be held in the prescribed manner.

Incorporation of Commissioners Clauses' Act.

Power to appoint a Secretary, Solicitor, and officers.

Power to send Precepts to the several Grand Juries, requiring them to provide for salaries of such officers and other expenses.[1]

Power to appoint Committees, and to pay their travelling expenses.

Casual vacancies.

Disqualification of Member to traffic with the Council.

Appeal to the High Court in case of invalid election.

The Commissioners of Education.

7. Dissolution of the Commissioners of Education. Transfer of vested schools.

Provision for officers of the Commissioners.

Lunatic Asylums.

8. The Provincial Council, instead of the Lord-Lieutenant, shall appoint the Board of Governors of Asylums.

9. Schedule. Rules as to Elections, etc.

----

[1] [The words "and other expenses" *In margin* in Mr. Gladstone's hand writing.]

CHAPTER XV

In the days of Whiteboy crime Cornewall Lewis recalled Bacon's story of the Spanish commander who vowed that when the Devil on the Mount showed Christ all the kingdoms of the earth he left Ireland out and kept it for himself. The history of a few short weeks in April and May, 1882, might seem to illustrate that melancholy truth. At the beginning of May, Ireland and England were near to a settlement. At the end of May they were more bitterly divided than ever. Yet it is easy to see that the event which brought this calamity might, had fortune been less implacable, have helped the two nations to understand each other.

The history of these momentous weeks is complicated, but it is easy to avoid confusion if the reader remembers how the Irish problem and the Irish prospect looked to Gladstone. In his view everything depended on the success of the Land Act. The case for coercion was not that it might be expected to cure Ireland, but that it might be expected to remove conditions under which the Irish Land Act was obstructed and might be defeated. Parnell had been put in prison as the chief agent in that attempt to obstruct and defeat it. Once there was evidence that he nursed that intention no longer, the case for keeping him under lock and key was gone.

Gladstone knew nothing of Parnell's private life and at this time he had not even heard the first rumour of his relations with Mrs. O'Shea. Those relations were now becoming an important political disturbance. In February Mrs. O'Shea had given birth to their first child, a daughter, so poor in health that her life only lasted a few weeks. On April 10, Parnell was released on parole to attend his nephew's funeral in Paris, and he was with Mrs. O'Shea for a short

time on his way through England. After the funeral on
April 19, he returned to the O'Sheas, and the child died
whilst he was there. Haunted by the sad face of his mistress,
he could not bear the prospect of a long and indefinite
separation. On this ground he was ready to consider some
accommodation with the Government. But he had public
as well as private reasons for desiring his freedom.

In Ireland the Land Act had beaten the Land League,
with the result that some of the critics of the policy of
repression had anticipated. For secret societies were growing
and gaining power, and thus an anarchy was spreading
more dangerous to the Government than the agrarian
agitation, but dangerous also to Parnell and his influence.
Parnell the leader had thus, like Parnell the lover, a strong
motive for wishing to leave his prison.

It happened that an accommodation was made easy by
the circumstances of the moment. Parnell had predicted,
when the Land Bill was under discussion, that it would come
to grief over the question of arrears. The Government had
tried to meet him, but their method was incompetent and
it had failed. This was as clear now to Gladstone and to
Forster as it had been to Parnell and Healy a year earlier.
Parnell and his followers wanted to amend the Act in such a
way as to solve this problem; Gladstone and Forster wanted
the very same thing. In Gladstone's view the moment
that Parnell showed himself willing to amend the Act,
instead of seeking to wreck it, he ceased to be an obstructive
force and had every right to come back into the light of
day. When his follower, John Redmond, introduced a
a Bill with that purpose Gladstone welcomed warmly the
evidence of a change of temper.

This was not the only indication that had reached Gladstone of a change in the Irish leader. His son Herbert, who
had served in Ireland under Forster since October, 1881,
had been brought into touch with an Irish member, F. H.
O'Donnell, and had learnt from him that there was hope
of an Irish peace, if the Government would pass an Arrears
Bill. His notes of this meeting had been put before Forster
and read to the Cabinet on April 22. In the bitterness of

the Home Rule quarrel after Forster's death the *Times* accused Herbert Gladstone of concealing his negotiation from Forster. The Gladstone papers show that the accusation was false. Forster knew of the negotiations but had no hope of any good result.

If Gladstone had been all powerful in his Cabinet, and his mind had been free, Parnell, Dillon, and O'Kelly might have been let out of prison at this moment without any kind of negotiation, an Arrears Bill passed, and the Government might then have proceeded with its programme of Provincial Councils and Land Purchase.

Circumstances unhappily were not simple but complicated. Gladstone was not all powerful. He had been defeated outright in his Cabinet over his first plan for Irish reform. He had been worsted in the first struggle over coercion. Nor was his mind free. He was still Chancellor of the Exchequer. He apologized for the delay in answering an important letter in April on the ground that the week in which he received it was for him the financial week of the year. When, six months later, he gave up this office he wrote to Granville (November 27, 1882) deprecating the combination of the two offices that he held himself. He was thinking of his successor in the leadership, and he wrote, " It would be a great mistake in any Government (as it was in the last) to have the leadership tacked on to the leadership of the Exchequer as being an easy office. I certainly never worked harder than for over nine years as Chancellor of the Exchequer." This fatal mistake of his was still exacting grave penalties.

In other ways too the conditions were unfavourable. For a change was in process at Dublin Castle. Gladstone had for some time wanted to put Spencer there in place of Cowper who had seemed to him unequal to his task. Gladstone had great confidence in Spencer and proposed to appoint him as Viceroy with a seat in the Cabinet, though no Viceroy had sat in the Cabinet since the Reform Bill. The correspondence on this subject suggests that Gladstone had not thought out all the consequences with great care. For with the Viceroy in the Cabinet the Chief Secretary's position would be altered. Forster, it is true, had himself expressed the view that the best successor to Cowper would be Spencer, and after him, Carlingford, but he naturally had no intention of surrendering any of his power and he wanted some rearrangement by which he should have more time in Parliament. Spencer, as his letters show, was uneasy about his relations with a Chief Secretary whose many fine qualities did not include a modest or accommodating disposition. The change no doubt helped to make Forster less anxious to keep his disagreeable office. But, what was more important, Forster was worn out and no longer capable of sober and steady thinking on Irish politics. His judgment as well as his temper had given way under his long strain.

As Forster's behaviour during the next few weeks was one of the main causes of the shipwreck of a most promising movement towards an Irish settlement, it is important to grasp this truth. The best proof is to be found perhaps in a long paper he sent to Gladstone on April 17, 1882. In this paper he stated that there was no open resistance to the law, that the Land League had been beaten, that the November rents, generally speaking, had been paid, but that there were important exceptions, the most important of these being the poor districts of Connaught and elsewhere where the tenants were unable to pay owing to the accumulation of arrears. On the other side there had been an alarming increase in violent crime in the last six months, and a great growth of secret societies. " In some counties such as Westmeath, where Ribbonism has long existed, it is more active ; and in other counties, such as Mayo, associations, mainly for rebellion, but also available for murders of individuals, are spreading and taking hold of young men."

Any statesman whose judgment was still fresh and clear would surely have seen the significance of these facts and of the figures that Forster gave in this letter. In the nine months between January and October, 1881, there had been 46 agrarian outrages, consisting of 9 murders, 5 cases of manslaughter, and 32 of firing at the person. On October 14 Parnell was sent to prison. In the six months between

October, 1881 and April, 1882, there had been no less than 75 agrarian outrages, 14 murders, and 61 cases of firing at the person. This increase of crime had been accompanied by the growth of secret societies—societies of men owning no allegiance to Parnell, and eager to undermine his authority. Forster noted another sinister symptom. He reported that the money sent to Egan in Paris from America was used much less than before for the evicted tenants; it was being spent on agitators or being reserved for an election or a possible rising. These facts explain Parnell's anxiety to leave his prison. He had no desire to see Ireland pass from his control into such hands as these. And any Minister with these reports before him should have seen that every reason that could have been given in October, 1881, for putting Parnell in prison could now be given for letting him out. The two chief causes of disorder on Forster's own showing were first the failure of the Arrears Clauses of the Land Act, and secondly the growth of secret societies that were almost as hostile and as obnoxious to Parnell as they were to the Government.

How little Forster, tired and weary with his hateful task, was able to judge Irish politics, can be seen from a single fact. On the question whether Parnell should be released he had the whole Cabinet against him. Even Selborne could not support him. When it is remembered that the Cabinet included Whig noblemen like Kimberley and Northbrook, and men like Harcourt and Hartington, to whom any tenderness to Irishmen was as distasteful as to a die-hard Tory, this fact has a striking importance. It may be said that so far as sympathy went, there were only two men in that Cabinet who were capable of judging Parnell fairly, Gladstone and Chamberlain. Bright, whose fearless attacks on coercion had brought down on him so often the angry looks and the bitter invective of Tories and Liberals alike, could never speak of Parnell except in the language that had then been used of his own behaviour. Gladstone had all the power of his character, his age, and his personal ascendancy. Chamberlain, on the other hand, was less likely to help than to hinder a bold cause by supporting it in that cautious and conservative circle where he was at once disliked and feared. Indeed, he was more suspect than ever to his Whig colleagues at this moment in consequence of an ill-advised outburst by Morley in the *Pall Mall Gazette*, for Morley in demanding Forster's resignation had been so imprudent as to name Chamberlain as his successor. The Whigs thought Morley was writing under Chamberlain's inspiration, which was true of much that he wrote, but not true of this proposal. Chamberlain's support was in these circumstances a doubtful help to Gladstone.

Forster's view was thus rejected by a Cabinet that was strongly inclined by its general sympathies to agree with him and to distrust his opponents. His case looked as weak to his friends and colleagues at the time as it must look to anybody who studies the documents to-day.[1] His reasoning shows how completely his judgment had lost its balance. He wanted a penitential public declaration from Parnell that he would discountenance intimidation. Yet a moment's reflexion should have made it clear that such a declaration would do more harm than good. Parnell's power to help in restoring order in Ireland rested on his moral authority. What could shake that authority more than a declaration which would mean to most of his fellow countrymen that he had bought his freedom by promising obedience to the Government, that just as other Irishmen had sold their country for office he had sold it for his liberty; that this proud and fastidious leader, whose bearing towards his followers illustrated Sir Walter Scott's dictum that the Protestants in Ireland reminded him of the Spaniards in Mexico, had failed before an ordeal that obscure and ragged peasants had faced with the patience and courage of martyrs?

---

[1] " I cannot comprehend W. E. F.'s position," Spencer wrote to Granville on May 18, 1882, " considering that had the letter from Kilmainham been turned a little one way or the other, and been satisfactory to him, he would not have gone. The whole thing is in a nutshell or two nutshells.

" 1. There was no condition or bargain whatever.

" 2. We were only doing with Parnell what Forster did with every man he had let out—got some assurance—I believe he hardly ever got a promise—that he (Parnell) would not relapse into ways of disorder, but support those who were attacking the Laws. . . . Does he forget too that these men were not convicted, but were only ' suspects '."

Gladstone always denounced the use of the word " Treaty" as applied to the arrangements under which Parnell left Kilmainham jail. His critics regarded his fierce protestations as merely another instance of his enjoyment of confusing and darkening dialectic; his dislike of calling anything by its naked name; his incorrigible casuistry. Yet his case for his own view of the transaction, put more concisely than was his habit, in the *Nineteenth Century*[1] a few years later, was unanswerable. He pointed out there that the Act under which Parnell was in prison enabled the Government to lock up a man " on reasonable suspicion " of inciting to violence and disturbing the maintenance of law and order.

" What the Executive Government had to do was simply to ascertain, or rather to receive through the unsolicited office of a friend, what was the state of Mr. Parnell's mind on the subject which had led to his imprisonment. A physician does not negotiate with his patient but examines him. The simple fact of scrutiny into the present did of itself, according to the view of the Ministry, determine the future."

But there was a good reason for Gladstone's vehemence in resisting the use of the term " Treaty." He was one of the two men in the Cabinet who expected a good deal from Parnell's co-operation in Ireland and he knew that once Parnell could be represented as a renegade his power to co-operate would be gone.

To have kept Parnell in prison after what had happened would have been equivalent to claiming the right to shut up a political leader indefinitely at your pleasure. It was one thing to put in prison the man who had made the Wexford speech. It was another to keep him there six months afterwards when he had made it known that he was anxious for a settlement of the agrarian question. Forster had indeed been so much demoralized by the use of his arbitrary power that he had ceased to think of his prisoner as a man with rights that a constitutional Government had to keep in mind. Gladstone had heard enough about the Naples Government and its prisoners from his taunting critics to

[1] September, 1888.

shrink from this view that when once a man was in your power, you could treat him as you pleased.

Nobody reviewing the facts and documents to-day can doubt that the Government acted justly and wisely in releasing Parnell. Unhappily, actions that are wise and just in themselves may end badly from mistakes of method. In this case a blunder ruined the good effects of the release, and added a new element of strife to the Irish problem. This blunder was the use of a most unsuitable agent. The release of so important a prisoner as the Irish leader was a delicate matter, and the conduct of the Government was certain to be scrutinized in a hostile and suspicious spirit. Chamberlain, who acted for the Cabinet, put the negotiation into the worst hands, the hands of a man who was considering from first to last, not how he could serve Ireland, or how he could serve either or both of the principals between whom he was carrying messages, but how he could serve his own ambition. His chief desire was to convince the Government that he was a man of weight, suitable for office.

Gladstone, owing to his folly in taking on himself the burden of the Budget, had his hands full at the critical moment, and the management of the affair was left to Chamberlain. Chamberlain was duped by O'Shea (Forster took his measure), but some of the blame must fall on Parnell. If Parnell had been a free man he would certainly have refused to accept O'Shea in this capacity from the first. But Parnell was not a free man. O'Shea was the husband of his mistress, and Parnell, who could be ruthless enough in his treatment of the courtesies when he liked, shrank from distressing Mrs. O'Shea who now, as always, was anxious to flatter O'Shea's vanity and to find opportunities for making him seem important. Parnell, therefore, half accepted this arrangement though, as we shall see, he took steps very soon to get rid of this impostor and substitute McCarthy. If he had acted as wisely from the first, and firmly refused to discuss terms or plans with O'Shea, a great calamity would have been averted.

Negotiations began whilst Parnell was in Paris on parole with a long letter from O'Shea to Gladstone on April 13 offering to mediate between the Government and Parnell. He said that Parnell had no part in this " initiative " but he laid great stress on his own influence over him:

" The person to whom Mr. Parnell addresses himself in many cases (much as I differ from him in serious matters of politics and policy) is myself. Eighteen months ago Mr. Parnell used every effort to induce me to take over the leadership of the Party. I mention these things (the last one is known only to two or three besides ourselves) as an explanation of what would otherwise appear to be fatuous officiousness."[1]

Gladstone in answering this letter (April 15), told O'Shea that he had sent his letter on to Forster, adding:

" Whether there can be an agreement upon means or not, the end in view is of vast moment and your letter is not the first favourable sign I have observed. Assuredly no resentment, or personal prejudice, or false shame, or other impediment extraneous to the matter itself, will prevent the Government from treading whatever path may most safely and shortly lead to the pacification of Ireland, I should rather say of the districts to which that term, strong as it is, may be thought applicable."

In sending the letter on to Forster in Ireland (April 15) Gladstone showed the right spirit of caution about his correspondent. " In a correspondence of this kind," he wrote, " very much depends on the personality of the correspondent, and I have very little knowledge on this matter. You have more, or can easily get it." Forster, in answering this letter on April 18, described O'Shea as " a clever fellow, but vain and untrustworthy," adding, " I do not believe he has the influence either with Parnell or the priests which he claims." By the time Forster's letter reached London Gladstone, as Chancellor of the Exchequer, was immersed in the financial week of the year, and the matter was in Chamberlain's hands. For O'Shea had written to Chamberlain on April 15, addressing him as " a Minister without political pedantry " and enclosing his letter to Gladstone.[2] On April 18 Chamberlain sent Gladstone a letter full of admirable sense:

[1] Garvin, I, 350.
[2] Garvin, I, 350.

" . . . I believe the time is opportune, if you think it desirable, for something like a reconciliation with the extreme Irish party—who are unfortunately the representatives of the great majority of the Irish people. . . . Might it not be worth while to open negotiations? I have not liked to speak to any of the Irish members for fear of embarrassing Mr. Forster, but I could, if permitted to do so, approach Healy, Gray, O'Shea and others of the party—without committing the Government—and ascertain in what humour they are—that is to say whether they are still anxious to make all Government impossible in Ireland, or whether they are now ready to unite with us to secure the good government of their country."

He added one of those criticisms on the Government's past policy which a Prime Minister will often make himself, but does not always welcome from a colleague. " I have always thought that we made a mistake, in the first instance when we came into office, in not taking any steps to communicate with any member of the Irish Party outside Ulster."

" I cannot but think that Mr. Parnell and his friends might have been committed to our policy—or at least precluded from active opposition—if some show of consulting them, before that policy was finally decided on, had been made." Chamberlain also suggested that Parnell should be offered an extension of his parole.

On Wednesday, April 19, Parnell returned from Paris. He went straight to Eltham, to Mrs. O'Shea, and wired to O'Shea, who had not expected him so soon, to tell of his arrival. Through O'Shea Chamberlain offered him an extension of his parole, to which Forster had agreed, but Parnell refused it. On the night of the 21st, Parnell and O'Shea sat in one room, working together over possible terms of agreement with the Government, whilst Mrs. O'Shea in another room tended her dying child. Next day, Saturday April 22, the Cabinet authorized Chamberlain to enter into negotiations at his own risk,[1] and that evening O'Shea came up to see him. Chamberlain then wrote out a memorandum afterwards produced before the Parnell Commission, which is important as giving the first version of possible terms:

[1] Gwynn and Tuckwell, *Life of Dilke*, I, p. 438.

" If the Government announce a satisfactory plan of dealing with arrears, Mr. Parnell will advise all tenants to pay rents and will denounce outrages, resistance to law and all processes of intimidation, whether by boycotting or in any other way.   No plan of dealing with arrears will be satisfactory which does not wipe them off compulsorily by a composition—one-third payable by tenant, one-third by the State—from the Church Fund or some other source—and one-third remitted by the landlord, but so that the contribution of the tenant and the State shall not exceed one year's rent each—the balance, if any, to be remitted by the landlord.

Arrears to be defined as arrears accruing up to May 1, 1881."[1]

A negotiation had thus been started between Chamberlain and Parnell conducted by O'Shea.   Mr. Garvin's account when read with Parnell's account of the incident before the Parnell Commission, gives the impression that O'Shea began at once to play the tricks that he played later when acting in the same capacity between the same principals, for Chamberlain seems to have complained that Parnell was raising his terms.   But one of those principals was already anxious to change his intermediary.   On his way through London, when returning to Kilmainham, Parnell had an interview with Justin McCarthy (April 23) and asked him to put his views orally before Chamberlain.   On Tuesday, April 25, he sent a long letter to McCarthy embodying those views, to be shown at once to Chamberlain, if McCarthy approved.   The letter was as follows:

" We think in the first place that no time should be lost in endeavouring to obtain a satisfactory settlement of the arrears question, and that the solution proposed in the Bill standing for second reading to-morrow (Wednesday) would provide a satisfactory solution, though the Church Fund would have to be supplemented by a grant from Imperial resources of probably a million or so.

" Next as regards the permanent amendment of the Land Act, we consider that the Rent-fixing clauses should be extended to as great an extent as is possible, having in view the necessity of passing an Amending Bill through the House of Lords; that Leaseholders who have taken leases either before or since the

---

[1] Garvin, *op. cit.*, I, 354.

T

Act of 1870 should be permitted to apply to have a fair rent fixed, and that the purchase clauses should be amended as suggested by the bill the second reading of which will be moved by Mr. Redmond to-morrow.

" If the Government were to announce their intention of proposing a satisfactory settlement of the arrears difficulty, as indicated above, we on our part would make it known that the No Rent Manifesto was withdrawn, and we should advise the tenants to settle with their Landlords. We should also then be in a much better position than we were ever before to make our exertions effective to put a stop to the outrages which are unhappily so prevalent. If the result of the arrears settlement and the further ameliorative measures suggested above were the material diminution of outrages before the end of the session and the prospect of the return of the country after a time to something like a normal condition, we should hope that the Government would allow the Coercion Act to lapse and govern the country by the same laws as in England."

The most suspicious and malicious critic of the Government could have found nothing sinister or dishonourable in this letter: its suggestions were reasonable and practicable. It is well described in the words Chamberlain used later about these dealings. " The communications . . . were in the nature of information as to the terms on which Parnell would make an agreement. They contain the conditions on which he alleged his influence for good depended. ' Unless the arrears question is settled in the way I point out, I shall be powerless '."

Parnell had thus taken steps to replace O'Shea by McCarthy. He had given McCarthy a letter for Chamberlain. He had written both to his mistress and to O'Shea. To Mrs. O'Shea he wrote on the same day, April 25, enclosing a letter from O'Shea obviously urging him to act, and asking advice about his answer. " I told my friend in Jermyn Street,"[1] he wrote, " what steps to take, so that the matter referred to in enclosed will probably go on all right without, or with, the further participation of the writer."[2] The answer he actually sent O'Shea was produced before the

[1] McCarthy.
[2] K. O'Shea, *Charles Stewart Parnell*, I, 253.

Parnell Commission. It was written on Thursday, April 27.

"My dear O'Shea,

Wednesday's proceedings were very promising so far as they went. I think it would be well now to wait and see what proposals are made, as any appearance of anxiety on your part might be injurious. The journey to London was very fair and quiet, and I got as far as Holyhead without being recognized. If you come to Ireland, I think you had best not see me, for reasons which I will explain hereafter.

Yours very truly,
CHARLES S. PARNELL."

It is not certain on which day Chamberlain received Parnell's message from McCarthy, but we know that it was before the Cabinet met on Tuesday afternoon, April 25. If Chamberlain had proceeded to treat this message as the basis for further discussion all would have been well. McCarthy would have taken O'Shea's place ; Ireland would have got a good Land Act, and England a bright hope of an Irish settlement. For Parnell would have left his prison not only anxious, but able, to forward reform and encourage peace, and a new atmosphere would have been created in the House of Commons. But Chamberlain now made two blunders. He defeated Parnell's plan for putting O'Shea on one side and substituting a man who could be trusted. It was perhaps not very easy for Chamberlain to drop O'Shea. He had taken his pretensions and assurances at their face value, and, like many Englishmen, he found O'Shea an agreeable person, with the kind of Irish temperament that impresses Englishmen more than Irishmen. But Chamberlain might obviously have followed up McCarthy's conversation. Instead of this he paid but little attention to it—" I received it without any reply," he wrote to Gladstone on April 25, " except thanks and an acknowledgment of its importance "—and sent O'Shea to Parnell on a new and extraordinary errand. " Chamberlain put it to O'Shea," says Mr. Garvin, " that it was high time now for Parnell to make some binding and public declaration. At the Radical Minister's suggestion apparently, though without any direct request of his to Forster,

the emissary at once asked the Chief Secretary for permission
to visit Parnell in gaol."[1] What induced Chamberlain to
take the view that Forster had taken that Parnell must be
persuaded to make a public declaration? The effect of
such a declaration would have been to damage gravely
Parnell's influence in Ireland and his prospect of making
head against the secret societies that had grown up and
spread during and in consequence of his imprisonment.
Chamberlain's judgment was perhaps deflected by the
exciting prospect of a great personal success, or perhaps
O'Shea, who was so ready with his promises, misled him on
this point as on others.

The letter sent by Parnell to Chamberlain through
McCarthy did not come into Chamberlain's hands till he
had taken this false and fatal step. For it was on Friday
evening, April 28, the evening that O'Shea left London, that
McCarthy read the letter to Chamberlain, and Chamberlain
did not receive a copy till the 29th or the 30th. Thus while
Parnell was urging O'Shea by letter and telegram not to
come near him, and hoping that the negotiations would
now be in McCarthy's hands, O'Shea was hastening to
Dublin on this extraordinary errand. Parnell, though
anxious not to use him, did not dare to break with the husband of his mistress, and when O'Shea came had to admit
his unwelcome visitor. He wrote to Mrs. O'Shea the next
day, April 30, " He came over to see me, so I thought it
best to give him a letter, as he would have been dreadfully
mortified if he had had nothing to show. Everything is
going very well, and I hope will continue straight."[2]

The last sentence referred, no doubt, to the letter he had
sent to McCarthy.

The letter that Parnell had given to O'Shea to save his
face was, of course, the letter that did all the mischief. It
was as follows:

" My dear O'Shea,
I was very sorry that you had left Albert Mansion before I
reached London from Eltham, as I had wished to tell you that

[1] *op. cit.*, I, p. 355.
[2] K. O'Shea, *op. cit.*, I, 255.

after our conversation I had made up my mind that it would be proper for me to put Mr. McCarthy in possession of the views which I had previously communicated to you.

I desire to impress upon you the absolute necessity of a settlement of the arrears question which will leave no recurring sore connected with it behind, and which will enable us to show the smaller tenantry that they have been treated with justice and some generosity.

The proposal you have described to me, as suggested in some quarters, of making a loan, over however many years the repayment might be spread, should be absolutely rejected for reasons which I have already fully explained to you. If the arrears question be settled upon the lines indicated by us, I have every confidence, a confidence shared by my colleagues, that the exertions which we should be able to make strenuously and unremittingly would be effective in stopping outrage and intimidation of all kinds.

As regards permanent legislation of an ameliorative character I may say that the views which you have always shared with me as to the admission of Lease-holders to the fair-rent clauses of the Act are more confirmed than ever. So long as the flower of the Irish tenantry are kept outside the Act there cannot be the permanent settlement of the Land question which we all so much desire.

I should also strongly hope that some compromise might be arrived at this session with regard to an amendment of the tenure clauses.

It is unnecessary for me to dwell upon the enormous advantage to be derived from the full extension of the purchase clauses which now seems practically to have been adopted by all parties.

The accomplishment of the programme I have sketched out to you would in my judgment by regarded by the country as a practical settlement of the Land Question and would I feel sure enable us to co-operate cordially for the future with the Liberal Party in forwarding Liberal principles and measures of general reform, (sic) and that the Government at the end of this Session would from the state of the country feel themselves thoroughly justified in dispensing with further coercive measures.

Your's very truly,

CHAS. S. PARNELL."[1]

[1] The copy of the letter that O'Shea brought over is among the Gladstone Papers.

It was obvious that this last paragraph, with its reference to the Liberal Party, though it clearly meant that Parnell hoped to work with the Government in its Irish programme, might be so interpreted as to give a sinister look to the whole negotiation, and the bitter suspicion and ill-will of party politics at that time made it certain that if the opportunity was given such a construction would be put upon it. If the opinion could be spread out of doors that Parnell had bought his freedom by a promise to support the Government, the brilliant prospect of peace and co-operation in Ireland which Chamberlain offered the Cabinet would be swept from the sky.

O'Shea had not got out of Parnell the promise to make a public declaration, but he had got something that he thought would please the Government even more. So instead of returning to Chamberlain he took his prize straight to Forster, the last thing Parnell wanted,[1] and probably the last thing Chamberlain wanted. Not content with showing him the letter, he gave him an account of his talk with Parnell, and, as he was chiefly anxious to advertise his own importance, he spoke in a large irresponsible way, explaining that if Forster were dissatisfied the wording of the letter could be altered but the important point was that " the conspiracy[2] which has been used to get up boycotting and outrages, will now be used to put them down, and that there will be reunion with the Liberal party." Forster dictated an account of this conversation to Mrs. Forster and sent a copy of his record, together with a copy of Parnell's letter for circulation to the Cabinet.

The incident naturally made the worst impression on Forster. And the letter O'Shea had brought did not contain the one thing that Forster cared about, for there was no promise of a public declaration. He, Forster, had written the day before to Gladstone to say that unless O'Shea could bring back such a declaration, he could not be a party to Parnell's release or to the release of other suspects. Forster therefore writing to Gladstone said that the result of the visit

---

[1] See his speech, House of Commons, May 15, 1882.
[2] O'Shea said that he had used the word " organization " not " conspiracy."

was " less even than I expected." Gladstone had always
seen the folly of expecting or desiring such a declaration, and
he received the letter in a very different spirit. " I own
myself," he wrote to Forster (April 30), " at a loss to gather
your meaning when you say ' the result of his visit to Parnell
is less even than I expected '." He pointed out the importance of the division of the letter into two sections. In the
first part Parnell expressed his belief that if the arrears
question were settled satisfactorily, then he and his friends
would be able to stop outrages and intimidation. In the
second part " With great sagacity, Parnell goes on to state
his other aims under the amendment of the Land Act. But
he carefully abstains from importing any of them as conditions of the former remarkable statement.

" He then proceeds to throw in his indication or promise
of future co-operation with the Liberal Party. This is a *hors
d'œuvre* which we had no right to expect, and, I rather think,
have at present no right to accept. . . . Upon the whole,
Parnell's letter is, I think, the most extraordinary I ever
read." He ended with a sentence that has a grim humour
for those who know the sequel. " I cannot help feeling
indebted to O'Shea."

To Granville he wrote the same day (April 30), " It would
hardly be possible to describe the amazement with which
after reading Forster's note I perused Parnell's letter.

" The promise seems to me if anything wider than we
wanted, and the sole condition is the settlement of the
arrears. The only question perhaps for to-morrow is the
release of the three: about which, as at present advised, I
see no remaining room for doubt."

Whilst the O'Shea-Parnell letter was causing this excitement in London on Sunday, April 30, Chamberlain, from
Birmingham, was sending Gladstone a copy of the Parnell
to McCarthy letter of April 25. But its importance was
overshadowed by the O'Shea document.

On Monday, May 1, the Cabinet met to discuss the
question of the release of the Kilmainham prisoners and
adjourned till next day. After the Cabinet meeting
Gladstone wrote to Cowper, still acting as Viceroy:

" No decision has been actually taken: but the Cabinet meets again to-morrow at twelve, and it is probable that a telegram may then be sent to you requesting you to give directions for an immediate liberation of the three.

" The information we have had is in the briefest words shortly this. We know authentically that Parnell and his friends are ready to abandon No Rent formally, and to declare against outrages energetically, intimidation included, if and when the Government announce a satisfactory plan for dealing with arrears. We had already as good as resolved upon a plan and we do not know any absolute reason why the form of it should not be ' satisfactory '."

On May 2, the Cabinet decided to release the three prisoners. It is important to remember that every member of the Cabinet had seen the unfortunate O'Shea documents before coming to that decision. On the same day Forster, the only Minister against release, resigned. His biographer, Sir Wemyss Reid, says that he resigned because the Cabinet would not agree to introduce at once the Coercion Bill that had been drafted. But on the next page Wemyss Reid prints a letter to an unnamed colleague, probably Kimberley, which is so confused that it is not unreasonable to conclude, as two of his colleagues, as different as Chamberlain and Selborne, concluded, that Forster wanted to leave the Irish Office and took this opportunity.[1] It is sometimes said that Forster was deserted and ill used by his colleagues, but Forster himself always protested—even after his relations with his old colleagues had become bitter—against the view that he had any grievance, or that his colleagues had given him less support or consideration than he was entitled to expect.[2]

On Forster's resignation, Chamberlain wrote to Gladstone suggesting the appointment of Shaw as his successor. It was a curious suggestion because Shaw and Parnell were on bad terms, and Chamberlain perhaps alone among Gladstone's

[1] On August 10, 1888, after Reid's book had appeared, Morley wrote to Gladstone, " I have been comparing notes with Chamberlain about Forster's resignation. His impressions quite fall in with my own. *Before* the Kilmainham communications were opened, Forster told him that he thought he had had enough of it—that he was tired out—and that he was entitled to a change."

[2] See, e.g., his speech on May 11, 1882.

colleagues wanted the Government to act with Parnell. O'Shea wrote to Gladstone deprecating Shaw's appointment on this ground and pressing for Chamberlain, promising Parnell's support. Chamberlain himself expected the offer. On May 3 the *Times* mentioned Shaw Lefevre as a likely successor, but next day it named Chamberlain with confidence. Chamberlain's chances had been prejudiced by the unwise article in the *Pall Mall Gazette*, already mentioned, in which Morley had recommended his friend after a furious attack on Forster. But did Gladstone ever think of him? Nobody who knew what is revealed in Gladstone's diary, the composition of the " conclave " at which the choice of a successor was discussed, would have expected it to be Chamberlain. The members were Spencer, Hartington and Richard Grosvenor. It would be difficult to say which of these eminent Whigs would have disliked Chamberlain's appointment most. The *Times* observed sarcastically on Cavendish's appointment, with an eye perhaps to the Whig temperament so strong in Gladstone's circle, that Lord Frederick Cavendish " is not exposed to the adverse influence which tells against a statesman who attains to such a position by mere merit."

Gladstone had his reasons for this choice. Frederick Cavendish had been working with Welby at the finance of Land Purchase, and as this was to be one of the main reforms of the immediate future, Gladstone was delighted to have in Dublin a man who had prepared his scheme under the vigilant Treasury eye. Frederick Cavendish also served a purpose of great importance within the Liberal Government as the link between Gladstone and his brother Hartington. This is made very clear in Lady Frederick Cavendish's diaries; Gladstone and Hartington were never happy or comfortable together, and Frederick Cavendish could make things easier. As Irish affairs raised problems on which these differences were sharp, there were obvious advantages in putting this peace-making influence at Dublin Castle, for a good deal of Gladstone's time had been spent in reconciling Hartington to Irish plans that he detested. There was also a third reason. No man was more completely under Gladstone's spell, and thus Gladstone would have for the first time an Irish secretary who would go to Dublin ready and eager to be the agent of Gladstone's ideas, with no rival ambitions of his own.

The sequel is well known.   On May 4 Frederick Cavendish was appointed; on the 5th he crossed to Dublin; on the night of the 6th Gladstone, as he stepped into his house in Downing Street, after a party at the Austrian Embassy, was told by his secretary that the man he loved as a son had been stabbed to death in Phoenix Park.

CHAPTER XVI

In January, 1858, Orsini, the Italian conspirator, threw a bomb at the Emperor Napoleon in Paris, killing eight people and wounding 150,[1] but missing altogether both Napoleon and the Empress. Orsini died for his crime, but by a strange irony his attempt succeeded in its purpose. Either some sudden impulse or some deeper calculation prompted Napoleon, whom Orsini had wrongly imagined to be the obstacle to French intervention against Austria, to choose this occasion for deciding to befriend Italy; to give form and substance to his Carbonari memories. A letter from Orsini appealing to the Emperor to give liberty to twenty-five millions of people was read at his trial; it was printed in all the French newspapers, and by Napoleon's own request in the Piedmontese Official Gazette. Napoleon's strange erratic mind, of which nobody could say at any moment whether it would look up or down, whether its mood would be generous or cunning, turned to a romantic adventure. In July he met Cavour at Plombières and planned with him the war of liberation.

On May 6, 1882, four men armed with long knives threw themselves on Burke, the chief official of Dublin Castle, walking with the new Chief Secretary, Cavendish, in Phoenix Park. Cavendish tried to defend Burke and both men lost their lives. This terrible murder, if the English Parliament had had more imagination or foresight, might have helped to make peace between England and Ireland. One English-woman at any rate would have made her private calamity into a public blessing. Lady Frederick Cavendish sent a

---

[1] Trevelyan, *Garibaldi and the Thousand*, p. 73 *seq.*, 156 men wounded, of whom eight dead. The figures differ in different accounts.

message to the Viceroy deprecating " panic and vindictive vengeance," which was read in many Irish Catholic Churches and quoted in many Irish speeches. Sexton well said in the House of Commons when the old passions were raging bitterly again, that he wished that English statesmen had " accepted the catastrophe in the noble and heroic spirit of the bereaved lady from whom that tragedy took the light of life."

For a few days after the murder an observer might have thought that Lady Frederick Cavendish's prayer was to be answered, and that good was to come to both countries from this catastrophe. A French journalist remarked on the self possession of the English, " calculated to produce a high opinion of their political character and spirit." Ireland exhibited an unusual spectacle. Her leaders, the men who had signed the no rent manifesto, were cabling not only to Irish Mayors but to America and the distant colonies their detestation of the crime and their sense of the shame it had brought on the Irish people. Public meetings were held to denounce the murderers, and when a priest in Connemara read Lady Frederick Cavendish's letter from the altar, the whole congregation fell spontaneously on their knees. Gladstone and Chamberlain might have hoped for one brief hour that their policy of reconciliation might survive the calamity. For it was clear that if England could act with magnanimous common sense, the Irish people might be won and coercion might be avoided.

Unhappily this was not long the mood of politicians. The temper of too many of them found expression in an article that Gladstone justly called " diabolical," in which the *Times* sought, as he put it, " to fasten this hellish crime on the Irish people." The Irish leaders had done everything to show their horror. Parnell wanted at first to retire from public life altogether, and Chamberlain and Gladstone, as well as the other Irish leaders, had to dissuade him. It was known that it was while Parnell was in prison that the secret societies had grown up, and that they were as hostile to Parnell as to the Government. Parnell half expected the fate of Lord Frederick. Yet in a sentence which for concentrated injustice and mischief it would be hard to beat, the *Times* remarked, " Mr. Gladstone's prospect of keeping the peace in Ireland by the aid of Mr. Parnell has endured just four days with what results we see."[1]

To any cool observer the significance of these murders was not that they showed that there were murderers in Ireland (that fact was only too well known), but that Dublin Castle with its immense power over Irish life was so inefficient and casual that it could not even protect a civil servant and a Minister within sight of its own windows. Ministers in England were followed by detectives. In Dublin Cavendish and Burke had been allowed to walk across the Park alone. A cynic might have observed that, if Forster had spent a little of the time he spent in putting people in prison in instilling a little order and system into his own police, Frederick Cavendish would have escaped. But Forster had left the police in a condition of which Spencer, writing to Gladstone on May 8, reported, " The case I have against the Police is overwhelming. To-day brings fresh evidence of incapacity and want of co-operation. I am obliged to see each Head to ensure his knowing what the other has done or is doing. That of course cannot go on." The moral to be drawn from the Phoenix Park Murders was not that Ireland needed a new coercion law but that she needed a new broom in Dublin Castle.

But the cynic would have been less than just. It must be remembered that Forster had had his hands full with agrarian problems from the moment of his taking office, and that the task thrown on his shoulders was the double task of reforming the law and reforming Dublin Castle. This was a capital difficulty. An Irish Secretary combined half a dozen offices in his own hands. Under the task Forster had broken down.

It might have been supposed that the murder of a man so well liked and esteemed in the House of Commons would have sobered party passion and softened for a week or two the bitterness of the House of Commons. Unhappily it had no such effect. Gladstone himself had received a blow from

[1] *Times*, May 8.

which he did not recover his full strength in this Parliament. On May 8 he dragged himself to the House where he spoke with white face and " by the help of God forced out what was needful."

" But, sir, the hand of the assassin has come nearer home, and though I feel it difficult to say a word, yet I must say that one of the very noblest hearts in England has ceased to beat, ceased at the very moment when it was just devoted to the service of Ireland, full of love for that country, full of hope for her future, full of capacity to render her service."

If we wish to understand the atmosphere of politics in these harsh and ruthless days, we have only to note the tone and temper of the House of Commons eight days later. Party spirit has never been so pitiless as it was during the debates on May 15 and 16 on the Kilmainham Treaty. And party spirit has never done more public mischief.

Nobody who has studied all the documents on the question can think that there was anything in these transactions of which Ministers had cause to be ashamed. Their decision was indeed unassailable except by persons whose judgment was completely blinded by the passions roused in the Irish agitation. Parnell, Dillon, and O'Kelly were leading Members of Parliament all returned by Irish constituencies. The Government were about to propose Irish legislation. In a country under constitutional rule the detention of these men would have needed some special justification even if Parliament had not been engaged on Irish business. But in this case a Government that kept these men in prison a day longer than was necessary would fall justly under the suspicion of keeping formidable critics in prison, because it was more convenient to the Government that they should be in prison than that they should be in the House of Commons, when laws were being made for Ireland. Forster seems to have been quite unable to grasp the constitutional aspect of his problem. What could be more unjust or more unwise than to lock up an opponent under a special law which gives you this arbitrary power, and then refuse to open the door again unless he would give you a promise in the face of the world that he would obey you?

The historian to-day is able to see how completely Gladstone's view of the spirit and character of the proceedings was shared by the two men who most of all disliked Parnell in his Cabinet. Months afterwards (November, 1882) Gladstone, smarting under Randolph Churchill's taunts, challenged the Opposition to set up an inquiry by committee into the circumstances under which Parnell was released. The Cabinet had to consider whether, if this committee was held, they should produce all the letters that had passed at the time. Harcourt strongly objected, on the good ground that if once a precedent was established Cabinet Government would become almost impossible. In the end the whole project died away, but the Gladstone Papers include two papers on the subject by Hartington and Harcourt in which the events of the time are described and discussed. Hartington gives this account:

"My recollection of the communications which took place is that they were mainly for the purpose of ascertaining the intentions of Parnell and his Colleagues at the time, what course he would probably pursue if he were released, and consequently whether it would be safe to release him or not. I do not think that the first communication from O'Shea could have been disregarded. Parnell had at that time no public or official means of communication open to him. But, although the first letter indicated, if it were confirmed, a great change in Parnell's sentiments it was scarcely possible to act upon it without taking some steps to ascertain how far it did really represent his opinions, and what course of conduct he was likely to pursue if released. It is probably the case that these further steps did assume something of the character of a negotiation, and that although there was no pledge, there was an understanding that an Arrears Bill would be brought in based on certain principles."

Harcourt's paper is fuller, but it agrees with this account, and it includes what, coming from him, is a notable statement. "The result has been what we expected and desired, and I believe Parnell's release has greatly conduced to the better state of Ireland."[1]

[1] Even the *Times* when commenting on this squabble in the House remarked "The promises made on behalf of the Land League have been at least in part performed." (November 17, 1882.)

Unhappily, owing to Chamberlain's fatal blunder in using O'Shea, an honourable and proper transaction could be made to look like a party manœuvre. If your intermediary's interest in such a transaction is nothing more or less than the interest of a self seeker and self advertiser, accidents are likely. This was a delicate situation, for Parnell's power to help in keeping order would be seriously endangered if his release could be interpreted as a surrender. The best thing that could have happened would have been for the Prime Minister to make a simple statement taking full responsibility for the release of the three members, and for the House of Commons to have accepted that decision. But when a Minister resigns, he makes a statement of his reasons. Forster made his statement on May 5.   The Opposition was eager for disclosures that would discredit the Government, and Forster, whose resignation had been greeted on the Irish benches with an enthusiasm that was natural but indiscreet, found himself in an atmosphere in which the temptation to mistake your pride for your conscience is specially strong. He made no revelations, but his appeals to the Government to avoid blackmail arrangements and not to buy obedience, received with delight by the Opposition, prepared an atmosphere of suspicion that was dangerous for the future. At the moment Hartington restored the fortunes of the Government, and even the *Times*, much as it disliked the new policy, admitted that his speech was " practically conclusive."

With an ex-Minister talking about blackmail in the House of Commons and an intriguer talking about his exploits in the Lobbies, suspicion was certain to spread.   After the Phoenix Park murders Ministers were pressed for documents and two days (May 15 and 16) were given up to discussion of the " Kilmainham Treaty."   O'Shea and Parnell themselves precipitated the disaster.   Parnell, hearing a rumour that his letter was going to be read in the House of Commons, decided to read it himself.   Unfortunately he read a version of it handed to him by O'Shea in which the sentence about working with the Liberal party was omitted.   Strictly speaking Forster was not entitled to reveal documents that had passed within the Cabinet, but it would have taken a larger man to resist the temptation that was now before him. He forced the reading of the full text of the letter as it had come to him,[1] and he read himself his own memorandum of O'Shea's conversation. O'Shea's rambling and irresponsible language was taken by Forster and others as proving that Parnell had admitted that he had taken part in organizing crime. (It was made the basis of such a charge by the *Times* in 1887 and the charge was examined and dismissed by the Parnell Commission.) Forster was thus able again to win the delighted applause of the Opposition benches by making the release damaging both to the Government and to Parnell.

His conduct could scarcely serve any other turn. Parnell was out of prison and Forster himself would not have been ready to put him back. The Government were about to pass two Bills, both of which Forster approved, a Coercion Bill and an Arrears Bill, and Forster's intervention could only make both these tasks more difficult. It is easy to find excuses for Forster whose noble work in Ireland's service as an agrarian reformer had been forgotten in the odium his coercion had excited, but if he still acknowledged a duty to the nation, that duty should have made him less ready to add to the difficulties of the problem he had left to his successors. He had been treated by Gladstone with great consideration and loyalty as long as he was in office, and he came forward more than once to rebuke Conservatives who alleged that he had been let down by his leader. The fact that he was willing to exasperate this problem still further shows what a moral disturbance he had suffered in the weary and anxious hours during which he had wrestled with his difficulties in Dublin Castle.

The opportunity was seized by Balfour to make an attack on Gladstone which would have attracted notice for its bitterness, even if it had come from a personal enemy. He began with a happy hit from Molière, but as he proceeded his temper got the better of him and he struck at last a blow

---

[1] Curiously enough the version of the letter printed in *Hansard* omits the words " and measures of general reform " after " Liberal principles."

U

that caused Gladstone such pain that he wrote about it to his daughter, for the relations of Balfour and the Gladstone family were intimate.[1]   " I do not believe that any such transaction can be quoted from the annals of our political or parliamentary history. It stands alone—I do not wish to use strong language—it stands alone in its infamy." It is not surprising that even in that bitter House of Commons there were some who remembered that not ten days before an old man had stood at his place at the table, with drawn face and shaking body, whose speech for once was slow and stumbling because to master his words he had first to master his misery.[2] Forster told Balfour he would regret his charge and even the *Times* blamed him for a false note.[3]

To understand the bitterness spread by this suspicion it must be remembered that during the first months of the year the Parnellites and the Conservatives had been drawing together. On March 30 they had combined against the closure Resolution and brought the Government's majority down to thirty-nine. One Conservative member, Sir John Hay, had given notice of a motion for bringing all Forster's suspects to trial. A Conservative Ex-Minister, Sir Richard Cross, had put down an amendment calling for the release of Parnell, Dillon, and O'Kelly. Anybody who had before him all the documents describing and revealing the state of mind of Ministers can see that Gladstone's action was not in any sense influenced by these facts, but a Conservative outsider who heard Forster declaiming against compromises, who had been present at the scene when the full letter from

---

[1] " Are his notions of conduct and social laws turned inside out, since the days when I knew him, enjoyed his hospitality, viewed him with esteem and regard, nay was wont to mate him with the incomparable F. Cavendish, now lost to our eyes but not our hearts, as the flower of rising manhood in the land? "

[2] Hicks Beach wrote to his wife that when he saw the look on Gladstone's face after Cavendish's murder, for the first time he pitied him. *Life*, I, p. 204.

[3] The *Spectator*, then in the hands of R. H. Hutton, observed on this debate (May 20, 1882), " We wonder whether there is a single Tory of any mark who believes genuinely in the ' scandal ' to the so-called exposure to which Monday and Tuesday were devoted." But it is only fair to Balfour to mention that Goschen took in private an equally severe view of Parnell's release. Such was the violence of suspicion. See Fisher, *Bryce*, I, 206.

Parnell was read, might suspect that the old Parliamentary hand had snatched a party advantage. Balfour's speech showed that an uncomfortable sense that his own Fourth Party had been discredited by its approaches to the Parnellites was rankling in his mind when he made his savage attack on Gladstone's conduct.

All this ill will was fomented by the leader of the Conservative party. Salisbury's utterances on Irish policy might be collected to make an anthology of sparkling fallacies. No man was so ready to use his taunting tongue for brilliant mischief. For Salisbury was two men, and Meredith's reflexion about Gladstone, that he excited at once both admiration and contempt, would have applied to his opponent. The trouble about Salisbury was that he was one day the wise and careful Foreign Minister, the best Foreign Minister who served England in his lifetime, thinking of the needs of the future, and another the rash and violent Saturday Reviewer enjoying the excitement of the hour. From the training in bitter and caustic invective he had received on a paper where every pen was a knife, he never recovered. Ireland almost always found him in the second mood and not the first. The *Spectator* compared him at this time to Coriolanus, and the scorn of the Roman recalls the temper of the speeches made by the English patrician on Irish reform. " Let them not lick the sweet that is their poison," and

> " In soothing them we nourish 'gainst our senate
> The cockle of rebellion, insolence, sedition"

are phrases into which could be packed the spirit and substance of all Salisbury's speeches against the Compensation for Disturbance Bill, the Land Bill, and the Bill for the Treatment of Arrears. He now produced an explanation of Gladstone's Irish policy since 1869 which might pass in an irresponsible paragraph under an editor who was only concerned to make somebody smart the next morning. He told his audiences that every step Gladstone had taken, had been taken in order to gain votes; that Disestablishment, the two Land Acts and now the release of Parnell had no deeper or more creditable origin than his greed of office.[1]

It was in this exasperated atmosphere that the Government now entered on its double task. For history was to repeat itself; 1882 was to follow the precedent of 1881, though in this case Coercion and Reform were to proceed side by side. On May 10, directly after the funeral of the murdered Minister, the House met for the introduction by Harcourt of the Coercion Bill. On May 15 Gladstone introduced the Arrears Bill. For the rest of the session the House was immersed in Ireland.

Parnell had expressed the hope in his letter to O'Shea that the reform of the arrears question would make coercion unnecessary. A ruler of imagination might have seen in the Irish outburst of horror and sympathy over the Phoenix Park murders a reason for taking the Arrears Bill first. A leading Irish member said in the House after listening to the debate on Harcourt's Bill that it would have been worth while, when Irish sentiment was in sympathy with English, to give that sentiment fair play. This opportunity had been destroyed by the Bill and by Forster's violent speech in support of it. If this policy looked too romantic, the Government might at least have tried to meet the difficulties of the Irish members, for Parnell showed how ready he was to meet the Government's difficulties by the moderation of his first speech.

" I do not deny that no Government has ever been pressed so much to step aside from the straight path and I do not wonder that they have so stepped aside; but the result they cannot foresee and we cannot be responsible for. . . . Your confident statesmen when they have to come to this House again at the end of twelve months for perhaps more stringent, more determined and more desperate coercion, will have once more to confess that England has not yet discovered the secret of that undiscoverable truth—the task of the government of one nation by another."

Parnell did his best to moderate Irish feeling both in public and behind the scenes. But his task was beyond him. An

[1] After one of Salisbury's outbursts the *Spectator* observed that he had as much chance of becoming leader of the Conservative Party as O'Donovan Rossa. April 23, 1883.

Irish member, referring to Forster's demand that everything should be put aside to pass the Coercion Bill, reminded the House that there were hundreds of innocent men, women, and children starving on the hillsides; a fact of which, as we know from his letters, Forster was aware. But Forster who had never forgotten a poor peasant whom he had seen dying in agony from gunshot wounds, victim of the Land League war, could never speak without bringing violence into a debate. There was this perpetual dividing line in the House of Commons. An Irishman thinking of Ireland thought first in terms of eviction; an Englishman first in terms of outrage. Each side thought the other callous and every debate on coercion soon passed beyond the short reach of reason.

When Harcourt described the Bill he was to introduce, Chaplin remarked that no Coercion Bill had ever been more stringent or severe. In one particular the new form of coercion was an improvement on the old for the power of arbitrary imprisonment was withdrawn. Trial by jury was to be replaced in certain cases by trial by three judges, and the Lord Lieutenant had power to forbid public meetings and to suppress newspapers. Increased powers were given to magistrates for convicting. Incitements to crime could be summarily punished and the police were given extensive powers of search. The impression made by the Bill can be seen by the comments in the *Times* which observed that it could only be justified on the ground of supreme necessity and described the state of Ireland as " veiled civil war." The incapacity of Englishmen to understand the strong and well grounded suspicion of the judges by the Irish members was illustrated by the contention of the same paper that " it cannot be seriously pretended that any innocent man would be placed in peril by having three judges to try him instead of a common jury."

Gladstone was alive to the importance of making the Bill as little provocative as possible.

" I have willingly consented," he wrote to Spencer on May 9th, " to take the question of crime in Ireland at once for Parliamentary handling and I am also quite ready for strong legislation against all capital offences reasonably believed by the Executive to spring out of treasonable or other secret societies.   What I desire to avoid is special legislation, on this occasion against the people of Ireland.   The tide of their feelings is now running in the right direction and we must try not to repress it. . . . We have certainly an opportunity *for* taking hold of Irishmen on their good side such as has never before offered itself to an English Government."

If Gladstone could have had his way the history of the next few years would have been very different.   Unhappily in the struggle that now began between him and Chamberlain on one side and Harcourt on the other, Harcourt was able to defeat his main purpose.   In this struggle Harcourt was helped by the excusable but unfortunate violence of Dillon's speeches, and still more by Irish crime.   For on June 8 an Irish landlord and his escort, a soldier, were murdered near Gort, and a few days later Harcourt announced the discovery of twenty-five cases of revolvers, five barrels of ammunition and other warlike material in a stable in Clerkenwell.   The effect of these events on the temper of the House of Commons is seen in a defeat Gladstone suffered at the hands of his own party.   The new Coercion Bill allowed houses to be searched for arms and Gladstone, after obtaining Spencer's assent (though Harcourt was against the concession), proposed to amend the clause by forbidding search at night except in special circumstances.   Harcourt declined even to be present when the concession was announced, and asked that Gladstone himself or Trevelyan should move the amendment.   Gladstone undertook the duty.   But twenty-five Liberals voted against him and the Government was thus defeated (July 7, 1882) in this attempt to soften its own Bill.[1]   Harcourt was triumphant.

Gladstone and Chamberlain realized as they listened to

---

[1] The *Times* remarked, " The sudden attempt of the Government or rather of the Head of the Government to weaken the Bill in direct opposition to the expressed wish of the Minister in charge of it, met with a sharp and decided defeat, so that for a short time the air was full of rumours of a Ministerial crisis." The votes were 217 to 194.   The Irish did not vote for they had withdrawn in disgust by this time.

Harcourt's defence of the Bill and to Forster's passionate attacks on the Irish that they were in danger of losing all that had been gained by the release of the suspects. "Parnell has thus far run quite true," Gladstone wrote to Spencer on May 24, " but it seems doubtful whether he can hold his ground. The Tories, and I am sorry to add Forster, have done much to increase his difficulties."

Parnell understood the difficulties of the two men who wanted an effective Irish peace and he put his own views of the Bill privately before them. As early as May 16th, Labouchere sent Chamberlain some amendments suggested by Healy, aimed chiefly at what he called " constructive intimidation." These he had discussed with Parnell. " He [Parnell] says that if the Government will meet him and his party in the conciliatory spirit of the amendments, he will promise that the opposition to the Bill shall be conducted on honest Parliamentary lines." Parnell was anxious also that the Bill should be in operation only until the close of the next session.

" He puts this on two grounds: (1) That the Tories may possibly come in at the end of that time. (2) That he may be able to advise the Irish to be quiet in the hopes of no renewal of the Bill. He says that he is in a very difficult position between the Government and the secret societies. . . . I really think that he is most anxious to be able to support the Government; he fully admits that a Bill is necessary on account of English opinion, but he does not wish to have it applied to himself, and he doubts whether it will be really effectual against the outrage mongers. Healy goes so far as to say that if the Prime Minister or you were to administer the Bill it would do no harm, and that he is not greatly afraid of it in the hands of Lord Spencer, but that it would be a monstrous weapon of oppression in the hands of Jim Lowther."[1]

A few days later Parnell took a further and most important step. On May 23, Gladstone received a letter from Mrs. O'Shea asking if he would have a private talk with Parnell.

[1] Thorold, *Life of Labouchere*, p. 161. Dilke says in his Diary that on May 22 Gladstone " was very strongly in favour of accepting Parnell's privately suggested amendments to the New Coercion Bill, obtained through O'Shea, but Hartington going with Harcourt against touching the Bill, Mr. Gladstone got no support except from Chamberlain." *Life*, I, 445.

Mrs. O'Shea was the granddaughter of Sir Matthew Wood, the famous Lord Mayor of London, the ardent friend and champion of Queen Caroline, the first of her subjects to receive an honour from Queen Victoria. Her father, Sir John Page Wood, was chaplain to Queen Caroline and afterwards to the Duke of Sussex; for most of his life he was Rector of St. Peter's, Cornhill. Her uncle, Lord Hatherley, had been Lord Chancellor in Gladstone's Government from 1868 to 1872, being succeeded in that office by Selborne, and one of her brothers was the famous soldier, Sir Evelyn Wood. She was thus well known in English society. Her interest in Irish politics was confined to her interest in her lover's fortunes and her desire for his society.

Gladstone answered this letter and sent a draft of his proposed reply to Granville. His letter was as follows:

10 Downing Street,
Whitehall.
May 23, 1882.

My dear Madam,

I thank you for your very frank letter, and I will be equally frank in reply, nor will I be less secret than you ask of me—no one being aware of your letter but myself.

I have no prejudice, and no recollection, which should hinder my seeing Mr. Parnell for a public object.

I have thought it my duty, ever since arriving at the conclusion that there was no longer any warrant for detaining him within prison doors, carefully to avoid any act or word that could injure his position or weaken his hands in doing good.

But, applying this criterion to your request, I am clearly of opinion, as at present advised, that a private interview between him and myself would have this very effect. It might also impair my means of action, but of this I see less cause to think at the present moment.

On this ground only, and because I can see no countervailing advantage to compensate for a serious mischief, I do not think I ought to see him in the manner you have described.

I remain, my dear Madam,
faithfully yours,
W. E. GLADSTONE.

Mrs. O'Shea replied regretting Gladstone's decision and asking if he would see her and learn from her what Parnell would have liked to say. Gladstone agreed and saw her at Thomas's Hotel in Berkeley Square on June 1. On June 3, Labouchere wrote to Chamberlain urging the exclusion of treason felony from the Bill, and on June 9, O'Shea wrote to Gladstone asking if he might see him. On O'Shea's letter Gladstone's private secretary minuted that he had been told to go to Chamberlain. On June 11, Spencer wrote to Gladstone about the outrages of the secret societies after the murders of the 8th, urging the dangers of delay with the new Coercion Bill. On the 16th, Mrs. O'Shea wrote to Gladstone asking to be allowed either to see him or to send him a proposal. Gladstone replied asking to see the proposal, and on June 17 it was sent.

The events of the next few days are a remarkable revelation of the bad temper that had been created in these weeks and the incapacity of the Government to keep its head and control that temper. From the beginning there had been serious efforts made by a few lawyers on the Liberal side, supported by the *Spectator*, to make the Bill less dangerous to liberty and less obnoxious to Irish sentiment. The Bill had two large objects; one to make it easier to obtain information about the secret societies and to obtain the conviction of guilty persons; the other to prevent incitement and intimidation by speech and writing. The provisions directed to this second purpose went much too far for Liberal minds, and great lawyers like Horace Davey, afterwards Lord of Appeal, Charles Russell, afterwards Chief Justice, Arthur Cohen (afterwards Judge), and Serjeant Simon, together with Bryce, the most distinguished academic lawyer in the House, all criticized the Bill from this point of view, moving amendments and voting against the Government. The mass of the Liberal party seems to have been little moved by their scruples and fears, but Gladstone managed with their help to soften the Bill in some important particulars. Thus a great many of the restrictions on the press were removed; a clause was inserted providing that the intimidation clause should not be so interpreted as to deprive the Irish of such liberties as were secured to the English workman by the Trade Union Act of 1875, and it was stipulated that the magistrates, when administering the Act, should have the assistance of trained assessors.

Gladstone thus contrived to make the Bill a little less obnoxious, and the *Spectator*, which regarded the committee stage as a duel between Gladstone and Harcourt (who had, the editor observed, plenty of courage and sangfroid but cared too little about the abuse of power) congratulated him on his success.   But the very fact that Gladstone secured some improvement of the Bill makes the Government's treatment of Parnell's proposal sent by Mrs. O'Shea on June 17 all the more unintelligible.   For Parnell made an extraordinary offer.   He offered, if Mrs. O'Shea correctly represented him, to withdraw opposition if the Government would make two concessions.[1]   One was to omit treason-felony[2] from the Bill; the other to provide that the duration of the Act should be limited to three months after the assembly of a new Parliament, if the present Parliament were dissolved within three years.   Gladstone, after receiving this offer, put it before Harcourt and Spencer.   On June 17, 1882, he wrote to Harcourt as follows:

" It was I think understood in the Cabinet that the Law Officers were to look into (and) state for us the exact value of the words ' treason felony ' in the Bill and what we should lose by omitting them on report.

" I am of course an ignoramus on the matter but I am very desirous to be informed, not because I have formed any opinion adverse to the words, but simply to know *whether* or not it would be worth while to keep them at a heavy cost or in other words desirable to part with them *if* parting with them were to be productive of great advantage.   I will tell you on Monday my reasons for asking."

The other point about the duration he referred to Spencer, saying that three months was too short, but that otherwise there was much to be said for the proposal.   The real motive was fear of Jim Lowther.

---

[1] On June 22 he would have been satisfied with one concession only.

[2] Certain offences formerly reckoned as treason but not directed at the person of the sovereign nor now punishable with death.

Harcourt replied at once rejecting the proposal. " Even if the legal value of this matter were small I think the political objections to yielding on such a point at this moment are conclusive." He went on to say that public opinion would be greatly exasperated by a large seizure of arms made in London the previous night, that the root of the whole thing was a treasonable conspiracy backed by assassination: the Land League was only the veil; that O'Shea had called on him the previous day and told him that Labouchere was the main source of obstruction and that he, Harcourt, gathered that the Irish wanted an " excuse to collapse." Spencer cabled on June 19, the next day, " I have strong objections as to suggested proposal; and regret I do not see how I could assent to it. Besides other reasons, the uncertainty created in Irish minds would be mischievous. I decidedly prefer even delay of Bill to the acceptance of the proposal."

The opinions of a Minister in charge of a Bill and of a Viceroy responsible for order in time of disturbance must always carry exceptional weight, but the acceptance of these objections must be counted Gladstone's chief tactical blunder in this disastrous summer. Harcourt was in this case against Davey, Bryce, Cohen, Serjeant Simon, and Charles Russell. In what state was he to judge the proposal? Two days before (June 16) he had written to Gladstone about the obstruction in Parliament: " These men are not only *sans loi* but *sans foi* and the more concessions that are made the less is the progress accomplished." Spencer was under the shadow of a crisis for two days (on June 17) before he had written, " We have general information from sources which have been generally correct, that a great blow is to be struck, many say on the 20th, probably by some concerted murders of officials or others in different places, or by some dynamite operations." It was hardly likely that a man with this on his mind would be able to think out all the consequences of the decision to repel Parnell. Of those consequences Gladstone himself could appreciate the importance, for on June 9th he had written to Granville:

" My opinion is that if Parnell goes, no restraining influence will remain; the *scale* of outrage will again be enlarged, and no repression Bill can avail to put it down.   The wretched murders yesterday have produced a temper in the House of Commons which would lead them to vote almost anything we ask however strongly; but this in truth is a danger as well as a temptation."

Why then did Gladstone accept defeat?   The answer is to be found probably in the account given by Harcourt, writing to Spencer on June 12, of the battle fought in the Cabinet on the preceding Saturday between himself and Chamberlain.[1] " In spite of some disposition in one influential quarter to support the other side," Harcourt had gained the day. Harcourt had stood out successfully against any negotiations. " If any other decision had been arrived at I would no longer have taken any responsibility for the Bill, and I believe the greater part of the Cabinet shared my determination." Thus, at the time Gladstone put Parnell's offer before Harcourt and Spencer, the Cabinet had already taken a fatal decision and Gladstone had no hope of carrying any proposal that was not supported by these two colleagues, one of them a die hard.   Whether under these conditions any good purpose was served by his interviews and correspondence with Mrs. O'Shea may be doubted.

The Irish did not think that they could be expected to give more consideration than they had received, and whereas in the early stages Parnell had regretted and blamed the violence of Dillon, in the later the whole party went into strenuous opposition.   This in turn exasperated Ministers, and even Chamberlain lost patience.   Writing to the slippery O'Shea on June 28, Chamberlain said:

" Your letter of the 28th and the previous one on the same subject fully justify the confidence I have always felt in your good faith and honour.   I wish I could say the same of Mr. Parnell's conduct, which is most disappointing to me. . . . I consider he is bound, in honour, to make a public effort to bring the debates in Committee on the Crimes Bill to a close. . . ."

Mr. Garvin points out that there was no pledge binding Parnell to accept increased and unprecedented coercion in Harcourt's sense, and that none of Chamberlain's constituents were in danger from the Bill.[2]   Parnell might have retorted

[1] Gardiner's *Life*, I, p. 446.   [2] *Life of Chamberlain*, I, 373.

that if the Government had listened to him on the Arrears question in 1881 they would not now be engaged in making the reform he had then pressed upon them, and that in that case the disorder that had made it necessary to pass a coercion Bill would not have arisen. He would have been fortified in such an answer by the comments on June 17 of the *Spectator* on a speech made by Trevelyan in the House of Commons, a speech which attracted the hostile notice of the Queen. Trevelyan stated that some 500 or 600 persons were being evicted every week, and the *Spectator* called on the Government either to lop off all provisions in the Crimes Bill that were not necessary, or else to proceed at once with the Arrears Bill and put the Crimes Bill on one side till that Bill had become law.

The history of this struggle in the Government is like the history of the last. Then Chamberlain, Gladstone, and Bright, were engaged against Forster and were beaten. Now Chamberlain and Gladstone were engaged against Harcourt, and they were beaten. Harcourt was so self-confident that he upheld his own favourable view of the resident magistrates against Gladstone, though Gladstone could quote against him the opinion both of Spencer and Forster.[1] Spencer, though he did not go so far as Harcourt, was nearer to him than to Gladstone, and his Whig fears were stiffened by his dislike of Chamberlain. If the Cabinet had been less illiberal a Bill might have been passed that would have satisfied the needs of order and yet not put the Irish people in revolt again. But the Whigs were indifferent to this prospect so distressing to Gladstone and Chamberlain. As Harcourt wanted the Arrears Bill to be defeated, it is easy to understand that he welcomed every opportunity of exasperating the Irish party over his Coercion Bill.

Fortunately, if Harcourt got his way on Coercion,

[1] The *Spectator* criticizing the proposal to put so much power in the hands of the resident magistrates remarked, " Say what we will the Magistrates belong to a caste who feel very little sympathy with the people; they are not highly trained lawyers; they are not, as a rule, persons of judicial mind, and they are pretty certain, without intending it, to strain the interpretation of an ill defined offence in a manner that may prove exceedingly injurious to the right of political combination." June 10, 1882.

Gladstone got his way on Arrears. Harcourt wrote to him, on July 9, with the confidence he always felt in his opinion on Irish questions, to say that nobody in Ireland cared about the Bill, that it would perish certainly in the House of Lords or possibly in the House of Commons, and that there remained only one remedy for Ireland, " and that is in the most resolute and sternest determination to enforce the law and to exercise to the utmost the powers of repression." Gladstone circulated these observations in the Cabinet. " I might have been more struck with Harcourt's letter if it had not been so like Lord Salisbury's speech of this afternoon," was Granville's reply. Carlingford dissented utterly from Harcourt's despairing view. Selborne on the other hand remarked that he wished there were less ground for Harcourt's letter than he feared there was. " I acquiesced, not without difficulty, in the lines on which it [the Arrears Bill] is drawn; and, having done so, I must abide by what the Cabinet has decided, or may decide." The Cabinet, though they had supported Harcourt against Chamberlain on Coercion, were not prepared to agree with his view that Disestablishment and the Land Act had been " worse than useless " and encouraged disorder. So the Government held on its course and the Arrears Bill became law by August, a month after the Coercion Bill.

The Arrears Bill followed the lines of the Parnell proposal. The Bill, which applied only to holdings valued on Griffith's valuation at £30 or under, provided that if the tenant paid one year's arrears and satisfied the Land Commissioners that he could not pay his antecedent arrears, the State would make a gift to the landlord of half the arrears and the rest were to be cancelled. The money required for the purpose was to be provided out of the Irish Church Fund supplemented if necessary from the Exchequer. The scheme was compulsory on both landlord and tenant. Gladstone in introducing the Bill pointed out that the permissive arrangement provided in the Act of 1881 had failed, that vast numbers of tenants could not use the Act because they were overwhelmed by debts that they could not pay, that they were threatened with eviction on a large scale, and that this was an obstacle both

to the success of the Land Act and to the preservation of
order.   In the course of his speech he let fall one of those
moral observations that showed the Irish that he could
see their history with Irish eyes.   " Eviction in the
exercise of a legal right may be to the prejudice of
your neighbours, may involve the highest reprehension,
may even imply deep moral guilt.   There may be outrages
which—all things considered—the persons and the facts—
may be less guilty in the sight of God than evictions."

The Bill was fiercely attacked by the Opposition.   Chaplin
called it confiscation; Hicks Beach an encouragement to lawlessness; Balfour a Bill to pauperize the tenants of Ireland by
remitting debts that ought to be paid in full.   All of these
speakers ignored the truth that the Bill was like Solon's
seissachtheia; a bill to relieve a burden of debt that was
crushing a society.   Trevelyan in a most telling speech
pointed out that tenants were being evicted in great numbers,
who were as little able to pay the arrears of three bad
years as to pay the National Debt.   Seven hundred
and fifty persons had been turned out of their homes in
three days in Connemara.   There were estates on
which arrears were outstanding since 1847.   The
second reading was carried on May 23, 1882, by 269
votes to 157, but on one important division there was a
serious drop in the majority.   On July 6, Chaplin's motion
for rejection when going into Committee was supported by
208 votes to 283.   On the third reading on July 21 the
party recovered its strength, the opposition being defeated
by 285 to 177.

In the Lords, Salisbury said common honesty demanded
that the Bill should only be applied with the consent of the
landlord.   Carlingford and Derby both pointed out that
this would destroy the Bill.   They had an unexpected ally
in Lansdowne, whose support was specially valuable as he
had left Gladstone over his first Land Bill.   In spite of Lansdowne's support the Government were defeated by 169 to
98.   When the Lords' amendments came before the
Commons Gladstone stood firm.   It looked as if the House
of Lords would act again as it had acted in the case of the

Compensation for Disturbance Bill. But in this case Gladstone was resolved to fight it out at the polls, and he wrote to Harcourt asking him to discuss with the Law Officers the arrangements for a dissolution. The Lords however gave way. The pressure of the Irish landlords was strong, for they knew that under the Bill many landlords would get two years' rent who otherwise would get no rent at all. Salisbury made a last fling. The Bill was a most pernicious Bill; an act of simple robbery. But he had consulted the Peers who had carried his amendment, and he found that they thought that in consequence of the state of affairs in Ireland and Egypt it was not expedient that the Arrears Bill should be thrown out. " I do not share in the opinion. If I had the power I would have thrown out the Bill." It is easy to understand the difficulties Gladstone had to overcome in pushing his agrarian reforms through Parliament when it is realized that politicians who knew nothing of Ireland were so ready to overrule those who knew a good deal. It was not likely that any upper class Englishman or Irishman would start with much sympathy with this revolutionary Bill. Yet the Arrears Bill was regarded as necessary by Carlingford who had been Chief Secretary in 1870, by Cowper and Forster, the late Viceroy and Chief Secretary, by Spencer and Trevelyan, the present Viceroy and Chief Secretary, and by Lansdowne, a great Irish landowner to whom Gladstone's temperament and convictions were alike obnoxious. Selborne who disliked it had no experience of Irish administration. The men who opposed it were men like Salisbury who had never had anything to do with an Irish measure and looked back regretfully to the age of Palmerston, and Harcourt who once boasted that he had never set foot in Ireland.

The first two Land Acts, 1870 and 1881, had been disappointing in their immediate results. The third Act, the Arrears Act of 1882, succeeded at once. Lord Monck, a man of great experience both at home and in the Colonies, was appointed an additional Land Commissioner to administer the Act. Out of 135,997 claims under the Act no less than 129,952 were allowed. The Act contained another provision which was much less agreeable to the Parnellites. This was a clause making a grant of £100,000 on which Boards of Guardians could draw to help tenants who wished to emigrate. The Irish members obtained an amendment restricting the amount of help to be given to an individual emigrant to £5. Under this arrangement some 20,000 poor emigrants left Ireland.

The agreement for a drastic settlement of this question under which Parnell had left prison was thus carried out by the Government, and the results that Parnell had expected followed the reform. In another sense, too, the transaction was completely justified by the event.

Gladstone had believed that it would be easier to keep order in Ireland if Parnell left Kilmainham for the House of Commons. Two days after his release the great hopes based on the new policy were shattered by the murders in Phoenix Park. In a few days the House of Commons was ringing once again with party strife, and Forster was denouncing Parnell as bitterly as if the Wexford speech was not months old but an outburst of yesterday. Then followed weeks of bitter argument over the new Coercion Bill, in the course of which Harcourt indulged to the full his dislike of the Irish leaders and the Irish people. The Irish members had good ground for disappointment and resentment. Yet Parnell kept his head and kept his word. His behaviour in Ireland in the next few months is perhaps the finest proof of his capacity for leadership.

Parnell, as we have already said, had made a serious attempt to come to terms with the Government over the Coercion Bill, an attempt which was rebuffed. Gladstone, who had been overruled, told Mrs. O'Shea on June 23 that it was useless to continue the correspondence.

" Reflecting on the subject, I have come to the conclusion that there would be no advantage in my calling on you again with reference to the Crimes Prevention Bill. I have had much at heart the purpose of expediting proceedings on this Bill, in order that we might go forward with the Arrears Bill, and with other business, of which also part is Irish: but I have failed: and the loss of time on the Crime Bill will be I fear repeated and cumu-

X

lated by a similar loss on the Bill which follows it, and which appears to be menaced with obstinate resistance. All that remains to me is to work for the best on each case as it arises, with a steady aim at the good of all classes of the community. When the present strain is relaxed, there may be greater freedom of communication, with less suspicion."

But Mrs. O'Shea was not easily discouraged. She asked on June 26 that she should not be " boycotted," and sent a message from Parnell to the effect that though the Coercion Bill would probably make it impossible for him to take further part in the Irish Land movement, he still hoped to be able to co-operate over land legislation and other measures of general reform. But Gladstone sent a depressing answer (June 29), " The news of another double murder in Galway again darkens the horizon. This exacerbation of the Fenian passion is terrible.

"I do not doubt that your friend does all he can, and I observe that what we may call ordinary outrage declines. . . .

"But these savage murders exhibit an open unstaunched source of mischief which goes far to destroy all confidence.

"I am afraid the Irish World party are not without complicity.

"Time too slips away. ' When is the Arrears Bill to become law? ' I ask myself in vain."

(On Friday, June 30, scenes of obstruction ended in the suspension of twenty-five Irish members.)

Through July, August, and September, Mrs. O'Shea continued to write, explaining Parnell's position, and making suggestions for co-operation. On August 29 she obtained an interview (the second of the three occasions on which she saw Gladstone[1]) of which Gladstone sent a full account the same day, to Spencer. " Davitt and Dillon," she had explained, " are both in great dudgeon with Parnell by reason of his restricted action on the land and national questions. She speaks of him as thoroughly bent on legality (which I tell her is the whole question) and does not say they are otherwise; but she impeaches Davitt for vanity and Dillon for being a *tête montée*." A sentence from

[1] The third meeting was on Sept. 14, 1882.

a letter of Parnell's which she sent on September 12 (which is also printed in her *Life of Parnell*) gives the situation as Parnell saw it.

" Some recognition ought to be extended to those who have done so much to restore peace in Ireland during the last few months and who are willing and *anxious* to do more if the Irish Government gives a chance by the Suspension of proceedings which are alike irritating to the popular mind and destructive of that understanding between the Irish members and the Liberal Party (so necessary for the stability of the latter and for the carrying of measures of reform").

Mrs. O'Shea's efforts were not confined to explaining Parnell's position. She took the opportunity to press O'Shea as a successor to Hamilton, as Under Secretary. (O'Shea himself was quite aware of her dealings with Gladstone. " I see G.O.M. got back to town yesterday," he wrote to his wife on August 26, " but I daresay he smells a rat and will not see you yet awhile. . . . I am greatly afraid the G.O.M. will leave us in the lurch.")

Spencer, to whom all Mrs. O'Shea's letters were sent, made short work of this proposal.

" I cannot for a moment conceive it possible," he wrote on August 31, " to entertain the idea of O'Shea being fitted to succeed Hamilton.

" The Post is one which requires the highest administrative qualities of an experienced Official, and if I were to judge of Captain O'Shea from the volumes of letters which he pours in to the Chief Secretary and to myself on every conceivable subject, I can hardly think of a man more unfitted for the Place.

" But I do not understand you to be of a different opinion: it is quite right that Mrs. O'Shea should have unbounded faith in her husband."[1]

Communications of any kind with Parnell seemed to Spencer undesirable and even dangerous.

" I am unpleasantly struck by Mrs. O'Shea's letter," he wrote on September 18.

" I confess that interesting as it is to get at the opinions of a man

[1] Gladstone thought that O'Shea deserved some reward for his services and recommended his claims to Ministers who had patronage at their disposal, in a Memorandum on November 3, but without result.

like Parnell on these subjects I feel that it is playing with edged tools, and entering into indirect communication with one who indirectly by his own confession has influence with the worst men in the Kingdom, those who can stop or commit atrocious murders."

Gladstone's answer to this letter was written next day, September 19.

" I will only say on your letter of yesterday that I for one cannot take exception to your view of Parnell (you are aware that Mrs. O'Shea's communications are wholly uninvited).

" My own opinion is pretty distinct to the effect

" That he fomented outrage under the No Rent manifesto for a considerable time, perhaps not with direct knowledge about the Secret Societies.

" That when he made up his mind that the Land Act would win the day, he determined to bow his neck to facts and no longer encourage crimes which would not attain the desired end.

" That since his liberation he has acted on this basis with as much consistency as he could, and has endeavoured to influence his friends in the same sense."

Spencer made another protest on September 25: " I return Mrs. O'Shea's letters. I wish she would not write to you. I quite dread the fact of her communications leaking out. I say this knowing she writes without your invitation." To this Gladstone replied on September 26: " Some time ago I signified to Mrs. O'Shea that we had better not meet again. Her letters I cannot controul but do not encourage. I think she has been of some use in keeping Parnell on the lines of moderation: and I imagine he prefers the wife to the husband as an organ."

On October 6, as on June 17, an exceedingly important offer from Parnell was sent through Mrs. O'Shea, and again Gladstone was overruled by his colleagues and forced to send a cold answer. Parnell suggested a method of settling the Land question in Ireland. All Irish Bills should be referred to a Grand Committee of the Chief Secretary, the Law Officers for Ireland and all the Irish members, the Committee stage in the whole House should be, as a rule, dispensed with, and a Bill to amend the Land Act should be introduced next session by the Irish members and read a second time by aid of the Closure, giving the Land Commission further powers of staying proceedings, breaking leases, and dealing with questions of improvement, etc. " If he were assured that this programme were likely to meet the views of the Government, he would feel justified in urging his party to support the Closure and other proposals of the Government." Parnell was anxious for an answer before speaking at the Convention on October 17.

Gladstone drafted at once a guarded but friendly letter in answer (October 7):

" I will make known the purport of your communication and its inclosure to one or two of my colleagues, without waiting for the assembling of the Cabinet which may not be for a fortnight.

" I do not think that the Government would consent to mix together the questions of Irish Land and Procedure. Were they known to do so, the fact of such a *tack* would injure, in the view of Parliament and the country generally, any proposals which they might make on either subject.

" As regards the points still remaining open under the Land Act, I think those interested in them should for the moment estimate our probable future conduct by what is known of the past, whether for evil or for good. As regards procedure, it is certainly my personal opinion that, in any plan of Devolution which Parliament ought or is likely to adopt, regard should be had to the local principle, and a reasonable scope be given to it. One of the powerful arguments in favour of such plans is their tendency to promote the passing of measures in which particular parts of the United Kingdom are particularly interested.

" In sending you this limited reply, I allow myself the satisfaction of acknowledging the spirit and intent of the memorandum which, in the exercise of his right, as a member of Parliament, Mr. Parnell has framed and transmitted."

But this limited reply did not meet with approval from two of the colleagues to whom it and Mrs. O'Shea's communication were sent. On Sunday, October 8, Granville wrote to Gladstone: " My dear Gladstone, I fancied that you had already put an end to the correspondence with Mrs. O'Shea. I quite agree that Dick Grosvenor would be the right channel.

"Would not the first two paragraphs of your answer be sufficient, if there is an objection to your replying to the present communication through Grosvenor.

"Spencer is here, and agrees that the remainder of the letter goes further than is prudent in a communication from you to Mrs. O'Shea.

"I will send on the correspondence to Hartington."

On receipt of this letter Gladstone altered his draft letter. He did not strike out the third paragraph as Granville and Spencer suggested, he merely altered "regard should be had" to "regard may be had" and inserted a "may" after "reasonable scope." But the last pleasant paragraph he cut out, substituting for it:

"I am doubtful whether the circuitous mode of communication which you have so kindly favoured, may not lead if it were to become known to suspicion and misapprehension. And I am inclined to think that, if Mr. Parnell in the exercise of his discretion is disposed at any time to make a communication to the Government, the best channel would be that which is also the most usual, viz., the channel supplied by the intervention of my friend Lord R. Grosvenor."

After drafting the new letter Gladstone the same day, October 10, wrote to Granville:

"I have struck out the last or complimentary paragraph of my letter to Mrs. O'Shea, in deference to your and Spencer's opinion (for I do not think it exceptionable): and I have substituted a paragraph proposing that in future R. Grosvenor should be the medium of intercourse if any be desired.

"I would not strike out (but have a little qualified) the paragraph about the local principle, for without it the letter would have been hardly civil and absolutely repellent. I feel quite certain that the local principle is essential to any scheme of devolution: and I have only given it as my personal opinion.

"In my opinion Parnell has behaved on the whole well for the last five months, and his improved behaviour has been of real value to the cause of law and order."

This chilling answer to Parnell's overtures was duly sent (with a further slight qualification in the third paragraph adding after "plan of Devolution" the words "if the plan is to have any pretension to completeness "). Had another member of the Cabinet to whom the correspondence was sent had his way the letter would have been decidedly uncivil and repellent. Hartington earnestly hoped that the letter had not gone, for he objected to any private communications with Parnell:

" I go further than Granville," he wrote on October 14, "in deprecating any such communications even through Trevelyan or R. Grosvenor. . . . I venture to think that there exists now no sufficient reason for any communication with Parnell, other than across the floor of the House, either as to Procedure, or as to amendment of the Land Act; and I sincerely hope that no legislation on the latter subject may be necessary in the next Session. It further appeared to me that some of Parnell's suggestions were of so objectionable (a) character, that I should regret even a simple acknowledgment of them without a protest."

Gladstone's answer to this was emphatic. He refused to make private communications from Parnell impossible.

" The reply to Mrs. O'Shea," he wrote, " is gone, with modifications, and with a paragraph proposing that any further communication, should there be such, should come through another channel.

" My recollection about the Cabinet is that there was informal conversation about it, but not any decision of any kind; much less that no communication should at any time be held with Parnell except across the table.

" In my opinion, as a general rule, every member of Parliament is entitled to make communications to the Government, at any time, and even though he be in avowed opposition to it; the exceptions to this rule, if any, would I think have to be founded on very definite grounds. I hold advisedly that this is a *right* of a member of Parliament as such, and not a mere matter of policy. I cannot help thinking you may be inclined to allow some force to the consideration of the character with which a member of Parliament as such is invested.

" I think with you it would be very advantageous if Parliament could let Irish land lie fallow for a season. I should be glad, however, if circumstances were to allow of the passing of a good measure for local Government in Ireland next year."

Mrs. O'Shea received the redrafted answer to Parnell's

suggestions and only observed in reply that it had taken her nearly two years to penetrate Parnell's reserve and his suspicion of the Saxon, and to detach him from the undesirable set by whom he was surrounded. She also enclosed telegrams from him sent shortly before the Convention of October 17, promising not " to be drawn or pushed beyond the limit of prudence and legality."

Gladstone's view of Parnell's intentions was correct and it was a calamity that his colleagues prevented him from turning them to account. He was using his influence steadily to discourage outrage and to keep the Irish agitation on constitutional lines. He lost in consequence the support of the Irish World and Patrick Ford. He regained his control of the Irish movement by setting up the Irish National League in October, 1882, with four objects, three of them political; the restitution of the Irish Parliament; the establishment of local government on a popular basis; franchise reform. The other reforms were agrarian ; Land Purchase; the amendment of the Healy clause of the Land Act and the inclusion of leaseholders under the Act, and legislation to improve the housing and other conditions of the labourers. Davitt who was dissatisfied with Parnell's programme, refused to use his great influence in America against him and gave him his loyal support. Under his influence outrages declined. Eversley gives the figures:

" It is to be observed that in the last half of 1882, agrarian outrages were, month by month, greatly and progressively reduced. The average of such offences, including threatening letters, for the first five months was 462. For the next two months it was 257. For the next three months there was a further drop to an average of 139, and for the last two months of the year, generally the worst for such cases, the average was only 89, and this low rate was maintained during the next two years."[1]

No doubt the credit for the improvement must be divided between the Coercion Act, the arrears reform, and the conduct of Parnell. But nobody can refuse credit to Parnell who had put down the Ladies' League and re-established

[1] *Gladstone and Ireland*, p. 246.

his authority. After the Home Rule split, in 1886, his old colleagues accused Gladstone of changing his mind about Parnell. There are several letters of his among the Gladstone papers to show how false was the charge. Gladstone changed his mind in 1882. From that time he held the view that Parnell was an influence for peace.

Parnell thus proved, as Gladstone had expected, a support to the cause of order in Ireland, and in this sense Forster was shown to be wrong and Gladstone right. The idea that he had been let out to support the Liberal party in the House of Commons, repudiated by Gladstone, but believed by some of his opponents in consequence of O'Shea's blunders, was also completely discredited by the event. In November, 1885, somebody prepared for Gladstone a list of the important divisions in which the Irish party had voted with the Opposition. There were no such cases in 1880 and 1881. In November, 1882, they voted with the Conservatives against the Government on the closure resolution; in 1883 on Balfour's amendment to the address on Egypt and the Oaths Bill; in 1884 on the Votes of Censure on the Sudan and Gordon; in 1885 on five important occasions. Thus, if Gladstone had released Parnell, expecting his support in the lobbies when his Government was in danger, he would have had reason to be disappointed with the result. But though he more than once praised Parnell for playing fair in his treatment of Irish agitation, he never complained of his conduct in trying, and at last with success, to destroy his Government.

Gladstone's belief that it would be easier to govern Ireland and to make the necessary reforms in her government with Parnell in the House of Commons, than with Parnell in Kilmainham jail, proved to be right. Unfortunately, the good results for which he looked were not achieved. At the beginning of April, 1882, everything was in train for Irish reform; Land Purchase and Provincial Councils. At the end of April, 1882, everything was in train for a new relationship with the most powerful Irish party, which would make it far easier to put down disorder and govern Ireland on constitutional principles. In June, 1885, Gladstone went out of office without Land Purchase, without Provincial Councils, after three more years of office in which all his hopes of co-operation with the Irish members in the government of Ireland had been baulked. What were the causes of this failure?

CHAPTER XVII

THE MAAMTRASNA MURDERS

THE FAILURE OF 1883

In August, 1882, a crime was committed in the wild mountains of Connemara which had almost as much importance as the murders in Phoenix Park. It is worth while to study its circumstances and its consequences, for they illustrate vividly the nature of the problem set to Gladstone's Government in 1882 and the reason why it was left unsolved when he went out of office in 1885.[1]

On the 8th of that month a number of men entered a house by night to murder not a single man but a whole family. The father, mother, and three children were killed; one young son survived his wounds and recovered. About the motive of a crime which, as Davitt said, was " almost without a parallel for its atrocity in the annals of agrarian outrage " there is room for doubt. Some six months earlier two bailiffs had been murdered and their bodies, tied in sacks, had been thrown into Lough Mask. Davitt believed that one member of the murdered family was supposed to know something about the crime and that the assassins had decided to destroy the whole family in order to bury the deadly secret.[2] Parnell gave a different account. In a debate in the House of Commons two years later he said that the murdered man was the treasurer of a Ribbon Society who had been accused of making away with some of the funds and that he was involved in consequence in a quarrel with other members of the society.[3] To

---

[1] Readers of Trollope's last and unfinished novel, *The Land Leaguers*, will remember that these murders are described in its pages.

[2] *Fall of Feudalism*, p. 381.

[3] H. of C., October 21, 1884.

Englishmen it was a most confusing story. The victims, and most of the men accused of the crime, were all called Joyce; those not called Joyce were almost all called Casey. None of them spoke English. The quarrels of the little secret society were complicated by other quarrels over sheep, for all these peasants had rights of pasturage in the mountains, causing frequent and violent disputes among them.

The murdered and the murderers were all living in conditions hardly to be matched this side of the Balkans. Here is the account given by the *Times* of the house in which the murders were committed.

" His home was a building of about twelve feet square, absolutely destitute of anything that could be called furniture. A hole in the wall served at once for chimney, window and ventilator. The fire was made by burning peat on the floor. In this miserable den lived six human beings, or when all were at home, seven. Their sustenance was derived from a bit of land for which they paid a rent of six pounds per annum together with the right of grazing a couple of cows on a mountain side."[1]

A month after the murder, Spencer rode over these mountains and sent Gladstone an account of his travels (September 20, 1882). " The degradation of the poor people living in the hovels which we visited is terrible. The house where the Maamtrasna murders took place would not be used for pigs in England."

Here then was one element in the Irish problem; the problem of a destitute peasantry. But destitution was not the whole of the agrarian problem.

Spencer then went on to describe the peasants of Arran whom he visited on the same tour:

" Arran was very curious. The people much better off there, indeed their cottages were equal to those I have seen in Perthshire, and the people looked well dressed and well fed. They have however been very turbulent, have not paid rent and thrown cattle and sheep valued at £900 over the Cliffs within the last year or so."

Thus, apart from the destitution problem, there was the

[1] The *Times*, August 12, 1882.

problem of the agrarian war and the " black and savage atrocity of mind," as Burke would call it, left by its passions and memories. Davitt, who, if the Die Hards Liberal and Tory had had their way would have spent his whole life in prison, had written about such outrages a few months before the Maamtrasna murders. " No injustice in the power of Irish landlordism to perpetuate upon our people can justify in the least degree the unfeeling brutality which inflicts injuries on harmless and defenceless animals in return for wrongs done to man." Here then were two problems; destitution and agrarian strife.

The next thing to note is that after the Maamtrasna trial had been held at Dublin by a special jury the verdict gave at first satisfaction to the Government's strongest critics. O'Brien's hostile paper *United Ireland* remarked, " We believe the public are satisfied that a disgusting butchery has been avenged upon convincing evidence by juries comparatively fairly chosen."[1] The same paper said that there were at least five or six Catholic jurors in the box. The evidence on which three men were hanged and five were sent to penal servitude for life was the evidence of two brothers, supported by the son of one of the two, who asserted that they had seen the murderers and had followed them, without being detected, for a considerable distance. Of the accused, two turned approvers or King's evidence. The five men whose death sentence was commuted to penal servitude all pleaded guilty on the advice of a friendly priest. The Irish members asserted that the accusers and some of the accused were bitter personal enemies.

This was not a case of the murder of a landlord or agent or of a tenant who had taken a farm from which another tenant had been evicted; it was the murder of one set of peasants by another in the course of something like a tribal quarrel. The oaths, perjuries, accusations and confessions through which the Court was taken in its search for the truth were the oaths, perjuries, accusations and confessions of men among whom, so far as the Government or the British people were concerned, there was no reason to distinguish one from another. The

[1] Quoted by Trevelyan in debate, October 21, 1884.

ordinary motives that made all Irish justice look like British oppression were absent. Yet this case became one of the burning grievances of Ireland and in the autumn of 1884 it occupied no less than four days of the time of Parliament. It became in fact a political event of high importance influencing, as we shall see later, the fortunes of both English parties and the course of Irish history.

The trouble over the case arose in a characteristic way. It was whispered that more than once when going his rounds in the prison a warder had seen the ghost of Miles Joyce, one of the three men who had been hanged. It then became known that after their conviction the two other men had admitted their own guilt but had exonerated Miles Joyce, and that Miles Joyce himself had died protesting his innocence.[1] Suspicion was excited and some Irish M.P.'s went to Connemara to inspect the scene of the murders. After seeing the country, they found cause for doubting the story of the men whose account of their own movements on the night of the 18th of August, when following the murderers, had been accepted by the Court. Then followed another characteristic Irish incident. An Irish barrister found thrown away on one side in a room in Green Street Court-house, Dublin, a number of Crown briefs and among them the briefs for the prosecution in this case. When these documents were examined, it became clear that papers that should have been shown to the defence had been withheld. An agitation was set on foot and other grounds for complaint were soon discovered. For the only survivor had been kept out of court on the ground that he was not in a condition to give evidence, though the statement he made when describing the dress and appearance of the assassins discredited the story of the accusers.

At last something happened that for most Catholic minds was decisive. A mission or revival was being held in the parish in which one of the two approvers lived.

---

[1] An account of the executions is given by an eyewitness, the only English journalist present. He says that Miles Joyce " a younger man of comely features of the Spanish type common in his native valley " bore himself with courage but protested his innocence in a vehement speech in Gaelic. The other two made no protest. See *The Vivid Life* by F. J. Higginbottom, p. 42.

This man named Casey startled the crowded church by standing up with a lighted candle in his hand and confessing that he had given false evidence. Miles Joyce, he said, was innocent as well as the three men who were serving sentences of penal servitude. Describing his crime, he brought a terrible charge against the prosecution, alleging that when he turned approver he was told that unless he denounced Miles Joyce as well as the other prisoners his evidence would not be accepted, that in other words he could only save his skin if, after committing one murder by violence, he committed another by perjury. The Archbishop of Tuam who was present at the scene sent the confession to Spencer who promised to hold an inquiry. Spencer himself, as we know from a letter of his to Gladstone, had not approved of the way in which the law officers had managed the prosecution, but his inquiry satisfied him that no injustice had been done and that the charge brought by Casey was false.

These were the facts that formed the subject of a long debate in the House of Commons in October 1884, when Timothy Harrington reviewed the conduct of the trials in a powerful speech. His contention that the venue should not have been changed from Galway to Dublin will not impress those who read Parnell's account of the local animosities, but he put the general case against the methods of the prosecution with effective moderation. He and his colleagues could not accept the results of Spencer's inquiry as satisfactory, for they maintained that Spencer had really done little more than refer the complaints to Brady the R.M. and Bolton the solicitor for the prosecution, the men whose conduct had been impugned. Healy pointed out that Brady was new to his work and that he did not know Irish, the only language the prisoners spoke. The first form of the amendment to the Address was softened down to a demand for an inquiry by a Select Committee and in this form it received the support of Charles Russell, afterwards Chief Justice and three important Conservative members, Randolph Churchill, Gorst, and Sir Edward Clarke.

The most violent speech in the debate was made by Clarke,

who used startling language about Bolton. Bolton was the
solicitor who, if Casey spoke the truth when he made his confession in church, had given Casey twenty minutes in which
to make up his mind either to denounce Miles Joyce as well as
the other prisoners, or stand his own trial. " Discredited as
Casey had been and infamous as a witness, he did not think
that the balance would be greatly in favour of Mr. Bolton."
The *Times*, commenting on the debate, admitted that it
would have been more satisfactory if Bolton's private character had been above suspicion, but tried to take the sting out
of Clarke's attack by pointing out that in two libel actions
he had brought against O'Brien's paper, Bolton had successfully defended his integrity as a public official.[1] The debate
lasted four days. The Solicitor General for Ireland made a
bad and violent speech, but the case for the Government
was put with effect by Trevelyan, Harcourt, the Attorney
General (Henry James), and Gladstone himself. They
refused to admit that Spencer's inquiry had been superficial,
and they pressed the strong general objections to making the
House of Commons a court of appeal. Though they were
not supported by their party, the intervention of Churchill
and his friends had most important consequences later.
For the rest the debate, though it satisfied the House of
Commons, had done nothing to satisfy Ireland.

In the House of Commons Gladstone had stood by colleagues whom he trusted, but he was less at his ease about the
case than his Attorney General and his Home Secretary.
Before the debate, according to Healy, he had sent for Peter
O'Brien, the Attorney General who had conducted the case.[2]
After the debate he wrote to James (October 29) to ask
whether there was " an unexceptionable method such as that
suggested by C. Russell and (I understand) by Gorst in
to-day's *Times* which might be accepted for further judicial
action of any kind." Gorst had argued that the three men
who were still in the convict prison had been tried for the
murder of one man and had pleaded guilty. It was possible
then to re-open the question by trying them on a different

---

[1] October 28, 1884.
[2] Healy, *Letters and Leaders of my Day*, p. 106.

charge, that of murdering one of the other victims. It is perhaps not surprising that James gave Gladstone no encouragement and that he saw "almost insuperable difficulties both technical and substantial in the way of constituting an inquiry of the character suggested by you." He pointed out that the state of excitement in Ireland would render any trial of these men by jury at present almost valueless. The question had a grave bearing on the position not only of Spencer but on that of the Government at home.

Spencer wrote at the same time (November 4, 1884) to say that the Irish Lord Chancellor and Irish Attorney General agreed with James and Harcourt and that he concurred in their opinion.

" I do not think that there is any ground whatever for re-opening the case and I feel that to do so would be disastrous to the future administration of the law of Ireland. I am sorry to say that I am convinced that the Irish members of extreme views are determined, if possible, to make English Government in Ireland impossible. Their attacks on the decisions of the Courts is part of this policy. The Maamtrasna case was their chief point of attack, but it is only one of several. They showed reason for doubt in one case (Kilmartin) and without having any fault to find with the conviction I gave the prisoner the benefit of the doubt. They are making similar attacks in a Clare case (Delahuxby), the Barbarilla case, the Crosmaglen case without any such reason. I am bound carefully to examine each memorial, but they are not satisfied with that but make each case the subject of political attack. The elaborate manner in which memorials are got up and printed show that they are not sent forward in the ordinary manner."

Spencer's letter shows that he was less able than Gladstone to understand that in a country living under exceptional law, the administration of justice is bound to become a political issue.[1]

The hint of a miscarriage of justice and still more of a

---

[1] Spencer's letters show that he took infinite trouble about such cases. After his retirement he said that of 40 capital sentences passed while he was Viceroy 21 were executed and 19 commuted; and that in considering his duty with regard to the prerogative of mercy he had had the patient advice of the three Irish Lord Chancellors, Law, Sullivan and Neish. Speech at dinner in his honour. August 24, 1885.

Y

police plot against a prisoner awakens immediate suspicion even under ordinary conditions. Ireland was not living under ordinary conditions. The critics of the Government seized on this case knowing that it had an importance beyond itself. The Coercion Act had thrown great power into the hands of men like Brady and Bolton, and if justice had been treated with negligence in this case, it was not unreasonable to hold that justice had suffered even worse treatment in others. For in this case no disturbing motive could be found except the professional desire to secure convictions. In other cases the men on trial were men who had denounced Dublin Castle; men engaged not in some obscure quarrel between lean and starving peasants but in a struggle with the Government itself. Men like O'Brien and Harrington, who had found themselves in jail under the Coercion Act, had every reason to wish to bring home to public opinion the grounds for refusing confidence to the British administration of justice.

In Ireland then the Maamtrasna murders which had begun by exciting anger against the murderers ended by exciting anger against the Government in England. In England their effect was to confirm the detestation and despair which Irish crime had spread far and wide. There was, however, one important exception. These murders took to Ireland one of the most striking and interesting figures in English life. This was Arnold Toynbee; the man who had broken the spell of the old rigid tradition in economic thinking and had brought to the interpretation of economic history the large imagination that was to revolutionize its study. He returned from the wilds of Connemara a man with a mission. It is significant of his large and courageous mind that the Irishman to whom he went as soon as he was back in Dublin was Davitt, the ex-convict whom Englishmen regarded as an untouchable. These two men, one an Englishman steeped in the large tragedies of great movements, the other an Irishman, victim as well as student of Irish misery, swore a noble oath like that of Wilberforce, that they would bring the quarrel of their two countries to an end.

Toynbee and Davitt were both men haunted by the sorrow of the world and better able than their fellows to see beyond the passions of class and race to its deeper causes. They had more than this in common. Davitt's *Leaves from a Prison Diary* show that he was moved by the large spirit and sympathy that inspired Toynbee's treatment of economic history and that ultimately these two men, one an Oxford don, the other an Irish labourer, had the same view of human happiness. In that fascinating book Davitt discusses as one of the urgent needs of the time a plan for giving to the common man the opportunity of enjoying great art; for bringing into the villages, Irish and English, the light of great sculpture, great music and great literature. Toynbee and Davitt were more intelligible to each other than either of them would have been to the " beefwitted lords " in Parliament who denounced the release of this dangerous felon; for Davitt's ideas of the place of culture in life would have seemed to them as preposterous as his idea that Ireland was something more than England's unruly subject.

Toynbee returned to Oxford and he wrote to Davitt from Balliol a letter that reveals the rare charm of his character.

" I was delighted with your speech at Haslingdon. If you could allow such a humble person as myself to co-operate with you I should be most grateful. I am not a politician but a student who loves books, but I am dragged out of my seclusion by the turmoil that is going on around me. I cannot be quiet while this terrible crisis in the history of the English and Irish nations is before my eyes. On Thursday I am going to speak on Ireland. I shall strain every nerve to make the English understand what is going on. My visit to Maamtrasna this summer opened my eyes."[1]

Toynbee wrote on January 16, 1883. Two months later he was dead.

It is difficult to overestimate the loss that Ireland suffered by the death of Arnold Toynbee in March, 1883, following on that of T. H. Green in November, 1882. Green had exposed in his lectures the fallacy underlying upper-class confidence in freedom of contract as a guiding formula for Irish politics. He had pointed out that a peasant farmer

---

[1] *Fall of Feudalism*, p. 382.

holding fifteen acres in Ireland confronted with his landlord was about as free in making a contract as a starving labourer confronted with an employer. " To uphold the sanctity of contracts is doubtless a prime business of governments but it is not less its business to provide against contracts being made which, from the helplessness of one of the parties to them, instead of being a security for freedom becomes an instrument of disguised oppression."[1] Toynbee was just about to bring the most original and enterprising mind in Oxford to bear on a problem for the study of which he was specially fitted by knowledge, sympathy, and freedom from every kind of enslaving prejudice. Toynbee's influence in Oxford was not merely that of a young and brilliant teacher; it was that of a remarkable personality. Even the cold *Times* observed on his death that his influence in Oxford was " extraordinary." His pupils Milner and Ashley have left on record their vivid impression of his power. Anybody who wants to see the difference between a rich and imaginative mind and a narrow and doctrinaire mind will find the contrast in the spirit in which the Irish question was treated by two Oxford men: Toynbee and Goldwin Smith. If the next generation of Oxford men had been under Toynbee's spell, England would have been far readier in 1885 for a bold and generous Irish policy.

The history of the Maamtrasna case and all its incidents and developments illustrates vividly the conditions of Irish life and Irish politics and it shows how and where Gladstone's Government, after putting on the Statute Book two important measures, the Land Act of 1881 and the Arrears Act of 1882, failed either to carry further Irish reform or to gain the gratitude and the confidence of the Irish people. In fact it helps us to answer the question with which the last chapter ended.

The fundamental difficulty of the Irish problem in 1882 can be put into a simple form. The Irish Government was faced with a great mass of undetected and unpunished crime. Trevelyan said that down to the time of the execution of Hynes in the autumn of 1882 some sixty murders

[1] T. H. Green, *Works*, Vol. III 382.

had been committed in succession, for which nobody had paid the penalty. It was faced also with great social problems, having on its hands a population disabled by poverty and embittered by strife. For it had on its hands the problem represented by Spencer's picture of the poverty of the peasants of Connemara and the problem represented by his picture of the passions of the peasants of Arran. Gladstone and Chamberlain hoped by reforming the government of Ireland to bring to an end the state of things under which the punishment of crime was mixed up with the politics of religion and race. A Government co-operating with the Irish people in setting up popular institutions would soon find coercion unnecessary. On the other hand, a Government drawn into a quarrel with the Irish people would be unable to enforce respect for the law because its methods for obtaining justice would spread mistrust, and those methods would absorb all its energies to the neglect of reform. This was the vicious circle outside which Gladstone and Chamberlain hoped to keep their Irish policy; it was the vicious circle in which it became fatally entangled. Thus a Prime Minister who aimed at the proud title of *auctor* went down in 1885 under the weight of hatred he had earned in the grim character of *vindex*; a Government of reconstruction looked to Ireland like a Government of punishment.

The failure is easy to understand when we turn to the temper of the English people and of the House of Commons. For Gladstone's purpose it could hardly have been worse. To the ordinary Englishman Ireland was a nation steeped in crime which had answered concession after concession by outrage after outrage. Almost every month brought its own murders, sometimes of landlords, sometimes of agents, sometimes of constables, sometimes of peasants. Two years had been spent in Irish problems while English reforms had been put aside. Parliament had given up to Ireland in 1881 the most strenuous session that had ever tried the nerves and the endurance of the House of Commons. In 1882 the Local Government Bill and the London Government Bill had been postponed once more that Parliament might pass the Arrears Act and give to Irish peasants rights unknown in England.

The autumn had been devoted to the reform of procedure and the setting up of two Grand Committees on legal and commercial questions. The Irishmen, so far from showing gratitude for their own measures, had made this work as difficult as possible by obstruction and bad temper. Irish manners in the House of Commons, Irish crimes in Ireland, Irish plots in the English towns had exasperated English opinion. Thus to the power of the vested interests that dreaded Irish reform there was added the force of dislike or apathy in the English mind; what the *Spectator* called a growing impatience of Irish questions because they were Irish questions. When Ireland was mentioned, England was like a man with the gout.

Active and resolute reform is not as a rule to be expected from an exhausted Government uninspired and undirected by public opinion. Gladstone's Government had never been, as a body, a Government with a vigorous desire for action. It was too heavily burdened with Whig lethargy for that. Circumstances, used by a leader whom it feared more than it trusted, had forced two great reforms upon its natural reluctance. It was now two years old as age is measured by time; much older if age is measured by exhaustion. It had been distracted by difficult and unexpected tasks in South Africa and Egypt; the first had cost it much of its strength, the second the support and prestige of an important Minister, for Bright had left when the fleet had shelled the forts of Alexandria. Tragedy and failure in Ireland had darkened its horizon. In the House of Commons it had been pursued without mercy by a little Tory band of brilliant debaters and tacticians whose spirit of faction and combat was equally active and resourceful whether they were attacking from the right or from the left. Two of its most powerful Members were Hartington and Harcourt; the one man who might have persuaded Hartington to support Reform had been struck down in Phoenix Park; Harcourt's dislike of the Irish was fed by the perpetual irritation caused in the Home Office by the Fenian plots. Where was Gladstone to find the power and energy that were needed to overcome the hostility of some of his colleagues and the apathy of others; to set out again on reforms as to which the English electorate were alike ignorant and indifferent?

The need of the moment then demanded from Gladstone himself a superhuman effort. In what condition was he to make it? Just as in his first Government he paid in the last two years of office for the immense exertions he had made in carrying his Irish Church and Irish Land Bills, so now he was finding out how much of his strength had gone in those triumphs in the House of Commons in 1881 that had given such an impression of power. The physical strain was severe; the moral strain almost intolerable. For the Irish struggle, so distressing to a man of his temperament, was now made still darker by a desolating personal sorrow. So long as he was in the House of Commons, with its life of daily battle, his amazing vitality in debate kept him from collapse and concealed the ravages of shock and misery. In the autumn the full effects of all that he had done and suffered came home to him. He turned his mind most seriously to retirement.

Gladstone never regarded himself as irrevocably committed to politics between 1875, when he first retired, and 1886, when he accepted the last great summons of his life. As we have seen, he touched constantly on his desire to withdraw for an evening of contemplation in which he might " unburthen'd crawl towards death." But in the letter that he wrote to Spencer in October, 1882, there is a new note of fatigue and failing power. He felt that he was no longer equal to the great constructive tasks that the time required.

" The principal reasons, then," he wrote, " for accomplishing it [his retirement] say before the close of the year, will be:

" 1. To restore the natural and normal state of things, which existed up to 1880.

" 2. To allow a man of seventy-three years (next December) old, and fifty of public service, to relieve himself from a life of contention which has been unusually sharp, and to devote whatever time may still be allotted him, in the main at least, to employments more appropriate, and less violently imperious than those of his present public life.

" These reasons, each of which ought to suffice, are backed by another yet more commanding: namely that increase of disinclination to work, and disposition (in homely phrase) to scamp it, which I think and know to be a sign of diminished power, I mean of power diminished below the point at which I ought to stand, in order to master in any tolerable degree the most difficult parts of that work. This I consider to be the supervision, and often the construction, of weighty legislative measures, which are duties I fear inseparable from my present place in the House of Commons and in the Government.

" The work of that kind, which is to come on as soon as the House recovers its liberty, is great and formidable. There is in the Government and the party plenty of energy, fresh and yet mature, to cope with it. I cannot and dare not face it as I have been accustomed to do. It would be of no good to anyone that I should remain on the stage like a half-exhausted singer, whose notes are flat, and everyone perceives it except himself. Such a condition of things ought to be met by prevention, and not by remedy; and kind Nature, if we give her fair play, helps us with premonitory signs, of which the persons concerned should always be the first interpreter. I do not contemplate immediate Parliamentary extinction. A part may yet remain, the part of independent co-operation upon occasion, which may be sought when it is desired, and which can be, and has been, safely and usefully discharged by many public men after they have bid a final adieu to office. . . .

He arranged that this letter should be seen by the two most important of his colleagues; Granville and Hartington. They both demurred. As Gladstone's view was that he had taken over the leadership from Hartington in 1880 for a temporary purpose and that the leadership would naturally revert to Hartington when he stepped down, Hartington's answer has a special importance. Hartington (November 12, 1882) gave two arguments against retirement:

" As to your reasons for retirement, I will only say, that without venturing to dispute any opinion which you have formed, which rests on your own feelings and your sense of your own powers, I am convinced that there does not at this moment exist in the party any man possessing a fraction of those mental powers which you consider so necessary to future constructive legislation."

His second argument was that Gladstone's retirement would be fatal to the Government and to the party. No one else could keep the moderate and the advanced section together.

' My letter of last month on Procedure and other matters must have proved to you how unfit, and how indisposed I am to take charge of such legislation especially in regard to Ireland as I conceive you anticipate as necessary, and which certainly the advanced party have been led to expect; and I more than doubt whether I should be justified in attempting to resume the leadership in the House of Commons under such circumstances. It would be no sacrifice to me to see it placed in the hands of others, who would not feel the same difficulties, but I cannot pretend to think that such an arrangement would have any prospect of success."

Gladstone did not easily relinquish his proposal. He wrote to Granville on November 26:

" I feel myself incapable of grappling with the hard constructive work that is coming on. It need not however, if I judge rightly, come on until after Easter 1883. Whether I should go now, i.e. before the new session, or at Easter, is open, as far as I am concerned; and it is for those chiefly concerned in any new arrangement to say whether it shall or shall not be now; I am willing to be guided by them, or (as I conceive) in other words by you and Hartington."

In the same letter he said that he would give up the Exchequer at once and that he proposed to offer it to Childers. This change was made in the following month. He then prepared to go to Cannes and nurse his broken health. The arrangements he had to make for admitting Dilke to the Cabinet at this time were troublesome, because of the Queen's strong feelings against accepting as Cabinet Minister a man who had made republican speeches. These vexing negotiations cost him his sleep and made him realize more strongly than ever that his nerves were worn out.

Gladstone's talk of retirement was often treated, not unnaturally, as if it were affectation or self-deception, but there is no doubt that on this occasion he was in earnest. Harcourt, whose cynical view of human nature never spared the dignity of his leader, wrote to Ponsonby on

January 10, 1883, " We have had great difficulty to prevent his bolting, and I do not feel that we are at all safe yet. There are some people I think who have not realized how much more uncomfortable things will be for *everybody* when he is gone, After all, he is the linch-pin of the coach."[1] A week later after seeing Gladstone off to Cannes, he wrote to Granville, " I fear his mind is more than ever turned towards retirement."

Gladstone went to Cannes on January 17, 1883, and stayed there about six weeks. He had meant to be away for a fortnight but he was not fit to return till the beginning of March. Those six weeks were fatal to his plans. If reform was to get ahead of coercion in Ireland, if, that is, the Government was to enlist the new Irish force on its side and thus avert a great quarrel, it was essential that the next great step should be taken in 1883. Gladstone was wide awake to this truth. One of the last letters he wrote before leaving was to Trevelyan (December 30, 1882). After expressing his wish that the House of Commons would take his plan for using Grand Committees " for portions of the United Kingdom," he went on :

" The subject of Local Government eclipses all the rest in importance. As long as the portentous centralization of the present system continues, Government will be to the common Irishman, I am afraid, an exotic, a foreign thing, and he may for long look upon it with a consequent aversion, which will extend even to its simplest and most needful and beneficial acts. I hope it will be founded upon the four Provinces . . . such Provincial bodies would I hope be capable of rendering far greater service than any weaker bodies could."

It is easy to imagine the consternation with which the writer of that letter read at Cannes on January 22, 1883, the report of a speech by Hartington in which the man on whom the leadership would devolve on his retirement protested against giving Ireland local government, " unless we can receive from the representatives of the Irish people some assurance that this boon would not be misused for the purpose of agitation and for the purpose of wrecking the power and

---

[1] A. G. Gardiner, *Life of Harcourt*, I, 469.

authority of the Government." Gladstone sent a strong protest to Granville who told him in reply that he and Hartington had very nearly quarrelled over this speech. Gladstone wrote also to Hartington, February 3, 1883. " Your contention cuts deep down into my elementary and fixed ideas: it seems to me to revive in principle the opposition offered in 1836-8 to the establishment of elective municipalities in Ireland." But Hartington had behind him not only the dead weight of Cabinet reluctance for action, but also the energetic personality of Harcourt and so far as the year 1883 was concerned, the opinion of Spencer. For Spencer, though he blamed Hartington for his speech, had reached the fatal conclusion that for the moment Ireland needed rest.

While Gladstone was still at Cannes, the influences against which he was struggling were strengthened by events in Ireland. For all the suspicion and ill-will that filled the English mind found new material in the revelations that followed the unravelling of the murders in Phoenix Park. By a combination of luck and skill the detectives employed to investigate an attempt on the life of an Irish judge in Dublin in January, 1883, lighted on important clues to the Phoenix Park murder. Twenty men were arrested, and when these men were brought into court on January 20 it was made known that one of them, a labourer named Farrell, had turned informer. Farrell gave astonishing details of the secret society that had been organized for the assassination of Government officials and others. On February 10 his information was supplemented by that of the man who drove the murderers to Phoenix Park, and on February 17 his example was followed by a more important prisoner, James Carey.[1] Carey, who had been a Fenian from 1861 to 1878, had become leader in 1881 of a secret society, the Invincibles, which planned assassinations, including that of Burke. Carey was a builder and a member of the Dublin Town Council. The world learnt from his disclosures all about the murders in Phoenix Park and also

---

[1] Carey was the principal criminal and it was with reluctance that the Cabinet agreed to let him turn King's evidence.

about earlier abortive plots against Cowper and Forster. The prisoners were tried in April. Five were hanged, and the rest sentenced to penal servitude, two of them for life. Carey went to South Africa, but was shot on the boat between Cape Town and Natal.

The Government ought to have been strengthened by these trials, for the revelations showed how wise and proper had been the release of Parnell. The murder society to which Carey belonged had been formed after Parnell had been put under lock and key, and the diaries that were read showed that its members hated the Irish leader. The Government by this discovery put down political assassination in Ireland; it had brought to light a dangerous conspiracy of which Forster, allowed to arrest on suspicion, had never heard, and secured a conviction, on unimpeachable evidence, by a jury and under a judge who took their lives in their hands. Moreover it had obtained these results by using that part of the Crimes Act to which no strong exception had been taken by its critics. It might then have been supposed that it would be easier to proceed with reform and to carry out Gladstone's policy.

Unhappily the result was far different. This moral was not the moral drawn by most people from the revelations. The revelations had not implicated the Land League, but they had implicated some of its leading officials. Frank Byrne who was directly incriminated was the secretary of the London branch and he had been in constant contact with Parnell and McCarthy. Patrick Egan, the treasurer, had got Carey his first job under the Dublin Corporation. Sheridan was also involved, the man whose name had been brought into the talks between O'Shea and Parnell as reported by O'Shea to Forster. In all revolutionary movements there are three sets of men and women; those who are innocent of crime and violence; those who are guilty, and those who are in both worlds. It was inevitable that a link could be found between Parnell and men who had blood on their conscience, just as it would no doubt have been possible to find a link between Cavour and some dark conspirator creeping, stiletto in hand, though the streets of

Milan. The English had never lived in the atmosphere of revolutionary conspiracy, nor did they understand that in Ireland the crimes of the peasants were set against the crimes of the landlords. They therefore concluded that Parnell's apparent indifference to outrages implied an active share in murder. Nor was the detached view of the relation of politics and crime in Ireland, that might be reached in the philosopher's study, encouraged in the ordinary man by the Fenian explosions.

The view of Gladstone and Chamberlain was that Parnell, whatever his past, was now ready and anxious to keep down disorder and crime, and that a wise Government would accept that disposition as an important fact. Most people unhappily thought that he ought to be held to his past and that these revelations should be used to discredit him still further. This was the spirit in which Forster made what was generally regarded as the most effective speech of his career in February 1883. Forster, brooding over his failure in Ireland, had come more and more to regard Parnell as Cicero regarded Catiline, and temper and vanity both prompted him to use the revelations and the atmosphere of the moment for a Philippic which would damage his enemy and delight the strong anti-Irish sentiment of the House of Commons. When he sat down, after an exhaustive and impressive indictment of Parnell's past, recalling all the crimes of the last two years, some discovered and punished, but most of them " unwhipped of justice," the Government's task of reforming and pacifying Ireland had been made much more difficult. The only answer a Minister could have made would have been the answer Hector made to Troilus, in *Troilus and Cressida*, warning him against " bad success in a bad cause," when Troilus, " with his blood so madly hot," had made his passionate speech against restoring Helen.

Worse was to follow. Parnell replied to Forster next day with a speech that delighted Ireland as much as Forster had delighted her enemies. For he affected to regard with indifference any accusations that came from Englishmen on the ground that he had to answer to his own people for what he did and said and to nobody else. His tone gave as much satisfaction to the Tory and Liberal anti-Irish sentiment as to the high spirit of his own followers. Any Minister who wanted to reform Ireland and not merely to punish her was desperately embarrassed by a speech which left the House of Commons under the impression that Forster was right, not only in his view of Parnell's past, but also in his view of the way of treating him. Politics were back in the spirit of the old Kilmainham controversy. All the passions that had bewildered and distracted the generous common sense needed for a statesmanlike policy in Ireland were raging in their old fury. The *Spectator*, in an article on March 3, 1883, criticizing Randolph Churchill's violence, quoted from a speech in which he had said of the Government, " In their government of Ireland they have abandoned the path of political imposture and have entered on the high road of political crime. . . . At a particular time, so base was their policy, that they forced the Crown to rely for their authority in Ireland on the assassins of Phoenix Park." A speech at Birmingham on June 14, 1883, by John Bright, which led afterwards to violent controversy in the House of Commons, turned the tables on Churchill, but in language which shows what kind of temper a Minister who wanted to serve the cause of peace with Ireland had to meet. " They (the Fourth Party) are found in alliance with an Irish rebel party, the main portion of whose funds for the purposes of agitation come directly from the enemies of England and whose oath of allegiance is broken by association with its enemies."

A few Liberals in the House of Commons, of whom the most important was Bryce and the most active Herbert Gladstone, tried to counteract this dangerous force by setting up a Committee for the study of Irish problems. They issued a manifesto and collected a few members but little seems to have come of their efforts. For politics were moving rapidly to the struggle over the franchise which was to absorb most of the Radical energy of the time.

Against such a body of feeling an old, tired, and disheartened man could not hope to make headway. There was a general agreement that Irish reform was impracticable, as we know from a letter Granville sent to Gladstone, then at Cannes, on February 6, 1883, describing the views of the Cabinet on the Queen's Speech then in preparation.

" On the question of the Irish Local Government Bill there were three shades of opinion. Harcourt and Hartington who are evidently hostile to extending local Government in Ireland. The majority of the Cabinet who are in different degrees favorable to the plan, but doubtful of the expediency or possibility of passing a measure for the purpose this year. Chamberlain and Dilke are both strong as to the impossibility of passing either an English or Irish local Government Bill this session. But anxious that both should be mentioned in the Queen's Speech. It was argued against them that it was absolutely dishonest to promise Bills which were not prepared and which no one present today at the Cabinet thought it possible to pass."

Nor less significant is a letter sent by Gladstone to Spencer a month later when Parnell had introduced a Bill making some necessary amendments to the Land Act. Spencer had sent a long letter in which while urging the objections against anything that would encourage new demands in Ireland, he thought that the Government should agree to two amendments to the Act. One was to change the date from which a tenant should pay the judicial rent, the other to make some provision to put an end to certain injustices that were found in practice in the treatment of leaseholders. Neither amendment went as far as Parnell proposed to go, and for the rest no further change should be allowed. To this letter, dated March 9, Gladstone replied on March 12 giving an account of the decisions of the Cabinet who were afraid of opening the subject and held that " the state of business and of demands other than Irish precludes our undertaking any new engagement in this direction."

This letter from Gladstone to Spencer, followed as it was by a speech of Gladstone's in the House of Commons opposing Parnell's Bill, curiously stiff and unfriendly in tone, showed that the Government had neither nerve nor patience for the task that was before them. In this case they refused to make amendments in their Act which the Land Commission considered necessary.   The third reason given by Gladstone in his letter was undoubtedly a cogent reason and it is not surprising if by itself it determined the decision of the Cabinet.   Anybody who compared what had been done in the way of Irish Legislation and of English legislation in the last two years would think that Ireland's claims on the time of the House of Commons were exhausted.   But there was another element in the problem.   When Gladstone said that he no longer felt equal to constructive legislation, he was putting his finger on a real weakness.   There is a limit to the amount of revolution that an old man can take into his blood and Gladstone, who had banished political economy to Saturn, was not for the moment ready for any fresh adventure.   He was in fact now in a dilemma, and a dilemma from which he did not escape for four years.   If Ireland had been his only responsibility he would have done well to persist in his decision to retire.   It would have been like his retirement in 1875.   It would have been an example of the law of the conservation of energy described by Toynbee in his *Study of History*[1] as the process of withdrawal and return; a law of which Toynbee quotes as examples, not only prophets like Moses and St. Paul, but statesmen like Solon and Julius Caesar.   If Gladstone had been out of politics for the next two years, and had then returned as a crusader for Home Rule, he might have swept the country in 1886 as he did in 1880.

It is not surprising that this plan was unattractive to his prospective successor.   Hartington would have found himself again in the uncomfortable position that he occupied in the late 'seventies.   The arrangement that Gladstone described as " opportunities for co-operation " might wear rather a different look to the weaker partner.

But Gladstone's responsibilities were not only Irish.   He was leader of the Liberal party.   In his view he had stepped into the leadership in an emergency, meaning to retire when the duty of the moment had been accomplished.   His successor would be the man who had made way for him. Unfortunately his successor held strongly that his retirement

[1] *Study of History*, Vol. III, 248, etc.

would mean the break up of the Liberal party. This difficulty faced him now; it faced him again in 1885, and, as we shall see, it explains a great deal that seemed obscure in his conduct. So he remained, head of a Government whose troubles came thick and fast in its last years of life, watching with distress and foreboding the steady loss of its power to help Ireland.

CHAPTER XVIII

TWO LOST YEARS, 1883 AND 1884

The decision to postpone the next step in Gladstone's programme in the spring of 1883 involved, so far as Ireland was concerned, the loss of the rest of the lifetime of this Parliament. For in Gladstone's mind Land Purchase was an unsafe and impracticable policy unless it was accompanied or preceded by the creation of Irish authorities strong enough and responsible enough to take the risk off British shoulders. He was very conscious of the grave political dangers that would follow if the British Government were confronted with a general repudiation of liabilities on the part of the Irish farmers. So long as the liabilities repudiated were liabilities from tenant to landowner, a British Government could manage the difficulty, partly by revising those liabilities and removing injustice, partly by upholding the administration of the law. But a repudiation of liabilities from peasant to Government, of liabilities accepted solemnly in the course of legislation, would be rebellion. If this happened the British Government would find itself involved in a new quarrel between England and Ireland; a quarrel of which the discomfort would affect Gladstone more than other politicians. For he had at the back of his mind a sense that Ireland's historical grievances were so serious as to excuse almost any extravagance of passion, and a conviction that no Government could fight successfully against the Irish people.

The Conservatives were much less anxious on this point. In their view the chief evil of what was happening in Ireland was the shock given to the sense and rights of property, and the ruin that threatened the landlord class. They were therefore far readier to take risks with Imperial credit, and, as in their view the State had shrunk from the duty of defending the rights of the landlords, they did not think that the plight of the world would be worse if the State were put in a position in which it would have to choose between defending or waiving rights that were its own rights and not the rights of others.

With this view Lord George Hamilton moved a resolution on June 12, 1883, asking for immediate revision of the Purchase Clauses of the 1881 Act.   He proposed a reduction in the annuities, the extension of the repayment period and the advance by the State of the whole purchase price.   Purchasers and vendors would appear before a local authority which would report on their application to a central board in Dublin.   If the Central Board approved, the intending purchaser would be entitled to borrow the whole of the purchase money from the local board.   This fund would be raised by debentures issued by the local authorities, bearing interest at three per cent. and repayable in forty years, with the rates as security backed by a State guarantee.   The purchase price was not to exceed twenty-three years' purchase of the legally ascertained rent.   Gladstone asked the House to substitute *early* for *immediate*, arguing that in its original form the resolution asked Parliament to put aside the work on which it was engaged (this included, as it happened, an important English Agricultural Holdings Act) in order to throw the Irish Land question again into confusion.   In commenting on the resolution he said that the Government were reluctant to abandon the principle of demanding the payment of part of the purchase money by the tenant; he laid stress on the absence of local authorities of higher standing than poor law guardians, and the danger of making a mass of tenants direct debtors of the Exchequer.

The Conservative initiative was warmly welcomed by Parnell and by Irishmen of all schools.   Next year Dickson, an Ulster Liberal, introduced (April 30, 1884) a Bill amending the purchase clauses by permitting the establishment of a land corporation with power to purchase estates and resell them to tenants. In the debate Trevelyan announced that the Government would bring in a Bill of their own and on May 7 he explained its proposals. The fall in prices, the reductions of rents and the general uncertainty had produced a slump in land and Trevelyan said that the " block " was almost as great as it had been before the passing of the Encumbered Estates Acts. The Government Bill divided prospective purchasers into two classes. Those who would pay one quarter of the purchase price would be required to repay the State in annuities of $4\frac{1}{2}$ per cent.—which should not exceed their present rent—for 40 years; those who advanced no part of the purchase money would repay in annuities of 5 per cent. for 33 years. But purchasers of the second class would have to satisfy a local board of 16 members (drawn from the Boards of Guardians and the Grand Jury) of their ability to pay and in the event of default this Board would have to make good the deficit from the local cess. The landlords would be paid in 3 per cent. debentures and the total issue was to be limited to twenty million pounds of which not more than five millions would be issued in any one year.

The Bill was criticized by the Parnellites on the ground that 20 years' purchase was too high a price in a falling market and that the local board would consist mainly of landlords who could wreck the scheme. The Government had little enthusiasm for the project. Spencer sent Gladstone a memorandum by Hamilton putting the objections to taking any action. Gladstone told Spencer, May 13, 1884, that he would himself prefer to advance the whole purchase price with an effective guarantee to giving three-quarters " with nobody between the Consolidated Fund and the debtor." He ended the letter with the remark that the " whole subject is one which I regard with misgiving, when once we get beyond the idea of facilitating a real purchase by select cultivators." It is not surprising that the Bill was dropped. Parliament had its hands full with the Franchise Bill and the Irish members were dissatisfied with the scheme.

Gladstone was uneasy about taking what should in his view be the second step until he had taken the first, and his

Government had decided in the early months of 1883 against his Provincial Councils.   But by this time he had lost heart about Irish reform and regarded it as a great problem which he would have to leave to his successors. This was made evident by the attitude his Government assumed towards his own policy when that policy was presented to the House from the Irish benches.   On April 11, 1883, Barry, acting for Healy, introduced a Bill for setting up county councils in Ireland.   In his speech he pointed out that the Government had promised this reform in the Queen's Speech in 1881.   Trevelyan on behalf of the Government had to oppose the Bill on the ground of the want of time.   Again, in March, 1884, Parnell proposed in the House of Commons that a Grand Committee should be set up for Irish Bills.   He made a most moderate speech, in the course of which he admitted that some of his followers were against him because they held that this reform would damage the cause of Home Rule.   In the previous session Parliament under the Government's guidance had set up two Grand Committees; one on Commerce and the other on law.   It was by their means that the Government passed Chamberlain's reforms of Bankruptcy and Patent Law. Gladstone had to answer a proposal which followed the lines he had suggested in his plan of reform in 1880.   He made a curious speech in which he said that he hoped that some day the experience of the working of the Grand Committees would induce Parliament to use them in the way Parnell proposed.   For the moment it was his duty to resist the proposal.   Another example of his reluctance to face any Irish question was more disastrous.   Though Spencer had been against legislation in 1883 he had been convinced by the Land Commissioners that two amendments were necessary and urgently desired in the Land Act; one was an amendment changing the date from which a judicial rent was paid; the other one to bring leaseholders into the Act.   These amendments he pressed on Gladstone in 1883 and 1884.   In March, 1883, Gladstone replied, as we have seen, by telling him that the Cabinet had decided against any reopening of the Land Act.   On February 28, 1884,

Spencer wrote again, but Gladstone never answered his letter. Gladstone was ill and only half doing his work for several weeks, and in this case an amendment that was urgently needed was neglected. It was in fact made later by a Conservative Government.

In spite of their difficulties the Government managed to give some help to Ireland. The first of a series of Bills for improving the housing of the labourers was passed into law in 1883. A Bill introduced by T. P. O'Connor, making provision for the first time for building cottages for agricultural labourers, was supported by the Government and pushed through Parliament. This Act, the Labourers (Ireland) Act, authorized the Boards of Guardians to build cottages, after inquiry, with a plot of land to be let at a rent that would pay the interest on the money borrowed for this purpose. The Bill in its first form would have added a national rate in aid to the resources of the local rates but this was struck out. It was a modest measure in its final form but it was the first of a series of good measures of this kind and was important as a beginning. Gladstone, throwing over Courtney who took the Treasury view, accepted a Bill from Blake to spend some of the Irish Church Fund on Sea Fisheries. Late in the session Trevelyan passed a useful Tramways Bill.

The Tramways Bill gave a State guarantee to encourage the opening up of agricultural districts beyond the reach of railways, increased the emigration grant and provided for lending money on easy terms to companies to enable them to purchase estates and resell to tenants. Parnell wanted to substitute for the emigration grant a plan for migration, and he said, what was true, that all the Government's plans in Ireland were prejudiced by the belief that their main remedy was emigration.[1] The Bill though

---

[1] This was indeed a constant cause of friction. The Irish believed that the English wanted to get as many Irishmen out of Ireland as possible, for their own convenience. The English that the Irish, like the Roman plebeians (*cetera multitudo poscere Romae agrum malle quam alibi accipere. Livy*, III, 1, 8), preferred to demand land at home rather than receive it elsewhere, from sentimental obstinacy. Neither of them recognized that what was wanted in Ireland's interest was a combination of the two plans.

introduced so late was passed into law by means of the new Grand Committee system.[1]

A debate on the Irish vote a few days after this Bill was discussed showed how bitter was the feeling at this time between the Irish members and the Government. Healy said that as long as Irish members were sent to the plank bed by the Irish Government for their speeches, there could be no peace in the House of Commons. The Irish Secretary treated the Irish members in Ireland as his enemies and could not expect them to treat him otherwise than as their enemy in Parliament. It was as much a war between the two countries as it had ever been. Gladstone, in what the *Annual Register* called " a dignified and pathetic speech," said that his own personal interest in the question could only be of short duration, but if it were to be the last time he were to speak in that House, he would use the language not of rebuke but of appeal and ask the Irish members to question their consciences and decide whether it was really incumbent on them to use deliberately such inflammatory language and so retard the establishment of peace between England and Ireland. It was as if the fierce strife of the hour had been broken by a voice that could speak, as Achilles spoke to Priam, of the merciless destiny that held in its sad grasp Greek and Trojan, English ruler and Irish rebel. Healy rose to his feet to declare his sympathy and admiration for Gladstone's character and extraordinary genius, but he could only reiterate his grim view that in this atmosphere no man could make peace.

By this time Gladstone had clearly made up his mind that Irish reform was beyond his strength, and that his immediate duty was to carry the Franchise Bill and to avert the domestic quarrel that was threatening to break up the party. In the early months of 1884 the Cabinet was divided

[1] It was one of the few Irish measures on which Chamberlain spoke. In the debate on the second reading he asked Irish members to bear in mind the great sacrifices the Government had been obliged to make of their economic principles in proposing such a scheme. No such grant had ever been proposed for public works in England. " He had always recognized that in dealing with a poor country such as Ireland, where commerce and enterprise had for a long time been at a low ebb, it would be absurd to apply the principles which had been found to apply to this country." (August 8, 1883.)

on the Franchise Bill. Hartington was against it, both on its merits and also because he dreaded the consequence of strengthening Parnell in Ireland. He was unfortunately dissuaded from resignation by Harcourt.

The two Ministers who agreed with Gladstone about Irish reform, Chamberlain and Dilke (Dilke had entered the Cabinet in December, 1882) were now absorbed in Radical politics at home. The whole of the year 1884 was taken up with two great controversies in both of which they were closely concerned; the controversy over Egypt and the controversy over the Franchise. In May the prestige of the Government had fallen so low in consequence of its mistakes and its misfortunes in Egypt that a vote of censure in the Commons was only defeated by 303 votes to 275. The Franchise Bill, extending household franchise to the counties and thus enfranchising the agricultural labourers, was introduced on February 29 and it did not reach its final stage till December. The struggle over the Bill became in the summer and autumn a struggle over the House of Lords and thus a fierce domestic strife was added to the bitterness caused by the life and death battles over Egypt.

Gladstone said in October, 1882, when pressing his desire to resign, that he drew a distinction between his capacity for constructive reform which he believed to be failing and his capacity for the regular House of Commons work which he believed to be maintained. This was a very important truth. In one sense it was a cause of weakness. Gladstone's unrivalled power in debate and moral authority enabled him to keep his Government alive after disasters that would have been fatal to Governments that had to trust to the leadership of ordinary talent. Such success, impressive at the moment, is dangerous for the future. A Government that survives its blunders and calamities by such means is apt to fall into all the greater discredit when the spell is lifted. That is what happened to Gladstone's Egyptian tragedies.

In the case of the Franchise Bill the course of history was very different. Here the Government gained a great triumph and a triumph that brought it credit and gratitude.

Gladstone's energy was inspired and invigorated by conflict on ground where he felt certain of himself. The man who had told Shaw that he could not devise an economic plan for helping the Irish labourer, much as he deplored his plight, had no difficulty in finding a hundred arguments, as they were needed, for giving the franchise to the labourer, Irish and English. In this way he strengthened the cause of Irish nationalism, for the new franchise raised the Irish electorate from 200,000 to 700,000[1] and the new electors followed Parnell.

The wisdom of enfranchising this large body of Irishmen was fiercely disputed in the House of Commons. Most of the Conservatives agreed with Hartington in disliking it. Churchill was an exception and his brilliant speech against the amendment to omit Ireland made a great impression. The amendment was Lord Claud Hamilton's but it was moved in his absence by Brodrick. Brodrick argued that if the Bill was allowed to include Ireland " the Government would concentrate in that House all the evil passions, all the patriotic follies, all the delusive sentimentalities which were now wasted at public meetings throughout Ireland." He was supported by Plunkett who said " it was madness to give increased power to those who wished to break up the Empire." Churchill in his vigorous reply to these speakers committed himself to an unhappy prophecy, for he predicted that the class to be enfranchized in Ireland would favour the landlords and strengthen the British connexion. If any member of the Government was entitled to regard himself as the father of this reform, that member was Trevelyan who had pressed the claims of the village labourer to the vote with a most honourable persistence ever since 1872. He ridiculed the idea that a Liberal Government could exclude Ireland and declared that he would not have remained a Minister for five minutes if the Government had decided on that course. On this issue Forster's democratic sense proved stronger than his fear of Parnell and he supported the Government. Gladstone's

---

[1] The Irish electorate was 92,152 in 1832; 222,450 in 1868; 742,120 in 1886. Paul Dubois, *op. cit.*, p. 8.

speech was characteristic. He argued that fifty years before England had stood " in the face of the civilized world as a culprit with regard to Ireland." The civilized world had now changed its judgment, recognizing that for a course of years there had been an honest and energetic attempt to solve Ireland's problems. " There is one way of making England weak in the face of Ireland and that is to apply to Ireland principles of inequality and injustice." Brodrick's amendment was rejected on May 20, 1884, by 332 votes to 137.

This is not the place to describe or discuss the history of the Franchise controversy, with its fierce storms and its peaceful ending. Gladstone's handling of his difficulties was a triumph of courage, of wisdom and of temper. He won golden praise from both sides in his Cabinet.

" Nothing was, in my opinion," said Selborne writing after the quarrel over Home Rule, " more honourable to Gladstone during the whole of his great career, than the resolution which, under his guidance, the Cabinet adopted, to come, if possible, to an agreement with the heads of the Conservative party as to a scheme of redistribution which both parties might accept."

Chamberlain sent him a letter on his birthday.

Highbury,
Moor Green,
Birmingham.
Decr 28 1884.

My dear Mr. Gladstone,

I hope I may be allowed to add my hearty and most sincere congratulations to those you will be receiving tomorrow from so many quarters. I can not doubt that the admiration and affection, justly felt for your character and work, by the vast majority of the people you have served so long, will be some compensation for the toils and anxiety of a life of political struggle.

I should like to add the expression of my sense of the magnitude of your latest triumph, and of the genius, the patience, and the resolution with which you have surmounted all the obstacles which might well have daunted any one less courageous. The new Reform Bills are the greatest Revolution this country has undergone—and, thanks to you, it has been accomplished peacefully and with general assent.

I am sure that the results will justify your policy, and will strengthen and unite the Nation in all that makes for its true interests and real greatness.

With kind regards and all good wishes

Believe me Yours very sincerely

J. Chamberlain.

It is easy then to see why Gladstone's Irish plans went wrong after 1882. Gladstone was not only a man of imagination and sympathy with a conscience and something like second-sight about Ireland. He was head of a Cabinet in which Ireland had very few friends, with a House of Commons that was much more ready for coercion than reform. Moreover he was Prime Minister of England and he was leader of the Liberal Party. In the first capacity he believed he owed two great duties to his country at this time; one to extricate her from her difficulties in Egypt, the other to pass a large reform Bill without public confusion or such violence as would shake the constitution. In the second capacity he believed he had a special duty to keep the peace between Hartington and Chamberlain and to leave his party intact when he handed it over to the man whom he had in 1880 displaced as leader. This duty was complicated by the wide difference between his views and temper and those of Hartington. Thus his disasters, his difficulties, and his triumphs all took him from Ireland to other pressing tasks. Yet if we are to judge his responsibility for the fate of his Irish plans, we must consider the record of those years in another aspect. There were three men who wanted to reform the government of Ireland and to keep down disorder without coercion. They were Gladstone, Chamberlain and Parnell. It is important to consider Gladstone's relations with the other two and to see how far he took or missed his opportunities of using their goodwill.

CHAPTER XIX

GLADSTONE, CHAMBERLAIN AND PARNELL

When Forster resigned in May, 1882, it was generally expected that Chamberlain would take his place. To the general astonishment Gladstone chose Lord Frederick Cavendish, known in the Treasury as an able and conscientious Minister, in the House of Commons as a good Liberal and a bad speaker, and in society as a man who combined high principle with great charm and sincerity of character.[1] When Cavendish was murdered Gladstone passed over Chamberlain again. In this case he offered the post to Chamberlain's ally, Dilke, but as he would not put him in the Cabinet—thinking that Spencer's position would be made difficult—Dilke refused. The office, now a post in which a man risked life as well as reputation, was then taken by Sir George Trevelyan.

Spencer and Trevelyan would in ordinary circumstances have been an admirable combination in Ireland. Their sense of duty did not fall short of the highest standard set by the noblest of England's public servants. They had personal courage and minds that were naturally generous and tolerant. Trevelyan was a first-rate speaker and debater, qualities needed in a Minister who had to answer such masters of guerilla warfare as Healy and Sexton. Spencer was an impressive figure whose dignity of carriage reflected dignity of character. They regarded the Orangemen and landlords, whose influence had made Dublin Castle so obnoxious and suspect, without fear or favour. Trevelyan's

---

[1] Writing to Acton, August 16, 1891, Gladstone said, "I won't admit politics to be so bad as all these big wigs make them, or they could not attract and hold two such men as Frederick Cavendish and the last Dalhousie, two men whose minds were in political action of a truly angelic purity." *Acton's Correspondence*, Figgis and Laurence, I, 258.

incisive tongue did not spare harsh landlords and Lord Rossmore, an Orange Peer, was removed from the Commission of the Peace for his truculence.

But if the view taken in these pages is correct, the view, that is, that it was essential that the Government should proceed at once with large reform, and not allow politics to be immersed in the strife that must follow coercion, these two Ministers were deficient in certain necessary qualities. Morley has drawn an admirable portrait of Spencer:

" No man of high social station or low was ever more disinterested, more unselfish, more free from the defects incident to either patrician pride or plebeian vanity. He was of too lofty a nature to have a trace of the covetousness of place that disfigured the patrician Whig caste even down to such days as these. He had a slow mind and was an awkward speaker; in fact he could not speak. But he always took sound practical points in deliberation, could weigh the force of an argument even if he bethought him of a decisive answer to it and he could be a useful critic of the clauses of a Bill. . . . Of no leading man of that time could it be more truly said that he was the soul of honour; or that the instinct of devotion to public duty was in his inmost fibre."[1]

Spencer was thus a man of good critical judgment but without constructive force, placed in circumstances in which nobody who had not great constructive vitality, and an exceptionally alert, enterprising, and confident mind, could hope to break through his difficulties. For he had on his hands the problem of keeping order. His troubles were complicated in the autumn of 1882 by a serious police strike in Dublin and though his coolness and presence of mind extinguished what might have been a most dangerous disturbance, the experience was bound to make him less inclined for bold measures. He was living among continual rumours of Fenian plots, faced with the difficulty of securing convictions for crime, and obliged again and again to decide whether to prosecute or ignore violence of speech and pen. The government of Ireland was like managing half a dozen public departments in a turbulent country, most of it under exceptional law, without local help or confidence. It is not

---

[1] *Recollections*, I, p. 220.

surprising that a man given that task shrank from the responsibility of initiating reform, and from adding new schemes and experiments to his huge and unmanageable burden. Spencer, as we have seen, was definitely on the side of Harcourt and the *Times* in the winter of 1882-3, believing that Ireland needed a rest.

Trevelyan brought to a strange and bewildering task a mind steeped in English ideas and trained in administration in a department where a good Minister was a man who kept down waste. Irish problems were new to him, and for such problems such experience as he had was disabling rather than encouraging. He was a reformer in spirit, but a reformer without plan, and therefore a reformer without scope or opportunity. What enthusiasm he took to Ireland had to struggle against an odious atmosphere of suspicion and misunderstanding. His letters to Gladstone show better than Spencer's the effect on a man's patience and vigour of the intense strain of his office. Writing to Trevelyan's father in December 1882, Gladstone spoke of his son's fast-growing reputation. But the atmosphere soon began to tell on him, as it was bound to tell on any sensitive and sympathetic nature. A Conservative Irish Secretary might be hated by Nationalist Ireland, but he had the backing and friendship of powerful classes. A Liberal Irish Secretary, administering coercion, lived for ever between two fires. Orange Ireland hated him as the representative of Liberal ideas; Nationalist Ireland hated him as the agent of English power.

At the same time Dublin Castle was strengthened by the introduction—as successor to Burke—of one of the best Civil Servants in Whitehall, Robert Hamilton, the permanent Secretary of the Admiralty. Hamilton's consent to this change was a notable act of self-sacrifice, and it had important results, for his influence on Spencer and Carnarvon in 1885 was undoubtedly one of the causes of their adoption of a Home Rule policy. But though he was a man of first-rate ability, his own experience, like that of Trevelyan, was in conservative and traditional administration. Thus there was nobody in the Irish Government who started with constructive plans or great confidence in measures that would have been considered daring and even revolutionary in Whitehall.

As Mr. Garvin has shown, there was one Minister who would have gone to Ireland with large plans of his own, determined to make reform his governing purpose and to prevent that purpose from being swallowed up in the problem of keeping order. Chamberlain had constructive schemes in his mind; he was also on good terms with Parnell's party and he had all the driving power that comes from a strong will and success tasted early in life. The case for his appointment was thus almost overwhelming. Yet Gladstone's choice of Lord Frederick Cavendish is intelligible. It must be remembered that the Gladstone who left his bed on the morning of May 6 was a very different man from the Gladstone who went to his bed that night. Phoenix Park did not kill him, as Austerlitz killed Pitt, but it robbed him of half his power. When he appointed Cavendish he was still confident and vigorous, and he thought that if his Irish secretary was a man who reflected his own wishes he would be able to push his ideas on Irish reform. He would be master in his Irish house.

It is impossible to say whether or not this plan would have succeeded if Cavendish had not been murdered. For Gladstone would have had the Irish Government behind him in his demand for Irish reform and the Irish Party would not have been driven into bitter opposition by the angry debates on coercion. It was the murder and its sequel that turned Spencer against reform in the winter of 1882 when delay was dangerous, besides crippling Gladstone's strength and hardening all the adverse influences in the Cabinet.

Gladstone then may be supposed to have appointed Cavendish with the intention of keeping Irish policy in his own hands. But there was another consideration that affected him both in passing over Chamberlain and in refusing to take Dilke into the Cabinet when offering him the office of Chief Secretary. Gladstone had chosen Spencer and, for the first time since the Reform Bill, put the Viceroy into the Cabinet, because he knew his great strength of character and he thought he would stand out against the social influences that so often demoralized English administration in Ireland. So far as knowledge and judgment of constructive politics went, he was a light weight compared with Dilke, the most serious and methodical student in public life. Now Spencer's appointment had undoubtedly made Forster discontented with his position as Chief Secretary and Gladstone feared that if Spencer and Dilke were both in the Cabinet there would be friction and difficulty.[1] This would have been a still greater objection in the case of Chamberlain. Thus the view Gladstone took of Spencer's importance for the success of his Irish policy excluded the use at Dublin of the two ablest men in his Government.

One of Chamberlain's brothers wrote to him after the Phoenix Park murder, to say that he did not think Gladstone could be so mean as to ask him then to take the post that he had not offered when it seemed his due.[2] That was one way of looking at public life. But there was another. The case for the appointment of a resolute reformer as Chief Secretary was stronger after the murder than before. The difficulties were greater; the danger of drifting into a quarrel with Ireland was increased. Gladstone's own power had been shaken. It is more difficult to justify Gladstone's failure to make use either of Chamberlain or of Dilke after the murder than to justify the choice of Cavendish when Forster left Dublin.

Chamberlain would not have gone to Ireland as the agent of any other ideas than his own. But on the main question his ideas were Gladstone's and if he had gone to Ireland he would have been a much more effective ally to Gladstone as Irish Secretary than as President of the Board of Trade in the perpetual struggle in which he was engaged within the Cabinet.

[1] The *Times* put it that Trevelyan was kept outside the Cabinet partly that Gladstone might control Irish business, partly that Spencer should not be overshadowed " just as the National Gallery was kept in its unimposing dimensions not to dwarf St. Martin's Church." May 10, 1882.

[2] Garvin, *op. cit.*, I, p. 366.

The views of Irish policy that Gladstone had to upset were put by Harcourt in a letter of July 7, 1883:

" The more I see of Ireland the more I am convinced that there are two things essential to the maintenance of the tranquillity that Spencer has established, viz., the belief in the minds of the people that the English Government have made up their minds
(1) As to the finality of the Land Act.
(2) As to permanence in its integrity of the Crimes Act."

Chamberlain, seeing Ireland in Ireland, would have had an easy task in answering Harcourt who saw Ireland from the windows of the exasperated Home Office. Gladstone supported by Chamberlain, the Irish Secretary, would have been in a much stronger position for overcoming Harcourt and Hartington than Gladstone supported by Chamberlain, the President of the Board of Trade. Indeed it is probable that Gladstone's only chance of proceeding with his programme of Provincial Councils was thrown away when he passed over Chamberlain. Chamberlain working with Hamilton would have mastered the problems of Irish reconstruction, and armed with all his knowledge and energy he would have been more than a match for Whig obstinacy and caution.

One doubt will occur to anybody who has followed the working of Gladstone's mind. Would he have accepted Chamberlain's programme? That programme was based on social ideas of which Gladstone was distrustful. Chamberlain, taught in a school where none of his colleagues had learnt any lessons, saw that Ireland needed much more help and initiative from her rulers than England, and he was ready to act on that knowledge. If Chamberlain had worked out his Irish plans with the help of Hamilton, as he worked out his British plans with the help of Farrer in the Board of Trade, if he had put the case for Government loans or guarantees or grants or guidance with all the skill that he possessed and the knowledge he would have acquired, it is not improbable that Gladstone would have been converted to his schemes. For Gladstone in the autumn of 1880 had misgivings as we have seen about the three F's that were almost as serious as his misgivings about social experiments with Government grants.   In that case he had shown that when once he was convinced of the necessity of a reform he could argue for it with greater power than those who had desired it from the first.   Even if Chamberlain had not been altogether successful in that attempt, the reform plan that he and Gladstone wanted would not on that account have broken down.   For Chamberlain's programme did not only include such measures as these; it included the reform of Dublin Castle and the development of local government on Gladstone's lines.   Chamberlain might have been quite willing to postpone his schemes for the development of Ireland until he had created these institutions, and in this part of his struggle, at any rate, he and Gladstone would have been in close co-operation.   Nobody can say whether Chamberlain would have succeeded.   He was a man with a good deal of gout in his character and the Irish people and the Irish problem provided ample material for irritation.   He might have fallen out with Parnell.   He had made a fatal blunder in his use of O'Shea at the time of the Kilmainham Treaty.   Healy indeed is said to have warned him against taking the office on the ground that the conditions made it impossible for any Englishman, however full of sympathy, to avoid a bitter quarrel with the Irish people. On the other hand J. K. Cross, a Radical M.P., wrote to Gladstone to say that several Irish M.P.'s, including Sexton, held that Chamberlain was the only man strong enough for the task.   Nobody can say whether he would have succeeded.   But it is probably safe to say that Gladstone's plans had no chance of success if the Irish Office was in the hands of anybody else.

If this view is correct it must seem strange that Gladstone did not appoint him or even think of him.   But this conclusion seems less strange when we remind ourselves of the political atmosphere of the time.   The best description of Chamberlain's position in the Whig world and the Cabinet is that given by Trollope in *Phineas Redux* of the position of Bonteen who, it will be remembered, was made President of the Board of Trade because the Whig Dukes would not have him as Chancellor of the Exchequer.   Lord Richard Grosvenor is well presented in Trollope's picture of the Duke of St. Bungay.

" He was wise enough to know that exclusiveness did not suit the nation, though human enough to feel that it would have been pleasant to himself. There must be Bonteens; but when any Bonteen came up who loomed before his eyes as specially disagreeable, it seemed to him to be a duty to close the door against such a one if it could be closed without violence. A constant gentle pressure against the door would tend to keep down the number of Bonteens."

When a successor to Forster had to be chosen, Lord Richard Grosvenor wrote to Gladstone " to say that he hoped he would not think of Shaw Lefevre, and still less of Chamberlain who would be very glad to try his prentice hand." Chamberlain had reformed the government of one of the largest cities in England; he had made that city the model of vigorous and constructive administration; for two years he had been the head of an important department in Whitehall. Yet his was "a prentice hand." What was wrong with him in Grosvenor's eyes was that he had neither the social traditions nor the stagnant mind of the Whig. If it had been left to the Whigs there would have been no reform, and to Grosvenor a man who had no ideas was better fitted than a man who had bold ideas, for public life. The choice of Chamberlain for the chair at the Cobden Club dinner was followed by a stampede from the Club of its Whig notables.

The relations of Whig and Radical were discussed a good deal during that Parliament. Salisbury offered a condescending sympathy to the Whigs who had to solve their difficulties by combining public loyalty with private imprecation; a description not ill suited to Hartington who accepted without approving the Land Act of 1881 and the Franchise Act of 1884. Hartington himself declared that the Whigs had never been leaders of reform and that their function was to accept reform in time and to prevent it from being too abrupt or violent.[1] To the Whigs Chamberlain was a dangerous man because he was inciting the discontented to demand reforms that were wild and mischievous. They had to put up with him because the alternative was to let the

[1] *Annual Register*, 1883, p. 184: speech, Manchester, November 27.

control of the Liberal party pass into his hands.[1] But they trusted him as little as they liked him.

Chamberlain increased this mistrust and dislike by his methods. In the political world he stood for the caucus and the use of the press; for the organization of forces that would be fatal to independence and integrity, and for co-operation between individual Ministers and editors to promote purposes on which the Minister desired to put pressure on his colleagues. The first method was public and everybody could see it at work. It was the regimentation of politics, the organization of the party system on new and democratic lines. The second was the object of deep suspicion and continual protests within the Cabinet. That Chamberlain got the discredit of all the leakages, even of those for which others were to blame, is not surprising to those who have read Dilke's diaries. For Dilke admits and defends such a method of putting pressure on colleagues and argues that on one occasion he was able to defeat a mischievous measure by a disclosure to the *Daily News*.[2]

It followed that Chamberlain was looked on with suspicion even by those who did not hold or admire the Whig prejudice in favour of exclusiveness. The *Times*, as it has been noted, was critical of the Whig predominance in the Cabinet that Gladstone formed in 1880 and Cavendish's appointment was the subject of a caustic note. But the *Times* regarded Chamberlain as a man who demoralized politics by his electioneering instincts. He was accused of acting from the basest motives in the Kilmainham Treaty.

" The Prime Minister immersed in the complexities and subtleties of his constructive legislation has lost touch of the facts of executive government in Ireland. He has lent too ready an ear to advisers whose political sagacity does not rise above the level of

---

[1] " The prospect of Gladstone's retirement kept Hartington in the Cabinet, who felt that, if he himself resigned, the leadership might in a few months pass into the hands of a Radical successor." Holland, *Life of Devonshire*, Vol. I, p. 377.

[2] That Gladstone suspected Chamberlain in all these cases is clear from a letter he wrote to Granville, May 25, 1885, when some Cabinet secrets were published in the *Birmingham Daily Post*. " The case of leakage is the most scandalous that has yet occurred and has most appearance of *purpose*. Shall I speak of it in Cabinet when we meet in rather strong language? "

the smallest electioneering arts and whose finest strokes of policy consist in squaring 'suspicious' interest and enlisting this or that vote for a consideration."[1]

This reputation injured Chamberlain's influence in his own party, and the bad impression created was not modified by his violence in party warfare, for just as Churchill's violence against Gladstone was half aimed at Northcote, so Chamberlain's violence against the Conservatives was half aimed at Hartington. Hartington, like Salisbury, belonged to the class that toiled not neither did they spin,[2] and the sins that Chamberlain painted in such vivid colours—the enclosures, game preserving and other forms of selfish pleasure—were the sins of landlords, whether Whig or Tory. The famous speech about the lilies of the field provoked Argyll to write a letter to the *Times* in which he argued that if Chamberlain was not removed from the Cabinet for a speech declaring sentiments that the Cabinet was known to disapprove, Cabinet Government would cease to exist. The *Times* supported Argyll in a long leader and called on the Cabinet to act.[3] Even so warm a friend as the *Spectator* complained of another of his speeches (June 25, 1883). In the autumn of 1884 after the Aston riots, his speeches at Birmingham were attacked by Churchill in an amendment to the Address, and though Gladstone gave Chamberlain his powerful support, the amendment was only defeated by 214 votes to 178. The *Annual Register* observed that this majority was far smaller " than a member of the Cabinet, commanding the confidence and sympathy of its supporters had a right to expect." His present violence encouraged his critics to recall his past. In February, 1882, Sir Edward Clarke reminded the House of Commons that Chamberlain had said of Disraeli that he never spoke the truth except by accident, and he warned him that Disraeli's friends would never forget his gibes.[4]

[1] May 17, 1882.

[2] " Lord Salisbury constitutes himself the spokesman of a class—of the class to which he himself belongs, who toil not neither do they spin. . . ."

[3] April 16, 1883.

[4] By a curious chance one of the best of Clarke's speeches in later life was the speech attacking Chamberlain's Transvaal War policy in October 1899.

There were three public men whose speeches at this time were specially sharp and stinging, Chamberlain, Churchill and Salisbury. They were all criticized severely by men of moderate or neutral minds. Gladstone defended Chamberlain skilfully by pleading Salisbury's provocation, but no leader of a Government is grateful to a colleague who adds to his difficulties by his irresponsible outbursts. In this case Gladstone had to defend both Chamberlain and Dilke against continual attack from the angry Queen. It is pitiful to contrast the benefits that Chamberlain and Dilke brought to the causes they believed themselves to be serving with the burdens they threw on their hard-pressed leader. It is indeed under these conditions that Gladstone's magnanimity is most evident. The generous trouble that he took to soothe the Queen's displeasure, the skilful defences he found for his colleagues, the tact and sympathy with which he treated those colleagues, must strike anybody who has read the numerous letters he was compelled to write on this subject. Both Chamberlain and Dilke were troublesome as men are apt to be who take themselves seriously as men of principle among colleagues who seem to them to be men of habit. The liberty they claimed was not always consistent with consideration for their colleagues, and though Gladstone spared himself no trouble to defend the rights of the Minister against the authority of the Crown, he was equally anxious to defend the rights of the Cabinet against a Minister who flouted them. In this case too he might reasonably hold that these young Ministers were wanting in respect not only for the authority of the Cabinet but for the authority of his " stretched out life."[1] For if he regarded his years as a reason for retirement, he never regarded them as a reason why his authority should be discounted so long as he remained in office.

---

[1] Gladstone's letter to Spencer (May 8, 1882) when Dilke refused the Irish office is interesting and characteristic. " Various motives, which I think you would have appreciated inclined the Cabinet (whom under all the circumstances I consulted) to Dilke, but he has refused, plump and positively, on account of the non admission to the Cabinet. Very wrong indeed I think. The notions of right, as between party and person, have greatly changed since I was young."

There is however another reason that may have influenced him. In the remarkable speech he made on Home Rule in February 1882, he had said that his views were held by very few persons in the House of Commons. He was probably looking to the left as well as to the right. A few weeks earlier Chamberlain had made the speech at Liverpool in which he used the analogy of the North and South and spoke firmly against anything like separation. At this time, with the exception of Dilke, the leading Radicals all spoke in this strain, often reproducing Chamberlain's analogy. Courtney and Fawcett made speeches that were almost like an answer to Gladstone's, and Leatham, a leading Radical Yorkshire member, said that the country that begins to parley with its own dissolution is lost. Gladstone may have made up his mind that Chamberlain was likely to be stiff on questions on which he himself desired to keep an open mind and, if that were so, every argument that would otherwise favour his appointment—that he was a man of character, energy and decision—would be an argument against it. The fact that Chamberlain had the Radicals and the Caucus behind him would only add strength to this objection.

How far Gladstone was moved by the Whig hostility, how far he shared it, how far the raw self-confidence of this new Minister rasped an old man's sensibilities,[1] how far his democratic manners and methods seemed a danger to party unity, how far a leader with his own path before him was afraid of adventures into which he might be drawn, how far he feared to find in Chamberlain an opponent of the more liberal policy to which his mind was moving, these are questions that nobody can answer. But it is difficult not to regret his action, for Chamberlain, who had all this energy ready for construction, spent much of it on violent speeches recommending a policy on which he was later to turn his back. England was not so rich in this kind of vigour that she could afford to waste the best years of such a man.

The waste of Chamberlain and the waste of Parnell could both be traced to the blunder over the Kilmainham Treaty.

---

[1] Gladstone once described himself as " censorious and fastidious."

If Parnell had been released without the clumsy manœuvres of O'Shea, the Government would have escaped the odium of suspicion and misunderstanding in which a factious Opposition contrived to envelop their action. After the bitter debates of that spring and the anti-Irish sentiment provoked by the Phoenix Park murders and other outrages, Gladstone, Chamberlain, and Parnell, were each of them in a very difficult position. Gladstone as conciliator was working in a hostile medium. "The wretched murders of yesterday," he wrote in June to Granville, "have produced a temper in the House of Commons which would lead them to vote almost anything we ask, however strong." His horror of the House of Commons atmosphere is well expressed in the letter he wrote to Spencer when he was beaten in trying to soften the search clause of the Coercion Act.

"July 19, 1882.

"In my eyes, as Liberty, especially in the form of domestic security (and in this you would agree) is a very sacred thing, and as the House of Commons is the special guardian of liberty, while the Government is the special guardian of order, it is a great offence, or I should call it an outrage, for the House of Commons while it has confidence in the Government, to force upon it provisions restrictive of liberty, which it does not think necessary for the fulfilment of its proper duty, the maintenance of order."

Chamberlain for his part was more than ever mistrusted by his Whig colleagues who thought he had involved them in an unpleasant mishap. Harcourt was indignant that he still had any relations with Parnell or his friends. Parnell himself was also greatly embarrassed because he had to consider his position in Ireland—seriously affected by the rumours of an agreement over his release—while he was anxious to help the Government to carry reforms on which he and they were agreed. His position he put to Labouchere, who wrote to Chamberlain in June, 1882:

"Parnell says that he wishes Mr. Gladstone would understand his position. He would like him to know (in the strictest confidence) that he has laid an embargo on the funds of the Land League and that he is at daggers drawn with Egan. He says that if he cannot show that he gets anything from adopting a

conciliatory policy he will have to retire from all present connexion with his party and that he will probably be shot."

Gladstone wrote on this to Granville:

" Please consider with care what should be said in the Cabinet
tomorrow on the subject of the enclosed letter. I take it upon
me to let you know the case as it stands between Parnell and
Egan but I beg of you to be kind enough not to let it go further.
The question is what can and what should be said in the Cabinet
tomorrow. My opinion is that if Parnell goes, no restraining
influence will remain; the scale of outrage will soon be enlarged
and no repression can avail to put it down."

A letter written a few days later by Spencer to Granville
shows how difficult it was for Gladstone to manage the
opportunities and the dangers of co-operation with a man
whom he rightly considered indispensable. On June 21,
1882, Spencer said in the course of a letter to Granville:

" What I wish to write to you is that I am greatly alarmed at
rumours which reach me from independent sources as to Mr.
G's either directly or through the Rt. Hon. Joe carrying on something like negotiations with Parnell as to the Bill. I heard it
recently from Mundella and I heard it from the Irish Chancellor
who met Shaw M.P. for Cork County t'other day in Dublin.
Shaw was very irate about this and said, ' Parnell has put his
finger in the Old Man's eye,' meaning that Parnell was hood-
winking Mr. Gladstone. I do trust that this is not the case.
Parnell may now be anxious for peace but his antecedents are
not such as to make him trustworthy and there is a real danger in
alienating the loyal Liberals like Shaw and the Ulster men. I
never for a moment regret our releasing the M.Ps, every day
shows me it was right but if we could have done it without O'Shea
etc. it would have avoided much ill blood etc. Do not let us
drift into a similar mess."

This letter reveals one important difficulty of these years.
Gladstone trusted Parnell and continued to trust him;
Spencer mistrusted him and continued to mistrust him.

Parnell himself was in a very difficult position. For he
wanted two things; to regain and consolidate his authority
in Ireland and to help the Government to carry Irish reform.
The second purpose could not be pursued too openly and
directly for the debates over Kilmainham had spread the

view that he had bought his freedom. He had thus to be more friendly to the Government in private than in public. This explains why from time to time he would throw into the middle of a reasonable speech a violent sentiment that undid all the good he had gained by moderation. Thus in March, 1883, he introduced, as we have seen, a Bill to reform the Land Act.[1] His Bill contained some excellent and urgently needed provisions supplying serious deficiencies in the Act and Gladstone's uncompromising and warlike reply was a disappointment to some good Liberals. That answer is partly explained by a wild sentence in Parnell's speech. For Parnell spoke of the judicial rents then being fixed by the Land Commission as rack rents. Gladstone was always inclined when he had passed an Act to regard any criticism of it as a sort of lèse majesté and for this reason he had agreed with his colleagues in the Cabinet that the Act was not to be re-opened. But if Parnell had wanted to harden the heart of the Government and of its head he could not have chosen a phrase more likely to serve his purpose. Gladstone had exhausted his energy and spent a good deal of his popularity in his own party in carrying first the Land Act of 1881 and then the Arrears Act of 1882. If Parnell was going to represent the judicial rents as rack rents and to repudiate the whole principle of this bold reform, everything that the enemies of this legislation had said would seem to be justified. For Parnell's words sounded in Gladstone's ears as a new declaration of war on the Land Act. Yet a few months later, speaking in Ireland, Parnell almost went out of his way to express his gratitude to the Government for the legislation of that session, the Fisheries Act, the Labourers Act and the Tramways Act and predicted the early passing of a measure of local self-government.[2]

The Irish situation was so complicated as to ruin the hope of co-operation by the method of communication through Mrs. O'Shea. Gladstone wanted Parnell to regain his influence in the agitation, rightly regarding him as a force on the side of order. But Gladstone was not allowed by his colleagues

[1] See Chapter XVII.
[2] Dublin, August 29, 1883.

to meet Parnell's honest and generous overtures in the spirit in which they should have been met, and in which he himself had wished to meet them. Parnell, on his part, though he could restrain and did restrain outrage by displacing leaders who liked violence, could not rule the temper of all his followers. His unhappy entanglement was already weakening his influence. Consequently many Irish members went to great lengths in their attacks on Spencer and the Government. Gladstone was anxious that the Government should abstain as far as possible from prosecutions for articles and speeches, but Spencer lost patience and he made the mistake of prosecuting Davitt, Harrington, Healy, Biggar and others. Gladstone wrote on one occasion trying to dissuade him from prosecuting Biggar for a speech, arguing that speeches attacking the Executive must not be treated in the same way as speeches attacking the Judges. In this case the prosecution ended in fiasco. It followed that there was perpetual war between Parnell's Party and the Irish Government.

This tension was increased by a strange incident arising out of an unhappy device that has already been mentioned for using the good offices of Rome to discourage Irish crime. Gladstone had asked Newman to urge the Pope to throw his influence against violence in Ireland and Newman had replied with some scepticism about the success of such a plan. A mild Home Ruler named Errington had been living in Rome as a kind of unofficial envoy to the Vatican. At his instance the Vatican now intervened in Irish politics with results very surprising both to the Vatican and to England.

Parnell was in financial difficulties. His rents had suffered—he said once that his own tenants were the only tenants in Ireland who responded to the No Rent manifesto—and his various plans for making money by quarrying for gold and minerals in the Wicklow Hills had brought no relief. He had been obliged to raise a mortgage of £14,000 on his Avondale estate. It was known in the autumn of 1882 that the mortgagees threatened to foreclose. Archbishop Croke came forward with a proposal to raise a

National tribute to Parnell " for the splendid public services by which he has earned the bitter hatred of every enemy of his country." The project was disliked at Rome and not content with censuring the Archbishop, the Vatican decided to place its veto on the plan. A papal rescript condemning the subscription was signed by the Prefect and the Secretary of the Sacred Congregation de Propaganda Fide and sent to the Irish Bishops. The result was astonishing both to the Pope and to the English. The English would have applied to the Irish the remark of Montesquieu about tyrants: " The prince who is actuated by the hopes and fears of religion may be compared to a lion, docile only to the voice and tractable to the hand of his keeper." The keeper had been called in, but the lion only roared the louder. Davitt called on the Irish people from his prison cell to show its indignation, and Healy called on it to defeat an English conspiracy. The fund, which stood at seven thousand when the rescript was received, reached in the end forty thousand.

The story of the presentation is well known. The Lord Mayor of Dublin, who was to make the gift, began a speech, but Parnell interrupted him, remarking: " I believe you have got a cheque for me." The Lord Mayor replied that he had, and was preparing, though a little chilled, to resume his speech when Parnell interrupted him again to ask whether it was made payable to order and crossed. With that he put out his hand, took the cheque, and put it in his pocket. Of the manner in which this haughty Protestant received from a Catholic people a large present given in defiance of the Pope, Sexton observed that a labourer would have shown more gratitude for the loan of a penknife. Others, applying what Thackeray said of Swift and his ungraciousness, might argue that there was very little of the Irishman in the Irish leader, and that no man could show such contempt for the Irish people who had not a good deal of the Englishman in his character.

This triumph was soon followed by another. In July 1883, Parnell's Party won a seat at Monaghan in Ulster. Parnell's candidate was Healy, and he is said to have won the seat on the prestige he had gained in the debates on the

Land Bill. Yet in March of this year the *Times* had written of " Mr. Parnell and his friends " as " a dwindling and discredited band " and " the Rump of the Land League."

During the years 1883 and 1884 Parnell's influence was thus growing in Ireland, partly at the expense of the wild and violent men who had usurped authority when he was in prison, but partly too at the expense of the Government. The hope of co-operation for purposes of Irish reform, which had inspired and encouraged Gladstone and Chamberlain when Parnell came out of prison, seemed to have been destroyed. The adverse influences in the Cabinet and Ireland had been too strong.

After the rebuff to Parnell in October 1882 Mrs. O'Shea had made various attempts to get into touch with Mr. Gladstone in connection with amendments to the Land Acts or minor matters of business, but these communications were now sent on to Lord Richard Grosvenor, and she was merely told by him that the matter would be looked into, or would receive careful attention, so that there was little encouragement to persevere. On June 15, 1883, she pleaded earnestly for an interview. But it was not granted.

" I hope," wrote Gladstone to her, " you will indulgently let me ask you to substitute tomorrow a letter for an interview. I have not great faith in my power of carrying accurately in my memory points perhaps of nicety, in which others besides myself are interested and have a joint responsibility, though if it were a matter known to be within my own discretion I would not interfere with your choice of a medium for communication."

The letter she wrote in answer contained a proposal from Parnell for helping in Government business on certain conditions, and a suggestion from Mrs. O'Shea that Gladstone should put Lord Richard Grosvenor into communication with Parnell. Whether this was done does not appear from the Gladstone Papers. At any rate nothing came of it. But in the winter of 1884 and the spring of 1885 hopes of co-operation revived, and a new and serious effort was made to solve the main Irish problem by Chamberlain. This effort came near to success, and yet, as it happened, it was a calamity that it was ever made, for the negotiations incidental to it poisoned the relations between Chamberlain and Parnell, owing to the double dealing of O'Shea who acted as intermediary between the two.

The Crimes Act was due to expire in September 1885. The Radicals in the Government and the House of Commons were against any renewal of coercion, but Spencer considered it necessary. He wanted, as he wrote to Gladstone on January 26, 1885, certain provisions of the Crimes Act to be re-enacted, but he wished this repressive measure to be accompanied by a remedial measure, establishing a representative system of Local Government so that Irish administration should be decentralized.[1] Meanwhile, as Mr. Garvin shows in his full account of Chamberlain's part in the transaction, Chamberlain had already in the winter of 1884 had several conversations with O'Shea, who told him that Parnell was sick of the agitation and would gladly bring it to an end, if he could get reasonable concessions from the Government. Chamberlain and Dilke worked at a scheme for giving Ireland Local Government, of which Chamberlain gave an outline in a letter to a friend, W. H. Duignan of Walsall, on December 17, 1884. Chamberlain would not let Duignan publish the letter, but he gave him leave to show it to any friends, and these friends included a good many of the Irish leaders. In the letter Chamberlain announced that whilst objecting to Home Rule, in so far as it meant separation, he considered that Ireland had a right to a far-reaching and representative system of County Local Government:

" But," he went on to say, " for myself I am willing to go even further. I believe that there are questions, not local in any narrow sense, but which require local and exceptional treatment in Ireland and which cannot be dealt with to the satisfaction of the Irish people by an Imperial Parliament.

" Chief among them are the education question and the land question, and I would not hesitate to transfer their consideration and solution entirely to an Irish Board altogether independent of English Government influence. Such a Board might also deal

[1] He also wanted the Viceroy to be superseded by a Secretary of State.

with railways and other communications, and would, of course, be invested with powers of taxation in Ireland for these strictly Irish purposes. . . ."

This plan sketched by Chamberlain was too ambitious to suit Parnell, who was afraid that so large a scheme would stand in the way of a National Parliament. He wished the Central Board to have administrative without legislative functions and he did not wish to give it power to deal with the Land question. His own plan, as handed to Chamberlain by O'Shea on January 15, 1885, provided for County Boards for all county business, and a Central Board, elected by the County Boards, which would perform the work of various public departments connected with public works and education. All the Boards would have "weighted" representation for landowners. The Central Board would have power to levy national rates for public purposes. Parnell did not wish the police to be under Irish control. Parnell's proposals were thus much more moderate than Chamberlain's. Unfortunately O'Shea, the go-between, concealed from Chamberlain the letters in which Parnell told him to explain to Chamberlain that he regarded the scheme not as a substitute for an Irish Parliament, but solely as an improvement in the system of Local Government, and O'Shea gave Chamberlain to understand that the scheme was Parnell's own proposal for a final settlement, his speeches in favour of Home Rule notwithstanding.

Chamberlain, full of hope, set himself to convert his colleagues in the Cabinet to the idea, and to work out an acceptable scheme. Even Spencer, who had, as we have seen, his own proposals about Local Government, seemed sympathetic, and wrote to Chamberlain on April 14, " I do not think that we are far apart in our views. I shall lean to some Central Board if we can work it out, but the difficulties are very large. . . ." Gladstone, though he took no part in framing the scheme, was strongly in favour. By the end of April everything promised well. Chamberlain's proposals were liked by the Irish Bishops, and in April Chamberlain had had a talk with Manning. Before seeing him Chamberlain consulted Gladstone who approved.

Parnell also saw Manning. Manning and the Bishops preferred Chamberlain's Central Board scheme to Home Rule, and were prepared to support it heartily. Parnell accepted it as a useful minor reform. At last it looked as if the Government might end its days in honour, after giving Ireland a reform that Irish opinion would approve.

Chamberlain's plan, as discussed in the Cabinet, was to involve the practical disappearance of " Castle " administration. There were to be County Boards elected by the Irish people, and a Central Board elected by the County Boards. On both Central and County Boards property would have a " weighted " representation. The Central Board would take over at once from the executive the charge of primary education (and possibly higher education), of Poor Law and Sanitary administration, and of Public Works of all kinds. It would be mainly an executive and administrative body, with certain powers to create bye-laws and raise funds granted by Parliament. Justice, Police and Prisons would be outside its scope.[1]

The first promise of success was soon clouded. The Irish Government, represented by Spencer, Campbell-Bannerman[2] and Hamilton, decided against the scheme. Spencer after reviewing the matter, as he had promised Chamberlain, wrote on April 30 that the only Central Board he could consider would be a Board of Education elected by School Managers and Guardians, and even that might have to have a nominated element. Hamilton and Campbell Bannerman both believed that a plan which combined an Irish administrative body in Dublin with executive control under a British Minister would lead to friction. Spencer himself (May 7) held that Chamberlain's scheme " would only lead to difficulty in the administration of the country and would certainly make even more bitter than now the relations between England and Ireland." Consequently when the Cabinet came to discuss it the plan was defeated, for all the Ministers in the Lords, except Granville, were on Spencer's

[1] Guedalla, *op. cit.*, pp. 356 and 357.

[2] Campbell-Bannerman had succeeded Trevelyan as Irish Secretary in October 1884.

side and voted against it. Harcourt was at first strongly opposed to it, but he was converted, and in the end the only Minister in the Commons who was hostile was Hartington. Gladstone observed to Chamberlain, when the decision was taken on May 9, " These men have rejected this scheme, but if God spares their lives for five years more they will be glad to accept something infinitely stronger."

What was Gladstone's position with regard to the Central Board scheme? He has been criticized for not giving Chamberlain fuller support. He found himself, as so often before, in sympathy with Chamberlain on Irish questions and in disagreement with the majority of his colleagues. He agreed with the scheme on the whole, though he would have liked to put the Police under the Central Board. In order to make the scheme more palatable to its opponents, Gladstone made two suggestions: (1) that a Bill embodying it should be introduced too late in the year to pass and the question left to the electorate; (2) that the Board could be suspended during the existing Parliament at any time by Act in Council. Neither suggestion seems to have pleased either side. But he looked on himself as on the brink of retirement. He thought it impossible that the scheme could be carried through the Cabinet without Spencer's concurrence, and in this case it seemed likely that Chamberlain and Dilke would resign. As he was himself retiring from politics, he did not want so to resign as to appear to be acting with Chamberlain and Dilke against their colleagues. In this he was well justified, for the party would clearly break up if the Prime Minister resigned with two of his colleagues in protest against the decisions of his Government.

The situation in which he found himself was clearly described in a memorandum of an important conversation with Granville on May 6.

" My opinions, I said, were very strong and inveterate. I did not calculate upon Parnell and his friends, or upon Manning and his Bishops. Nor was I under any obligation to follow or to act with Chamberlain. But independently of all questions of party, of support, and of success, I looked upon the extension of a strong measure of Local Government like this to Ireland, now that the question is effectually raised by the Crimes Act, invaluable in itself, and as the only hopeful means of saving Crown and State from an ignominious surrender in the next Parliament after a mischievous and painful struggle. (I did not advert to the difficulties which will in this session be experienced in carrying on a great battle for the Crimes Act.) My difficulty would lie not in my pledges or declarations (tho' those, of a public character, are serious) but in my opinions.

" Under these circumstances I said I take into view the freedom of my own position. My engagements to my Colleagues are fulfilled: the great Russian question is probably settled: if we stand firm on the Soudan we are now released from that embarrassment: and the Egyptian question, if the financial Convention be safe, no longer presents any very serious difficulties. I am entitled to lay down my office as having done my work.

" Consequently the very last thing I should contemplate is opening the Irish difficulty in connection with my resignation should I resign. It would come antecedently to any Parliamentary treatment of that problem. . . ."

It was to prevent any misunderstanding on Chamberlain's part that Gladstone wrote a letter to him embodying this view of his own position (May 6, 1885). " I have no reason to think," he wrote to Granville, " he supposes me in any way bound to act with any section of men or opinions on the impending Irish questions. Yet he may think so; and if he does it is desirable to remove such an idea from his mind, which is the aim of this letter." To Chamberlain he wrote:

" I think that to my conversations with you on the merits of the case as regards Crimes Bill and Local Government Bill for Ireland I ought to add a word on my personal position, which is peculiar at this moment.

" I consider that my interposition in these questions is that of an *amicus curiae*. My covenant with my colleagues about Redistribution is substantially fulfilled, and our foreign difficulties are as I conceive (if the Financial Commission for Egypt can now be regarded as safe in France) effectually relieved.

" Such at least are the appearances and probabilities of the case. The result is that I am a free man, and am entitled to claim my release without either rendering or having a reason, except that my work is done.

" My opinions about Local Self-Government in Ireland have I think long been well known; but I have preserved an entire liberty of action as to the time and circumstances of their application. Still, I shall be most happy if in the smallest degree I can aid those who are less free than myself towards the solution of a problem soon to come fully into view. . . ."

The Central Board scheme had been rejected by the Cabinet, but the problem of Coercion remained:

" I am not going to bore you," wrote Gladstone to Spencer on the day of the rejection, May 9, " with doses of persuasion about a Central Board in Ireland—that subject is dead as mutton for the present, though as I believe for the present only. It will quickly rise again and as I think perhaps in larger dimensions.

" But how as to the immediate future? Some members of the Cabinet, I do not know how many, will resign rather than demand from Parliament (without a Central Board Bill) the scheme of penal or repressive provisions which you desire.

" In what way, after such resignation, are such provisions to be carried through Parliament in what remains of the session."[1]

---

[1] The intensity of Gladstone's feelings against coercion is shown in a letter he wrote to Spencer next day, but withheld, probably in consequence of pressure from Granville.

Secret.   Downing St.
        (cancelled)   May 10–11. 85.
My dear Spencer,
     I think that on this unhappy Irish matter my convictions have passed beyond the stage of argument and in the Cabinet of yesterday leaving argument to others I . . . only at what in my belief are facts.
     It is always well, and the more so in proportion as the case is difficult, to narrow the field by noting fixed points that are to be taken for granted.
     One of these I have already stated—the Central Board Scheme is dead and buried.
     Another I thought you knew that my fixed convictions make it simply *impossible* for me to be responsible for a fresh Crimes Act, such as you at present desire without the Central Board Scheme.
     Consequently the only alternatives open to me would be
       1. to resign with those who have the same opinion
       2. to resign antecedently, on grounds partly personal and peculiar to myself.
     Between them my choice is made, and I have described it you and Granville and *not to any of those*, with whom I agree on the case.
                         Ever your's
                         W. E. GLADSTONE.
     If and when you think the time has come for a Cabinet please to let me know. But that will be a formidable gathering, unless preceded by an understanding.
     (The word omitted in the first paragraph is illegible.)

The Radicals, deprived of their own scheme, were unwilling to allow any minor remedies. Just as Parnell did
not wish the Central Board to have powers which might
prejudice the creation of an Irish Parliament, so they did not
wish for any scheme of Land Purchase since it might prejudice the creation of a Central Board. How far would
Spencer modify his repressive measure? How far would
the Radicals allow remedial measures? Ministers wrangled
over the Crimes Act and Land Purchase. Gladstone tried
hard to bring the two parties to a compromise, and on one
occasion his efforts nearly broke up the Cabinet, for Chamberlain and Dilke both held that he had treated them
unfairly in announcing, in spite of their disagreement, the
Government's arrangement for a Land Purchase Bill. His
action, as the papers show, was due to a genuine misunderstanding. The controversy has little bearing on the main
issue of the time except for its effect in increasing the strain
on temper and confidence.

Gladstone's own views at this time are given very frankly
in the course of a long letter to Hartington on May 30.

" What if Chamberlain and Dilke, as you seem to anticipate,
raise the question of a prospective declaration about Local
Government in Ireland as a condition of their remaining in the
Cabinet?

" I consider that question as disposed of for the present (much
against my will) ; and I do not *see* that any of us, having accepted
the decision, can attempt to disturb it. Moreover their ground
will be very weak and narrow, for their actual reason of going, if
they go, will be the really small question arising upon the Land
Purchase Bill.

" I think they will commit a great error, if they take this course.
It will be straining at the gnat. No doubt it will weaken the
party at the election; but I entertain no fear of the immediate
effect. Their error will however in my view go beyond this.
Forgive me if I now speak with great frankness on a matter, one
of few, in which I agree with them, and not with you. I am
firmly convinced that on the Local Government for Ireland they
hold a winning position; which by resignation now they will
greatly compromise. You will all I am convinced have to give
what they recommend; at the least what they recommend.

" There are two differences between them and me on this subject. First as to the matter; I go rather further than they do; for I would undoubtedly make a *beginning* with the Irish Police. Secondly as to the *ground*: here I differ seriously. I do not reckon with any confidence upon Manning or Parnell: I have never looked much in Irish matters at negotiation or the conciliation of leaders. I look at the question in itself, and I am deeply convinced that the measure in itself will (*especially* if accompanied with similar measures elsewhere, e.g., in Scotland) be good for the country and the Empire; I do not say unmixedly good, but with advantages enormously outweighing any drawbacks.

" Apart from these differences, and taking their point of view, I think they ought to endeavour to fight the election with you; and, in the *new state of affairs* which will be presented after the Dissolution, try and see what effect may be produced on your mind, and on other minds, when you have to look at the matter *cominus* and not *eminus*, as actual and not as hypothetical."

Gladstone was here writing as an *amicus curiae*, looking forward to an election in which he would not himself take part, and he feared that if Chamberlain resigned he would prejudice the chances of co-operation between him and Hartington on a forward Irish policy. With an optimism that had survived disappointment after disappointment, he believed that events would educate Hartington.

Early in June it became obvious that, apart from the quarrels in the Cabinet, the new Crimes Bill, though considerably modified, would have no chance of getting through the House of Commons, without further change. Spencer was standing out for the Bill as it was. Gladstone urged him not to face his colleagues with " an ugly and a sorry choice." The question was still unsettled when, on the night of June 8-9, the Conservatives joined forces with the Parnellites to defeat the Budget. The voting was 264 to 252. Thirty-nine Parnellites voted against the Government and there were seventy-six Liberal abstentions. To some members of the Government defeat seemed not too high a price to pay for the end of internal discord.[1]

[1] Acton states that " the defeat was prepared by the Birmingham wire-pullers to evade the impending collision between the two wings of the Government; and they induced their people to stay away and bring the Tories in for a time. If you do not know or believe this, let me say that I have it on the best

Defeat was no disaster, but for a man less Olympian than Gladstone in his sense of public duty it might well have left a bitter sting. For the spectacle that Ireland presented might have broken the heart of any man whose power and spirit depended on human gratitude. What had Gladstone accomplished for Ireland? In 1879 Parnell had declared that what was wanted for the solution of the Irish problem was that the tenants should pay reasonable rents for thirty years and then become the owners of their farms. This was treated as a proposal so ridiculous that it was cited by the *Times* to show that Parnell could not be regarded as a serious force. Gladstone by his stupendous exertions had given Ireland the most difficult half of that programme. He had given her too a series of social reforms of which it can be said that, though they were tentative and modest in themselves, they were the key to all the reforms that have followed since: reforms for the labourers, reforms for the Congested Districts as well as reforms for the farmers. He had failed in his further projects but his failure was due largely, perhaps wholly, to the murders in Phoenix Park. He had resisted the strong pressure for leaving Ireland out of the Reform Bill and had taken the risk of adding half a million to the Irish electorate, though he had been warned that such an extension of the franchise would put an end, as it did, to his own party in Ireland.

This was an heroic record. Of the gratitude of Ireland we have a grim picture given by Dilke who went to Dublin in May, 1885, of a walk with Spencer.

" In the course of the whole long walk but one man lifted his hat to Spencer, who was universally recognised, but assailed by the majority of those we met with shouts of ' Who killed Miles Joyce? ' while some varied the proceedings by calling ' Murderer ' after him. A few days later, when I was driving with Lady Spencer in an open carriage, a well-dressed bicyclist came riding through the cavalry escort, and in a quiet, conversational tone observed to us ' Who killed Myles Joyce? ' " [1]

Birmingham authority. . . ." (Chamberlain was Acton's tenant at the time at Princes Gate. Acton wrote this letter (June 16, 1885) to Mary Gladstone from that address.) *Acton's Correspondence*, I, 265, edited by Figgis and Laurence,
[1] Gwynn and Tuckwell, *Life of Dilke*, Vol. II, p. 138.

[*Stewart & Co.*]

LORD SPENCER

No country can rival Ireland as the home of the surprises and perversities of history. Spencer, taunted and shunned in the streets of Dublin, was to face the hatred of the English upper class for the Ireland that hated him, showing to the fashionable world, of which he had been a favourite, the firm integrity that had seemed to Irishmen the mark of a man without feeling.[1] Of the other chief actors in this chapter Chamberlain had given Ireland his last service, and was soon to become her most obstinate and merciless enemy. Parnell, because he had lacked the moral strength to tell his mistress that she must choose between him and her aunt's fortune, was already wasting in a life of squalid intrigue and was soon to destroy by a stupendous blunder, his power to help the nation that had trusted him. Gladstone, who had thought of himself as on the brink of retirement, was to spend seven years in the most arduous and heroic struggle of his long life, for the sake of Irish freedom.

[1] Chamberlain afterwards derided Spencer for supporting Home Rule after refusing the Central Board. But Spencer's position is quite intelligible. He took Hamilton's view that the Central Board scheme would not work, and that Home Rule would. Mr. Spender has pointed out that C.B. opposed the Central Board on the ground on which he disapproved of the Lyttelton constitution for the Transvaal in 1906. See his memorandum of April 30, 1885. *Life of Campbell-Bannerman*, I, p. 84.

CHAPTER XX

In the winter of 1884, while Chamberlain was negotiating with Manning and Parnell through the unfortunate medium of O'Shea, a distinguished Irishman was discussing the Irish problem with a leading Conservative. The Irishman was Sir Charles Gavan Duffy who in his youth had suffered imprisonment as an Irish patriot and had emigrated to Australia in 1856, disgusted by the failure of his effort to form and keep together an independent Irish Party in the House of Commons. In Australia he had had a successful career, being Prime Minister of Victoria from 1871 to 1877. In 1880 he had returned to Europe and settled at Nice. He had followed the new movements in Ireland with great sympathy and had written in favour of Gladstone's Land Act in 1882. The Conservative was Lord Carnarvon who had been Colonial Secretary twice, first under Derby in 1867, and then under Disraeli in 1878. He was a man with a mind of his own and he had left office on both occasions over a disagreement on policy. He had resigned in 1867 in protest against Disraeli's Reform Bill and in 1878 in protest against Disraeli's decision to send the Fleet to Constantinople.

Carnarvon and Duffy had made friends in 1883 and from that time the two had corresponded on the Irish question. Gavan Duffy had urged Carnarvon to consider whether the Conservative Party could not find a settlement. In October 1884, Duffy stayed with Carnarvon and put before him a scheme for an Irish Parliament. He declared that if there was the least chance of its being adopted by the Conservative Party he would return to England and devote to it all that he had of strength and life remaining. He would canvass the Roman Catholic Bishops and all the moderate Party, and he felt certain that, though Parnell and many of his demagogic supporters would not like the proposal, they could not withstand it. It was agreed between him and Carnarvon that Duffy should write an article on these lines in the *National Review* and that Carnarvon should sound his friends on the subject. In February 1885, Carnarvon wrote to Salisbury calling his attention to the article and saying that it represented the opinion of the moderate Roman Catholic Party:

" For my own part I have little doubt that in the general interests of the country and of the Irish Loyalists—whose safety is the great difficulty and the principal consideration to which we are bound in point of honour and policy—our best and almost only hope is to come to some fair and reasonable arrangement for Home Rule with their protection guaranteed as strongly as constitutional characters and fundamental laws can guarantee it." In his letter he suggested several modes of action—a speech, a committee, a secret committee, a joint committee, " or it might be perhaps possible to repeat the experiment of the last session and to come to an understanding with the Government, . . . or to move for a committee to consider Imperial relations and under cover of this to deal with the relations of Ireland to England. . . . Turn it as one may, the whole question is most thorny. But I still incline to believe that it is our wisest policy to take the initiative."[1]

Salisbury replied saying that it was possible that such a scheme could be devised but he was not hopeful. In any case it would need plenipotentiaries. " The Irishmen who offer it must represent a majority of the Irish members and the Englishmen who accept it must command a majority in Parliament. From that point of view I think we have plenty of time for reflection before us." But the time was shorter than Salisbury supposed, for in June Salisbury found himself Prime Minister,[2] compelled to appoint a Viceroy and to form some plan for Irish policy. Carnarvon discussed Duffy's scheme with Stafford Northcote who thought

---

[1] Hardinge, *Life of Carnarvon*, III, p. 151.

[2] The Conservative Government could not dissolve Parliament till the autumn, because they had to wait for the new register including the voters enfranchised by the Act of 1884.

it vague but worth consideration.   On June 15 Carnarvon put his view before a meeting of Cabinet Ministers.   He suggested that the Government should appoint Sir Garnet Wolseley Viceroy, select an Irishman for every Irish office, make it clear that a full and permanent settlement was going to be attempted and drop Coercion.   The next day Salisbury entreated and persuaded Carnarvon to take the office of Viceroy himself.

One of Carnarvon's first visitors was Manning who came to give him the views of the Irish Bishops.   They were in favour of self-government for the different provinces but against a Central Parliament which they feared would weaken the Church.   He urged Carnarvon to see the four Archbishops and promised that such a meeting would have an excellent effect, for the relations of the Viceroy in the previous Parliament had been those of " control " and " contempt."   Carnarvon readily agreed.   On June 30 he took the oath as Viceroy, Gibson being sworn in at the same time as Irish Lord Chancellor with the title of Ashbourne and a seat in the Cabinet.   Carnarvon returned to London for a Cabinet on July 4 at which he put his immediate policy before his colleagues.   Coercion was to be dropped; the Liberal Government's Bill to amend the Labourers Housing Act of 1883 was to be taken up and passed, and a Land Purchase Bill introduced.   This Bill, afterwards known as the Ashbourne Act, proceeded on a new principle in advancing from the State to the tenant the whole purchase price of his farm.   The Government accepted this policy.

Gavan Duffy, finding his friend in office was anxious to do his part in helping the cause of Irish reform under Conservative auspices.   He arranged an interview between Carnarvon and Justin McCarthy for July 6.   McCarthy assured Carnarvon that Parnell, whom he described as " cold, narrow and unimaginative," was against violence and confiscation, and said that he would like a gradual scheme of self-government.   He urged Carnarvon to see him.

Fresh from his talks with Manning and McCarthy, and

cheered by the atmosphere of Dublin where he had been received as a second Fitzwilliam, Carnarvon went to the House of Lords, July 6, 1885, to describe his policy. There could be no mistake about its character. He condemned Coercion and he put his alternative policy into some generous and striking phrases:

" Just as I have seen in English colonies, across the sea, a combination of English, Irish and Scotch settlers bound together in loyal obedience to the law and the crown and contributing to the general prosperity of the country, so I cannot conceive that there is any irreconcilable bar here in their native home and in England to the unity and amity of the two nations."

The reference to the colonies and the use of the word nation made the meaning of this sentence clear and showed what was in his mind when he went on to say that " with honesty and single-mindedness on the one side, and with the willingness of the Irish people on the other," it was not hopeless to look for some satisfactory solution of this terrible question. " My Lords," he added, " these I believe to be the opinions and the views of my colleagues."

The *Spectator*, commenting on the speech, remarked that Conservatives listening to it must have felt like the man in the sedan chair without any bottom who said that if he did not know he was riding he would think he was walking, and some of Carnarvon's colleagues must have shared the surprise of these Conservative listeners, particularly when they came to the sentence describing their agreement with his views.

Carnarvon's adventure had started well. He had behind him the good will of the Bishops, and something almost resembling confidence in the Irish Party where Gavan Duffy and Justin McCarthy could speak of his manifest sympathy. He had a still greater advantage. The leader of the Opposition, himself the most powerful man in England, was anxious for his success. Consequently though this volte-face offered a splendid target for his ridicule and invective, Gladstone made a speech on that new departure in the House of Commons which Randolph Churchill himself described as " magnanimous." But within a fortnight the prospect had been clouded. For that great misfortune the chief blame falls on Salisbury and Hicks Beach, who showed themselves wanting in moral strength, but some of it on Parnell who showed himself wanting in wisdom.

Parnell gave notice of a motion attacking Spencer's administration of the criminal law and calling for an inquiry into the Maamtrasna case. It was a temptation to exploit the new Conservative sympathy in this dramatic manner but a wiser man would have seen its dangers. Carnarvon saw at once that his whole policy might be imperilled by a false step at this moment. The House of Commons had rejected such a motion in the previous autumn. Ashbourne, the Irish Lord Chancellor, then in the House of Commons, had spoken against it and the present Ministers, with the exception of Churchill and Gorst, had taken the same view. He wrote at once on July 1, to Salisbury:

" Gibson and I, as well as Dyke [the Chief Secretary] are, I think, quite agreed as to the course to be pursued, which should be not so much a defence of Spencer as a support of his defence by his own friends. On them really rests the chief burden, and if we support them in this, we do I think what is right and fair."[1]

The Cabinet accepted this view on July 7, but before the debate came on Hicks Beach re-opened the question. He wrote to Carnarvon urging him to reconsider the answer to be given. Carnarvon said that he infinitely preferred to hold to the Cabinet decision, but that if great care was taken in the language used, he could not object to an intimation that the Viceroy would examine any case in which a prisoner presented a memorial to him. How strongly he dreaded any appearance of attacking Spencer he made clear to Salisbury.

" It is, as you will see, of *vital* importance involving personal and collective honour, and if great care is not taken, perhaps leading to the most serious difficulties and risks here. . . . It is well to turn a parliamentary corner, but it can be done at too great a cost sometimes, and the day of reckoning in this case will come very rapidly if any unwise promises are made or implied. . . . If we shake confidence amongst the Government here—I mean the

[1] Sir Arthur Hardinge, *Life of Carnarvon*, Vol. III, p. 168.

executive and judicial—we shall open a chapter of disaster and discredit."

Salisbury replied:

" I have written to Beach stating my view that he ought not to depart from the resolution of the Cabinet without consulting it again—that personal honour was involved in the matter— and that we should lose confidence as a Government if we seemed to allow Parliamentary tactics to interfere with the administration of the Criminal Law."[1]

Salisbury's views, Prime Minister though he was, had as little effect on Beach as Carnarvon's. The debate in the House of Commons (on July 17), so far as Ministers went, turned into a general attack on Spencer: into a display, in fact, of the very spirit that Salisbury said would destroy confidence in the Government.[2] The Irishmen were so much delighted that they never raised the Maamtrasna case again, although Carnarvon left it where Spencer had left it. But they paid a heavy price for a few hours' satisfaction. For with this debate began the Conservative revolt against Carnarvon to which Salisbury later surrendered. It was said at the time that many Conservatives looked as if they had been sentenced to death as they listened to these speeches; Brodrick (afterwards Lord Midleton) made an energetic protest. The *Times* remarked next day:

" The Chancellor of the Exchequer, the responsible spokesman of a Ministry which proposes to rely in the government of Ireland on the ordinary law, was surely under an obligation to have said something to show that he had neither sympathy with nor belief in the monstrous accusations of Mr. Parnell and his associates, which the House of Commons and the public opinion of Great Britain indignantly and unhesitatingly repudiated last year. It is not Lord Spencer alone whose good faith has been impeached, but the Irish judiciary, the law officers of the Crown, the public prosecutors, the magistracy and the police."

The disastrous effect on the temper of the Conservative party was noted at once by the friends of the new policy. Carnarvon wanted to meet the wishes of the Bishops and

---

[1] Hardinge, *op. cit.*, Vol. III, p. 169.

[2] Salisbury tried to counteract this impression by a speech in the Lords on July 21 in which he gave Spencer warm praise for his " high and manly courage."

make a grant to University College. Hart Dyke wrote to him that " the whole political position " had " been transformed by the debate," and Harrowby, the Privy Seal, wrote to him:

" The Roman Catholic vote of money is, I fear, really impossible. I have no doubt it would ruin our prospects at the general Election.   Already there is a growing distaste for our supposed Irish Alliance, distrust has been excited by Randolph's and Gorst's unfortunate speeches on the Maamtrasna affair[1] (which have altered the situation since you were here). . . ."[2]

Thus the ghost of Maamtrasna still worked mischief. For this debate had two disastrous consequences. It roused Conservative feeling against Carnarvon's policy and it helped to mislead Parnell.   For Parnell naturally knew nothing of the strong protest that Carnarvon had sent to Salisbury, and he believed that the speeches of Beach, Churchill, and Gorst, represented his views.   It is not surprising that he afterwards read more into Carnarvon's language to him than Carnarvon meant.

Carnarvon, having obtained Salisbury's consent,[3] had agreed to McCarthy's suggestion that he should meet Parnell.   The meeting took place at 15 Hill Street on August 1.   Salisbury and Ashbourne were the only members of the Cabinet who knew of it.   Salisbury, remembering doubtless the use that had been made of Parnell's unhappy letter from Kilmainham, urged that there should be the minimum of writing.   Carnarvon went straight from his talk to Hatfield where he drew up a memorandum of his talk and showed it to Salisbury.[4]   This memorandum contained a passage of great significance:

[1] To complete the Maamtrasna story it should be added that Carnarvon left the convicted men in prison and that the last survivor was released in 1903. His wife made a personal appeal to Queen Alexandra when she and the King visited Ireland and the Government released her husband.   Healy says that the Irish M.P.s had never pressed his case because it was noticed that he did not go to confession when the priest visited the jail and this was taken as an admission of guilt.

[2] Hardinge, *op. cit.*, Vol. III, p. 172.

[3] By an extraordinary blunder Balfour stated at Stockport on July 15, 1893, that Salisbury had not been consulted about the interview.   Hardinge, *op. cit.*, Vol. III, p. 248.

[4] The memorandum is given in full. Hardinge, *op. cit.*, III, 178–181.

" In the course of conversation I raised the question of a removal of the Irish members from the House of Commons, if the representation in an Irish Parliament should be considerable. He replied in such a way as to show that he would regret it, but also that he would accept it, if it was an inevitable or necessary condition of Self-Government."

It is interesting too to notice that there was no mention of any special provision for Ulster. " Lord Salisbury read and accepted the memorandum, and said that the conversation seemed to him to have been conducted with perfect discretion, and that he agreed in the line Lord Carnarvon was pursuing."[1]

It is curious to compare the account that Carnarvon gave to Salisbury of his conversation with the account that Balfour gave later in the House of Commons of Carnarvon's instructions. On March 10, 1890, Balfour said:

" As the Right Honourable Gentleman (Harcourt) has challenged me, I will tell him what the facts are. Lord Carnarvon wrote to Lord Salisbury that the Hon. Member for Cork desired to speak with him, Lord Carnarvon, on certain matters relating to Ireland ; Lord Salisbury said in my presence, and, if I may express an opinion, said rightly, that if the Hon. Member for Cork desired to see Lord Carnarvon, Lord Carnarvon must see him; but Lord Carnarvon on his part was to listen to what the Rt. Hon. Member for Cork had to say and to say nothing."

There was afterwards a sharp controversy between Parnell and Carnarvon about what happened at the interview, but Carnarvon, on his own showing, as anybody will see who reads his memorandum, did not confine himself to listening. The point of controversy between him and Parnell was not whether Carnarvon said something or said nothing, but whether he gave Parnell to believe that he was making promises for the Government.

On October 6, 1885, at the first of the autumn Cabinets, Carnarvon laid his views again before his colleagues. He thought local county boards were the most dangerous form of local government, for they would mean government by the lowest class of administrators; there was an undeniable

[1] Hardinge, *op. cit.*, Vol. III, p. 181.

danger in a local parliament, but he was disposed to believe that there might be less danger in it than in any other solution.[1] The influence of these suggestions on Salisbury's mind was seen in the speech he made the next day at Newport. In this speech Salisbury defended the dropping of coercion on two grounds. Coercion was inconsistent with the grant of a popular franchise and it had failed to stop boycotting, the chief of the grievances of which loyalists complained. He referred to what he called Parnell's remarkable speech about the arrangements of Austria-Hungary and said that he did not wish to discourage a plan in which the fondest hopes of high Imperial greatness for England in the future may be realized. "But with respect to Ireland I am bound to say that I have never seen any plan or any suggestion which gives me at present the slightest ground for anticipating that it is in that direction that we shall find any substantial solution of the difficulties of the problem." Spencer once pointed out to Gladstone that much greater importance had been attached to the words " for the present " in one of his speeches than to everything else he had said.

But another passage in this speech had a still greater significance for those who knew of the controversies between the partisans of the small and of the large settlement:

" Local authorities are more exposed to the temptation of enabling the majority to be unjust to the minority when they obtain jurisdiction over a small area, than is the case when the authority derives its sanction and extends its jurisdiction over a wider area. In a large central authority the wisdom of several parts of the country will correct the folly and mistakes of one. In a local authority that correction is to a much greater extent wanting, and it would be impossible to leave that out of sight, in any extension of any such local authority in Ireland."

If these sentences mean anything they might be supposed to support Chamberlain's scheme against Hartington's, and to offer considerations that might even support Gladstone's later scheme against Chamberlain.

But Salisbury, as we know from Carnarvon, was not giving

[1] Hardinge, *op. cit.*, III, 194.

as much attention to the Irish problem as his audiences might have been led to expect. Iddesleigh had suggested a month earlier that the party should put a constructive and sympathetic policy before the electors and he had pointed out, what Gladstone had pointed out once to his colleagues, that you could call the same thing Home Rule if you wished to frighten people away, or local Self-government if you wished to attract support.[1] He argued that the electors had the right to expect a definite declaration from Ministers before they cast their votes. Nothing however was decided. Carnarvon was still pressing for a constructive policy, urged not only by his own interest in such a scheme but by the growing sense of danger in Ireland. On November 18 he proposed to Salisbury that the Cabinet should adopt one of two plans. The first was that a joint committee of both Houses should be set up to consider the government of Ireland, and the second that a powerful educational council should be set up for all Ireland. He himself favoured the first plan. Salisbury replied that he could not act like Peel nor remain a member of the Government if it adopted such a policy, but that he was ready to facilitate it by retiring.[2] For the moment this was of course decisive, but Carnarvon did not despair. At a Cabinet on December 14, after the elections, he returned to his plan for a Joint Committee and suggested that the Government should ascertain by very private negotiations whether the support of any or all the Opposition leaders could be obtained. The Cabinet rejected his policy, and the Carnarvon adventure was at an end.[3]

Of Salisbury's behaviour Carnarvon has left an account that should in fairness to him be given here.

" I had several conversations with Lord Salisbury in private on the subject. Indeed, I felt it necessary for my own sake as well as for the sake of the question itself to lay my ideas clearly before him: and I am bound to say that he was consistent in his refusal to entertain them. But his main objection to any such proposals

[1] Hardinge, *op. cit.*, III, 191.
[2] Hardinge, *op. cit.*, III, 197.
[3] Hardinge, *op. cit.*, III, 206.

2C

was his fear of repeating the conduct of Sir Robert Peel at the time of the Corn Law Repeal. In addition to this he was so engrossed with the management of the Foreign Office that it was with very great difficulty that any other subject could be brought before him."[1]

Carnarvon was giving all his mind to Ireland and none of it to the tactics of party. Salisbury regarded Ireland as only part and a less important part of his problem. He was less afraid at that moment of Irish disorder than of the disestablishment of the Church. By a curious irony it was Chamberlain, who was to be his ally for nearly twenty years, who had frightened him into refusing to consider an active Irish policy. In his Newport speech he attacked Chamberlain's speeches as the chief danger to our civilization.

" The Church would be stripped and bare. In every part of the land the machinery by which God's word had been preached, by which Christianity had been upheld, by which all the ministrations of religion had been carried to suffering humanity would be put an end to. We can talk in no ambiguous language. It is a matter of life and death to us. Our party is bound up with the maintenance of the Established and Endowed Church of the country."

In this world of wild attacks on religion and land, with a statesman as reckless as Chamberlain, with a colleague as unscrupulous as Churchill, party safety was the first of his cares. To that everything had to be subordinated. A dissatisfied Ireland might be a danger to the Empire but the wicked Radicals were threatening something older and more sacred still: they wanted to undo the work of Theodore of Tarsus and throw England back to the fifth century.

It was widely believed at the time that the Government had thought seriously of a constructive policy in Ireland designed to meet the demand for self-government. This is clear from the language of the Unionist papers after the elections were over.

The *Spectator* (January 2, 1886) commenting on a speech by Sir R. Webster declaring that there should be no truckling with ideas that tended to separation, remarked:

[1] Hardinge, *op. cit.*, III, 219.

" That means we suppose that the suggestions thrown out in Lord Salisbury's Newport speech have been warmly repudiated by his colleagues, for assuredly the comparison between the Hungarian Diet and Home Rule for Ireland was not thrown out as a mere straw to see which way the wind was blowing but did represent some political speculation to which Lord Salisbury was at the time more or less inclined."

The *Economist* (February 20, 1886) said: " Lord Salisbury was turned out because after much vacillation he had at length definitely pronounced against Home Rule and in favour of the immediate strengthening of the law."

The best and the most illuminating explanation of the Newport speech is given by Lady Gwendolen Cecil.

" He had to place clearly on record the principles and limitations by which the Irish policy of his party would be controlled without using such quotably provocative phrases as would, at the moment, make Lord Carnarvon's administrative task harder, or needlessly interfere with Mr. Parnell's vindictive purpose against the Liberals."[1]

Salisbury had to consider his own views, Carnarvon's different views, and the electioneering importance of Parnell's sympathies. He wanted to encourage Carnarvon without encouraging the hopes raised by Carnarvon; to warn Parnell without estranging him from the Conservative party or, as Lady Gwendolen puts it, without needlessly interfering with his vindictive purpose against the Liberals. It is not surprising that even a master of diplomatic phrasing failed to produce precisely the effect he desired on public opinion, and that Hartington read the speech with disgust, thinking it an unscrupulous bid for the Irish vote and Gladstone with pleasure, thinking it meant that Salisbury was moving towards Carnarvon's policy.

Salisbury's conduct during these six months was harshly judged both by opponents and supporters at the time.

" Certainly it is Lord Salisbury," said the *Spectator*, " whose unscrupulous abandonment of his own principles has brought about the present state of anarchy. If he had not allowed Lord Randolph Churchill to intrigue for the Parnellite vote by the

[1] *Life of Salisbury*, Vol. III, p. 271.

surrender of the renewal of the Crimes Act we should not be where we are in Ireland." (January 27, 1886.)

Thus the *Spectator* took in January, 1886, the view that Shaftesbury had taken in June, 1885.

" June 9th.—Have just seen defeat of Government on the Budget by Conservatives and Parnellites united ; an act of folly amounting to wickedness. God is not in all their thoughts, nor the country either. All seek their own, and in their own is party-spirit, momentary triumph, political hatred, and the indulgence of low, personal, and unpatriotic passion."[1]

The *Times*, though anxious to say nothing to weaken Salisbury, was scarcely less caustic in its comments on Churchill's attempts on February 13, 1886, to justify his vagaries to his constituents.

The history of this blunder is not so simple as this analysis would make it. But of those who would have found a less harsh explanation of the motives that had inspired the conduct of Salisbury's government, few would not have deplored the consequences. It was obvious that Salisbury's first term as Prime Minister was as disastrous in its Irish policy as it was brilliantly successful in its foreign policy.

Salisbury's mistake over Carnarvon was not unlike Gladstone's mistake over Gordon. Gladstone summed up the truth in his later years when he said that Gordon was a hero and therefore quite unfit to be employed by men who were non-heroes. Henry Sidgwick put it that Gordon's appointment was a speculative stroke which might have been a brilliant success. " If it had turned out well what an achievement to have pacified the Sudan without wasting a soldier."[2] In both cases the mistake was in making the appointment without facing the consequences or realizing what it involved. No Ministers should have sent out a hero like Gordon, with all the virtues and all the drawbacks of that character, unless they had made up their minds to trust his judgment even when it crossed theirs. No Ministers should have sent Carnarvon to Ireland, knowing, as Salisbury knew, that his ideas were not theirs, unless they had made up

---

[1] Hodder's *Shaftesbury*, Vol. III, p. 501.
[2] *Memoir*, p. 402.

their minds that his views were to be given the most serious and sympathetic consideration. On no other basis was Salisbury justified in raising the expectations that were excited by Carnarvon's appointment and his sensational speech in the Lords. Salisbury's treatment of Carnarvon was less excusable than Gladstone's treatment of Gordon in one respect. For whereas Gordon changed his mind and often bewildered Ministers by his conduct, Carnarvon from first to last held to the views that he had put before Salisbury. Thus Salisbury was only asked to support Carnarvon in the ideas he knew Carnarvon to hold when he appointed him, whereas Gordon put a great strain on Gladstone's confidence and finally lost it by urging ideas, that he had condemned when he discussed the problem of the Sudan in London. On the other hand Salisbury was doubtless impressed by Carnarvon's failure to convince his colleagues of the wisdom of the advice he gave them. He might argue, with reason, that he had given Carnarvon the opportunity to put his case and that he had to accept the result.

Gladstone and Salisbury were both victims of the same illusion. Englishmen live so much and so successfully by compromise that they came to look for the spirit of compromise in the processes of fate. They think that nature shares their dislike of sharp alternatives and will adapt herself to the formulas by which dexterous men soften and disguise their disagreements. Nature does not often so act; she never so acts in Ireland. There cause and effect stand in too bleak a relationship to allow a man to get the good without the bad, by playing with words and principles. Gladstone paid Salisbury the compliment of supposing that he had not made over Carnarvon the mistake he himself had made over Gordon. His belief that Salisbury was thinking seriously of a constructive policy and was ready even to risk the fortunes of his party for an Irish peace, is the key to his conduct between June and December 1885.

CHAPTER XXI

". . . The question with me now is whether I am to march any more or not.

" I can neither march with a party which is simply a party, nor with a party which is in schism against itself.

" Not that I undervalue the interests which are involved in the regular and standing contention between Liberalism and Toryism, especially the Toryism of the present day and the miserable imposture termed Tory democracy. But the life of tension and contention which I have been living is an awful life, eminently unsuited to old age; and hence it is that I leave the strife of party to my successors who have not yet served out their time.

" Nothing can withhold or suspend my retirement except the presentation of some great and critical problem in the national life, and the hope, *if* such a hope shall be, of making some special contribution towards a solution of it.

" No one I think can doubt that, according to all present appearances, the greatest incident of the coming elections is to be the Parnell or Nationalist majority. And such a majority is a very great fact indeed. It will at once shift the centre of gravity in the relations between the two countries.

" How is it and how are its probable proposals to be met?

" If the heads of the Liberal party shall be prepared to unite in rendering an *adequate* answer to this question, and if they unitedly desire me to keep my present place for the purpose of giving to that answer legislative effect, such a state of things may impose upon me a formidable obligation for the time of the crisis. I cannot conceive any other form in which my resolution could be unsettled. . . .

" I have not considered the question what will the Tories do with Ireland. But they may solve all these questions for me, and for us all, if it be true that they are really to grant Parnell's motion for an inquiry into the actual trial of the Maamtrasna case, not merely the conduct of the political authorities in regard to it." *Gladstone to Spencer, June 30, 1885.*

Gladstone and Salisbury were in some respects in similar circumstances as party leaders, for both the great parties were in considerable internal discomfort. Gladstone had to defend one party against the dangerous energy of Chamberlain and Dilke as Salisbury had to defend the other against the dangerous energy of Churchill and Gorst. Chamberlain and Churchill had both created party organizations about which their leaders had misgivings and suspicions. Churchill's dislike of Northcote and Cross was not greater than Chamberlain's dislike of Hartington and Spencer. There were resemblances of temperament as well as of method and conduct, for Chamberlain and Churchill were equally impatient of the restraints that public men observed as a rule in criticizing one another. Nobody can read Churchill's letters and speeches without seeing that he was a difficult force inside a party; nobody can read Dilke's diaries without seeing that neither he nor Chamberlain were strong at that time in the qualities that help men to work together, modesty, consideration or tolerance. A man may like Chamberlain's ideas and dislike Hartington's and yet read with some sympathy the letters in which Hartington complained to Gladstone of Chamberlain's views of what was due from one colleague to another.

For Chamberlain hardly recognized any obligations to a Whig colleague. As far as he was concerned the Whigs would be better out of the party. Everything that he disliked about the Whigs, their opinions and their temperament, found the most complete expression in Hartington. Hartington was the typical Whig. He looked on politics as a field of duty for his class, in which a man needed above all things the reasonable habits of mind that come from a life of leisure and ease. The problems of government had to be met as they arose. Those problems were not too difficult, if agitators like Chamberlain did not stir up trouble, for the English character seemed to him to resemble that given to the Roman by a French historian " bon pour administrer et être administré."[1] Chamberlain looked on politics not as the art of governing by one moderate and

---

[1] M. Ferdinand Lot in *Histoire du Moyen Age*, Vol. I, p. 112.

cautious expedient after another, but the art of reconstructing by one bold and generous reform after another. He
resented both the wrongs of the poor and the selfishness of
the rich; both the slums of the towns and the great game
preserves of the countryside. He spoke of the enclosures as
robbery and he had no respect for the sacred principles of
property that ruled and limited the imagination of the
governing class. Salisbury said that his doctrines were the
common property of all barbarous governments. His
speeches were violent for two reasons. In the first place his
feelings were violent. In the second he was afraid that unless
he was violent he would not be able to assert himself against
the dead weight of Hartington's complacency. He tried to
shake the self satisfaction of the Whigs by the self confidence
of the intruder. This made him one of the politicians whose
bark is worse than his bite. The convenience or the dignity
of his colleagues and his leader meant nothing to him.

Gladstone himself occupied a difficult position. He was
not a Radical in the Chamberlain sense but neither was he a
Whig in the Hartington sense. Unlike Hartington he
sympathized with passion and energy, and he certainly
did not like Chamberlain the less for being in earnest.
When Chamberlain said that he wanted to do for the
English labourer what the Gladstonian government had done
for the Irish peasant, Gladstone, though cautious about any
plan proposed to him, was attracted by the spirit of such
language. Hartington, like Salisbury, thought it the reckless mischief-making of the demagogue. On the other hand
Gladstone preferred Hartington's manners to Chamberlain's,
for Hartington was under no suspicion of using the press
against his colleagues. It sometimes looked as though
Gladstone did not mind Radical ideas as much as he disliked
Radical methods. During the five years they had been
colleagues he had agreed more often with Chamberlain
than with Hartington. It is significant that both Chamberlain and Dilke wanted him to remain leader after the fall of
his Government. At other times he was estranged by
Chamberlain's class warfare. " His socialism repels me,"
he said once to Granville. Though he never had much

personal or political sympathy with Hartington he looked on
him as his successor, and he recognized certain obligations
to him.[1] Hartington had led the party under most difficult
conditions after his own resignation in 1875, and had then
handed over the party to him when he had won the Election
of 1880. Hartington had thus an overwhelming claim
on the succession. Gladstone found himself under a moral
obligation to preserve the unity of the party with the prospect
of handing it back to a man with whom he had often disagreed in his first Government, and with whom he had very
rarely agreed in his second.

Gladstone's letter to Spencer on June 30, 1885, showed
how his mind was moving. He had no wish to lead the
Liberal party at the General Election and after it, but he was
not ready to see the break up of the party if he could avert it.
And it looked as if his immediate retirement would have
that consequence.[2]

Gladstone went to Norway in August, and it was still
uncertain when he returned in September whether he would
lead the party at the General Election. Before going he
had an interview on August 7 with Hartington, and read
him a memorandum giving his sketch of a programme. The
domestic programme he outlined in this form:

1	Procedure	
2	Local Govt. (Liquor Laws)	For all
3	Land	
4	Registration	
5	Economy	For such as please:
6	Reform of Lords	and *as* they please
7	Established Church	

[1] The record of his conversation with Chamberlain when a visitor at
Hawarden in October 1885, which Gladstone sent to Granville contains this
passage: " He spoke of the constant conflicts of opinion with Hartington in
the late Cabinet, but I reverted to the time when Hartington used to summon
and lead meetings of the leading commoners, in which he was really the least
antagonistic of men." Morley, Vol. III, p. 226.

[2] Canon Maccoll wrote to Salisbury at this time: " My own conviction is
that, if the Session had died a natural death, Mr. Gladstone would have
retired. It is believed now that he will not leave the party in the lurch,
but will lead in the dissolution, and perhaps for the first session of the new
Parliament. A Liberal told me yesterday that this would make a difference
of over a hundred seats to the Liberals. I am not sure that this is an exaggeration." *Malcolm Maccoll*, by Russell, p. 115.

His notes on Ireland are discussed in the next chapter. Hartington was quite frank. He wrote that he was doubtful whether he could serve under Gladstone, knowing as he did that Gladstone's views on Ireland were very different from his. On the other hand, though he was doubtful whether the unity of the party could be maintained under Gladstone's leadership, he was certain that it would not be maintained under anybody else. Chamberlain was also doubtful whether the party could hold together under any conditions, for his differences with Hartington seemed to him almost irreconcilable. On the other hand he was certain that party unity was only possible under Gladstone's leadership. Gladstone called on, not too confidently, to avert a party split, prepared an address to the electors of Midlothian. The spirit in which he accepted the task is shown in his letter to Granville on September 9.

" . . . I think it impossible to make through my mouth or pen a formal manifesto to which all the leaders of the party shall be pledged as if it were a Queen's speech.

" I find the bulk of matter such that any address from me must amount to a moderate pamphlet. This helps towards the solution of any difficulty connected with a speaking campaign, and what is more important exhibits the document as mine and leaves others more free.

" The problem for me is to make if possible a Statement, which will hold through the Election and not to go into conflict with either the right wing of the party for whom Hartington has spoken, or the left wing for whom Chamberlain I suppose spoke last night. I do not say they are to be treated as on a footing, but I must do no act disparaging to Chamberlain's wing. Dilke for the moment is under his mantle.

" After the Dissolution things will define themselves. There is no very threatening difficulty unless one arise from Ireland. We shall then know whether there is one and what it is. If my darkest Estimate continue, and if the party and I are at variance, as to the means of meeting it, I am fixed in my determination not on that account to enter into a schism or aggravate the difficulties of others.

" I have spent much time and reflection on the Irish part of my address, and indeed you will not be surprised, when I say, I find the whole, in every line and word a trouble."

On September 12, soon after his return from a sea trip, he wrote to Harcourt to say that he was preparing his address to his constituents.

" I have communicated with Granville who thinks me right in not attempting to make others responsible for the terms of this address—and with Hartington and Chamberlain. By both of them I am a good deal buffeted, perhaps the former even more than the latter. They are in states of mind such as if they were put in contact would lead to an explosion."

Gladstone then undertook to keep the leadership of the party for the election with two objects in his mind. The first was to prevent the immediate and open disruption of the Party; the second to take part, if occasion arose, in the settlement of what he believed to be the most urgent problem of the time. The first purpose was achieved. It is not necessary here to go into detail on the domestic issues of the election. Gladstone's course was opportunist as it was bound to be. It was opportunist in the sense that it met the difficulties of the party over disestablishment by postponing them. Its constructive policy was contained in four reforms: reform of procedure of the House of Commons, reform of the Land Laws, reform of rural government, and creation of County Councils. The differences between Hartington and Chamberlain could wait until the time came to give effect to that programme and to settle its details. Salisbury said in his final speech at St. Stephen's Club, November 21, 1885:

" Mr. Gladstone had gone to Scotland to secure the unity of the Liberal party; but as they were not agreed upon a set of opinions, they were not a party, and an exhortation to unity was an exhortation to hypocrisy." If Salisbury had seen a letter Hartington sent to Gladstone on November 8 he would have been confirmed in his view.

" Chatsworth,
Chesterfield.

November 8, 1885.

" My dear Mr. Gladstone,

" Although I do not like troubling you, there are one or two things which I should wish to say before you begin your speeches in Scotland.

" I feel that my position in the party is becoming every day more difficult. I have tried as much as I could to minimise the difference between Chamberlain and myself in the hope—I believe a vain one—of averting an open split in the party or incurring the responsibility for causing it. But I feel that the only effect of this has been that while I have incurred the violent abuse of the Tories and the patronising protection of Chamberlain and Dilke which is more difficult to bear, my own friends are losing confidence, and are slipping away from me. They are probably right, and the Radicals are so forcing on their opinions that there will soon be no place in the party for less extreme men, who will have to be either for or against the new doctrines.

" The only possibility of keeping the moderate men in the party seems to lie in your taking a strong and decided line against the radicals. If you are unable to do this, my firm belief is that they will go; and whether I go or not does not much matter, as I shall be left alone.

" The other point is that if you are determined not to resume office it seems hardly fair to allow this to be kept secret. Thousands of votes will be given under the impression that you will come back as Prime Minister, which would not be given if it were known that after the election, the Liberal party would fall into the state of disruption which it inevitably will on your retirement.

" I hope you will excuse my making these observations. I do not at all wish to try to influence you in the line you are going to take. More than ever it would be the happiest moment of my life if I could see the prospect, as I begin to see it, of the possibility of my giving up any further part in politics.

" Yours very truly,
" HARTINGTON."

Gladstone in his reply, November 10, said:

" I wish to say something about the modern Radicalism. But I must include this that, if it is rampant and ambitious the two most prominent causes of its forwardness have been 1, Tory democracy, 2, The gradual disintegration of the Liberal aristocracy. On both these subjects my opinions are strong. I think the conduct of the Duke of Bedford and others has been as unjustifiable as it was foolish, especially after what we did to save the House of Lords from itself in the business of the franchise.

" Nor can I deny that the question of the House of Lords, of the Church, or both, will probably split the Liberal party. But let it split decently, honourably, and for cause. That it should split now would, so far as I see, be ludicrous.

" I am sorry that Chamberlain raises and presses his notion about the compulsory powers for the local authorities. I should have said, try freedom first. But when it is considered how such a scheme must be tied up with safeguards, and how powerful are the natural checks, I hardly see, and I am not sure that you see, in this proposal *stuff* enough to cause a breach.

" I am no partisan in fine of Chamberlainism, but I think that some ' moderate Liberals ' have done much to foster it; and that if we are men of sense, the crisis will not be yet."

As Gladstone was never at his best when dealing with men, the success with which he managed this difficult problem in the summer and autumn of 1885 is a proof of his moral ascendancy. The Liberal party was in danger of breaking into two. The cause of discord was partly Chamberlain's social programme; partly the acute feeling over disestablishment. Salisbury as we have seen, argued in his own mind that the integrity of the Conservative party was the only safeguard against Chamberlain's hatred of the Church[1] and that therefore he must put aside any scheme or reform to which his party was disinclined. The *Guardian* said on September 12, that 374 Liberal candidates were in favour of disestablishment. A number of Liberals at the same time put out a manifesto declaring that the establishment was so important that they would vote against any Liberal candidate who shared Chamberlain's views on that question. This manifesto was signed by Selborne, who had been Lord Chancellor in the Government that had just resigned, by Halifax who had been in Gladstone's first Cabinet, by powerful Whigs like the Duke of Westminster, father of the chief Liberal Whip, and by a well-known Radical, Tom Hughes, author of *Tom Brown's School Days*.

Gladstone's leadership prevented the immediate break up

[1] If Salisbury had seen a letter Chamberlain wrote to Dilke in November, 1885, he would have been confirmed in his fears. " It does not look as if the Tories would have the chance of doing much mischief: but I should much like them to be in for a couple of years before we try again and then I should go for the Church." *Life of Dilke*, II, p. 193.

of the party but the acute differences had an inevitable effect on the elections. In the boroughs the Liberals lost heavily. London, which in 1880 had returned 14 Liberals and 8 Conservatives, now returned 25 Liberals and 37 Conservatives; the boroughs, which in 1880 had returned only 85 Conservatives in 287 seats, now returned 118 in 232 seats. There were various reasons for the change. One was the influence of the Parnellite vote.[1] The disgrace and disaster of Gordon's fate must have had considerable influence. Gladstone, writing to Grosvenor on November 27, said: " Fair Trade+Parnell+Church+Chamberlain have damaged us a good deal in the boroughs. . . . I place the *causae damni* in what I think their order of importance." Hartington writing on December 3, said: " There is no doubt that Fair Trade has made a considerable number of converts in Lancashire. Your great majority is one of the few satisfactory events of the Election." Grosvenor wrote on November 17 to a correspondent: " things are *not* looking as well as they did 6 weeks or 2 months ago, Fair-trade and J.C. are both doing us harm, the latter more particularly." Selborne, who had so often disagreed with Gladstone, wrote warmly (November 25) about his majority at Midlothian.

" I trust I need not assure you, that I rejoice, as much as anyone can, in the renewed and splendid testimony borne by the electors of Midlothian to yourself and your services. Whatever may be the causes of recent events in other constituencies, it is my firm conviction, that diminution of the public confidence in yourself, personally, is not one of them."

It would probably have been better if the counties had followed the boroughs but here the Liberals gained a great many seats, raising their numbers from 54 to 133. It looks as if the agricultural labourers had done what Chamberlain said he hoped they would do; lie to the Tories and vote for the Liberals. The total result could not have been worse if it had been arranged by the worst enemy of England and Ireland. The new House contained 333

[1] St. Cyres, son of Sir S. Northcote, wrote to Algernon West on October 15: " I hear we are to win 40 seats in England by the Parnellite vote." West's *Recollections*, II, p. 250. This was probably an exaggeration.

Liberals, 251 Conservatives and 86 Home Rulers. Grosvenor, writing to Lyttelton on November 17, 1885, had expected 358 Liberals, giving the party a majority of 46 over all parties: writing to Gladstone on December 12 he divided the Liberals into 232 Liberals and 101 Radicals. This new party was hardly likely to be a happy family. The feelings of the Whigs were well expressed by the *Times* in a leading article on the borough losses.[1]

". . . The opposition have to thank Mr. Chamberlain, not only for their defeat at the polls, but for the irremediable disruption and hopeless disorganization of the Liberal party, with its great historic past and its high claims to national gratitude. We have freely recognized Mr. Chamberlain's ability, the development of his powers as a speaker, the energy and persistence with which he pursues his ends, and the sincerity of feeling which may be held to excuse his violence, his rancour, and his disregard of scruples. But he has now accomplished something which, even a few months ago, seemed to be far beyond his reach. His achievement in destroying the Liberal party as an organized and united power in the State may give him such immortality as was won by the man who burned down the temple of Diana at Ephesus."[1]

History was to give to this language an unexpected interpretation.

[1] *Times*, November 26, 1885.

[1] The *Times* which made Chamberlain responsible for all the borough losses gave him no credit for the county gains. These it attributed in the main to the fear of Protection. "Sir William Harcourt attributes the success of the Liberals to the revolt of the agricultural labourer against his Tory patrons—against the dictation of the squire and the intimidation of the parson. These causes may have had something to do with the general result. But we believe that the doctrines identified with the name of Mr. James Lowther have contributed more to the Tory defeat in the counties than any other single cause whatever." (December 12, 1885.)

CHAPTER XXII

GLADSTONE AND THE IRISH ISSUE, JULY, 1885—DEC., 1885

ADDRESS TO THE ELECTORS OF MIDLOTHIAN, September 17, 1885.
XVIII.—IRELAND.

I have reserved until the close the mention of Ireland.

The change just effected in our representative system is felt to have been a large one even in Great Britain; but it is of far wider scope in Ireland, where the mass of the people in boroughs as well as counties have, for the first time, by the free and almost unsolicited gift of the Legislature, been called to exercise the Parliamentary franchise. They will thus, in the coming Parliament, have improved means of making known, through the Irish members, their views and wishes on public affairs. Without doubt we have arrived at an important epoch in her history, which it behoves us to meet in a temper of very serious and dispassionate reflection.

Those grievances of Ireland, with which we had been historically too familiar before and since the Union, have, at length, been happily removed. The poison of religious ascendancy, in its various forms, has been expelled from the country; and the condition of the cultivators of the soil, constituting the majority of the people, which had been a scandal and a danger to the Empire, has been fundamentally improved, at the cost of no small effort, by the action of Parliament.

But the wants of Ireland have to be considered, as well as her grievances. Down to this hour Ireland has continued greatly in arrear both of England and of Scotland, with respect to those powers of local self-government which associate the people, in act and feeling, with the law, and which lie at the root, as I believe, of political stability, of the harmony of classes, and of national strength. This is a serious evil; and it is the more to be regretted, because both the circumstances and the geographical position of Ireland may appear to invest her, as a portion of the Empire, with special claims to a liberal interpretation and application of the principles, which the people of Great Britain have traditionally held so dear.

Whatever be the obligations of the party now in power to those known in the existing Parliament as Irish Nationalists, the Liberals of England and Scotland will have to draw the inspirations of their future policy from a higher source, and to cast aside the recollections of party action during the last few years, which ought not to prejudice in any way any just claim of the Irish people. Neither should those claims be hindered on account of any premature and prejudicial words which may have been spoken in the acutest, that is the electioneering, stage of a long and too bitter controversy.

Nothing can be easier than to mar and intercept, by narrow prejudices and by appeals to passion, any adjustment of this important question; which cannot be satisfactorily handled unless it be approached, on the one side and on the other, in a spirit of enlightened moderation.

Should such a spirit happily prevail, I cannot believe that the political genius of these nations, illustrious in the history of the world, will prove inadequate to the solution of the problem, without the heavy drawback of embittered civil strife. If such strife should now unhappily arise between Ireland and Great Britain, the one may readily reproach and condemn the other, but the broader opinion of the civilized world, will, I conceive, alike censure both.

In my opinion, not now for the first time delivered, the limit is clear, within which any desires of Ireland, constitutionally ascertained, may, and beyond which they cannot, receive the assent of Parliament. To maintain the supremacy of the Crown, the unity of the Empire, and all the authority of Parliament necessary for the conservation of that unity, is the first duty of every representative of the people. Subject to this governing principle, every grant to portions of the country of enlarged powers for the management of their own affairs is, in my view, not a source of danger, but a means of averting it, and is in the nature of a new guarantee for increased cohesion, happiness, and strength.

We have no right to expect that the remedial process in human affairs shall always be greatly shorter than the period of mistakes and misgovernment. And if in the case of Ireland, half a century of efforts at redress, not always consistent or sustained, and following upon long ages for which as a whole we blush, have still

2 D

left something to be attempted, we ought not to wax weary in well doing, nor rest until every claim which justice may be found to urge, shall have been satisfied.

The main question is, whether it is for the interests of all the three countries that the thorough and enduring harmony which has now been long established, but only after centuries of manful strife, between England and Scotland, should include Ireland also. My personal answer to the question is this: I believe history and posterity will consign to disgrace the name and memory of every man, be he who he may, and on whichever side of the Channel he may dwell, that, having the power to aid in an equitable settlement between Ireland and Great Britain, shall use that power not to aid, but to prevent or to retard it. If the duty of working for this end cannot be doubted, then I trust that, on the one hand, Ireland will remember that she too is subject to the authority of reason and justice, and cannot always plead the wrongs of other days in bar of submission to them; and that the two sister Kingdoms, aware of their overwhelming strength, will dismiss every fear except that of doing wrong, and will make yet another effort to complete a reconciling work, which has already done so much to redeem the past, and which, when completed, will yet more redound to the honour of our legislation and our race.

Gladstone, as we have seen, had been in a difficulty ever since 1874 in speaking about Home Rule. For he occupied a position of his own. He did not want to encourage the demand for Home Rule, for he saw that that demand would raise a problem which would tax all the statesmanship of the two countries. He hoped down to 1885 that it might be possible to satisfy Irish national sentiment with something short of a special Parliament. On the other hand he alone among public men held from the first that Great Britain could not resist that demand if it were seriously made by the great majority of the Irish people. With his large European outlook, he had no mind to see England in the place that Austria had held in Italy and still held in Poland.

With the unexpected turn that Conservative policy took in the summer of 1885 a new difficulty arose. That change created at once an opportunity and a danger. Nobody knew better than Gladstone that a Conservative Government, able to control the House of Lords, would have great advantages over a Liberal Government in trying to solve the Irish problem, and he hoped that the new mood of the Conservative party might signify a serious purpose. He was therefore much more moderate in his criticisms of Conservative policy than others. Hartington called that policy a " great blow to public morality." Chamberlain, though he was glad to see coercion dropped, was not less severe on the motives of the Government whom he called hungry office seekers who had trampled in the mire " the consistency of our public life, the honour of political controversy, and the patriotism of statesmen which should be set above all party considerations." Gladstone made what Churchill himself called " a magnanimous speech." But there was an obvious danger; the danger that Parnell, finding the Conservatives so strangely amenable, might try to make the two parties bid against each other for the Irish vote with consequences fatal to the integrity of British government.

Gladstone's correspondence makes it clear that, though he was in great perplexity, he was guided by three principles of action. In the first place he wanted to educate himself and his chief colleagues on the Irish question. In the second place he wanted in his public speeches to do justice to his strong conviction in favour of a generous Irish policy without saying anything that might invite Irish support. In the third place he wanted to help the Conservative party in any Liberal plans for Ireland it might have in mind.

After the Home Rule split it was often alleged that Gladstone had changed his views in order to take office with the help of the Parnellite vote. Even Bright, though he did not charge him with this motive, believed that had happened to him. The only explanation that can be given of Bright's extraordinary mistake is that Bright, like Gladstone himself, was too apt in conversation to think that the person with whom he was talking agreed with him and to read his own mind into a mind that was quite differently affected. Gladstone could persuade himself after a talk with Goschen that Goschen was a Home Ruler, because, as Acton once said, he was apt to think that when a man with whom he was arguing ceased to resist, silence meant conversion. Bright had left Gladstone's Government in July 1882, after the bombardment of Alexandria. But there was no excuse for Bright's blindness in the case of any of his colleagues. Hartington admitted publicly that none of them had any ground for surprise or resentment when Gladstone adopted Home Rule.

Hartington's comment is readily understood when we turn to his conversation with Gladstone on August 7 and the letters that had passed between them during the autumn. The memorandum described in the previous chapter, which Gladstone read to Hartington on August 7, 1885, contains this note on Ireland:

" Ireland. An epoch: possibly a crisis. Grievance in the main gone, but Administration development remains. Considerable changes may be desired; and may be desirable if effected with a due regard to the unity of the Empire. I cannot treat the people of Ireland as foes or aliens, or advise that less sh^d be done for them than w^d in like circ^s be done for the inhabitants of any other portion of the U.K.

" These are my opinions. What to say publicly must be most carefully cons^d on my return.

" Had party been agreed, and other circ^s favourable, on the Central Board Scheme, I sh^d have been ready to offer myself at the Dissolution on that basis.

" N.B. (Granville and Derby view)

" But of this little chance."

What impression Hartington received at the conversation on this memorandum we know from the letter he wrote to Granville the next day. " He (Gladstone) seems to consider the Central Board plan the minimum which might have sufficed; but that as that plan seems to have collapsed, a separate Legislature in some form or other will have to be considered."

Nobody can look at the letters that Gladstone wrote after his return from Norway to Hartington and Chamberlain without seeing that it was perfectly plain to them that his mind was moving to a definite Home Rule policy. Early in September he wrote to Hartington deprecating an uncompromising speech Hartington had made on Ireland, and a few extracts from letters that followed speak for themselves.

September 8, . . . " In conclusion I earnestly hope that our friends will give to the Irish case a really historical consideration. Depend upon it you cannot *simpliciter* fall back on the important debate of 1834. The general development since that time of popular principles, the prolonged experience of Norway (I might perhaps mention Finland) and the altogether new experience of Austro-Hungary, along with them the great power we have placed in the hands of the Irish people, require the reconsideration of the whole position. And in *one* point Parnell gives some ground of hope, for he seems to contemplate a constitution for Ireland *octroyé* by Parliament.

" I have laboured very hard at the Irish portion of my (possible) Address."

Hartington replied on September 10:

" . . . What I said in my previous letter was that I did not know whether unity could under any circumstances be secured, but that I felt certain that it could not be secured under any other condition than that of your leadership. Whether I desire that such unity should be secured must depend on what the party is likely to do, if in a majority after the election.

" You do not refer to the attitude which you would take in regard to Chamberlain's projects relating to Land, Education and Taxation, but I assume that it would be generally in the direction of restraint and moderation. It would however be difficult if these matters are dealt with at all, as I assume they must be, to avoid all conflict with the declared opinions of either Chamberlain or myself. But passing by this for the present, I come to Ireland. I assume that your Address would not indicate any new Irish policy; as in your former letter you said ' that every object is gained for the present by declaring substantively our views as to the unity of the Empire ' and in your last that you ' are strongly in favour of waiting.' But I find some difficulty in reconciling this with what you say of the labour you have given to the Irish portion of your (possible) Address. But however this may be, I must acknowledge that the references in your letter to Norway, Finland, Austria-Hungary, and to one point in Parnell's speeches give me the greatest uneasiness, and lead me to fear that the return to power of the Liberal party whether pledged or not beforehand would involve the adoption of an Irish policy for which I at least am not prepared. I acknowledge that the danger of what the Tory party may do under the inspiration of R. Churchill is considerable; but I doubt whether he can carry his party with him in any very serious concessions; and in any event the fear of what the Tories may do on their responsibility would be no justification to me for doing what I disapprove of on my own. My desire therefore for the unity of the party under your leadership is under present circumstances subject to very serious qualifications."

Gladstone, replying to this letter, September 11, said:

" I had no other purpose than that of promoting, what I think dangerously deficient in many quarters, an historical and therefore a comprehensive view of the Irish question. . . . What I say on Ireland is simply an expansion and adaptation of what I have already said often, namely that Ireland may have all that is compatible with the unity of the Empire. When I said it would have sufficed for you to declare the unity of the Empire, I meant it would have sufficed for *your* purpose. But I have had to say much more than you on the Irish question, and could not now hold back from what I have frequently promised." Hartington replying, remarked " Of course I know that you are and have long been in favour of granting to Ireland a larger measure of self government than I think I could ever agree to."

Two letters that passed between him and Chamberlain on the questions which Chamberlain thought vital show that he was urging Chamberlain also to take a larger view of the Irish question.

> Hawarden Castle,
> Chester.
> September 26, 1885.

My dear Chamberlain

I felt well-pleased and easy after receiving your note of the 21st, but there is a point I should like to put to you with reference to your self-denying ordinance making the three points conditions of office.

Supposing Parnell to come back 80 to 90 strong, to keep them together, to bring forward a plan which shall contain in your opinion adequate securities for the Union of the Empire, and to press this plan under whatever name as having claims to pre-

cedence (claims which could hardly be denied even by opponents)
—do you think no Gov^t should be formed to promote such a
plan unless the three points were glued on to it at the same time?
Do you not think you w^d do well to reserve elbow-room for a
case like this?

I hope you will not think my suggestion—it is not a question—
captious and a mantrap.   It is meant in a very different sense.

A Liberal majority is assumed in it.

Yrs sincerely,

W. E. GLADSTONE.

Highbury,

Moor Green,

Birmingham.

September 28, 1885.

My dear Mr Gladstone

I had certainly not contemplated the contingency you suggest
in your letter of the 26th.   I had supposed that the first work of a
liberal ministry would be Local Government, and I thought
it probable that Bills for the three countries would be brought in
together.   In consequence of Mr. Parnell's change of front I
assumed that these Bills would not go beyond County Councils,
and that any further proposal would be left over till a more
favourable time.   In this case the Irish Bill must necessarily
contain powers to Local authorities to acquire land, since this is
already included in the Land Act and Labourers' Acts and it
would be necessary to transfer the powers from existing bodies
to the new Councils.   The only question would then be whether
similar powers should not be given in the English and Scotch
Bills and to this I feel myself pledged.

I may remind you that as regards taxation, I expressed myself
as entirely satisfied by the terms of your manifesto and I have no
wish to go beyond it.

As regards Free Schools, I should be very glad if the Gov^t saw
its way to take the question up—but if it did not I should feel
that I was bound to support by speech and vote any resolution
that might be moved on the subject.

I can hardly think it probable that Parnell will bring forward
any scheme that a Liberal Gov^t could support.   He has so
entirely put Local Govern^t in the background, and has so plainly
declared for a separate and independent Parliament that I have
little hope of his action.

If however he did take the course suggested in your letter, I should be bound to strain every nerve to assist the Government in dealing with it.

I am not however certain that I could not render more help from outside than as a member of the Cabinet.

I should at all times be greatly influenced by any opinion you might form as to the way in which I could be of most service.

Believe me,

Yours very Truly,

J. CHAMBERLAIN.

Hartington was hostile and Chamberlain was becoming hostile—under influences to be described later—to Irish self-government. Another of Gladstone's colleagues, Childers, had moved the other way, and in September he wrote to Gladstone to say that he proposed to make a Home Rule speech at Pontefract. Gladstone answered him on September 28.

Private.

My dear Childers,

I have a decided sympathy with the general scope and spirit of your proposed declaration about Ireland.

If I offer any observations, they are meant to be simply in furtherance of your purpose.

1. I would disclaim giving any exhaustive list of Imperial subjects, and would not " put my foot down " as to Revenue but would keep plenty of elbow room to keep all Customs and Excise which might probably be found necessary.

2. A general disclaimer of particulars as to the form of any Local Legislature might suffice without giving the Irish expressly to know it might be decided mainly by their wish.

3. I think there is no doubt Ulster would be able to take care of itself in respect to Education, but a question arises and forms I think the most difficult part of the whole subject whether some defensive provisions for the owners of land and property should not be considered.

4. It is evident you have given the subject much thought and my sympathy goes largely to your details as well as your principle. But considering the danger of placing confidence in the leaders of the National party at the present moment, and the decided disposition they have shown to raise their terms on any favourable indication, I wd beg you to consider further whether

you should *bind* yourself at present to any details or go beyond general indications.   If you say in terms (and this I do not dissuade) that you are ready to consider the question whether they can have a Legislature for all questions not Imperial this will be a great step in advance; and anything you may say beyond it I should like to see veiled in language not such as to commit you.

Believe me sincerely yours,

W. E. GLADSTONE.

Gladstone's own view of his position was made clear by the following letter to Granville.

Hawarden,

October 5, 1885.

Private.

My dear Granville,

I need not make a long story of the threatened letter, which now descends upon you.

The Speech, in which Chamberlain announced, to my great surprise, that he could not take office unless his three points were adopted by the incoming Government, rather cut across my purpose.   But his answer to a note which I wrote to him seems sufficiently to open the door, so I proceed.

You hold a position of great impartiality in relation to any divergent opinions among members of the late Cabinet.   No other person occupies ground so thoroughly favourable.

I turn to myself for one moment.   I remain at present in the leadership of the party, first with a view to the Election, and secondly with a view to being, by a bare possibility, of use afterwards in the Irish question, if it should take a favourable turn: but as you know with the intention of taking no part in any schism of the party should it arise, and of avoiding any and all official responsibility, should the question be merely one of Liberal v. Conservative, and not one of commanding Imperial necessity such as that of Irish Government may come to be after the Dissolution. . . .

During these weeks Gladstone was trying to educate himself as well as his colleagues.   On August 6 he wrote to Granville: " For my own part I have seen my way pretty well as to the particulars of the minor and rejected plan, but the idea of the wider one puzzles me much.   At the same time *if* the Election gives a return of a decisive character, the sooner the subject is dealt with probably the better." The day before he had written to Knowles, the editor of the *Nineteenth Century*, urging him to publish a series of articles on the Irish question.

" The Chapter of grievance, properly so called, is pretty well closed. The Chapter of material aid, eleemosynary aid, cannot close too soon. The Chapter of competent adminis-trative development is the one which remains to be treated. I can only indicate two sections of the question; a searching and impartial article on the history of the Union; and a careful account of the novel and critical Austro-Hungarian experiment, its terms and its actual working. . . . As to plans, I can say nothing. I take it to be very doubtful whether the Nationalist party at this moment know their own plan or are in any way of one mind."

His own judgment naturally depended a good deal on the temper of the Irish leader. There were times when Parnell's reckless language made him doubt whether any settlement was possible. Parnell, intoxicated by his glimpse into the Viceroy's mind, believed that he was in a position to choose whether to take what he wanted from the Con-servatives or the Liberals. In this unfortunate mood he made speeches that did widespread harm to his cause, like the speech that frightened Chamberlain away and provoked the retort at Warrington on September 12 in which the Radical leader announced his firm intention to resist Parnell's demands. Parnell impressed Gavan Duffy on his return from Australia by his power over his Irish colleagues, men, as Duffy put it, who were naturally individualists. Duffy, recollecting the failure of his plans in the 'fifties, naturally attached great importance to this gift. Unhappily Parnell was as unskilful in handling Englishmen and English minds as he was effective in controlling Irish politicians and Irish peasants. A wiser man would have seen in the readiness of leaders like Carnarvon, Churchill, Chamberlain, and Gladstone to consider a bolder Irish policy a reason for treating English opinion and English prejudices with care and sympathy. Parnell seems to have drawn just the oppo-site conclusion.

From time to time, however, he made a good speech and

one of these speeches—on October 9—had a reassuring
effect on Gladstone's mind.   There was one argument that
was used against every scheme for giving Ireland self-
government.   It was the argument that Ireland would use
any such institutions for the purpose of extorting greater
concessions and ultimately complete independence.   This
argument Hartington had used in January 1883 against
Gladstone's scheme for provincial Councils.   It was used
in 1885 against Chamberlain's central Board scheme.   It
was used later by Chamberlain against Gladstone's scheme.
On October 5 Parnell addressed himself to this argument.
He said that it was preposterous to expect England to give
Ireland an engine which Ireland meant to use for the
purpose of bringing about the separation of the two countries.   On the other hand it was impossible to ask a counter-
guarantee from Ireland, for nobody could forecast the
future.   All that he could do to satisfy England was to point
out that the present arrangement, tried for eighty years, had
produced a disaffected Ireland and that other arrangements
might be imagined under which England's capacity to
draw out the affection of the Irish people would have a
better chance.   He pointed to the good will of the colonies
and the successful working of the Austro-Hungarian scheme.
This was really the answer, and it was a complete and a
statesmanlike answer to Chamberlain's unimaginative
treatment of this difficulty.   Gladstone saw its importance
at once.   " The Irish subject in my mind," he said to Granville at the end of a letter on October 10, " altogether over-
shadows all this, *I* considered Parnell's last as a *step* not in the
wrong direction, perhaps as much as he dared.   I think
you, and all, should read Gavan Duffy's letter to Carnarvon."
A few weeks later unfortunately Parnell made a wild speech
which caused Gladstone further anxiety.   He wrote to
Granville on October 22:

" As to Ireland I have reserves myself, for I do not pretend as yet
to see my way to a due protection for the landlords; against them
Parnell seems to have issued a new proclamation of war, and how
can we make over the judicial rents to his mercy?   I am trying
to familiarize my mind with the subject and to look at it all round.

but it still requires a good deal more looking at before I could ask myself to adhere to anything I had conceived. I adhere however to this one belief; there is great advantage in a constructive measure (which would be subject to change or recall) as compared with the repeal of the Union."

There was a very serious obstacle to the success of Gladstone's plan for educating the English mind on the Irish question. In the earlier controversies of 1882 he and Chamberlain had had the powerful help of the *Spectator*. Unhappily the *Spectator* was now hostile to all Irish reform. The editor had become convinced, partly no doubt by Parnell's unwise and intemperate behaviour, that concessions to Ireland were so many bribes that failed. There was nothing for it but stern resistance and if necessary a determination by English politicians to put everything on one side in order to unite to convince Ireland that she would get nothing by agitation. This might involve ten years of concentration on this issue to the neglect of all questions on which English politicians were not agreed at home. Thus the scheme for a Central Board which had attracted the interest if not the sympathy of Salisbury and had apparently been put aside because Carnarvon wanted something larger,[1] was obnoxious to the chief Radical weekly as well as to the *Times*. The *Spectator*, which had been anxious for local government in 1882, now looked on every such plan as a concession to men who would use it only for mischief. This view was put bluntly by the *Times* in an attack on Chamberlain and Harcourt—for during the election Harcourt had come out strongly on the side of Chamberlain—on October 6.

" A National Council or four provincial Councils such as Mr. Chamberlain and Sir W. Harcourt were quite ready to concede —if only there were customers to be found for the offer—would be organizations of the National League—abundantly provided with the means of crushing, and castigating individuals who dared to oppose the will of the despots."

The summary of Liberal opinion on Parnell's demand for an Irish Parliament that the *Spectator* gave when praising Chamberlain's famous speech at Warrington on September

---

[1] Whibley, *Lord John Manners and his Friends*, II, p. 307.

12—" There never was any doubt about the opinion of the Whigs, or of the Moderates and now there is no doubt about that of the Radicals "—shows that Gladstone had an uphill task in educating his party to a larger view of the question. Radical opinion, so far as it was represented by Chamberlain and Trevelyan, was hardening against concession.

There were personal reasons for Chamberlain's growing hostility. In the negotiations of the winter of 1885 he had been in touch with O'Shea and Manning; O'Shea representing Parnell and Manning the Irish Bishops. The duplicity of O'Shea, who deceived both Parnell and Chamberlain, thereby creating the bad temper and suspicion that poisoned their relations ever afterwards, has been described in Mr. Garvin's pages. Parnell was ready to take the National Council but not ready to substitute it for an Irish Parliament; Chamberlain understood from O'Shea that Parnell would want nothing more; Parnell that Chamberlain offered this concession without prejudice to Parnell's larger ideas.[1] This was the first cause of discord. Chamberlain's idea had been that he and Dilke should conduct a campaign in favour of this plan. Soon after the fall of the Government, on June 27 or 28, he wrote in great spirits to Dilke:

" On the greatest issue between us and the Whigs Mr. G. is on our side, and has told Harcourt that if he stands at the General Election he will make this a prominent feature in his platform and will adopt in principle our scheme—Local Government and devolution. This will immensely strengthen our position if we finally decide to press the matter. I say ' if ' because I wait to have more positive assurances as to Parnell's present attitude. If he throws us over, I do not believe that we can go further at present, but O'Shea remains confident that matters will come right."[2]

The reference to the danger of a change of mind on Parnell's part was inspired not by any suspicion of the facts that O'Shea had concealed, but by the uncertainty created

[1] The discrepancy was not discovered until the revelations before the Parnell Commission when the truth was dragged out of O'Shea. Chamberlain learned for the first time how he had been duped.

[2] Gwynn and Tuckwell, *Life of Dilke*, II, 152.

by the new Conservative departure.   In fact that departure
had already settled the fate not only of Chamberlain's
reform but also of a plan that he and Dilke had in mind for
a visit to Ireland.   When Chamberlain's scheme had first
been mooted, there had been two views of it in the Irish
party.   Some welcomed it but others regarded it as an
insidious manœuvre against Home Rule.   Consequently
when it became known that the two Radicals were to visit
Ireland, the *United Ireland* edited by William O'Brien and
Healy made a strong attack on them.   Davitt, the wisest
head in Irish politics wherever the relations of England and
Ireland were concerned, wrote to Chamberlain assuring him
that O'Brien and Healy did not represent the Irish party,
but the truth was that Parnell and Manning had both
lost interest in Chamberlain's policy, holding that they
had now a more powerful friend in Carnarvon.   They
threw over the Radical Chamberlain for the Conservative
Viceroy, entirely mistaking the extent and character of
Carnarvon's influence in his party, and of his personal
tenacity in pursuing his ideas.   Parnell wanted if possible
to get more than Chamberlain had offered and he believed
he could get it from the Conservative Government.   Manning
and the Irish Bishops preferred the Central Council to Home
Rule.   Both alike believed that they could get what they
wanted more easily from the Tories than from the Liberals.
The two Radicals were thrown over.

It is difficult not to believe that Parnell's gross stupidity
in making an everlasting enemy of the man who had the
most bitter and unscrupulous tongue in England was partly
due to his personal circumstances.   Chamberlain was in
his eyes not only the Radical leader; he was the friend of
O'Shea.   So while Chamberlain was being poisoned against
Parnell by O'Shea's duplicity, Parnell was learning to hate
Chamberlain, as the power behind the husband of his
mistress.   In this strange Irish tragedy everything comes
back in a fatal circle to the same ultimate cause.   It can
safely be said that rarely in the history of the world have two
commonplace persons been able to do greater public mischief
than O'Shea and his wife.   Chamberlain cannot be held

free from responsibility. Both his judgment and his taste must suffer in estimation from his failure to see through O'Shea's shifty self-importance and his persistence in this curious and unlucky friendship.

Chamberlain, whose combative instincts and personal pride had thus been provoked by Parnell, was still under this fatal influence during the General Election. " O'Shea, who was here last week," he wrote to Gladstone on October 26, " says there are internecine conflicts in their ranks. Healy and Campbell (Parnell's Secretary) actually came to blows at a recent convention. If we have a good majority it may be possible to divide them and secure some support for our proposals." In the same letter he used language that warned Gladstone of the obstacles he would find in his path.

" I cannot see my way at all about Ireland.   Parnell has shown that he is not to be depended upon.   He will not stick to any ' minimum ' even if he could now be induced to formulate another. After his recent public utterances he must go for a separate independent Parliament.   For myself, I would rather let Ireland go altogether than accept the responsibility of a nominal Union.   But I think that a great number of Liberals probably the majority, are not willing to give more than English Local Government.   National Councils would have tried them very severely, and beyond that I do not believe they can possibly be pressed at present.   If the Tories are in a minority, they will join malcontent Liberals in resisting concessions.   If they were strong enough to hold their own with Parnell's support, I do not know that there is any limit to the price they would pay. In this case however the responsibility of proposing anything would not lie with us.   On the whole I think the only chance is to let the Irishmen ' stew in their juice '."

This letter was in answer to a letter from Gladstone which contained this sentence: " An instinct blindly impresses me with the likelihood that Ireland may shoulder everything else aside."   It was pretty clear from Chamberlain's answer that Gladstone could look for little support from the only one of his colleagues who had been in active sympathy with him on Irish questions in the Cabinet.

Chamberlain's mind was revealed further in the letters

he exchanged with Labouchere at this time.   Labouchere had been in communication with Herbert Gladstone, who wrote to him on October 12, 1885, giving an account of his father's ideas.

Hawarden Castle,

Chester.

Private.   October 12, 1885.

Dear Mr Labouchere

Many thanks for your interesting letter.   I can go so far as to give you my own impressions as to my Father's view derived from observation and from conversations with him at times but I doubt whether he has as yet communicated largely on this matter with his late colleagues.

I feel sure that he has thought much before using the words of his address which relate to Ireland, and that he means to stand by them in both the main particulars, i.e. first, to uphold the unity of the Empire and surrender or compromise nothing that is essential for it; and secondly that there is no limit to the powers he would gladly see compatibly with this condition, given to Ireland for the management of all affairs which are properly her own.   Further, he, as I think, in no way disapproves of the efforts of the Nationalists to get the Tory party to take up their question, as if that could be done it might be the shortest way to a settlement.   I have however heard him say that unless they wish permanently and unconditionally to sink or swim with the Tories, they had better bring the matter to a very speedy upshot.

I doubt whether supposing he could see his way, he would consider the gratuitous launching of a plan by him at the present stage to be the best way to forward it; and from his Address he seems to expect that Ireland may through her representatives speak plainly and publicly for herself.

I have heard him speak of the protection of the minority in a country so long torn by dissensions as a difficult point requiring careful consideration.   But I do not believe that procedure would stand in his way as to this particular subject.

I go today to Leeds where my direction will be Gledhow Hall, and I come back here on Saturday.   I should be glad to hear again from you if you think I can throw any light on points of difficulty.   If you do go to Ireland will you let me know, as if I am at home I can easily go into Chester at any time.

Yours very truly

HERBERT J. GLADSTONE.

Labouchere had a bad influence on Chamberlain for he made him suspect, what was far from the truth, that Gladstone's interest in the Irish question was largely or chiefly inspired by the desire to get rid of Chamberlain's troublesome enthusiasms for social reform and disestablishment and he confirmed him in his dislike of Parnell.   In writing to Chamberlain, Labouchere said on October 18: " My own experience of Parnell is that he never makes a bargain without intending to get out of it, and that he has either a natural love of treachery, or considers that promises are not binding when made to a Saxon."   He gave this as the opinion also of Churchill.   " By the way, I do not think that the alliance of Randolph with the Irish is going on very smoothly.   He complained to me that it was impossible to trust Parnell and that the Maamtrasna business had been sprung as a surprise."[1]   Chamberlain replying said (October 20):

" Mr G himself was cautious with me at Hawarden, though he did not conceal that his present interest was in the Irish question, and he seemed to think that a policy for dealing with it might be found which would unite us all and which would necessarily throw into the background those minor points of difference about the schools and small holdings which threaten to drive the Whigs into the arms of the Tories or into retirement.   But I agree with you that the *modus vivendi* cannot be found.   First, because all Liberals are getting weary of making concessions to Parnell, and will not stand much more of it, and secondly, because Parnell cannot be depended on to keep any bargain.   I believe, therefore, that Mr G's plans will come to naught."[2]

Gladstone, by his method of argument and his curiously complicated habits of mind, often laid himself open to the charge of deliberate obscurity.   Gavan Duffy, describing his speaking in 1852 said: " His speeches gave the impression that the process of adopting a conclusion was not always complete when he rose to speak."[3]   By some strange per-

[1] Thorold, *Life of Labouchere*, p. 237.

[2] *ibid.*, p. 239.

[3] Gladstone's curious style exasperated Archbishop Whateley.   " What they can see in Gladstone," he wrote in January 1846, " I can't think.   His mind is full of cul-de-sacs.   He takes up a principle and defends it plausibly and follows it up to some absurd conclusion and then scrambles away one cannot tell how." *Life* by E. J. Whateley, II, 92.

versity the deepest suspicion has fallen on him in a case where every letter that he wrote in private shows that his public utterances exactly represented the state of his mind. This letter from Herbert Gladstone reflects the desires and difficulties of which Gladstone spoke in writing to Hartington, Chamberlain, and Granville. He wanted the Irish question settled not because he wanted to get rid of party difficulties or because he had some ambition of his own to serve, but because he thought it the most serious of all public problems. He thought he had good reason for believing the Conservative Party might try seriously to settle it. Gavan Duffy's article had been printed in a Conservative review. The Conservative Government had thrown over coercion and had spoken of bringing a new spirit into Irish administration. Carnarvon had been received as a second Fitzwilliam. It is probable that Gladstone knew that Salisbury had asked Lord John Manners two days after the fall of the Gladstone Government if he would consider whether Ireland could be divided into four Provinces with a central Court of Appeal for local and private Bill purposes.[1] It happened that Gavan Duffy was a friend of Ripon as well as of Carnarvon and Duffy went to Studley in August 1885 to put his ideas before him. Ripon listened with great sympathy. On November 10 Gladstone notes in his diary that he saw Ripon and he puts in brackets " (Ireland)." Gladstone must thus have known pretty well what had happened between Duffy and Carnarvon, even if he had not known earlier. Gladstone had thus to consider his words with unusual care. His own views which, as Hartington said, had long been known to his colleagues, were well summed up in a letter he wrote to a challenge from a Conservative member, Sir F. Milner, on October 19. " My own opinion is what it has often been declared to be, that everything should be freely granted to Ireland which she may prove to desire and which is also compatible with the unity of the Empire." But he was determined to say nothing that would seem to bid for the Irish vote, and he held that the duty of putting forward a

[1] Whibley, *Lord John Manners and his Friends*, Vol. II, p. 307.

scheme rested on the Government and the Irish party. He had already before the end of the session, if Labouchere is to be believed, urged the Irishmen to work at the question seriously and constructively and they had so far taken his advice that Sexton, T. P. O'Connor and others had formed a committee to study federations, but " Parnell hardly spoke to his followers upon political matters, beyond such as concerned the Irish elections. . . ."[1]

The sincerity of Gladstone's refusal to bid for Irish support was proved by the communications that passed this autumn between him and Mrs. O'Shea. Of these a full account must be given here.

When Chamberlain received from O'Shea on January 15, 1885, a document in O'Shea's handwriting which contained, as he told Chamberlain, Parnell's scheme for a Central Board, Chamberlain took it to Gladstone who was less astonished than Chamberlain had expected him to be. " Mr Gladstone told me that he had received a similar scheme embodying Mr Parnell's views through Mrs O'Shea." In her book Mrs. O'Shea published " A Proposed Constitution for Ireland," a scheme for Home Rule which she described as " a document of tremendous import," sent by her to Gladstone on Parnell's behalf early in 1884.[2] Mr. Garvin suggests that this was the document referred to by Gladstone as " a similar scheme."[3] But even Gladstone with his power of putting unexpected interpretations on words could scarcely have called this ambitious scheme for Home Rule a similar scheme to the scheme for a Central Board, and the Gladstone Papers show that a scheme giving Parnell's views on a Central Board was sent to Gladstone early in 1885, and that the " proposed Constitution for Ireland," said by Mrs. O'Shea to have been sent early in 1884, was not in fact sent to Gladstone till October 30, 1885.

After the fall of his Government, Gladstone wrote to Spencer (June 27, 1885):

---

[1] Thorold, *Life of Labouchere*, p. 237.
[2] Vol. II, pp. 18–20.
[3] *Life of Chamberlain*, Vol. I, p. 582.

" I suppose you to be in possession of a paper said to contain Parnell's views on Local Government for Ireland, which was privately forwarded to me several months ago, and which (if my memory serves me right) I sent on to you.   Will you kindly let me have it, or a copy of it, that I may (for the first time) peruse it."

This paper was clearly the paper mentioned by Gladstone to Chamberlain; he had glanced at it, but given it no special attention, for, as we have seen, the negotiations about the Central Board scheme were in Chamberlain's hands and Gladstone thought himself on the eve of retirement.   In the summer, when he began to think of remaining in politics for the election, he wished to examine the paper and asked Spencer for it.   We know that at this time Gladstone was considering the possibility of fighting the election on the Central Board scheme.[1]   After writing to Spencer he wrote also to Grosvenor,[2] to whom, as he remembered, he had sent the original paper, suggesting that he should find out from Mrs. O'Shea whether Parnell still adhered to his scheme. Mrs. O'Shea did not answer Grosvenor till July 21, and then her letter was curt.   Speaking for herself only she thought that nothing less than a scheme on the lines of Herbert Gladstone's speech at Leeds would now be considered.[3] But she suggested writing more fully later, if Grosvenor wished her to do so.   Two rather urgent letters from Grosvenor on July 23 and July 28 elicited no further reply, but her letter of the 21st seems to have convinced Gladstone that Parnell was going to ask for something more ambitious than a Central Board.   On July 23 he wrote to Granville: " In writing to Derby I said that present appearances were not favourable to the plan called Chamberlain's, but that a larger demand seemed to be taking its place. He reserved his judgment but the larger seemed to repel him less than the smaller."

[1] See Chap. XXI.

[2] " You will remember that early in the present year Mrs O'Shea was good enough to send me a paper which as she informed me contained the views of Mr Parnell on Local Government."

[3] Herbert Gladstone on July 14 had declared for a Parliament on College Green on a Federal basis.

In August, after seeing Carnarvon (August 1), Parnell hoped to persuade Gladstone to put out a large policy for Ireland. Mrs. O'Shea, early in August, in answer to a letter from Gladstone, sent what she calls in her book " a long and comprehensive reply " offering at the same time to send him a paper setting out Parnell's views. Mrs. O'Shea's letter, unfortunately does not survive. Gladstone replied to it on August 8.

" I have to thank you for a very interesting letter. Too interesting, almost, to be addressed to a person of my age and to weakened sight, since it substitutes for a limited prospect a field almost without bounds.

"You do not explain the nature of the changes which have occurred since you sent me a spontaneous proposal, which is now, it appears, superseded. The only one I am aware of is the altered attitude of the Tory party, and I presume its heightened biddings. It is right I should say that into any counterbidding of any sort against Lord R. Churchill I for one cannot enter.

" If this were a question of negotiation, I should have to say that in considering any project which might now be recommended by Mr Parnell I should have to take into view the question whether, two or three months hence, it might be extinguished like its predecessor, on account of altered circumstances.

"But it is not a question of that kind, and therefore I have no difficulty in saying it would ill become me to discourage any declaration of his views for Ireland by a person of so much ability representing so large a body of opinion. I have always felt, and I believe I have publicly expressed, my regret that we were so much in the dark as to the views of the Home Rule or Nationalist party; and the limit I assign to the desirable and allowable is one which I have often made known in Parliament and elsewhere. I should look therefore to such a paper as you describe, and appear to tender, as one of very great public interest."

Gladstone was thus careful to make it clear to Parnell that he was not going to counterbid against the Government, and as a result the Parnell paper was not sent. But in the autumn on October 23 Mrs. O'Shea, writing about getting O'Shea a seat, added a remark that she had the Parnell paper if Gladstone would like to see it. This probably meant that Parnell was less confident of getting what he wanted from the Conservatives. Gladstone said he would like to see it and on October 30 the paper was sent. It was as follows:

A PROPOSED CONSTITUTION FOR IRELAND.

An elected Chamber with power to make enactments regarding all the domestic concerns of Ireland, but without power to interfere in any Imperial matter.

The Chamber to consist of three hundred members.

Two hundred and six of the number to be elected under the present suffrage, by the present Irish constituencies, with special arrangements for securing to the Protestant minority a representation proportionate to their numbers; the remaining ninety-four members to be named in the Act constituting the Chamber.

The principle of nomination regarding this proportion of members to last necessarily only during the duration of the first Chamber.

The number of elected members, suffrage, and boundaries of constituencies for election of succeeding Chamber to be capable of alteration by the preceding Chamber, excepting those special arrangements for securing to the Protestant minority a proportionate representation, which arrangements shall be fixed and immutable.

The first Chamber to last for three years, unless sooner dissolved by the Crown.

The Chamber shall have power to enact laws and make regulations regarding all the domestic and internal affairs of Ireland, including her sea fisheries.

The Chamber shall also have power to raise a revenue for any purpose over which it has jurisdiction, by direct taxation upon property, by Customs duties and by licenses.

The Chamber shall have power to create departments for the transaction of all business connected with the affairs over which it has jurisdiction, and to appoint and dismiss chief and subordinate officials for such departments, to fix the term of their office, and to fix and pay their salaries; and to maintain a police force for the preservation of order and the enforcement of the law.

This power will include the constitution of Courts of Justice and the appointment and payment of all judges, magistrates, and other officials of such Courts, provided that the appointment of judges and magistrates shall in each case be subject to the assent of the Crown.

No enactment of the Chamber shall have the force of law until it shall have received the assent of the Crown.

A sum of one million pounds sterling per annum shall be paid by the Chamber to the Imperial Treasury in lieu of the right of the Crown to levy taxes in Ireland for Imperial purposes, which right would be held in suspense so long as punctual payment was made of the above sum.

The right of the Imperial Parliament to legislate regarding the domestic concerns and internal affairs of Ireland will also be held in suspense, only to be exercised for weighty and urgent cause.

The abolition of the office of Lord Lieutenant of Ireland and all other offices in Ireland under the Crown connected with the domestic affairs of that country.

The representation of Ireland in the Imperial Parliament might be retained or might be given up. If it be retained the Speaker might have power to decide what questions the Irish members might take part in as Imperial questions, if this limitation were thought desirable.

Such Naval and Military force as the Crown thought requisite from time to time would be maintained in Ireland out of the contribution of one million pounds per annum to the Imperial Treasury; any excess in the cost of these forces over such sum being provided for out of the Imperial Revenue (i.e. by Great Britain).

The Militia would also be levied, controlled, and paid by the Crown, and all the forts, military barracks, posts, and strong places of the country would be held and garrisoned by the Crown forces.

No volunteer force to be raised in Ireland without the consent of the Crown and enactment of the Imperial Parliament, and, if raised, to be paid for and controlled by the Crown.

Gladstone wrote two answers to this communication. The first and fuller answer was not sent, but is amongst his papers. It was as follows, dated " circa Nov. 3, 1885.

" I thank you for the interesting paper which you have sent me on the part of Mr Parnell.

" You are already aware that I could not enter into any competition with others upon the question how much or how little can be done for Ireland in the way of self-government. Before giving any practical opinion, I must be much better informed as to facts and prospects on both sides the water and must know with whom and in what capacity I am dealing.

" Further I have seen it argued that Mr Parnell and his allies ought to seek a settlement of this question from the party now in office, and I am not at all inclined to dissent from this opinion, for I bear in mind the history of the years 1829, 1845, 1846, and 1867, as illustrative of the respective capacity of the two parties to deal under certain circumstances with sharply controverted matters. In this view no question can arise for those connected with the Liberal party until the Ministers have given their reply upon a subject which they are well entitled to have submitted to them.

" I am aware that important questions arise as to the dispositions of Liberal candidates and members to-be, and as to the effect the circumstances of the Election may have upon them. But these questions are not under my controul.

" One observation only I will hazard on the form of the plan here presented. It would have been of advantage, if it had been as fully and carefully developed as the former paper on the Central Board. I observe for instance that finance is only touched at a single point and that no provision is offered for the Irish share in the National Debt, in Naval Defence, or in Royal Charges. This is only by the way.

" If the Government are asked, I shall be glad to know their reply so soon as it can legitimately become public property. What I think essential to any hope of a satisfactory issue is that any answer given on behalf of either party should be given on its own ground, and quite independently of the other party.

" I return the paper herewith."

The natural conclusion to draw from this letter would be that Parnell would be wise to support the Conservatives if he could get what he wanted from them. But Grosvenor, bitter Unionist though he was when the split came, was too much of a Whip to like the idea of losing votes, even Irish votes, and the letter was not sent. Instead a letter was sent from Grosvenor, drafted by Gladstone:

" Mr. Gladstone wishes me to thank you for the paper which you have sent him containing the views of Mr Parnell on the subject of Irish government. The important subject to which it relates could best be considered by the Government of the day, but all information in regard to it is of great interest to him. He will strictly observe your injunction as to secrecy; and intends to take a very early opportunity in Midlothian of declaring his views of the present position of the Liberal and Conservative parties in relation to Mr Parnell and his friends, and to the policy they may propose to pursue."

On November 9 Gladstone carried out his promise and spoke at Edinburgh on the Irish question. He asked for a majority large enough to enable a Liberal Government to deal independently with the question; he reaffirmed the essential importance of the preservation of the unity of the Empire and he insisted on his desire to give Ireland all means of local self-government. Parnell replied at Liverpool next day declaring that his speech, though vague and unsatisfactory, was the most important declaration ever made by an English Minister on the Irish national question and he invited him, Gladstone, to draw up a constitution for Ireland which no man could do better " subject to the conditions and limitations which he had stipulated for regarding the supremacy of the Crown and the maintenance of the unity of the Empire," and to let them see what his proposals were. Gladstone replied on the 17th, rallying Parnell on this method of confidential communication through the public press and putting two objections to his proposal. Until Ireland had declared her wishes at the Election, there was no authoritative representation of her opinion and Gladstone was not a Minister and therefore had no kind of right to assume a function belonging to Ministers alone. Thus his public speeches were exactly in accord with his private letters both to his colleagues and to Mrs. O'Shea. Parnell, unable to extract anything more from the Liberals, told his countrymen to vote Conservative.[1] Davitt was strongly against this advice. But Parnell went much further. For he approved of a manifesto in which the Liberals were abused with extreme violence. Irishmen were called on to vote against " the men who coerced Ireland, deluged Egypt with blood, menace religious liberty in the school, the freedom of speech in Parliament, and promise to the country generally a repetition of the

[1] November 21.

crimes and follies of the last Liberal Administration." It is difficult to understand the play of Parnell's mind at this juncture. If Gladstone had made a die-hard speech and it was clear that the Irish would either get what they wanted from a Conservative Minister or not get it at all, such tactics were intelligible. But Parnell must have known that this was not Gladstone's state of mind. Sexton had seen in 1881 where Gladstone's speech on Home Rule must lead him; all his utterances for four years had shown where his sympathies lay; his Edinburgh speech had been welcomed by Parnell himself. Parnell's misunderstanding of English politics, revealed in the levity with which he made a mortal enemy of Chamberlain, led him now to create in the most wanton manner an obstacle to Home Rule that even Gladstone could not overcome, for when the Home Rule Bill was introduced, Gladstone had to commend it to men who had been denounced three months earlier by the Irish Party to their constituents as murderers and tyrants. For Gladstone the issue at stake was so important that he never gave a thought to the abuse he had received but it was less easy for men who had not been immersed in Irish history to forgive and forget the treatment they had suffered. When Sir Henry James was offered the Woolsack the recollections of his bitter encounters with the Irishmen at Bury were still rankling in his own mind and that of his supporters.[1]

It is safe to say that if everything Gladstone wrote between July and December 1885 on the Irish Question had been published at the time, no suspicion could have fallen on his motives or his conduct. Whether he was writing to colleagues who were hostile like Hartington, suspicious like Chamberlain, or sympathetic like Granville and Spencer, or to Mrs. O'Shea representing Parnell, his tone and argument never varied. His one dominating desire was the settlement of the Irish problem and no thought of personal or party advantage ever turned him aside from the course he had marked out for himself. We shall see in the next chapter that when the Election was over he acted consistently in the same spirit.

[1] See Herbert Gladstone's statement in *After Thirty Years*, p. 289.

CHAPTER XXIII

In the autumn of 1885 there were two men who thought the Irish question the most urgent of all the problems of politics. They were Carnarvon and Gladstone. Salisbury, Chamberlain, Hartington, and Churchill, were all more interested, from one point of view or another, in the fate of the Church and of property. Carnarvon among the Conservatives had only joined Salisbury's Government because he believed that the constructive settlement of the Irish problem was a vital need. Gladstone had written frankly that he would not lead the Liberal Party after the election for any of the ordinary purposes of public life, but that if he could help the two nations to solve this problem he would think it a duty to give what help he could. These two men arrived at the same conclusion; that a settlement could best be found by co-operation between men who differed in domestic politics. The plan of a union of men of all parties to resist concessions to Ireland had occurred both to the *Spectator* and to Hartington. Carnarvon and Gladstone took just the opposite view. They looked for a union of men of all parties not to defeat Home Rule but to grant it; not to convince Ireland that however often she asked for self-government it would be refused, but to convince her that if she was ready to consider England's difficulties, England would try to satisfy her wishes.

Neither of these two men knew what was in the other's mind, but, as it happened, they acted within a few hours of each other. Carnarvon suggested at a Cabinet meeting on December 14 that Salisbury should find out whether he would get the support of some of the Liberal leaders if he decided for an inquiry into Home Rule. On the very next day Gladstone met Balfour, who was then Secretary for Scotland but not in the Cabinet, and said, as he puts it in his Diary, " what he will probably report in London."   On December 20 he wrote to Balfour about this conversation, authorizing him to speak to Salisbury and saying that he wrote for himself and without consultation.   In the course of this letter he said that he thought it would be a public calamity

" if this great subject should fall into the lines of party conflict. I feel sure that the question can only be dealt with by a Government and I desire specially on grounds of public policy that it should be dealt with by the present Government. If therefore they bring in a proposal for settling the whole question of the future Government of Ireland, my desire will be, reserving of course necessary freedom, to treat it in the same spirit, in which I have endeavoured to proceed with respect to Afghanistan and with respect to the Balkan peninsula."

Gladstone acted, as he said, without consultation, though as soon as he had acted he told Granville, Hartington, Spencer, and Rosebery, what he had done. His action shows how lightly his sense of what was due to his party sat upon him at a time when the Irish issue overshadowed everything else in his mind. It is not surprising that his independent advance to Salisbury added to the suspicion and ill will in which his relations both with Hartington and Chamberlain were soon involved. Spencer, who like him was dominated by the sense of the urgency of the Irish question, rejoiced to hear of his overture, but Hartington passed it by without comment. Gladstone was not only Gladstone: the most powerful Englishman alive with strong views of his own on Ireland. He was leader of the Liberal party, and in that capacity owing something to the views of his late colleagues. At the time he did not hesitate but he had some doubts later whether he had treated those colleagues quite fairly. In February 1888 Bessborough wrote a letter to Granville in which he complained that Ireland had been made a party question. In replying to Granville Gladstone wrote (February 16, 1888):

" I pass by his reproach about keeping Ireland as a fighting ground for parties because the only reproach I can make to myself is that in 1885, from anxiety to settle the Irish question, I committed myself to Salisbury in defiance of party interests more than (perhaps) was justifiable without a greater amount of concurrence from friends and colleagues."

Mr. Churchill's Life of his father tells us how Gladstone's offer was regarded in Conservative circles. " His letter was treated with contempt. No other word will suffice. ' A public calamity ' forsooth! ' His hypocrisy ', wrote a Minister to whom this letter had been shown, ' makes me sick '. In the Tory Cabinet there was but one opinion about him. He was ' mad to take office ', and if his hunger were not ' prematurely gratified ' he would be forced into some line of conduct which would be ' discreditable to him and disastrous '." Of the decision of the Cabinet to refuse to consider Gladstone's overture, Mr. Churchill justly remarked: " Thus idly drifted away what was perhaps the best hope of the settlement of Ireland which that generation was to see."[1]

If Ministers could have seen the correspondence that was passing between Gladstone and Mrs. O'Shea they would have seen that they grossly misunderstood his action. Five times during December, Mrs. O'Shea pressed him on Parnell's behalf to disclose his intentions; five time he refused in language that grew steadily more blunt. He used all his influence to encourage Parnell to work with the Conservatives, and to make it easy for the Government to satisfy him. Not only did he refuse to make any offer himself, but he made it clear that he thought that the best chance of an Irish settlement was for the Government to take the initiative and for him to support them. On December 12 he wrote in answer to Mrs. O'Shea's first appeal:[2]

" I am glad to hear that Mr. Parnell is about to see ' Lord C,' (Carnarvon as I read it). I have the strongest opinion that

[1] Sir Henry Ponsonby's papers, which Lord Ponsonby has kindly allowed the writer to see, show that that wise adviser of the Queen approved warmly of Gladstone's proposal. He had thought of it independently as the best solution and deplored its rejection.
[2] Letter printed in full in Appendix.

he ought if he can to arrange with the Government, for the plain reason that the Tories will fight hard against any plan proceeding from the Liberals: all or most of the Liberals will give fair play and even more to a plan proceeding from the Tories."

On December 15 Mrs. O'Shea sent him a very important letter to her from Parnell, dated December 14, which is printed in full in her Life of Parnell.[1] Parnell wrote that he understood Gladstone's speeches to mean that he would admit Ireland's claim to autonomy, provided that the General Election showed an overwhelming majority of Irish members in favour of it. The General Election had done this, so that it only remained to consider, first, the details of the proposed settlement, second, how to pass it through Parliament.

" As regards the first matter, the rough sketch, which I sent you some weeks back, appeared then, and still appears to me, the smallest proposal which would be likely to find favour in Ireland if brought forward by an English Minister, but it is not one which I could undertake to suggest publicly myself, though if it were enacted I would work in Ireland to have it accepted bona fide as a final settlement, and I believe it would prove to be one.

" This proposal was carefully designed with a view to propitiate English prejudice, and to afford those guarantees against hasty legislation, interference in extraneous matters, and unfair action against particular classes, apprehended by many persons as a result of the establishment of an Irish Parliament. It did not involve a repeal of the Act of Union, an irrevocable step, and the Imperial Parliament having conferred the privilege by statute would thus always be in a position to recall it by a similar method, if the privilege was abused.

" It provided for a special proportionate representation for the large Protestant minority of Ireland. It also left to the Imperial Parliament the practical decision from time to time as to the matters which did or did not come within the province of the local legislature. These are all important concessions and guarantees, and some opinion must surely have been formed by now upon these and other details."

[1] Vol. II, p. 26 f.

" I have not seen Lord C., and shall probably not arrange to do so for a week or two, as I wish to know how the other side is disposed first. I have always felt Mr. Gladstone is the only living statesman who has both the power and the will to carry a settlement it would be possible for me to accept and work with.

" I doubt Lord C.'s power to do so, though I know him to be very well disposed. However, if neither party can offer a solution of the question I should prefer the Conservatives to remain in office, as under them we could at least work out gradually a solution of the Land question."

He urged that he should no longer be kept in the dark about Gladstone's views. Were there any details in the sketch to which he objected? What would be the best way of bringing about " that change of Government which would enable Mr. Gladstone to deal authoritatively with the Irish question? "

To this communication, Gladstone wrote on December 16 a long reply (printed in full in the appendix). " Any letters," he wrote, " now passing between us are highly confidential, I would almost say sacred. At the same time, I shall not write a word without being prepared to stand by the consequences, should it at any time become public." He explained again why he thought that " the Irish party ought at once to ascertain the intentions of Ministers . . . ", pointed out the dangers of playing off one party against the other, and discussed how he himself could best help towards a settlement, reminding Parnell of the difference in their positions:

" He has behind him a party of limited numbers for whom he is a plenipotentiary fully authorized. I have a large party behind me, whose minds are only by degrees opening, from day to day I think, to the bigness and the bearings of the question, and among them there may be what the Scotch call ' division courses'."

Parnell still refused to believe that he could get no offer out of Gladstone. He was not intending, he wrote to Mrs. O'Shea, to make the two parties compete. If Gladstone would only outline a scheme that seemed to offer the basis of a settlement there would be no need to approach the Tories at all. Gladstone on December 19 repeated in plain language, that under the circumstances it was Parnell's business to approach the Government.[1] He reminded Parnell too of the difficulties caused by his policy of supporting the Conservatives at the General Election:

" Let me too refer to facts public and patent. Up to this moment the Nationalists are the ostensible allies of the Government and opponents of the Liberals. By their means, the Government have gained and we have lost a majority in the towns. Under these circumstances as there is irritation to soothe, as well as prejudice to overcome, most of all there is novelty and strangeness to convert into familiar observation and reflection."

He added a postscript explaining the difficulties further, " My fear is that to open myself on this subject before the Government have answered or had full opportunity of answering, would probably be fatal to any attempt to carry with me the Liberal party." Three days later, on December 22, he sent a short letter confirming his first letter and referring to a possible course of procedure.

" I write again, but it is in confirmation of what I have before written. The Nationalists are in the face of the world in practical alliance with the Tories. Any communication of views from me to them would be certainly regarded as the offer by me of a bribe to detach them from the Tories. It is therefore impossible. The first step for me is to know, and that the world should also know, whether that alliance continues or not. This involves the course of procedure, to which I have already pointed.

"One thing I may add. Some talk of a Committee. A fishing Committee I should regard as a subterfuge perhaps even as a fraud. But a Committee to which a responsible Government undertakes to submit a policy or plan, ought not perhaps at this stage to be excluded from consideration, so great are the possibilities of fearful miscarriage, so high the obligation to put a ban upon no idea that has elements of hope. If the Government had in view a method of this kind, I should myself be disposed at any rate to think if it could be made workable.

" I will also add that I *have taken* steps to make known to them my personal disposition to give what aid I can should they take up the question."

[1] For full letter see Appendix.

The significance of this letter is that Carnarvon at the instance of the Chief Justice of Ireland had suggested this course to the Cabinet. Evidently a rumour had reached Gladstone who thought that Parnell might be influenced in its favour, and the Government encouraged to try such a plan, by the knowledge that he would treat it in this spirit. The only possible conclusion to be drawn from these letters is that drawn by a responsible historian who has studied them. " Whatever else Gladstone wanted at that time," says Mr. Ensor, " he obviously was not eager for office."[1]

Gladstone was always surprised that his proposal to co-operate with Salisbury was not given serious consideration.[2] He thought he had good reason for thinking that it might be accepted. In the first place he knew of course that Carnarvon and Parnell had been in touch and he knew from Ripon, who, like Carnarvon, was a friend of Gavan Duffy, what were Carnarvon's views. He thought, as we know from one of his letters,[3] that Salisbury agreed with Carnarvon, a not unnatural view seeing that Salisbury had chosen him as Viceroy and publicly

[1] *England* 1870–1914, p. 561.

[2] Lord Norton (formerly C. B. Adderley, and a member of Disraeli's Cabinet of 1874–1880) protested, though a Unionist, against the language of his fellow unionists in the House of Lords about Gladstone's motives in taking up Home Rule. Gladstone replied September 10, 1893: " My dear Norton, Thank you very much for your letter. It is just like yourself, that is to say, kind and generous throughout. Who are the aspersing Peers are I know not— and never shall know—for my eyesight disables me from reading the debates. All the better—I can neither wonder at nor complain of them when a man like Argyll, my friend for forty years and my colleague for twenty, accuses me (if I understand him aright) of having done what I did in order to get office. In face of the fact that my first act was shortly after the election to make known to the Government that if *they* would settle the Irish question, they would have the best support I could give them and that I never said a word against them (though they were a small minority) until they declared in February for coercion. No answer was ever made to my offer, but I know there are among them men, or a man, who lament that it was not accepted." Of one of Argyll's speeches the *Annual Register* remarked " So severe a condemnation of one living statesman by another, both for many years belonging to the same political party and sitting in the same Cabinet, has seldom been heard before and its very bitterness in some manner detracted from its authority." November 1893.

[3] Letter to Hartington, December 15, 1885: " So far as I can learn Salisbury and Carnarvon are rather with Randolph, but are afraid of their colleagues and their party." Gladstone was under the illusion that Churchill's alliance with the Parnellites meant that he was a Home Ruler.

praised his administration, when Tory newspapers were attacking it.

This belief naturally coloured his view of the meaning of the speeches on Ireland in which Salisbury's intentions were so differently interpreted by different readers. The *Spectator* said of the Newport speech that Salisbury could quote it afterwards if he wished to justify his consistency, whether he adopted a policy of Home Rule or a policy of coercion. Gladstone naturally put the most hopeful construction on it. In a later speech made on November 9 Salisbury, after praising Carnarvon, said that subject to certain conditions, the unity of the Empire and the protection of minorities, etc., " the policy which every English Government and I am sure the present Government would pursue would be to do everything possible to give contentment, happiness and prosperity to the Irish people." Gladstone wrote to Hartington calling his attention to this speech.

" You have I think courted the hostility of Parnell. Salisbury has carefully avoided doing this, and last night he simply confined himself to two conditions, which you and I both think vital; namely the unity of the Empire and an honourable regard to the position of the ' minority,' i.e. the Landlords. . . . I am much struck by the increased breadth of Salisbury's declaration last night; he dropped the ' I do not see how '."

This interpretation of Salisbury's views was fortified by letters he received from Maccoll. Maccoll, though a Canon, was an active politician who was on terms of friendship both with Gladstone and Salisbury and he had acted as a go-between in the negotiations over Franchise and Redistribution. He was anxious to fill the same rôle again and on December 22 he wrote to Gladstone: " I found Lord Salisbury, as I gathered, prepared to go as far probably as yourself on the question of Home Rule; but he seemed hopeless as to the prospect of carrying his party with him."[1]

There were further reasons why Gladstone might fairly expect his proposal to be considered seriously, for he knew

---

[1] *Malcolm Maccoll*, edited by G. W. E. Russell, p. 122.

that among the Government's advisers on Ireland there was strong pressure for such a policy. On December 12 he received a long secret letter from Jenkinson, the head of the Irish C.I.D., putting a strong case for Home Rule. Gladstone answered him saying that he agreed with his leading views, adding " if they [the Government] will not trifle with the subject but bring in a measure adequate and safe, I shall use them as I have used them about Afghanistan and about Bulgaria." He sent on the letter to Hartington, who replied (December 17) that he had shown it to Northbrook and Harcourt who were staying with him. " I find that they were both aware of his opinions on the subject of Home Rule, which however were previously quite unknown to me." Spencer was in communication with Sir Robert Hamilton who sent him in confidence a memorandum he had drawn up on Irish policy. Hamilton had been against the Central Board scheme and still was, but he was strongly in favour of a larger plan. This memorandum (dated October 21, 1885) had undoubtedly had a great effect on Carnarvon.

In this memorandum Hamilton put a strong case for the view that the new demand likely to be made by Ireland must be met in a generous spirit. He held, as he had always held, that it would be better to go directly to a large parliamentary settlement than to begin with the reform of local government. His argument was that if local government was started while the present agitation was in progress, all the local authorities would fall under the power of the more extreme parties and that the future of a parliamentary system would be prejudiced. He maintained that if Ireland returned a great majority for Home Rule it would be unconstitutional and inconsistent for the British Parliament to ignore that demand. And there was every reason to expect such a demand. Parnell's policy was supported by the Catholic hierarchy and candidates pledged to that policy were being adopted everywhere by conventions representing the priests and the people with extraordinary unanimity. He went on to consider the objection that removing the Irish members from Westminster would weaken imperial unity. The Irish members would leave Westminster but they would return in another form, for some kind of imperial federation was certain in the future:

" Whatever party may be in power after the election should in my mind take up the Irish question as of the first and supremest importance. A Resolution should be proposed to the House of Commons that the fullest measure of legislative independence should be given to Ireland consistently with maintaining the integrity of the Empire and the supremacy of the Throne, and with efficient safeguards for the rights of property and the liberties of the minority, and a joint Committee of both Houses, on which of course the Irish National Party should be strongly represented should be appointed to draw up a constitution for Ireland. . . ."

Thus the two most important officials in Dublin Castle were both of opinion that a serious effort should be made to meet the Irish demand. This was also the view of Sir Michael Morris, the Chief Justice of Ireland and a Conservative. It was he who suggested to Carnarvon the plan of a Committee which Carnarvon urged on the Conservative Cabinet.

There was thus important support for the kind of Irish policy that Gladstone hoped Salisbury might adopt among persons familiar with the state of Ireland from their official experience. We know too that there was a good deal of Home Rule in the air in London. We know this from a letter sent by Goschen to the Queen on December 22, 1885. The Queen was working hard at this time to create an anti-Gladstone party and urging Hartington, Forster and Goschen to unite for this purpose. The letters published in Mr. Buckle's volume show with what little foresight or imagination or sense of her constitutional duty the Queen acted from first to last in the final phases of the Irish question. She was accustomed habitually to speak of the Irish as George the Third spoke of the Americans and she imitated him in her conduct to her Ministers; if she had shown a trace of the wisdom and balance that she showed at the time of the Disestablishment of the Irish Church, she might have rendered an incalculable service to the Empire. Goschen, hostile though he was to Gladstone's Irish sentiments, was clearly alarmed by the lengths to which she was ready to go. In a letter on December 22 he wrote:

" Mr. Goschen ventures humbly to submit that, while in his own opinion it is the duty of the country courageously to face the certain perils involved in the refusal of the Irish demands, hesitation on the subject need not necessarily be ascribed to any care for party interests or desire for office, but may spring, in the case of many men, from a real apprehension of formidable consequences likely to follow from a policy of resistance. Mr. Goschen has seen with much regret symptoms of this frame of mind in some quarters where hostility to Mr Parnell's plans has hitherto been strongest."[1]

Gladstone then might reasonably hope that after appointing a Home Ruler as Viceroy and dropping measures for keeping order that Spencer had considered essential, Salisbury had in mind some political concession to the Irish demand. This belief was in one sense too flattering, for, as we know, Salisbury had never been ready to take the risk of upsetting his party for an Irish reform. But Gladstone was influenced by his strong personal feeling for Salisbury. In 1878 he had regarded him as upholding good views for Europe against Disraeli's dangerous ambitions.[2] When he took office in 1880 he found that Salisbury had entered into secret relations with France about Egypt and Tunis which tied his hands. He was indignant and for a time changed his views of Salisbury's capacity.[3] We know now that Salisbury had been invited by France to

[1] Buckle, *Letters of Queen Victoria*, Second Series, Vol. III, p. 715.

[2] Morley quotes (*Gladstone*, Vol. II, p. 560) Gladstone's description of Salisbury in a letter to a private correspondent at this time. " I think it right at once to give you my opinion of Lord Salisbury, whom I know pretty well in private. He has little foreign or eastern knowledge, and little craft; he is rough of tongue in public debate, but a great gentleman in private society; he is very remarkably clever, of unsure judgment, but is above anything mean; has no Disraelite prejudices; keeps a conscience, and has plenty of manhood and character. In a word the appointment of Lord Salisbury to Constantinople is the best thing the Government has yet done in the eastern question." This is the tenor of all Gladstone's references to Salisbury in his private letters, except for his comments on Salisbury's arrangements with France about Tunis, on which he commented with astonishment and indignation.

[3] Goschen, who so rarely agreed with Gladstone, took the same view of Salisbury's conduct over the Turkish convention and the arrangements he had made to satisfy France.

make a defensive alliance for the defence of Belgium and
Holland and that Salisbury held this proposal to be fantastic.
France got instead a free hand in Tunis and an engagement
for common action in Egypt. But Gladstone's confidence
in Salisbury, which had been cooled by this discovery, was
revived by the admirable manner in which Salisbury had
handled foreign questions during the summer and autumn
of 1885. Moreover his personal relations with Salisbury
had been very cordial on the negotiations over the Redistribution Bill. Unfortunately Gladstone's confidence in
Salisbury which in this case misled him, was only equalled by
Salisbury's equally misleading mistrust of Gladstone.   In
fact Salisbury might have said of Gladstone in 1885 what
Octavio Piccolomini said of Wallenstein in Coleridge's
drama:

> Since then his confidence has followed me
> With the same pace that mine has fled from him.[1]

A remarkable error in Lady Gwendolen Cecil's Life of
her father shows that Salisbury's delusions became a
family belief. She says, speaking of the winter of 1885,
" Mr Parnell maintained an obstinate silence. But it
was known that he had been a visitor at Hawarden."
Parnell never saw Gladstone until April 5, 1886, when he
met him in conclave with Morley on the Home Rule
Bill: he saw him a second time on May 27.   He paid his
first visit to Hawarden in December 1889.[2]

Salisbury's mistrust was intensified by the disastrous incident that has become famous in history as the Hawarden
Kite.   To those who knew the facts no description of the
incident could be less accurate.

Herbert Gladstone had long been a Home Ruler and his
Home Rule speeches had more than once been cited by
Gladstone's opponents, as evidence of Gladstone's own
sentiments. During the autumn of 1885 he had been
pressing his father to go further and to try to satisfy Parnell.

---

[1] Act I, Scene III.
[2] See Life of Salisbury, Vol. III, p. 282 and Morley Gladstone, Vol. III, pp. 305,
324 and 420.

Gladstone replied to all these suggestions in the spirit of his letters to his colleagues and to Mrs. O'Shea.[1]

Herbert Gladstone was also in touch with Labouchere. During the autumn of 1885 several letters passed between them. Labouchere was in touch with Chamberlain and Randolph Churchill. The air was full of suspicion and rumour, and Labouchere was not the man to dissipate this atmosphere or to create confidence between public men. The political situation was complicated by Dilke's personal difficulties. It was generally believed (by Richard Grosvenor among others) that Dilke and Chamberlain were both manœuvring at this time to prevent the early formation of a Liberal Government, holding that Dilke could not be included in a Cabinet until the Divorce case was settled. Herbert Gladstone was afraid that Chamberlain and Dilke were both spreading through the caucus ideas that would be fatal to the hope of adopting a Home Rule policy; the policy on which his own heart was set.

Whilst in this state of uneasiness Herbert Gladstone received a letter from Wemyss Reid, editor of the *Leeds Mercury*, which confirmed all his worst suspicions. Reid occupied a peculiar position. He was not at heart a Home Ruler at all, for his hero was Forster, but he admired Gladstone and gave him loyal support and he disliked and mistrusted Chamberlain. Reid sent Herbert Gladstone on December 13 a letter which he described as a " very confidential and serious communication." In his letter Reid told Herbert Gladstone that Chamberlain, Dilke and Morley[2] were resolved to prevent the formation of a Government by Gladstone; and that they alleged that Gladstone had come to an agreement with Parnell which they were determined to upset. Reid was himself determined to support Gladstone, all the more because he suspected that Churchill had a share in this intrigue.

---

[1] See the three letters published in Appendix.

[2] Reid was strangely mistaken about Morley, who wrote on December 15 to Spence Watson: " Much dirty intriguing is going on. I won't be a party to snubbing the Old Man." Hirst. *Early Life and Letters of Morley*, Vol. II, p. 272.

Rosebery wrote to Gladstone on January 7, 1886: " Chamberlain, I believe, is coming round though he has had a serious split with Morley."

" But it is impossible to fight in the dark. The present crisis is one of extreme gravity, and the forces which Chamberlain can command both in Parliament and the press are very formidable. If the independent Liberal papers (the *Spectator, Scotsman, Manchester Guardian* and *Leeds Mercury*) are left without any kind of guidance they can do nothing, and our party will come to something like shipwreck. . . . I do not ask you to commit your father in any way whatever; but I certainly think that you might be of great use to him and to the Liberal party just now, if you would give all the assistance you could to those who are anxious loyally to sustain Mr Gladstone in this great crisis, and who have infinitely greater faith in his power of dealing with the difficulties of the situation than in that of any other man."

Wemyss Reid added that he had himself a scheme in hand for bringing about joint action among the newspapers he had named.

This letter was an S.O.S. from a moderate Liberal, editor of the Liberal paper in the town for which Herbert Gladstone sat in the House of Commons, a person of special importance just because he was more likely from his Irish views to follow Hartington than Gladstone. But this letter was not the only appeal that Herbert Gladstone received. The manager of the National Press Agency, who supplied leaders, letters, etc., to 170 papers, was also pressing him for guidance. Lyon Playfair wrote at the same time to tell him that he had sat next to Dilke at dinner who had told him that he and Chamberlain were in action for the shelving of Home Rule, which meant the retirement of Gladstone.[1] Herbert Gladstone decided to go up to London.

In London he had a talk with Wemyss Reid on December 15 and on the 16th a talk with the editor of the National Press Agency, Dawson Rogers, in the presence of his two assistants, L. F. Austin and H. W. Massingham. Within a few hours the mischief had been done. The *Standard* came out next day with Gladstone's plan of Home Rule and the evening papers published a communication from the National Press Agency.[2] What Herbert Gladstone had regarded as purely private talk, had been treated as

---

[1] *After Thirty Years*, p. 308.
[2] This is given in an appendix to this Chapter.

if it was all for the public ear. He says of the interview:

" Excepting two essential and one or two lesser points the account of my interview was accurate. The interview was lengthy. I was cross-examined and in the course of it expressed opinions which were definitely my own. The unforgivable error was made in gathering everything up—personal as well as political—and publishing it as Mr Gladstone's own definite plans and opinions. I was asked my opinion of Lord Hartington's position and gave it as such. This opinion was quoted as Mr Gladstone's. I was made to say things I did not say."[1]

Gladstone, who of course had known nothing about his son's actions, hastened to announce that the paragraphs that had appeared were not an account of his view but speculations on them,[2] but this denial was of no help to him in his difficulties. Morley, writing in 1903, said: " There can be no doubt, whatever else may be said, that the publication was neither to his advantage nor in conformity with his view of the crisis." Nothing could in fact have been more damaging to him in the two tasks on which he was engaged at the moment, and nothing therefore that he was more certain to dislike. He was trying, first to persuade the Government to take up Home Rule, and secondly to coax his doubting colleagues out of their fears.

For it must have been obvious to Gladstone that this announcement was likely to destroy what hope there might have been of persuading the Government to adopt his plan of a non-party Home Rule settlement. Salisbury was anxious to go out of office. He was unhappy about the seven months during which he had had to defend the dropping of coercion and a general policy that Balfour, years afterwards, described to Mr. Garvin as a policy of eating dirt.[3] If he were to accept Gladstone's offer, he would find himself in a position of discomfort in two respects. In the first place he might well doubt how much freedom he

[1] *After Thirty Years*, pp. 312–3.

[2] Gladstone telegraphed to the Central Press " The statement is not an accurate representation of my views but is, I presume, a speculation upon them. It is not published with my knowledge or authority ; nor is any other, beyond my own public declarations."

[3] *Life of Chamberlain*, Vol. II, p. 9 n.

would have in fact when holding office with a minority Government, in co-operating with somebody of Gladstone's immense ascendancy, power, and self-will. In the second place he might well think of this announcement that it showed how Gladstone could use that ascendancy to create a public opinion that would still further handicap his independence. Thus this disastrous incident would make him more uneasy than before about the conditions under which he would receive the support of his powerful opponent. All this must have been clear to Gladstone when he read the fatal paragraphs.

We know, of course, what Gladstone did not know, that Salisbury's Cabinet had already rejected Carnarvon's proposals, and determined against Home Rule. Salisbury wrote to the Queen on December 14 giving an account of the meeting of the Cabinet which contained these words: " It was resolved . . . that it was not possible for the Conservative Party to tamper with the question of Home Rule." Mrs. O'Shea had written to Gladstone on December 10 saying that Parnell was to see Carnarvon in a few days' time. This visit never happened; presumably because Carnarvon had nothing to tell him. The fate of Gladstone's suggestion was thus settled before he sent his letter to Balfour on December 20, though under more favourable conditions Carnarvon might have been able to use the fact of this offer to get some reconsideration of his policy. But it is easy to see that the Hawarden Kite was bound to have a bad influence on the policy of the Conservative Government, even if its decision on the large question had already been taken. It is only necessary to glance at the position of the Government to understand this.

The Conservatives had hoped for a modest majority in the new Parliament, though not a majority without the Parnellites. Balfour told Henry Sidgwick in October that they expected a majority of about twenty.[1] Instead they would only have just half the House when the Parnellites supported them. The election was thus a disappointment. They had had the Irish vote and they were attacking a party whose

[1] Henry Sidgwick, *Memoir*, p. 427.

disasters had spread both indignation and mistrust. The appearance of the Kite gave them a new hope. Randolph Churchill knew well of the strong opposition to Home Rule in the Liberal party; he knew Chamberlain's view that the working men were hostile; he knew what Hartington and Goschen felt about it; he knew also that opposition to Home Rule would be a much stronger electioneering cry than the cries that had failed at the last election to rouse enough excitement to give their party a majority. Church and Property had failed. The Empire, national safety, all the passions that had been excited by Irish outrages, the Ulster sentiment, here was ample material for mobilizing rhetoric. Parnell had made a party by exciting the hereditary passions of an oppressed peasantry; but he had been equally successful in provoking the hereditary passions of the Ulster Protestants. And Churchill, like all orators, was given, when studying the arguments for and against a course, to put himself in fancy on the platform. If Salisbury had been afraid of accepting Carnarvon's advice in the autumn because he thought he would break up his party, his misgivings would be much stronger now when Churchill could use against him this powerful sentiment. All the arguments from party advantage were now on the side of rejecting Gladstone's overture and forcing him either to fight for Home Rule—a hopeless case as it looked—or to retire from politics and leave his party torn between Hartington and Chamberlain.

Gladstone then, who believed that Salisbury was thinking of Home Rule, could see at once that the effect of this disclosure must be to discourage him from any such plan. If he had known what was in Salisbury's mind, he would have seen that the publication of the Kite was likely to precipitate the disaster he wanted to avoid, and to drive Salisbury into coercion. For instead of thinking of making a large Irish settlement, Salisbury and Churchill were both thinking of drawing off Gladstone's Whig supporters. Churchill had written to Salisbury on November 29 offering to resign in order to make it easier for Salisbury to persuade Hartington, Goschen and Rosebery to join his Government. Salisbury replied putting Churchill's offer on one side and saying that the moment for bargaining had not yet come and that it would be wise to keep back some of the reforms Churchill suggested in order to offer them to Hartington as an inducement when the time arrived. " If we are too free with our cash now, we shall have no money to go to market with when the market is open." Salisbury, that is, was thinking already, before Gladstone had made any Irish announcement, of bringing about just the Coalition that was afterwards created, with the difference that he contemplated a coalition that was primarily intended to resist Chamberlain and was lucky enough to get one that included and disarmed him.[1] The Hawarden Kite thus would not only serve to confirm him in rejecting any idea of a Home Rule policy, but would make him all the more ready to precipitate a crisis by returning to Coercion. In a memorandum on Policy that he sent Salisbury about December 4 or 5, Churchill had spoken of coercion as impossible. After the Hawarden Kite coercion had a different look. For anything that tempted Gladstone to act in the spirit of that communication would make it easier for Salisbury and Churchill to draw Hartington, Goschen, James and other Whigs over to their side.

Not less serious was the effect on Gladstone's colleagues. They had good reason for holding that he had shown them little consideration. In private he had been urging them to take a larger view of the Irish question and they knew well how his mind was moving. In his letter of November 10 to Hartington he had said:

" You have opened a vista, which appears to terminate in a possible concession to Ireland of full power to manage her own local affairs. But I own my leaning to the opinion that, if that consummation is in any way to be contemplated, action at a stroke will be more honourable, less unsafe, less uneasy, than the jolting process of a series of partial measures. This is my opinion; but I have no intention as at present advised, of signifying it. I have all along in public declarations avoided offering anything to the Nationalists, beyond describing the limiting rule which must govern the question. It is for them to ask: and for

[1] Churchill, *Life*, Vol. II, pp. 6 and 15.

us as I think, to leave the space so defined as open and unencumbered as possible."

Later letters had made it clear that Gladstone was more and more inclining to a large policy, but nothing had prepared his colleagues to expect that he would disclose his mind to the public before he disclosed it to them. They had every right to resent the announcement of December 17. As soon as it appeared Gladstone wrote to Hartington (December 17), " The whole stream of public excitement is now turned upon me and I am pestered with incessant telegrams which there is no defence against but either suicide or Parnell's method of self effacement. The truth is I have more or less of opinions and ideas but no intentions or negotiations." He then went on to say that he thought the Government ought to make an effort to meet the Irish demand. Hartington's retort was unanswerable.

" When you say," he wrote on December 18, " that you are determined to have no intentions at present, I understand that you do not desire to take or prepare any action, before the Government have had the opportunity of acting. But the fact that you have formed the opinion that an effort should be made by the Government to meet the Irish demand, and that this opinion has been allowed to be made known and cannot be contradicted amounts in my view to action of enormous importance."

Gladstone wrote to him on the 20th to tell him of his meeting with Balfour, and of his subsequent letter. But Hartington's patience had given way and, disregarding Granville's entreaties, he wrote to his chairman on the 20th, to say that he had received no proposals of Liberal policy on the Irish question, and that he stood to what he had said at the election. Chamberlain, Harcourt, and Dilke, all assumed that Gladstone had inspired this revelation and stolen a march upon them. Spencer, though he agreed with Gladstone, was in consternation. " I have never felt so disgusted in my life," he wrote to Rosebery on December 30, " as I was by the *Standard* and *Pall Mall*, not to say Leeds revelations. The letter to the travelling artist was bad enough, but my hair well nigh bleached when I read the disclosures." Spencer went on to describe the mischief that had been done: distrust among colleagues, a storm in the London Press, the turning back of the commencement of concession among Irish Tories who had begun to say " This tension is intolerable, terms must be made, the sooner the better."[1]

It is not surprising that his colleagues pressed Gladstone for a meeting to discuss policy. Hartington wrote to him, January 1, 1886, on behalf of Harcourt, Dilke, and Chamberlain, (the combination was significant, for till then he had scarcely been on speaking terms with Chamberlain) making this demand. Thus the year ended in an atmosphere of bitter suspicion. Men who had held together through the dark days of the Gordon disaster were breaking angrily apart. Gladstone, who had kept the quarrel between Chamberlain and Hartington from wrecking the party, was now the centre of the storm. All his plans for keeping his colleagues together as long as possible had been upset by this shock. And the victim of the blunder was still suspected in important quarters of being its author.

APPENDIX TO CHAPTER XXIII

I. CORRESPONDENCE WITH HERBERT GLADSTONE

Hawarden Castle,
Chester,

October 18, 1885.

My dearest Herbert,

To return to the subject of our Irish conversations.

1. It is impossible to say whether a saving Liberal majority, if returned against a Coalition of Tories and Nationalists at the Election, could be kept *together* for a settlement of the Irish question—or to say what the effect of a split among them would be. This is a risk inseparable from the supposed Irish plan for the Election. The Irish ought to deal with the Tories and settle the matter with them before the Election. It is quite conceivable that, if this be not done, the Tories might then refuse or excuse from settling, and might be kept in by a Liberal secession of men, partly incorporated with the Irish, partly unwilling to concede to them.

[1] Crewe, *Life of Rosebery*, I, 255.

I know for myself what in these cases I should *not* do, but it is too soon to speak for others.

2. What I have said seems to assume that a plan could be devised, which would meet the two fundamental conditions. This as yet is not known. But I think the greatest difficulty in the way of such a plan is the protection of the Landlords, not of a Protestant minority. However I make the *assumption*.

3. The dilemma, which you put to me about the House of Lords, is not difficult of solution. Subject to (2) the assumption is that the H. of Lords fairly backed by popular opinion, as at one time the Jingoes seemed to be, rejects a plan carried by a sheer Liberal majority. In such a case the Liberals plainly, not being sure of the country, must resign. It is infallibly certain that the incoming Tories must at once make the concession.

3. An Opposition made up of Liberals and Nationalists (always subject to (2)) might work: but a Liberal Government could not stand on that basis to procure a settlement. This I take to be fundamental. Nothing but a sheer and clear majority in Parl^t could enable Liberals in Government to carry a plan. Personally I shake myself free of any other idea.

4. It is quite right to deal with the Tories. But they will avoid Aye or No and keep the thing dangling. If this is tolerated it is likely to spoil all hope of a settlement.

Your aff^{te} Father,

W. E. G.

Dalmeny Park,
Edinburgh, Forward.

November 14, 1885.

My dearest Herbert,

There is much to be said in favour of your suggestion: but it is dangerous for me to give out anything, however obvious it may be, which could be carried to the Government that they might outbid it.

It is beyond all doubt that if 1. the sense of Ireland be adequately declared in a certain direction, and if 2. the Liberal party is placed by the Election in a position to take up the question, then there ought to be early communication with those who would be the organs of Irish desire.

You might state your opinion to this effect, and your opinion also that this is my opinion. But remember to do nothing that can indicate a desire on our part to draw them off from communicating with the Government if they are so inclined.

I conceive that the obvious bases of any admissible measure would be 1. Irish Chamber for Irish affairs. 2. Irish representation to remain as now in both Houses but only for Imperial affairs. 3. Equitable division of Imperial charges by fixed proportions. 4. Protection of Minority. 5. Suspension of Imperial authority for all civil purposes whatever.

I send you herewith for perusal and return a letter in which I have given the conclusive reasons against my acting on Mr. Parnell's suggestion that I should produce a plan.

It was I think an error on his part to put forward the House [*sic*] Lords. *If* ever they were to be in a position to act as he suggests, they would put forward his authority, and make much of it.

Ever your aff^{te} Father,

W. E. GLADSTONE.

H. J. Gladstone, Esq., M.P.

Hawarden Castle,
Chester.

December 10, 1885.

My dearest Herbert,

1. The Nationalists have been in practical alliance with the Tories for years; more especially for six months; most of all at the close during the Elections which *they* have made us 335 (say) against 250 instead of 355 against 230. This alliance is therefore at its zenith.

2. The question of Irish Government ought for the highest reasons to be settled at once, and settled by the allied forces, (1) because they have the Government, (2) because their measure will have fair play from all, most, or many of us, which a measure of ours could not have from the Tories.

3. As the allied forces are half the House, so that there is not a majority against them, no constitutional principle is violated by allowing the present Cabinet to continue undisturbed for the purpose in view.

4. The plan for Ireland ought to be produced by the Government of the day. Principles may be laid down by others, but not the detailed interpretation of them in a measure. I have publicly declared I produce no plan until the Government has arrived at some issue with the Irish, as I hope they will.

5. If the moment ever came when a plan had to be considered with a view to production on behalf of the Liberal party, I do not at present see how such a question could be dissociated from another vital question namely who are to be the Government. For a Government alone can carry a measure; though some outline of essentials might be put out in a motion or Resolution.

You will be sure to be right as to my opinions while you keep on these lines.

Your affect. Father,
W. E. GLADSTONE.

II. THE HAWARDEN KITE

The statement issued by the National Press Agency on the night of December 16, 1885, as given in the *Pall Mall Gazette* of December 17, was as follows:

" Mr. Gladstone has definitely adopted the policy of Home Rule for Ireland and there are well-founded hopes that he will win over the chief representatives of the moderate section of the party to his views. Lord Spencer is practically convinced that no other policy is possible, and his authority as the Minister who has governed Ireland during a most troublous time is unimpeachable. There are only two alternatives—coercion and conciliation. Coercion has been made well-nigh impossible by the action of the Tories, its chief champions; and in no circumstances will the Liberal party ever consent to exceptional repressive legislation for Ireland again. Conciliation can be effectual on one condition—the support of Mr. Parnell, and this would be granted only to a measure for the establishment of a Parliament in Dublin. Mr. Gladstone is fully aware of the necessity of guarantees for the adequate protection of the minority in Ireland. It is not unlikely that Mr. Parnell would consent to a system of proportional representation; and in any case the position of the landlords would be thoroughly discussed and safeguarded by the new Act. It is not intended to exclude the Irish party from the House of Commons. They would still share in the deliberations of the British Parliament in Imperial affairs. Nor does Mr. Gladstone propose to give the Parliament at Westminster any veto on the proceedings of the Parliament at Dublin. Such a veto will be exercised by the Crown only on the advice of the Irish Ministry. It is not expected that there would be any necessity to revise the acts of the Dublin Parliament with regard to the commercial relations between the two countries. Mr. Parnell's suggestion of a protective tariff does not meet with the approval of all his colleagues; and if it were carried out the first to suffer would be the Irish people.

Mr. Gladstone holds none of the gloomy views prevalent in some quarters about the probable action of an Irish Legislature. It is not likely that the composition of that Legislature would be at all similar to the present personnel of the Irish party on the House of Commons. That party has been primarily elected to annoy and harass the British Government. It represents Irish unity on one great question—the recovery of Irish legislative independence. As soon as that question is settled, the unity will vanish, and all the sectional differences of the Irish people will reappear. The forces of intelligence, the wealth, and the interests of every class of the population, will assert themselves; and the members returned to the Parliament in Dublin will be vastly different in every respect from those who represent Ireland now at Westminster. The formation of a strong Opposition in the Irish Parliament will be comparatively easy; and Mr. Parnell will be entirely indisposed to take any steps in the direction of Separation. The strength of the Separatists is much overrated. There is probably not more than one of Mr. Parnell's parliamentary followers who wishes to see Ireland absolutely independent. Mr. Gladstone is sanguine that this policy of settling the Irish question once for all, will commend itself to the majority of his party and to the English people, when it is clearly understood that no other course can bring real peace. If he is enabled to eject the Government in this issue, he will have a large majority in the House of Commons for his Irish bill, and he believes that the House of Lords, weighing the gravity of the situation, will not reject it. Should there be a sufficient defection of the moderate Liberals to encourage the Lords to throw out the bill a dissolution would be inevitable, but except in the event of any serious explosion in Ireland that would have the effect of exasperating the popular feeling in England against the Irish the country would in all probability endorse Mr. Gladstone's policy and give him an unmistakable mandate to carry it into law. There is reasonable expectation that both Lord Hartington and Mr. Goschen will come round to Mr. Gladstone's view, and Mr. Chamberlain and Sir Charles Dilke, in spite of their present attitude, could not consistently oppose it."

Private and Confidential.

Hawarden Castle,
Chester.

December 12, 1885.

Dear Mrs. O'Shea,

1. I am glad to hear that Mr Parnell is about to see ' Lord
C. ' (Carnarvon as I read it). I have the strongest opinion that
he ought if he can to arrange with the Government, for the plain
reason that the Tories will fight hard against any plan proceeding
from the Liberals: all or most of the Liberals will give fair play
and even more to a plan proceeding from the Tories.

2. I am of opinion and all my public words and acts have
shown and will show that as matter of public interest this subject
is great, as matter of public honour is overwhelming, for all
concerned in it.

3. No plan can go forth as mine as or approved by me for
the plain reason that in my opinion no such plan can properly
proceed from any *British* source but one, viz. the Government of
the day. Rely upon it the issue will show that no resource can be
dispensed with, and certainly not the *authority* which waits upon
the Executive power.

4. If you ask me whether I think a plan based on the paper
you sent me can be adopted, I must ask what *is* its basis? Is it
(*a*) to deal not merely with all Ireland but with Ireland as a
whole
(*b*) to place Irishmen on a level of full political equality with
Englishmen and Scotchmen
(*c*) to make a fair not illiberal partition of *Imperial* charges
(*d*) to make an equitable provision for protecting the minority
(*e*) to give Ireland by Statute legislative and administrative
power over Irish as apart from Imperial affairs
I am dear Mrs. O'Shea,
faithfully yours,
W. E. GLADSTONE.

Hawarden Castle,
Chester.

December 16, 1885.

Dear Mrs. O'Shea

I have your letter of yesterday; and as, with my views of the

Irish question, I do not wish to be responsible for any loss of time that can properly be avoided, I reply at once.

Any letters now passing between us are highly confidential, I would almost say sacred. At the same time, I shall not write a word without being prepared to stand by the consequences, should it at any time become public.

Reading the able and comprehensive letter which you inclose *together* with your reply to my alphabetic inquiry, I remark as follows—

Communications *from* Mr Parnell and from his friends I have always desired, and for years I have publicly expressed my inability to pronounce upon Home Rule until it was explained to me. In this matter great progress has now been made.

Communication *with* Mr Parnell by the proper persons, as the chosen organ of five-sixths of the lawfully chosen Irish members, has now become not only warrantable but (as I think) imperative. The question remains who are the proper persons.

They are in my view, long ago stated publicly, the Government of the day. First because only a Government can handle this matter. Secondly because a Tory Government, with the aid it would receive from Liberals, might most certainly, safely, and quickly, settle it.

Mr Parnell's letter interprets with accuracy, and with moderation, my speeches in Scotland. It also states justly, as I think, the paramount claim of the question to immediate settlement—though I intend to avoid particulars, I will not scruple to say that in my judgment the point of urgency can hardly be overstated: that this matter lies in a region above and beyond that of Parliamentary procedure, as well as that of party, personal, and sectional interests and difficulties; and that my acts and words have been, and will be, governed entirely by the consideration of what is best for the " cause " by which I mean the settlement.

I do not know that my opinions on this great matter are unripe: but my position is very different from that of Mr Parnell. He acts on behalf of Ireland; I have to act for Ireland inclusively, but for the State. (Perhaps I should rather say *think*, or *speak*.) He has behind him a party of limited numbers for whom he is a plenipotentiary fully authorised. I have a large party behind me, whose minds are only by degrees opening, from day to day I think, to the bigness and the bearings of the quest on, and among whom there may be what the Scotch call " division courses."

I must consider my duties to the Government on the one side, to Ireland as represented by him, on the other.

With him, I can find no fault, if thinking it his duty to obtain the best terms he can, he tries to find out the terms our party will give, carry them to the other, and not decide upon them till he has compared so to speak the final terms of both.

Such a process could not be kept secret or disavowed. When before the world, it would damage a Tory proposal, it would ruin a Liberal proposal, if not as to the final issue yet as to all through which that final issue was to be reached.

Supposing the time had come when the question had passed legitimately into the hands of the Liberals, I should apprehend failure chiefly from one of two causes.

1. If it could be said that the matter had been settled by negotiation with Mr Parnell before the Tories had given their reply.

2. If the state of Ireland as to peace, or as to contracts, were visibly worse than when Lord Spencer left it.

I should do an ill service to Mr Parnell were I at this moment so to speak or act as to minister to any disintegration of the forces behind me, or to increase in any way the tremendous difficulties we should have to encounter, were we, the Liberals, called upon to act.

I will now bring together the threads of my letter.

Holding that the Irish party ought at once to ascertain the intentions of Ministers, I ask myself in what can I give legitimate help for this purpose.

I might make it known to the Government that if they will bring in an honourable and also an adequate measure, they shall have, with a fair reservation of opinion upon details, all the support I can give them. I should proceed in the same spirit as that in which I have already endeavoured to proceed with respect to Afghanistan, and to the Balkan Peninsula.

Secondly if I am asked to go beyond my public declarations, and to give my express concurrence to the basis of a plan, my present impression is that this could not be done safely except through some fresh public declaration. This, which would be no small matter, I might undertake carefully to weigh: but I must be first assured that the Government have had a fair opportunity given them.

There is much weighty matter in the latter portion of your

inclosure on which it would at this moment be premature to touch.

Believe me,

faithfully yours,

W. E. GLADSTONE.

P.S.   I am not in communication with Mr. L——.   Your inclosures are returned but I keep copies.

Private and Confidential.

Hawarden Castle,
Chester.

Dear Mrs. O'Shea   December 19, 1885.

1.   I accept absolutely the explanation as to the purpose for which Mr P. desires some development of the ideas I have often publicly expressed.

2.   But refer to the two things, either of which I said would probably be fatal.

3.   Let me too refer to facts public and patent.   Up to this moment the Nationalists are the ostensible allies of the Government and opponents of the Liberals.   By their means the Government have gained and we have lost a majority in the towns. Under these circumstances as there is irritation to soothe, as well as prejudice to overcome, most of all there is novelty and strangeness to convert into familiar observation and reflection.

3.   I think duty to the Government (as and while such) duty to my own party, and duty to the purpose in view, combine to require that I should hold my ground; should cherish the hope that the Government will act; and that Mr Parnell as the organ of what is now undeniably the Irish party should learn from them whether they will bring in a measure or proposition to deal with and settle the whole question of the future government of Ireland.

4.   Again I write at once, for as my suggestion would take some little time, I am desirous to lose none that I can save. Should I on reflection at all incline to modify what I have said, I will write in a couple of days.

Yours very faithfully

W. E. GLADSTONE.

I think I have not explained myself sufficiently under (2). My fear is that to open myself on this subject before the Government have answered or had full opportunity of answering, would probably be fatal to any attempt to carry with me the Liberal party.

I *retain* your inclosure.

CHAPTER XXIV

THE CHANGE OF GOVERNMENT

This being so I wish, under the very peculiar circumstances of the case to go a step further and say that I think it will be a public calamity if this great subject should fall into the lines of party conflict.

Gladstone to Balfour, December 20, 1885.

The prospect is very gloomy abroad; but England cannot brighten it. Torn in two by a controversy which almost threatens her existence, she cannot, in the present state of public opinion, interfere with any decisive action abroad.

Salisbury to the Queen, January 24, 1887.[1]

Continental observers have always been struck by the good fortune or the good temper that has enabled the British people to manage their most difficult problems without violence. Catholic Emancipation in 1829, the Reform Bill of 1832, the Repeal of the Corn Laws in 1846, the Reform Bill of 1867 all illustrated in their history a law that seemed to govern and to distinguish British politics. There seemed to be in public life some steadying power in reserve which came to the rescue when civil war looked inevitable, with the consequence that Great Britain had much less bloodshed in the nineteenth century than her neighbours. How far this was due to the British temperament, how far to personal accidents, it is not easy to say. Certainly it was a piece of good fortune that the leading figure in politics when the first of these crises had to be met was a soldier who made up his mind that civil war was the greatest of all calamities. Wellington and Peel established a tradition that survived for half a century, the tradition that governed and limited the range and methods of party conflict. It was agreed that it

[1] *Letters of Queen Victoria*, Third Series, Vol. I, p. 263.

was the duty of an opposition, when a controversy reached a certain point or a problem assumed a certain character, to seek to limit the mischief that might be caused by a reform that was distasteful, rather than to prolong resistance by methods that might provoke revolution.

This tradition lasted from 1828 till 1886. Gladstone had it in mind as soon as he saw that the Irish demand, of which he had said in 1884 that it would become a serious problem within ten years, was going, owing to the action of the Salisbury Government and the indication of Parnellite triumph in Ireland, to become a serious problem within ten months. He knew that if the Conservative Government decided on a constructive policy, he could assure to it the support of important elements in his own party. He was therefore sincerely anxious that the Conservative Government should make the attempt. If Carnarvon had been able to impress his own view and his own reading of the Irish problem on his colleagues and his chief, Gladstone's invitation would have resulted either in the setting up of a Commission to study the problem or the introduction of a Bill with the goodwill of the effective Opposition. By such methods the most difficult of the internal problems of Home Rule could have been treated and discussed dispassionately; the protection of Ulster and the protection of the landlords. Thus from Gladstone's initiative there would have come a serious deliberate non-party effort to solve the Irish problem. The question would have been kept, so far as that was possible, outside the passions and the tactics of party. It might have proceeded through the stages by which twenty years later the Union of South Africa was effected by agreement.

Unfortunately what happened in 1886 was exactly the opposite of what Gladstone wanted in 1885. He had desired a non-party settlement to be achieved by a combination of constructive forces, whereby the statesmen who realized what was needed could find enough support to carry a reform against the opposition of the forces in both parties that were obstructive from conviction or from mischievous motives. In this way an Irish settlement would be attempted with more power and prestige than the power and prestige of a single party.   The settlement would be British rather than Conservative or Liberal.   Events took just the opposite course.   An Irish settlement became the purpose not of something more than a party but of something less.   For the crisis created a combination, but a combination not to obtain reform but to defeat it.   Passions were not kept in abeyance; on the contrary two of the foremost men in politics were soon using their great gifts and their great prestige to incite part of Ireland to armed violence.   The Civil War which had seemed to Wellington the worst of evils seemed to these statesmen a lesser evil than Home Rule.

Nor was this the only tradition that disappeared in the storm.

The Queen, stepping away from all the habits and restraints that are the mark of constitutional monarchy in England, carried on a correspondence with the Leader of the Opposition on the methods by which she could help him to defeat the Prime Minister.   For the publication of the Queen's letters show that she even discussed with Salisbury the question of the date most propitious to his party for a dissolution.[1]

It has often been said that these calamities might have been averted or that in any case their bad consequences might have been modified if Gladstone had taken a different course.   To form an opinion on this subject it is necessary to recall the sequence of events.

The General Election, which began with the unopposed election of C. P. Villiers for Wolverhampton on November 23, ended early in December.   It resulted in the return of 335 Liberals, 249 Conservatives and 86 Home Rulers.

The Irish results were more emphatic than anybody had expected.   There was good reason for those outside the Cabinet circles to suppose that the demonstration of the strong feeling behind Parnell's demand would impress Ministers and incline them to develop the policy that Carnarvon had outlined in the Lords in July, 1885.   In the autumn Salisbury had justified the dropping of coercion on the

---

[1] *Letters of Queen Victoria*, Third Series, Vol. I, p. 135.

ground that it was inconsistent to give Ireland a popular
franchise and at the same time to use coercion against her:
an argument in the spirit of Carnarvon's new policy.   On
November 12, Churchill had derided Gladstone for asking
for a majority independent of the Irish vote.   This meant,
he said, " that seeing that the Irish people had now for the
first time obtained the means of speaking clearly, the people
of England, Scotland and Wales should give him an overwhelming majority in order that he might silence the Irish
vote."   On November 20, Churchill had said " that the
decision of the Government to preserve order by the same
laws as in England had been abundantly justified."   Thus
any person who had followed the speeches of Ministers would
have concluded, when the Election returned eighty-six
Home Rulers to Parliament, that an effort would be made to
continue the policy that had been adopted when Parnell's
following was much smaller.

Gladstone, as we have seen, thought this likely and was
passionately anxious to help the Government to follow this
course.   He declared this view to certain of his late colleagues, Hartington, Spencer, Granville and Rosebery.   To
Hartington he wrote on December 17:

" I consider that Ireland has now spoken; and that an effort ought to
be made *by the Government* without delay to meet her demands for
the management by an Irish legislative body of Irish as distinct
from Imperial affairs.   Only a Government can do it and a Tory
Government can do it more easily and safely than any other. . . .
As to intentions, I am determined to have none at present—to
leave space to the Government—I should wish to encourage them
if I properly could—above all on no account to say or do anything
which would enable the Nationalists to establish rival biddings
between us."

Gladstone, as we have seen, had already taken one step on
this path in speaking to Balfour.   On the 20th he followed
up his talk by a letter, and he told Spencer, Granville and
Hartington that he had so written.

On the very day when Gladstone wrote this letter to
Hartington, Chamberlain was speaking at Birmingham:

" We are face to face," he said, " with a very remarkable demonstration by the Irish people. They have shown that as far as regards the great majority of them, they are earnestly in favour of a change in the administration of their government, and of some system which would give them a larger control of their domestic affairs. Well, we ourselves by our public declarations and by our liberal principles are pledged to acknowledge the justice of this claim."

He went on to say a little later: " Mr. Parnell has appealed to the Tories. Let him settle accounts with his new friends. Let him test their sincerity and good will; and if he finds that he has been deceived, he will approach the liberal party in a spirit of reason and conciliation."

Thus Chamberlain agreed with Gladstone on two points; the first that the Irish elections could not be disregarded, the second that the Government ought to act.

Gladstone sent Balfour his letter on December 20, 1885. On the 23rd he wrote again, evidently realizing the difficulties of a position in which he was obliged to keep silence. He wrote to say that he was not himself acting:

" Time is precious, and is of the case. But, wishing them to have a fair opportunity of taking their decision, I have felt that *so long* as I entertained the hope connected with that wish (and how long[?] that will be of course I cannot say) I should entirely decline all communication of my own views beyond the circle of private confidence, and only allow to be freely known, my great anxiety that the Government should decide and act in this great matter."[1]

To this offer Gladstone did not receive an answer until January 4, 1886. Thus from December 15 when Gladstone made his proposal to Balfour to January 4, he was waiting for a reply to a specific suggestion, and his hands were tied in consequence.

It is interesting to compare with Gladstone's letter to Balfour of December 23, the letter he wrote to Mrs. O'Shea on December 24. Mrs. O'Shea, ignoring his repeated refusals to disclose his mind to Parnell, had written, after receiving his letters of December 19 and 22,[2] minimising

[1] Viscount Gladstone, *After Thirty Years*, p. 397.
[2] See p. 432.

the alliance between the Nationalists and the Tories, and asking again for guidance. Gladstone, on December 24, replied as follows:

Private and Confidential.

" Dear Mrs O'Shea,

" From the terms of your letter of yesterday, I think you wrote it with mine of the 22d before you. But it seems to me as if I had failed to make my position intelligible. Had I been in a majority, it, and my course, would have been different. I have made another effort in the Memorandum within. Observe I do not know what the Government will do, or what the Irish party will do. These are the two essential factors. The time is short.

Yours faithfully,

W. E. GLADSTONE."

The Memorandum ran:

" 1. My wish and hope still are that Ministers should propose some adequate and honourable plan for settling the question of Irish Government, and that the Nationalists should continue in amicable relations with them for that purpose.

My desire would be to use every effort to promote such a plan.

This course would be best for Irish and for Imperial interests. If it is adopted, I see my way.

2. I have no title to ask the Administration, whether they will adopt it.

Mr. Parnell has such a title. He has already made one arrangement with the Administration, on the basis of ' No coercion ' exchanged against the Irish Vote, which has worked satisfactorily to both parties.

There was an alliance, so to call it, during pleasure.

This alliance has not been dissolved. In the eye and estimation, therefore, of the world, it *exists* for every practical purpose.

3. The slightest communication of plans or intentions from me to Mr. Parnell would be irrefaceably stamped with the character of a bribe given to obtain the dissolution of the Alliance.

4. Foreseeing these embarrassments, I used every effort to obtain a clear majority at the Election; and failed.

5. I am therefore at present a man in chains.

Will Ministers bring in a measure such as described?

If ' Aye ' I see my way.

If No; that I presume puts an end to all relations of confidence between Nationalists and Tories. If that is done, I have then upon me, as is evident, the responsibilities of *the Leader of a majority*.

But what if neither Aye nor No can be had—will the Nationalists then continue their support, and thus relieve me from responsibility, or withdraw their support, and thus change essentially my position.

Nothing but a public or published dissolution of a relation of amity publicly sealed could be of any avail."[1]

In the middle of January the world learnt that Carnarvon had resigned, an event of ominous significance, though Carnarvon agreed that its political meaning should not at the moment be disclosed. When Parliament met there was no new Viceroy, but Hart Dyke, who had shared Carnarvon's views, had been replaced as Chief Secretary by W. H. Smith. On January 26, the full importance of the change of policy was revealed, for the leader of the House announced that two days later the Chief Secretary would introduce a Bill dealing with the Land League and the protection of person, property and public order. In July, 1885, Carnarvon had announced that his Government was going to try to govern on a new principle of conciliation. In December, 1885, Ireland had sent eighty-six members to ask for Home Rule. The Government which, six weeks before, on the eve of the poll, had told England that coercion was not needed, replied to this demand with the promise of a Coercion Bill, going much further than the Bill which it had refused to renew in the previous summer. The *Spectator*, judging the earlier policy in the light of the later, described the conduct of the Government in the previous summer as " the most barefaced dereliction of principle of which the political history of the century shows us any trace " (January 17, 1886). For Gladstone the event was worse than his worst fears, for he saw that the Government was answering Ireland's constitutional demand with a declaration of war.

[1] This very explicit statement did not prevent Parnell from attempting, a few days later through Mrs. O'Shea, to obtain a pledge from Gladstone that the Liberals would not bring in coercion if they returned to office. Gladstone's answer (December 31) does not survive amongst the Gladstone Papers, but Mrs. O'Shea states that he wrote a memorandum summarizing the position, refusing to give any pledge. *Life of Parnell*, II, 31.

A Leader of the Opposition whose chief desire was that he should be able to support the Government in a constructive policy, who knew that the Government were divided on that policy, was in a very embarrassing position during these critical weeks. Gladstone did not want to say a word that would make it less easy for the Government to take action. He had told the Government that he was not taking action himself. He could therefore do nothing for his own views or policy.[1] But his embarrassments did not end there. His own party was in a state of discord and confusion. Hartington and Chamberlain were hardly on speaking terms. On Ireland Hartington had, in Gladstone's opinion, gone beyond what was needed in justice to his own views and what was proper in justice to Gladstone's, in denouncing any Home Rule policy. Domestic and Irish issues were both causes of disagreement. When Granville wrote on December 27:

" I have been asked to request you to call a cabinet of your late colleagues to discuss the present state of affairs. I have declined giving my reasons, which appear to me to be good," Gladstone replied: " A cabinet does not exist out of office, and no one in his senses could covenant to call *the late cabinet* together, I think, even if there were something on which it was ready to take counsel, which at this moment there is not."

He had already, on December 26, sent Granville a secret memorandum giving his views of the situation.[2] He wanted the Government to act and he had let this be known; if the Government refused, then the Liberal majority could not consistently with the principles of parliamentary government leave the government to a minority. If the Queen sent for him he would only accept the commission if assured of the general support of the party to a plan of safely guarded Home Rule; if that support were withheld he would stand aside. It would then be the duty of the anti-Home Rule

[1] During January he was turning a deaf ear to Parnell's continued suggestions for co-operation and as late as January 24, he was still referring " to what he had said before about communications from him to Parnell before the Tory Government had had its chance": See *Charles Stewart Parnell*, by Mrs. O'Shea, II, 32.

[2] See Morley, *op. cit.*, II, 270.

Liberals to form a Government and that Government he would support, for though the Irish question would remain paramount in his view, he would prefer a Liberal Government without an Irish measure to a Tory Government without an Irish measure.

The Government's decision to revert to coercion and to drop all constructive plans put an end of course to the period of suspense. Gladstone made up his mind at once that it was his duty if he could to turn them out. His memory, as well as his imagination, filled him with fear for the future of the two peoples if England's only answer to the new Nationalist demand was to be a declaration of war. He felt, like Hamilton, that no society that professed any respect for popular government could so treat a demand made by constitutional methods on behalf of the Irish people. The best thing that could happen was the settlement of the Irish question by non-party methods, the worst was a combination of parties to use force against the declared will of Ireland. That would indeed put England in the place of one of the continental despotisms. For Gladstone to end his career by complicity with such a plan would be to belie the whole meaning of his life.

If the Government was to be turned out it might be done in one of various ways. Either some non-Irish amendment on the Address might be used, or its Irish policy might be directly challenged. The first course was adopted and on January 26, Jesse Collings' amendment, regretting that nothing was contained in the Address about allotments for agricultural labourers, was carried against the Government by 331 votes to 252. The figures of the Division were interesting, for eighteen Liberals, including Hartington, Goschen, James and Courtney, voted with the Government and seventy-four abstained. Some of the Liberals were voting against concession to Ireland, some were voting against Chamberlain's English programme, some like Hartington and Goschen were voting against both.

Gladstone had good reasons for deciding to turn the Government out on the first opportunity instead of waiting to raise a direct Irish issue. For his compulsory silence had prevented him from giving any instruction or persuasion on the Irish question, and he could not tell how Liberals would vote on that issue. He pointed out later that after three months' discussion, 300 Liberals voted for the Home Rule Bill: it was unlikely that so large a number would have voted for Home Rule without previous discussion. Also he knew well from bitter experience that when once coercion begins, calm and considered policy has little chance. If Home Rule was to be tried, it was essential to prevent the creation of a storm of passion between the two countries before debate began.

On the fall of the Government Gladstone acted according to the plan he had put before Granville and Spencer in December. He formed a Government whose main purpose was to be Home Rule. In inviting Liberals to enter his Government he described his intentions.

" I propose to examine whether it is or is not practicable to comply with the desire, widely prevalent in Ireland, and testified by the return of eighty-five out of one hundred and three representatives, for the establishment by Statute of a Legislative Body, to sit in Dublin, and to deal with Irish as distinguished from Imperial affairs; in such a manner as would be just to each of the three Kingdoms, equitable with reference to every class of the people of Ireland, conducive to the social order and harmony of that country, and calculated to support and consolidate the unity of the Empire on the combined basis of Imperial Authority and mutual attachment."[1]

Hartington and most of the Whigs declined to take office for this purpose. It may be doubted whether Hartington would have joined a Liberal Government, whatever its Irish policy, that included Chamberlain. Chamberlain on the other hand decided to accept, though with many misgivings of which he made no secret. Trevelyan was in the same position as Chamberlain. It was a disaster for the new Government that the only member of the little Radical group who agreed with Gladstone on Ireland, Dilke, was kept outside by the shadow of the Divorce Court.

Gladstone had taken the only course that a man with any

[1] Morley, *op. cit.*, III, p. 292.

sense of public responsibility holding his views could have taken. No doubt it would have been better if some way could have been found of postponing a direct struggle for Home Rule and of keeping the question as far as possible outside conflict. But it was not the fault of Gladstone that this struggle was precipitated and that these disasters followed. He would have liked, as we have seen, to settle the question by agreement or at any rate to begin by inquiry in a non-party spirit. When this offer failed, the alternative was not between reflection and action; it was between action of one kind and action of another, between construction and repression. Gladstone was not in the position of a man who was flinging into politics a question full of danger and passion; he was a man who, finding himself in an atmosphere of danger and passion, had to guide his country to a reasonable settlement of a most difficult problem. Here he was in agreement both with Carnarvon and Chamberlain, for when Carnarvon's proposals were rejected, Carnarvon said that he could only hope that Gladstone would act, and Chamberlain, though he had under O'Shea's influence moved further to the right in the last six months, was still a reformer.

For the issue between peace and war was forced at once not by Gladstone but by the powerful newspaper that was to play the chief part in destroying Gladstone's plans. The *Times* urged the British people to turn away from Gladstone to Gladstone's chief enemy in Europe. It happened that at this moment Bismarck was deep in his schemes for subduing discontent in Poland. In May of the previous year he had expelled some 37,000 foreign Poles, not on the ground that they were seditious but on the ground that the Polish population in East Prussia was increasing faster than the German, and reasons of State made it necessary to defend Prussian interests by this method. The brutality of his action excited strong indignation and the comments in the *Annual Register* are severe. Bismarck was attacked in Germany. In January, 1886, there was a debate on Polish policy in the Prussian Parliament, in the course of which Bismarck unfolded his view that Prussian policy towards the

Poles between 1815 and 1848 had been fatally and foolishly generous, that mistaken promises to respect Polish feeling had been made: that those promises relating to schools, language, administrative appointments and other matters, could not be kept: and that it was necessary now to correct the blunders into which Germany had been led by sentiment.   The number of Poles in the Eastern provinces must be diminished and the number of Germans increased; the first object could be secured by the expulsion of Poles; the second by introducing German settlers.[1]

Defending his drastic policy Bismarck compared the Poles to the Parnellite Irish.   The comparison was not lost upon the *Times*.   Gladstone's attention was drawn to the fact that confronted with a problem not unlike that of Ireland,

" a statesman who is no novice or visionary—who is unsurpassed by any of his contemporaries in practical wisdom and resources —finds the solution, not in laborious efforts to follow every winding and evolution of national sentiment, but in a vigorous application of stringent measures, buying out the disaffected, and settling in their place loyal subjects."[2]

A little later, the writer points out, that Bismarck is " not quite so simple as to seek the co-operation of the hostile Poles.   He wants Home Rule for Prussia, not Home Rule for Poland."   How completely the *Times* had absorbed Bismarck's spirit was shown in a leader on February 17. " We in this country have been far too much blinded by specious nonsense about justice and its infallible efficacy as a breeder of affection.   It is time to recognize the truth, written large in history, in contemporary events and in human nature, that there are antipathies which have to be accepted as ultimate facts, and which neither justice nor generosity

---

[1] A well-known historian has pointed out that this coercion with which this policy was accompanied was followed by the second and worse coercion of 1905, when it was found that the first plans had been a signal failure and he remarks that a policy of conciliation could not have had worse results for Prussia than the coercion Bismarck adopted.   Conciliation indeed might have had the effect of detaching to Prussia the whole of Poland with consequences of great importance in the Great War.   *Life of Bismarck*, by Grant Robertson, p. 391.

[2] *Times*, February 11, 1886.

can soften." Thus the *Times* thought about past concessions to Ireland as Bismarck thought about past concessions to Poland and drew the same conclusion that conciliation must be put aside for good and all.[1]

The same spirit was shown in quarters where a different tone had been held in the past. On February 22, 1886, Churchill went to Belfast and made the first of his famous violent speeches. The speech was followed by riots and the *Annual Register* remarks that the revelations that followed an inquiry into the riots were very unfavourable to the Orange lodges. Churchill in the eyes of the *Times* had been the villain of the piece. It was he who had attacked the administration of justice in Ireland in the Maamtrasna case; it was he who had denounced the rule of Spencer as harsh and unfeeling; it was he who had arranged the alliance of the Parnellites and the Conservatives; it was he who had declared just before the election, when reports of the state of Ireland were already causing anxiety to the Irish Government, that coercion was unnecessary. Yet Churchill was now prepared to start civil war in Ireland rather than consider a Home Rule settlement.

For it must be remembered that all this violent talk and writing preceded the production of Gladstone's scheme. Gladstone had formed a Government to inquire into the question and to see whether he could construct a scheme for Home Rule that satisfied the conditions he thought indispensable. No doubt a man might argue that when a politician of Gladstone's immense power, will and versatility starts out on such an inquiry he is pretty sure to find what he wants to find. It would no doubt have astonished everybody if Gladstone had said after three months that his inquiry had convinced him that no such scheme could be devised. But nobody knew, when these speeches were made and these articles written, what Gladstone's Home Rule scheme would be. It was possible

---

[1] Salisbury spoke in the same spirit. On February 17 he reminded Englishmen that the Irish majority was descended from a long line of ancestors who had never ceased to hate England, and on May 15 he said he would rather spend a million in helping Irishmen to emigrate than on Land Purchase. In his heart he was still in favour of the old policy of clearance.

for a man to hold that no scheme could be accepted. It was possible to argue that any scheme would be better than perpetual strife between the two countries. But it was also possible for a man to argue that whether or not a practicable scheme could be devised could only be ascertained by inquiry and discussion, and that he was prepared to suspend his judgment until a scheme was before him. To those who know what disasters followed from the controversy that was then beginning it seems strange that the leaders of the Opposition, who had been told by their Viceroy that some scheme was essential, met the decision of Gladstone to start an inquiry with this passionate hostility. Thus at the outset a powerful party committed itself to two views; one, that any kind of Home Rule would break up the Empire; the other, that the Irish were unfit for self-government.

It would have been difficult for anybody, speaking not to an intimate circle but to the whole world, to put this second view in such a way as to cause no offence to Irish sentiment. Bagehot indeed laid down a general law which would have softened the edge of this conclusion. He argued that parliamentary government worked with stupid peoples only and that a clever people like the French or the Irish, with their quick and subtle intelligence, could not endure its absurdities. It would be difficult to imagine a more unfortunate effort to put a delicate truth with a minimum of disturbance than the speech Salisbury made on May 15 at St. James's Hall: a speech that caused a great sensation at the time and left behind it bitter memories. The argument of the speech is well given in Lady Gwendolen Cecil's masterly biography of her father.[1]

"He was disputing the contention that we ought to show confidence in the Irish people by giving them independent representative government. The claim of any population to this precise expression of confidence depended upon their characteristics: 'You would not confide free representative institutions to the Hottentots, for instance.' Then going on, as he said, up the scale, he quoted the populations of India,—'although finer

---

[1] Vol. II, p. 302.

specimens of human character you will hardly find than some among them '—Russians, Greeks—as people for whom such institutions were unsuitable, closing with a more generally exclusive statement: ' When you come to narrow it down you will find that this—which is called self-government but is really government by the majority—works admirably when it is confided to people who are of Teutonic race, but that it does not work so well when people of other races are called upon to join in it.' The Irish would be naturally included and were probably intended to be included in this final negative, in dignified companionship with the Latin peoples. But the fatally vigorous suggestion conveyed in the opening sentence was ineffaceable, and for the next half-dozen years it would be safe to say that there was not one Liberal meeting in ten at which some speaker did not repeat the assertion, that Lord Salisbury had declared Irishmen to be on a level with Hottentots."

This speech is remarkably illuminating. It will be seen that so far as the general argument went there was no need to refer to the Hottentots. For Salisbury goes on to speak of developed peoples, including some of the most experienced people of Europe, who are unsuccessful with self-government. The allusion to the Hottentots was all the more provocative because it was superfluous. It was, as Lady Gwendolen Cecil well puts it, a " fatally vigorous suggestion." But the rest of the speech was also strangely tactless in the mouth of a man who a few months before had had to receive the Ambassadors of France, Italy and Spain at the Foreign Office and was certain to have to receive them again. A private person or an irresponsible politician might tell the Latin peoples that Germany was better at self-government than they were, but the information came strangely from an Ex-Foreign Secretary and an Ex-Prime Minister.[1] The contrast between Salisbury's conspicuous wisdom and address as a Foreign Minister and his recklessness and his taste as a

---

[1] The Queen's Diary contains an amusing allusion to this speech. She is reporting a private talk of Goschen's. " Lord Salisbury's speech had done harm, though it was unintentional. He (Lord S.) said there were different nations who could not govern themselves; the Hottentots couldn't, the Indians couldn't, and the Irish couldn't! Of course his opponents and enemies who did not know him say he compared the Irish to the Hottentots! Most unfortunate. He heard he intended to make another speech to put it right." *Queen Victoria's Letters*, Third Series, Vol. I, p. 132.

party combatant is one of the curiosities of history. As a Foreign Minister he had a great sense for the dignity of the British Empire; as a combatant he could sneer at a Parsee candidate for Parliament, a late Member of the Legislative Council for Bombay, as "a black man."[1] To understand the passion with which Gladstone threw himself into the Irish controversy we must remember that though there was an element of personal arrogance in his nature,[2] the insolence of race seemed to him the sin against the Holy Ghost. The secret of the intensity of the conflict that was now beginning was the violent opposition between the spirit of European sympathy that governed his outlook, and the spirit of national pride bred in the ruling class by a long history of success, and in the new business class by the ease with which it led and managed the enterprise and commerce of the world. Salisbury had one; Chamberlain the other. This was partly why Salisbury and Chamberlain, in spite of their great differences and mutual repulsion, found it easier to come together than either of them found it to work with Gladstone.

We can see an analogy in Roman history. The Roman senators had, like the English ruling class, a great tradition as the rulers of a State dazzlingly successful in war and politics; the Roman knights, like the manufacturers, merchants, and bankers, of England, had the immense prestige and self-confidence that come from brilliant enterprise and wealth. These two classes had a purely nationalist outlook on the world. But Roman society was gradually influenced by Scipio's Greek friend Panaetius who preached a universal philosophy. Cicero, Virgil, Livy all show the effect of this teaching on Latin literature. With Augustus this spirit comes into constructive politics. Gladstone belonged by birth to the same class as Chamberlain, by education and marriage to the same class as Salisbury. But what Greek philosophy had done for Cicero and Livy,

[1] The workmen of Finsbury showed more of the spirit of the old Roman Empire than this descendant of a long line of Senators, for they returned Mr. Naoroji in 1892 to Parliament.

[2] See the impression made on Grey as a young man. Trevelyan's *Grey of Fallodon*, p. 29.

his Hellenist culture had done for Gladstone. His large European spirit was now in conflict with the intense national pride of the ruling classes.

These passions were to play havoc with politics for many years. Gladstone did not raise them, for, as we have seen, they were brought into action by his opponents as soon as he formed a Government. Every step he took between June 1885 and January 1886 was a deliberate effort to obtain a solution by passionless co-operation among the leading statesmen. Whether he managed wisely the different problems that faced him when he became Prime Minister is a more difficult question to answer.

CHAPTER XXV

February 18. Gladstone's third Government meets Parliament.

March 26. Home Rule Bill brought before Cabinet. Chamberlain and Trevelyan resign.

April 8. Gladstone introduces Home Rule Bill.

April 16. Gladstone introduces Land Purchase Bill.

May 10. Gladstone moves second reading of Home Rule Bill.

May 27. Liberal Party meeting at Foreign Office on Home Rule Bill.

May 31. Chamberlain holds meeting of 55 members " who being in favour of some sort of autonomy for Ireland disapproved of the Government Bills in their present shape." Bright sends letter stating his intention of voting against the second reading. The meeting decides by a majority on voting against the second reading.

June 7. Home Rule Bill defeated on second reading by 343 votes to 313, 93 Liberals voting against the Bill.

The voting of the non-Irish Members was as follows:

	For		Against		Absent	
	L.	C.	L.	C.	L.	C.
England and Wales ...	191	0	70	223	9	1
Scotland	38	0	23	10	1	0
	229	0	93	233	10	1

July. Dissolution of Parliament and General Election.
Conservatives 316, Liberal Unionists 78, Home Rule Liberals 194, Irish Home Rulers 85.

The Cabinet with which Gladstone set out on his great task contained fourteen members. The leading Whigs had followed Hartington, and Selborne, Northbrook, Carlingford, and Derby, went into opposition. Eight members of the late Cabinet were in the new Government: four Peers, Granville, Spencer, Kimberley, and Rosebery; four commoners, Harcourt, Childers, Chamberlain, and Trevelyan.[1] Ripon, who went to the Admiralty, had been in Gladstone's first Cabinet and during Gladstone's second Cabinet he had earned a great reputation as a reforming Viceroy in India. Campbell-Bannerman, who went to the War Office, had been Irish Secretary, and Herschell, the new Chancellor, Solicitor General in the last Gladstone Government. The other two members of the Cabinet, Morley and Mundella, were new to office; Morley had made a great position as a critic of politics in the *Fortnightly* and the *Pall Mall Gazette*, and Mundella had made his mark in the House of Commons by his speeches on Housing and Factory reform. Shaw Lefevre, who had been a Minister in the last Government and had declined the Irish Secretaryship, had lost his seat at the election and was for the moment out of Parliament.

In the last Government Gladstone and Chamberlain had almost always been on the same side on Irish questions with Hartington and Harcourt as their chief adversaries. In the last crisis over the Central Board Harcourt had changed sides and supported Chamberlain; at the election he had come out as his strong ally. He now went beyond him. Like Spencer he had been greatly influenced by what he considered the purely factious treatment of the Irish question by Salisbury's Government, and he had made up his mind that after this exhibition of inconsistency and instability England could not hope to govern Ireland by force.[2] But though he despised the Conservatives, he disliked the Irish as much as ever, and he was a Home Ruler against the grain.

The division between Whigs and Radicals had been sharply defined and greatly embittered during the elections,

---

[1] Chamberlain and Trevelyan accepted office with great misgivings and they formally resigned on March 26. Stansfeld took Chamberlain's place.

[2] See his speech, April 13, 1886: "I was convinced at that time, I am more convinced now,—that those events and the course then taken by the Conservative party made Home Rule inevitable." Gardiner, *op. cit.*, Vol. I, p. 580.

and it is certain that even if the Irish issue had not arisen there would have been a considerable defection from the Liberal party. Hartington had made it clear that he could not remain in the party with the author of the Radical programme,[1] and Selborne did not dislike Gladstone's ideas on Ireland more than he disliked Chamberlain's ideas on disestablishment. Whig losses were inevitable if the Liberal party was to be a party of active reform. The real disaster was of course the loss of the Radical leader. Whether that loss could have been prevented, and how far Gladstone was to blame for it, are questions that have interested historians ever since.

Now that Hartington had gone, Chamberlain was in his own estimation, and in that of a great number of Liberals, the most important person in the party after the Prime Minister. The prudent course for a Liberal leader, who has been deserted by his supporters on the right would be to treat the leader of the left with great consideration, and so to adapt his policy as to get the most that could be got out of his enthusiasms and his popular strength. Gladstone, following the inscrutable workings of his mysterious mind, went on the opposite principle. He behaved as if he attached little importance either to Chamberlain's personality, or to the forces and ideas that he represented in public life.

Gladstone's problem was complicated by the uncertainty about the future caused by Chamberlain's Irish hesitations. When Gladstone asked him to join the Government Chamberlain made no secret of his difficulties. His letter on acceptance was carefully worded.

"January 30, 1886. You have been kind enough . . . to repeat your request that I should join your Government and you

---

[1] In 1889 (January 13) Gladstone writing to Granville said, " I think Hartington started in life as Liberal, if not a strong Liberal; but ' society ' and the life it lives have worn it out of him so that for many years he has had but little of it but he remained in the party from loyalty to family traditions and to colleagues, and from fear of throwing things increasingly into the hands of Chamberlain. It would be hard I think to name any of our Liberal measures of which he was a warm supporter." Dilke's Diaries describe the constant Tory pressure on Hartington from his mistress.

have explained that in this case I shall retain ' unlimited liberty of judgment and rejection ' on any scheme that may ultimately be proposed and that the full consideration of such minor proposals as I have referred to as an alternative to any larger arrangement will not be excluded by you. (A) On the other hand I have no difficulty in assuring you of my readiness to give an unprejudiced consideration to any more extensive proposals that may be made, with an anxious desire that the result may be more favourable than I am at present able to anticipate."[1]

The paragraph marked (A) was inserted at Gladstone's suggestion.

Gladstone had good reason to doubt whether the writer of that letter would remain very long in his Government. Slow as he was by temperament to recognize unpleasant facts, he could scarcely disregard its significance. This might be held a reason against giving Chamberlain the Exchequer, for the resignation of the Chancellor of the Exchequer would throw all the plans of the Government into confusion. But the course Gladstone took seems strangely perverse and wrong-headed. He offered Chamberlain the Admiralty. Chamberlain demurred on the ground that it was ill-suited to a man of his ideas.

" Gladstone. Then what office would you prefer?
Chamberlain. The Colonial Office.
Gladstone. Oh! a Secretary of State!"

The Prime Minister, says Mr. Garvin, " raised his head and dismissed tacitly—without one further syllable of comment—Chamberlain's desire for a department which had become to him, as we have seen, a subject of intense interest. The Radical at this slight controlled his anger."[2] Gladstone was in a difficulty about the Colonial Office. The Queen, after asking Salisbury's advice, had said that she would not agree to Granville's reappointment to the Foreign Office, and Gladstone, who had had to break this hard truth to the old man, had persuaded him to accept the Colonial Office. It happened that the best chance of getting Chamberlain to take a large instead of a small view of the

[1] Garvin, *op. cit.*, II, p. 172.
[2] Garvin, *ibid.*

Irish question was to give him the Department he wanted, for there he would have been in touch with Colonial opinion and its Home Rule sympathies.[1] It would have been better to make a great appeal to Granville to accept the Presidency of the Council in order to give Chamberlain what he wanted, and to put him in a place where his Irish outlook was likely to become more generous. What is remarkable about the interview is that Gladstone, if Chamberlain's account is accurate, did not make any effort to soften the refusal; did not even treat him with ordinary courtesy. His behaviour is difficult to understand. He might well have said about Chamberlain with his Irish doubts what Maurice of Saxony said of Charles the Fifth, " I have no cage big enough for such a bird." What he seems to have said was: " This is an uncommonly big bird with a difficult temper. I will therefore put him in one of my smaller cages."

Chamberlain had good reason for resenting such treatment. Yet if he had seen Gladstone's diary at the time he would have allowed something for an old man's distress. On the 30th Gladstone wrote: " A very long laborious day, from 9 a.m. to 8, with an hour's intermission. . . . Lord Spencer in evening, 11 to 12 on the sad question of the F.O." On the 31st he wrote: " My sleep for once gave way." Gladstone's interview with Chamberlain came at a moment when he was in no condition to do himself justice. He had had to wound deeply the feelings of his oldest colleague, a man who had served with him in six Cabinets, who had shared all his secrets, to whom he had turned in every difficulty, from whose wisdom, sympathy, and unselfishness he had drawn good sense and moral strength in all the quarrels of his Government. In the sad perspective created by memories that went back to the Crimean War he could not put himself for a moment in Chamberlain's place, or understand that he was making one of the most important decisions of his

---

[1] The Assembly of the Province of Quebec, e.g., passed a unanimous resolution in favour of Home Rule on April 17, 1886, as a method of solving the Irish problem without disintegrating the Empire, the wisdom of which had been proved by Canadian experience. In Australia there was, of course, a strong Home Rule sentiment.

career. The slight Chamberlain resented was really the aberration of a lonely old man, clinging to the friendships that linked him to his past.[1]

The slight Gladstone put on Chamberlain was followed by a pin-prick that shows him at his worst. With the business of recreating the British Empire on a new basis on his hands, he suddenly thought of an unhappy plan for saving £600 a year. This was to be done by cutting down the salaries of the Parliamentary secretaries to the Local Government Board and the Board of Trade. The first office had just been filled by Jesse Collings, Chamberlain's chief henchman, whose honourable efforts on behalf of the agricultural labourer had had a good deal to do with Liberal victories in the counties; the author of the amendment on which the Salisbury Government had been turned out of office. Chamberlain rightly resisted and held his own. If Gladstone had wanted to exasperate him he could not have chosen a more effective or more graceless method.

Chamberlain had received what he was entitled to regard as inconsiderate treatment in both these respects. There was still a method by which his smarting self-esteem could be flattered. Refused the Colonial Office, he took the Local Government Board. The Liberals had announced that local government reform would be one of their chief tasks if they won the election, and Chamberlain was obviously the most suitable Minister to take charge of this policy. It was closely related to the question of allotments which had been agitated in the election and used as the occasion for turning out the Salisbury Government. Chamberlain was ready with large plans. If the Government had allowed him to pursue them and had treated these Bills as a principal part of their programme, his office would have become at once, what it should always have been, an office second in import-

[1] We can see the same influence in Gladstone's treatment of Argyll. Argyll was a definite opponent and yet Gladstone would write long letters to convince him that Burke would have supported the Home Rule Bill at a time when men of influence and standing, such as William Rathbone, whose minds were not made up, could not secure his attention for the discussion of serious concrete points.

ance to no other, and he would have had the satisfaction of finding an opportunity for his talent for constructive reform.

The case for such a course was strong on every ground. Most of the Liberals who disliked Chamberlain's ideas had left the party with Hartington and Goschen; Chamberlain's energy and capacity would have been turned to good use; and the problem itself was urgent.

This plan was pressed on Gladstone both by individuals and by a large group of Liberals who sent him a memorandum urging the importance of pushing British land reform. Gladstone's neglect of this advice was one of the greatest mistakes of his life and it reacted seriously on the cause to which he devoted himself. The Irish controversy within the party would have lost some of its irritating power, if the party had been engaged simultaneously on a large English policy on which all the active elements in the party were agreed. Chamberlain would have seen a great reform on which his heart had been set brought within his reach. The prospect at the polls would have been better. The Irish issue was capable of being put in such a way as to enlist all the selfish elements in the electorate against it.[1] Many agricultural labourers had voted Liberal at the election of 1885 at great personal risk. The men whose speeches and promises had inspired them were Chamberlain and Jesse Collings. The Gladstone Government had taken office after turning Salisbury's Government out on the question of allotments. It is not surprising that at the election of 1886 the agricultural labourers for whom the Gladstone Government had done nothing, had a good deal less enthusiasm for the Liberal party, especially as Chamberlain and Collings were now on the other side. The Liberal losses in the election of July 1886 were very much heavier in the counties than in the boroughs.

Gladstone's unfortunate tendency to become absorbed

---

[1] A letter in the *Times* gave some extracts from the election literature of the Unionists in North Dorset in July 1886 (July 23, 1886): "If you vote for Mr Portman there will be fighting in Ireland. Swarms of poor Irishmen will come over to England and lower your wages. Mr Gladstone means to spend one hundred millions of your money in buying out the Irish landlords which will enormously increase the taxes on your tea, coffee and cocoa."

in one question to the exclusion of all others had thus a serious effect on the fortunes of his Home Rule policy. It was also in itself a grave public misfortune. Chamberlain was at this time the chief constructive force in social politics. Even those who think, reflecting on his career, that the passionate Radical was destined sooner or later to disappear in the business Imperialist, may well hold that if he had been treated differently England would have obtained some valuable social reforms from him before that conversion took place. Gladstone unhappily underrated both his capacity and the importance of the reforms on which his heart was set. This was all the more unfortunate because it confirmed Chamberlain in his suspicion that Gladstone wanted to use Home Rule to divert the party from social reform. This was not true of the reform of local government, and Gladstone in allowing Chamberlain a pretty free hand on measures for this purpose would have been only carrying out the programme he had himself laid down at the General Election.[1]

Gladstone's failure to enlist Chamberlain as a reformer on lines where co-operation was possible made everything turn on those questions on which it was not. On February 8 Gladstone wrote to Chamberlain asking him to come and talk about the Irish question. " I should like to have a good long exposition from you." On February 13 the two men met and on the 15th Chamberlain sent Gladstone the draft of a proposed scheme for Land Purchase which was circulated to the Cabinet. Gladstone must have been convinced at this interview that it was almost certain that he would lose Chamberlain, for Chamberlain instead of

[1] On one of the questions as it happened Gladstone was ahead of Chamberlain, for Gladstone wanted a large scheme for London Government whereas Chamberlain was against it. But there was some excuse for Chamberlain's suspicion. Gladstone thought that one of Chamberlain's reasons for wanting to keep the Irish M.P.s at Westminster was that he hoped for their support for his Radical schemes. We know this from the memorandum he sent to the Queen on March 23, 1886: " A solution in favour of Home Rule would appear likely to check very materially the onward movement of British Radicalism, as has probably been discerned by its leading promoter." (*Letters of Queen Victoria*, Third Series, Vol. I, p. 88.) Gladstone was no doubt thinking specially of Disestablishment. (See Garvin, Vol. II, p. 197.)

advancing from his policy of the preceding spring was retreating from it. His combative nature had been excited by Parnell's speeches, and thinking, as he told Gladstone in the autumn, that the issue was between twenty-two millions on one side and four on the other he wished to impose a scheme that Parnell would not like and take no notice of the demand made by the Irish at the General Election. " I urged him," Chamberlain recorded, " to deal first with the Irish land question, and then with education and municipal and county government, leaving anything more entirely for future consideration."[1] His mind poisoned by O'Shea and embittered by the stupid and ungrateful treatment he had received from the Irish leaders in the summer of 1885, he had abandoned the sensible view he had urged in 1881 that the Government ought to consider and consult the leader of Nationalist opinion. He was in fact less ready to consider and consult Parnell with eighty-five members behind him than he had been when Parnell had thirty supporters. Yet if four-fifths of the Members for Scotland had demanded a particular reform, Chamberlain could hardly have argued that no notice at all need be taken of their wishes.

If Gladstone's treatment of Chamberlain and his social programme reveals Gladstone at his worst, Chamberlain's treatment of Gladstone and his Irish problem at this interview reveals Chamberlain at his worst. Every letter Chamberlain had received from Gladstone since the fall of his Government in June must have shown him that Gladstone could not accept a modest programme of this kind, and it was mere obstinacy to present it as Chamberlain's only contribution. Gladstone, whatever his mistakes, had seized the fundamental truth that any Irish programme must aim at satisfying not merely Ireland's practical needs but her imagination as well. Chamberlain was as blind to this truth about the Irish problem as Gladstone was to important truths that Chamberlain had grasped about

---

[1] Garvin, op. cit., Vol. II, p. 182. According to a letter from Labouchere to Herbert Gladstone (January 22, 1886) Chamberlain had proposed this plan to Parnell via Labouchere. Parnell of course had rejected it outright.

English problems. In the second reading debate Chamberlain, then no longer a Minister, declared himself in favour of a federal solution of the Irish problem, giving Ireland an arrangement that could be extended to Scotland and Wales. Gladstone himself had inclined to such a plan at an earlier stage and there is nothing to show that he had abandoned it. It was a disaster that when asked for his ideas on February 13, Chamberlain was silent on this subject, and produced proposals that could not be given serious consideration unless the Prime Minister meant to abandon his whole policy.

Gladstone now set to work on the preparation of his Bills. His immense energy was ready to face all the problems this involved; land, finance, the tasks to be given to the Irish Parliament, the constitution of the Irish Parliament and the provision for the supremacy of the Imperial Parliament. Within a few weeks his ideas had taken shape. Great efforts were made to disarm the fears of property. The Irish Legislature was to consist of 309 members, in two orders, sitting together and voting together unless a separate vote was demanded. If the two orders disagreed the matter was to be vetoed for three years. If then carried by the second order it was to be decided by a majority of the two orders voting together. The first order was to contain 103 members, 28 of them the Irish representative Peers, the other 75 chosen on a £25 franchise with a property qualification. The second order was to consist of 206 members, elected on the existing franchise. A number of questions were reserved for the Imperial Parliament. The Irish Legislature was not to establish or endow any religion. There was to be no Irish representation at Westminster, but the Irish Parliament was to have control of customs and excise. The Land Bill was also of course an effort to allay the fears of property and to prevent the risk of injustice. Irish landlords were to have the option of selling at a price to be fixed by a Land Commission. The British Treasury was to advance a sum not exceeding £50,000,000 up to March 1890. The Irish State authority was to pay four per cent. on the loan and, to obtain security for the loan, the British Government was to

21

appoint a Receiver General through whose hands the whole of the Irish revenue would pass.[1]

In the preparation of these Bills Chamberlain had no share.   Mr. Garvin well describes him as " in a state of preventive detention—almost of solitary confinement."   A later correspondence between Gladstone and Rosebery shows how Gladstone regarded his view that he ought to have been taken into consultation.   Rosebery, who was at that time a convinced Home Ruler and a good adviser to Gladstone, wrote in August 1889 to suggest that a committee or quasi-committee of the Cabinet of 1886 should be appointed to take in hand the amendment of the Home Rule Bill of that year.[2]   Gladstone did not take to the proposal. In replying on August 7, 1889, he said that every measure that he had introduced, with the exception of the Succession Duty Act, he had framed himself.   He then referred to the Bill of 1886.   No Bill had been the subject of so much concert and collaboration with the most appropriate members as the Bill of 1886.   " Chamberlain's complaint was preposterous.   He (or his Department) framed one large measure (on Bankruptcy) and if my memory serves me right, never said anything at all either to the Cabinet or me."   This is a significant passage.   In fact Gladstone consulted Morley and through him Parnell.   That he was right in consulting Parnell nobody will deny, for it would have been useless to bring in a large Bill for Home Rule of which the leader of the party of eighty-five Irish members disapproved.   But his account shows that he did not consider that Chamberlain had any right to be consulted at this stage and that he regarded himself as standing to this Bill in the same relation as that in which Chamberlain stood to his Bankruptcy Bill.

Some notes that find a place among Gladstone's papers

[1] Early in January Parnell had sent Gladstone through Mrs. O'Shea a scheme for compulsory purchase, forwarded to him by the representatives of one of the chief landlord political associations in Ireland.   It was considered that this arrangement would make Home Rule acceptable to landowners. Under the scheme the British Treasury was to advance £70 millions, on which the Irish Parliament was to pay 4 per cent.   Parnell remarked that the sum suggested was excessive and might be reduced.

[2] Crewe, *Life of Rosebery*, I, 339.

explain why Chamberlain was so treated.   He was regarded, naturally enough, if his later description of his temper at the time has any truth, as an enemy on the watch.   If a man who is sitting at your table to-day is likely to-morrow to be attacking the plans you lay before him for discussion, it is hardly prudent to expose a large surface for his criticism. Gladstone, Spencer, Morley, and Granville, on one occasion had a meeting to consider this difficulty.   Harcourt had been asked to find out " if possible " what were his intentions.   How far was it safe to bring any scheme before the Cabinet, before it was known what Chamberlain meant to do?   All these anxieties were well justified, but Chamberlain, who had excited them, resented the result.

As soon as the Home Rule scheme was laid before the Cabinet, Chamberlain and Trevelyan wanted to resign. Chamberlain had four large objections.   He wanted to keep the Irish representation at Westminster; to keep in British hands the control of customs and excise, and the appointment of judges and magistrates, and to specify the things that an Irish Government might do instead of specifying the powers and duties that were withheld.   Trevelyan objected further to giving Ireland the control of the police.   Their resignations were kept in suspense and were not formally accepted until March 26.

Of the temper in which Chamberlain's resignation was received we have a picture from an eyewitness of the scene.

" Some supposed then, and Mr. Chamberlain has said since, that when he entered the Cabinet room on this memorable occasion, he intended to be conciliatory.   Witnesses of the scene thought that the Prime Minister made little attempt in that direction. Yet where two men of clear mind and firm will mean two essentially different things under the same name, whether autonomy or anything else, and each intends to stand by his own interpretation, it is childish to suppose that arts of deportment will smother or attenuate fundamental divergence, or make people who are quite aware how vitally they differ, pretend that they entirely agree."[1]

There is little doubt that Gladstone thought that even Chamberlain's open hostility would be less dangerous to his

[1] Morley, *op. cit.*, Vol. III, p. 303.

Bill than a perpetual struggle with him over details. He put this view clearly very early in the discussions. On March 20, he wrote to Harcourt, who was trying to mediate between him and Chamberlain, " It is not possible to work a Cabinet on the basis of universal discussion without purpose. At any rate aet. 77."

For Gladstone knew well where he was strong and where he was weak. In the last Cabinet he had seen his most cherished schemes destroyed in an atmosphere of divided councils and bitter debate. What had not been lost in the conflicts with Hartington and Harcourt on this very question of Ireland? If he was now to spend his strength fighting point after point against a man twenty years younger, with Chamberlain's energy, address, ruthlessness, and skill, versed in all the arts of strategy indoors and out of doors, with power in the caucus and spokesmen in the press, disaster was certain. Chamberlain could do less harm attacking him outside than wearing him down inside his Cabinet. Chamberlain himself took the same view. When he was about to leave the Cabinet he was present at a dinner at which an anti-Gladstonian Liberal remarked with glee: " At any rate the old man is down at last." " On the contrary," said Chamberlain, " you will never know how strong he is till he has parted from all his colleagues." Chamberlain had seen enough to know the difference between Gladstone discovering the strength of the orator in the passionate leadership of noble causes, and Gladstone discovering the weakness of the orator in the management of his Cabinet. If the Queen had known what Chamberlain knew, instead of inciting and begging all moderate Liberals to leave Gladstone at the first moment, she would have urged them to stay with him to the last.

It is probable then that Gladstone's decision to let Chamberlain leave his Government was deliberate. In his view there were two alternative methods of settling the Irish problem. The first and the best was a dispassionate non-party effort. If Salisbury had been ready to make this effort, Gladstone, as we have seen, would have given him his best help and secured him from the risk of factious opposition.

That method rejected, what was left? If war between England and Ireland was to be averted, the imagination of the English people must be roused, and the bitter anti-Irish sentiment to which the Unionist leaders had appealed must be met by a counter appeal to English generosity. This Gladstone could only do by the use of his special power. He had not wanted to act on this plan. When he made his offer to Salisbury he had some presentiment of the consequences that would follow if he pitted his immense moral authority against all the powerful interests that were consolidating themselves behind the sincere alarm that Home Rule excited. But his motive is plain. He knew that he was the only man who could persuade England to give Ireland Home Rule, and he could only persuade England if he could appeal to her imagination. He could draw the bow of Odysseus but no other. If he was to make a nation want what he wanted, if he was to put the problem on the high plane on which his own mind moved, he had to give his undivided strength to his task. That was why it was easier for him to go on alone than to spend weeks on argument, to set the generous impulses of a people on fire than to disperse all the doubts and difficulties of critics, to put before the nation a large idea rather than to wrestle with colleagues who wanted to turn it into a small one.

Gladstone knew what were the conditions under which his strength could be used to the best advantage. But he had to do something besides persuading England. He had to prepare a scheme. The Irish problem was not one problem but several. There was the land problem. There was the finance problem. There was the constitutional problem. There were the questions of protecting minorities, of keeping some community of interest and purpose between the two peoples, of preserving the ultimate authority of the Empire over all its parts. What equipment did Gladstone's Cabinet provide for the construction of such plans in a few weeks? For answer we have only to note that the Cabinet Minister with whom Gladstone shared his task was Morley, a man of most distinguished mind but a Minister who had never held even subordinate office, who had never taken part in drafting a Bill, whose political experience was confined to speaking, writing and discussion with his friends. Chamberlain on the other hand had drafted and carried important legislation, and he had taken an active share in the work of a very busy Cabinet for five years. Certain Irish questions—Ulster in particular—he understood much better than either Gladstone or Morley. Chamberlain's help, if he would and could have given it, would have been invaluable. This fact made his exclusion from Gladstone's councils a greater grievance, and made him a more bitter opponent.

Gladstone at first underrated his strength as an opponent. It is perhaps the measure of Gladstone's ascendancy that men who worked with him never developed their full power in debate until they were in conflict with him. This was true of Chamberlain as it was of Hartington. But Chamberlain's hostility had its own special importance. In the autumn of 1885, when urging Parnell to try to come to terms with Salisbury, Gladstone had pointed out to Mrs. O'Shea that whereas a Conservative Government that attempted to make a Home Rule settlement would not have to face the opposition of the Liberal party, a Liberal Government engaged on such a task would certainly have to face the opposition of the Conservative party. He had stressed this point to Rosebery (November 13, 1885), as a reason why the Liberals should not produce a plan so long as there was still hope of a Conservative plan. " This opposition and the appeals with which it will be accompanied will render the carrying of the measure difficult even by an united Liberal party; hopeless or most difficult should there be serious defections."

Chamberlain's opposition was specially serious not only because, as Gladstone soon discovered to his surprise, Chamberlain was a more formidable debater than any of the Conservative leaders, but also because the Home Rule policy was now exposed to a Radical as well as a Whig attack. Gladstone was thus preparing a large revolutionary plan under raking fire from the left as well as from the right. The Whigs and Conservatives who, it was hoped, would be conciliated by the concessions to property, were so intent on defeating the whole policy and so hopeful of success that those concessions never softened their hostility. Radical critics on the other hand could use these concessions with immense effect. Chamberlain made great play with the arrangement for the two orders and the generous terms offered to the landlords. The arguments about ransom and the wickedness of the House of Lords lately used against Salisbury could now be turned against Gladstone. A significant incident shows how heavy a burden the Land Bill put on the back of Home Rule. Forster died on April 5 and Shaw Lefevre went down to Bradford to contest the seat. He was elected by a majority of 740, about half of Forster's majority, which was not in itself discouraging. But he found it necessary to promise to vote against the Land Bill; a Bill that seemed to the workmen of Bradford a sop to landlords and to those landlords who of all their class were the least deserving.

Chamberlain's resignation was not followed by open war. He had no desire to break up the Liberal party with which both his ardent desires and his personal fortunes seemed to be bound up. Nor was he openly against Home Rule. He did not agree with Hartington who had disliked his plan the year before and was no more inclined to it at this time. Contact with the constituencies had made an impression on his mind and he appeared to be moving towards Gladstone. He said in the House that two things had become clear in the controversy; one was the passionate devotion of the British democracy to the Prime Minister; the other, the display of a sentiment out of doors, " the universality and completeness of which, I dare say, has taken many of us by surprise, in favour of some form of Home Rule to Ireland, which will give to the Irish people some greater control over their own affairs."[1] The weeks between his resignation (March 26) and the fatal division on the second reading (June 7) were spent in indirect negotiation and tactical manœuvres.

The decisive questions to which the controversy

[1] Morley, *op. cit.*, III, p. 330.

was reduced were the representation of Ireland in the
House of Commons and the treatment that the Government would give to proposals for amendment in Committee. On May 27 Gladstone called a meeting at the
Foreign Office of Liberals who, while retaining full freedom
on all particulars in the Bill, were in favour of the establishment of a legislative body in Dublin for the management of
affairs specifically and exclusively Irish. Some 220 members attended. Gladstone made a speech lasting an hour in
which he said that members might vote for the second
reading with a view to its amendment in committee, and
that they would not be committed by that vote to supporting
the Land Bill. As to procedure the Government could
either after a second reading hang up the Bill and defer
committee till the autumn or they could wind up the session
and introduce the Bill afresh with proper amendments in
October. The Cabinet inclined to the latter course. He
was ready to consider any plan for the retention of the Irish
members, provided that it did not interfere with the liberty
of the Irish Parliament or introduce confusion at Westminster. Bryce held afterwards that if nothing more had
happened before the second reading the Bill would have been
carried. But the Opposition challenged the Government in
the Commons and in the debate that followed Gladstone,
losing patience under cross fire, seemed to take back much
that he had offered at the Foreign Office meeting.[1]

[1] Just before the meeting Gladstone circulated the following paper: " 10,
Downing Street, Whitehall, May 26, 1886. Irish Gov^t Bill. Question of
time. Our view at the Cabinet yesterday was that I should apprise the meeting
tomorrow that, on account of dates, there could be no effectual progress with
the Bill within the limits of the ordinary Session, and that we should therefore
propose to take no further steps at present, but that we looked forward to
proceeding with the Bill, on the subject, in the early autumn.

" I am however distinctly informed that the effect on the division will be
much more favourable if I am able to inform them that our proposal will be
to introduce in the early autumn a new bill with any necessary amendments or
perhaps *better to introduce the Bill afresh with the necessary amendments*.

" Accordingly, I am very desirous (being in much doubt whether this is
not on all grounds the *best* form of proceeding) to be at liberty to announce
accordingly to-morrow.

" I agree K[imberley]"

" I fear that such an announcement will be taken to mean that we are going

The debate was indeed an illustration of one of Gladstone's most serious weaknesses. It may indeed be said of him that nobody else could have gained for Home Rule anything like the support it received in the House of Commons and in the country in 1886; that was the result of his moral power and intellectual ascendancy. But it may also be said that a man with gifts far inferior to his could have obtained a second reading for his Bill if once that Bill had reached the position that Home Rule Bill had reached by April 1886. Eloquence, imagination, moral force had done their part and gained a triumph which had astonished Chamberlain: what was wanted now was tact, patience and the power of dealing with men, the very qualities that Gladstone lacked. We get the same impression of his failure from two friendly sources. Bryce wrote of the successful tactics of the Opposition:

" Their cue was to taunt Gladstone with having gone far in the way of concession, and they attacked him in a way which provoked his anger, and, as it seemed to me, disturbed his judgment. In repelling their charges he seemed to virtually withdraw or minimise the concessions he had made at the meeting, partly, I think, out of pride, partly because he did not wish to awaken suspicions among the Irish. The result was to lose all that he had gained by the meeting. The waverers fell away from him. I felt from that evening that we should be beaten."[1]

Herbert Gladstone described the scene and its consequences in a letter to his brother written on June 10.

" The meeting at the F.O. was a marked success but it made the Whigs furious for by the terms of the invitation they were excluded. Chamberlain refused to come I imagine because he

to bring in a new bill on different lines—and that, if we are not, then when the time comes, our last state will be worse than our first. But if Mr. Gladstone believes that this announcement is the only way of getting the second reading, I agree. J. M[orley]"
" I agree with what Mr. Morley has written, but I am content to leave the matter to Mr. Gladstone. H[erschell] "
" ' To introduce the Bill afresh with the necessary amendments ' commends itself I think   A. J. M[undella]"
" I believe that the phrase last quoted is the best: and I think it ought to be listinct and unmistakeable. H. C. B[annerman]."
[1] H. A. L. Fisher, *James Bryce*, Vol. I, p. 214.

had agreed on joint action with Hartington. So good was the spirit of our fellows at the meeting that it was thought that the second reading was safe beyond doubt; and this was the belief of Whigs and Tories alike. Consequently the Tories resolved on a desperate move. All turned or seemed to turn on the exact wording of Father's amendments with reference to the crucial difficulties of the Bill, and Beach moved the adjournment of the House in concert with the Whigs in a violent and irritating speech in order to goad Father into the use of incautious language such as would undo the effect of the F.O. Speech. And in my opinion he succeeded."

Why Herbert Gladstone should have called Hicks Beach's party manœuvre a desperate move, it is difficult to say; it was the sort of move that any man who had Gladstone against him, generous on large matters, obstinate and irritable on small, would be tempted to make. And it was made not for the first time with complete success.

Gladstone's loss of temper gave Chamberlain his opportunity. He had refused to attend Gladstone's meeting at the Foreign Office, giving his reasons in a letter to Labouchere, which Labouchere sent to Herbert Gladstone:

Private	40 Prince's Gardens, S.W., May 26, 1886.

My dear Labouchere

I am pledged by public declarations to vote against 2nd R unless 24th Cl. is withdrawn to secure the complete and continual representation of Ireland in Imperial Parlt. I have given up everything else at the 2nd R stage in order to confine myself to a single point. I am very sorry that the Gov^t are unable to meet me, but I can do no more.

Under the circumstances I think it will be better for me not to attend Thursday's meeting. I have no doubt however that many of the dissentients will be present.

Yours very Truly,
J. CHAMBERLAIN.

On the day after the debate, May 29, Chamberlain called a meeting of members who " being in favour of some sort of autonomy for Ireland disapproved of the Government Bills in their present shape." The decision of the meeting, which was attended by fifty-five Liberals,[1] to oppose the second reading was determined by a letter from Bright saying that he was going to vote against the second reading, though he hoped that every member would use his own mind. Bright was against every kind of autonomy, including the scheme Chamberlain had proposed in the spring of 1885, and though as an illustrious man his judgment might influence anybody, his special authority over men with whom he was thus in fundamental disagreement throws an air of unreality over the proceedings. That decision of course settled the fate of the Bill.

Chamberlain himself in his letters to Labouchere had reduced his own conditions to a single amendment.[2] On May 2 he wrote to Labouchere:

" I consider that Mr. Gladstone's action has in any case destroyed the Liberal Party as a controlling force in politics for a considerable time. I am willing however in deference to the views of yourself and others to do my best to bring about an immediate reconciliation. With this view I have asked for more than I am ready to take so that there may be no appearance of surrender on either side. I have asked for supremacy of Imperial Parliament, separate assembly for Ulster, abolition of all the restrictions and minority representation devices. All these I am ready to leave to their chance in Committee, if the Government will say before second reading that they will retain Irish representatives on its present footing. Less than this I cannot possibly accept."

Two days later he wrote to Labouchere saying that he was replying to those who asked him how he would vote on second reading that he would vote against second reading, unless he knew that the Government would keep " the Irish Representation on its present footing."[3]

This was a dangerously simple offer. Chamberlain knew that there was strong opposition to the retention of the Irish members. Freeman the historian, who was a powerful supporter of Home Rule at a time when the support of men

[1] According to Herbert Gladstone, 22 of these Liberals were followers of Hartington. Letter to Henry Gladstone, June 10.

[2] The Government had given up the Irish control of customs and excise to which Chamberlain had objected in the Cabinet.

[3] *Life of Labouchere*, by Thorold, p. 305.

of his standing had a scarcity value, held that any such plan was inconsistent with a sound constitutional scheme. There were others who held that the removal of the Irish Members whose conduct in the House of Commons had broken down its traditions was a benefit that would outweigh many inconveniences. Bright said bluntly: " I would do much to clear the rebel party out of Parliament and do not sympathise with those who wish to retain them," though unfortunately his strong desire stopped short of voting for Home Rule. Granville wrote to Gladstone on April 12 when Gladstone raised the point: " You know how strong I am on the point you have told Spencer to mention to Kimberley and me. If we had retained the Irish Members there would have been a howl, and I believe no one excepting Chamberlain for obvious reasons, is anxious to retain them."[1] The difficulty created by Chamberlain's demand was summed up by Gladstone writing to Granville on April 30: " I scarcely see how a Cabinet could have been formed, if the inclusion of the Irish Members had been insisted on. And now I do not well see how the scheme and policy can be saved from shipwreck if the exclusion is insisted on as an absolute preliminary condition." The difficulty about keeping the Irish members was that there was no plan to which there were not obvious objections and though a Bill can be passed with several provisions that are open to criticism if all parties are agreed upon it, a Government fighting against strenuous opposition cannot afford to expose too vast a surface to attack.

No Government could have promised, as Chamberlain asked, that there should be no change in the Irish representation at Westminster, for such a promise would have tied its hands. Gladstone went as far as anybody could go in the offer he made at the meeting at the Foreign Office.[2]

Chamberlain affected to think that his one demand was so simple and modest that nothing but malevolence could

[1] A colleague more important, in the sense that he was now Gladstone's best fighting lieutenant, Harcourt, was as strong against retention as Chamberlain against exclusion. Gardiner, I, p. 576.

[2] On the problem of preserving the association of the two nations he threw out, as we shall see later, a statesmanlike solution.

JOSEPH CHAMBERLAIN

have caused its refusal. Was this his real view? It would be difficult to believe this, and suspicion is justified by his later language. In considering the part he played and the impression he made on Gladstone, it is impossible to overlook the strange account of his own conduct that he gave many years afterwards. Barry O'Brien in his *Life of Parnell* describes an interview with him in February 1898.

" I should now like to talk about the Home Rule Bill. I have come to the conclusion, after giving the matter—your speeches and all that has been written and said upon the subject—the best consideration I could, that you were never a Home Ruler in our sense; but there are some points which I should feel obliged if you would clear up for me. You opposed the exclusion of the Irish members from the Imperial Parliament. I thought at that time, and I think a great many other people thought too, that you were in favour, or that ultimately you came to be in favour, of the principle of Mr. Gladstone's Bill, but that you objected to the exclusion of the Irish members as a matter of detail. What I should like to ask is, if you objected to the exclusion as a matter of detail, or if you really used that clause for the purpose of attacking the Bill? Was it really your aim to turn Mr. Gladstone's flank by attacking that point?

" *Mr. Chamberlain:* ' I wanted to kill the Bill.'

" And you used the question of the exclusion of the Irish members for that purpose?

" *Mr. Chamberlain:* 'I did, and I used the Land Bill for the same purpose. I was not opposed to the reform of the land laws. I was not opposed to land purchase. It was the right way to settle the land question, but there were many things in the Bill to which I was opposed on principle. My main object in attacking it, though, was to kill the Home Rule Bill. As soon as the Land Bill was out of the way[1] I attacked the question of the exclusion of the Irish members. I used that point to show the absurdity of the whole scheme.'

" Well, I may say, Mr. Chamberlain, that that is the conclusion I have myself come to. It was strategy, simply strategy.

" *Mr. Chamberlain:* 'I wanted to kill the Bill. You may take that all the time.'

" Mr. Jeyes, in his short life of you—which seems to me a very

[1] Mr. Gladstone introduced a Land Purchase Bill at the same time as the Home Rule Bill, and suddenly dropped it.

fair as well as a clever book—says you were once on the point of
being converted to Home Rule.

"*Mr. Chamberlain :* 'He is wrong.   I was never near being
converted to an Irish Parliament.   The national councils was
my extreme point.   There I stood.'

"I should like to talk to you about what you said on the subject
of Canadian Home Rule.   I am satisfied that you attacked the
exclusion of the Irish members to kill the Bill, but I think you
said things about Canada which are open to the interpretation
that you might favour the establishment of an Irish Parliament.
The matter is not quite clear to me.

"*Mr. Chamberlain :* 'I do not think you should press me too
hard.   I stated my object was to kill the Bill.   I have no doubt
that I said many things that may have been open to some such
interpretation as you suggest. . . . However open I may be to
criticism in whatever I said, my aim was, as I say, to kill the Bill'."[1]

In the same interview Chamberlain gave O'Brien his
view of Parnell and it has some bearing on the question
discussed in this chapter:

"Did you think him [Parnell] a remarkable man?

"*Mr. Chamberlain :* 'Very   remarkable.   A   great   man.
Unscrupulous, if I may say so.   I do not wish to be misunderstood
in my meaning of the word "unscrupulous."   I mean that he was
unscrupulous like every great man.   I have often thought Parnell
was like Napoleon.   He allowed nothing to stand in his way.
He stopped at nothing to gain his end.   If a man opposed him,
he flung him aside and dashed on.   He did not care.   He did
not harbour any enmity.   He was too great a man for that.   He
was indifferent about the means he used to gain his object.   That
is my view'."[2]

When Chamberlain gave O'Brien this interview he was
the idol of the Unionist party.   He had made his peace with
property and the Church; he was the colleague of Salisbury,
Hartington and Goschen, the three men whom he had hated
most in 1885; he stood in the public mind not for ransom
from the landlords and disendowment for the Church but
for big business and a defiant Empire.   It was difficult for
him, secure and at his ease, his ambition and his conscience
satisfied, to remember how he felt in those anxious weeks,
when his future was in doubt, and it was hard to decide

[1] *Life of Parnell,* Vol. II, pp. 139–141.   [2] *Life of Parnell,* Vol. II, p. 131.

from hour to hour how best he could serve his sense of duty and his strong natural desire for a great career. It was difficult too for that later Chamberlain to do justice to the anxieties and scruples of his earlier Radical self. It was said of Pythagoras that of all his previous incarnations he could remember best his life as a peacock. To ask Chamberlain to recall his Radical past would have been like asking a dignified peacock to recall the disreputable view that he had taken of the world in an earlier existence when he was a noisy and impudent jackdaw. But if it would be unfair to Chamberlain to take this as a complete account of his motives and aims in 1886, it would be unfair to Gladstone to disreregard it. We may doubt whether Chamberlain was right in 1897 in saying that every offer he made to Gladstone in 1886 was only made to destroy him, though his definition of an unscrupulous man might give colour to that view, but it is not unreasonable to hold that Gladstone was right in suspecting that those offers, had he accepted them, would have proved a fatal embarrassment.[1]

[1] Writing to Dilke on May 6, 1886, Chamberlain said: " To satisfy others I have talked about conciliation, and have consented to make advances, but on the whole I would rather vote against the Bill than not, and the retention of the Irish members is only, with me, the flag that covers other objections." *Life of Dilke*, Vol. II, p. 222.

Gladstone wrote to Arnold Morley on April 20, 1886: " With men like most of my colleagues it is safe to go to an extreme of possible concession. But my experience in Chamberlain's case [is] that such concession is treated mainly as an acknowledgment of his Superior greatness and wisdom, and as a fresh point of departure accordingly."

It is interesting to note that Chamberlain seemed to Harcourt, who was at that time more intimate with him than with Gladstone, to be overbearing. " You must see," he wrote on April 18, " that you cannot settle with the G.O.M. on the terms of an absolute surrender, in which you shall assume the position of saying that from the first you have been all in the right and he all in the wrong. This is not compromise but capitulation." The next day he wrote: " I don't think Mr. G. is nearly as hostile to you as you are to him, but after all he is the master of the Party, and must be treated as such." Gardiner, *op. cit.*, Vol. I, p. 582.

On May 13, Harcourt wrote to Gladstone: " I am sure you will be deceived if you think Chamberlain is to be conciliated on any terms. He has no thought but war to the knife." From a letter that Herbert Gladstone wrote to his brother Henry in India on May 21, we know that Gladstone took at that time the view of Chamberlain's conduct which Chamberlain himself took in his interview with Barry O'Brien. " He (Father) is much incensed with Chamberlain and thinks that he has designedly worked to throw him and the Bill from the first. In spite of Chamberlain's fair words to me I fear it is only too true."

So far as the contest was a clash between two wills, it is easy to see how strong was the clash; how irreparable the discord. Gladstone was an old and tired man, doubtful whether his own great power would last (" such light as I have," he wrote to Ponsonby on May 27, 1886, " is fast burning out, I constantly feel in listening to speakers in the House of Commons how they are doing what I cannot do "), impatient by nature, surrounded by men who were unable to do justice to Chamberlain's sincerity, himself specially liable to be irritated by Chamberlain's personality and methods of controversy.[1] Chamberlain's dashing and irresponsible performance at the Election of 1885, which seemed to his friends a splendid stroke for Liberalism, seemed to Gladstone's friends an outrage to his authority as leader of the party. Gladstone was in addition a self-willed man, magnanimous in the range of his spirit, but tenacious and stiff when concessions were to be made to a colleague, suspicious and alert if that colleague behaved like a rival. Morley once compared him to Bossuet but there is perhaps a closer resemblance to an earlier and greater Churchman. The character of St. Ambrose has been drawn by a recent French writer in a few sentences that well describe Gladstone's temperament.

" Sans doute il a la passion de l'autorité et dans son corps débile un invincible besoin d'activité; tous ses écrits, toutes ses idées sont orientées vers l'action; il lui faut persuader, entrainer, diriger. Mais ce primat de l'action n'a pas sa fin en soi; cette flamme dévorante ne se consume pas vainement; elle est au service d'une cause qui dépasse de beaucoup les personnes en présence; ce passionné est au fond un désintéressé."[2]

Against him was pitted a man of immense force and courage, who had first set foot on the ladder of success as a boy of eighteen, who had made his way in business by his

[1] He wrote to Morley, April 20, " I cannot write *Kootooing* letters to C. and I doubt as to their effect. He views his speech as a great effort at conciliation. I could only reply by a ' note of admiration '. . . . Decency, principle, and policy alike forbid me to enter into private arrangements about alterations of the Bill in Committee. My proceedings in this matter must be public proceedings, and my public proceedings must be governed by a view of all the considerations in the case."

[2] *St. Ambroise et l'Empire Romain.* Palanquin, p. 394.

strength of will, his resourcefulness in method, his power of wearing down rivals; who was in fact the embodiment of the rough qualities by which England had gained the leadership of the Industrial Revolution. Indulgence, sympathy, consideration, these are minor virtues in such a career, and even the moments when Chamberlain seemed to yield were followed by speeches that revived suspicion and anger. Gladstone had never done him justice, for he had never seen through that defiance and self-confidence to the strong human feeling behind them. On the other hand his quick and sensitive nature had discerned what it was that divided him from Chamberlain, even when they were co-operating in a Government. Chamberlain was in temper a Palmerston, facing in the same spirit one day the landlord, another day the Church, another the foreigner. No Nonsense from the Landlords, No Nonsense from the Church, No Nonsense from the Foreigner: these were the mottoes of his fighting career. Gladstone found it difficult to appreciate the fine qualities that were combined with this temper, and in consequence he had made too little use of all the energy and courage that Chamberlain had brought to his first Cabinet. Chamberlain thus entered on this new relationship with his old chief under most unfavourable conditions. He was a man with a grievance, well aware that Gladstone underrated him; very conscious of the qualities that Gladstone had overlooked; very confident in the powers that Gladstone had wasted.

When their purposes were the same these two men had never been cordial allies. Gladstone's natural subtlety looked to Chamberlain like artifice; Chamberlain's hard efficiency looked to Gladstone like insolence. Now that their purposes were different there was nothing in their memories or their sympathies to soften their disagreement. If will was in conflict with will, conscience was in conflict with conscience, the conscience of a man seeking truth in a large world with the conscience of a man seeking truth in a small. In the bitterness of the quarrel many Liberals imputed insincerity to Chamberlain, but nobody can read Mr. Garvin's moving account of his perplexities and fore-

2 K

bodings and think that charge true. Both men were self-willed; both men were men of action; both men had strong convictions. And unhappily events had brought to a sharp point just those issues on which they were in conflict.

Down to 1885 Chamberlain had seen Ireland, as he had seen Birmingham, with the eyes of the reformer; he had been revolted by its misgovernment; its wasted resources; its hideous poverty; its manifest wrongs. Gladstone and he, though in some important respects their views of Ireland were different, were agreed in wishing to put an end to this scandal. Chamberlain had his remedies just as he had had his remedies for Birmingham. But in 1885 he found that Parnell would not take his remedies, and owing, as we have seen, to O'Shea's duplicity, he believed that Parnell was not merely obstinate but treacherous. A new problem then had arisen: a problem of discipline. Parnell must be taught to take what was good for him. Ireland was in one sense a victim; but in another an obstacle. It was as if one of the Birmingham slums had refused to accept his great scheme for reconstructing Birmingham and putting an end to its squalor, and wanted some plan of its own, inconvenient to Birmingham and disrespectful to its rulers. In that case Birmingham would be faced with rebellion. England was now faced with rebellion: an impudent rebellion, for it was the rebellion of four millions against twenty, and the rebellion of men who were offered handsome remedies for all their wrongs but were so perverse as to want a remedy that would do them more harm than good. There could be only one answer. No Nonsense from Parnell.

Thus Gladstone found himself once more fighting with a Palmerston. With his large historical view he had no patience with this insular arrogance: with this unimaginative treatment of something so delicate and so important as the relations of two peoples to each other. But he was partly to blame for this fatal development. He had refused to use Chamberlain's great qualities as a statesman and give him a large domestic task, and now those qualities in which he had justly discerned a public danger were making Chamberlain his most formidable opponent. As a man of action he should have foreseen that the energy of this other man of action, if left unemployed, would not lie meekly at his service, waiting on his moods, following his directions, accepting his orders. It is possible that if Chamberlain had remained in the Government with important and absorbing duties, facing the hostility of Conservatives and Whigs to his domestic reforms, Gladstone's spell would have brought him to a less intolerant view of the Irish demand. That spell had little power when he had left the Cabinet, and the controversy in which he was engaged was not a controversy with his old opponents, but a controversy with his old allies. The breach may have been inevitable under any conditions; it was certainly inevitable from the moment when Gladstone put Chamberlain's scheme of local government in his drawer, thinking that the best service he could give to Home Rule was to forget everything else. It would have been better for his Irish plan if, for a few days, he could have forgotten Home Rule itself.

CHAPTER XXVI

THE FIRST HOME RULE BILL

Events had brought the British people in 1886 face to face with a great constitutional problem. Ireland was governed, as Lord Crewe has put it, like a Crown Colony.[1] The election had returned to Parliament a solid party of eighty-five Irish Members who demanded self-government for Ireland. Was it possible to put an end to Crown Colony Government and to substitute a form of government that would be workable, tolerable to the Irish, and compatible with the political unity of the peoples of the two islands? If the answer to this question was favourable, how should the several problems involved in this great change be treated? These were the questions that presented themselves for decision as soon as Parnell found himself at the head of a party which spoke for three-fourths of the people of Ireland.

When Campbell-Bannerman decided to give the Boer States self-government, important statesmen like Balfour, Lansdowne, and Milner, protested, but the Unionist party of that day, badly reduced at the General Election, was not united and British opinion supported the Government's action. It was therefore easy to take the steps that led up to the Union of South Africa without a violent explosion of feeling. There was indeed much more contention over the Education Bill of 1906 than over this great and daring decision. If in January 1886 there had been no more hostility to the grant of self-government to Ireland than there was in 1906 to the grant of self-government to the Boers, it would have been easy to proceed by discussion, conference, and all the

---

[1] " The presence of Irish Members in the House of Commons did not really contradict this, highly inconvenient as they could make themselves there." Crewe, *Rosebery*, Vol. II, p. 429.

processes for obtaining a considered and temperate deliberation.   Unhappily the conditions were very different.   To
understand the course that events took in 1886 it is necessary
to see what those differences were.

There was in the first place a great difference of temper.
The Boer War had a remarkably chastening effect on
British public opinion.   When it broke out Imperialism was
in its most self-confident and high-flying mood.   Lord
Crewe writing to Canon Maccoll well put it, speaking of
" the curious *entêtement* of the time," that the country " would
have gone into any war during the last four years, with
France, Germany, Russia or the U.S., with the same light
heart."[1]   If anybody thinks this an extravagant description
he should turn to the letter Chamberlain wrote to Esher on
October 11, 1899, on the eve of the great military disasters in
South Africa.

" I am not in the least anxious about foreign complications.
It is a pleasant habit of our dear friends on the Continent to show
their teeth when we are engaged with another dog.   But in
certain tempers of the British public these demonstrations are
dangerous, and if I were ' a Frenchman or a Roosian or a
Proosian ' I should be inclined not to twist the lion's tail at this
precise juncture."[2]

After the war there was a great revulsion.   It had brought
little military glory; the enemy had won sympathy and
admiration by his gallant struggle; Chinese labour was very
different from the kind of prize that the nation had been led
to expect after its losses and exertions, and it seemed to
symbolize the part played by cold-blooded finance in an
adventure in which many high-minded men had seen
nothing but disinterested duty.   The English were ready for
a generous policy.

In 1886 recent history had been of a different kind.   The
event that stood out in men's minds was the death of Gordon,
" the man of England circled by the sands."   The disasters
that were fresh in men's minds were not the disasters that
had overtaken pride, but the disasters that had followed

[1] Russell, *Memoirs of Maccoll*, p. 385.
[2] Esher, *Journals*, Vol. I, p. 240.

vacillation. The lessons to be drawn from those disasters seemed to many to be the need for firmness, for the stubborn maintenance of rights and privileges, for presenting to the world the stout face of an obstinate Empire that kept, and meant to keep, what it had got. To men in such a mood generosity looks like weakness. Two of the chief statesmen of the time held that whether Home Rule was right or wrong, human nature would make its concession impossible. Chamberlain wrote to Labouchere in October 1885:[1] " My proposal " (he referred to his Central Board) " is the maximum that the Radicals will stand and a great deal more than the Whigs will accept." Salisbury wrote to Maccoll on April 12, 1889:

" As to Home Rule in your sense—which is Federation—I do not see in it any elements of practicability. Nations do not change their political nature like that, except through blood. It would require a subordination of all ordinary motives, a renunciation of traditions and prepossessions, a far-reaching and disciplined resolve, which is never engendered by mere persuasion, and only comes after conflict and under the pressure of military force."[2]

This was a fundamental difference. In all other respects too the conditions were as adverse in the second case as they were favourable in the first. In 1906 the Liberal Government took office after the greatest victory won at the polls since the Reform Bill; in 1886 the Liberal Government had a good deal less than the full strength of its own party and it faced an Opposition that had a good prospect of becoming the Government. The mass of the press was doubtful or hostile. Thus there was every reason, so far as political motives and conditions went, why this question should become what Gladstone had dreaded, the subject of a party conflict.

When once party conflict arises over a question that touches to the quick men's hopes and fears, their pride and anger, reason is about as comfortable as a fish out of water. For it is the business of politicians to use and

---

[1] Thorold's *Life of Labouchere*, p. 241.
[2] Russell, *Memoirs of Maccoll*, p. 137.

stimulate all the emotions that can serve their purpose, not to bring those actions into an atmosphere in which they cease to be deciding forces. When men sit round a table to draw up a constitution, they try to keep in their place the emotions that might disturb their spirit of co-operation, and make it less likely that they will create something that will last. The less passion is about, the better. When men try to destroy a plan of public policy, whose destruction is in their judgment both an advantage in itself and the means to a party victory, they look for passion, they foment it and they play upon it. Are men afraid of the policy? Then make them more afraid. Do they resent what they think a loss of strength and importance? Make them resent it more. Do they suspect the motives of those who propose it? Make them think that you share their suspicion. Is there fuel in the question for the hatreds of race, of religion or of class? Make it red hot. No question lent itself so easily to such inflammatory management as the question of Home Rule, for race, religion, and class, were all blazing below the surface.

The great majority of the Englishmen of the time who were eminent in literature or science were afraid of Home Rule for one reason or another, or for more reasons than one; thinking it would bring disaster to England, to Ireland, to the landlords, to the Protestants, to Catholic Ireland unable to govern herself, to Ulster unable to protect herself. Nobody could say of such fears that they were baseless, any more than he could say that the instinct that made men dread the surrender of British power was always selfish and had nothing noble and high minded about it. The man who wanted to persuade England to give Ireland Home Rule had to meet this body of fear; to show either by argument, or by producing a scheme that could prove his case, that the last word in this argument should not be spoken by fear. If it had been possible to put the Home Rule issue before the public after it had been considered by a committee which had itself put passion on one side, it might have been possible to get a fair hearing even for a policy exposed to all this fear and animosity. But if the policy had to be discussed without any such preparation, as a burning party question, fear and animosity would be all-powerful once the leaders of opinion blew the bellows. Thomas Hardy, visiting London in the early days, observed that this was a contest between the strongest impulses that can govern man.

Could this have been avoided if Gladstone after taking office had acted differently ? It was sometimes said that he might have proceeded by resolution. But would his opponents have been more ready to consider the policy if submitted in this form? Chamberlain said on February 15: " As for passing Home Rule resolutions at the present time, I utterly disbelieve in its possibility."[1] When the troubles of the Liberal party were causing men who wanted above all to keep the party together to cast about for a method, some of them turned to the idea of dropping the Bill and substituting a resolution. Gladstone wrote to Sir J. Pease on May 21 saying that a Government could not make such a confession of failure. " I will not say Aye or No to the question whether a Resolution *by consent* as in 1858, i.e. supported at least by the United Liberals and the Nationalists (418 against 252 Tories) would have been admissible. It is not before me. Lord Hartington, to speak of no one else, has killed it." Two days earlier he had written to Arnold Morley: " Events appear now to have made a Resolution unavailable. Hartington has stated with great force (in an ultra speech) the arguments against it; and I think it plain it could only be adopted as a practical solution by consent." Perhaps if he had acted at once on another plan, if he had set up a committee or a commission, he might have got over this difficulty. Rosebery remarks in his diary that at a conversation in February 1888 he remarked to Gladstone " that if we had proposed a Royal Commission we should have carried our measure through the House of Commons after the pause of a year that it would have given us. He generally concurred."[2] There is nothing in Gladstone's letters at the time to suggest that he thought this practicable. Presumably the proposal would have been met by the same flood of rhetoric from the Conservative

---

[1] Garvin, II, 153.   [2] Crewe, *Rosebery*, Vol. I, p. 318.

leaders as a Home Rule Bill, but it might have enabled a number of persons to keep their minds open until the Commission had reported. The best thing would have been no doubt a Commission on which Carnarvon was a member, but it is unlikely that Carnarvon would have consented to co-operate in this way as his party had rejected his policy and declared against Home Rule in any form.

Whether this would have been practicable or not is a question difficult to answer. But short of this, Gladstone might well have set up expert committees to manage certain of his problems, notably that of finance. He worked hard at finance himself and produced an arrangement with which he was better satisfied than the Irish. Indeed Morley admits that if the Bill had passed its second reading, the Irish might have thrown it out on the financial clauses. It is difficult to see why Gladstone did not take the step he took later of setting up a committee or commission to study the financial relations of the two countries. This question remained an unsolved problem till the last, and, as we shall see, it played a part in the later clash with Parnell. It was unfortunate that Gladstone's taste for finance led him to prepare this part of the Bill himself, without any formal Irish assent, for there was no part of the Bill on which it was more important to reach conclusions that would stand; conclusions, that is, that would seem just to the Irish not only at the time but afterwards.

During the French Revolution Windham attacked Fox and Grey who wanted to reform Parliament on the ground that they were trying to rebuild a house in a hurricane. This is precisely what Gladstone found himself doing in the spring of 1886. He had to persuade the country to give Ireland Home Rule by producing a scheme that showed that his view of the effects of Home Rule was right and the view of his opponents wrong. This he had to do in the midst of the most violent hurricane that had raged in English politics since the Reform Bill. His plan has to be judged in the light of his difficulties. If there had been an overruling body of opinion behind Home Rule drawn from both parties, such as he looked for when he made his proposal to

Salisbury, it would have been possible to discuss every part of the scheme on its merits. As it was the Bill had to be prepared with an eye to the tactics of a determined and vehement Opposition.

Gladstone was ready himself, for example, to give Ireland the right to impose protective duties on British goods, and there was a great deal to be said for the view that the bolder policy was in this case the safer. But it was soon evident that the opponents of Home Rule would use such a provision with great effect in the English towns. Chamberlain marked down this as one of his objections to the Bill in its original form, and it is easy to see how he would have played on the selfish fears of the electorate if Ireland had been given this power. On March 31, after an attack in the *Scotsman*, Gladstone wrote to Rosebery that he and Morley thought this power should be withheld. But this change affected the question of Irish representation at Westminster and made it more difficult to defend exclusion against Chamberlain.

This question as we have seen became the final battleground between Chamberlain and the Government. He told Labouchere that he had let his friends know that he would vote for the second reading if Gladstone promised to keep the Irish representation untouched. As the Bill was defeated on second reading by Liberal votes after a division in which one teller was a Liberal and the other a Radical, this issue was obviously one of great importance. When the negotiations on this point were in progress Gladstone sent to his colleagues a most interesting paper discussing the problem both as it affected taxation and as it affected the larger question of political unity.

May 5, 1886

Memorandum on
Bill for Irish Government 2nd *Reading*
Division

2 R OF IRISH GOVERNMENT BILL.

In anticipation of the Cabinet on Friday, I will endeavour in this Memorandum to bring before my colleagues the exact state of the case, as it stands before us, with respect to the exclusion of Irish Members from the Imperial Parliament, and the condition of Ireland as to Imperial affairs.

I. UNDER THE BILL AS IT STANDS.

1. The whole Irish representation in both Houses is to be recalled, if any alteration is to be made in the Statutes itself on which there has not been a previous agreement between the two Legislatures.

2. The Imperial contribution being fixed, and based upon peace charges, Great Britain can only obtain aid from Ireland towards a war expenditure by the free action of the Irish Legislative Body upon a Message from the Crown, which aid of course might be withheld.

3. It is impossible to restrain the right of free speech on any subject Imperial or other, or to refuse it to the Body while allowing it to the members. The Addresses of the Legislative Body, if founded in reason, would on excluded subjects have no power, but they might have a great deal of influence.

Such is the provision already made, and, whether from imperfect comprehension or not, deemed insufficient.

II. The question then arises, what more can we rightly and safely do, in order to secure against risk the second reading of the Bill?

(1) and first let me exclude what I think the Cabinet believe we cannot safely do. We cannot agree to the simple retention of the Irish Representation in the two Houses as it stands under the Act of Union?

Nor, I assume, can we agree to its retention with the condition of reduced numbers?

(I observe in passing on the question of reduced numbers that it would involve a new legislative machinery to provide for the choice of them: while the 103 and the 28 would be those entitled under the Act of Union.)

(2) Mr Stansfeld has suggested that perhaps the case might be met by a simple form of Federation, with division of subjects, for Scotland and Wales as well as Ireland. Whether or not this method might have been originally entertained I will not say: but at the present stage it would involve the withdrawal of the Bill, and to this I do not see my way. I mention the point however in case others should think we can work in this direction?

I will confine myself to suggesting changes which though

undoubtedly important would not alter the principle of the Bill, nor extensively modify its framework.

1. The first point to be considered is the force of the argument against taxation without representation. Volenti non fit injuria; and we have the consent of the Irish members.

But it is a very large interpretation of their mandate, if we take this consent as binding Ireland to bear all changes of Excise and Customs Duty which may be enacted at Westminster during a long and not absolutely limited future.

When the exclusion of Irish members was originally proposed by me, there was to be no Parliamentary taxation of Ireland.

We imported Parliamentary taxation of Ireland into the plan, in order to gain the great object of fiscal unity.

I for one must plead guilty to having at the moment partially lost sight of the bearing of this change on the exclusion of Irish members. Both on principle, and as matter of policy, I am prepared to agree that the Irish representation (even if need be in both Houses) shall revive, so as to give the Irish members a *right* of attending at Westminster on any question of *altering* taxation for Ireland. (It would be needful to exclude the unusual renewal of the Tea Duty and to have some special enactment for Bills simply of reduction or repeal.)

There would be some inconvenience in this, as there might be intrigues with the Irish to overthrow a Ministry through its Budget.

But we know the worst of this inconvenience now. Since the Act of Union, I think that only two Ministries (one of them already in a minority) have been overthrown, i.e. driven out, on Budgets. These cases were in 1852 and 1885. The Ministry of the day would have full opportunity of forecasting consequences in determining on its finance.

At the worst, whereas it has to deal now with Irish members who have no other legislative avocation, it would then have to deal with Irish members whose place of ordinary duty, and of preference, would be in Dublin.

I commend this proposal to careful consideration: especially if it is likely to have considerable influence on the coming division; which is of the most vital moment.

2. But undoubtedly it would not satisfy the whole craving that exists.

Can anything more be done? Taxation being so far disposed of, there remain, in threefold division

(a) The Crown, and Defence.

(b) Foreign and Colonial relations.

(c) Subjects reserved on practical grounds such as Patents, Copyright and so forth.

On (a) I do not see how to modify the Bill with any sort of advantage.

On (b) the ' sentiment ' presses for a change. But how could Irish members, unless always here, be enabled to participate in dealing with a class of subjects which are mainly in the hands of private members, (at least I should say in the proportion of twenty occasions against one) and perfectly uncertain as to the time and method of handling? (For instance: Irish members would have had to be " notified " for the motion of Sir J. Pease last night, on which the House was *counted* out.)

Two suggestions however have been made which might conceivably cover both (b) and (c).

The first is that provision might be made in the Act for regular communication between the British and Irish Executives on the (b) and (c) subjects. Foreign policy is thus managed as between Sweden and Norway; but their system is even now not quite determined, and it is founded on discussion in the presence of the Sovereign. I do not as yet see that much could be made of this. Time and convenience would bring about these communications spontaneously. Nor would the plan do much to meet the ' sentiment ' now operative.

Another perhaps less unhopeful suggestion has been made from an unofficial source. It is that a Standing Committee or Delegation might be appointed, to meet from time to time during the (London) Session; to be composed (1) from and by both Houses here, and (2) from and by the two Orders of the Irish Legislative Body, in some reasonable proportion such as *perhaps* one third; to have power to report and make recommendations upon any of the subjects reserved in the Statute (except the Crown and Defence?) On the class of matters reserved, which are embraced in (c), I can conceive that such a Committee might be very useful. As to Foreign and Colonial questions, it might afford some safety-valve, if any be needed. But further: I am inclined to think it might go some considerable way towards meeting the *sentiment* which craves for symbols of Imperial Unity, while it would have no dangerous connection, under any ordinary circumstances, with the great and delicate question of the responsibility, and the stability, of Ministries here.

In conclusion; I conceive that whatever we adopt, or whatever we open as admissible, at this juncture, will hardly leave room for much farther change, except in details.

W.E.G., May 5, 1886.

P.S.   Very early in the day, I suggested that Irish members might be allowed to appear on particular subjects, if the Irish Legislative Body should ask it *pro hac vice* by Address to the Crown. There would however be difficulty I fear in framing a proposal on this basis and while in principle it is not inadmissible (as I think) the plan of a Committee or Delegation appears to me easier and better.[1]

The most interesting part of this paper is, not that which refers to taxation, but that which discusses new plans for preserving the political unity of the two countries by a system of delegations. At this time Imperial Federation was in the air, and Sir Robert Hamilton in the memorandum

---

[1] There is another paper of Gladstone's dated May 11, as follows:—

Draft.

Secret

HOUSE OF COMMONS

(Each House to be dealt with separately).   Irish members (103) shall be invited by Mr Speaker to attend

1.   When the Gov^t makes a proposal for the alteration or repeal of any tax now levied in Ireland by the authority of Parliament, or for the imposition of any new tax.   (This might be framed to include the regular annual renewal.)

2.   When on the proposal of any member of Parl^t the House of Commons shall have once voted for a Bill to repeal or reduce a tax; and (in order to give sufficient notice) after such first vote an interval of not less than one week shall be allowed before a second vote is taken.

3.   When the Joint Commission appointed by this Act shall have reported that in its judgment a change in the law touching any of the reserved subjects, on which it is statutably authorised to report, is expedient, and any proposal shall be submitted to the House in conformity with such report.

4.   When the Irish Legislative Body shall have signified by Address to the Crown its desire to promote an alteration in the Law on any of the reserved subjects.

N.B.   Query add after " Law " " or in any Treaty with a Foreign Power."

5.   When the Irish Legislative Body shall have signified by Address to the Crown, Her Majesty assenting thereto, its desire either to initiate or to share in any proceeding in Parliament on any of the reserved subjects.

Alternative for 4 and 5.

Another plan, simpler and perhaps safer, would be to omit No. 4 altogether, and leave its matter to be covered as it would be covered by No. 5.

W.E.G., May 11, 1886.

he wrote for Carnarvon argued that removing the Irish from Westminster looked like a step back but was really a step forward, for some form of federation was probable in the future, and Ireland would then take her place with the other partners in the Empire. We can see that there were three ways of preserving political unity. One was to leave things as they were with the Irish at Westminster in sullen and permanent revolt. The second was to make some arrangement for Home Rule all round with subordinate Parliaments for England, Ireland, Scotland and Wales. Chamberlain thought that if the Government went beyond his Central Board scheme this was the only plan that could be accepted. The third was to make the Empire a Commonwealth in which the several Colonies found their place, not by sending members to Westminster, but by associating with the Imperial Government in conference as sister States, and to put Ireland in this category. Gladstone's suggestion pointed in this direction; the direction that the Empire has taken.

The first effect of Gladstone's paper as it happened was to alarm the chief spokesman of Imperial federation in the Government.

Rosebery wrote in reply (May 6):

" I cannot attend the Cabinet on Saturday and therefore beg to enter my humble protest against the delegation on foreign and colonial questions. On Foreign Affairs it would be mischievous and on colonial affairs derisory unless you admitted a colonial element. You could not have a special arrangement in order to enable Irishmen to discuss colonial affairs from which you excluded colonists. You would then have a body which might be useful but which would no longer be the British Parliament and would no longer therefore satisfy that sentiment. In any case it would be a project outside and beyond this Bill."[1]

Gladstone replied (May 7):

" I am sorry to have made your hair stand on end, and I think you have used the word protest in some haste, as it usually follows rather than begins discussions, but I am comforted in thinking

[1] Granville was also uneasy. (May 6.) " It seems to me unadvisable to introduce anything quite new in its character and likely to puzzle people not very anxious to understand."

that there is no necessity probably for raising any disputable point. The idea of a Joint Commission may be reasonably entertained without stereotyping at the first moment the precise limit at all points of its office."

Gladstone clearly had in view a possible extension to include the Colonies.

It is curious to reflect that if Gladstone had given Chamberlain the Colonial Office, this hint of a plan for Imperial co-operation might have caught his fancy and the energy that was spent on contesting detail after detail in the Bill might have been given to a piece of constructive statesmanship. The first step might thus have been taken towards the shape that the Commonwealth has since assumed under the guiding hands of Gladstone, Rosebery, and Chamberlain, with Ireland satisfied and interested in this common enterprise. Whatever the first misgivings of his colleagues, Gladstone was not prevented from putting this idea before Parliament in his speech on the second reading on May 10.

(Mr. Gladstone): " . . . Then I take the first objection that has been made to the proposed exclusion of the Irish Representatives from this Parliament. It is that the principle that representation should accompany taxation would thereby be violated. Now, what I am about to say involves a considerable responsibility; but the question whether and how far the difficulty may be met has been considered; and I am prepared to say that we can give full satisfaction to those who advance this objection. If agreeable to the House, we will meet it in Committee by providing that when a proposal is made to alter the taxation in respect of Customs and Excise Irish Members shall have an opportunity of appearing in this House to take a share in the transaction of that Business. It will then be impossible to urge against the Bill that it is proposed by the Government that representation should not accompany taxation.

" In regard to such matters of common interest between Great Britain and Ireland as those which form the subject of Foreign Treaties, no doubt the objections urged from some quarters may be met in some considerable degree by the adoption of a system of executive communications, which is the system adopted in certain foreign countries. There are cases in which two countries are disunited in their Legislatures, but united in national action and feeling. They find themselves able, by executive communications, to provide for the common handling of common subjects. But we do not feel that the plan of executive communications need of necessity be the only one. There are various plans which have been proposed in order to indicate and maintain common action on Imperial subjects, and which are well worthy of consideration. For example, it has been proposed that a Joint Commission should be appointed representing the Houses of Parliament on this side of the water and representing the Irish Legislative Body in due proportion of Members, and that that Commission should meet from time to time, as occasion might arise, during the Session of Parliament to consider common questions and report their opinions to both Legislative Bodies upon many, at any rate, of the Imperial matters that are reserved by the Bill as it stands. I hesitate to say upon ' any ' of those questions, for I incline to the belief, for example, that the question relating to the succession of the Crown—in all the different branches of the subject—ought not to go to any secondary authority. But I can conceive that many subjects, such, for example, as Treaties of Commerce, might well be considered by a Commission of this kind. I do not say of this plan as absolutely as I do of the plan as to taxation, that we are quite ready to propose it if it be the wish of Parliament, for it has been little canvassed, and objections may be raised to it which we have failed to anticipate; but I can say that we look at the proposal as one which might satisfy jealousies, might have other advantages, and is not open, so far as we know, to serious objection.

" Another proposal is that a Joint Committee of the kind which I have described could be appointed to consider how far and upon what conditions other than those provided in the Statute Irish Members should come here. There is yet another suggestion, that Irish Members might be entitled to come to Parliament—I assume generally that corresponding opportunity would be given to Irish Peers—upon occasions when the Legislative Body should, by an Address to the Crown, have expressed a desire that they should do so. I do not say that that is open to objection on principle. At the same time, I see considerable difficulties as to the particular way of making it a practicable plan. I will, however, state broadly that it is our duty to give an unprejudiced ear to proposals which others may make for the purpose of insuring the continued manifestation of common interest between Great Britain and Ireland in Imperial concerns. That end, we say distinctly, is a good end; means for attaining it we regard with favour, subject to the condition that they shall not be so handled as to introduce into this House the principle of confusion, nor so handled as to impose on the Irish Legislative Body limitations of its liberty in any matters except such as affect high Imperial policy."

In the excitement of battle not much notice was taken of this passage. The *Times* received it with profound mistrust.

" What Mr. Chamberlain has demanded as the indispensable condition of his assent to a Home Rule scheme is ' the maintenance of the united representation of the three countries in one supreme Parliament,' retaining for Ireland not only ' full representation ' at Westminster, but ' full responsibility for all Imperial affairs.' Instead of this Mr. Gladstone proposes a system of casual and partial interference in Imperial affairs by the representatives of the Irish constituencies, complicated with a still more curious constitutional innovation, which, as Lord Hartington shows, establishes the Irish Legislature as a power in the State co-ordinate with the Imperial Parliament."[1]

The *Spectator* was equally hostile. The plan was " either futile though injurious or in the highest degree dangerous to the Empire."

The *Manchester Guardian*, on the other hand, which had started in a very critical mood, was enthusiastic over this particular proposal.

" It will supply a ready means of communication on the matters of common interest between responsible men on both sides. It will keep the English Government in touch with the Irish. . . . We should be disposed indeed to enlarge the scope of this Commission and to include in it representatives also of the colonies, against whose interests ignorance and inattention in high quarters have so often told with damaging effect. The scheme is a stroke of genius and should win the approval of all parties."[2]

If the exact character of the relations of Ireland to the Empire was one great problem, the relations of Ulster to

[1] *Times*, May 11, 1886.

[2] It is pretty safe to conclude that this expressed the opinion of W. T. Arnold who was deeply interested in Home Rule as a means to Imperial unity.

Ireland was another.   It is often said that Gladstone did not grasp the full gravity of this problem.   This doubtless is true.   He thought that the minority that chiefly needed protection was the landlord class.   Parnell himself had used violent and threatening language about the landlords at one time during the General Election, and Gladstone believed that a Land Bill enabling landlords to sell was essential to his scheme, both to make it secure against injustice and to persuade English people to accept it.   The Ulster difficulty and the Ulster protests he took less seriously.   He had in mind perhaps the difference between the threats and the behaviour of the Established Irish Church before and after disestablishment.   Of Presbyterian Ulster he knew little. He might have recalled Swift's description of the Irish Presbyterians as an angry cat at large.[1]   For Ulster had deep roots of strength and tenacity of character.   She had supplied the best rebels Ireland had known; her land system with the Ulster custom had encouraged personal independence; her religion, with much of the old Covenanting spirit, was much fiercer than the religion of the Anglican houses where Gladstone had spent his time on his only visit to Ireland.   And Ulster, as Mr. Stephen Gwynn has pointed out, had little respect for law.   Southern Ireland looked on law as the weapon of her oppressors; Northern Ireland looked on law as something that existed for her convenience.   This was the inevitable consequence of Irish history.   It was certain that if Ulster had to choose between law and her liberties she would give as little attention to law as any moonlighter or Fenian in the south. After Chamberlain resigned there was only one man among Gladstone's colleagues who understood Ulster.   Bryce was himself an Ulsterman.   In December 1885 he gave Gladstone a paper containing his impressions of opinion and feeling after a visit to Ireland, and in March 1886 he gave him a paper on the Ulster question which has unfortunately been lost.   It was a misfortune that Gladstone did not take him into the Cabinet, for his special knowledge was worth more than the prestige the Cabinet gained from the

[1] Stephen Gwynn, *Irish Literature and Drama*, p. 29.

experience and the reputations of Ministers who were better known.

It is true that Gladstone did not give its full importance to the Ulster difficulty. On the other hand it is not true that he ignored it. In his speech on introducing the Home Rule Bill, April 8, 1886, he said that though the Government had made no special provision for Ulster, they were prepared to give sympathetic consideration to any proposal made to them.

" I will deviate from my path for a moment to say a word upon the state of opinion in that wealthy, intelligent, and energetic portion of the Irish community which, as I have said, predominates in a certain portion of Ulster. Our duty is to adhere to sound general principles, and to give the utmost consideration we can to the opinions of that energetic minority. The first thing of all, I should say, is that if, upon any occasion, by any individual or section, violent measures have been threatened in certain emergencies, I think the best compliment I can pay to those who have threatened us is to take no notice whatever of the threats, but to treat them as momentary ebullitions, which will pass away with the fears from which they spring, and at the same time to adopt on our part every reasonable measure for disarming those fears. I cannot conceal the conviction that the voice of Ireland, as a whole, is at this moment clearly and Constitutionally spoken. I cannot say it is otherwise when five-sixths of its lawfully-chosen Representatives are of one mind in this matter. There is a counter voice; and I wish to know what is the claim of those by whom that counter voice is spoken, and how much is the scope and allowance we can give them. Certainly, Sir, I cannot allow it to be said that a Protestant minority in Ulster, or elsewhere, is to rule the question at large for Ireland. I am aware of no Constitutional doctrine tolerable on which such a conclusion could be adopted or justified. But I think that the Protestant minority should have its wishes considered to the utmost practicable extent in any form which they may assume.

" Various schemes, short of refusing the demand of Ireland at large, have been proposed on behalf of Ulster. One scheme is, that Ulster itself, or, perhaps with more appearance of reason, a portion of Ulster, should be excluded from the operation of the Bill we are about to introduce. Another scheme is, that a separate autonomy should be provided for Ulster, or for a portion of Ulster. Another scheme is, that certain rights with regard to certain subjects—such, for example, as education and some other subjects—should be reserved and should be placed, to a certain extent, under the control of Provincial Councils. These, I think, are the suggestions which have reached me in different shapes; there may be others. But what I wish to say of them is this—there is no one of them which has appeared to us to be so completely justified, either upon its merits or by the weight of opinion supporting and recommending it, as to warrant our including it in the Bill and proposing it to Parliament upon our responsibility. What we think is that such suggestions deserve careful and unprejudiced consideration. It may be that that free discussion, which I have no doubt will largely take place after a Bill such as we propose shall have been laid on the Table of the House, may give to one of these proposals, or to some other proposals, a practicable form, and that some such plan may be found to be recommended by a general or predominating approval. If it should be so, it will, at our hands, have the most favourable consideration, with every disposition to do what equity may appear to recommend. That is what I have to say on the subject of Ulster."

The difficulty was that the hostility of Ulster was to the whole scheme of Home Rule and that the Ulster opponents wanted, not concessions to their special circumstances, but the destruction of the Bill. If the Ulster leaders had ever taken the view taken by a distinguished Unionist thinker, Henry Sidgwick, the solution would have been simpler. " Ulster," he wrote at a later phase of the controversy, " has strong claims to have any arrangement it may like as between Great Britain and herself but no right to determine the conditions of the arrangement between Great Britain and the rest of Ireland."[1] As the Ulster leaders made the larger claim and had good reason to think that they could defeat the whole scheme, they were not ready to consider any plan for securing their own liberties. With Ulster in this mood any spontaneous concession would clearly expose a new surface to attack. For every such arrangement would inevitably involve anomalies and put new arguments in the hands of opponents. Thus there

[1] *Memoir*, p. 526.

was a strong objection to taking the initiative in such a proposal. On the other hand the objection to the policy of waiting for a remedy was almost equally strong. For nobody could deny the claim of Ulster to special treatment; or disregard her genuine fears. Ulster was indeed just the kind of problem that was insoluble until there was agreement on the principle of Home Rule.

Thus everything comes back to the same fundamental difficulty. Of most of the great reforms of the nineteenth century it might be said that in one sense they were agreed reforms. It is significant that hardly any of them were repealed. This is not to say that the Bills by which they were carried into effect were not often fiercely disputed, or that there were no party differences on this or that aspect of a measure. The divergent interests of religion and class caused sharp conflicts. But if we look back on the history of Local Government and Public Health during the last half of the century, we find that both parties when in office prepared schemes, and that schemes that came to nothing under one Government were often carried into law by another. If we compare the Acts passed and the Bills prepared for sanitary legislation by Stansfeld in the first Gladstone Government with those passed and prepared by Cross in Disraeli's last Government, or those prepared by Harcourt and Dilke for London and County Government in Gladstone's second Government with those passed by Ritchie in Salisbury's second Government, we might conclude that the same political party had been in office all the time. By 1886 Irish land had almost passed into this category, as anybody can see who traces the sequence of Acts that followed the first Land Act of 1870, and then notes the agrarian legislation that Salisbury's second Government passed, sometimes spontaneously, but in one important case against its will.[1] If Home Rule could once reach this stage,

[1] See a speech by Lord Cadogan, one of Salisbury's colleagues in the 1886 Government and afterwards Lord Lieutenant in the 1895 Government.

". . . Up to the year 1870 the land laws of Ireland were a disgrace to any civilised and well-governed country. And let me say, and say sincerely, that I think it is the greatest honour, that the greatest credit is owing to Mr. Gladstone, for his having undertaken, in the year 1870, to attempt to alter the laws

then the different questions it raised could be treated dispassionately, and the best constructive minds could work on its problems. But how was this to be done? How was England to be brought to think of Home Rule as a desirable or necessary reform?

Gladstone, as we have seen, had been trying in the autumn to educate his colleagues in his own Home Rule views. He had also prompted Knowles to let Barry O'Brien put the case for Home Rule in the *Nineteenth Century*. But when the Conservatives rejected his offer, and he found himself Prime Minister with a storm getting up against Home Rule, little had been done, for, as we have seen, his mouth had been closed until then by his sense of the danger of bidding for the Irish vote. What then could he do? This kind of crusade had always before been undertaken first by a man out of office. This was true of the Repeal of the Corn Laws, and the Disestablishment of the Irish Church. When later Chamberlain wished to persuade the country to change its fiscal system he went out of office and secured liberty to conduct his crusade as he liked. Could Gladstone have so acted in 1886? There was much to be said for such a course. Home Rule was his only interest, and nothing else attached him to public life. If he could have given up a few months to educating the country on this question, while a Liberal Government devoted itself to domestic reforms, there would have been enough support at the end of that time to make a strong case for setting up a Royal Commission. A long step forward would have been taken.

There were however strong arguments on the other side.

of Ireland so as to bring them more in harmony with civilisation. ('Hear, hear, and No, no.') There are those, I know, who differ with the policy of Mr. Gladstone's Acts of 1870 and 1881, and I think some gentlemen on this platform are of this opinion. I can only say that it having been my duty especially to direct my attention to these matters, I have come to the conclusion that Mr. Gladstone had no alternative, and that the legislation which he initiated in 1870, which he continued in 1881, and which we followed in 1887 was upon the only lines which could promise a peaceful solution of the land difficulty in Ireland, and that it is upon those principles and those alone that you will have to legislate." (*Leicester Daily Post*, January 22, 1890.) It is interesting to note that Stafford Northcote had changed his view of the Land Act of 1881 after a visit to Ireland in 1883. See *Life of Lord Iddesleigh* by Andrew Lang, II, 260.

In the first place Gladstone might well fear that a campaign for Home Rule, conducted by the most powerful man in England as a private mission, might create serious difficulties in the government of Ireland. He might be accused of refusing responsibility himself and embarrassing those to whom fell the task of ruling Ireland from day to day. Thus there existed in this case a difficulty that did not exist for the men who wanted to repeal the Corn Laws, and for those who wanted afterwards to restore them. It might fairly be argued by his opponents that if he wanted to throw this disturbing question into politics, he had no right to put the immediate inconvenience on to others. How far this argument should have been decisive it is difficult to say, but it is easy to understand the weight it would carry in Gladstone's judgment.

There was a second difficulty. Chamberlain was not a leader of his party when he started on his campaign for Tariff Reform. Gladstone had consented to remain leader of his party for the Election, after the Whig and the Radical Ministers had told him that the party could not hold together if he went. Could he now desert his party in order to conduct a crusade as a private member? Gladstone took a more indulgent view of the obligations of a leader to his party than Salisbury, and he had shown, as his colleagues rightly considered, too little respect for their claims to be consulted and informed. But however lightly he took such obligations he could hardly leave the party in such a manner as to cause it the maximum of inconvenience and perhaps the risk of disruption. Chamberlain's crusade was a considerable embarrassment to his party, but Chamberlain was not its leader nor, with all his power, was he as powerful in 1903 as Gladstone in 1886.

It has always seemed to critics since that Gladstone underrated the task he had set himself. That is probably true. Gladstone was thinking much more of the Irish difficulty than of the English. He thought that the temper of Ireland for the future would depend on the action taken then by England. He was persuaded by his correspondence with Mrs. O'Shea that Parnell had a hard task to hold his own

against his extreme men, and that, if she did not get constitutional reform from England, Ireland would become
irreconcilable. He was steeped in Ireland's past, and he
knew that a rebel with all this angry history in his heart
was not just a peevish man, ready to be charmed out of his
ill humour by this or that gift or boon. The difference
between him and Chamberlain was partly that Chamberlain
took his impressions from O'Shea, an irresponsible trifler,
whereas his came from his knowledge of the part imagination
and memory play in national discontent. He knew that
the sort of fire that was smouldering in the Irish mind was not
of a kind to be put out with a bucket of the best Birmingham
water.

At the same time he was much more hopeful than he had
been that Ireland could be reconciled. Among his papers
there is a memorandum describing a visit to Ireland in the
autumn of 1885. It is unsigned, but it is pretty clear that it is
written by Bryce. The writer reported among other
things a conversation with Davitt, who was regarded as a
man on the extreme left, who had told him that Home Rule
would satisfy all but a very few, and that he was certain
that if it were granted there would be very little feeling for
separation. Gladstone had been haunted by the fear that
Parnell might take his eighty-five men to Dublin, and set
them up as a Parliament defying England. How then
would England look in the eyes of the world: England the
mother of free institutions: the friend of Italy in her struggle:
the nation that had read the tyrants of Europe so many a
lesson? He believed that Ireland was now in a mood to
accept what England could afford to give, and his chief
anxiety was that nothing should happen that could shake
her confidence.[1] And, as it seemed to him, he often had to

---

[1] The importance of the impression made on him by the discovery in
December 1885 that the Irish party might co-operate on a practicable plan of
Home Rule can be seen from a letter he had written to Rosebery in the early
autumn, when the hostility of that party to his Government was fresh in his
mind.

September 10, 1885:

" It is no pain to me to be relieved of the will of the wisp idea of satisfying
the Irish party, as I have never had that expectation or acted with such a view.

choose between increasing his difficulties in England and increasing the risk of that loss of confidence in Ireland. The delay that would have helped him in England seemed to him dangerous in Ireland, and, in this sense, Churchill's hit at him as " an old man in a hurry " was to the point. He overrated one risk, and underrated the other. And, by a curious irony, he made this mistake just because he understood the character of the Irish problem better than anybody else.

Some critics have thought that if Gladstone had been less anxious to satisfy the full Irish demand, he could have secured from England a measure of self-government which, if at first it disappointed Ireland, would in the end have proved workable and brought contentment. On this point later events have justified Gladstone rather than his critics. He put the case against this view in introducing his Bill:

" There have been several plans liberally devised for granting to Ireland the management of her education, the management of her public works, and the management of one subject and another—boons very important in themselves—under a Central Elective Body; boons, any of which I do not hesitate to say I should have been glad to see accepted, or I should have been glad to see a trial given to a system which might have been constructed under them, had it been the desire and the demand of Ireland. I do not think such a scheme would have possessed the advantage of finality. If it had been accepted, and especially if it had been freely suggested from that quarter—by the Irish Representatives —it might have furnished a useful *modus vivendi*. But it is absurd. in my opinion, to talk of the adoption of such a scheme in the face of two obstacles—first of all, that those whom it is intended to benefit do not want it, do not ask it, and refuse it; and, secondly, the obstacle, not less important, that all those who are fearful of giving a domestic Legislature to Ireland would naturally, emphatically, and rather justly, say—' We will not create your Central Board and palter with this question, because we feel certain that it will afford nothing in this world except a

What I do think of is the Irish nation and the fame, duty and peace of my country. Some of you—to speak freely and without this why speak at all?— seem to me not to have taken any just measure of the probable position of a serious dispute with the Irish nation. Chamberlain says what are 4 millions against 32? The answer depends wholly on the case."

stage from which to agitate for a further concession, and because we see that by the proposal you make you will not even attain the advantage of settling the question that is raised '."

The method Gladstone then rejected was put before England twice afterwards; once under the most favourable conditions. Towards the end of Wyndham's most successful term of office as Chief Secretary, there was a movement in Ireland, promoted by the group of moderate men who had produced the Land Conference of which Wyndham's Land Act was the outcome, for devolution, on the general lines of Chamberlain's original scheme. But the Conservative party rejected it at once, and Wyndham was obliged to resign in May 1905, on the mere suspicion of liking it. In 1907 the Liberal Government produced an Irish Councils Bill. The Bill was rejected in Ireland, but before it was considered there it had been attacked in the House of Commons by the leader of the Unionist party as warmly as if it had been a Bill for full Home Rule. There is something to be said for the view that if Home Rule had grown up from such a beginning the Ulster question would have been simplified. But it was just because it seemed like a beginning and not the end of a reform that Unionists fought it as fiercely as Home Rule. Thus it looks as if by adopting the smaller instead of the larger plan Gladstone would have lost a great deal of support in Ireland, without gaining any in England.

Gladstone then allowed his tactics to be determined by a single consideration; the importance of keeping Ireland's new confidence in the English power to do her justice. To most people it seems extraordinary that he could persuade himself that he could sweep to one side a great mass of fear and prejudice by a simple appeal to England's conscience. The adverse forces included not only the wealth and social power, but the intellect of England. In the 'seventies he had that force behind him; in the 'eighties he had begun to lose it, and Home Rule stripped him bare. Herbert Paul gives a list of men eminent in science and literature who now declared against him, most of whom had been his supporters: Huxley, Tyndall, Tennyson, Browning,

Lecky,[1] Seeley, Froude, Goldwin Smith, Martineau, Jowett, Herbert Spencer. The old man was undaunted. A sentence from his superb speech on the Bradlaugh controversy gives the secret of his courage. What, he asked, was the value of the Oath taken in Parliament, merely a Theistic oath, " embracing no acknowledgment of Providence, of divine government, of responsibility, of retribution." These resounding names describe the setting in which he saw the dealings of nation with nation; they represented the great forces that govern human destiny, and marked the difference between insolent strength and obedient power. The case against him was thrown by the *Times* into a single sentence: " We cannot make Ireland like Canada, first because Canadians are our friends, whilst the majority of Irishmen are our enemies, and second because Canada is 3,000 miles away, and Ireland is at our doors."[2] He could have put his case into a single sentence: " Ireland has great wrongs, and those wrongs will be redressed by the generous wisdom of England, if the English people accepts its responsibility, or righted by the desperate violence of the Irish, if England waits for retribution." Dazzled by his amazing power over great audiences, he believed that England had only to be told this truth to be as anxious as he was that reparation should be made and justice done.

---

[1] Lecky, though an anti-Home Ruler, was of course the cause of a great deal of Home Rule in others. His *Leaders of Public Opinion in Ireland* and *History of England in the Eighteenth Century* made a profound impression on Gladstone, and made a Home Ruler of Roosevelt, otherwise a strong Imperialist. Roosevelt wrote to Bryce: " I have been a Home Ruler ever since reading Lecky's account of Ireland in the eighteenth century." (Fisher, *Bryce*, Vol. I, p. 338.)

Trevelyan wrote to Gladstone on May 28, 1887, after the publication of the fifth and sixth volumes of Lecky's *History of England in the Eighteenth Century*: " I am glad to have just finished Lecky's volume in time for your article. I am immensely struck with what you describe as his honesty. The foolish and unworthy references to modern politics lie on the surface, and are in no sense justified by, or even connected with, the texture of the narrative, which is the most convincing case for a new treatment of Ireland that ever I read."

[2] December 19, 1885.

APPENDIX TO CHAPTER XXVI

THE ABORTIVE NEGOTIATIONS OF MAY, 1886

Labouchere published in *Truth* on October 14, 1908, under the title " The Secret History of the First Home Rule Bill " an account of the negotiations in which he took a leading part on the eve of the debate on the Second Reading. Gladstone made his speech on the Second Reading on May 10, and it disappointed Chamberlain's expectations and destroyed the hope of a settlement. Labouchere gives the events leading up to this speech. He says that on May 8 when the Cabinet was sitting he sent in to Gladstone a memorandum asking him certain questions about the concessions he was ready to make; that he received a satisfactory answer which he communicated to Chamberlain; that Chamberlain then telegraphed to some of his friends to say that Gladstone had capitulated; that among these friends was O'Shea; that Parnell heard in this way of the proposed concessions. Mr. Garvin, who supplements Labouchere's account from the Chamberlain Papers, thus describes the consequence. " One of these messages went to O'Shea who was in high feather since he had forced the Irish leader to return him for Galway. Parnell was told and at once communicated the telegram to Downing St. Indignantly Mr. Gladstone informed an inquiring journalist that he had yielded nothing."[1]

The Gladstone papers throw a new light on these events and they show clearly two things; the first that Gladstone believed that the concessions he announced on May 10, which Chamberlain found so unsatisfactory, gave Chamberlain what he asked through Labouchere; the second that Parnell did not influence the speech or lead Gladstone to change his mind or tactics.

The sequence of events is as follows. On May 5 Gladstone drew up the Memorandum on his Bill for Irish Government, 2nd Reading Division, and sent it first to Morley and Granville and then had it circulated to the Cabinet. In this paper he provided for the return of the Irish members when questions of taxation affecting Ireland were discussed. On May 6 Labouchere wrote to Chamberlain stating that Gladstone had drawn up this scheme and urging Chamberlain to accept it.[2] " I don't believe that you will get more." On May 8 the Cabinet met and accepted Gladstone's scheme. On May 9 Gladstone, then out of London, wrote to Arnold Morley thanking

[1] Garvin, Vol. II, p. 227.   [2] *Life of Labouchere*, p. 305.

him for sending him a memorandum from Labouchere. This memorandum is not in his papers but it is summarized in the letter as follows:

1. That the Government will assent to full representation on all questions of taxation.

2. That some means will be found by which the Irish opinions on questions excluded from the Dublin Parliament shall be conveyed to the Imperial Parliament, such as a Joint Committee representing England, Scotland and Ireland.

3. That the Irish Parliament has the right by address to claim representation upon any question of Imperial Policy.

Such modifications as are needed to give full effect to above will be made in Bill.

Gladstone was well pleased with this memorandum for it seemed to him to agree with the scheme he had put before the Cabinet. He wrote to Arnold Morley on May 9:

" Point 1. Taxation. I am instructed, from yesterday, to promise this shall be done if agreeable to the House.

" Point 2. I have authority to speak of this with favour.

" Point 3. To the principle of this I am favourable and I have no reason to believe the Cabinet are hostile. I am not so certain, as with respect to the two former, that a practical proposal can easily be put into shape. But I may refer to the subject in no adverse spirit."

Thus on May 9 Gladstone thought that what Labouchere, who was acting as mediator between Chamberlain and the Government, was proposing was in conformity with the decisions taken by the Cabinet on May 8. His speech follows these lines.

The second question that arises is the intervention of Parnell.

Before submitting his scheme to the Cabinet Gladstone was naturally anxious to learn Parnell's view of it. But Parnell was always elusive and Morley's first efforts to see him failed. Gladstone then sent an S.O.S. to Mrs. O'Shea telling her that Morley wanted urgently to see Parnell. As the Cabinet meeting was to be held on the 8th the urgency is easily understood. Morley saw Parnell that day just after the Cabinet meeting. Here is his account of the interview.

Secret.   Irish Office,
                                                         Gt. Queen St.,

                                                 May 8, 1886. 5.20 p.m.

Dear Mr Gladstone,

I have seen my friend. He is much more stiff against the

retention even than he was before.   His new argument is that their presence would be used as a justification for raising their imperial contribution, and an excuse for varying it, and getting more out of theirs " in our usual rapacious fashion."

However, he sees no decisive sort of objection to any of the points which you intend to throw out on Monday.   He would rather not have the proposal that Irish members should come over if any alteration of taxation were on foot.

But neither that, nor the two other possible suggestions—Standing Committee, and Dale's proviso to Clause 24—will make any difference in their support.

He thinks that we shall win the second reading, but of course he only goes on general probabilities and his instinct—the latter, no bad instrument in his case.

Your's sincerely,
JOHN MORLEY.

Now Gladstone's concessions to Chamberlain were said to have been made during the meeting of the Cabinet.[1]   Gladstone's diary mentions that the Cabinet lasted from 2.30—4.30. Morley's letter is dated 5.20 p.m. of the same day, May 8.   If then any concession had been made outside the concessions suggested in Gladstone's scheme and Parnell had objected to those concessions, Morley would have mentioned this.   But what he says is that Parnell, though more stiff against retention than before (there was no question of yielding on this point on which, as Gladstone said, his Cabinet would split), sees no decisive sort of objection to the concessions Gladstone is to throw out and that the support of his party won't be affected.   In other words what had happened up to this point was that Gladstone had, as he thought, met Chamberlain's objections by the concession he was making on the readmission of Irish members on questions of taxation and Parnell had assured Morley that the Irish party would support him.   No doubt Chamberlain's telegrams of self-congratulation on Gladstone's concession did not make the older man more enthusiastic about concession in itself and therefore when he came to make his speech he threw into three sentences, short and ungracious, what if his temper had been different would have occupied twenty, and assumed a different look.   It was the manner of his speech as much as its matter, that offended Chamberlain.

We get an interesting picture of what happened in Herbert

[1] Garvin, Vol. II, p. 227.

Gladstone's letters to his brother Henry then in India. On May 2 Herbert Gladstone wrote to Labouchere:

Private.   Hawarden,
                                                             May 2, 1886.
Dear Mr. Labouchere

I had to go to Scotland last Tuesday for a funeral and only came back last night when I found your letters.

I think things look a little more hopeful. Tomorrow appears in the Scotch papers a letter from my Father which I have not seen which from what I hear is in the direction of peace. You state his mind on the Exclusion question with perfect correctness and it is true that no working method of retention has yet been propounded. It is of course impossible for the Government to give in to a wish however widely expressed when no one has yet produced a working plan. And as you say a further split in the Cabinet must be avoided at any rate for the present.

Personally I am strongly for retention and I believe that a basis for agreement on this point can and ought to be found. I look on this as the real bone of contention for if the innumerable ultimata have all to be accepted Heaven only knows how the question stands.

The matter must now stand over for a few days so that it may be further considered in London. But I sincerely hope that adjectives will be omitted by all who wish to come to terms when they are dealing in public with the motives and policy of political allies whether in speech or letter. It is not over pleasant when one wishes to be friends to see oneself taunted in public with folly, absurdity, insanity and general wickedness. Unconditional admission cannot be conceded. It would not only give the Irish an absolute predominance in Imperial but also in Scotch and English affairs. If they did not exercise this power the wish to obtain the benefit of it might be too much for the honesty of political parties and Gov^{ts} English and Scotch and to make no attempt to meet these palpable dangers would be incredibly foolish.

But representation should go with taxation and Ireland should have a more or less direct voice and power in relation to those subjects excluded from the cognizance of an Irish Parliament. I don't believe this problem is insoluble but for God's sake let us have a little patience. It is one of the hardest nuts to crack in the whole business and it cannot be done to order at a day's notice or a month's.   But I agree that no time should be lost.

Yours very truly,

HERBERT J. GLADSTONE.

I don't think the ' open ' question will do.   It will be best to arrive at a definite basis of agreement.   Whitbread's plan of an interval spoken of favourably by Morley on Friday doesn't settle but postpone the difficulty.   But it might be adopted so far as direct representation for taxation goes and other machinery might be set up to give Irishmen authority in relation to Imperial and excluded matters at once.

Letter to Henry Gladstone.

House of Commons,

May 7, 1886.

. . . The Whigs declare they are going to win even if we conciliate Chamberlain.   I don't believe it, for much depends on what the Govt. does and no one knows what concessions are likely to be made.   Chamberlain holds out for the principle of the retention of Irish members, and has put himself at the head of about 30 men who have taken this view.   He has a following of 6 in the House personally, and nothing to speak of in the country.   In fact he c^d not make a speech out of B'ham at present. Therefore he may be expected to give in, but he is vain and obstinate.   I found that Father on Wed^y proposed to readmit Irish members for taxing matters where I^d is concerned.   I got him to circulate two other proposals for tomorrow's Cabinet. (1) Irish members (100) to come back here on specific questions and for a given time upon an address to the Crown.   Such an address to be carried by a majority in the Irish Par^{mt}.   (2) Standing Committee of Eng. Scotch and Irish to consider Bills and motions of a secondary character affecting Ireland wh. are excluded from the cognizance of the Irish Par^{mt}.   It appears to me that these 3 proposals meet all the main objections of C. and his friends and from what I have heard about C. and from a long talk with Caine I am inclined to think that we may unite on them if the Cabinet agrees to them.   Father approves of them. If the concession is not made the Bill is dead for the present.   I think however that in all probability this particular difficulty will be overcome. . . .

2 M

Letter from Herbert Gladstone to Henry Gladstone.

War Office,
May 14, 1886.

Since writing things have considerably changed. I give a short history of what has happened since I wrote last week. I told you that Father suggested to the Cabinet some proposals relating to the exclusion of Irish members. On Sat^y they decided to readmit Irish members on taxing matters—and to consider favourably plans for a standing joint Commission to watch Irish interests relating to reserved matters and admission of Irish Members on Address. I knew this w^d not meet Chamberlain's views. I went down to Wolverton's on Sunday and that evening Father told me he had had a letter from A. Morley to the effect that C. was satisfied and w^d come in after Father's speech moving the 2nd R^g on Monday. Knowing what the Cabinet had settled I was surprised but had no grounds for discouraging the idea. The speech on Monday was in many respects a great one especially as against the Tories and Whigs. But the net result was distinctly unfortunate. Everybody had run off with the notion that a basis of agreement had been found and it was a g^t shock to find that there was an uncertainty and an amount of reservation about the Gov^t concessions wh. made C. furious and bitterly disappointed a number of men who had hoped to come in. Much of this was unreasonable. At the same time I c^d not help feeling that the Govt. had not gone far enough, and that Father had not been as clear and forcible as usual in expounding what he proposed to concede. The misunderstanding arose between C., Labouchere and A. Morley but I think it was mostly L's fault. C. immediately seized his advantage and set to work to get the malcontents around him. The meeting at his house was a clever move and secured for him something in the shape of a party, but it was by no means altogether hostile to the Govt. The debate yesterday went off quietly and without special event. James made a moderate and very clever speech. C. Bannerman also very good. Dillon spoke with great force later. Today there has been a meeting at Devonshire House, and I understand H^n and C. have resolved on something like a plan of common future action; and they resolved at all costs to vote against the 2nd R^g. . . .

These letters explain a sentence in the letter that Labouchere wrote to Chamberlain just after the debate when Chamberlain was angry and, as Labouchere thought, angry with good reason. " The funny thing is that Mr Gladstone has walked off under the conviction that his speech was most satisfactory."[1]

[1] Letter to Chamberlain, May 10, 1886. Thorold, *Life of Labouchere*, p. 310,

CHAPTER XXVII

GLADSTONE AND THE EDUCATED CLASSES

A former worshipper of the ex-Prime Minister said to me some time ago " Never in the history of England was there such a consensus of intellect arrayed against statesmen as is now arrayed against Mr Gladstone. What a fall. I rejoice to find this unanimity of judgment so specially illustrated among scientific men." . . .

> John Tyndall: Letter to the *Times*, June 1887.

It may seem a paradox to say that Gladstone's isolation at this time and his confidence came from the same cause. Yet if his position is examined it will be seen that this is true. He was isolated because his fundamental outlook differed from that of the intellectual Liberal; he was confident because he put his faith in the very ideas and beliefs that created that difference between them.

Let us take two statements that describe the perplexity of his intellectual contemporaries about him. One by Leslie Stephen writing on Fawcett; the other by Courtney writing about the Cambridge of the 'sixties.

" Mr Gladstone, if I may say so, was as typical a representative of the Oxford which obeyed the impulse of Newman, as Fawcett of the comparatively plain, practical, and downright Cambridge. Mr Gladstone's astonishing versatility of mind, the power of interesting himself in ancient Greece or in modern theology which relieves his political energy, was a source of wondering amusement to Fawcett's strong, but comparatively limited, intellect. He was rather scandalised than amused by the singular subtlety and ingenuity in presenting unexpected interpretations of apparently plain doctrines which makes the history of Mr Gladstone's opinions so curious a subject for the psychologist."[1]

Courtney, writing after the death of Stephen, described the atmosphere of Cambridge in the 'sixties: " Mr Glad-

[1] Stephen's *Life of Fawcett*, p. 244.

stone was a rising politician whose conclusions were generally right, though it was often difficult to understand how
he had reached them, and in whose future there could be no
certain faith, since it is impossible to say upon what lines it
would be pursued."[1]

Most persons would agree that the masters of Liberalism
as an intellectual force in the days of Gladstone's ascendancy
were Locke, Adam Smith, Bentham and Mill. For how
much (apart from Adam Smith's *Free Trade*) did they count
in Gladstone's development? For nothing of which Gladstone was conscious. Gladstone, writing to an old friend,
Francis Doyle, in 1880, said:

" I was born with smaller natural endowments than you and I
had also a narrower earlier training. But my life has certainly
been remarkable for the mass of continuous and searching
experience it has brought me ever since I began to pass out of
boyhood. I have been feeling my way; owing little to living
teachers, but enormously to four dead ones (over and above the
four gospels). It has been experience which has altered my politics."

Morley adds in a footnote the four dead teachers, " Aristotle,
Augustine, Dante, Butler."[2] Indeed, just as Gladstone
differed from Shaftesbury in diverting to Homer much of the
importance that Shaftesbury would have reserved for the
Old Testament, so he differed from his fellow Liberals in
giving to Butler the importance they gave to Locke and
Bentham. Just as he defended Homer against " the
fanatical Christians " who disparaged Greek culture, as
part of God's manifestation of truth, so he spent his last years
in defending Butler against the criticisms that had been
passed on him by Bagehot, Matthew Arnold, and Leslie
Stephen.[3] Thus his fellow Liberals found him difficult to

---

[1] *The Speaker*, Feb. 27, 1904.
[2] Morley, *Gladstone*, Vol. I, p. 207.
[3] Here he and Newman were on the same side. For whereas James Mill
found the *Analogy* " sceptical in essence " and Martineau called it " one
of the most terrible persuasives to atheism ever produced," Newman spoke of
Butler's " profound investigation," and said that Butler " formed an era in
his religious opinions," and taught him that " the world was a sacramental
system." See *Difficulties felt by Anglicans*, Vol I, p. 3, and Leslie Stephen's
article on Butler in the D.N.B. Gladstone published his *Studies subsidiary to
the Works of Bishop Butler* in 1896.

understand, not merely because of the subtlety and mysti-
fication of his language, but because his opinions were
derived from sources so different and in some aspects so
hostile. Bentham taught him as little[1] as Butler taught
Fawcett.

The full extent of this difference was described in a letter
in which Acton took him to task for some of his observations
in his review of *Robert Elsemere*. He complained that
Gladstone had been much too kind to the Christian Church
and overlooked its crimes:

"There is much to deduct from the praise of the Church in
protecting marriage, abolishing slavery and human sacrifice,
preventing war, and helping the poor. No deduction can be
made from her evil-doing towards unbelievers, heretics, savages,
and witches. . . . It was the negation not only of religious
liberty, which is the mainspring of civil, but equally of civil
liberty, because a government armed with the machinery of the
Inquisition is necessarily absolute. So that if Liberalism has a
desperate foe it is the Church, as it was in the West, between 1200
and 1600 or 1700. The philosophy of Liberal history which
has to acknowledge the invaluable services of early Christianity,
feels at the same time rather more strongly the anti-liberal and
anti-social action of later Christianity, before the rise of the
sects which rejected, some the divinity of Christ, others, the
institutions of the Church erected upon it. Liberalism, if it
admits these things as adiaphora, surrenders its own *raison
d'être*, and ceases to strive for an ethical cause. To speak with
unabated reverence of the actual Christianity as it prevailed
from Innocent III to Bossuet and Oates, would imply that the
moral evil bore no proportion to the dogmatic merit, that so
orthodox an institution could not be employed to do the devil's
work and people hell. Whatever we think of the faith, we must
condemn the works."

He concludes that it might be said that " you do not work
really from the principle of Liberalism, but from the cognate
though distinct principle of Democracy, Nationality, Progress
etc." " If I had to put my own doubts instead of the

---

[1] Of course as a pupil of Peel he owned a great deal to Bentham, but this
was not a direct or conscious influence.

average Liberal's, I should state the case in other terms, but not altogether differently."[1]

Gladstone remained a heretic on Locke to the end of his days. Morley reports in his *Life* a conversation in December 1891 in which he tried to get Gladstone to admit that Locke must be regarded as one of the great Oxford names of the eighteenth century.

" This brought on a tremendous tussle, for Mr G was of the same mind, and perhaps for the same sort of reason, as Joseph de Maistre, that contempt for Locke is the beginning of knowledge. All very well for De Maistre, but not for a man in line with European liberalism. . . . From the point of view of influence Locke was the origin of the emancipatory movement of the eighteenth century abroad, and laid the philosophic foundations of liberalism in civil government at home. . . . To minds nursed in dogmatic schools, all this is both unpalatable and incredible."[2]

If Acton and Morley saw how wide was the divergence between Gladstone and the intellectual Liberals, it is not surprising that those Liberals were very conscious of it. For the truth was that Gladstone's letter to Doyle summed up very truly what had happened to him. His liberal views were not a body of truth acquired from the study of masters like Locke, Bentham, and Mill; they were the effect of experience on a mind nursed on Aristotle, Augustine, Dante, and Butler. When a young man he had written to his father:

" New principles prevail in morals, politics, education. Enlightened self-interest is made the substitute for the old bonds of unreasoned attachment, and under the plausible maxim that knowledge is power, one kind of ignorance is made to take the place of another kind. Christianity teaches that the head is to be exalted through the heart, but Benthamism maintains that the heart is to be amended through the head."[3]

Those sentences were written by Gladstone in 1832; he

---

[1] Letter from Acton to Gladstone, May 2, 1888. *Acton's Correspondence*, Laurence and Figgis, pp. 217–218.

[2] *Gladstone*, Vol. III, p. 476.

[3] Morley, *Gladstone*, Vol. I, p. 82.

could have written them in 1892.[1] But whereas in 1832
his adaptation of these ideas to politics made him a Conservative, in 1892 it made him a Liberal.   It had made him
accept conclusions which others had reached from quite
different premises.

To understand the broad difference between Gladstone
and the intellectual Liberals it is useful to glance at Bergson's
work, *Les deux sources de la réligion et la morale*.   Bergson
argues that nature teaches man to live in small societies,
and that it needs something more than nature and reason
to give him the impulse to desire the unity of the world.
This love of man belongs to his spiritual nature.   Man can
only find the spirit of brotherhood by grasping a relationship
that comes from the common fatherhood of God.   Gladstone's strongest feeling was for the unity of the world, and he
found this taught and symbolized by the Christian religion.
God, after teaching the world a great deal about civilized
life by Greek culture and Latin politics, had taught this
supreme lesson of universal brotherhood by the Incarnation.[2]
This was the light that guided Gladstone's politics.   Whereas
many dreamed of the unity of mankind as the final triumph
of the recognition of the rights of man, he dreamed of it
as the final triumph of the recognition of the common
fatherhood of God.

Now the Liberals who deduced their principles from
Locke and Bentham were often men of Christian belief
but their political ideas did not come from their Christianity.
Gladstone, as we have seen, seemed to Acton to exaggerate

---

[1] For his whole life rested on the belief that Bridges put into the *Testament of Beauty*:

> " In truth ' spiritual animal ' wer a term for man
> nearer than ' rational ' to define his genus;
> Faith being the humanizer of his brutal passions,
> the clarifier of folly and medicine of care,
> the clue of reality, and the driving motiv
> of thatt self-knowledge which teacheth the ethick of life."
>
> Book IV, 1132.

[2] Most of Gladstone's religious writings are to be found in his *Gleanings from Past Years*, published in 1879.

In writing this chapter I have been greatly helped and guided by reading in type the important discussion of this large theme in Mr. Arnold Toynbee's *Study of History*, Vol. VI.

the part played by Christianity in civilizing the world, and to ignore what had been done by Liberalism. Bergson himself observes that the Christian idea spread slowly, and that it was not until the American Declaration of Independence that it received a formal acknowledgment. In that declaration the rights of man are traced to God. But all the emphasis that Liberals would put on the Revolutions, American and French, in the assertion of large human ideas, Gladstone put on the Christian religion. Here, as Acton showed, he came into conflict with the intellectual Liberals. For the history of Christianity was the history of institutions as well as of ideas, the Church had often been one of the Secular Powers, seeking the same ends as her rivals, using the same means, and committing the same crimes, and the liberties Liberalism had won for mankind had been won, often by sacrifice and suffering, from a persecuting Church professing the principles that Gladstone cherished as the source of his large and generous sympathies. It is not surprising that, as Morley listened to his disparagement of Locke, he regarded Gladstone as the prisoner of dogmatic systems.

But the prisoner of the dogmatic systems did not receive help or countenance from those politicians who regarded the defence of the Anglican dogmatic system as their special care. Gladstone, who was losing the confidence of the intellectual Liberals in the 'eighties, had lost the confidence of the educated Churchmen long before. It was not that they could convict him of shifting or shaken faith. " The fundamentals of Christian dogma," says Morley, " so far as I know and am entitled to speak, are the only region in which Mr Gladstone's opinions have no history."[1] But on the spirit in which a man holding those dogmas should look on politics his opinions had of course an important and exciting history. He had begun his political life thinking that " men who have no belief in the divine revelation are not the men to govern this nation."[2] For, as he explained in his early book *The State in its relation to the Church* (1838)

---

[1] Morley, *Gladstone*, Vol. I, p. 207.
[2] Morley, *Gladstone*, Vol. I, p. 138.

he believed that "the State should and could propagate religious truth and discourage religious error." His Christian dogmas had remained but his Christianity had learnt tolerance and wisdom from his experience of life and man. His enlightenment was slow and sometimes reluctant, as was shown in the course his mind took on University tests, for, though he consented to make abolition a Government measure in 1871, he had been strongly hostile as late as 1865. Gradually he had surrendered one after another of the privileges that the Established Church enjoyed, as he found that those privileges were a weakness rather than a strength to her spiritual influence. Thus, though his attachment to Christian dogma was as deep as that of Salisbury and Carnarvon, he seemed to them and to men like them a bad friend to the Church, because he took a different view of the value of its political and legal privileges. The Bradlaugh case brought out this contrast very clearly, for the whole Conservative party in the House of Commons voted against him, though his speech exposing the worthlessness of the Parliamentary oath was the most solemn and moving defence of Christian doctrine ever heard in the House of Commons. It is at once a measure of his magnanimity and his sincerity that the finest speech made in Parliament on a religious controversy was made by the most devout of its members, in defence of the rights of a man who was chiefly known to his fellow countrymen as a militant atheist.

Bradlaugh, on his election to the House of Commons in 1880 as Member of Parliament for Northampton, claimed the right to make an affirmation of allegiance instead of taking the Parliamentary oath. Then followed a series of blunders in which weakness, cowardice, party spirit, and religious passion all had their share. The Speaker referred the question to the House of Commons which appointed a Select Committee. This Committee reported by a majority of one against Bradlaugh's claim. The minority included such names as Sir Henry James, Herschell, afterwards Lord Chancellor, John Bright, and Whitbread. Bradlaugh then proposed to take the oath, but the Speaker, in answer to an appeal from a member who recalled Bradlaugh's earlier statement that the oath would not bind his conscience, would not allow him. A second Committee was then set up, and this Committee reported that Bradlaugh should not be allowed to take the oath, but recommended that he should be permitted to affirm at his own risk: the risk that is of an action in the Courts. But the House of Commons rejected this plan by 275 votes to 230. For the Fourth Party had seen the great opportunities of the case for party tactics, since Bradlaugh was known far and wide as an atheist and a preacher of birth control, and Churchill and his friends saw that they had here an issue on which they could mobilise, not only religious sentiment, but respectable sentiment, against the Government. The *Daily Telegraph* had already accused Ministers of the " open patronage of unbelief and Malthusianism." There thus began a struggle between Bradlaugh and a majority in the House of Commons, which was not unlike the earlier struggle between another House of Commons and John Wilkes. The House of Commons would not let Bradlaugh take the oath or affirm, and expelled him whenever he attempted to take his seat. His constituents stuck to him, and re-elected him as often as the House expelled him.

In April 1883 the Government brought in a Bill to put an end to this scandal by amending the Parliamentary Oath and allowing affirmation. The Oath had already been amended, first to admit Catholics, and then to admit Jews. But the Fourth Party, representing what Churchill called the " unerring instinct of the House," was not going to surrender the advantage of Bradlaugh's unpopularity, and, as its noise and truculence dominated the Opposition, the Bill was fought by every device that was possible and was ultimately defeated by three votes.

In defending this Bill Gladstone spoke as Morley had said under circumstances of unexampled difficulty. " There was revolt in the party, the client was repugnant, the opinions brought into issue were to Mr Gladstone hateful." Nobody could vote for the Bill without the risk of being branded in his constituency as an atheist and a neo-Malthusian, and in those days it was as great a sin to advocate birth control as to deny the existence of God. No less than 3,000 petitions were presented to the House of Commons against the Bill. In the House of Commons the Radicals had often helped the Irish Nationalists, and Bradlaugh had been one of eight English Members to support Parnell's amendment to the Address. But Manning had called on the Catholics to reject the Bill, the Catholic Bishops had condemned it, and the Irish members, almost without exception, voted against Gladstone.[1] It was under all these difficulties that Gladstone made the speech which was described by so cold a critic as the *Times* as not only a great speech but as the only great speech produced by the long struggle over the Bill.[2]

Gladstone was thus isolated in the educated and leisured world because few Christians in that world gave to Christianity, and few Liberals gave to Liberalism, the form and colour that he gave to them. Now the Irish case happened

---

[1] Newman differed from Manning and the Bishops. He stated at the time to a friend that he would have signed the petition but only not to be singular. " For I think it a piece of humbug and no good would come of the Bill's being rejected and no harm by its passing. . . . I was obliged to write a letter to say that I neither approved of it nor disapproved,—that it was a mere political bill with which I had nothing to do." Ward, *Life of Newman*, Vol. II, p. 521. During the debate on Bradlaugh's Bill in 1888 a Catholic Member, De Lisle, speaking against the Bill, quoted a declaration by Newman on the Bill of 1883 which resembled very closely Gladstone's own argument. " I cannot consider the Affirmation Bill involves a religious principle for as I had occasion to observe in print more than thirty years ago, what the political and social world means by the word God is too often not the Christian nor the Jewish nor the Mahommedan God nor a personal God. . . . Hence it little concerns religion whether Mr Bradlaugh swears by no God, or by an impersonal material, or an abstract or ideal something or other." *Hansard*. March 14, 1888.

[2] The sequel is a bitter comment on the passions and artifices of the House of Commons. For the storm that had raged so violently fell as suddenly as it had risen. The new Parliament of 1886 had a new Speaker, Peel, and when Hicks Beach on behalf of the Government contended that Bradlaugh should not be allowed to take his seat, Peel, a man of decision, brushed him aside, and Bradlaugh who had gone out of the last House of Commons as a lion, entered the new House as a lamb. In 1888 the man who had so often been expelled from the House had the satisfaction of passing a Bill to abolish the oath, and in January 1891, when Bradlaugh was on his death bed, the House of Commons unanimously rescinded the original resolution excluding him. The second reading of Bradlaugh's Bill was carried by 250 to 150 on March 14, 1888. On this occasion the Irish voted with Bradlaugh.

to bring to a sharp issue the difference between his outlook and that of the enlightened and scientific mind of that age. There were many reasons why a man who was neither reactionary nor illiberal in his general view might mistrust the Home Rule policy. There were many arguments that might be brought against it. Was the passionate desire of a small people to be set against the convenience, perhaps the safety, of the British Empire? Did the doctrine of the greatest happiness of the greatest number teach you to consider the four millions of Irishmen or the twenty millions of Englishmen? Would not Home Rule spread confusion, strengthen the power of a Church that many Englishmen held to be a danger to liberty, and throw back this small people into a smaller world of its own, making it still more insular. Was not the influence of education and enlightenment in the government of the world likely to diminish? Was not Gladstone who urged this reform a man apt to be carried away by sentimental ideas and insufficiently protected by scientific principles?

Gladstone had his own answer to these questions, but his fundamental argument would have been that to deny this desire of a small people was to deny something that Christians could not deny, if they were to be obedient to the spirit of their religion. For Gladstone saw in the world on one side power, force, and violence, all the influences that divided mankind. He saw on the other the movement towards the moral unity of the world, based on mutual respect between peoples. That unity has inspired teachers of one kind or another from early times. Mr. Tarn traces it to Alexander; others trace it first to the Stoic philosopher Zeno. Gladstone found its first great message to mankind in Christianity. For him then the issue was between these two principles, between living with another people in the spirit of Empire and repression, or living with that people in the spirit of fellowship and sympathy. Thus the last great struggle in which he was engaged represented more dramatically than any other struggle in his career the dominant passion of his mind.

This caused not only his isolation but his confidence. He

was not daunted by the overwhelming hostility that surrounded him. For in this encounter between his mystical temperament and the scientific mind, there was on both sides a certain tendency to disparage the other. The men of science, judging him by his rash excursions into fields where he was weak and ill equipped, could neither understand nor appreciate his moral and intellectual power: when they understood him, they often found him wrong: when they did not understand him, they thought him, as Acton thought Newman, a sophist.[1] His schoolman's delight in fine drawn distinctions, his equal readiness to fight for the shadow or the substance, a comma or a creed, his controversialist's skill in twisting and doubling, his obstinacy in acknowledging error and persistence in defending it, Gladstone's besetting sins in contention,[2] seemed to them the signs of a man without principle. And the solemn religious cast of his life and mind aggravated this suspicion. Leslie Stephen told how F. D. Maurice, lecturing at Cambridge on the character and conduct of Jacob, remarked:

" After all, my brethren, this story illustrates the tendency of the spiritual man in all ages to be a liar and a sneak." " Nobody," says Stephen, " it is superfluous to add, was less of a liar or a sneak than Maurice. But the ' tendency ' may lead the spiritual man to do quite innocently what in other men can only be done by deliberate self-mystification. I, not being a spiritual man, must have deserved one or both of these epithets had I continued to set forth as solemn truths narratives which I could not spiritualise and which seemed to me to be exploded legends implying a crude and revolting morality."[3]

Gladstone was a spiritual man, but he was also a subtle and indirect man. In the fierce contests of the time, it was not surprising that some of his opponents judged him shifty and insincere. If he thought, as he told Mrs. Gladstone, that the battle between Christian belief and this challenging science was more important than any political issue, it is not

---

[1] " That splendid sophist." Letter to Gladstone, August 18, 1890.
[2] Both Edward Hamilton and Kilbracken noted this weakness.
[3] *Leslie Stephen* by Desmond MacCarthy, p. 30.

strange that those engaged on the other side took an equally serious view of that issue. The Church, in whose history Gladstone found such noble pages, had committed crime after crime against freedom, reason, and justice. Acton had put this aspect plainly and bluntly when he said that the great Liberals of the past had " swept away the appalling edifice of intolerance, tyranny and cruelty which believers in Christ had built up to perpetuate their belief." In obeying the teaching of the Church man had often accepted false ideas and missed the light. Science was destroying one after another of these false notions and guiding man out of the dark. Gladstone sought to keep him in the dark. Both his integrity and his wisdom were under a cloud.

But, if the men of science despised him, Gladstone on his part did not attach considerable importance to their judgment. The Irish issue was, so far as they were concerned, a political issue and a political issue alone. They could not follow him into the transcendental mysteries in which he had found the ultimate reason for his policy. For them there was no question of religious truth behind the proposal to set up a Parliament in Dublin. But was their judgment of politics not affected by their cold science? Perhaps we get a glimpse into Gladstone's mind on this question in the very interesting article he wrote on *The Courses of Religious Thought* in the *Contemporary Review* in January 1876. In this article he discusses five main schools or systems which he divides up thus:

1. Those who accept the Papal monarchy or the Ultramontane school.

2. Those who rejecting the Papal monarchy believe in the visibility of the Church; or the Historical School.

3. Those who rejecting the Papal monarchy and the visibility of the Church, believe in the great central dogmas of the Christian system, the Trinity and the Incarnation. These will be here termed the Protestant Evangelical School.

4. The two other systems were the Theistic and the Negative. By " Negative," that is to say, as to thought which can be called religious in the accustomed sense.

In his discussion of the last category he has some interesting reflexions, on the value a man may find in Pantheism or Positivism as an object of reverence, a restraint on tendencies to evil, a consolation in adversity and so on. He then proceeds:

" But, as in wines, it is one question what mode of composition will produce a commodity drinkable in the country of origin, and what further provision may be requisite in order that the product may bear a sea voyage without turning into vinegar, so, in the matter of belief, select individuals may subsist on a poor, thin, sodden, and attenuated diet, which would simply be death to the multitude. Schemes, then, may suffice for the moral wants of a few intellectual and cultivated men, which cannot be propagated, and cannot be transmitted; which cannot bear the wear and tear of constant re-delivery; which cannot meet the countless and ever-shifting exigencies of our nature taken at large; which cannot do the rough work of the world. The colours, that will endure through the term of a butterfly's existence would not avail to carry the works of Titian down from generation to generation and century to century. Think of twelve agnostics, or twelve pantheists, or twelve materialists, setting out from some modern Jerusalem to do the work of the twelve Apostles!"[1]

In another passage in the same article he contrasts Christianity with Monotheism, " a system dry, abstract, unattractive, without a way to the general heart."

" We live, as men, in a labyrinth of problems, and of moral problems, from which there is no escape permitted us. The prevalence of pain and sin, the limitations of free will, approximating sometimes to its virtual extinction, the mysterious laws of our independence, the indeterminateness for most or many men of the discipline of life, the cross purposes that seem at so many points to traverse the dispensations of an Almighty benevolence, can only be encountered by a large, an almost immeasurable suspense of judgment. Solution for them we have none.

" But a scheme came eighteen hundred years ago into the

---

[1] *Gleanings of Past Years.* Vol. III, p. 127, In his article on Leopardi he writes more severely of what Wellington called " fancy religions," for he says of Leopardi that he had not " the presumption of those who, having hidden from their view the sun of the Gospel and created a darkness for themselves, light some farthing candle of their own in its stead." *Gleanings*, II, p. 105.

world, which is an earnest and harbinger of solution: which has banished from the earth, or frightened into the darkness, many of the foulest monsters that laid waste humanity; which has restored woman to her place in the natural order; which has set up the law of right against the rule of force; which has proclaimed, and in many great particulars enforced, the rule of mutual love; which has opened from within sources of strength for poverty and weakness, and put a bit in the mouth, and a bridle on the neck, of pride. In a word, this scheme, by mitigating the present pressure of one and all of these tremendous problems, has entitled itself to be heard when it boldly assures us that a day will come, in which we shall know as we are known, and when their pressure shall no longer baffle the strong intellects and characters among us, nor drive the weaker even to despair."[1]

In judging Gladstone's criticisms of the intellectuals on politics, we must note that in the first of these passages he is defending Christianity, not as a body of truth, but as a great civilizing power in the world. He was conscious, of course, of the crimes of the Church, even if he gave them less than their due importance. But he is thinking of Christianity as a moral force, looking at its influence on the habits and conduct and emotions. And the men of science seemed to him to want to substitute for this powerful civilization, powerful in its appeal to men and women in great societies, a dry abstract scheme that could not touch the imagination or fill man's dreams. Thus, while they distrusted him for his crude treatment of problems on which they had expert knowledge, he distrusted them for taking, what seemed to him, too limited and bare a view of the range of the problem with which man's moral teachers are concerned, and too ambitious a view of the place science could claim in the interpretation of moral consciousness. And here, as it happened, one of the leading Liberals agreed with him. After the General Election of 1880 Morley wrote to him:

" I am sorry to say that it is quite true that Huxley (and also

[1] *Gleanings of Past Years*, Vol. III, p. 124. It is interesting to contrast Gladstone's hopeful reading of history with the gloom into which meditation on the past of man threw Newman, Newman with whom he had so much in common. " If I looked into a mirror, and did not see my face, I should have the sort of feeling which actually comes upon me, when I look into this living busy world, and see no reflexion of its Creator." (*Apologia*, p. 241.)

Tyndall) did not wish well to the liberal cause. Darwin, on the other hand, was staunch throughout. For myself, I have always felt that the scientific specialist is most likely of all men to lose the useful and human point of view. His mind is inevitably narrowed, I fear, by the narrowness or minuteness of the specialist's conception of Truth; and this narrow view of Truth chokes his care for Freedom and Humanity. It would be interesting to consider how, by different paths, the men of science and their foes, the priests (Anglican no less than Roman), have come to the same disregard for political morality."[1]

Gladstone then would have said of the men of science that they were apt to take the narrow view of the specialist. But he would also have held that they lacked certain faculties and faculties of importance for judging questions of politics. " A man may be partially or wholly deity blind," says Alexander, " as he is stone deaf, or has no attunement with scientific truth; he may lack the emotional suggestibility for deity."[2] The same truth is put by Delisle Burns: " Clearly the sense of deity is not universal. At any rate, some men and some groups of men seem to have very little of it. The acuteness of the sense varies from the vague feeling that something strange is near, which may exist in conventional churchgoers and temple worshippers, to the insight of religious genius. Those who have had the sense of deity in an exceptional degree have evidently added not merely to religious but to the whole of experience; for just as the passion of love for a person may irradiate the whole of a situation, and improve the sight of common things, so the insight of religious genius may deeply affect morality and social policy."[3] Gladstone regarded men who lacked his own mystical sense as suffering from this kind of blindness: a kind of mental deficiency.[4] There is a letter from him to Döllinger in 1889 who had expressed a fear that their difference of view on Home Rule (Döllinger took the conventional German view) might disturb their enjoyment of their friendship. " Tolerance of differences of opinion," he replied, " is for me a

---

[1] Hirst, *Early Life and Letters of John Morley*, Vol. II, p. 89.
[2] *Space, Time and Deity*, II, 378.
[3] Delisle Burns, *The Horizon of Experience*, 288.
[4] See *The Nature of the Physical World*, p. 322.

much easier matter than you might possibly suppose. My profession as a politician has both great dangers and great advantages. One of its advantages is not only to inculcate this tolerance, but to make it a matter of first necessity. It is part of my daily practice, in cases infinitely more searching, than a difference between you and me on Home Rule in Ireland. For instance; I am in close, harmonious, and daily political co-operation with a man who is not a Christian. And I do not find even this burden to be severe, or at least intolerable, because I have confidence in his rectitude and believe (able as he is) in his ' invincible ignorance.' The only case where the trial becomes too formidable is where the conflict of opinion seems to be traceable to some misconception of the first principles of right."[1]

Now Gladstone did not think it surprising that men should be found who combined great gifts with the lack of this mystical sense. As early as 1850 he had discussed in an article on Leopardi the " conjunction, so paradoxical to us, between the moral and intellectual gifts of Leopardi and his blindness to the Christian faith " and he argued that when you considered all the tragical circumstances of Leopardi's life, you could see that the " genius, attended commonly with a highly acute and susceptible nervous organization, would, in all probability, render him not more, but far less, able to maintain the perfect equilibrium of his mind than one who had less weight to carry in his ever-labouring brain, a fire less intense burning within him."[2]

Here we can detect a resemblance to Newman. Newman, looking out on the world and on history, threw up his hands in despair. " Here," he said in substance, " is a world so wicked that we can only conclude that it has been discarded by God. All that He can do for it is to set up the Catholic Church as a witness to the truths it has abandoned." Gladstone, in one sense, went to the other extreme. Here, he said, we can see what Christianity has done for the world, putting down or mitigating abuses of the pre-Christian world, in respect of the treatment of women, of slaves, of the poor, and of the behaviour of nation to nation. But Gladstone

---

[1] Quoted Hammond, *Shaftesbury*, 4th edition, Appendix: " Shaftesbury and Gladstone," p. 287.
[2] *Gleanings*, II, 116.

agreed with Newman that the first revelation of the truth by God to man had been confused and degraded in the interval between that revelation and the Incarnation. " The heathen religion," said Newman, " was a true religion corrupted; the Jewish a true religion dead; Christianity the true religion living and perfect."[1]   Newman spoke of

" the all-corroding, all-dissolving scepticism of the intellect in religious inquiries. . . . I know that even the unaided reason, when correctly exercised, leads to a belief in God, in the immortality of the soul, and in a future retribution; but I am considering the faculty of reason actually and historically; and in this point of view, I do not think I am wrong in saying that its tendency is towards a simple unbelief in matters of religion. No truth, however sacred, can stand against it, in the long run; and hence it is that in the pagan world, when our Lord came, the last traces of the religious knowledge of former times were all but disappearing from those portions of the world in which the intellect had been active and had had a career."[2]

Gladstone in his Homeric studies had also drawn a contrast between the survival " of the truth brought by our first parents from Paradise " in Homer's Olympus with the speculations on religion in the time of Cicero.   The abstract gods in Cicero were far more elevated than the personal gods of Homer, but in the course of this change the belief in a real Providence, overseeing the affairs of men, had been lost.   The starting point was belief in a Moral Ruler of the universe; then came the deterioration in the character of Olympus and man, finding his gods so unsatisfactory, took refuge in the Lucretian theory that the gods take no interest in man.   Then comes " the transition . . . from gods with a sinecure to no gods at all: and Paganism ends in nullity, just as a moving mass finds its final equilibrium in repose."[3]

Readers of Gladstone's great speech on the Bradlaugh case will remember that part of his argument was that the oath which Parliament wished to force on Bradlaugh was

---

[1] *Parochial Sermons*, Vol. V, p. 170.

[2] *Apologia*, p. 243.   Cp. Donne, *The Litany*.

"Let not my mind be blinder by more light
Nor Faith, by Reason added, lose her sight."

[3] *Homer and the Homeric Age*, Vol. II, p. 392.

an oath that could be taken by a man who held the view described in the famous lines of Lucretius, and that it was the shallowest kind of reasoning that could see in such an oath any defence of the Christian religion.   For that oath embraced no acknowledgment of providence, of divine government, of responsibility, or of retribution.   The great danger of the time was not atheism but the form of opinion " which would teach us that, whatever there may be beyond the visible things of this world, whatever there may be beyond this short span of life, you know and can know nothing of it, and that it is a bootless undertaking to attempt to establish relations with it." This tendency Gladstone found more general among the upper ruling class and intellectual class than among the common people.   And when he found that popular audiences were more ready to listen to arguments in which self-interest and pride were subordinated to higher principles, he associated their emotions with their mysticism. He thought they had escaped the mistake, which he described in his early criticism of Bentham, as that of overestimating the power of the head to amend the heart.   Huxley said that Gladstone had the greatest intellect in Europe, and that he degraded it by following majorities.   Nobody could say this of his Irish crusade.   But educated men looked with suspicion and resentment on this belief that the highest wisdom was to be found in what Meredith called " the God in the conscience of multitudes."

This combination of Liberalism and mystical Christianity, which separated Gladstone from the educated classes, explains what is at first sight the strange affinity between this High Churchman and the Nonconformists.   For one reason why he was so powerful a popular leader was that his religion had something in common with the religion of the poor, whereas it had nothing in common with the religion of the rich.   Neither rich nor poor would have been very much interested in his general outlook on Christian history, or his admiration of the Fathers, or his eager solicitude about the theology of Homer.   But Christianity as a spiritual power, a bond between men and nations, a great principle to which all reasons of empire and state must give way, in other words, Christianity in all those aspects for which it hardly existed in the politics of the upper classes, had a vital significance for the Miners' Leaders, who were trade union secretaries in the week and local preachers on the Sunday.

In all religious history we can discern two forces: the missionary force and the conservative force; the fervour that marks the crusader, and the prudence that marks the guardian of institutions. The Established Church, steeped in the second spirit, regarded Gladstone's view of Home Rule, that it was a debt England owed to her Christian conscience, as the House of Lords regarded it; it was a dangerous and unreasonable doctrine. In these circles Christianity had long since lost the character it possessed when first it made its way in the Roman Empire, a religion, as Toynbee puts it, of the proletariate. This spirit so strong in the Church was found also in the organized religious life of England outside it, for the Nonconformist world had its conservative leaders, and its conservative churches with the same statesmanlike suspicion of absolute values, of moral disturbance, of rash impulse. But the other religious force was also active for the fervour of a proletarian religion still survived, rekindled a century earlier by the man of genius whose power and courage had led Newman to compare him to St. Francis.[1] It survived in the simple

---

[1] " The Established Church may have preserved in the country the idea of sacramental grace, and the movement of 1833 may have spread it; but if you wish to find the shadow and the suggestion of the supernatural qualities which make up the notion of a Catholic saint, to Wesley you must go and such as him. Personally I do not like him, if it were merely for his deep self-reliance and self-conceit; still I am bound in justice to him, to ask, and you in consistency to answer, what historical personage in the establishment, during its whole three centuries, has approximated in force and splendour of conduct and achievement to one who began by innovating on your rules and ended by contemning your authorities." *Difficulties felt by Anglicans*, Vol. I, p. 90. Cp. Gladstone's first talk with Döllinger in 1845: " What I like perhaps most, or what crowns other causes of liking towards him, is that he, like Rio, seems to take hearty interest in the progress of religion in the church of England, apart from the (so to speak) party question between us, and to have a mind to appreciate good wherever he can find it. For instance, when in speaking of Wesley I said that his own views and intuitions were not heretical, and that if the ruling power in our church had had energy and a right mind to turn him to account, or if he had been in the church of Rome I was about to add, he would

humanity of the small chapel and in great numbers of workmen, some of them professing Methodist principles, others not Methodist in name but living in the Methodist culture inherited from their fathers. Thus, when Gladstone summoned the nation to a Christian duty, he found himself, like a second Wesley, mistrusted by the religion of the upper classes, followed by the religion of the common people.

Gladstone, then, was not afraid of the great solid hostility of the educated classes. His confidence was not shaken. They on their side liked his rhetoric all the less because of the religious atmosphere of his life. For he could not be better described than by inverting what Mr. Desmond MacCarthy said about Leslie Stephen. " He had never associated religion with his most valued emotions towards nature and man." If the word " never " is changed to the word " always " the sentence will give the most important truth about Gladstone. Now a man who practises a spiritual life with such devotion and ardour will often seem either ridiculous or egotistical to the man who is without this spiritual faculty, whether he rejects Christianity, or has what Gladstone described as " the commonplace and every-day Christianity of the lip." The man who lacks the mystical sense may in some cases envy and admire the man in whom the sense of a divine presence irradiating the soul is, not only one of the obvious facts of experience, but the most important of those facts. Gladstone, for whom " the unseen thus took shape to common eye," was no doubt passionately admired by many who had no share in his religious ideas or his religious sense. But to a great many this side of his character was unintelligible and alien.

For the importance Gladstone attached to his spiritual life, to the ordinances and ritual by which concentration on religious study and religious meditation was encouraged, seemed to them excessive and unbalanced. He

then have been a great saint, or something to that effect. But I hesitated, thinking it perhaps too strong, and even presumptuous, but he took me up and used the very words, declaring that to be his opinion." Morley, *Gladstone*, Vol. I, p. 319.

only spent three weeks in Ireland, in Ireland with all her problems, and during those three weeks he was vitally interested in the sermons he heard in Anglican pulpits, and in the habits of the great houses where he stayed in respect of family prayers. We have remarked one characteristic that he shared with Shaftesbury, the belief that God was taking special care of him because he had been given a mission. In his diary he carries this belief to great lengths, noting how often he had a fine day for a great monster meeting, and wondering why men in face of such facts can doubt the existence of Providence. This kind of conviction gave him great strength, but it is easy to see that it is a kind of egotism for which a man must suffer. Gladstone's character and mind were such a labyrinth, his nature was so full of surprises, his actions were often so difficult to understand, that men in the circle of cynical politics found it hard to believe that his mysticism was as simple as it seemed. Gladstone told the Queen in 1880 that he would not have allowed himself to use the language about the Eastern question of which she complained, if he had been a leader of a party, or had looked upon himself as a man about to take office. He justified, first his violence to Austria as a private politician, and then his acceptance of power, on the ground that in both cases he was obeying a divine summons. As, in their view, he acted on both occasions as he would have acted if he had consulted his own feelings, they found it difficult to believe that he was always able to distinguish between the will of Gladstone and the will of God.

Thus, in his last great battle for a great cause, he found himself, mistrusted and disliked, fighting against the class in which he was born and brought up, what seemed to most educated men a desperate cause, and yet he was confident of victory. But his confidence did not blind him to the character of his task. In many of his controversies he was unskilful, imperious, sophistical, and impatient. Readers who turn to the little volume he published on the Irish question in 1886 will be struck by his moderation and care, by his avoidance of doubtful arguments, by the impression he gives of a wisdom that was neither discouraged, nor embittered, as he saw his long life setting, not in gentle peace, but in such storms as he had not had to face in the days of his unabated strength. For never in his career had he been so certain that his judgment was right and his conscience clear.[1]

APPENDIX TO CHAPTER XXVII

GLADSTONE ON NEWMAN AND BUTLER

To Sir F. Rogers (afterwards Lord Blachford).

Windsor Castle,

February 25, 1866.

My dear Rogers,

I have read, or rather reread, those fine sermons, and will return the volume tomorrow, which you so kindly lent me; but, though with a great deference to your opinion, I hold firmly to my own, that the ' Ecce Homo ' cannot be by Dr Newman. I please myself with thinking that in this busy age, quick at sapping and dissolving, but commonly not masculine enough in thought to construct, the author of this volume may have been sent among us as a builder, and may perform a great work for truth and for mankind.

I have called the two sermons ' fine.' It is a poor word for them. I do not know if Newman's style affects others as I find myself affected by it. It is a transporting style. I find myself constantly disposed to cry aloud, and vent myself in that way,

---

[1] Early in the struggle Tennyson had sent him a few lines from Pindar, which might be read as a warning from an old friend against pulling down a constitution. Gladstone replied that he regarded Home Rule as essentially conservative in character. He went on:

" According to the laws of human nature it is difficult to suppose that at seventy-six, with senses gradually closing in, and memory for all things recent failing fast, I can have thrown myself into the midst of these tempestuous billows without these two things, first a clear conviction and secondly a strong sense of personal call. For 42 years out of the 54 years of my public life Ireland has had rather a dominant influence over it; which is there of my opponents that has had occasion to study it as resolutely and for the same time? . . . I feel a strong assurance that the subject of In Memoriam would have been with us and I cannot surrender hope of the author."[2] Letter to Tennyson, April 26, 1886.

as I read. It is like the very highest music, and seems sometimes in beauty to go beyond the human.

It is a *kind* of beauty far above the ordinary beauties of style, like the drawing of Raphael compared with the drawing of ordinary painters. It calls back to me a line in which I think (but it is long since I read it) Dante describes his own *religious* ecstasies: " Che fece me da me uscir di mente."

And yet (I do not know if you agree with me) I think Newman is not, and never was, a philosopher—a philosopher, I mean, in the sense of Butler.

He has not the balance of mind, and his aspects of truth are partial: he is not well settled on a centre of gravity, his plumb-line is not true.

I think there is nothing more characteristic of the unphilosophic mind than impatience of doubt and premature avidity for system. That seems to me (especially after the revelations of the " Apologia ") to have been Newman's snare all along. No man can grasp truth entire. Butler took it in fragments, but his wise instinct enabled him so to lay each stone that it would fit in with every stone which might be well and truly laid in the double light of thought and of experience. He is now in his second century, and his works are at once younger and older than when he wrote them: older, because confirmed by the testing operations of other minds, younger, because with not only fuller and broader, but with, so to speak, more flexible foundations adaptive to the present and the coming needs of the human mind. Newman also laid his stones; but at every period of his life he seems to have been driven by a fatal necessity to piece them all together, to make a building of them, and he has made half a dozen; and when the winds blew and the floods beat they gave way, and if the one he now inhabits seems to him firmer than the rest, I do believe it may be the result of little else than weariness of mind at so many painful efforts and (to a man of his intense feelings and perceptions) so many sad collapses. And yet, for one, I say boldly that since the days of Butler the Church of England reared no son so great as Newman.

It would seem the Almighty, ever bringing good from evil, has given him a work to do where he is: may it prosper in his hand!

Believe me,

Most sincerely yours,

W. E. GLADSTONE.

CHAPTER XXVIII

" Mr. Gladstone has reserved for his closing days a conspiracy against the honour of Britain and the welfare of Ireland more startingly base and nefarious than any of those other numerous designs and plots which, during the last quarter of a century, have occupied his imagination."

From Churchill's Election Address, June, 1886.

The Home Rule Bill was introduced on April 8, 1886. The second reading debate began on May 10, and ended on June 11, when the Bill was condemned by 341 votes to 311. Parliament was dissolved and the General Election was held in July. The Government were severely defeated for in Great Britain only 193 Home Rulers were returned. Thus in five months Gladstone's plan for solving the Irish question by Home Rule was formed, discussed, and rejected, first by the House of Commons, and then by the country.

The chief impression made at the time was the impression of crushing defeat. Most people thought of the collapse of the Liberal party and the disaster in which Gladstone's long career seemed to have reached its end. The *Spectator*, rejoicing in the general verdict, could not refrain from a lament over its personal aspect, drawing a sad picture of the " great consul deserted by his legions." To-day it is more natural to be surprised, not that so many Liberals deserted Gladstone, but that so many more stood by him. For this was no ordinary occasion. The electorate had to pronounce on a question which to the great majority was novel and disturbing. What it had known of the earlier history of the Irish question had not attracted its sympathies to the Irish people, and Liberals had a grudge of their own. The view taken by some of the party managers of the electioneering value of the Irish vote was exaggerated, as the *Annual Register* showed. But the damage done to the Liberal party by the Irish opposition at the election of December, 1885, was not to be measured by the number of seats that it gave to the Conservatives, but by the bad blood it created between the Irish and the Radicals. The working men who were now asked to put everything on one side in order to do justice to Ireland had listened only six months earlier to violent attacks made on their leaders by Irish speakers and writers in the towns of England, Scotland, and Wales. Davitt had tried to counteract this impression, but one man, how-ever sincere, could not put up much resistance to the organi-zation that was active in every British town.

The only election with which the election of 1886 can be compared is that of January, 1906. In both cases a revolutionary proposal was made to the electors; in both cases the party in power was divided on it. At no other election since 1867 was the electorate pronouncing on a new issue of capital importance, and not merely giving a vote of confidence to this or that set of politicians.

When the figures are studied it is seen that the Liberal defeat after the introduction of Home Rule was nothing like as severe as the Unionist defeat after the introduction of Tariff Reform. The Home Rulers held 193 seats, in July, 1886, in Great Britain against the 138 seats held by the Unionists in January, 1906. If the returns for the thirteen towns with more than two members are compared, it will be seen that except for Birmingham and Salford, there was no town in 1886 in which the Liberals were left without a member, whereas in 1906 the Unionists lost every seat in Manchester, Leeds, Bradford, Salford, Nottingham, and Wolverhampton. If the figures of voting are considered, the comparison is also more favourable to 1886. The total vote polled in July, 1886, was much smaller than the total vote polled in December, 1885. There was a fall of nearly a million and a half; the total being in December, 1885, just under four millions and in July, 1886, just over two millions and a half. This fall was partly accounted for by absten-tions, partly by the number of unopposed returns. Of these there were 152 against 23 in December, 1885. The 152

were made up of 110 anti-Home Rulers and 42 Home
Rulers.   If these constituencies are given votes in proportion,
the total vote polled would be increased roughly by a
million.   If it were supposed that two-thirds of these votes
should be given to the party holding the unopposed seat, the
Liberal Home Rule vote would be about 1,440,000 and the
anti-Home Rule vote should be about 1,750,000.   In 1906
the difference between the Unionist and the anti-Unionist
vote was nearly twice as great.

In certain important respects the Tariff Reformers in
1906 had an advantage over the Home Rulers in 1886.
Home Rule was an absolutely novel idea to the British
electorate and it had only been discussed for a few months.
There had been an active Protectionist propaganda in
England for twenty years before 1906, and Chamberlain, as
an ardent free trader, had noticed its influence when
President of the Board of Trade in Gladstone's Government.
All these forces had been mobilized by the most powerful
man in England, and for two or three years there had been
an incessant agitation on the question.

In a second respect the second campaign had advantages
over the first.   Chamberlain by his honesty and courage
had excited against his cause the fear of dearer food, but
there were large interests and large sections of the population
who stood to gain by the success of his campaign.   In
1886 there were no voters who had reason to think they were
consulting their own interests or the interests of their class in
voting for Home Rule.   Gladstone's ill-devised procedure
had made the election a plebiscite on Home Rule.   No
elector who wanted anything else had much reason for
voting for him.   He seemed to have dropped with Chamberlain all Chamberlain's schemes, and the man who stood in
the popular eye for great social reforms was urging all whom
he could influence to vote for the hardest reactionary rather
than for a Home Rule Liberal.   The great drop in the
Liberal county vote showed what Gladstone had lost when
he lost this force.   There the Liberal vote fell from 1,113,693
to 524,508.   In December, 1885, a great many agricultural
labourers and small men had voted Liberal at great risk to

themselves but it could hardly be expected of them that they should run that risk again in order to give Ireland a Parliament, at the instance of a Prime Minister who had done nothing in his six months to improve the bad conditions of their village life.

It was this fall in the Liberal vote in the counties that caused the great Liberal defeat. In the boroughs outside London the Home Rulers held their own. Chamberlain proved to be much less strong in his hold on working-class confidence than Gladstone. In Birmingham and its area he was all powerful. Five of the Birmingham seats were not contested. But in the English, Welsh and Scottish boroughs (if London is excluded) the recorded Liberal vote and the anti-Home Rule vote were almost equal (491,685 and 491,098). (In these boroughs there were 18 unopposed Unionist and 11 unopposed Liberal returns, so that some addition should be made to the Unionist vote.) After the election of December, 1885, Grosvenor, writing to Gladstone, estimated that of the 335 Liberals returned, 101 were Radicals. The *Annual Register* estimates that of the 78 Liberal Unionists returned in July, 1886, only 12 were followers of Chamberlain. The great majority of the Liberal votes lost in 1886 were thus the votes not of Radicals but of Whigs and moderate Liberals. It is clear then that the majority of working men voters followed Gladstone and not Chamberlain, though Gladstone offered them nothing but Home Rule, and Chamberlain offered them social reforms. The result is a striking proof both of Gladstone's personal ascendancy and of the strong feeling for justice in the working man.

The rest of Gladstone's life can be divided into two chapters. He was engaged on a supreme effort to gain and mobilize the conscience of the British people on behalf of a cause that was condemned by the judgment of the educated classes. The first chapter is the record of the steady success of the effort for four years; the second that of the catastrophe that destroyed it.

To understand what Gladstone was trying to do, and the temper in which he acted, it is useful to turn to that other large European question which had had so large a part in making him a Liberal. In the 'fifties Austria was trying to force her rule on five million Italian subjects. She hung, flogged, tortured, court-martialled, imprisoned and made it a capital offence to possess a revolver or to withhold information about a conspiracy. The Italians replied by appeals to Europe, by a boycott, by insurrections, and by plots and murders. The Austrian of the time thought that the whole world must be horrified by the outrages of the rebels. He never dreamed that it was the punishment of outrage that would make the chief impression and prepare for the war of liberation in 1859. Nor did he imagine that when history was written few people would notice this tale of crime, that Italy would be forgiven the plan for assassinating unsuspecting soldiers by the hundred in the cafés of Milan which Mazzini compared to the Sicilian Vespers, that the last thing that people would remember of Garibaldi was that this tenderest and kindest of men had said of the murder of Rossi that " a young man had recovered the spirit of Marcus Brutus," or that it would be seen that amid all this crime there was a spirit that would make the Italian struggle one of the epics of history.

The English were in some respects in a position like that of the Austrians. They had four million unwilling subjects: these subjects, like the subjects of Austria, used murder, outrage, boycott, and other cruel and wicked weapons; they on their part used methods of coercion and helped the landlords to evict peasants. On neither side was there so much crime or cruelty as in Austrian Lombardy. Coercion was less brutal; rebellion less violent. But the ordinary Englishman felt towards this problem as the ordinary Austrian felt towards his problem. For him the fact that stood out was the wickedness of the people he was trying to rule; the justice of his rule either in its principles or its methods seemed of minor importance.

What distinguished Gladstone from most of his countrymen was his power of putting himself into a larger perspective. He had so often thought of the Italian problem in the Italian sense that he could not think of the Irish problem purely in the English sense. He could not think that crime

absolved a ruler from the duty of governing with justice or
that the mere repression of crime could extinguish the force
of national sentiment. In Ireland, as in Italy, he believed
that the wrongs of a people would be redressed by wise
reform or righted by desperate violence.

A good example of his success in emancipating himself
from the ordinary English view was his treatment of the
support given to the Irish nationalist movements in the
United States. Unionists of all schools joined in resenting
this and in thinking that it brought discredit on the Irish
cause. Chamberlain taunted the Irish party with living on
subscriptions from Irish servant girls in the United States,
Yet the United States contained thousands of Irishmen
and Irish women who, themselves or their fathers,
had been driven from Ireland by a land system so unjust
that the English Government had been compelled to destroy
it. What right, Gladstone asked, had Englishmen who had
given a home to Mazzini and other exiles, who had given
moral help and more than moral help to more than one
fierce underground struggle for national freedom, beneath
whose shelter, as it was commonly believed, refugees had
plotted the assassination of despots, to complain of American
sympathy with Ireland or of the sacrifices made by the Irish
in the United States for the Irish in Ireland?

It will be seen that even when full allowance has been
made for the uncontested seats at the General Election, the
difference between the number who voted in the two elections of 1885 and 1886 is about half a million. Gladstone
was justified in thinking that this meant that a great many
people had not made up their minds on Home Rule. His
task was to gain this element and to win back as many as he
could of the Liberals who had left him. For four years he
made such progress with this task that it is generally agreed
that if Parliament had been dissolved in the summer of 1890
instead of the summer of 1892, he would have had a majority
of 100.

The Salisbury Government began by committing one of
those blunders, so common in Irish history, which seem at

the moment much less serious than they prove to be.   They took two steps, both of them, so far as they went, sensible and useful.   They set up a Commission under Cowper to inquire into the working of Land Purchase, and another to inquire into arterial drainage.   At the same time they sent Sir Redvers Buller to take charge of certain agrarian districts, a wise and happy choice.   But they proceeded to show that they had learnt nothing from the history of the last few years.   Parnell came forward with a most reasonable proposal, advanced in a most reasonable speech.   He showed that there had been such a fall of prices as to make it necessary to apply some immediate remedy. He proposed that eviction proceedings should be suspended for two years in cases where the tenant paid up a half of his arrears; that tenants whose rents had been fixed before 1884 should be granted abatements, and that leaseholders should be admitted to the benefits of the Act of 1881.   In August, 1887, the Government, under pressure from Ulster and the Cowper Commission, had to concede the greater part of these demands, but in September, 1886, they rejected them outright, for no better reason than that they were afraid of appearing to take Parnell's views into account.

Hicks Beach, who had with a rare magnanimity resigned the leadership of the Commons to Churchill and taken the Irish Secretaryship, was not altogether out of sympathy with Parnell's wishes.   For he had been put out by the uncompromising pro-landlord language of the Prime Minister. Churchill wrote to Salisbury about his dissatisfaction: "What he is afraid of, is being forced to administer Ireland too much on a ' Landlords ' Rights' basis, and he does not believe in the possibility of governing Ireland so as to afford complete and perfect protection for those rights as they exist now."[1] Hicks Beach's misgivings were increased by the letters he received from Buller, on whom the state of Ireland made the same kind of impression that it had made on General Gordon.   Buller was soon writing letters to Hicks Beach in the spirit of the evidence he gave afterwards to the Cowper Commission.   He found that in a great many cases where

[1] *Life of Hicks Beach*, Vol. I, p. 280.

20

evictions were carried out, the rents demanded were exorbitant in view of the rise in prices, and that the peasants were quite unable to pay them. He put the truth bluntly to the Commission: " You have got an ignorant poor people and the law should look after them, instead of which the law has looked after the rich." Buller urged Hicks Beach not to lend troops for evictions in cases where the eviction was obviously unjust. Hicks Beach listened to him and proposed to the Lord Chancellor and the Attorney General that the Government might arrange to be represented by counsel at the hearing of ejectment processes with power to suggest the suspense of eviction, in cases where he thought this the right course. But to defend an Irish peasant against a landlord by a method that seemed to question the rights of property seemed to Sir Richard Webster, the Attorney General, an outrage, and this wise project was dropped. Hicks Beach also received something like a public censure from an Irish judge, Chief Baron Palles.

The Government's decision to refuse any concession to Parnell was explained in a letter Hicks Beach sent to Buller, as due to the suspicion that Parnell was trying to stop the operation of the Ashbourne Act, which was quite untrue, and the fear of seeming to yield anything to him.[1] The incident recalls the early history of the Gladstone Government of 1880. The Liberal Government wanted to have the power of suspending evictions to meet an emergency. The House of Lords destroyed their Bill and by refusing that power brought on Ireland the agitation and the disorder which occupied so much of the Government's time and attention afterwards. That was the view, as we have seen, not only of Chamberlain and Gladstone, but of Forster. In this case the Government had to meet the same kind of emergency but they did not dare to apply this remedy. The consequence was precisely the same. In the winter of 1880 the Land League started its sweeping campaign among the peasants evicted or threatened with eviction for the non-payment of rents that within a few months were declared by courts of law to be exorbitant. In the winter of 1886 the

[1] *Life of Hicks Beach*, Vol. I, p. 284.

Plan of Campaign was set on foot among the peasants whose treatment by their landlords had excited the indignation of Buller, in order to obtain concessions which were shown by the Cowper Commission a few months later to be reasonable and just.

One of the best speeches for Parnell's policy was made by Chamberlain, who recalled his view of the similar state of things in 1880. " We have to deal with a crisis," he said, " which is apparently imminent with the general inability to pay rents, with the numerous evictions and consequent suffering and with great danger to social order." He went on to say that the price of produce had fallen by 20 or 30 per cent. since the judicial rents had been fixed and to deny that there was any sanctity about judicial rents. Unfortunately, though Chamberlain spoke in this sense he voted with the Government, in his new character of a supporter of Hartington, in rejecting Parnell's Bill. The Government's majority was 297 to 202.

Five months later Parnell's view of what was needed received striking confirmation from the Cowper Commission. This body appointed by the Government, with a strong Unionist at its head, recommended the extension of the 1881 Act to leaseholders, and agreed with Parnell that the judicial rents must be revised. This was too hard a truth at first for Salisbury who said that to interfere with judicial rents would be laying the axe at the root of the fabric of civilized society, and the Government's Bill was much weaker than the Report. But there was such a tempest in Ulster that the Liberal Unionists, who would not make any concession to Parnell, insisted that the concessions refused to him should be made to this new agitation. The Bill as amended provided that all rents judicially fixed before 1886 should be revised in accordance with the changes in agricultural prices.[1]

The folly of the Government in refusing, when Parnell proposed it, a reform that was forced on them a few months

[1] Balfour had said in March, after he had taken Hicks Beach's place as Irish Secretary, that it would be folly and madness to break these solemn contracts. Morley, *Gladstone*, Vol. III, p. 374.

later, was all the greater because Parnell was anxious that Ireland should keep quiet. His view was that Gladstone, and Gladstone alone, could carry Home Rule and that nothing should be done in Ireland which would make his task of converting England harder. The Liberal alliance was thus a steadying force, and if the Government had been wise instead of small-minded, it would have helped them in their Irish task. But it was hardly likely that a state of things which seemed intolerable to Buller and unjust to Hicks Beach would be accepted by the peasants on whom ruin was falling. The answer to the Government's rejection of reform was the Plan of Campaign.

The Plan of Campaign was invented by an able Irish member, Timothy Harrington. It was in many respects an excellent scheme. The November rents were about to fall due, and the Government had refused to take any step to protect the tenants from being forced to pay rents that by Chamberlain's admission would be 20 or 30 per cent. too high. The peasants were invited to take steps for their own protection. The tenants on an estate where no voluntary abatement was offered were to act as a body. They were to wait on the landlord and ask for an abatement. If it was refused, they were to resolve to pay him no rent but to put into " a campaign fund " the reduced rent that they had offered him. If he relented under this pressure the sum would be handed to him; if not, it was to be used for the fight in the courts and for the protection of the evicted. " The estates fund if properly utilized will reduce to reason any landlord in Ireland." All tenants deprived of their holdings through sale or ejectment were to be supported from the fund, and if it were not sufficient it became the duty of the National League to replenish it as long as the struggle lasted. Blacklegs were to be boycotted. The scheme was thus a method of applying the principle of the collective bargain to Irish agriculture. To the educated Englishman it had as ugly a look as the early trade unions had worn to the upper class mind half a century before. To the Irishman it seemed a simple plan for using the spirit of loyalty and co-operation to prevent injustice.

The plan really grew out of the action of the tenants on the estate of an absentee landlord, Clanricarde, who made himself notorious. Clanricarde, who had been a Whig member until he revolted against the Land Act of 1871, was one of the largest landlords. He had 52,000 acres, 1,900 tenants and a rent roll of £25,000 a year. He came into the estate in 1873, and when Shaw Lefevre was in Ireland in 1882 he learned that Clanricarde had never visited his estate except to attend his father's funeral.[1] His agent, Blake, was murdered in that year, the suspicion having spread that it was at his instance that Clanricarde had held out against all remission of rent. His widow wanted after his death to publish his letters to show that this was false, and that he had urged Clanricarde to make abatements, but Clanricarde got an injunction to prevent her.[2]

In 1886 Clanricarde was acting in the same spirit against the advice of his agent. His rents were fully 25 to 30 per cent. above the recent judicial rents. A large body of his tenants met and asked him to accept a reduction of 25 per cent., stating their willingness to pay such a rent. They were supported by the priests and by the Bishop who was well-known for his moderate views. Clanricarde's agent strongly urged him to agree, but he was told peremptorily to take " full and drastic measures to secure the full amount." The tenants then entered into a combination binding themselves to pay no rent until a reasonable abatement was conceded. Hicks Beach authorized the employment of 500 constables to support the eviction of a selected number of the tenants; the tenants resisted and seventy-five men were sent to prison, many of whom were sentenced to hard labour for a year or eighteen months, though no person had been injured in the struggle. Clanricarde then asked for more constables for another series of evictions, but Hicks Beach, having learnt from the agent that the agent himself had recommended the reductions, wrote Clanricarde a stiff letter in the course of which he observed that he had considered the agent who lived in Ireland

---

[1] Lord Eversley, *Gladstone and Ireland*, pp. 179–180.
[2] *ibid.*, pp. 183–184.

a better judge than the landlord who never went there.[1]

The plan was put into operation on eighty-four estates and on no less than sixty the landlords and tenants came to an agreement. It had an undoubted influence in reducing rents and in this way it contributed to peace. But landlords like Clanricarde refused to reinstate evicted tenants and thus, when the Government went out of office in 1892, there was a great body of evicted tenants maintained by public subscription and demanding reinstatement. This long standing wrong was not righted until 1907 when Birrell was Chief Secretary.[2] Thus the consequences of the refusal of the Government to do in September, 1886, what it was forced to do a few months later left a legacy of suffering and disorder for twenty years.

The Cowper Commission reported in February, 1887, and the Land Act, which in its final form incorporated proposals rejected in 1886 and again in June, 1887, passed into law in August, 1887. In the interval two important things had happened. Churchill, making a false estimate of his power, resigned in December, 1886, because Salisbury had not supported him in his quarrel with the Ministers for the fighting departments whose estimates he wanted to force down. He thought that he was indispensable, but Salisbury persuaded Goschen to take his place, and Churchill's career came to an abrupt end. No man ever fell more strictly on a question of principle, but his impulsive act showed that he had as little judgment as Fox in managing his personal relations with difficult or disapproving colleagues. Churchill's resignation made Chamberlain uncomfortable about his personal position, for he and Churchill were friends, and he feared that Churchill's departure would throw the Government more and more into Tory hands. He turned again in consequence to the idea of making his peace with the Liberal party. Harcourt, to whom he made advances, was eager for reconciliation, and Gladstone readily agreed to the proposal that there should be a discussion between a few leading Liberal leaders on both sides.

[1] Eversley, *Gladstone and Ireland*, pp. 320–323. *Life of Hicks Beach*, I, 293.
[2] Pomfret, *op. cit.*, p. 308.

The first meeting of the Round Table was held at Harcourt's house on January 14, 1887, the members of the Conference being Harcourt, Morley and Herschell, on one side, and Chamberlain and Trevelyan on the other. Chamberlain told Morley that he had tried to persuade Hartington to join but Hartington refused on the ground that he was afraid of upsetting his Tory allies. He had just been urging Goschen to come to Salisbury's aid, so his refusal was not surprising. Three meetings were held. Unfortunately as the fact of the meetings became known, Radicals and Nationalists made bitter attacks on Chamberlain, though Chamberlain himself had made promising speeches: Chamberlain retorted, and in the end he broke off the discussion after sending an angry letter to the *Baptist*. His own account of his position was given in a letter to the *Times* on July 30, 1887. He said that there were four points on which he (with Hartington in agreement) had insisted:

(1) Full and continuous representation of Ireland at Westminster.
(2) Separate treatment of Ulster.
(3) Reservation of criminal legislation and appointment of judges to Imperial Parliament.
(4) Definition and delegation of specific subjects to be dealt with by any new Legislative authorities hereafter to be created.

Harcourt told Morley afterwards that the Round Table Conference would have kept Chamberlain and saved the party but for Morley's quarrels with Chamberlain. " It was his irritation at something said in a speech by you that led to the fatal *Baptist* letter."[1] It is true that Morley's relations with Chamberlain were tense (Chamberlain had not wanted him to be a member of the Round Table), that Morley wrote in alarm to Gladstone that he thought Harcourt much too ready for concession, and that he had little hope of a genuine reconciliation, but there is little reason to think that Chamberlain was prepared to make any substantial concession for peace.

Gladstone was never very hopeful of what he called " large

[1] Morley, *Recollections*, I, 297.

and final arrangements " but he thought, as he told Acton, that the conference might do some little good.   He combined a sense of uncertainty about Chamberlain's temperament with a real insight into the substance of his quarrel with Home Rule.   He wrote to Acton on January 13, 1887:

" His character is remarkable, as are in a very high degree his talents.   It is one of my common sayings that to me characters of the political class are the most mysterious of all I meet, so that I am obliged to travel the road of life surrounded by an immense number of judgments more or less in suspense, and getting on for practical purposes as well as I can."[1]

He had two or three friendly meetings with Chamberlain at the time.   On February 21, four days before Chamberlain's sharp letter to the *Baptist*, Gladstone met him at the Devonshire Club at dinner, their host being Canon Maccoll. He records in his diary," Much conversation with C. who was very friendly."   On March 15 they met at a dinner party and Gladstone notes," Easy general conversation with Chamberlain."   On April 5 they had a meeting, at Chamberlain's suggestion, to discuss politics.   Mr. Gladstone records " Conversation with Mr. Chamberlain 12–1.30. Ambiguous result, but some ground gained."   Chamberlain left an account of this meeting, at which Gladstone proposed that the Liberal Unionists as a party should bring forward a plan of local government but Chamberlain did not think this possible.   Chamberlain ended:

" The general impression left on my mind by the interview was that Mr. G. confidently counts on the unpopularity of coercion to bring about an early appeal to the country and to secure a decision in his favour, and that under these circumstances he does not desire to proceed further in the direction of conciliation and does not believe that the Party would allow him to do so."[2]

Now, as before, Gladstone was determined not to turn what he thought a good Bill into a bad Bill in order to obtain the support of politicians who would prefer to have no Bill at all.   But at this moment he and Chamberlain were much

---

[1] Morley, *Life of Gladstone*, Vol. III, p. 355.
[2] Garvin, Vol. II, p. 296.

closer to agreement on Land Purchase, and though Morley had written to Gladstone while the Round Table Conference was in session, denouncing the idea of the severance of Ulster, Gladstone made a speech at Faringdon Street on July 30, 1887, with Morley in the Chair, at which he repeated with emphasis his offer to consider any scheme for separating Ulster from the government of the rest of Ireland.[1]

Gladstone's belief that coercion would bring over a great mass of opinion to Home Rule was soon justified. This is not difficult to understand. Balfour, who was received with derision by the Nationalist members when first he stood up in the House of Commons, soon showed that he was their match in spirit, in determination, and in the cut and thrust of debate. The office of Chief Secretary had often thrown a man back in his career, and in one case at least had proved fatal. Balfour, finding his opportunities in its difficulties, entered it an untried man, and left it likely to be his party's next Prime Minister. He had, besides his amazing dexterity in debate, courage that never failed, and a nerve that was never weakened by compunction. Ireland had never had a Chief Secretary who was less able to understand nationalist sentiment, and he looked upon his opponents as men using wicked means to foolish ends. But his rapid reputation in the House of Commons did nothing to reconcile English opinion to coercion.

For the coercion of 1887 differed from all previous coercion in one most important respect. It was directed against a form of action and combination that was not only intelligible but congenial to the English working classes. In 1881 coercion had been applied against a movement to bring about a universal combination to refuse all rent. The English working classes, who did not hold with Proudhon that all property was theft, were not drawn into any passionate sympathy with that movement. Then followed the coercion administered by Spencer which was an attempt to put down murder and outrage and the secret

[1] " We have said over and over again from the first to the last that if there be a disposition to sever some portion of Ireland which may fairly be called a protestant portion of Ireland if the public mind is in favour of that severance, we will not stand in the way. I cannot say more."

societies that organized them. In this case again the working classes, though suspicious of coercion, had no liking for the victims. But in 1887 coercion was directed against men doing precisely what they did themselves, using their own methods and fighting their own battles. The Plan of Campaign was a method of collective bargaining which seemed to them, as it seemed to the Irish peasants, just and reasonable. After it was organized the Government passed a Bill which recognized the justice of the demand behind the Plan. Most landlords accepted the Plan and came to terms with their tenants, but on twenty-four estates the Plan was resisted, in some cases evictions continued and in most there were a number of evicted tenants whom the landlords refused to reinstate. Here was a state of things with which the English working classes were familiar enough. After every strike the question of victimization is a serious legacy. If after the settlement of the great Coal Strike of 1893 the coal owners had declined to re-employ men whom they regarded as ringleaders in the agitation, there would have been an agitation throughout the trade union world. A miner or engineer who was told that the question at issue was whether the landlord should be compelled or not to take back the evicted tenants, was in no doubt about the answer.

The most striking example of the manner in which Gladstone was learning to take a larger view of working-class questions from his Irish experience is to be found in his treatment of this new issue. The ordinary Conservative regarded the Plan of Campaign as an outrage. But then the ordinary Conservative would have liked to be in a position to treat English trade unionists as Balfour proposed to treat the Irish peasants. That a mass of workmen should be able to compel their employer to pay a higher wage than he thought reasonable, and able to prevent him from refusing to reinstate men who had been active trade unionists, seemed to him full of danger for the State. In Ireland it was possible to enforce a view of the relation of the State to the rights of property which unfortunately could no longer be upheld in English industry, with its democratic franchise and its powerful Unions.   In the case of the agricultural labourers, the landlords in the 'seventies had been strong enough to treat the labourers out on strike under Joseph Arch as the Irish landlord treated his peasants.   The Plan of Campaign was fighting a battle that the workmen in the large unions had won, and the labourers in Arch's movement had lost. The English workman, whether he belonged to the successful or the unsuccessful class, had nothing but sympathy with the Irish struggle, and nothing but admiration for the principles and the spirit that inspired it.[1]

The English upper class then supposed that to say a word that might look like approval of this conspiracy against property would damage any statesman beyond hope of recovery.   With this view Hartington now challenged Gladstone to say what he thought of the Plan of Campaign. Gladstone replied:

" The Plan of Campaign was one of those devices that cannot be reconciled with the principles of law and order in a civilized society.   Yet we all know that such devices are the certain result of misgovernment.   With respect to this particular instance if the plan be blameable (I cannot deny that I feel it difficult to acquit any such plan) I feel its authors are not one tenth part so blameable as the government whose contemptuous refusal of what they have now granted, was the parent and source of the mischief."

Gladstone and Parnell had agreed in regretting the organization of the Plan, for they both held that disorder in Ireland would make it more difficult to convert England. But, as it happened, this method brought home the realities of the Irish question to the Englishman more vividly than anything else.   For the coercion by which Balfour now sought to suppress it was palpably a method of coercing a people under circumstances in which the law was maintaining injustice.   " What they call a conspiracy now," one of the leaders of the Plan of Campaign said at the start, " they will call an Act of Parliament next year."[2]   That is pre-

---

[1] The total sum spent by the National League over this campaign was £230,000 in seven years.   Davitt, *Fall of Feudalism*, p. 529.

[2] Morley, *Gladstone*, Vol. III, p. 373.

cisely what had happened.   Coercion was now to be applied
not to compel recalcitrant landlords to accept what the law
had declared to be justice, but to punish anybody who tried
to save the peasants from the ruin that the injustice of the
landlords had brought upon them.   No fewer than 150
persons were now sent to prison for offences in the agitation
for the reinstatement of Clanricarde's tenants, some for
speaking[1] at meetings, some for attending meetings, some for
refusing to serve the planters who had been introduced to
take the place of evicted men and some for resisting their
own eviction.   Yet we know that it was the view that the
peasants took of Clanricarde and not the view that Clanricarde took of himself that had been taken by Hicks Beach.

The Bill that Balfour introduced in March, 1887,[2] differed
from all previous Bills in that it was unlimited in time and
could be brought into effect whenever a Lord Lieutenant
decided to proclaim a district or districts.   It was made, as
Morley put it,[3] a " standing instrument of government."
Gladstone had been insistent when the question of coercion
was under dispute in his Government in the spring of 1885
that as far as possible there should be no difference between
Ireland and the rest of the United Kingdom.   The new
Bill proposed to make a permanent separation between the
criminal law of Great Britain and that of Ireland.   Trial by
jury disappeared.   The trial of conspiracy was given to the
Resident Magistrates.   They could treat a public meeting
in a proclaimed district as an illegal assembly and punish
anybody who attended it.   The Resident Magistrates, as
the *Spectator* had pointed out in an earlier discussion, were
quite unfitted for such duties.   We know as it happens what
the Irish judges thought of them.   An appeal was brought
to the High Court against the conviction of four men for
conspiracy.   Their conviction was quashed, for the Court
found in one case that the Magistrates had convicted a man
who was the victim rather than the agent of intimidation.
The magistrates had refused to state a case.   On this Baron

[1] One of these was Wilfrid Blunt.
[2] In its original form it proposed to bring Irishmen to England for trial, but
Balfour had to drop that extraordinary project.
[3] Morley, *Gladstone*, Vol. III, p. 376.

Dowse, one of the judges who considered the appeal, remarked that of course a Resident Magistrate was unable to state a case. "He might as well be asked to write a Greek ode. He would have to be made over again before he could do it."[1] Herbert Paul remarks: "When these facetious remarks were made, one of the four men, the intimidated one, had served the whole of his term, and the other three had undergone more than half their punishment."

Under a system of justice, so administered, nearly 3,000 men and women were sent to prison, many of them with hard labour, all of them compelled to wear prison dress, to sleep on a plank bed, and to suffer all the indignities of prison life for offences connected with the movement for helping the evicted tenants. No man could open his mouth in their defence without the risk of a sentence. Thus coercion was directed primarily not against crime[2] but against an agitation. And as Balfour refused to make any distinction between a political and a non-political prisoner, agreeing with Salisbury who spoke of the "strange maudlin effeminate doctrine" that had grown up on this subject, men who made a speech that was disliked by a Resident Magistrate, a man with no legal training, found themselves wearing prison dress and suffering all the indignities of a convict prison. The Government made a strange miscalculation. They thought this would have a deterrent effect. Its only effect of course was to increase the popular indignation both in Ireland and in England. Harrington, the Member of Parliament for Tralee, had to appear in his own constituency when he was summoned as a witness, wearing his prison dress. If there are nations in the world that can be cowed by such methods, Ireland is not one of them.

More than twenty Members of Parliament were sent to prison. It had been held, when Forster locked Parnell up, that the imprisonment by a Government of its critics in Parliament had an invidious and objectionable look. Few

---

[1] Herbert Paul, *History of England*, Vol. V, p. 152.

[2] "No agrarian movement in Ireland was ever so unstained by crime." Morley, *Gladstone*, Vol. III, p. 373.

will think now that the imprisonment of Parnell was not a mistake. But it was made after a deliberately defiant speech by Parnell in support of a movement to withhold all rent, and Parnell made it, wishing at the time to be arrested and shut up. Forster shut him up without a trial. Balfour was shutting up political opponents after a trial that was a farce, for supporting a movement of which nobody could say that its object was unjust. Parnell had nothing to complain of in his treatment, whereas Balfour's opponents were subjected to gross indignities. Balfour himself enjoying the fight, took to fighting for fighting's sake. Randolph Churchill soon detected the truth about it. " He discovered, as time went on, that special legislation was not regarded by the Government as a hateful necessity; but as something good in itself, producing a salutary effect upon the Irish people and raising the temper of the Ministerial party."[1] Balfour had no qualms or scruples for he thought that having been forced to pass a land law that he did not wish to pass, he must restore respect for authority by making authority dreaded. Intimidation was thus his object, and in pursuing it he did not flinch from any action however arbitrary, or any method however careless of justice. He had behind him a majority that enjoyed his ruthless use of force and fear as much as he did, and his brilliant display of skill, courage, and coolness, gained for him in parliamentary reputation as much as it lost his party in popularity in working-class England. Passion was running so high that Chamberlain, who had been ready to break up the 1885 Government rather than assent to a moderate coercion Bill, supported the most violent suppression of liberty that Ireland had ever suffered.

For the English working class the battle was clearly taking the form of a battle for rights they themselves had won, they or their fathers, by such sacrifices as those that Irish peasants, priests, journalists, and Members of Parliament, were now making in Ireland. Mitchelstown was the Peterloo of this struggle. A monster meeting was invaded by the police who wished to escort a government note taker

[1] Churchill, *Life*, Vol. II, p. 342.

to the platform. A struggle arose and soon became a battle between police and mob in which three men were killed. It was a complicated incident, and it was clear that the facts could only be elicited by careful inquiry, but just as Sidmouth sent his famous message of congratulation to the Manchester Magistrates without waiting for inquiry, so Balfour told the House of Commons on Monday, speaking of the events of the preceding Friday, that " looking at the matter in the most impartial spirit, he was of opinion that the police were in no way to blame."[1] This was characteristic of his treatment of all those cases where he had to choose between blind support of his officials, and the administration of impartial justice. It answered his purposes, but it added immensely to the force of the passion that his policy was exciting. English Members of Parliament went over to Ireland, witnessed evictions, and brought back to their constituencies accounts of the great fight for the right to combine, the right to free speech, and the right to a fair trial. Irish Members became great favourites on English platforms, and the fight for Home Rule, which had begun as a fight for an Irish cause that had no direct connexion with English history, was now a fight in which democrats recognized a battle against the old Combination Laws, the Treason and Sedition Acts and all the other measures that had once stood between the English workman and his liberty and self-respect.

[1] A full account of the struggle is given by an eyewitness in *The Vivid Life*, by F. J. Higginbottom, pp. 80-113. Mr. Higginbottom was the correspondent of the Press Association and his long despatch was as important an exposure as the famous despatch from the *Times* correspondent after Peterloo. Gladstone made great use of it. It appeared in over fifty papers and though its revelations were very damaging to the police, their truth was never shaken.

CHAPTER XXIX

In the autumn of 1885 Lord Richard Grosvenor was occupied in two transactions, the combination of which must make a strange impression on anybody who has followed the events of the time. He was corresponding, as we have seen, with Mrs. O'Shea, partly about Parnell's plans, partly about finding a seat for O'Shea; at the same time he was corresponding with a gentleman of the name of Pigott who had asked him to find money for the publication of a pamphlet called *Parnellism unmasked*. For the last three years Pigott had been supplying anti-Irish papers in England with articles attacking Parnell, and this pamphlet attempted to give its full concentrated effect to the energy that had been dispersed over these several publications. Grosvenor ended by putting Pigott into touch with a young man named Houston, a gentleman who had been on the staff of the *Times* correspondent in Dublin, and was at this moment secretary of a body called The Irish Loyal and Patriotic Union.

Houston saw pretty soon that to treat Pigott merely as a man of letters was to waste him. For Pigott had had a long and interesting career, in the course of which he had been Fenian and anti-Fenian, Leaguer and anti-Leaguer. Almost his first success in the world of blackmail and plot where he was most at home had been in drawing money out of poor Butt by threatening to set the Fenians on him in all their fury. Since that time he had sponged on men of all parties, intrigued with men of all parties, and he had known everybody who was to be known in the revolutionary movement, in Ireland or the United States. He was just the man to dig out secrets.

At first Houston found him a little diffident. Fortune

had been hard to him and he was in low spirits. But when Houston suggested that he should have the maintenance allowance of a first class civil servant while he travelled about the world, he saw the prospect of escape from a life of mean shift and sorry adventure into a life of ease and pleasure, in which he could make himself comfortable, one week in Paris, another in Lausanne. He began to think that what Houston asked, the means of enabling Houston to prove Parnell a rogue, and to drive him out of public life, was not really out of his reach. As he had in his possession the handwriting of everybody of importance in Irish politics and knew their habits, he soon persuaded himself that as Titus Oates he could make a fortune that would have been beyond him as a writer of pamphlets, even if his pen had been not that of Pigott but that of Swift. It might be said of him—such had been his advantages in this respect— " Capax fabricandi nisi fabricasset." Grosvenor might perhaps console himself for his failure to find O'Shea a seat by his success in finding Pigott a career.

The extraordinary events that followed from the meeting of Houston, then a young man in the twenties, with this veteran sponger and blackmailer, are well known to all who remember the excitements of the Parnell Commission. It is probably difficult for those who were not living at the time to make the allowance that must be made if the behaviour of the Government is not to remain inexplicable. For nobody who cannot understand the atmosphere of the Irish struggle, with its violent passions and its genuine fears, can understand how the Government was tempted into its fatal misconduct.

At no time was the Irish agitation free from crime and disorder. This was inevitable. For that agitation sprang from two impulses, two causes of discontent, and each of them is associated in history with violence. One was the sense of social wrong; the other the sense of thwarted national feeling. Whenever a class has had to fight for justice, or a people for liberty against overwhelming power, violence has been either a weapon or an incident of the struggle. The Luddite movement, the Rebecca movement, the

2 P

Chartist movement, all the great social dissatisfactions of the working classes have followed this law. So with the nationalist movements. There indeed the violence has been greater. There are many dark pages in the history of the Risorgimento.

A man who wishes to judge the moral issues raised by such events will weigh provocation against crime, and take into account all the antecedent and contemporary circumstances. Some may hold that the crime of the insurgent class is no greater, or even that it is less, than the crime of the class whose power it attacks. Was a miner who inflicted brutal wounds on a blackleg in the Tyne and West strikes of 1831 and 1832 worse than the parson colliery owner who turned women out of their homes in the midst of an epidemic of cholera? Was a peasant who murdered a neighbour who took a farm from which he himself had been unjustly evicted worse than the landlord who turned a hundred families out of their houses to starve because they could not pay him a rent pronounced by the law to be unjust? Jesse Collings once declared boldly in the House of Commons that Lord Leitrim was a worse man than any of his moonlighting tenants. The allowances a man was prepared to make for provocation depended on the incidence of his sympathies. Collings was naturally on the side of the peasant just as most Peers were naturally on the side of the landlords. Gladstone's feeling for Irish sentiment about Irish history made him better able to understand a violent and lawless patriotism than the Conservative who had no respect for this spiritual discontent. In 1887 Manley Hopkins, a Jesuit who was hostile to the Nationalists, wrote in alarm and indignation to Newman about the outrages of that time. Newman held, of course, a grave view of rebellion as a sin. His answer is therefore specially interesting:

"The Irish patriots hold that they have never yielded themselves to the sway of England, and therefore have never been under her laws and never have been rebels. This does not diminish the force of your picture, but it suggests that there is no help, no remedy. If I were an Irishman, I should be (in heart) a rebel."[1]

[1] Ward, *Life of Newman*, Vol. II, p. 527.

Newman, as a Catholic, realized how much injustice Ireland had suffered at the hands of Protestant England. It is obvious that in this state of things the fact of outrage can be used with great effect against any reformer. The violence of the Sheffield trade unions in the 'sixties, the series of explosions with which the different Grinders Unions had tried to coerce and terrorize recalcitrant workmen, the lynch law they put into force, could be turned as a weapon in debate against all trade union leaders and their friends. Any man who spoke up for the Chartist petitions was liable to be treated as an accomplice in disorder. Chamberlain himself was attacked with great severity by the *Times*, as condoning and encouraging crime, for a speech he made in the autumn of 1881, because he said that the objects of the Land League were not in themselves improper. In Irish politics this was a permanent incumbrance. For Irish discontent was not like the discontent of a Roman legion, frightened back to discipline by an eclipse of the moon, but something rooted in history and habit.

Of the fact and the effects of all this violence in Irish history and British politics there was of course no secret. It is often said that when a society is making its discontents known by such methods, concession is a mistake. But nobody could pretend that this principle had been observed. Every Government had yielded to this pressure. The Land Act passed by the Conservative Government in 1887 contained provisions which Salisbury and Balfour had denounced in the strongest terms a few weeks before the Bill became an Act, because the demand for those provisions had been emphasized by violence. Successful violence was indeed the one permanent fact of Irish history. The only question on which there was any doubt was to what extent and in what form Parnell and his followers had encouraged or countenanced such methods. That they had encouraged such movements as the Land League, and that the Land League set up law of its own and usurped an authority that should belong only to a Government, was well known. That some of them (though not Parnell himself) had taken part in starting the Plan of Campaign was no secret. That in the past Parnell had recommended boycotting and the refusal to pay rent was known to all who remembered the speech at Wexford for which Gladstone and Forster had put him in prison. That the Irish leaders had in fact made use of disorder, for pressing their reforms in Parliament and making government difficult until those demands were heard, was all part of history. But when Houston started Pigott on his task he was not thinking of things like these. What he wanted was to connect Parnell and his followers with murder, by knife, by gunshot, or by dynamite. He wanted, that is, to connect the Irish leaders with those secret societies that had gained such power when Parnell was in prison, and to prove that, while saying one thing in the House of Commons, he was planning something very different outside.

If a man thinks a reform so objectionable that it must be resisted at all cost, he will not be too careful about his methods of discrediting its friends. In 1886 there was a powerful set of politicians who took this view of Home Rule. They regarded it as so dangerous that every effort should be made to put obstacles in its way, and they were glad that every waste-paper basket in Europe should be turned inside out to find some document that would convict its leaders of crime. The *Times*, acting in this spirit, received Houston and his documents with open arms. It published a series of articles on Parnellism and Crime. The series made a great impresison on Bright, and on others like him, whose minds were now so hard set that they had lost all power of criticism and discrimination. But the articles did not make a great impression on the world at large until the morning of the day on which the division was to be taken on the second reading of the Coercion Bill. On that day the *Times* published, with a violent leading article, a letter purporting to be written by Parnell on May 15, 1882, in which he apologized to his correspondent for denouncing the Phoenix Park murders in the House of Commons. The letter was as follows:

Dear Sir,   15/5/82.

I am not surprised at your friend's anger, but he and you should know that to denounce the murders was the only course open to us.   To do that promptly was plainly our best policy.

But you can tell him and all others concerned, that though I regret the accident of Lord F. Cavendish's death, I cannot refuse to admit that Burke got no more than his deserts.

You are at liberty to show him this, and others whom you can trust also, but let not my address be known.   He can write to House of Commons.

Yours very truly.

CHAS. S. PARNELL.

Parnell declared in the House that the letter was a " villainous and barefaced forgery," but the *Times* refused to withdraw.   Most Unionists, thinking that the *Times* had, and Parnell had not, a character to lose, believed that Parnell was lying.

The forged letter, printed on April 18, 1887, had been shown to various persons and offered to other newspapers but in all these cases it had been regarded with suspicion. Buckle, the editor of the *Times*, was against publishing it, but he was overborne by MacDonald the manager.   For this blunder the *Times* paid heavily in reputation.   Nobody would have suspected that a paper of its standing would publish, to gain a party advantage, a letter of this kind without doing all that it could to make sure that it was genuine.   It turned out that the manager had made no effort at all to secure himself against fraud, and that a very little trouble would have been needed to put him on his guard.   A paper that strikes such a blow at a public man with such levity forfeits the respect as well as the confidence of its readers.   On the other hand, though the *Times* claimed, and has often deserved, the reputation of a paper that was not a mere party organ, it did not stand in the position of a great impartial public authority.   The worst that could be said was that this indiscretion, involving cruel injustice to a public man, owed something to malice. MacDonald admitted afterwards that he took the letter because he thought it was the kind of letter that Parnell would write.

The Government were of course in a very different position.   Parnell, though at the Election of 1885 he had been treated by Ministers as an ally with sympathy and respect, was now the formidable leader of a party in angry opposition. In this sense Ministers were eager for his fall. But these Ministers were also the Government of the country, and in that sense an accusation brought against Parnell should have been in their eyes on exactly the same footing as an accusation brought against Randolph Churchill or Lord Selborne. Unhappily from the first moment to the last they overlooked this plain truth and treated Parnell, not as if they were the Government and he a citizen, but as if the power and authority of the Government had been put into the hands of a political party with licence to use them to inflict as much damage as possible upon its opponents. Everybody who has read Morley's *Recollections* will see that in its pages he treats his political opponents with great generosity. Nothing could be handsomer than his tributes to Chamberlain and Balfour. If, therefore, writing of these incidents nearly half a century after they happened, he finds himself compelled to draw a parallel " with some of the episodes of the contemporary affair of Dreyfus in the French Republic," we may be sure that he was not merely throwing out an extravagance in a fit of temper. The calm recital of the facts is enough to provide his justification.

Parnell's enemies said at the time that his remedy was simple. He had only to sue the *Times* for libel. Many of his friends regretted at the time and afterwards that he did not take this course. That was a remedy certainly, but not a simple remedy. If Mazzini had been libelled in a paper in Vienna he could no doubt have sued the paper before a Vienna court. Parnell suing the *Times* for libel was not in the position of Hartington or Chamberlain suing the *Times*. That fact itself ought to have made the *Times* specially scrupulous in attacking him by this method. Whether Parnell could have obtained justice from a London jury is much like the question that was so important last century in industrial history: the question whether a trade union could obtain justice from an English judge. The ideal tribunal for such a case would have been an international court, but no such court existed.

Parnell contented himself at the moment with a repudiation of the charge that he had ever written such a letter. Within forty-eight hours, before it was known whether or not Parnell would bring an action, Salisbury made a public speech in which he accepted the authenticity of the letter.

" You may go back," he told the Primrose League, " to the beginning of British Government, you may go back from decade to decade, and from leader to leader, but you will never find a man who has accepted a position, in reference to an ally tainted with the strong presumption of conniving at assassination, which has been accepted by Mr. Gladstone at the present time."[1]

Can anybody suppose that if a grave charge had been brought in this form by the *Times* against Churchill or Lord Selborne, the Prime Minister, speaking twenty-four hours later, would have dreamt of using such language ? If ever a court had to decide whether or not Parnell had written that letter, every juror would step into the box knowing that the Prime Minister had already made up his mind that there was a strong presumption of Parnell's guilt. That speech was proof enough to Parnell that he could not look for justice from English minds.

The next episode in this· extraordinary story was an action for libel brought against the *Times* by a man, F. H. O'Donnell, who had been, but was no longer, one of Parnell's followers. O'Donnell sued on the ground that he had been mentioned in the articles on *Parnellism and Crime*. The *Times* replied by denying that the charges referred to him, and by pleading that the statements in the articles were true in substance and in fact. In those days the evil system obtained by which a law officer of the Crown could appear in private practice. The Government allowed the Attorney General to appear for the *Times*. In other words, a man whose duty it might be to advise the Government whether Parnell or other persons should be prosecuted in con- nexion with circumstances arising from this publication, now appeared against him as the advocate of a newspaper that had brought charges against him, intent in that capacity on proving that these charges were true. This was

[1] *Times*, April 21, 1887.

an extraordinary position. In one capacity, that of counsel for the *Times*, it was his duty to try to persuade a court, and incidentally the world, that this political opponent was a scoundrel. In another capacity, that of Attorney General, it was his duty to keep his judgment in suspense on all these charges, and only to decide on the fullest investigation whether or not that political opponent ought to be prosecuted. It is not surprising that Morley wrote to Gladstone on June 1, 1888: "I understand there is a pretty strong feeling at the Bar that Webster ought not to undertake to lead the defence."

Thus, on the day after the publication of the forged letter, the Prime Minister tells the country that there is a strong presumption that Parnell had connived at assassination. As soon as a case is brought into court, the Chief Law Officer of the Government appears for the paper that has made these charges. Whether any law officer so placed could have done justice at once to his duty to his client, and his duty to the State, is a nice question. Webster resolved it easily and simply. He was convinced that his duty to the State was the same as his duty to his client; his duty was to ruin this dangerous political opponent. He therefore spoke for two days describing the terrible charges that he was about to bring home to Parnell, and then he pulled himself up with the reflection that as Parnell was not a party to the action, and was therefore not represented in court, it would be fairer to him not to prove these charges, but to content himself with telling the world that they were true. In the course of these remarkable proceedings he read out a number of other letters which he said had been written by Parnell. One of them from Kilmainham jail was in these terms:

9/1/82.
"Dear E.

"What are these fellows waiting for? This inaction is inexcuseable; our best men are in prison and nothing is being done.

Let there be an end of this hesitency. Prompt action is called for.

MR. PARNELL BEFORE THE SPECIAL COMMISSION

From a drawing by Sidney P. Hall

You undertook to make it hot for old Forster and Co. Let
us have some evidence of your power to do so.
My health is good, thanks.

> " Yours very truly,
> " CHARLES S. PARNELL."

This was a more shocking letter than the letter already
published, for it was an incitement to assassination.[1]

[1] Of the other letters some were undated. They were printed in an
Appendix to the Report of the Special Commission in this order:

Dear Sir,   Tuesday.
    Tell B. to write me direct. Have not received the papers.
> Yours very truly,
> CHAS. S. PARNELL.

Dear Sir,   Tuesday.
    Send full particulars. What amount does he want? Other letters to hand.
> Yours very truly,
> CHAS. S. PARNELL.

Dear Sir,   Tuesday.
    I see no objection to your giving the amount asked for. There is not the
least likelihood of what you are apprehensive of happening.
> Yours truly,
> CHAS. S. PARNELL.

Dear sir,
    I am leaving for Cork tomorrow morning, but should be glad to see you
for some time today if you will fix an time convenient to yourself to call. Just
at this moment and for an hour or two I shall be engaged on matters of pressing
importance.
> Yours truly,
> CHAS. S. PARNELL.

In the original the word *for* was crossed out, and *hour* was substituted for time.
Richard Pigott, Esq.

Dear Sir,   June 16th, 1882.
    I shall always be anxious to have the good will of your friends, but why do
they impugn my motives. I could not consent to the conditions they would
impose, but I accept the entire responsibility for what we have done.
> Yours very truly,
> CHAS. S. PARNELL.

Dear Sir,   June 16th, 1882.
    I am sure you will feel that I could not appear in Parliament in the face of
this thing unless I condemned it. Our position there is always difficult to
maintain; it would be untenable but for the course we took. That is the truth.
I can say no more.
> Yours Very Truly,
> CHAS. S. PARNELL.

Pigott also furnished 8 letters signed by Egan, one by Davitt, one by James
O'Kelly.

Parnell now made up his mind that he could no longer sit still. Morley tried to dissuade him but he persisted. His first plan was to proceed against the *Times*, and run the risk of anti-Irish prejudice. His second to ask for a Select Committee to inquire into the authenticity of the letters. He suggested that it should be a committee without any Irish members. This committee would have power to compel the production of witnesses, a fact of some importance, since Webster had declared that the *Times* " would never disclose from whom these letters came."

The Government refused Parnell's demand but offered instead a " Commission to inquire into the allegations and charges made against members of Parliament by the defendants in the recent action." Thus the Attorney General, in his capacity of counsel for the *Times*, spends two days flinging charges against certain of his political opponents, and reading forged letters imputed to their leader. The leader asks for a select committee to inquire into the authenticity of the letters. The Government refuse but offer instead a commission to be appointed by themselves to inquire into a mass of allegations which their own Law Officer has brought against his opponents when acting as counsel in a private case. It came out that before making this suggestion the Leader of the House, W. H. Smith, had had a long visit from his old friend John Walter of the *Times*. So far gone were Ministers in the moral confusion into which their party spirit had brought them, that he told the House that he thought there was nothing odd in this behaviour.

The Government first treated this proposal as an offer. Among Parnell's friends there was a division of opinion. Some, looking first at the credit and the future of English government, thought that so grave an innovation ought not to be allowed. Gladstone was afraid that reluctance on Parnell's part might be misunderstood by English opinion. But the Government soon took the choice out of Parnell's hands. For, after appearing to consult the Irish leader's wishes, they proceeded to act as if he were not there. By a flagrant trick they changed the whole scope of the inquiry.

After offering an inquiry into the allegations made against Members of Parliament, they added to the notice " and others," so that, when the Bill came before Parliament, Parnell found that this monstrous addition had been made to the field of inquiry. The Government, having presumably started with the intention of providing for a judicial inquiry, were now openly seeking a method of propaganda. As Courtney, a strong Unionist, Chairman of Committees put it, they had taken sides. Their object was to discredit Parnell, and for that purpose it was not enough to turn a searchlight on to the secret conduct of his eighty members; they wanted to explore the whole mass of Irish crime and disorder, in the hope of incriminating the Irish Party. They pushed the Bill through Parliament, as if it were a mere formality, by the use of the closure. Having got their Bill, they nominated three judges, all of them strong opponents of Home Rule, and one of them well known for the violence of his feelings.

The best account of the proceeding was given in a short speech by Herschell in the Lords on August 10, 1888.

" Charges of the gravest character are made against men taking an active part in political life. Charges no doubt of a serious character are made and to test these charges and inquire into them a tribunal has been appointed at the absolute discretion of their most vehement political opponents, who have always been bitterly opposed to them, and those who entertain these feelings towards them have also determined what shall be the limit and scope of the inquiry, as to which they have listened to no one word of remonstrance or protest whatever."

" Herschell's speech last night," wrote Morley to Gladstone the next day, " was admirable. . . . He says not a single lawyer in the House of Lords dissents from his view. FitzGerald would not have voted for it nor Lord Watson and Macnaghten took care to be away."

The case had now been turned into a State prosecution. The counsel for the *Times* was the Attorney General. The chief law officer of the Crown was to spend the next eighteen months in trying to convince a Court that Parnell and his friends were men who had encouraged murder and fraternized with assassins. The Court consisted of three judges, all of the same political complexion as the Attorney General, chosen specially by the Government of the day to try these allegations without a jury. Well might Herschell speak of the danger to the State of such a confusion of executive and judicial functions and powers. As Herbert Paul has well put it, the law was a privilegium; " a special law directed against individuals obnoxious to the majority."[1] Home Rule seemed to Ministers such a public danger that in order to defeat it they were ready to put aside all the safeguards of constitutional custom. They had seen their opportunity in Parnell's embarrassment. For Parnell, whose cold blood had at last been stirred, was now set on an inquiry, and they saw that they could use their majority to force this infamous arrangement on him. By the simple device of setting up a Commission, not to decide whether or not the letters were forged but to review the general mass of Irish disorder, they could organize a great political campaign and throw over it a fraudulent look of public justice.

For Parnell and his friends the letters were of course the all important issue. For the general indictment of his party as a party mixed up with disorder and intimidation was no new thing. It had been brought by Forster himself in a striking speech as early as 1883. Salisbury and Carnarvon knew, when they treated with Parnell in 1885 on the footing of an honourable man and accepted his support, that he had made violent speeches recommending boycotting and asking Irishmen to treat a blackleg as a leper. The important thing that had happened since that time was, not some new outrage by Parnell, but the publication by a newspaper bitterly hostile to him of letters, which, if they were his, convicted him of direct association with murderers. Under any just plan those letters would have been taken first. But that would not have suited the purpose of the prosecution. Webster was allowed to postpone this part of the case for four months, while he brought one witness after another to give evidence of the connexion of the Land League and crime. With the Government's help he staged with effect all

[1] *History of Modern England*, Vol. V, p. 162.

the horrors of agrarian life under moonlighters and boy-cotters, bringing pitiful victims into court as well as spies, constables, informers, and smart detectives. In fact the Commission was being used for a great demonstration against a political party, much as the Hungarian Government used the trial at Agram in 1908 of fifty-eight Nationalists from Croatia: the trial that first brought out Masaryk's great qualities as a Nationalist leader.

At last on February 14, 1889, the Court was allowed to come to the letters. The manager of the *Times* explained that when the first letter was shown to him he thought it was just the sort of letter Parnell would write; without making any inquiry into the source from which it had come, he had decided that it was his duty to the public to print the letter at the moment most likely to influence the division on the second reading of the Coercion Bill. In the early part of 1888 he had received two other batches, the letters with which the Attorney General had made such play in the O'Donnell case. After these revelations had been made about the charges that Webster had said in the O'Donnell case he could prove against Parnell, if he had not felt that it would be unfair, Webster brought O'Shea into court to say that he thought Parnell had written the letter. O'Shea had more reason than anybody else in the world to desire the ruin of Parnell. Webster wanted to be allowed to bring a number of handwriting experts, but the Court, though it had given him all the license he wanted in delaying the trial of the letters, had now lost patience, and insisted on hearing where the letters had come from. Houston was thus brought into court, and he disclosed the name of Pigott. In a few weeks after a most dramatic sequence of events the truth about the forgery was out and Pigott had blown his brains out in Madrid.[1]

When the whole squalid story was known, it is not surprising that the ordinary man asked himself what

[1] Pigott had a fatal weakness for the letter e. He made Parnell spell hesitancy and likelihood with two e's. It was this that betrayed him to the Irishmen though Parnell suspected somebody else (Barry O'Brien, *Life*, II, 211). Russell made him write down a number of words in court and Pigott gave himself away by at once writing these two words with this spelling.

Webster had meant when he told the House of Commons that he could prove these letters to be authentic. Either he knew where the *Times* had got them, or he did not know. On either assumption it was difficult to see how an honourable man could have used such language about them.

There were some who thought that Sir Charles Russell, who was Parnell's leading counsel, should have withdrawn from the case as soon as the letters had been proved forgeries, but he had other plans. He made a speech lasting seven days in which he reviewed Irish history with an eloquence and a power that neither Webster nor James, the opposing counsel, could rival. Long speeches became one of the chief features of the proceedings. James spoke for twelve days. Davitt, who defended himself, for seven. To students of social history a comparison of these documents has all the interest that belongs to a revelation of the difference between the point of view of a ruling race, and that of the race that was twisting under its paw, and gradually twisting itself free.

Soon afterwards Russell and his colleagues, Asquith, Reid, and Lockwood, retired from the case. H. H. Asquith, R. T. Reid (afterwards Lord Loreburn), F. Lockwood (afterwards Sir Frank Lockwood), were counsel for the Irish members. Asquith's brilliant performance in this capacity had a good deal to do with his rapid rise to political eminence. Russell had asked that the books of the Irish Loyal and Patriotic Union should be produced. There was as much reason for suspecting this body of illegality and conspiracy on one side, as for suspecting the Land League on the other. The Commission refused this demand, though Asquith urged that an inquiry " into charges and allegations " might fairly be supposed to include an inquiry into the origin and circumstances of the charges, as well as into their truth and substance. The decision of the Commission increased the suspicion that was left behind in the Irish mind by these proceedings. This danger should have been evident. In the early days of the century Sidmouth was believed in Radical circles not only to have employed a bad man in Oliver the spy, which was true, but to have employed him because he was a bad man in order to trap working men into crime, which was false. The revelations that ended in Pigott's exposure had made it highly desirable that more should be known about the proceedings of this body, in order to dissipate the suspicion of the complicity of Ministers which was settling down into a firm belief in Ireland. As the Commission persisted in their refusal, on July 16, 1889, Russell and his colleagues withdrew from the case.

For the most part the general effect of these proceedings was exceedingly favourable to the Irish Party. There were however two exceptions. Parnell's manner was at times uneasy and constrained, and onlookers imagined he was trying to conceal something. They were right as to the fact but wrong about the cause. Parnell's discomfort was due to his fear, not of some political danger lurking in the background, but of the light that might be thrown on his private life. The other exception was the answer that he gave on one occasion to Webster, who asked him why he told the House of Commons on January 7, 1881, that secret societies had ceased to exist: " It is possible that I was endeavouring to mislead the House of Commons on that occasion." The judges found in fact that Parnell had not been misleading the House, but the answer gave a shock to public opinion at the time. It was probably prompted by Parnell's contempt for Parliament, which, though an integral part of his character, was a weakness to him as an advocate of his cause in England. Whether it was worse for him to confess that he might have tried to mislead the House of Commons, than for Chamberlain to accuse himself of trying to trick Gladstone into ruining his own Bill by a pretended co-operation is a question for casuists.

The Commission reported on February 13, 1890. So far as Parnell was concerned, the grave charges brought against him were all dismissed.

" We consider that there is no foundation whatever for the charge that Mr. Parnell was intimate with Invincibles, knowing them to be such, or that he had any knowledge, direct or indirect, of the conspiracy which resulted in the Phoenix Park murders, and we find the same with reference to all the other respondents. We do not think it necessary to enter into the question whether or not any persons other than those who were convicted were guilty of participation in those crimes, because we are clearly of opinion that none of the respondents were aware at the time that any persons with whom they associated were connected with these murders."

This was the judges' verdict on the charge of which the Prime Minister had said that there was a strong presumption that Parnell had connived at assassination. The Commission absolved Parnell on every charge that had been brought against him, for the first time, in this set of articles. They also reported that some of the respondents, and Davitt in particular, did express bona fide disapproval of crime and outrage; that they did not directly incite persons to the commission of crime; that it had not been proved that they were intimately associated with notorious criminals. On the other hand they found that the respondents did enter into a conspiracy by a system of coercion and intimidation to promote an agrarian agitation against the payment of agricultural rents, for the purpose of impoverishing and expelling from the country the Irish landlords who were styled " the English garrison "; that crime and outrage were committed by persons whom they had incited to practise intimidation; that they made payments to persons who had been injured in the commission of crime. On the question of the connexion of the Nationalist movement with the party of violence in America, they stated that Davitt had received money to start the agitation that led up to the Land League from a fund which had been contributed for the purpose of outrage and crime, and that he returned this money out of his own resources.

" With regard to the further allegation that he was in close and intimate association with the party of violence in America and mainly instrumental in bringing about an alliance between that party and the Parnellite and Home Rule party in America, we find that he was in such close and intimate association for the purpose of bringing about, and that he was mainly instrumental in bringing about, the alliance referred to."

Gladstone moving the adjournment of the House of Commons
after the Phœnix Park Murders, May 8, 1882

From the drawing by Harry Furniss

Thus the whole problem was brought back into the old circle. In the early nineteenth century Ireland, as a result of England's usurpations and confiscations, was in the hands of a small and, for the most part, selfish and irresponsible landlord class. In the twentieth century she had become a society of peasant agriculture. How was this conversion effected? If all the circumstances had been favourable, it might have been effected without violence. Unhappily they were all unfavourable so that conversion was only made possible by the violence of the victims of the old system. The grip of the landlord, his ability to screw out rents, and his enjoyment of power, had to be shaken. The first blows to the landlord's position came from peasant conspiracy. Gradually English statesmen learned that the old system was untenable but English opinion was indifferent and the Irish landlord had an almost controlling influence over one of the English parties. It was therefore only by combination to break the law that the peasant could force England to make this reform. What were the consequences of such a combination? Violence, murder, boycott, cruelty to rich and poor. The Commission reported that the Irish party had denounced crime and outrage but that " they did not denounce the system that led to crime and outrage and persisted in it with knowledge of its effect." That is a grave charge, and the charge was true. The Irishman's only defence was a tu quoque. How long had English Governments persisted with knowledge of its effects, in a system that brought upon thousands of men, women and children the cruelties of eviction, famine, intimidation, and exile?

So again with Irish self-government. In the spring of 1885 Chamberlain had compared the government of Ireland to that of Poland. If Davitt had sought to bring into combination all the forces that were in revolt against a government that Chamberlain could so describe, was he more guilty or the different Governments that had left Ireland in that plight? Students of Davitt's life will see that he used these tactics, as he used his influence, not to spread the power of the party of violence but to restrict it. He succeeded. In some respects the most interesting speech in the debates that followed the report was a speech of remarkable courage made by Bryce. He said that Parnell and Davitt must be looked on as leaders of a nationalist movement, subject in that respect to all the difficulties that had beset the efforts of Mazzini and Kossuth; that in all the nationalist movements there had been a party of violence and assassination, and that men in the position of Parnell and Davitt would probably have been less successful in restraining violence and strengthening the constitutional movement if they had attacked that party. Anybody reading the history of the time in cool blood to-day can see that this was true. But it was the kind of truth that only a brave man would have told a House that contained such ruthless debaters as Balfour and Chamberlain and all the passions that they could so easily whip into a storm.

The Government proceeded to make every mistake they could. As soon as the Pigott forgery appeared in the *Times*, the Prime Minister had taunted Gladstone with associating with a man against whom there was a strong presumption that he connived at assassination. When the forgery was exposed he made another speech in which he said the letters were of no consequence except as proofs that one Nationalist could forge the signature of another. This was the high water mark of Salisbury's patrician insolence. Pigott and Parnell, Parnell and Pigott, what was the difference between them? When " Rome and her rats are at the point of battle,"[1] one rat is very much like another. The Prime Minister's caustic tongue was a fatal gift, for all the arrogance of a ruling race, and a territorial class, towards a subject nation of peasants found in consequence phrases that were remembered, rankling in the Irish mind long after the speaker had passed to some new butt for his brilliant wit.

When the Report was presented to Parliament the Government erred again from lack of generosity. They proposed a motion to the effect that the House adopted the Report, thanked the judges for their just and impartial

[1] *Coriolanus*, I, 1, 159.

conduct and ordered the reports to be entered on the journals. The wrong done to the Irish members was passed over in insolent silence. When it is recollected that in the same House the Ministers' Chief Law Officer had stated that he could prove Parnell to be guilty of complicity with murder, and that the judges had found that his statement was baseless, it is not surprising that men of all parties held that something was due to the victims of calumny. Moreover the report, though just and impartial to individuals, contained some remarkable and provocative political reflexions. For the three judges had expressed opinions which were worth no more when they were delivered from the Bench than they would have been if delivered in the smoking-room of the Carlton Club. They believed that distress and extravagant rents had had nothing to do with crime, that the rejection of the Disturbance Bill by the Lords had not been a cause of the disorder of the winter of 1881, and that the Land Bill of 1881 had not mitigated the condition of Ireland. Some spoke of the impartiality of the three judges as if it was some kind of Olympian quality, which enabled them to survey a whole field of history and politics with the wisdom of complete detachment. This, of course, is an absurd view. Herbert Paul once pointed out that when six judges had to decide whether Hertford College, Oxford, could shut Nonconformists out of its fellowships, four decided that it could and two that it could not; the four were Churchmen and the two Nonconformists. Does anybody suppose that if the three Judges had not been Unionists the report would have been similar in all respects? The Lord Chief Justice of the time, Coleridge, was a Home Ruler; so were Herschell and Davey. If those three had reported on these facts, they would not have been fairer to individuals than the three Judges, Hannen, Day, and Smith, but their observations on the general issues would certainly have been different.

The Government were merely concerned to get these strange and startling views into print with the support of the House of Commons. They treated the report as if they were not the Government of the day responsible for justice to the people of Great Britain and the people of Ireland, but as a party caucus concerned only to put the report to the best party use. But party spirit is a bad guide even to tactics, and their refusal to make any kind of reparation to the Irish leader was keenly resented on their own back benches. The *Annual Register* states that the influence and reputation of Ministers suffered from the debate. " In order to preserve discipline in the ranks of the party, the severest pressure was put on those Unionist M.P.s who honestly sympathized with Mr. Parnell, and felt that to him and his colleagues some reparation was due." The same authority adds that the relations of the Government and its supporters were affected for the rest of the Session by the conduct of the Government on this occasion. This view receives support from the private conversation of a young Conservative member destined afterwards to great distinction. Curzon said at the time that half the party would have liked to vote for an amendment censuring the *Times*.[1] Curzon himself abstained.

This discontent found brilliant expression in a speech by Churchill which missed its mark at the moment, because he could not control his indignation, and his onslaught on the Government was too direct and passionate to gain the support of men who resented their meanness but did not wish to turn them out of office. A few sentences from his speech gave a summary of the Government's action:

" The procedure which we are called upon to stamp with our approval tonight is a procedure which would undoubtedly have been gladly resorted to by the Tudors and their judges. It is procedure of an arbitrary and tyrannical character, used against individuals who are political opponents of the Government of the day—procedure such as Parliament has for generations and centuries struggled against and resisted—procedure such as we had hoped in these happy days, Parliament had triumphantly overcome. It is procedure such as would have startled even Lord Eldon; it is procedure such as Lords Lyndhurst and Brougham would have protested against; it is procedure

[1] Gooch, *Courtney*, p. 285

which, if that great lawyer Earl Cairns had been alive, the Tory party would never have carried."[1]

It was of course impossible for Gladstone to accept the ungenerous course proposed by the Government. He resented it on three grounds. In the first place he was sensitive for the honour of the House of Commons. The whole spirit of parliamentary government was involved in his mind in the recognition of the equality of its members. To the Government the place of the Irish members, noisy and unwilling guests at the common table, was below the salt, and no courtesies were due to them. The Prime Minister saw little difference between Parnell and Pigott, and his colleagues in the Government denied to Parnell what they could not have denied to any British member. Nor could Gladstone, who had been at the head of the Government that passed that Land Act of 1881, sit down under the absurd extravagances into which their social prejudices had led the judges. How could he agree that they had read Irish history with greater insight than all the different Ministers who had taken part in the government of Ireland between 1880 and 1885; Forster and Chamberlain had disliked and mistrusted each other, but they had agreed in taking the view that the judges condemned; Cowper was a strong Unionist, but on those questions he had been in agreement with Gladstone.

But Gladstone resented the conduct of the Government for another reason. He felt that England's reputation was at stake in Ireland and in the world at large. Nothing is more striking to anybody who reads this strange history than the

[1] Churchill, *Life*, Vol. II, p. 416. The subject was debated first on a motion by Harcourt of February 11, 1890, declaring the conduct of the *Times* a breach of privilege. He made a brilliant attack on Webster and was only defeated by 48: then on an amendment moved by Gladstone recording reprobation of the false charges and expressing regret at the wrong inflicted which was defeated by 71 (the *Annual Register* noted that among the deliberate absentees were Churchill, Hanbury, J. S. Gathorne Hardy and T. W. Russell), lastly on an amendment moved by Caine (the Liberal Unionist who had been chiefly active in securing the fatal decision to vote against the second reading of the Home Rule Bill on May 31, 1886) and seconded by Edward Grey, then a very young member, condemning the conduct of those responsible for the accusation of complicity with murder, which was defeated by 62. Both those divisions were taken on March 11.

complete failure of the Government to think of Irish opinion. If it was desired to keep Ireland in the Empire, what could be more unwise than to give her reason to suspect that the Government was behind the conspiracy against Parnell ? The refusal of the Commission to allow the inspection of the documents of the Loyal and Patriotic Union led to the suspicion, widespread in Ireland at the time, that certain Ministers had started Pigott on his career, and arranged the whole plot with the *Times*. Ministers, by now refusing to show common generosity to the man who had escaped the snare, gave new strength to these dangerous illusions. Gladstone then was inspired by the strongest passion in his nature—his desire to make peace between England and Ireland—in this great appeal. The *Annual Register* describes his speech as a masterpiece which could bear comparison with some of his most celebrated achievements. To the reader to-day it has only one fault. The temptation to remind the Conservatives that they had used the help of Parnell to defeat his Government and to win the election, and that at that time they had thought lightly of Irish disorder and had attacked Spencer, was almost irresistible, but the speech would have been a greater speech and he would have been a greater man if he had withstood it. Yet such was his power that he could pass from these just but wounding criticisms to an appeal, based on something far deeper than party passion, which moved the whole House. It was rare in those days for men to cheer their opponents, but the *Annual Register* records that when he sat down there burst from all sides " applause . . . unstinted and unrestrained by party feeling."

How could men of the high character of the leading Unionists have behaved with such disregard to justice and such want of generosity ? The answer is to be found in the facts and atmosphere of their position. They were afraid of Home Rule much as the Dual Government of Austria-Hungary was afraid of the Nationalist movements within their borders before the Great War. The demand for Home Rule was a demand that no Great Power would have conceded in 1886. They would all have looked upon it as disintegration. Very few of the foreign statesmen of the time thought it good policy for England, though the few included one of the most respected names of the Italian Revolution, Marco Minghetti. Men nursed in the politics of power took such a view of the Irish problem by instinct. And the Unionists were afraid of Home Rule, not only as a danger to the Empire, but as a danger to the Irish minority. " I believe, " wrote Sir Henry James to Maccoll on December 3, 1886, " that the two-thirds of the Irish people to whom the Government of Ireland would be confided are not fit to govern the three-thirds. I believe that to place the executive and legislative power in the hands of these two-thirds —such as they are and will be—would be a positive crime."[1] That was a sincere view and it was held with passionate conviction by many Unionists. Such a calamity must be resisted at all costs. Unionists saw a chance by setting up this irregular tribunal of making that calamity less probable. They had in their view to choose between one crime and another; one crime seemed a little one; the other a great one. A man choosing between a little crime and a great crime soon comes to think of the little crime as no crime at all. Everything that Churchill said was true, but when so much was at stake you could not keep too close to conscience or principle.

To anybody who looks back to-day to these scenes, who thinks of them as a chapter in the history of the relations of England and Ireland, there is one consoling reflection. The Government were striking at a political enemy, at a subject race, under the influence of fear and passion. They had used all the means in their power to help a great newspaper to maintain what proved to be a slander upon their political opponents. As soon as the report was issued the Attorney General had hastened to declare that it was a complete justification of the Government's Crimes Bill. How had the incident started? In the publication of a letter by Parnell's enemies to make the world think that Parnell had incited to assassination. How did it end?

[1] Russell, *Memoir of Maccoll*, p. 375.

In the loud assertion that the Government's case for coercion had been vindicated before a court of three judges.   Such was the influence of fear and passion, that Ministers never stopped to ask how their conduct must look to men who had not lost their balance or, as Courtney put it, lost their head. Against this mass of fear and passion Gladstone brought all the fire and power of his great imagination, and the superb courage of his large European sense.   If Parliament ratified this nefarious abuse of power, there was still to stand on its records the noble protest of the greatest living Englishman.   And if Ministers forced their discipline on their party, that party too was alive to the dishonour done to Parliament and their nation.   The Government had done a great wrong, but the nation resented it.

For the effect on the country was seen in the rapid return of Liberal Unionists of the rank and file to their old party. Their leaders had seemed to justify Gladstone's prophecy that the danger of conceding Home Rule was less than the danger of withholding it.   Resistance clearly meant more and more coercion, and new and mischievous abuses of power.   The Liberal Unionists in Parliament by their own conduct had given colour to the view that a man could no longer combine Liberal ideas and   Unionist politics. Grosvenor had been discovered as a prime mover in the squalid story of Pigott.   Webster, hard driven by Harcourt's merciless exposure, took shelter under his learned friend, Sir Henry James, with whom he said he had consulted at every step; Liberals were not the more inclined to put their trust in James' leadership.   Hartington had rushed into the original controversy with the remark that it was true that Parnell denied that he had written the letters but on the other hand the *Times* asserted that he had.   Chamberlain, now that he had abandoned all idea of returning to his party, threw himself into the cause of his new allies with all the energy of his combative nature, and no man held more stoutly that the interests of empire came before justice. According to Sir Edward Clarke it was he who had pressed most strongly for the Commission.   One Unionist, Leonard Courtney, repelled by the Irish character and hostile to Irish ideas, had too strong a sense of constitutional rectitude to follow his party, but no other Unionist leader joined him in voting against the Government. Trevelyan, a man of integrity and courage equal to his, and admired by all Radicals for his brilliant crusade for the agricultural labourers' franchise, had returned after the Round Table Conference, and was now Liberal member for a Glasgow seat. Chamberlain's own following was thus limited to the Birmingham circle. He had made a last effort in 1888 to persuade Hartington to move towards his own ideas for a constructive settlement, but Hartington would not budge. Thus the alternatives for Liberal Unionists in the country seemed to be Home Rule, or the kind of warfare with Ireland of which the Pigott scandal was an ugly incident. Between the day of Pigott's exposure and that of the Parnell divorce the Liberals captured 9 seats in 21 bye-elections.[1]

" On this great day," Gladstone wrote in his Diary on Easter Sunday, 1887, " what are my special prayers? They are three. 1. For the speedy concession to Ireland of what she most justly desires. 2. That the concession may be so timed and shaped as to be entirely severed from all temptations to self-glorifying as far as I am concerned. 3. That thereafter the tie between me and the contentious life may at once be snapped. But now one prayer absorbs all others—Ireland—Ireland—Ireland."

On Easter Day, 1890, it looked as if his prayer would be answered.

---

[1] Ayr, which they had won in a previous bye-election in 1888 by 53, was lost by 130, but in 1886 the Unionist majority had been 1,175. In these 21 seats the Liberal vote increased by over 12,000 and the Unionist vote fell by about 500. The Liberal accession thus came from the return of men who had abstained in 1886. In all the bye-elections during the whole period between the beginning of coercion and the Parnell divorce the Liberal vote increased by 32,000 and the Unionist by 10,000.

CHAPTER XXX

CATASTROPHE

In the summer of 1889 Gladstone wrote to Döllinger in reply to a letter in which Döllinger had been expressing his Unionist views and his reasons for them. " It is most touching," replied Gladstone

" that your misgivings as to Home Rule in Ireland should spring from the high value you set upon the vocation of England. It is in truth, my completely accordant estimate of that vocation which makes me almost more anxious for Home Rule on England's behalf than on Ireland's. Ireland is at present a source of military weakness, as well as of moral discredit. It is fearful to reflect that, when Bonaparte was threatening us with invasion, we had to keep 140,000 armed men in Ireland, for which, six or seven years before, 50,000 had sufficed. However I cannot complain of the march of opinion in this country. I may die, and (which would be more serious) Parnell may die; but the end will come so soon as the people have an opportunity of giving judgment."[1]

Thus in the summer of 1889 Gladstone thought that the worst disaster that could befall Home Rule would be the death of Parnell. He learned in the winter of 1890 that he was wrong. Parnell's death would have been a small disaster compared with Parnell's disgrace. Home Rule might have survived the first; it was destroyed—for Gladstone's lifetime and long after—by the second.

Between the close of the Commission and the issue and discussion of the Report Parnell made his first and only visit to Hawarden. Everything promised well for the success of the Liberal party and it was obviously desirable that the details of a Home Rule settlement should be carefully examined as the time for action approached.

[1] Gladstone to Döllinger, July 13, 1889.

Gladstone had invited him in August, 1889. Parnell was unable to go to Hawarden then and Gladstone wrote again in October:

Private

Hawarden Castle,
Chester.
October 4, 1889.

Dear Mr Parnell,

I have been in hopes of hearing from you. Perhaps you cannot yet propose a time for coming here. If however you could come within the next ten days I should be glad: because soon after that time I should expect to have personal communication with several of my ex-colleagues and I could make good use of the results of any conversations between us.

The subjects on which I desire to speak with you as fully as may be are:

1. Changes in the Home Rule plan of 1886.
2. The Land question.
3. Your and our position under the commission, and the matters therewith immediately connected.

I should look to you, here, for all the information you can properly give me. I hope that the actions will in no case have the effect of losing another Parliamentary campaign. And I hope nothing may occur to give occasion for a days unnecessary delay in the Report of the Commission.

Believe me,
faithfully yours,
W. E. GLADSTONE.

Parnell did not find time to go to Hawarden till December 18. He spent two days there and Gladstone sent his colleagues the following account of his visit:

Secret.

After very long delay, of which I do not know the cause, Mr. Parnell's promised visit came off last week. He appeared well and cheerful and proposed to accompany (without a gun) my younger sons who went out shooting.

Nothing could be more satisfactory than his conversation; full as I thought of good sense from beginning to end.

I had prepared carefully all the points that I could think of, or recall from the suggestions of others, as possible improvements (as to essence or as to prudential policy) in the Irish Government Bill or Land Bill.

I did not press him to positive conclusions, but learned pretty well the leaning of his mind; and ascertained that, so far as I could judge, nothing like a crotchet, or an irrational demand, from his side, was likely to interfere with the proper freedom of our deliberations when the proper time comes for practical steps.

The points were numerous, and I propose to reserve the recital of them until we meet in London, which, if (as I assume) the Judges have made their report, I think we ought to do not later than the Saturday, or perhaps the Friday, before Tuesday the 11th when the Session opens.

I may say, however, that we were quite agreed in thinking the real difficulty lies in determining the particular form in which an Irish representation may have to be retained at Westminster. We conversed at large on the different modes. He has no absolute or foregone conclusion.

He emphatically agreed in the wisdom and necessity of reserving our judgment on this matter until a crisis is at hand.

Will those of my late colleagues who may see this paper kindly note the fact by their initials.

W.E.G.   D. 23. 89.

S.   24.12.89.
R.   27.12.89.
W.V.H.   29.12.'89.
G. rec^d and forwarded 30.12.89.
H.   1.1.90.
K.   2.1.90.
J.M.   3.1.90.
R.   4.1.90.
J.S.   7.1.90.
A.J.M.   8.1.90.
H.C.B.   20.1.90.
A.M.   25.1.90.

(Spencer, Ripon, Harcourt, Granville, Herschell, Kimberley, John Morley, Rosebery, Stansfeld, Mundella, Campbell-Bannerman, and Arnold Morley.)

This account can be supplemented by that given by Gladstone in his Diary.

Dec. 18, 1889.   Reviewed and threw into form all the points of possible amendment or change in the plan of Irish government, etc. for my meeting with Mr. Parnell.[1] He arrived at 5.30 and we had two hours of satisfactory conversation; but he put off the *gros* of it. 19. Two hours more with Mr. P. on points in Irish procedure plans. He is certainly one of the very best people to deal with that I have ever known. Took him to the old castle. He seems to notice and appreciate everything.

It is important, in view of the controversy that arose later, to note that, immediately after leaving Hawarden, Parnell made a speech at Liverpool full of enthusiasm and confidence in Gladstone.

Five days after this visit the first step was taken in the proceedings that destroyed Parnell and Gladstone's Home Rule plan, for it was on Christmas Eve, 1889, that O'Shea's solicitor filed his petition for divorce. The case itself did not come into court until November 15, 1890. Two days later O'Shea got his decree. Parnell and Mrs. O'Shea both denied the adultery and neither of them offered any defence. But Mrs. O'Shea in her pleadings had brought counter charges and this gave O'Shea's counsel, who was one of Parnell's bitterest opponents, Sir Edward Clarke, Solicitor General, full scope. He used his opportunity and Parnell was ruined.[2]

After the verdict on the Parnell case, Parnell said in a speech that when his own side of the divorce suit was known, a very different view would be entertained concerning him. The *Spectator* quoting this observed: " When have we heard anything else from anybody who has been the subject of universal condemnation ? " Parnell's side was not made

---

[1] These notes are given in an Appendix to this chapter.

[2] " Under ordinary circumstances, where no defence is forthcoming, the proceedings in the Divorce Court are often purely formal, and the matter is despatched without speeches or oral evidence. But in the present case counter-charges of connivance and condonation enabled the Solicitor General (Sir E. Clarke) who appeared for Captain O'Shea, to make a long statement as to the relations which had existed for many years between his client's wife and Mr. Parnell, and this statement was subsequently supported by evidence of which the credibility was not called in question by cross-examination. The outcome of this course was to show that for years Mr. Parnell had resorted to every device and subterfuge to conceal from the man he continued to call his friend the dishonour he had inflicted upon him. The facts as substantiated revealed a course of conduct more than usually base, and proved Mr. Parnell to be wholly without sense of honour or truthfulness." *Annual Register*, 1890, p. 231.

known to the world until 1931, when Mr. Henry Harrison published his important book *Parnell Vindicated*.[1] The significance of those revelations must be considered later. For the moment it is important to understand how the divorce court proceedings looked at the time.

A useful summary of the impression is to be found in the review of those proceedings given by the *Spectator*.

". . . it was shown that in spite of constant denials from both the accused, Capt. O'Shea had been persistently deceived by his friend and his wife for six years, and that so far from Capt. O'Shea conniving, he had challenged Mr. Parnell and that Mr. Parnell had on one occasion only avoided a personal collision through a discreet descent by a fire escape, from a window in Mrs. O'Shea's house, after which he presented himself at the front door, as a guest just arrived." (Nov. 17, 1890.)

Hardly a word in this account is true, yet it is the account that any man, friend as well as enemy of Parnell, would have given if he had followed the proceedings in court and known nothing more. All of these statements were made and none of them challenged. For two days anybody could say what he liked about Parnell, for Parnell did not appear and he was unrepresented by counsel. The view that an ordinary man would take of his conduct in appearing to shirk this ordeal was given by Clarke: " For some persons the criminal law had terrors which the moral law had not, and it was perhaps not to be wondered at that Mr. Parnell did not venture to add a criminal offence to the course of faithlessness and falsehood by which during these years he had betrayed the wife of a friend who trusted him." In court, O'Shea, free from the danger of cross-examination, stated that his wife had told him that Parnell was secretly married, and that his suspicions first roused in 1881, when he had sent Parnell a challenge to a duel which Parnell had declined, had been composed by assurances and denials. The documents produced included a letter from Parnell to O'Shea written in 1884, saying, in answer to remonstrances, " I do not know of any scandal, or any ground for one," and another from Mrs. O'Shea to her seventeen-year-old son,

---

[1] Mr. Harrison's revelations are the basis for this chapter.

written in 1887, promising to have " no further communications direct or indirect " with Parnell.

Even a friend who sat through these proceedings in court would have found it difficult at the end to think Parnell a man to be trusted. In the powerful and educated world Parnell had many more enemies than friends. Among his enemies was of course the *Times* newspaper, smarting under its terrible defeat. It is not surprising that the opportunity Parnell had given to his enemies was used to the utmost. Here is a description of these revelations given by the *Times* on November 18, a description artfully drawn to engage against Parnell every single prejudice in the British character:

" Domestic treachery, systematic and long continued deception, the whole squalid apparatus of letters written with the intention of misleading, houses taken under false names, disguises and aliases, secret visits and sudden flights make up a story of dull ignoble infidelity, untouched, so far as can be seen, by a single ray of sentiment, a single flash of passion, and comparable only to the dreary monotony of French middle-class vice, over which M. Zola's scalpel so lovingly lingers."

Thus the trial had created an atmosphere in which the *Times* could declare that there was no single flash of passion in an attachment of which the truth was that it was so completely governed by passion that Parnell let it ruin his life. But " middle-class French vice " was a stroke almost as telling as Pigott's letter—with the advantage that it could not be parried.

A few months earlier Parnell had appeared to the public a man of courage and character who had escaped a shameful conspiracy on the part of his rich and powerful enemies. He now appeared, apart from his adultery, a liar and coward, afraid both of O'Shea's boot and of the strong hand of the law. Morley writing on November 17 to Gladstone within a few hours of the decree, remarked: " What a perversion of character must have been worked by all that mean hiding, lying and the rest of it."

How had Parnell given this fatal impression ?

When Parnell and Mrs. O'Shea fell in love there were

two methods of treating their problem that would have rendered unnecessary all " that mean hiding, lying and the rest of it," which were fatal to his reputation. O'Shea was himself a faithless husband who was no longer living with his wife, and Mrs. O'Shea might have brought an action for divorce. Whether she could have obtained it is of course doubtful, for adultery and desertion were not at that time sufficient ground, without cruelty, for divorcing a husband. If the divorce was granted, Parnell's difficulty was gone. If it failed, the manly course for him was to carry her off openly and leave O'Shea to take action. Parnell would have been condemned by those who think it wrong for a man to be the lover of a woman who has a husband in law though not in fact, but there would have been nothing disgraceful to his reputation for honesty and courage. He would certainly have survived what would have been in comparison with the disturbance of 1890 something less than a storm in a teacup.

Unfortunately romance was in this case mixed up with finance. Mrs. O'Shea had a rich aunt with whom she was on most affectionate terms. The niece visited the aunt every day, and the aunt, it was well known, was going to leave her a fortune. In her lifetime she gave her generous help amounting to £3,000 a year. A scandal would put an end to this income and these expectations, and therefore both the O'Sheas wished to avoid a disclosure. O'Shea as well as Mrs. O'Shea would suffer if this old lady, then nearly ninety years of age, discovered that her niece had " looked outside her wedding ring." O'Shea had been living for some time in a flat provided by this aunt. It was easy then for Parnell to see a great deal of his wife without inconvenience or embarrassment to her absent husband, and he and Mrs. O'Shea regarded themselves as man and wife. Three daughters were born to them. O'Shea used to visit her house at Eltham from time to time to keep up appearances. He had a letter from Mrs. O'Shea promising him £600 a year if he left her free.[1]

All the facts with which Clarke made such play wear, of

[1] Harrison, *Parnell Vindicated*, p. 192.

course, a different look when this clue is in our hands. There was a conspiracy, but O'Shea was as much a conspirator as his wife and her lover. The victim, if there was a victim, was this old lady who provided both O'Shea and his wife with their livelihood and cheered them both with a prospect of a fortune. The secret of this affair had to be kept from her and kept also from the public. This was necessary for two reasons. In the first place if the facts became known they would reach her ears. In the second they would injure O'Shea's reputation and self-esteem.

Parnell's assurances and denials were thus not meant to deceive O'Shea but to enable him to deny the rumours that began to spread about Parnell's relations with his wife. They were given him to save his face. And the disguises that Parnell assumed—one day he was with a beard, another without it, one day he would drop his own not undistinguished name for the noble name of Fox—were meant, not to mislead O'Shea, but to mislead reporters. Parnell, O'Shea, and Mrs. O'Shea, had all a common interest in defeating the curiosity of the press.

Unfortunately for Parnell, O'Shea wanted more out of the arrangement than income to-day and a share in a fortune to-morrow. He wanted place and consequence in politics. Parnell had given him prestige by using him or accepting him as an intermediary, and on the strength of this prestige he importuned both Gladstone and Chamberlain for appointments. In the summer of 1885 he had to ask something that it was harder for Parnell to give. He found that he was going to lose his seat in Clare and he therefore asked Parnell to use his influence with the Liberals to get him a seat elsewhere. Parnell, putting his pride in his pocket, made a remarkable offer. He offered, through Mrs. O'Shea, if the Liberals would give O'Shea a Liberal seat in Ulster, to secure the Nationalist vote for four Liberal candidates in Ulster and for Henry Fowler in Wolverhampton.[1]

Gladstone replied to this offer as follows :

Dear Mrs. O'Shea.   October 24, 1885.

    I have received your letter together with one from your

---

[1] Letter from Mrs. O'Shea to Gladstone, Oct. 23, 1885.

2 R

husband of the same date.   I rely on your kindness to convey my answer.

The suggestions you have made lie wholly within the province of Lord Richard Grosvenor.   I will at once forward them to him and may perhaps see him: in any case I will not fail to tell him what I think however he already knows, that I shall be very sorry if Captain O'Shea should fail to obtain a seat in the new Parliament.

You will I am sure understand me in saying that if I were to go beyond this it would lead to much inconvenience and confusion of duties.

With regard to the paper you so kindly offer, if it is intended for me I shall be happy to receive it. . . .

He wrote the same day to Grosvenor:

October 24, 1885.

My dear R.G.

I inclose two letters from O'Sheas, *he* and *she*, together with copy of my reply.   The subject matter of the letters is very curious.   If I am to see the " paper " the sooner I see it the better.

Ever yours,

W. E. GLADSTONE.

Grosvenor tried to oblige him, but the local difficulties proved too great.   Parnell then offered help in the other Liverpool constituencies if the Liberals would give O'Shea the Exchange Division.   O'Shea was thus adopted as Liberal candidate.   Parnell's method and behaviour show how far he had to do violence to his feelings in so acting.   To get the Irish vote for O'Shea he had himself nominated and then withdrew in O'Shea's favour.   He then spoke for O'Shea to whom he paid compliments whose extravagance was only matched by their insincerity.   As the Irishmen had been ordered to vote against the Liberals throughout the country, some reason had to be given for the strange course Parnell was taking in recommending this exception.   He said that he recommended O'Shea because he had voted against coercion.   O'Shea was an Irishman and a Catholic, and he had performed important services in respect to the passing of the Arrears Act under which fully 100,000 tenant farmers were saved from the risk of eviction and extermination. He knew from his own knowledge that had it not been for the exertions of Capt. O'Shea that Act would never have been passed.[1] But O'Shea was beaten by fifty-five votes. Parnell was then driven to the last extremity. A vacancy occurred at Galway and Parnell forced O'Shea, who was, if the Nationalists had known, even more odious to him than to them, on this most unwilling constituency. But there was a struggle, and Healy and Biggar openly accused Parnell of compelling Irishmen to take a man they mistrusted in order to keep his mouth shut about Parnell's relations to his wife.

In 1890, when O'Shea was anxious to clear himself of the suspicion of collusion, he got Chamberlain to write him a letter in which Chamberlain said that Parnell had only taken up O'Shea's cause out of deference to the strong wishes of himself and " another person."[2] This statement was supplemented by a statement from Grosvenor to the effect that he had run O'Shea as a Liberal candidate.[3] It is difficult to understand how anybody could have believed that Parnell had put himself out and made himself bitter enemies in Galway by overriding the local choice and forcing O'Shea upon his party, merely in order to please the Liberal leaders whom he had just denounced savagely in his election manifesto. Grosvenor's statement was true, but it would have had rather a different look if he had added that Parnell had been so urgent in pressing the Liberals to find O'Shea a seat that he had offered them the Irish vote in four or five other constituencies. The truth was, of course, not that Parnell took up O'Shea at the request of the Liberals, but that the Liberals took up O'Shea at the request of O'Shea and Mrs. O'Shea strongly backed by Parnell.

Thus Parnell ruined himself by his fatal weakness in assenting to the O'Shea scheme. He put himself in the power of a man who had every reason to dislike him, and no reason to spare him, once his interest in sparing him had ceased. Master of his party, and at one time almost master

---

[1] *Times*, November 25, 1885.
[2] *Charles Stewart Parnell*, by K. O'Shea, II, p. 232.
[3] *ibid.*

of the House of Commons, he had given himself a master, and that master a man in whose hands no man of sense would put anything he valued. He suffered tortures as a lover and a father, wore out his sensitive nerves, and ruined his health, his career, and his cause, because in his first infatuation he had not had the strength of mind to tell his mistress that she must choose between him and her aunt's fortune. Few men have paid such a cruel price for a mistake. It was easy to yield to the woman he loved when he thought that his false position was only to last for a short time. Mrs. Wood was eighty-eight when Parnell became the lover of her niece. But as time went on this proud man found his plight intolerable. His double life involved him in one sacrifice after another, sacrifice of his dignity, sacrifice of his party's interests, neglect of his duty as a public man, neglect of his duty to his colleagues. The strain on his nerves helped to produce the final catastrophe, for, when at last O'Shea took action, he behaved like a man who had nothing to lose. For what is exasperating about this disaster is that even at the last Parnell could have averted the full blow if he had behaved with common sense.

The mutual hatred and contempt of these two men had grown steadily under the influence of their strange relationship. For the lapse of time made it more and more difficult to keep secret a makeshift arrangement designed to hold together for a few months. Parnell might take off his beard, borrow another name, try one method of concealment after another, but disguises that will serve an emergency become a danger when they become a habit. Parnell's mysterious absences from the House, from party meetings, from his Irish home and his Irish connexions, all the strange circumstances of his lonely life, spread talk and rumour. Parnell felt the strain in one character; O'Shea in another. Parnell had no hold over O'Shea except this prospect of a fortune; O'Shea, knowing himself the object of a good deal of ridicule and scorn behind the scenes, was like a man tempted and strained, fingering a loaded revolver. He knew that he could destroy this haughty man when he wanted. And every day, as talk spread, he became more conscious of his inglorious position. Here was a man who had believed not long before that he was going to step into some prized appointment.[1] When Mrs. O'Shea pressed Gladstone to find him a post, Gladstone, notoriously unsuccessful in judging men, passed on her request to his colleagues with his good wishes, believing that it was O'Shea who had got the Government out of their difficulty when Parnell was in Kilmainham, whereas O'Shea's part in the transaction had been the cause of their disaster. O'Shea had no longer any hope from the Liberals and his temper and his patience not unnaturally suffered when he heard everywhere of the rumours that were in movement all round him.

Mrs. Wood had defeated her niece's plans by her stubborn tenacity in defying death. When at last she died in 1889 she defeated her plans by her excessive generosity. For she left almost all her estate to Mrs. O'Shea in her own right. This unfortunately brought the other members of the family into litigation, for the brothers and sisters (one of them the soldier, Sir Evelyn Wood) held that the old lady had outlived her sanity, had been subject to undue influence, and had in consequence made an invalid will. Consequently Mrs. O'Shea could not put her hands on the money left her when she most needed it. For by this time the tension of the difficult position between Parnell and O'Shea had become intolerable. Parnell could not conceal his contempt for O'Shea ; O'Shea could not bridle his hatred for Parnell. The fortune, which it was supposed would come to him in a few months, had hung fire for some years, and there was now the prospect of delay, and further delay, and even the risk of its loss.

Moreover O'Shea's political importance no longer depended on Parnell. When Chamberlain left Gladstone and broke with Parnell, O'Shea naturally followed his friend and patron. He did not vote for the Home Rule Bill. He had then moved further and further away from Parnell into Chamberlain's confidence and friendship.

---

[1] See his flamboyant letter to his wife in 1885, to whom he said that Chamberlain had promised to make him Chief Secretary for Ireland. *Charles Stewart Parnell*, by K. O'Shea, II, p. 205.

It was Chamberlain who introduced him to Buckle when the *Times* wanted him as a witness against Parnell. That attempt to destroy Parnell had failed. There was another method that could not fail. A disclosure made nearly forty years later throws an interesting light on the final chapter. As early as September, 1889, when the forged letters had been exposed, Sir Alfred Robbins, the London correspondent of the *Birmingham Daily Post*, the great Liberal Unionist paper, was asked by " one on the inside of the Liberal Unionist ' machine' whether Parnell would be politically ruined by a divorce, the then recent Dilke instance being given as a promising precedent, and Capt. O'Shea, it was added, being believed to be willing to take proceedings."[1] Robbins strongly deprecated any such plan. The sequel he tells in a short and significant sentence. " But counsels of caution proved unavailing; and the die was soon cast." O'Shea agreed to take his loaded revolver out of his pocket.

As the day of the trial approached there was a good deal of uneasiness in Liberal circles. Gladstone wrote to Arnold Morley on November 4: " I fear a thundercloud is about to burst over Parnell's head, and I suppose it will end the career of a man in many respects invaluable."[2] But at the last moment he received a reassuring message from John Morley. On the 13th Morley had a talk with Parnell who dined with him at his house. In the course of his letter to Gladstone he said:

" I was bold enough to ask him, with due apologies, whether there was any chance of certain legal proceedings resulting in his disappearance, temporary or permanent, from the political stage. He took it graciously enough, though he showed no inclination to discuss the subject. ' Oh, no '—he said, ' nothing in the least leading to disappearance, so far as I am concerned, will come out of the legal proceedings. The other side don't know what a broken-kneed horse they are riding.' I said—' My notion is that unless something pointing to disappearance comes to pass, then you ought intrepidly to come to the H. of C., and take a part in business on the earliest occasion.' ' That,'

---

[1] *Parnell, the Last Five Years*, p. 132.
[2] Morley, *Life of Gladstone*, Vol. III, p. 429.

he replied, ' is just what you may depend on my doing. I assure you there will be nothing to prevent it.' I did not feel at liberty to go further into this delicate branch of my business."

At the same time Parnell gave a similar assurance to Davitt, who passed it on to the Irish Bishops. It was characteristic of Davitt that he found it harder to forgive Parnell for his perfidy to a friend than to forgive England for her brutality to an enemy.

What was Parnell's motive in making this strange statement? It was bound to increase the feeling against him if things went wrong and there seemed no reason on the face of it why he should want Morley not to know on November 13 what the whole world would know on November 17. Mr. Harrison's book and Sir Edward Clarke's allusions suggest a solution. By " the other side " Parnell meant of course his political enemies; by the " broken kneed horse," O'Shea. Mrs. O'Shea seems to have believed to the last that O'Shea would be bought off.[1] This would explain not only Parnell's statement but also her extraordinary behaviour.

Both Parnell and Mrs. O'Shea met the charge at first with simple denials. But Mrs. O'Shea then took a course of her own, a course that Clarke justly described as very remarkable. In fact a mistress resolved to ruin her lover would have acted as she did. She threw over her solicitor, Sir George Lewis, denied adultery and yet accused O'Shea of connivance, and then proceeded to charge him with adultery with her own sister, Mrs. Steele, who had been an opponent in the family litigation.[2] If Parnell had allowed O'Shea's collusion to be proved and the facts put before the Court, opinion of his own conduct would have been much less severe. But Parnell wanted to be rid of all the life of pretence and disguise to which he had been condemned, and to live openly with

[1] Mr. Harrison (p. 128 f.) thinks that Mrs. O'Shea could have bought her husband off and induced him to be divorced instead, if she could have touched Mrs. Wood's legacy and given him £20,000 and Sir Edward Clarke's book gives some colour to this view.

[2] This charge was probably connected with Mrs. O'Shea's hopes of divorcing O'Shea, against whom she would have had to prove cruelty as well as adultery.

the woman he loved and his children. He would not therefore do anything that would make it difficult for O'Shea to get his divorce. He did not defend the case. But obviously he ought to have restrained his mistress and compelled her to take the same course. If she had acted as he acted, the proceedings would have been brief and simple, and there would have been little for the sensational press and nothing for the music halls. It was Mrs. O'Shea's behaviour that enabled Parnell's enemies to say whatever they liked about him, for Clarke was of course entitled to call witnesses to rebut her charges, charges that seemed all the more outrageous because she made no attempt to sustain them. Parnell never tried apparently to check her fatal violence, and he took no single step to see that his own interests and reputation should count for anything in her decision. So he appeared to the public eye as a treacherous and cowardly fellow, slinking from the anger of an ill-used husband, living under one name here, another there, reduced to ludicrous shifts and tricks to save his skin. It was thus largely his own fault that the world only knew about his conduct what his enemies liked to say about it.

It was difficult for anybody to believe that Parnell could have exposed himself to such a misunderstanding from wilful negligence, and the conclusion that he was, in fact, what he appeared to be, followed inevitably for most minds. There seems little doubt that his negligence was due to his pride, and thus, by a strange irony, he owed his ascendancy and his fall to the same cause. He was a typical member of the Irish landlord class, inheriting its arrogance and its self sufficiency. When Gavan Duffy returned to Europe from Australia, he put his finger at once on the secret of Parnell's power over his followers. He saw that, whereas the Nationalist members were all men who found it difficult to work together, Parnell had the character that could impose its will. He was really a member of the garrison ruling the native Irish. But he had the reckless and imperious self confidence of that class. This quality had shown itself in his blunders as well as his successes. The speech in which he replied to Forster in 1883 was one example; the answer before the Parnell Commission, in which he spoke lightly of deceiving the House of Commons, was another. It was in that spirit that he treated from first to last all the problems raised by his relations with Mrs. O'Shea. That quality that Mr. Stephen Gwynn has described as so important an element in the landlord class, the spoilt children of Irish history, the belief that they are above the law and can follow their own impulses, gave Parnell in this last crisis the self-confidence that ruined him.

Thus his wilful recklessness destroyed his dignity in the public eye and there was no man who could less afford the loss of his dignity. It gave him his place in English esteem, as it gave him his place in Irish loyalty. Anybody in the House of Commons would have said of him what Abergavenny said of Wolsey:

> " I can see his pride
> Peep through each part of him: . . ."[1]

The *Spectator* once compared him to Napoleon III, of whom it was said that his external calm lowered the intellectual pulse of every man who came into contact with him. Dufferin had noted this as a secret of Napoleon's power. " It is this tranquillity of manner which gives him such ascendancy over the volatile French."[2] Mr. Henry Harrison says that Parnell could hold Irish audiences during long speeches of dry and hard argument, untouched by the rhetoric on which Irishmen live. If Fox had lost his dignity, there would still have been something for men to prize in him, for he was loved and not only respected. Parnell reminded his age of the saying about Pitt: " The lion walks alone; the jackals herd together." Once his dignity was gone, there was little left. His face was his fortune.

There was another reason why Parnell was in a specially vulnerable position. He was not only the leader of a party, he was also the man into whose control, as all England believed, Ireland would pass if Home Rule was carried. A

---

[1] *Henry VIII*, I, i, 67.
[2] *Helen's Tower*, by Harold Nicolson, p. 147.

great many Englishmen had regarded him as a man who was indifferent to means so long as he obtained his ends, who had used outrage as a political weapon; whose word was not to be trusted and whose sense of right and wrong was dusty and confused. Many of these Englishmen felt after the Parnell Commission that they had wronged him, that their own nation, as represented by its Government and its most powerful journal, had behaved meanly and unfairly, and that this cold and resolute Irishman had defeated a conspiracy in which all the wealth and social influence of a great party had been used without scruple for his ruin. For a few weeks Parnell was an English idol.

Then the idol had his great fall. He was tripped up, not by profligacy but by fidelity. If, instead of loving one woman with passionate constancy, he could have said

" What though a hundred lips shall meet with mine
A vagabond I shall be as the moon is "[1]

he might still have stood before the world a man of virtue. Unfortunately he appeared in court, not as the faithful lover but as the faithless friend. He allowed it to be believed that he was a liar, a trickster, and a coward. Cavour is reported to have said, when he was engaged in his plots for the liberation of Italy, " What rogues we should be if we did for ourselves what we do for our country." Of Parnell a man might well say as he read this story, " What a rogue he must be as a politician, if he does for his country what he does for himself." All the fear of putting Ireland under his power revived among men and women who had thought yesterday that Parnell was an honest man wronged, and believed to-day that for six years he had lived the kind of life described by Sir Edward Clarke. Webster and James had spent days in trying to prove that Parnell was a man whom nobody could trust. They had failed. In a few hours Clarke, using the opportunity Parnell's weakness had put into his eager hands, shattered his character, exposing him not only to the pulpit violence of the Puritans, but to the wicked laughter of the music halls.

ge Moore, *A Sicilian Idyll*

APPENDIX TO CHAPTER XXX

GLADSTONE'S NOTES FOR HIS CONVERSATION WITH PARNELL

IRISH GOVERNMENT. Points prepared for Conversation, December 18, 1889.

1. LAND.
   Irish Guarantee. Secured as in '86.
   Russell's compulsory purchase.
   q^y leave open to Dublin Parlt? (Or *allow* this to be introduced?)
   Point out that the question of guarantee is a question of
   economy—
   of free choice—
   not of risk.
   Compulsion is twofold.
   a. from the State.
   b. from the landlords *or* tenants.

2. CONTRACTS.
   Shall the Irish Legislature be inhibited from voting a law against contracts, in the same manner as the American States are now restrained?

3. SUPREMACY.
   Shall there be a Clause explicitly reserving the supremacy of Parliament over Ireland in common with the rest of the Empire?

4. MODE OF DELEGATION.
   Shall the imperial questions be enumerated as in 1886? or Shall the delegated powers be fixed by enumeration?

5. JUDICIAL APPOINTMENTS.
   (7 or 10).
   Fix x years from the passing of this Act, no Judge of the Superior Courts of Ireland except under an instrument signed or countersigned by one of Her Majesty's Principal Secretaries of State.
   The present salaries and pensions of all persons being such Judges at the time of passing this Act, and the salaries and pensions which may be appointed for all such other judges as above mentioned, to be charges upon the Consolidated Fund of Ireland and to be a lien on that Fund preferably to all voted charges.

6. AN IRISH REPRESENTATION AT WESTMINSTER.

    1. To be retained—in *some* form—if the public opinion, at the proper time, shall require it.

    2. Cardinal conditions of a retention.

       a. Clause for their reappearance in full numbers to consider any alteration of the Act shall be retained.

       b. Outside of this, the question to be *British*, not *Irish*, in honour as well as in law. Parliament to retain a free hand.

       c. So much will depend upon experience that the first legislation should be marked as *tentative*, in the form supplied by the Bank Act of 1844.

Practically perhaps the selection is to be made among three modes of proceeding:

    1. All Irish, voting on all questions.

    2. All Irish voting on some, i.e. Imperial questions.

    3. Some Irish, voting on all questions.

(A mode if full number retained)

Duplicate the Irish M.P.s to form the Irish House.

Senior M.P. to have seat in British Parlt.

And to vote on all questions *reserved* to that Parlt.

Speaker aided by a small Committee to decide in case of doubt.

So to continue for x years and thereafter until Parliament shall otherwise provide.

House of Lords. May decide upon notice given (or taken at the time) whether any particular question is or is not Imperial and if not may inhibit Irish Peers from voting, whether such Peers hold Peerages of the U.K. or not. But any Peer being also Peer of U.K. may renounce his Irish Peerage if he think fit.

PEERS.

    1. Irish Peers at Westminster: to follow the analogy of the plan which may be adopted for the House of Commons.

    2. If a *selection* has to be made, provision would be necessary to regulate the mode of voting, as Irish Peers are not necessarily connected with that country or any part of it.

MODES.

    1. Election.

    Shall there be a separate *Election* for Westminster? No.

    2. Numbers.

    Shall all Irish M.P.s have seats at Westminster? or a

selection? If a selection shall the Irish House choose them?
Under what conditions? In provinces.

3. Voting Powers.
    a. On all questions? or
    b. on all Imperial questions ? or
    c. on all except *delegated* questions?
    d. In case of doubt who decides?
4. Permutations and combinations of these.

FINANCE.

1. Relative amount of burden in respect of Imperial charges
   to be considered by a Commission, and estimated with
   reference
       a. to capacity
       b. to history
   for the decision of Govt. and Parlt.
2. When decided, shall it be embodied (as in 1886) in a fixed
   annual sum? or shall it be a fixed percentage of the total
   Imperial charge, varying in amount only with the variation
   of that charge?
3. Shall the sum, or percentage, thus fixed, be liable to reconsideration at Westminster, after a (sufficiently long)
   term of years?
4. The fixed proportion of Imperial Expenditure would be a
   first charge on all Irish Receipts.
5. Shall the machinery of the Receiver Generalship be
   retained? As matter of policy, for both sides of the water (i.e.,
   for British opinion now and the Irish *credit* hereafter) I
   attach to it the utmost value.
6. The Commission would have to consider:
       a. What items of charge are Imperial.
       b. How to deal with duties levied in one country for
            consumption in the other.
       c. Whether Ireland has any financial claim in respect of
            bygone transactions
7. Imperial Parliament to tax Ireland only in Customs and
   Excise: direct and mixed taxation resting with the Irish
   Legislature.
       Or can power of extending poor rate beyond Counties
   (or Provinces?) be withheld.

CHAPTER XXXI

GLADSTONE'S DILEMMA

" The political situation was never more grotesque than at the present moment. The enthusiasts for Home Rule are moving heaven and earth to deprive the Irish majority of their right to choose their own leader; while the opponents of Home Rule can hardly conceal their passionate desire that Mr. Parnell may remain where he is, in order that the party which he leads may lose all the English and Scotch sympathy which it had gained."

Spectator, November 29, 1890.

" Mr. Parnell doubtless trusts greatly to the effect of time; but the Home Rule party is now called by his name, and at the Election England and Scotland will be placarded with the charge of the Judge in the Divorce Court."

Spectator, November 22, 1890.

" The Gladstonian party have gone to deplorable lengths already in countenancing scandals for which only the defence of revolutionary expediency could be set up; but they will court moral destruction for themselves if they continue to maintain even political intimacy with one who rests under so grave and so ineffaceable a stigma."

The Standard, November, 1890 (quoted in the
Annual Register, 1890, p. 232).

To understand the difficulty that now overwhelmed Gladstone in the state to which the collapse of Parnell had brought politics we cannot do better than observe a remark that was made at the time by Hartington, recorded in the Queen's Journal. " I never thought anything in politics could give me as much pleasure as this does."[1] Hartington,

[1] *Queen Victoria's Letters*, Third Series, Vol. I, p. 658. November 29, 1890.

if any man, might have been expected to show a little sympathy with his ruined opponent. For Hartington had long been living in what the law would call adultery with a married woman. His mistress was a free woman in the sense that Mrs. O'Shea was a free woman. Like Mrs. O'Shea she was active in intriguing on her lover's behalf, and his colleagues regarded her influence as one of the forces that were drawing him to the Right. Yet he was as merciless to Parnell as if instead of being a Philistine fox-hunter, lover of a married woman, whose husband could have brought him into the Courts as O'Shea had brought Parnell, he had been an anchorite, a man of fasts and vigils, worn and emaciated by the austerities of one of the desert religions. He had been in two Cabinets. He had shared in some of the greatest reforms in his age. He had helped to give England Cardwell's Army and Forster's Schools, to give Ireland Gladstone's Land Acts. He had tasted in the course of his career the delights of unexpected victory and the satisfaction of difficult success. He had worked side by side with the greatest man of his time. Yet in this long and exciting career he had never known such pleasure as the pleasure he now enjoyed because a man of his own circumstances had been caught in the toils of the law. Parnell, whom he had always hated, had been taken in adultery, and Gladstone, for whom his steadily growing dislike by this time hardly fell short of hatred, was involved in his ruin. This was the high moment of the career of this proud patrician. Never in history has chivalry been at a lower ebb in the English upper classes.

The explanation is simple. Passion was allied with fear. To men like Hartington Parnell had always been a repulsive figure.[1] The cause he represented which had seemed merely insolent and ridiculous, was now, they believed, a grave danger to the British Empire. Consequently there had happened to British politics what has happened to war. The contrast is often drawn between the temper of modern war and of war before the French Revolution. In the eighteenth century Sterne

[1] The Phoenix Park murders had made Hartington more bitterly anti-Irish.

might wander about France not knowing whether at the moment England and France were at war or peace. In the twentieth century such a state of things was inconceivable. The Germans, who treated Belgium with whom they had no shadow of a quarrel with such barbarous cruelty, believed that they were fighting for existence. The Allies, whose sea power was used to make a blockade much more inflexible than the blockade that Cobbett thought too brutal a century earlier, believed that they were fighting for their existence. To men like Salisbury and Hartington the struggle over Home Rule differed from previous struggles as the Great War of 1914 differed from the dynastic wars of the eighteenth century. In such a struggle it is only in rare minds that there is still place for chivalry or for the graces and generosities of politics. Thus Parnell's calamity could not have come at a time when his enemies would have been more determined to use it for his ruin.

Nor could it have come at a time when it was more certain to make him a fatal incubus to his friends. To understand this it is only necessary to consider what had happened between 1886 and 1890.

Unwisely, as we have seen, Gladstone had put aside all question of English reform in 1886 in order to concentrate on the Irish issue. He had said to the nation, " You have the opportunity if you act quickly of winning the friendship of the Irish people; if you lose the opportunity it may never come again. I ask you to make a great contribution to the peace of the world and to the happiness and self-respect of the British Empire." That was his appeal. It was rejected by the comfortable and leisured classes; accepted by the majority of the workmen and the Nonconformists in the Liberal party. It was accepted, that is, as a great moral act of friendship and justice.

During the last three years the Liberal agitation for Home Rule had been helped first by coercion and then by the scandal of the Parnell Commission. English M.P.s had gone to Ireland to witness evictions; Irish members had come to England to speak in all the English towns. These joint meetings had become a regular feature of Liberal politics. Gladstone by his policy had succeeded in bringing about an alliance between British democratic sentiment and Irish popular feeling; a success that was of lasting value. All the strength and purpose of the Liberal movement had been concentrated on a great display of friendship and generosity. In a letter to Parnell Gladstone, long before the crash, had paid a tribute to the warmth with which British Nonconformists had taken up the grievances of a Catholic people. There has never perhaps been a time when there was more chivalry in the popular feeling. It was this that had upset the calculations of Chamberlain.

In these demonstrations Parnell was of course the hero of British Liberalism. He was like a Kossuth or a Garibaldi; the leader of a small people seeking its freedom; the protector of the peasant crushed by landlords like Clanricarde; the victim of the plots of powerful enemies, pursued by Salisbury and Chamberlain as Garibaldi and Mazzini had been pursued by Italy's Austrian oppressors. To understand the plight in which the Liberal Party found itself, it must be remembered that it stood for one thing only, Home Rule, for it had gambled, under Gladstone's inspiration, on its chance of persuading the English people to do a generous thing. All its eggs were in Parnell's basket at the moment when O'Shea kicked that basket over.

To understand the public opinion of a party it is necessary to study its component elements. An important part of the strength of the Liberal party was of course its Nonconformist following. This was still considerable, though some leading figures like Dale[1] and Spurgeon had followed Chamberlain. In a controversy where the Established Church was pretty solid on one side, in a country where organized religion has always had political interests, the tone and temper of this Nonconformist element counted for a good deal. It was clearly and loudly hostile to a man who had broken what it considered a moral law of great consequence.[2] Its leaders held that such behaviour as that of

[1] Dale tried to act as peacemaker in April, 1886, and Gladstone warmly appreciated his efforts. See letter from Gladstone to Dale, April 29, 1886.
[2] With a few notable exceptions such as Jacob Bright and Alfred Illingworth.

2 S

which Parnell had been found guilty should disqualify a public man for a great position in politics.[1]

On any large view of history this contention seems wrong and dangerous. The government of a society is not like the government of a monastery and a man's capacity for serving its highest purposes must be judged by the sum of his qualities. It would be generally agreed that Fox, Grey, Melbourne, Wellington, and Palmerston had qualities that far outweighed the evil that the public suffered from their habits. Gladstone would not admit, when he discussed Sheridan's treatment at the hands of the Whigs, in an article in the *Nineteenth Century* in 1896, that his drunkenness excused his exclusion from the Cabinet of 1806. If private virtue is the only criterion of public usefulness, we should be driven to conclude that Fox who did more than any other English Minister to put down the slave trade should have been kept out of power, and Sidmouth who supported the trade with the ingenious argument that it enabled the slaves in the West Indies to receive news from time to time of their relations in Africa, should have been upheld as a Minister. Sidmouth was an Evangelical, but he was also one of the most mischievous influences in public life; if it had not been for the little band of Liberals who followed Fox and learnt from him their sense for liberty, he would have brought England almost to civil war. The authors of the infamous Combination Laws were the most virtuous men of the day (one of them was Wilberforce); they were resisted with immense courage and public spirit by Sheridan, a drunkard, and Lord Holland, convicted of adultery and living in great state with the woman whom he had tempted away from her lawful husband. It is easy then to see that if men of irregular life had been shut out from politics in the eighteenth century, England would have been worse governed and the classes and races, who were at the mercy of her rulers, would have been worse treated.

No doubt even in those days such men paid for their habits in some loss of power and influence. Of none of them

---

[1] Dr. Clifford wrote to the *Star*, " Men legally convicted of immorality will not be permitted to lead in the legislation of the kingdom."

was it truer than of Fox. That was inevitable and not unjust. Price, the famous Nonconformist philosopher, supported him, but he was distressed by his conduct. " Oh that I could see," he wrote, " in men who oppose tyranny in the State, a disdain for the tyranny of low passions in themselves." Some dissenters actively opposed him on the ground that Wilkes had given a bad name to the " immoral patriot," and one poet of the time put the feeling against such characters into some biting lines:

> " Amaze the Welkin with an empty cry
> of ' Justice, Rights of Men and Liberty '
> As if the villain whom no ties can bind
> In private life can cherish all his kind."[1]

Most people now would agree that the destruction of Parnell in consequence of the divorce case was a stupendous calamity both for England and Ireland. But to treat the Nonconformist sentiment on the case as a trifle that a political leader could disregard is to forget the plain facts. In 1890 the Nonconformist leaders were active politicians as well as preachers of the gospel and their power as political leaders came from the confidence that their followers gave to their authority as moral teachers. This had helped the cause of Home Rule but it was now a strong obstacle to Parnell's leadership. On what ground was Dr. Clifford a Home Ruler? On the ground that Home Rule raised in his judgment a moral issue. But the same set of convictions that made him a Home Ruler made him take a stern view of Parnell's conduct, and of the effect of his example. Salisbury made great play with the difficulties of the Irish party, hesitating between Parnell and the Seventh Commandment.[2] If he could have twitted the Nonconformists with throwing over the Seventh Commandment what would have been their answer? After asking England to put Parnell into power in Ireland in the name of a great moral principle, they could hardly reply that Parnell's character was a matter of

[1] See Lincoln, *English Dissent*, p. 147.
[2] " The Dublin agitators at first backed Mr. Parnell: later on they backed the Seventh Commandment."

indifference.   It is one thing to judge them right in their conclusion and their refusal to consider other aspects of the problem; it is another to think that their objection was merely a fugitive mood or that holding the views they held they could have suppressed them without loss of self respect.

The Nonconformists were supported by the Catholics. The Catholics in England were divided on Home Rule but the poor Catholics were an important element in the Home Rule movement in the towns of England and Scotland. Their leader was Manning.   No man had done more to win and justify their confidence.   If it is one of the chief tasks of a Christian leader to help the weak and downtrodden, Manning was the leading Christian in England.   He had stood by the agricultural labourers in the days of Arch when a leading Anglican bishop had incited the farmers to violence against them; he had been the friend of the docker; all his letters to Gladstone show what he said to him at the end of his life that he had never forgotten the echoes of Peterloo and the cruel treatment of the English poor in the days of Sidmouth.   Manning made up his mind at once. As soon as the case was over he wrote urgently to the Archbishop of Dublin and his agitation is shown by the letters that followed one another in quick succession to Hawarden (Nov. 21, Nov. 22, Nov. 27, Nov. 29, Dec. 4, Dec. 5).

Mr. Robert Graves has given a delightful picture of the adventure of the great whale that made its way into the Black Sea in the time of Justinian, causing a great deal of damage and spreading terror among fishermen.[1]   Both Orthodox and Monophysite bishops went down to preach to him from the shore and pamphlets and texts were put into the sea to warn him of the displeasure of the Trinity.   The Catholics and Nonconformists now combined as Orthodox and Monophysite combined in that emergency.   Parnell took as little notice of them as the great whale Porphyry took of the sixth-century bishops but unhappily their weapons were more effective.

If the Nonconformists were one element in the party, the Radicals were another.   How did they stand?   They had

---

[1] *Belisarius*, by Robert Graves, p. 82.

allowed all their special causes to be postponed for a single purpose. They had seen all the force of their party, its new popular organization, and the power and energy of its great orator and leader, diverted from domestic needs of the most pressing kind to this Irish revolution. Parnell had put his country's interest so definitely below his own desires as a lover as to destroy a great body of enthusiasm in England at the moment when it seemed on the brink of triumph. What then should the Radicals do? Return to their own neglected causes and put this shaken and broken enterprise aside. That was the argument of men like Atherley Jones, the son of Ernest Jones the Chartist.

The Nonconformist and the Radical were both men with a special interest in the Liberal movement. But there were also, of course, a great number of men who were Liberals, either from tradition, or because their general outlook had kept them on that side when the split came. They did not share the special views either of the Nonconformist or the Radical. For them the important question was what was going to become of their party. It had suffered one great defeat. Was it now, after all its confident hopes of coming victory, to suffer a second? Whether Parnell should suffer for his private life was one question; whether he would suffer another. A man might think that it was wrong and foolish to throw over a man of genius because he had stolen another man's wife, and yet recognize that if enough people took the other view Parnell's leadership could only mean the destruction of the Party that was allied with him. It might be that somebody ought to come forward to defend the view that a man's private life should not be considered by the public when he asked for its confidence, but it could hardly be said that a political party should put all its prospects and programmes aside for this purpose.

For the Liberals were challenged directly on this issue.

" No statesman aspiring to control a powerful party, and to share the responsibilities of office, could survive the blow of having such a charge proved against him in open court. The Gladstonians and the Parnellite party may, if they like, ignore the finding of the Divorce Court and the charge of Mr. Justice Butt as they pretended to ignore the report of the Special Commission, but they cannot prevent the British public from drawing its own conclusion."

In that sentence the *Times* made it clear that all the force with which his opponents had assailed the character of Parnell, the politician, was now to be turned against his character as a man. The unhappy Liberals were not in the position of men who could pass over this event in silence; they had to meet a challenge. Nearly sixty years before, a politician more powerful than Parnell had been attacked in the courts on a similar charge. In June, 1836, Melbourne, then Prime Minister, was served with a writ by George Norton who accused him of adultery with his wife. The case ended with a triumph for Melbourne, but it cost him several sleepless nights and before it came into court he informed the King that he was ready to resign. But William IV, though he hated Melbourne's Government, was too much of a gentleman to take advantage of this opportunity for injuring him. " People may discuss," he replied, " the public acts of my Ministers, as much as they please, but I will never countenance an attempt of any party to turn to its advantage an error of conduct of this description. We have all had our faults in this way."[1] A person even more important than the King gave Melbourne his support. Wellington let him know that he would not take a place in any Government that was formed to succeed him if he was compelled to resign on account of this incident.[2] Unfortunately Queen Victoria was not King William IV, and there was nothing of Wellington's temper in Salisbury, Hartington, or Chamberlain. One of them might have said with William IV, " We have all had our faults in this way," but they were all three intent on Parnell's ruin, and the destruction of the Home Rule cause, and they welcomed eagerly this turn of fortune.

Politics are to-day so much gentler than they were at that time that it is not easy for us to understand what the prospect of the next election looked like to a Liberal

---

[1] Newman, *Melbourne*, p. 216.
[2] Torrens, *Memoirs of Melbourne*, Vol. II, p. 191.

without studying the speeches made against Gladstone and Parnell before the divorce case was heard of. The Liberals of the time were under no illusion. They knew that, as the *Spectator* saw, the Parnell divorce would be the topic of the next election. The Unionist party literature would have been full of its ignominious revelations or fictions. The invented fire-escape would have played a large part. Gladstone, of whom the *Times* said when the divorce occurred that he occupied a position more humiliating than any man had occupied before in history, would have been pilloried as the ally of the hero of these squalid intrigues. Salisbury had the most caustic and Chamberlain the most bitter tongue in politics, and neither of them was capable of letting such an opportunity slip. We have only to look at their speeches at this time to see how little self-restraint they would have shown. Salisbury joked in the House of Lords about the fire-escape.[1] Chamberlain attacked the Liberal leaders for their delay in denouncing Parnell's adultery. " Even the disclosures in the Divorce Court did not shake the loyalty of the Gladstonian politicians and it was not until there was agitation among the Nonconformists and that it was evident that the party were going to lose votes, that any of the party leaders uttered a word of condemnation."[2] He described Parnell's followers as " mercenaries paid by foreign money," and declared that there was no pin to choose between " these two rival bands of mercenary patriots."[3] A passage in the report of another speech

---

[1] November 25, 1890. The *Annual Register* remarks: " The House was greatly amused but somewhat astonished," p. 250.

[2] *Times,* January 14, 1891.

[3] " These men call themselves Nationalists. They now—some of them—have even ventured to assume the title of patriots. (Laughter.) They are neither one nor the other (Cheers.) But they are mercenaries paid by foreign money. (Loud Cheers.)" It is curious to reflect on the difference between the Irish party leaders to whom Chamberlain denied the name of patriots and the leaders of other parties. Parnell, Dillon, Sexton, William O'Brien, Redmond, and Healy all spent several months in prison. No Unionist leader was ever called upon to pay that price for his patriotism. Moreover, all of those men, if they had chosen to enter the House of Commons as Liberals or Conservatives or to change their party, would have been certain of office. They were all men of Front Bench rank. But every Irish Nationalist had to put this, which most politicians regard as one of the attractions of a political career, outside

of his gives us the atmosphere of these meetings. " Is there any price that Mr. Gladstone would not pay for eighty-six Irish votes? What is it that Mr. Parnell wants? (A voice: A 'Fire escape.') Laughter."[1] Every Liberal candidate would have to face a campaign of ridicule and abuse, such as no man had faced since Fox faced Gillray, at the outset of an election of which he had hoped, until this disaster, that it would give Home Rule a triumph. What sort of hearing would the case for Home Rule get from audiences offered these personal entertainments? For, if Parnell was leader, everything would turn on his claim to the public confidence, as the man into whose hands England was to put the destinies of Ireland. The only chance for Home Rule, for Radical causes, and for the Liberal party, was to eliminate the personal issue, to give the party a domestic Radical programme, and to trust to Gladstone's eloquence to keep alive some of the old fire on the wrongs of Ireland. These would seem to the ordinary Liberal the plain tactics of the hour. Yet how could the personal question be eliminated unless Parnell withdrew for a time into the background?

When the blow fell, Gladstone wrote to Acton (November 17):

" The Parnell business is terrible. It seems that he is to go on, and that he has been accepted by his party as prospective leader. There comes back upon my mind the saying of the old Aberdeenshire peasant ' It'll na dae (do).' We have never had a case quite like it. His intellect has some singular and admirable qualifications of statesmanship but it seems to me that all moral force is gone and what a man can do when publicly deprived of it we have now to know by an experiment heretofore untried."

In other words Gladstone had no intention of helping to hound Parnell out of public life, but he was pretty sure that these revelations had destroyed his power. Gladstone's interest in the experiment was that of the man who had

---

his mind altogether. One Irishman who had been associated with Parnell's party tried to feather his own nest. This was O'Shea, the man of whom Chamberlain made an intimate friend and ally.

[1] *Times*, January 28, 1891.

staked all that was left of his career on carrying Home Rule, and had led the Liberal party into this perilous cause. He watched events, as a Home Ruler and as Liberal leader, not as a censor of morals. A man who had served under Palmerston, and under whom Hartington had served, could not take the view of the Nonconformists that in itself adultery was a bar to public office.

Morley's first letter was hopeful, for he thought that " the ugly thing might quickly recede into the background," a view that seemed to overlook the strong interest that Parnell's opponents had in keeping " the ugly thing " before the public eye. The *Times*, having discovered, as it put it, that " Mr. Gladstone occupied the most pitiable and humiliating position that can possibly be conceived for the trusted chief of a historic party," was hardly likely to turn aside to tamer topics. Moreover the divorce had come at the worst possible moment. The case ended on November 17. On November 21 there was to be the annual meeting of the National Liberal Federation and on the 25th Parliament was to reassemble. There was little chance of sober and quiet reflexion and discussion, with, first a party meeting, and then the meeting of Parliament, following immediately upon this political shock.

On November 18 Morley wrote to Gladstone saying he had to speak at Sheffield and that his own disposition was to " give our passing disaster the complete go bye " and asking if Gladstone had anything he wished said. Gladstone replied sending a paragraph as well as his private comments on the position.

Copy.   Hawarden,

Secret.   November 19, 1890.

My dear Morley,

Your appeal as to your meeting to-morrow gives matter for thought. I feel 1. that the Irish have abstractedly a right to decide the question 2. that on account of Parnell's enormous services—he has done for Home Rule something like what Cobden did for Free Trade, set the argument on its legs—they are in a position of immense difficulty; 3. that we the Liberal party as a whole, & especially as its leaders, have for the moment nothing to say to it, that we must be passive, must wait & watch. But I again & again say to myself the words I have already quoted, say them I mean in the interior & silent forum " It'll na dae."

I should not be surprised if there were to be rather painful manifestations in the House on Tuesday.

It is yet to be seen what our Nonconformist friends, such a man as Guiness Rogers for example, or such a man as Colman, will say.

On reading your note, I can only find my way to an answer by asking myself what *I* should do were I in your or Harcourt's place. And I certainly think that I should use such words as the inclosed, or should say something in that sense.

If I recollect Southey's *Life of Nelson* was in my early days published & circulated by the Society for promoting Christian Knowledge. It wd. be curious to look back upon it & see how the Biographer treats his narrative at the tender points.

What I have said under figure 3 applies to me beyond all others & notwithstanding my prognostications I shall maintain an extreme reserve in a position when I can do no good (in the present time) & might by indiscretion do much harm.

You will doubtless communicate with Harcourt & confidential friends only as to anything in this letter & inclosure.

ever yours sincerely,
W. E. GLADSTONE.

The thing, one can see, is not a *res judicata.* It may ripen fast. Thus far, there is a total want of moral support from this side to the Irish judgment.

ABBOZZO.

We meet to-day, as heretofore, in the prosecution of a great cause, which our opponents endeavour to darken and discredit by misstatement, or by mixing it with matter either irrelevant or secondary. Our duty is to keep it apart from what does not belong to it and hold it aloft in the public view. This happens to be difficult at a moment when, as within the last week or fortnight, the country has been peculiarly stirred by anxious or painful incidents and disclosures. None of these derogate in the slightest degree from the justice, or the urgency, or the sacredness, of our great cause. It is as sound to-day as it was yesterday; and it becomes from day to day more urgent, as it draws nearer to the final issue; so that it is more than ever necessary to look at it on the merits and to allow nothing else however grave, however material to be considered in its proper time and place, to slacken for a moment our devotion to it.

Unfortunately for Gladstone's peace of mind, it was not only his opponents who were mixing Home Rule with "matter either irrelevant or secondary." Among them was a journalist of whose capacity for mischief every politician was painfully aware. Morley wrote on November 19 that Stead had been to see him, and had told him that he was going to raise his fiercest whoop against Parnell remaining in the post of leader on the ground that " we shall never be able to persuade the public that any bargain made by him will be kept." Stead had also given him information about persons more important than Stead himself.

" He saw Davitt this morning. Davitt is furious with Parnell who, as he asserts, assured him that the charge was utterly false. Davitt has written to Croke (Archbishop of Cashel) to warn him that Parnell's leadership will not be endorsed by his (Davitt's) section at any price. . . . Stead had also seen Cardinal Manning. The Cardinal said ' I have expressed my views in quarters where it is proper that they should be first known. Until there has been time for their consideration, I must decline to say a word.' This means, no doubt, stern condemnation of Parnell's leadership in Ireland and at Rome."[1]

Gladstone thus knew that there would be Irish opposition to Parnell, partly from the Left and partly from the Church. A few days later Gladstone received a letter from Manning himself. Manning had sent Gladstone proof of an article that he was writing for the *Nineteenth Century* on a scheme of Carnegie's for organizing private charity and, after thanking Gladstone for his promptness in returning it he went on:

" I have written twice since Monday most urgently to the Archbishop of Dublin. Mr. Parnell cannot be upheld as leader. No political expediency can outweigh the moral sense. I trust that the Irish people will see this. The politicians will not but I

---

[1] This shows that Miss Haslip is incorrect in stating that Manning took his lead from Gladstone. *Parnell*, p. 375.

hope the Bishops, Priests and the " sanior pars " of the people will. I suggested the appointment of five as the leaders in Commission, Justin McCarthy, Sexton, Healy, Dillon and O'Brien. These would represent the extremes and the Centre. Mr. Stead tells me to-day that Archbishop Croke is for Parnell's retirement. If Archbishop Walsh agrees I think it will be done. But it rests more with you than with any man. If you say "do not fetter my freedom of action and take away my strength by putting the cause of Ireland in opposition to the public feeling and instinct of England and my chief supporters," Mr. Parnell would retire from leadership and still give all aid as before to the Irish cause. I have not spoken publicly for fear of clashing with the Irish Bishops, but I have let them know my mind."

The next day Manning wrote again:

Gratitude, blind loyalty and just anger at English violence will make the Irish people refuse to forsake Parnell.

" I feel for them and in a sense with them. But I hope their Bishops and Priests will bid them be silent.

" My belief is that when Parliament meets and you and the Irish Members are face to face Mr. Parnell will quietly leave you and the Irish Members to act together. But to this end you must let the weight of your words be felt. Do not efface yourself."

On the 22nd Morley sent him an alarming account of the atmosphere of the Sheffield meeting.

Private.

95 Elm Park Gardens,
South Kensington, S.W.

November 22, 1890.

Dear Mr. Gladstone,

I was very grateful for your letter at Sheffield.

The feeling there was as strong as strong could be, that Parnell's leadership is, for a time at least, intolerable. Some declare that they would rather vote for a Tory, than for H.R. under Parnell. Most, however, take the more moderate line that his installation as leader now would be a piece of bravado, and that he must at any rate subject himself to a period of quarantine.

Abp. Croke has written to Davitt, approving his line. But I do not expect Dr. Croke or any of his confreres to say as much in public. The ground won't bear, to use your own expression.

Guinness Rogers, I hear, is as strong as Clifford or Hughes, the Wesleyan.

. . . . .

Always your's sincerely,

JOHN MORLEY.

Parliament was to meet on the 25th and on the 24th Gladstone came to London. The Irish party was to meet next day to elect its leader for the session. There had already been enthusiastic meetings of support for Parnell in Dublin, one on the 18th a meeting of the National League, the other a meeting on the 20th, a demonstration over which the Lord Mayor had presided. But there were also signs of opposition, for, of the five delegates at that moment in the United States, Dillon, William O'Brien, Harrington, T. P. O'Connor, and T. D. Sullivan, the last named, taking the same view as Davitt of Parnell's offence, had refused to give his signature to a message of confidence.

Gladstone had now made up his mind that the hope of carrying Home Rule was desperate if the Liberal party had to defend at the General Election not only Home Rule but Parnell's mismanaged divorce case. Mr. Francis Birrell, in his brilliant little book on Gladstone, observed that it was a pity that neither Gladstone, nor Harcourt, nor Morley, were Nonconformists, for if they had been they would have rated at its true value the Nonconformist bluster. But Gladstone might fairly reply that he disregarded Nonconformist bluster over the Forster Bill in 1870, and that the Nonconformist defection was everywhere believed to be one of the chief causes of his disastrous defeat in 1874. An election like that of 1874 would finish Home Rule for his lifetime.[1]

Gladstone had, as it happened, given Parnell a year earlier a warning about the importance of the Nonconformist vote to Home Rule. At the end of the session of 1889 Balfour had surprised the House of Commons by a speech in which he intimated that he hoped to be able to give the Irish Catholics a University. Parnell had given the speech what the *Annual Register* called " a cautious approval," but

[1] In 1874 the Liberals were 244 to the Conservatives 350.

there was an immediate outcry from some of the Radicals. The inside history of the proposal and its abandonment is told in the *Life of Balfour*.[1] Gladstone wrote to Parnell in August warning him that there were limits to his influence over the Liberal Party and that the Nonconformists were the backbone of the party.[2]

Gladstone was thus drawn into a problem of how to treat, not a question, but a man, and almost all his failures in politics came from his want of skill and judgment for such purposes. He began wisely enough. Parnell and Morley had always got on well together, and even after the bitter quarrel Parnell continued to say that he regarded Morley as an honest man. Morley was, therefore, the obvious person to act as an emissary and Morley undertook the task. But Parnell was better able than most men to avoid a meeting that he wished to avoid, and the nearest that Morley could get to him was his secretary, Campbell. From him he learned that Parnell, at first unyielding, had later been more ready to consider the difficulties of his allies and the risk of losing Home Rule.[3] Unhappily this mood did not last. Meanwhile Gladstone was being pressed by Harcourt to write directly to Parnell and to break with him. Harcourt differed of course from Gladstone and Morley on Home Rule; they were Home Rulers before they were anything else, he was a Home Ruler against the grain.[4] He wrote to Gladstone in this sense on November 22, " whether it means a severance from the Irish party I know not, but any other course will certainly involve the alienation of the greater and better portion of the Liberal party of Great Britain—which after all, is that which we have mainly to consider." Gladstone's answer written on November 23 put his own position and asked that McCarthy should be invited to call on him (Gladstone) on the 24th when Gladstone was to

---

[1] *Life of Balfour*, by Mrs. Dugdale, Vol. I, 1, 168.

[2] The letter is printed in an Appendix to this Chapter.

[3] *Recollections*, Vol. I, p. 259.

[4] He wrote later, December 18, to his son: " Like Grattan we can say ' we sat by its cradle and we followed its hearse '. And I at least suffered quite as much from the pangs of its birth as I ever can from the agony of its decease." Gardiner, *Life*, Vol. II, p. 91.

arrive in London.[1] He explained what he wanted said to
McCarthy, for McCarthy to pass on to Parnell. After
referring to the week spent in observing the movement of
public opinion, he went on

" The effect of that observation, corroborated by counsel with my
friends, is to convince me that the continuance of Mr. Parnell
in the leadership of the Irish party at the present moment would
be, notwithstanding his splendid services to his country, so to
act upon British sentiment as to produce the gravest mischief
to the cause of Ireland; to place those who represent that Party
in a position of irremediable difficulty; and to make the farther
maintenance of my own leadership for the purposes of that cause
little better than a nullity.

" It should be understood that in what has been said I do
not constitute myself a judge, in any respect or degree, of the
merits of the case, but simply take note of the facts, as I conceive
that I am bound to do by my duty to the Irish party and to
Ireland at large."

Gladstone thus asked Harcourt to ask McCarthy to pass
on to Parnell a tactful and friendly warning. He could
scarcely have done less. He and Parnell were engaged in
the battle for Home Rule. It would have been fair neither
to Parnell nor to Ireland for him to conceal from Parnell his
belief that if Parnell did not withdraw he, Gladstone, could
not carry Home Rule in England. That after all was
Gladstone's part of the alliance. Parnell himself might
have complained of such concealment. Up to this point
Gladstone was engaged only in the attempt to communicate
his views privately to Parnell through a friendly medium,
and the views that he wished so to communicate were his
views of the political effects, not of the moral implications,
of the proceedings in the Divorce Court. Harcourt would
have liked him to pronounce on both, but he resolutely
declined.

" Harcourt was very strong that in the communication to Parnell
Mr. G. should express his own opinion that the immorality
itself had made him unfit and impossible, and not merely found
himself on the opinion of the party upon the immorality. ' The

[1] The letter is given in Gardiner, *Life of Harcourt*, Vol. II, p. 84.

party would expect it,' he said,' would not be satisfied otherwise; Mr. G's moral reputation required it.' Mr. G. stoutly fought any such position. ' What,' cried Mr. G., ' because a man is what is called leader of a party, does that constitute him a judge and accuser of faith and morals? I will not accept it. It would make life intolerable '."[1]

On the 24th McCarthy called on Gladstone who had with him Harcourt, Granville, Morley, and Arnold Morley. Gladstone went upstairs and saw McCarthy who told him that he did not know where Parnell was but that he hoped to see him next day and would then show him a short letter that Gladstone was to prepare. This letter was given later to McCarthy. But Morley also expected to see Parnell the next day, and it was agreed that Gladstone should also write a letter to Morley which he would show to Parnell. Thus Parnell would learn Gladstone's views either from Morley or from McCarthy. That night the men who had met at Gladstone's house at the Ex-Cabinet dinner all dined at Arnold Morley's. Gladstone drafted his letter and showed it to Morley. Then followed a curious incident, thus described by Morley.

" While he read the Queen's Speech to the rest, I perused and reperused the letter; Granville also read it. I said to Mr. G. across Granville, ' But you have not put in the very thing that would be most likely of all things to move him.' Harcourt again regretted that it was addressed to me and not to Parnell, and agreed with me that it ought to be strengthened as I had indicated, if it was really meant to affect P's mind. Mr. G. rose, went to the writing table, and with me standing by, wrote, on a sheet of Arnold M's grey paper, the important insertion. I marked then and there under his eyes the point at which the insertion was to be made, and put the whole into my pocket. Nobody else besides H. was consulted about it, or saw it. After the letter came to be printed, Mr. G. remarked to me that he thought the insertion was to be a postscript. He did not complain or care but was it not so? ' No,' I said, ' it really was not; I marked the place in pencil at the moment'. Just imagine— ' P.S. By the way, I forgot to mention that if he does not go, my leadership of the Liberal Party is reduced to a nullity.' What a postscript, to be sure."[1]

The next day Parnell managed to elude Morley till after the Irish meeting but McCarthy saw him and brought back bad news. When Morley saw Gladstone after lunch he learned that McCarthy had told Arnold Morley that he had seen Parnell, that he had delivered Gladstone's message and that Parnell meant to stick to his guns. Meanwhile John Morley's attempt to see Parnell before the meeting of the Irish party had miscarried. They met after the meeting when the Irish party, ignorant of Gladstone's warning, had re-elected Parnell. Morley has given an account of their conversation and its sequel.

" November 25. I had taken the usual means of sending a message to Mr. Parnell, to the effect that Mr. Gladstone was coming to town on the following day, and that I should almost certainly have a communication to make to Mr. Parnell on Tuesday morning. It was agreed at my meeting with his emissary on Sunday night (November 23) that I should be informed by eleven on Tuesday forenoon where I should see him. I laid special stress on my seeing him before the party met. At half past eleven, or a little later, on that day I received a telegram from the emissary that he could not reach his friend. I had no difficulty in interpreting this. It meant that Mr. Parnell had made up his mind to fight it out, whatever line we might adopt; that he guessed that my wish to see him must from his point of view mean mischief; and that he would secure his re-election as Chairman before the secret was out. Mr. McCarthy was at this hour also entirely in the dark, and so were all the other members of the Irish party supposed to be much in Mr. Parnell's confidence. When I reached the House a little after three, the lobby was alive with the bustle and animation usual at the opening of a session, and Mr. Parnell was in the thick of it, talking to a group of his friends. He came forward with much cordiality. ' I am very sorry,' he said, ' that I could not make an appointment, but the truth is I did not get your message until I came down to the House, and then it was too late.' I

---

[1] Morley, *Recollections*, Vol. I, p. 261. Morley adds an interesting piece of information. " Had some talk with Spencer in the drawing room. He was the only man who doubted whether we were right in putting any screw at all upon Parnell."

2 T

asked him to come round with me to Mr. Gladstone's room. As
we went along the corridor he informed me in a casual way that
the party had again elected him Chairman. When we reached
the sunless little room, I told him I was sorry to hear that the
election was over, for I had a communication to make which
might, as I hoped, still make a difference. I then read out to
him Mr. Gladstone's letter.[1] As he listened I knew the look on
his face quite well enough to see that he was obdurate. The
conversation did not last long. He said the feeling against him
was a storm in a teacup and would soon pass. I replied that he
might know Ireland but he did not half know England; that it
was much more than a storm in a teacup; that if he set British
feeling at defiance and brazened it out, it would be ruin to Home
Rule at the election; that if he did not withdraw for a time, the
storm would not pass; that if he withdrew from the actual leadership now as a concession to public feeling in this country, this
need not prevent him from taking the helm when new circumstances demanded his presence; that he could very well treat his
re-election as a public vote of confidence by his party; that
having secured this, he would suffer no loss of dignity or authority
by a longer or shorter period of retirement. I reminded him
that for two years he had been practically absent from active
leadership. He answered, in his slow dry way, that he must look
to the future; that he had made up his mind to stick to the House
of Commons and to his present position in his party until he was
convinced, and he would not soon be convinced, that it was impossible to obtain Home Rule from a British parliament; that
if he gave up the leadership for a time, he should never return
to it; that if he once let go, it was all over. There was the usual
iteration on both sides in a conversation of the kind, but this is
the substance of what passed. His manner throughout was
perfectly cool and quiet, and his unresonant voice was unshaken.
He was paler than usual, and now and then a wintry smile passed
over his face. I saw that nothing could be gained by further
parley, so I rose and he somewhat slowly did the same. ' Of
course,' he said, as I held the door open for him to leave, ' Mr.
Gladstone will have to attack me. I shall expect that. He will
have a right to do that.' So we parted."[2]

Parnell's answer created a situation which clearly
demanded the most careful study and discussion. This was

[1] For the letter see Appendix II to this Chapter.
[2] Morley, *Gladstone*, Vol. III, p. 440.

evident from Parnell's last words. Parnell said that Gladstone could not avoid a struggle. What was involved in such a struggle for the future, near and distant? Unhappily that answer was considered under the worst possible conditions. Morley's narrative thus proceeds.

" I waited for Mr. Gladstone, who arrived in a few minutes. It was now four o'clock. ' Well,'' he asked eagerly the moment the door was closed, and without taking off cape or hat, ' Have you seen him? ' ' He is obdurate,' said I. I told him shortly what had passed. He stood at the table, dumb for some instants, looking at me as if he could not believe what I had said. Then he burst out that we must at once publish his letter to me; at once, that very afternoon. I said ' 'Tis too late now.' ' Oh, No,' said he, ' the *Pall Mall* will bring it out in a special edition.' ' Well, but,' I persisted, ' we ought really to consider it a little.' Reluctantly he yielded, and we went into the House. Harcourt presently joined us and we told him the news. It was by and by decided that the letter should be immediately published. Mr. Gladstone thought that I should at once inform Mr. Parnell of this. There he was at that moment, pleasant and smiling, in his usual place, on the Irish bench. I went into our lobby and sent somebody to bring him out. Out he came and we took three or four turns in the lobby. I told him that it was thought right, under the new circumstances, to send the letter to the press. ' Yes,' he said amicably, as if it were no particular concern of his, ' I think Mr. Gladstone will be quite right to do that; it will put him straight with his party '.''

A worse atmosphere for deliberation could not be imagined. Feeling was tense in the House of Commons. Gladstone was surrounded by men who, after looking forward a week before to an early victory, now found their party in desperate danger (Schnadhorst, the agent, reported that candidates were bolting); Liberals who had been held up to odium for their support of Parnell when the whole upper-class world was denouncing him as a rogue, his hands not even free from blood, now found, as they thought, that their own difficulties and humiliations counted for nothing in the Irish mind. Gladstone, whose strength and weakness were both associated with his excitable and impulsive nature, was less suited for managing such an emergency than men of Salisbury's cooler temperament. In this atmosphere Gladstone, Morley, and Harcourt made on November 26, 1890, the same mistake that Granville, Hartington, Northbrook, and Dilke made on January 18, 1884. For the decision to publish this letter was like the decision to send Gordon to the Sudan ; the decision of men who took a strong step without thinking out all its consequences. In both cases the problem looked at the moment simpler than it was.

It is obvious that a man cannot ignore the sentiment of the party he leads. Least of all, could Gladstone ignore the sentiment of a party he had led into this fine but perilous adventure. It is obvious too that a man who has set before himself and his party a single great purpose cannot sit down and see that purpose wrecked with his hands folded. If Gladstone had done nothing in this crisis he would have been negligent of his plain duty. But it was one thing to urge Parnell to withdraw; it was another to publish a letter, however polite and careful its tone, in which this course was pressed upon him. The first act was a warning; the second a threat. The first left a door wide open for further co-operation; the second almost closed it.

APPENDICES TO CHAPTER XXXI

I

Letter from Gladstone to Parnell on Nonconformist sentiment and a Catholic University. See p. 638

Most private.

Hawarden Castle,
Chester.

August 30, 1889.

Dear Mr. Parnell

I have been expecting for some time, as you are aware, to hear from you, and likewise from some of your friends, with reference to visits to this place, which I had taken the liberty to propose. Yesterday I telegraphed to mention that I was obliged to quit Hawarden next Monday on a visit to Paris. Observing the equivocal yet significant announcement made by the Government, within the last 48 hours respecting Roman Catholic University Education in Ireland, I am led, perhaps wrongly to connect with the approach of this announcement the silence which from post to post I had expected to be broken.

That you should accept from the Tories whatever you conceive to lie within the claims and rights of Ireland neither surprises nor displeases me. On the contrary I have in public and in private, since 1885, and even in 1882, held that the Irish party ought to hold itself independent of British Liberalism, in order to be in a condition to accept Home Rule for Ireland from the Tories, if need were, without our consent or even knowledge. The larger boon includes the smaller: and perhaps you have been acting to the fullest extent upon the view which I have taken and announced. I could wish it had been for the larger aim, rather than the smaller.

I felt no fear of your confronting, in the matter of the Royal Grants, a soreness among British Liberals, which I was certain must be momentary. But we have now come in sight of an issue of a different order, in regard to which many questions will press themselves on your consideration.

1. Do the Government seriously intend (they have I see refused the pledge) to place the question of a Roman Catholic University in the foreground, thrusting aside " all other ": or to dangle it before your eyes as a means of severing you from the bulk of the Liberals, treating it as they have dealt with (for example) the Tithe question and the Sugar Convention?

2. The back-bone of the Liberal party lies in the Nonconformists of England and Wales, and the Presbyterians of Scotland. These men have a higher level and a stiffer rule of action than the Tory party. As my own standing ground is not wholly theirs, I say this with some approach to impartiality. They have strong Protestant prejudices, which, on the Irish Church question, and again (with some exceptions in England) on Home Rule they have nobly overcome. I suppose you have well considered what may be the effect of the new development on this party. They will not become anti-Home Rulers. It is another question whether they will lose compactness and heart, as they did when they thought Forster betrayed them, and whether the effect would now follow which followed then: i.e. that Home Rule would lose the elections instead of winning them.

I think that for you this may prove the most difficult problem you have had to face: and I must say one word as to myself. If the Government know their own mind, and are resolute in your sense, they will probably patch up some arrangement to satisfy the small scruples of their followers, and I do not count upon a break up there. There is another thing which you ought not to count upon, and that is my possession of any influence with the Liberal party which I could exercise in your sense. They behave very well to me, but I could not expect this from them. As to my own opinions they are partly Utopian. I think for example, as I thought in 1873, that the proper place for the Roman Catholics of Ireland is in the national and historical University of Ireland. I think that it is an Irish Parliament which ought to settle the question. There is a further question which I have to ponder. Viewing the fixed policy of Parliament for the last half century, is the demand which (it seems) the Government are to make, a demand which it is fair to address to a British Parliament as such, however fair it may be that an anti-Nationalist majority *should* grant it.

I wish to raise these questions before you: they deserve to be weighed with other questions. For example there are different modes of supporting as well as of opposing. Beyond opening up the various matters, I wish to say nothing at this time, except to affirm (1) the gravity of the case; (2) my own impotence, which the recent declarations must increase; and (3) my duty to do justice, as well as I can, both to Ireland, and to the British Liberals, who have made me much their debtor.

Should you wish to see me (for Home Rule purposes I should be glad of it) I may say that I am to be in London on Monday afternoon, and again probably in the following week. I have written this letter as a debt to you; and I remain faithfully yours

W. E. GLADSTONE.

P.S.—One early duty of mine will be to look back to Hansard of 1868, when the Disraeli Government proposed concurrent endowment and I made an instant and strong declaration against it. I cannot yet judge how far the Government proposal will cover that ground, or how far it may raise anew the question of Trinity College. Or in truth of anything except that there is room for *great caution*.

W.E.G.

II
1 Carlton Gardens,
November 24, 1890.

My dear Morley.

Having arrived at a certain conclusion with regard to the continuance, at the present moment, of Mr. Parnell's leadership of the Irish party, I have seen Mr. McCarthy on my arrival in town, and have inquired from him whether I was likely to receive from Mr. Parnell himself any communication on the subject. Mr. McCarthy replied that he was unable to give me any information on the subject. I mentioned to him that in 1882, after the terrible murder in the Phoenix Park, Mr. Parnell, though totally removed from any idea of responsibility, had spontaneously written to me, and offered to take the Chiltern Hundreds, an offer much to his honour but one which I thought it my duty to decline.

While clinging to the hope of a communication from Mr. Parnell, to whomsoever addressed, I thought it necessary, viewing the arrangements for the commencement of the session to-morrow, to acquaint Mr. McCarthy with the conclusion at which, after using all the means of observation and reflection in my power, I had myself arrived. It was that notwithstanding the splendid services rendered by Mr. Parnell to his country, his continuance at the present moment in the leadership would be productive of consequences disastrous in the highest degree to the cause of Ireland. I think I may be warranted in asking you so far to expand the conclusion I have given above, as to add that the continuance I speak of would not only place many hearty and effective friends of the Irish cause in a position of great embarrassment, but would render my retention of the leadership of the Liberal party, based as it has been mainly upon the prosecution of the Irish cause, almost a nullity. This explanation of my views I begged Mr. McCarthy to regard as confidential, and not intended for his colleagues generally, if he found that Mr. Parnell contemplated spontaneous action; but I also begged that he would make known to the Irish party, at their meeting to-morrow afternoon, that such was my conclusion, if he should find that Mr. Parnell had not in contemplation any step of the nature indicated. I now write to you, in case Mr. McCarthy should be unable to communicate with Mr. Parnell, as I understand you may possibly have an opening to-morrow through another channel. Should you have such an opening,

I beg you to make known to Mr. Parnell the conclusion itself, which I have stated in the earlier part of this letter. I have thought it best to put it in terms simple and direct, much as I should have desired had it lain within my power, to alleviate the painful nature of the situation. As respects the manner of conveying what my public duty has made it an obligation to say, I rely entirely on your good feeling, tact, and judgment.—Believe me sincerely yours,

W. E. GLADSTONE.

CHAPTER XXXII

THE BREAK WITH PARNELL

Gladstone had before him on November 25, 1890, the sudden prospect of the destruction of all his high hopes for Home Rule. There was a danger that the Liberal party would drop the policy, satisfied that in these changed conditions they could not carry it. It is clear from Morley's account of a talk with Chamberlain that Chamberlain expected this to happen and was thinking of reunion.[1] If Gladstone could avert this danger, there was a second. The Liberal party might keep Home Rule and lose the election. In that case what would be the outlook for Home Rule? Two defeats in succession would be serious enough in themselves; they would be still more serious because they would involve the loss of the only Englishman, who, as Parnell himself had said, could persuade England to give Ireland self-government. Even Gladstone could hardly start a third campaign at ninety. If, on the other hand, Parnell would retire, Gladstone might still hope to win the next election. Everything, in so far as the prospect of saving Home Rule in England was concerned, seemed thus to depend on getting this personal issue out of the way of Home Rule. If Parnell withdrew Home Rule might still be won; if he stayed the cause was hopeless. Was it not therefore reasonable to take every step that might produce his retirement? Should anything else count against this supreme consideration?

To answer that question we must ask another.

Why had Gladstone taken up Home Rule? Because he alone had seen the Irish problem as a problem of the relations of two peoples. Salisbury, Hartington, Chamberlain,

[1] *Recollections*, Vol. I, p. 265.

had seen it as a collection of obstinate concrete questions; Gladstone had seen it as a state of mind, something alive, persistent and haunting in the Irish imagination. On this view the decision taken so suddenly in a moment of excitement on that fatal afternoon involved something infinitely serious and yet too remote from the burning trouble of the hour to arrest attention. How was that impulsive action going to affect Ireland ten years, twenty years, thirty years later? Unless Parnell relented at the eleventh hour, it would be followed by a quarrel between the Liberal party and the Irish leader, a breach between the man who had taught Ireland that an English statesman could do justice to her case, and the man who, whatever his faults and blunders, stood in the Irish mind for the national cause. In a calm hour Gladstone would have seen this danger; in that moment of excitement he only saw the other. Yet it would have been better, perhaps even to risk the defeat of the Liberal party and Home Rule than to risk peopling Ireland with the memories and the legends that this conflict would leave behind it.

It was dangerous to the whole cause of peace between England and Ireland either to tell England that Parnell's leadership was a question for Ireland alone; or to tell Ireland that Parnell's leadership was for the time a fatal obstacle to Home Rule in England. Between the two dangers Gladstone had to choose and he chose under conditions most unfavourable to a sound judgment.

For Gladstone's object in taking up Home Rule was to reconcile Ireland to Great Britain. Some Englishmen said, as the *Times* and Salisbury had said in 1886, that it was impossible to reconcile Ireland, and that it was better to abandon the hope, and imitate Bismarck's hard-faced realism. Others said that it was possible to reconcile her by bestowing material benefits, and that if this policy was carried out, sentimental desires would die down. Gladstone held that it could only be done by recognizing that the demand for Home Rule was now associated with Irish self-respect and with the lessons of her history, and that if this desire was met with generosity and courage, Ireland would remain in the British Empire, a willing partner instead of a sullen rebel.

But on this view Gladstone and his colleagues were taking a decision on that evening of violent emotions which was to affect, not merely the next election, but generations to come. For Gladstone's whole case rested on the importance of imagination, legend, history, in Irish politics. Was not Parnell's fall bound to take a great place in imagination, legend, and history? Could a people which dreamed so much of its past be expected to put out of its mind a man who had played such a part as his? If Englishmen compared Parnell to Grattan, to Wolfe Tone, to O'Connell, were Irishmen going to forget him? And if they did not forget him, how were they going to remember him? Would they not think of him as a great Irishman, destroyed by the malignity of England?

Parnell said to Morley when they parted that Gladstone would of course have to attack him. What he meant was that he would have to attack Gladstone. For what was his position? For two years, as Morley pointed out to him, he had taken a very spasmodic part in the Irish agitation. On one occasion when Morley wanted to know his views, Dillon had to tell him that none of his colleagues had seen Parnell for several months. On another occasion his colleagues had to ask Morley what he knew about Parnell's health, suspecting that he had some alarming secret that he was keeping from them. He had been all this time a moderating and a languid force. He denounced Dillon to Morley for his violent speeches; he was strongly opposed to the Plan of Campaign; in the very last talk he had with Morley before the divorce he recurred to this point.[1] In all the work that was done for the defence of the party before the Commission he had been much less active than Davitt. In the division of his interest between Ireland and Mrs. O'Shea, Ireland had come second.

Then the blow fell and the man who had had the chief part in helping him to build up the new party in Ireland made a public appeal to him to withdraw for a time;

---

[1] " He still thinks the plan of campaign a great error, and that all the turbulence incident to it has done great harm in England, where people don't like disorder." Morley to Gladstone, November 13, 1890.

Davitt had been bitterly hurt by what he regarded as Parnell's deliberate perfidy in lying to him on the eve of the proceedings.

"This crisis," wrote Davitt in his paper *The Labour World*, "has been brought about by no other agency than that of Mr. Parnell's own conduct; and we say emphatically that both Irish and British Home Rulers have a right to look to him, and to him alone, to deliver the cause of which he has been till now the trusted leader from the deadliest peril by which it has yet been assailed. Mr. Parnell is called upon to make a sacrifice, a comparatively small one, in return for the many sacrifices which the most confiding and generous people who ever followed a political leader have made for him. . . . He is urged by the highest considerations that could appeal to a leader to efface himself for a brief period from public life until the time which the law requires to elapse before a divorced woman can marry, enables him to come back, having paid the penalty which the public sentiment rightly inflicts for such transgressions as his."[1]

This appeal came from the man whose importance in the creating of the Nationalist movement in Ireland and the United States had been second only to that of Parnell himself. He now asked that Parnell should sacrifice his pride for his country. No man had a better right to make that request. For Davitt had put his own pride in his pocket rather than weaken the Irish movement at a time when he and Parnell had differed. Davitt held that Parnell's policy of moderation after Kilmainham was a mistake. As one of the two men who had made that movement, he was entitled to press his view. Parnell was firm and if Davitt had not yielded there would have been a split. An impartial historian has said of this decision: " It would not be an exaggeration to add that Davitt unlike many who have served the Irish cause was guided by a willingness at all times to sacrifice personal ambition and submerge purely personal views."[2] Barry O'Brien, Parnell's close adherent and biographer, is not less emphatic in describing Davitt's service to Parnell.

"He (Davitt) was a power. He had the Irish World at his

---

[1] *Annual Register*, 1890, p. 239.
[2] Pomfret, *The Struggle for Land in Ireland*, p. 191.

back. He could not, of course, have driven Parnell from the position of Irish leader, for all Ireland was now solid for the Chief—the Church, the farmers, and many of the rank and file of the Fenians,· who had, contrary to the direction of the supreme Council, joined the Land League, but he could have made division in the ranks. The Irish World was only too ready to dethrone Parnell, whom Ford disliked for his moderation and strength. Had Davitt only spoken the word, there would probably have been an internecine struggle full of peril to the national interests. . . . He did not speak it. He made no attempt at revolt. He tried to convert Parnell to his views. He failed and submitted."[1]

Davitt thus refused to excite a mutiny among the men of extreme views. He rejected, that is, the temptation to which Parnell in his wild anger with the Irish party now yielded. Yet Davitt had agreed with those extreme views whereas Parnell down to December, 1890, had been strongly hostile to them.[2] Of Davitt's single-minded sincerity nobody ever had any doubt. His character indeed won admiration in the most diverse circles. " When Davitt calls," said George Moore, " I run to open the door for him; the only man for whom I do that."[3] When he died the *Times*, which had pursued him so bitterly in his life, admitted that he had qualities that had gained the respect of his strongest opponents. And if a man's claims to be heard depend at all on his sufferings, nobody could stand higher than Davitt. Looking back on those sufferings he might well say that the sacrifice now asked of Parnell was " a comparatively small one."

Davitt spent more years in prison for Ireland than Parnell spent months. And what had his life in prison been like? Parnell received better treatment than the ordinary prisoner; Davitt received worse treatment than the ordinary felon. He began by serving a sentence of seven years in

[1] O'Brien, *Life of Parnell*, Vol I, p. 376.
[2] In his maiden speech in the House of Commons, which was admired by men of all parties, on the Home Rule Bill, April 11, 1893, Davitt declared: " It is quite true that I have been not only an enemy, but a sworn enemy, of this Empire during the greater part of my political career." The Parnell Commission reported that he had aimed at complete separation in founding the Land League.
[3] Hone, *Life of Moore*, p. 271.

1870, ten months in Millbank, and almost all the rest on
Dartmoor. His treatment there is a terrible commentary
on British methods of punishment. During the ten months
he spent in Millbank he was allowed in all twenty minutes'
conversation. During the whole time he was at Dartmoor
he was never allowed to receive a visitor. The ordinary
convicts were allowed to choose a fellow convict with whom
to exercise on Sundays; Davitt and another Fenian prisoner
were forbidden this privilege. He was a good conduct
convict given none of the privileges of the good convict. He
went to prison a strong man, six feet high; he came out
weighing eight stone ten pounds. He spent a hot summer on
Dartmoor, one of a working party, in a building 20 feet by
10, breaking up putrid bones for manure; he was harnessed
with his one arm to a team of eight convicts to drag stones
and manure over the moor; he was not allowed to walk
about in his cell; to get any sleep at all in summer he had to
lie on the floor with his mouth against the chink beneath the
door. On one occasion he was handcuffed to a man out of
his mind when travelling by train. All these tortures, of
which Parnell himself said that he could not have endured
them, Davitt suffered for his patriotism in trying to procure
arms for an Irish rising; the offence for which Mazzini
would have been punished if he had been caught by the
Austrians.[1] Davitt's specially cruel treatment was due to
the belief that he had incited to assassination. The truth
was just the opposite. He learned that a young Irishman
talked of assassinating a spy. Davitt wrote strongly dis-
suading him, but finding the youth obstinate, he wrote a
second letter, in which he urged delay, meaning to use the
delay to bring the organization into action to stop the youth.
In this he succeeded and he saved a boy of nineteen from

---

[1] Davitt was first selected for a plot to capture Chester Castle, seize
the arms there and send them to Ireland. But this plot was betrayed. Afterwards he had a depot at Leeds for storing arms to be sent to an Irish port. He
once pointed out in the House of Commons that his crime was like the crime
that Salisbury and Churchill had encouraged in Ulster. After his death the
parallel was closer except that the arms sent to Ulster came from Germany
instead of from Leeds.

For the description of Davitt's Fenian career see Chapter II, and for that of
his prison life see Chapter III, of Sheehy-Skeffington's *Life of Davitt*.

committing a crime and a man who, as it turned out, was not a spy, from assassination. But a copy of this second letter was found and it gave the police a wrong impression; an impression that Davitt could only have removed by telling all the facts and getting a fellow Irishman into jail. This he refused to do.

In all Davitt spent nearly nine years in prison. His other sentences, served in 1881-2 and 1883 for seditious speeches, were not served under the barbarous conditions of the first, and Gladstone himself urged Harcourt to give him what indulgences he could. In comparison with Davitt's sufferings for Ireland at Dartmoor in the 'seventies, Parnell's life in Kilmainham was that of a man living at his club, kept indoors by the orders of an old-fashioned doctor.[1]

Parnell, to whom this appeal was made, was unhappily little accessible to argument or suggestion from his followers. One influence alone moved him. It was that of his mistress, who had no Irish blood and no Irish interest except her interest in Parnell's fortunes. In her mind there was no struggle, as there might be in his own, between ambition and patriotism. She looked on Parnell's colleagues not as his comrades, but as his rivals. Her life for eight years had been devoted to the effort to keep Parnell's love and her aunt's fortune without endangering his political position. If now Parnell retired she would appear to herself and to him to have caused his ruin. We can well understand that this proud and lonely man, faced with this sudden summons, thought first and last of sparing the woman he loved the

---

[1] As early as 1873 there was a strong opinion in the Home Office that Davitt's case should be reconsidered. Lowe, then Home Secretary, was so much influenced by it that he wrote to Gladstone on November 25, 1873, that Davitt was a very dangerous character but that no great principle was involved in keeping him in prison. He and Wilson, the other Fenian guilty of sending arms to Ireland, " have been guilty of an act not criminal in itself but only made so by the object." Unfortunately, in the same letter Lowe added that he had just heard of a plot in Liverpool for buying revolvers and distributing them " among the low Irish." The news came to him from the Irish detective police. This may perhaps explain why Davitt was left in prison. He remained there till 1878. On January 13, 1878, he arrived at Dublin with three other liberated prisoners, and an address of welcome was presented to them. Two days later one of the three died of a heart attack.

pain such a belief must bring her. Thus the advice of a woman who had never made a sacrifice for Ireland counted for more in his mind than the appeal of the man who had been tortured in Dartmoor prison for six years. And there seems to be reason to think that besides giving him this fatal advice, she helped to push him to disaster by her own hand, for she is said to have intercepted and destroyed the first letter Morley sent to him at Brighton.[1]

How could Parnell justify such a refusal to himself? On what public ground could he put it? On the ground that he was indispensable and that among his eighty colleagues there was not one who could take his place? He had never concealed his contempt for his party; a contempt ill-judged, for his party included some of the readiest debaters in the House of Commons. But even Parnell could hardly say " I will not resign because I am the only man who can lead this party; " however strongly he might be convinced that this was true, he had to find some other ground to give to the public and to Ireland.

But he had an alternative expedient after Gladstone's letter appeared. It was to move quickly to the left and to denounce Gladstone as a false friend who meant to give Ireland as little Home Rule as possible. To give a plausible look to this view he now announced in a manifesto (November 29) that, when he visited Gladstone at Hawarden in November, 1889, he had found Gladstone's state of mind very unsatisfactory. He gave an account of the conversations from which he drew the conclusion that Gladstone wished to modify his plans for Home Rule, and to give Ireland less than she had expected. He referred in particular to the questions of the retention of the Irish members, to the settlement of the Land question, to the control of the constabulary, and the appointment of judges. He then discussed his confidential talks with Morley, whom he accused of trying to destroy the independence of the Irish party by offering him, Parnell, the office of Chief Secretary.

So far as Parnell's charges against Gladstone and Morley

[1] Robbins, *Parnell, The Last Five Years*, p. 159.

were concerned, answer was easy. Why, if Parnell had left Hawarden so profoundly depressed, had he made a speech at Liverpool immediately after his visit full of confidence in Gladstone and victory?

" You people of England," he said at Liverpool, on December 19, a few hours after leaving Hawarden, " now see under the guidance of your great leader the way to terminate the strife of centuries. You are convinced that there is nothing so radically wrong in the nature of Irishmen as to prevent an amicable and satisfactory settlement of our difficulties. . . . Irishmen can now pin their faith to the constitution as a remedy for their grievances." He had gone on to deprecate any idea of violence. " I know enough of my countrymen to know that brave as they are, they recognize and join me in recognizing that we are on the safe path to our legitimate freedom, and future prosperity, and that they will accompany me and accompany you on that path, until you have helped your great leader to win the battle which I trust we are on the eve of entering upon."[1]

This was strange language for a man full of misgiving about Gladstone's plans and intentions. Why for ten months had he never let his colleages suspect those misgivings? Why had he continued confidential discussions with Morley on the old footing?

It was fortunate for Parnell that the men whom he was attacking had a different standard of conduct. If Gladstone had treated confidential discussion with the same levity, he could have used a terrible weapon on his side. For Parnell in the extremities to which he had been reduced by the O'Shea entanglement, had offered the Liberals, as we have seen, the Irish vote in four constituencies in 1885 if they would find O'Shea a seat. Such a revelation would have damped the confidence of the staunchest Parnellite. It would have shown Ireland to what humiliations his secret weakness had brought the man who walked, like Shelley's Laud, " as if he trod upon the heads of men."

Parnell had now replied, by a mistake of his own, to the mistake Gladstone had made on the 25th. For Parnell's manifesto was as mischievous to his own interests, however

---

[1] *Times*, December 20, 1889.

narrowly conceived, as to the Irish cause. He must have
known that even if the Church had not moved already, its
hostility was certain and he had therefore every motive for
avoiding, or if he could not do that, postponing to the last
moment, any breach with his own parliamentary party.
He had beaten the Church before, but then he had the party
at his back. Now his party consisted of men who had been
in close association with Liberals for four years, on British
and on Irish platforms, for the Nationalist members were
favourite speakers in England and Scotland and in Ireland
Radical members were taking part in demonstrations of
sympathy with the tenants evicted in the great struggle
over the Plan of Campaign. In the House of Commons,
where Parnell himself had played a slight and intermittent
part, they had seen Gladstone fighting their cause with
indomitable spirit against all the arrogance of race and
class, aspersed and derided as bitterly as any Irishman.
The victory of Home Rule had seemed only three weeks
earlier certain and near, a victory to be won by this alliance
with the Liberals. Parnell now asked them to throw all this
on one side, to attack Gladstone and to break with the
Liberals just because he had mismanaged his love affair so
wantonly as to make himself at once odious and ludicrous
in the public eye.

It was a great deal for any leader to ask of his party.
Parnell had his enemies among his followers. Men treated
as they had been must often have said, as Ulysses said of
Achilles,

> "And we were better parch in Afric sun
> Than in the pride and salt scorn of his eye.[1]"

Opposition to his new policy from public motives was
certain to be reinforced and embittered by the animosities
lurking under that iron discipline. Parnell therefore
had every ground for acting with care and circum-
spection. The first protest against his wild outburst came
from two men whose distinguished and devoted loyalty to
their cause nobody could question. Dillon and O'Brien

---

[1] *Troilus and Cressida*, Act I, Scene iii, line 371.

travelling in America read the manifesto with consternation and telegraphed a protest to Ireland. The next day the Bishops came out into the open and the struggle began in which Parnell went down.

Thus one blunder had been answered by another. Unfortunately the second was now answered by a third. The Liberal leaders who had first lost their heads in panic, now lost them again in anger. Their anger was natural enough. Parnell's breach of confidence and his grave misrepresentation of the views both of Gladstone and Morley had spread both resentment and suspicion. The consequences were seen in the treatment by the Liberal leaders of the next phase. Parnell, finding that the opinion of the party was against him, now adopted a different tone. He said that he was ready to go if the party could get satisfactory assurances from the Liberals about the next Home Rule Bill. The Liberal leaders, resenting the treatment they had received, met these tactics with a stiff refusal. " I hear with alarm from Harcourt," Morley wrote on November 30,

" that Parnell is trying to obtain some sort of terms from you to cover his surrender. Surely after what has passed, and after the declarations we are making as to the impossibility of cooperating with a man capable of such shameless breach of faith and confidence, it would produce a terribly bad effect in the public mind. It would moreover be to recognise Parnell as actual leader—which is the very thing that we have protested we could not do. It will also enable him to make off with flying colours. It seems to me that any declaration as to the details of Home Rule in this moment of confusion would be very disadvantageous in every respect."

This letter shows into what disorder so clear a mind as Morley's had been thrown by Parnell's attack. For there is only one sentence, the last, that offered any argument at all for the course Morley was advocating.

For what was the position? The Liberal party and the Irish party were separate and independent parties, working together for a common object. The Liberal leader had informed the Irish party that in his opinion the Liberal party could not carry Home Rule if Parnell remained leader. The Irish party was considering how it should act. Parnell had refused a strong appeal from its chief leaders to withdraw. He was now arguing that the Irish party ought, before they dropped their leader, to know exactly what the Liberal party meant by Home Rule. Was that view unreasonable?

It was quite untrue to suggest that Gladstone was anxious to give Ireland less Home Rule than Parnell had thought desirable. On the other hand the details of the next Home Rule Bill were still vague and undefined. Rosebery had long been anxious that attention should be given to this task and in August, 1889, as we have seen, he had urged Gladstone to form a committee to draw up a Bill. He had also suggested the invitation to Parnell to Hawarden. But Gladstone had a constitutional objection—perhaps strengthened by age—to working out a scheme in this way before the moment had come for action. He was ready to discuss and talk round a policy, but he kept to the stage of preliminary speculation and debate. Consequently many points were still uncertain in 1890, and it was not unreasonable for Parnell to say to the Irish party, and for the Irish party to say to Gladstone, " We want to know a little more about your proposals on this and that detail." If Parnell had never launched his fatal manifesto, if he had met his party and said:

" I make no attack on anybody but I want to draw your attention to the following facts. The last Home Rule Bill was entirely unsatisfactory to us in respect of finance.[1] What is going to be done in the next ? The last Bill excluded Irish representation altogether from Westminster. At that time I was strongly for exclusion and only reluctantly agreed to Gladstone's reconsidering it in the hope of getting Chamberlain's vote. Now my views are the other way and I want to know what Gladstone proposes. Then there are the questions of the Judges and the constabulary. The Round Table Conference broke down partly because the

[1] Morley considers that the first Home Rule Bill might have been rejected by the Irish in Committee because of their dissatisfaction with its finance. See Morley, *Gladstone*, Vol. III, p. 306.

Liberals held out against Chamberlain on the question of the Judges. There will be strong pressure. Ought we not to be taken into Gladstone's confidence? Then again there is the Land Question. What is Gladstone's present plan? "

Can anybody doubt that if Parnell, without a word of abuse, had made a temperate speech on these lines to his party, he would have been acting reasonably and that the Liberals would have been greatly to blame if they had not tried to meet these difficulties ? No doubt, as Morley said, the moment was a bad one for such discussion but, if the Irish party was to take such a strong step as to ask its leader to resign, the Liberal leaders on their part might be asked to take a strong step to satisfy such apprehensions.

Was the fact that Parnell had launched his offensive and misleading manifesto a sufficient reason for refusing a discussion that would have been proper and necessary if he had not so acted? To anybody able to see the problem in the true perspective it was not, but there were two reasons why the Liberal leaders were in a bad position for answering that question. In the first place their dignity had been wounded by treatment which they had every right to resent. In the second place, with their inside knowledge, they might suspect that Parnell had chosen his ground with no other object than to put them in a difficulty. For Parnell proposed to the Irish party that they should appoint a sub-committee to wait on Gladstone, Harcourt, and Morley, to ascertain whether they agreed with the Irish parliamentary party that the Irish constabulary should be under the Irish Parliament, and that the Irish Parliament should have full power to deal with the land question. The Liberals resented the proposal that the sub-committee should meet three leaders instead of Gladstone alone. This was surely an unreasonable and petulant objection. Gladstone was 81. Harcourt, the most likely man to succeed him, was known to be a very lukewarm Home Ruler. But the sting lay in the end of the resolution. Parnell knew that the Liberal party was divided on the Land question; that Gladstone and Morley had differed, and that the Radicals still held the view Chamberlain had pressed in 1886 that no

English money should go into Irish landlord pockets.[1] Parnell knew this, but Gladstone and Morley also knew that he felt as strongly as Morley did, the danger of starting Home Rule with the land question left open.[2] Gladstone and Morley, that is, knew that Parnell was asking the Irish party to put a pistol at Gladstone's head for something that he himself had regarded with dread only a fortnight earlier. That knowledge might well make them suspect that his motives were wholly sinister.

Gladstone refused the request for an interview on these lines, but on December 5 he received Sexton, who read a memorandum, and he read a memorandum in reply in which he repudiated again Parnell's account of the Hawarden conversations. The Irish party then adopted a resolution appointing four members, Redmond, Healy, Sexton, and Leamy, who were to request a conference with Gladstone, to represent the views of the party, and to request from him an intimation of the intentions of the Liberal leaders on the settlement of the Land question and the control of the constabulary. Gladstone replied in a long letter in which he argued that the question proposed in the resolution had no proper connection with the question of the leadership of the party.

" When the Irish party shall have disposed of this question, which belongs entirely to their own competence, in such a manner as will enable me to renew the former relations, it will be my desire to enter without prejudice into confidential communication, such as has heretofore taken place, as occasion may serve, upon all amendment of particulars and suggestion of improvements in any plan for a measure of Home Rule."

This answer shows how false was the logic by which the Liberal leaders had allowed the temper of the moment to draw them to disaster. What was behind these refusals? The view that the issue was now between two men of strong will and that any concession to the difficulties of the Irish

---

[1] This of course had been a great difficulty in 1886. " Vivid pictures were drawn of a train of railway trucks two miles long, loaded with millions of bright sovereigns, all travelling from the pocket of the British son of toil to the pocket of the idle Irish landlord." Morley, *Gladstone*, Vol. III, p. 325.

[2] Morley's letter to Gladstone after his talk with Parnell.

party was really a concession to a dangerous and unscrupulous antagonist. Harcourt put this view with all his immense energy and force. He wrote on December 5: " Whatever you do, whether Parnell retires for the moment or not, upon your acceptance of his dictation, he will return long before you can bring forward a Home Rule Bill, and then you will have to deal with a man who has thus spoken of you."[1] This was an important point but to treat it as if it was the only point, or the main point, was surely a strange reading of the situation. The Irish members had to justify their conduct to the Irish people, and Gladstone might have taken the view that in meeting their delegates he was recognizing their right to discuss these questions with him. No doubt they were awkward questions, and Gladstone could see the danger that Parnell in his new mood would declare for proposals much more revolutionary than the policy he had favoured behind the scenes. But in such a discussion Gladstone could ask questions as well as answer them. The constabulary question had been raised by some of the Irish members in 1886, and Parnell had then replied that it would be wrong to insist on a concession that might imperil Home Rule. On the Land Bill the Irish members had their own difficulties and Gladstone would have been justified in asking for a more precise account of their views.[2]

---

[1] Manning, who by this time, had come to think that Parnell was " of unsound mind " was as urgent as Harcourt. He wrote to Gladstone on December 4, saying that Parnell's conduct recalled the case of Sir Henry Parnell " who made an end of himself when we were young." On December 5, he wrote:
" The P.M.G. says that the conference with the Irish Members may take place at 11 o'clock to night. I hope:
1 that you will refuse all discussion
2 that you will refuse all pledges except one
3 that your one pledge shall be
" I will endeavour to frame a scheme of Home Rule which shall be *acceptable to the people of Ireland. If they shall refuse to accept it* I will relinquish the work to other hands and leave public life." Do not hamper yourself with so much as a cobweb. Who can foresee the state and circumstances even of next year? Excuse my intrusion. I could not be silent."

[2] " In 1890 he (Parnell) was much exercised on land purchase. He once asked me to speak with him, having devised a very complex and impracticable set of notions of his own, which he slowly expounded to me. I asked would

Gladstone's answer went almost to the length of refusing to admit that the Irish party had any right to ask him any questions until they had got rid of Parnell. On what ground could such a refusal be justified? Such a claim on his part was an unwarrantable interference with the freedom of the Irish party and an unwarrantable slur on Parnell.

The refusal looks all the more wanton in the light of the sequel. When the second Home Rule Bill was introduced in February, 1893, both the Land questions and the Constabulary questions were treated on the lines suggested for discussion. The constabulary were to be replaced gradually by Irish police and the whole force was to come to an end within six years. The Land question was to pass to the Irish Parliament after three years. Redmond, the Parnellite leader in that Parliament, one of the delegates from Committee Room 15 in December, 1890, said on February 14, 1893, speaking on the Bill, that he welcomed these arrangements but he reflected sadly that if Gladstone had met the Irish request in this spirit in December, 1890, he would probably have saved Ireland two years of misery and strife. Nobody can say to-day whether Redmond was right in thinking that the negotiations which Gladstone declined would have been successful, but the Irishmen, the peace of their party at stake, might well complain that he never made any effort to help them.

The refusal of this request brought all Parnell's plans for prolonging the struggle to an end, and on December 6 the Irish party broke up, forty-five declaring against Parnell, twenty-two supporting him. The majority have been criticized bitterly by those who think that loyalty to a man is more important than loyalty to a cause, and that

his people like it? He did not care whether they did or not, he had thought it over for ten years. He presently unfolded it in the House of Commons in a speech which was slow, interesting, serious, but horribly obscure. It was lucky for me that I possessed the answer to the riddle. The House was profoundly still, but so, too, was the general confusion of mind profound. The most important of his lieutenants came to me at midnight; the speech had completely mystified them; could I explain? Mr. Gladstone laughed at the oddity of it all. ' It is difficult enough for him to be absent and inaccessible, but, if besides that, when he does appear—to plunge into unexplained politics, that is indeed too bad! ' " Morley, *Recollections*, Vol. I, p. 245.

the duty to stand by Parnell was a higher duty than to stand by Home Rule. Such criticism is cruelly unjust to men who found themselves faced with the most distressing dilemma ever presented to a body of serious-minded politicians. There were some who thought, when the grim choice had to be made, that the best way to serve Home Rule was to keep this man of genius, whatever the cost in Liberal and Catholic support, but most of the leaders believed that Parnell could not be kept without involving the whole Irish cause in his ruin. Both parties deserve respect and sympathy. The fight then passed to Ireland. In January and February, when Dillon and W. O'Brien returned from America, there were negotiations at Boulogne which broke down. The terrible sequel need not be described. Parnell, after making passionate efforts and appealing to the violent spirit which for eight years he had tried to overcome, was beaten in three bye-elections,[1] and the uncrowned king died in the hour of utter and bitter defeat. The politicians who had persuaded O'Shea to take his revolver from his pocket had done their work even more thoroughly than they had hoped. They had baulked Gladstone of his victory, thrown Parnell's party into confusion, and put an end not merely to his career but to his life.[2]

It is evident that in the fatal fortnight that had followed the decree in the divorce court the Liberal leaders had moved into a false position. Harcourt's letter makes this quite clear. He thought that if Parnell returned after an interval the consequences would be disastrous. Even Morley spoke of " Parnell covering his surrender " as if it was something to be dreaded. Yet surely, if the Liberals still occupied the position Gladstone had taken on November 25, both these views were wrong. Why had Gladstone wanted Parnell to retire ? Because he thought that Parnell's retention of the leadership at this moment would drive away so many voters as to defeat Home Rule in England. That was a simple, precise, and intelligible

[1] Pope-Hennessy who won the first of these elections was the original of Trollope's *Phineas Finn*. Paul, *History of Modern England*, V, 195.

[2] He died at Brighton on October 6, 1891.

view. On that view, taken both by Gladstone and
Morley on November 25, nothing would be better than
an arrangement under which Parnell could " cover his
surrender." And Morley himself, in his own account of
his talk with Parnell, had spoken of his retirement as
temporary, though Harcourt now argued that temporary
retirement would be disastrous.

Harcourt's influence at this time was a calamity. It
was a great pity that his place in Gladstone's counsels could
not have been taken by Asquith who made a courageous and
sensible speech, with no trace of temper.[1] Harcourt had
never liked Parnell; he had never liked Home Rule; he took a
ridiculously severe view of Parnell's conduct to O'Shea, for
though the divorce court story was of course accepted by
public opinion, he must have suspected that it was not the
truth, the whole truth, and nothing but the truth. He
now talked of Parnell with the sort of wild rage that Burke
had shown in the French Revolution, when he said that he
had decided to disinfect his house on reflecting that Mirabeau
had once stayed in it.[2] Harcourt was anxious to drop
Home Rule and for a few weeks he and Morley were hardly
on speaking terms. He was now urging a view of the relations of the Liberal leaders to the whole controversy that
was quite inconsistent with Gladstone's original view. He
seemed to think that it was the business of the Liberal
leaders to ruin Parnell, whereas Gladstone had merely
stated that if Parnell remained leader at the present moment
Home Rule would be beaten at the polls. Thus he was
soon in conflict with Gladstone and Morley on the whole
question of giving assurances at all.

In December, 1890, the Leaders had made the grave mistake of refusing to discuss details of Home Rule or to give
assurances while Parnell was leader. After the break up of

---

[1] At Manchester on January 8, 1891, " Speaking for himself, he distinctly
declared that to give Ireland Home Rule without putting the police entirely
under the local Irish control and without giving the Irish Legislature full
power to deal with the Land question as it pleased, would be absurd." *Annual
Register*, 1891, p. 5.

[2] " It was an ungoverned temper. I don't know whether he had ever tried
to govern it, but if he had, it beat him." Sir Lawrence Guillemard on Harcourt. Gardiner, *Life of Harcourt*, Vol. II, p. 207.

the parliamentary party, as has been said, there was a second attempt to make peace in Ireland. In January and February, 1891, negotiations were carried on at Boulogne (Dillon and O'Brien were under arrest and therefore could not set foot in England or Ireland) between Parnell, O'Brien, Dillon, McCarthy, with T. P. Gill as a liaison officer, with the Liberals, with a view to making terms and avoiding civil war in the Home Rule ranks. Harcourt was at first against giving any assurances, though Parnell was now no longer the accepted leader, on the ground that, though Parnell was not to be leader of the parliamentary party, he was to be president of the National League. Thus this Home Rule party was to go the length of telling Irishmen whom they could or could not have at the head of an Irish popular organization. Insolence could hardly go further. Morley remarked bitterly to Gladstone on January 16, after a talk with Gill, " I don't think our party at all realises the immense responsibility that they incurred when they insisted on the cashiering of Parnell."

Harcourt was worsted in this second struggle and the Liberal leaders gave assurances to McCarthy[1], but the difficulties at Boulogne proved too great and the negotiations broke down, on February 15. If Barry O'Brien is correct, Parnell himself changed from time to time, being seriously anxious at one moment for peace, and thinking only at another of making difficulties.

Parnell's case raised problems for the casuist, the moralist, the cynic, and the politician. Nobody pretended that every person in public life had always respected the Seventh Commandment. What then was Parnell's offence except that he had broken the Eleventh Commandment? The cynic might observe that Salisbury's speech on December 3, 1890, in which, according to the *Annual Register*, he said that " the proceedings and destiny of Mr. Parnell had brought out an uprising in favour of domestic purity which all must regard with the deepest satisfaction," was made to Hartington's

---

[1] Given by Gladstone, Spencer, Ripon, Morley, and Harcourt. Gardiner, *op. cit.*, II, p. 99. The assurances were on the lines of the 1893 Bill.

supporters in Rossendale. Salisbury would have replied:

" As I attach great importance to domestic purity I am naturally
glad that when a public man is proved guilty of an offence against
domestic purity, there should be a strong condemnation from
public opinion. On the other hand I have to draw a strong
distinction between such offences when proved in a court of law
and such offences when they are mere matter of gossip or private
knowledge. Otherwise the door stands open to all manner of
slander and scandal and public life becomes intolerable. In
this sense the Eleventh Commandment is for a politician the most
important of all."

It is possible to concede a good deal to this argument and
yet hold that there is something repulsive at once to the sense
of justice and the sense of decency in the haste with which
his enemies fell upon Parnell.

The case of the Liberals is different. They were not
Parnell's enemies but his allies. Some of the leaders knew
long before the case came into court that Parnell was Mrs.
O'Shea's lover and it has been argued that it was hypo-
critical of them to abandon him after his exposure. But
this overlooks the plain facts of politics. The character of
a man in public life is his own affair unless it becomes
notorious. Then it becomes public property. Cunning-
hame Graham said justly that a man is not more disqualified for public life by adultery than by vices that are
common enough among public men. Certainly avarice
or cruelty to those in his power, to take only two examples,
are worse faults in a man who is given influence in public
administration and the framing of the law. But a man who
was notorious for such vices would certainly find that
the door was closed against him. No Prime Minister would
have taken into his Government the Welsh peer, whose
obstinate oppression of his miners in the quarries was well
known from one end of England to the other, or Lord
Clanricarde whose treatment of his tenants had made him
a bye-word.

What kind of character had Parnell now acquired?
Many who had known that he was Mrs. O'Shea's
lover had been taken aback by some of the dis-

closures in the Court.   A man living with a married woman
is not necessarily a vicious or a dishonourable man.   George
Eliot and G. H. Lewes, who set up house together when
Lewes's wife was still alive, were received as guests by
the Master of Balliol and the Master of Trinity, and the
most distinguished of the dons at the two Universities
did them honour.[1] Parnell's treatment of O'Shea was
not essentially worse than George Eliot's treatment of
Mrs. Lewes, but a man who had only known of him that he
was Mrs. O'Shea's lover might well shrink from the
picture of his conduct that was painted in Court.
Parnell's character in the public eye was now that of a man
who was both cowardly and deceitful.   There was therefore
nothing inconsistent (whatever else can be urged against it)
in the behaviour of a man who had worked for Parnell's
success, with knowledge of his secret liaison, and then
despaired of that success when that secret was exposed to the
world.   From the moment a man's private life becomes
public property, it is as much an element in his success as
debating power or personal magnetism.   From that moment
his colleagues have to consider its effect on his position,
not as moralists but as realists.   There were some who
held that Parnell was so strong a man that he could live
this odium down but most of those who made their views
known thought it would overwhelm him.

Gladstone's own conduct has been blamed on another
ground.   It has been said that he knew of the relations of
Parnell and Mrs. O'Shea when he was in correspondence
with her about Parnell's plans.   Gladstone was in correspondence with Mrs. O'Shea between 1882 and 1886.   Her
first letter came to him on May 23.   Dilke states in his
diary that Harcourt told the Cabinet that Mrs. O'Shea was
Parnell's mistress, a fact he had discovered when his detectives were following Parnell's movements.   He adds that
he, Dilke, wrote to Grant Duff on May 18, 1882, telling him
about Harcourt's disclosure.[2] Now it may often happen

---

[1] Jowett received and answered a protest. See Jowett, *Life and Letters*, 2, 160.

[2] Dilke gives a wrong date (May 17) for the Cabinet. There was no
Cabinet that day.

that something is said at a Cabinet which is not heard by all the members. Harcourt may well have made this remark in a private aside. There is good evidence that Gladstone did not hear it. When Gladstone sent Granville Mrs. O'Shea's first letter on May 24, with his projected reply, Granville answered: " Your decision appears to me to be quite right and your letter excellent. G. She is said to be his mistress." Granville clearly thought that in adding this note he was telling Gladstone something he had not heard. If Harcourt had made his statement publicly at the Cabinet, Granville could hardly have written this note.

Gladstone then heard of this rumour from Granville. He also heard of it from his youngest private secretary, Sir George Leveson Gower, who was Granville's nephew. Sir George Leveson Gower has given an account of the incident, describing the stern face that Gladstone turned to him, when he admitted that he was speaking only of a rumour, and the stern voice in which he demanded whether he was to believe such a charge on such a basis. Gladstone certainly disbelieved the story then, and he continued to disbelieve it. Nor is this surprising to anybody who has studied the correspondence between Mrs. O'Shea and Gladstone. Many of her letters to Gladstone were letters asking for favours for O'Shea. Many of the questions that she raised were questions that interested O'Shea as well as Parnell. From time to time Mrs. O'Shea sent him letters from her husband, all in affectionate terms, beginning " My dearest wife." Sir George Leveson Gower's story shows that Gladstone was not the kind of man whose tolerance of gossip encouraged others to talk scandal in his presence. And he thought that Parnell had a motive for using her rather than O'Shea, after the catastrophe over the Kilmainham letter. On September 26, 1882, he wrote to Spencer who disliked his negotiations:

" Some time ago I signified to Mrs. O'Shea that we had better not meet again. Her letters I cannot controul but do not encourage. I think she has been of some use in keeping Parnell on the lines of moderation; and I imagine he prefers the wife to the husband as an organ."

At the time when the rumours began to spread in consequence of the episode of the Galway bye-election, Gladstone's negotiations through Mrs. O'Shea had come to an end, for after 1886 no intermediary was needed, since Morley was in direct touch with Parnell.[1] Gladstone evidently disbelieved the rumours until very near the end and then at the last he was completely reassured by Morley's message. There is a letter from George Russell describing the shocked atmosphere of the Gladstone circle. He wrote on December 3, 1890, to Lady Battersea:

" I have seen Mr. and Mrs. G. He was very grave, sad, quiet and dignified and entirely free from rancour or violence. Mrs. Drew is here. I make out from her that they all positively believed in P's innocence, and never doubted till they saw the reports of the trial. Imagine the shock and surprise to them."[2]

Few would doubt to-day that Parnell was judged much too harshly throughout. He committed from the point of view of most Liberals two offences. He appeared in the divorce court as a man who had deceived a friend, lied repeatedly to him, and carried on a liaison with his wife for several years. If the world had known the facts his position of course would have been very different. His life, from the time of his association with Mrs. O'Shea, was a life of moral fidelity to the woman he regarded as his wife. O'Shea was not his friend nor the husband, except in the eyes of the law, of his mistress. There was nothing of treachery or of cowardice in his conduct. Still he could hardly expect the world to judge him on facts that were known to him but not to it, as he refused to take any steps to enlighten its ignorance. He paid in this way, not for his love for Mrs. O'Shea, but for his folly or his obstinacy or his weakness in ever allowing himself to be put into so false a position. Looking much blacker to the world than he knew himself to be, and therefore all the more sensitive to criticism, he then proceeded to outrage Liberal feeling by his sudden attack on Gladstone

---

[1] A summary account of Gladstone's interviews and correspondence with Mrs. O'Shea is given in an Appendix to this Chapter.

[2] Lucy Cohen. *Lady de Rothschild and her Daughters*, p. 213.

after the publication of Gladstone's letter. It is not surprising that that attack was resented. It was resented because it was bitter and unjust to a man who had made great sacrifices for Ireland, and also because in making it Parnell had broken the honourable understanding which public men must respect or never discuss plans with one another. That was the case against Parnell, and it is easy to understand that men smarting under his sudden and violent offensive were unable to make any allowances for him.

Yet allowances were due to him even from those who did not know that the O'Shea result had been a shock to him as to others. He was in a very difficult position. He might fear that retirement, even for a few months, might be fatal to his career. He had his enemies, and, once his firm hand was gone, might he not find it difficult ever to recover his authority? The plan of temporary retirement, which, if it were successful, would reduce the danger to Home Rule in England without causing Ireland to lose the services of a man of genius, did not look quite so simple to him as to those who pressed it upon him. If Protestant England condemned him as the lover of a married woman, Catholic Ireland would be more severe on him as the husband of a woman who had been divorced. He was only allowed a few days in which to consider his policy. In the publication of the Gladstone letter he had a real grievance. Having this grievance he turned on a man who had stood most loyally by him, when most of respectable England was treating him as a bloodstained criminal, with savage ingratitude and injustice. Having thus put himself in the wrong with Liberal opinion, Parnell was suspected from that moment of bad faith and trickery in everything he did and said. This suspicion blinded Liberals to his case, for he had a case. Parnell might honestly think that he was the only man who could stand up to Gladstone if the Liberals and the Irish came to some sharp difference over Home Rule, as might well happen over finance, and that for this reason his retirement was dangerous for Ireland. In that case he was surely justified in asking for assurances.

Liberals forgot too that Parnell was not like an ordinary

party leader. He had been the leader of a revolutionary party and he had to be judged as such. Indeed Morley the historian gives the answer to Morley the politician. Because Parnell divulged private conversations and misrepresented Gladstone, Morley suddenly decided that Liberals could have no discussion with him. He was an outlaw who should not be allowed " to cover his surrender." But Morley the historian uses a very different tone. " Must we not, against our will agree with Green, our Oxford moralist, that the assertion of Cromwell's unselfish enthusiasm is quite consistent with the imputation to him of much unscrupulousness, violence, simulation and dissimulation— sins which no one has escaped who ever led or controlled a revolution?"[1] Parnell had made his way outwitting statesmen, politicians, officials, as he brought his revolutionary party from its shadowy beginnings to its power and importance. He should be judged with that past in mind. Yet Liberals now treated his offences as if they were more serious than similar offences committed by ordinary English politicians, as if it was now a kind of lèse-majesté for him to suggest that Gladstone had ever said anything that he did not remember having said. Salisbury declared that it was tolerably evident that Parnell's recollections were more accurate than Gladstone's because, if they were not, Gladstone would have produced documents to convict him of error.[2] Salisbury of course wanted to make as much party capital as possible out of this quarrel, and this was his way of doing it. But to men looking out for insults it was more offensive to Gladstone than Parnell's original accusation. Would then the Liberals have said that they could have no dealings with Salisbury? On the principle on which they acted to Parnell, they ought never to have admitted Chamberlain to the Round Table Conference. Parnell's character is a permanent mystery, but the hasty conclusion of the Liberal leaders that his character, as revealed in those weeks of strain, was such that it was better for Ireland to lose him than to use him, seems to-day preposterous and disastrous.

[1] *Recollections*, Vol. I, p. 244.
[2] At Cambridge, January 21, 1891. *Annual Register*, p. 10.

2 X

It is pretty evident that Gladstone himself repented of that view later.[1]

It looks as if sometimes a doubt crossed Morley's mind. On December 27, 1890, he wrote to Gladstone: " I wonder whether Parnell's betrayal of conversations is worse than O'Connell's explosion of Mr. Littleton in 1834." The parallel is interesting for O'Connell's disclosure of the private communications from the Irish Secretary had the effect by a series of connected incidents of driving Grey from office. What was the sequel? Between 1835 and 1840 Ireland was governed by Thomas Drummond with more justice and sympathy and better order than at any other time in the history of the nineteenth century. Yet that government reposed on an understanding with O'Connell. It is a pity that Morley's historical parallel did not come into his mind a few weeks earlier, for O'Connell ranked almost with Peel in Gladstone's regard after he had thrown himself into the Irish problem.

If Parnell was judged too harshly by Englishmen at the time, Gladstone has been judged too harshly by Irishmen since. For from these events there has sprung a legend that is as remarkable as it is mischievous. It is that Gladstone was glad to get rid of Parnell, because he feared that Parnell would press for a bolder form of Home Rule than he was ready to consider. Nothing could be further from the truth. Parnell represented to Gladstone not advanced but moderate Irish opinion. Mrs. O'Shea had so described him to Gladstone in the early days. She had appealed to him to recognize Parnell's difficulties as a moderate leader, against whom the extremists were plotting, and he had answered the appeal. The proposed Home Rule constitution which Parnell drew up reflected moderate views, and acknowledged the supremacy of the Imperial Parliament. Between 1886 and 1890 Gladstone was in touch with Parnell's views through Morley, and, as Parnell himself said after the quarrel that he trusted Morley, there is no reason to suspect the truth of the account Morley gave to Gladstone from time to time of Parnell's views. All through that time Parnell stood for

[1] See the interview with Barry O'Brien. *Life of Parnell*, II, 358.

moderate Nationalism against Dillon and Davitt. From the time of Parnell's release down to the thunderbolt of the Divorce Court Gladstone believed that Parnell was indispensable, both because of his gifts for leadership, and because of his practicable politics. That was the view of Parnell that he urged on his colleagues in 1883 and 1884. Those convictions are recorded in letter after letter. We have seen that in writing to Döllinger in 1887 he had spoken of Parnell's death as the worst catastrophe that could happen to Home Rule. After the crash he wrote to Acton (December 27, 1890), " the blow to me is very heavy—the heaviest I ever have received." The most malignant opponent can hardly find a reason for doubting his sincerity in so writing to his private friends.

To what is this strange delusion due? To the incidents and violence of the final struggle in Ireland. In that struggle Parnell was a desperate man, fighting, not to save Ireland, but to save his pride. He was sacrificing everything he had won for his country to revenge. He had one object only: the defeat of the party he had made and led. With that object he appealed to the wild men, to the forces he had himself resisted and overcome. To suppose that Parnell, in those frenzied months, with his nerves on edge and his bodily strength wasting, giving and receiving the most cruel blows in politics, took a more profound and a larger view of Irish interests than he had taken in the eight years since he left Kilmainham jail, is to suppose that Mark Antony was at the height of his power and wisdom when he said

"Let Rome in Tiber melt, and the wide arch
    Of the ranged Empire fall."

What hope had Ireland of taking her freedom by force at that moment? Davitt, who had never feared the English, for when his life behind the savage bars of his Dartmoor prison was fresh in his memory, he had found his way back to jail for seditious speeches, said justly that for Parnell to throw over the constitutional movement in Ireland and appeal to violence was to play a cruel trick on the ignorance of the Irish peasant. What chance had violence at the

moment? Parnell himself told Asquith and Morley that
one of his reasons for regretting and disapproving the Plan
of Campaign was that he believed that England could
conquer the Irish by coercion. He had said at Liverpool on
December 19, 1889, just after his long talk with Gladstone
at Hawarden, that " it would be madness for them to talk
of physical force or to turn from the ways of the constitution
to the ways of rebellion and of treason."

" Irishmen can now pin their faith to the constitution as a remedy
for their grievances, and they ought to do so because their
members had been faithful to them, and had been successful in
their efforts, and not only that, but the great Liberal party had
come to the help and the rescue of Ireland, and it would be madness for Irishmen, with these chances and aids in their favour,
with these prospects before them of all legitimate freedom, of
every power to do those things which are necessary for their own
success and the prosperity of their nation in the future—it would
be madness for them to talk about physical force."

This was the advice he had given Ireland just after the talk with
Gladstone of which he said now that it had made him anxious
about Gladstone's intentions. If even then he had thought
physical force madness, how could he think it anything else
now? What had happened since to make him believe that
the policy he had urged for eight years was wrong? Had the
scandal of the divorce court changed the whole character of
the Irish problem? No; but it had changed the character
of the Irish leader. He was no longer the leader of a people
but a desperate adventurer, fighting for his own hand and
for the happiness and peace of mind of the woman who had
ruined him, putting no doubt an Irish colour into purposes
so fatal to Irish unity. Great men have often broken down
under the strain of wounded pride, or thwarted desires, or
threatened loss of some cherished prize, or danger to some
important personal interest. Parnell was not the last nor
Themistocles the first. All that can be said of Parnell's last
months is that, if he was right then, he had been wrong for
most of his life. But to judge him by those months and not by
the rest of his life would be as stupid as it would be unjust.

From this struggle there has entered the Irish mind a view

of Gladstone's purposes and motives that is cruel and unjust. This view is put in Mr. Hackett's brilliant *Story of the Irish Nation*. " So long as Parnell was beaten in Ireland he had succeeded in his main object; reducing the Irish problem to a municipal problem."[1] Nobody who had studied Gladstone's letters on the Irish question could fall into this error. But many writers to-day forget what it was that Gladstone had tried to do. He had tried to persuade the British people to make a concession to nationalist sentiment that would have been refused by every other Great Power in the world, including the United States. He had struggled with this stupendous task for five years. If Ireland had now followed Parnell in his new and desperate mood the cause of Home Rule would have been hopeless. Gladstone was fighting to save the cause of Home Rule in England, to save something that Parnell, judged by all that he had said for the last five years, had wanted Ireland to have. Nobody but a man of his genius could have persuaded half England to put Ireland under Parnell sober; even he could not hope to persuade her to put Ireland under Parnell drunk.

For Parnell's final tactics were only intelligible on the assumption that he wished to wreck the Home Rule movement in England. He might in 1882 have joined with the extreme party and given to the men of violence a competent leader. What would have come of those tactics nobody can say. But he had thrown over the violent men and directed and led a constitutional movement; a movement not for separation but for autonomy. On this basis he had secured the alliance of the Liberal party. To go back on this policy at the moment when England was moving towards it, and revive the methods discarded eight years earlier when Ireland had moved away from them, was the policy of a madman. Others besides Manning might doubt whether his mind was still sound. Gladstone had no alternative, as a Home Ruler, except to desire his defeat. Once Parnell had decided to fight a wrecking battle the struggle could not be avoided. Gladstone's blunders had been made in the first weeks. He should have

---

[1] p. 328.

made greater and more patient efforts to avert that struggle·
If the view taken in these pages is correct, he is to blame for
his impetuous action in publishing the letter to Morley, and
his stiff refusal of negotiation when the parliamentary party
was considering the question of leadership. Those were grave
errors. But if Parnell was acting under a strain, was
not Gladstone? " Since the month of December, 1885,"
he wrote on November 26, 1890,

" my whole political life has been governed by a supreme regard
to the Irish question. For every day, I may say, of these five,
we have been engaged in laboriously rolling uphill the stone of
Sisyphus. Mr. Parnell's decision of yesterday means that the
stone is to break away from us and roll down again to the bottom
of the hill. I cannot recall the years which have elapsed."[1]

Something surely must be allowed to the man who had to
write thus at the age of eighty-one of his chief hope and
purpose in life.

For five years Gladstone had defended Parnell
against the whole weight of English prejudice and suspicion. Let anybody turn to the stinging leaders of the
Times of those days, or to Salisbury's caustic contempt, or
Hartington's patrician arrogance, or Chamberlain's bitter
malice, if he wants to know, what he will not learn from
English public life to-day, the power of hatred as a political
force. Gladstone's high courage had never flinched from
that storm. He had regarded Parnell as a man suffering
injustice at the hands of England, and he had faced all this
insolence and venom as readily as if Parnell's wrongs
had been his own. Yet Parnell gave as little consideration to his difficulties, from start to finish of the
proceedings, as if Gladstone had never lifted a finger in his
defence. It is not surprising that Gladstone's judgment was
misled by his temper. But even when the Irish quarrel
was at its worst he spoke of Parnell with sympathy and
dignity, without rancour or recrimination. Of his champion-
ship of Parnell he only said that he thought he had shown in
the Pigott affair that he had no desire to treat him without
justice.

[1] Morley, *Life of Gladstone*, Vol. III, p. 443.

For the mistakes of a few hours or days Gladstone has paid in the loss of fame and affection ever since among a people to whose interests he had dedicated most of his life. Where else in history can a man be found who has given to a people ruled by his race such sympathy and devotion as Gladstone gave to Ireland? If we read his speeches, his letters, his diaries, Ireland dominates his interests, his imagination, his conscience. If Parnell had never put his head into O'Shea's noose, he would probably have been Ireland's first Prime Minister. If Gladstone had been able to manage the crisis of 1890, he would be remembered to-day in Ireland for what he was, a giant who spent in the disinterested, and as it seemed to his age the romantic service of the Irish people, all the collected strength of his mind, his character and his fame. Never have men been so cruelly punished. Parnell's honourable ambitions ended in defeat and death, after a struggle in which his superb services to his people were half undone in the wild violence of revenge and despair. Gladstone, who was treated in England as a traitor to his nation for his mighty effort for Ireland's freedom, has himself become part of the evil legend that he had hoped to destroy.

APPENDIX TO CHAPTER XXXII

GLADSTONE'S DEALINGS WITH MRS. O'SHEA.

1881.

In June O'Shea made an offer on Parnell's behalf to support the Land Bill if certain amendments were made and if the Exchequer would make a grant to compensate the landlords. This plan was considered by the Cabinet and rejected.

1882.

In April O'Shea acted as mediator between Parnell and the Government in the Kilmainham Treaty affair. After Parnell's release, up to May 15, he was acting as an intermediary between Parnell and Gladstone; he wrote several times to Gladstone and also saw him. It was through him that Parnell sent his offer to resign after the Phoenix Park murders. After the disastrous debate on May 15 his credit sank, and his dealings between Parnell and Gladstone came to an end.

On May 23 Mrs. O'Shea wrote her first letter to Gladstone, asking that he should let Parnell have a few minutes' private conversation with him, and suggesting that she should first see Gladstone to explain matters to him. Gladstone refused to see Parnell, but after a second letter agreed to see Mrs. O'Shea. He did so at Thomas's Hotel on June 1.

On June 9 O'Shea again tried to get into touch with Gladstone, and was referred to Chamberlain.

On June 16 Mrs. O'Shea wrote the first letter of a series containing proposals for co-operation from Parnell, of which the most important were sent on June 17 and October 6. The substance and, in most cases, the text of these letters are given in the confused series of undated notes and memoranda printed in her *Life of Parnell*, Vol. II, pp. 1, 2, 7–10.

She twice intervened on behalf of two men condemned to death for murder. Altogether she wrote twenty letters to Gladstone during the year, and saw him three times, including the interview on June 1. The second interview was on August 29, and was described by Gladstone to Spencer. Besides explaining Parnell's position she put in a plea that her husband should be given a post as successor to Hamilton, as Under Secretary. The third interview on September 14 was probably about her husband, for a letter from her to Gladstone of September 15 thanks him sincerely, and encloses a letter from O'Shea to his " dearest wife " about his suitability for the position. In October Gladstone's colleagues objected to the correspondence, and it was intimated to Mrs. O'Shea that if Parnell wished to communicate with the Government he had better do so through Lord Richard Grosvenor. Mrs. O'Shea wrote six times to Gladstone after this (mostly about possible co-operation, once about her husband and his desire for an appointment). Gladstone's only answer was about O'Shea's appointment. The other letters were sent on to Grosvenor. Gladstone in 1882 wrote ten letters to Mrs. O'Shea.

1883.

During this year Mrs. O'Shea sent eight letters to Gladstone, one of them, written in April and cancelled by a wire, does not survive. Her first letter (March 13) enclosed a long extract of a letter from her husband criticizing the treatment of Parnell by the Government. It was endorsed by Gladstone. " He expresses himself anxious about action of Government to-day. Land Act *must* be amended sooner or later. Parnell indignant at certain members of Government speaking ill of him. Evidently thinks Parnell will be very violent in America." The letter was sent on to Grosvenor who answered it. On June 15 she pleaded in vain for an interview. On June 18, she sent Gladstone a proposal for co-operation from Parnell of which the details are given in her *Life of Parnell* (Vol. II, pp. 14 and 15). Gladstone answered this letter, saying that it had had his careful consideration and that he was looking into the matter. Other letters containing proposals for co-operation or information about a Reclamation Bill drawn up by Parnell were sent on to Grosvenor. A letter of October 27, making two suggestions about details of Irish administration, was endorsed by Gladstone. " Better I think express civilly my regret that I cannot do more than send letter to Lord S." Gladstone wrote twice to her during the year, once refusing an interview, once acknowledging her letter of June 18.

1884.

Mrs. O'Shea wrote twice to Gladstone this year, in March, sending messages from Parnell about the desirability of including leaseholders in the Land Act. Both letters were answered by Grosvenor. There are no letters to her from Gladstone.

1885.

Early in January, Mrs. O'Shea sent Gladstone a paper containing Parnell's views on Irish Local Government (the Central Board Scheme). After three letters from Grosvenor in July, asking her whether Parnell still adhered to the scheme, and a letter to the same effect from Gladstone on August 4 (mentioned in her book and noted in his diary but not amongst the Gladstone Papers) she wrote Gladstone what she describes in her book as a " long and comprehensive reply." This letter does not survive. Gladstone on August 8 answered this letter (see text) and asked to see a paper containing Parnell's views which she had offered to send. Mrs. O'Shea's next letter (October 23) dealt with the question of obtaining a seat for her husband, and contained Parnell's offer of Nationalist votes for certain Liberals in return for a constituency for O'Shea. She wrote a letter in similar terms to Grosvenor the same day, and O'Shea also wrote that day to Gladstone announcing the offer. Gladstone in answering her letter (October 24) told her that he was sending the letters on to Grosvenor, and asked for the paper which she had again mentioned. On October 30 Mrs. O'Shea wrote to Gladstone, sending the paper containing Parnell's Proposed Constitution for Ireland. Gladstone answered through Grosvenor on November 3. In December, Mrs. O'Shea wrote five letters to Gladstone urging him to disclose his intentions. In three of these letters she enclosed letters to her on the same subject from Parnell. Five letters from Gladstone in answer, refusing to make any bargain, are given in full in the text. A sixth letter from him to the same effect, written on December 31, is noted in his diary and mentioned in Mrs. O'Shea's *Life of Parnell* (Vol. II, p. 31), but does not survive amongst the Gladstone Papers.

Mrs. O'Shea sent nine letters to Gladstone, during the year, of which seven are among the Gladstone Papers. Gladstone sent ten letters to Mrs. O'Shea (one of them through Grosvenor) of which eight are among the Papers.

1886.

Mrs. O'Shea wrote three letters to Gladstone in January. The first (January 7) contained a proposal from Parnell for making Home Rule acceptable to landlords by a generous scheme of compulsory land purchase. To this Gladstone (whose letter does not survive though it is noted in his diary) replied according to Mrs. O'Shea in " vague terms." (See *Life of Parnell*, Vol. II, p. 32.) Her second letter (January 23) proposed co-operation with the Liberals in turning out the Government, provided Gladstone would form a Ministry. To this proposal, according to Mrs. O'Shea (Vol. II, p. 32) Gladstone replied on the lines of his December letters, but neither that letter, nor two other letters of January 26 and January 29, all three noted in his diary, survive. Mrs. O'Shea's third January letter, the last letter of any importance that she wrote him, was concerned with the question of how best Parnell and Gladstone could now interchange views. In discussing her own position as an intermediary, she explained that since the Kilmainham episode Parnell had refused to confide his views elsewhere.

As soon as the Gladstone Government was formed, Morley, as Irish Secretary, entered into direct communication with Parnell. During the rest of the year Mrs. O'Shea sent five letters and two telegrams to Gladstone, none of them of importance. They contained enclosures for Morley, or exhortations to Gladstone to stand firm, or information about Parnell's whereabouts.

One concerned an absurd attempt of a hostess to effect a meeting between Parnell and Gladstone at an evening party.

Mrs. O'Shea sent eight letters and two telegrams to Gladstone during the year. Gladstone sent Mrs. O'Shea seven letters, of which three are among the Gladstone Papers.

1888.

In April and May there are two letters from Mrs. O'Shea to Gladstone, enclosing one from Parnell, referring to a forthcoming Petition for an inquiry as to the unsoundness of Mrs. Wood's mind. (As an arrangement was agreed on out of court the petition was never heard.)

CHAPTER XXXIII

THE LAST BATTLE

Until a very recent period—certainly, I think, until within the last sixty years, until the epoch of the first Reform Act, the question between Great Britain and Ireland was a question between a nation and a class, or rather between a class and a nation; because I do not think that, except in a very limited sense indeed, we could call this country substantially a self-governing country until the period of the first Reform Act. During all the previous long, weary, deplorable centuries the question was, in the main, between a governing class on one side of the Channel and a nation on the other side. Sir, it is not so now. It is now a question between a nation and a nation. If there is, as we believe that there is, injustice in the present legislative relations between England and Ireland, and if that injustice be deliberately accepted and prolonged, it will not be inflicted by a class upon a nation, not by an aristocracy, not by a body of landed proprietors, not by a body of merchants and manufacturers, not by the property of the country, but by the people of the country. It has now become—and it appears to me a consideration of extreme importance—it has now become a question, in the strictest sense, between a nation and a nation, and not only between a nation and a nation, but between a great nation and a small nation, between a strong nation and a weak nation, between a wealthy nation and a poor nation. There can be no more melancholy and, in the last result, no more degrading spectacle upon earth than the spectacle of oppression, or of wrong in whatever form, inflicted by the deliberate act of a nation upon another nation, especially by the deliberate act of such a country as Great Britain upon such a country as Ireland. But, on the other hand, there can be no nobler spectacle than that which we think is now dawning upon us, the spectacle of a nation deliberately set on the removal of injustice, deliberately determined to break—not through terror and not in haste, but

under the sole influence of duty and honour—determined to
break with whatever remains still existing of an evil tradition,
and determined in that way at once to pay a debt of justice and
to consult by a bold, wide and good act its own interest and its
own honour.
Gladstone's speech on Second Reading of second Home Rule
Bill. *Hansard,* April 6, 1893.

In the first confusion of the winter of 1890–1 there were
many Unionists who advised Salisbury to seize the moment
for a dissolution. Even Acton thought that this would be
justified. The *Spectator* urged Salisbury to hold out against
the Whips and Wirepullers. If Salisbury had accepted their
advice he would have made the same mistake that Chamberlain persuaded him to make in 1900. For the Unionist
party paid in 1906 for yielding in 1900 to the temptation to
snatch the best moment for immediate victory. If Salisbury
had dissolved in the winter of 1890–1 he would probably
have won the election, but he would have provoked a great
Liberal reaction later. Instead he stuck to office, went
ahead with reform, and put himself in so good a position
that the Liberal victory in 1892 was, so far as Great Britain
was concerned, not a victory but a defeat. For if Ireland is
excluded, there were 277 Liberals returned against 290
Unionists. In votes the Liberals did a little better, polling
2,125,612 to 2,123,009.[1] Ireland returned 81 Home
Rulers to 23 Unionists, the 81 being divided into 9 Parnellites
and 72 Anti-Parnellites.

Such a result would have been a crushing disappointment
to Gladstone if it had come in 1890. Even as it was, he had
expected a much better result. Yet, if the conditions are
reviewed, it is perhaps surprising that the Liberals won a
victory at all. The conditions were adverse in almost
every respect. Apart from the scandal of the Parnell
Commission and Irish coercion, the Government had an
excellent record. The indignation excited by the Commission had died down after the Parnell divorce, and coercion

---

[1] *Recent Electoral Statistics,* by Corbet. The Liberal vote increased between
1886 and 1892 by 400,000: the Unionist by 200,000: a very much smaller
Liberal improvement than that reflected in the bye-elections of 1890.

had been followed by remedial legislation that might well reassure many who had meant to vote Liberal when it looked as if they had to choose between Home Rule and repression. It is true that Balfour had dropped his Local Government Bill, and that this reform was not passed until 1898. Morley indeed well described the fate of this measure when he said that " it had been laughed out of the House and nobody had laughed at it more heartily than its author." But the Land Act of 1887, already described, had been followed by the Land Purchase Act of 1888, voting ten millions sterling on the lines of the Ashbourne Act of 1885, by a Railways Act of 1890, and by the important Land Act of 1891 which included a reform of the greatest value, setting up the Congested Districts Board. The Bill of 1891 extended the credit facilities for land purchase by thirty-three millions and though this part of the Bill proved in fact a failure,[1] there was no reason why the ordinary observer should have expected this in 1891. The other part of the Bill setting up a Congested District Board was a success from the first and it became of course a most important instrument; it was a reform for which Balfour deserved and received the greatest credit at the time and afterwards. In the hands of his brother Gerald it was used later with striking effect. The Liberals were in difficulties about Land Purchase on which they disagreed among themselves, and the contrast between their ineffective discussions and the clear and bold reforms introduced by Balfour added to the prestige of the Government.

Those Liberals who had been inclined to revert to their party before 1889 and 1890, in their dislike of coercion, had good reason now to hope that Ireland might be pacified after all without Home Rule by such measures as these. Meanwhile the state of Ireland offered a further argument for holding back. In 1890 there had been a single Irish nationalist party led by a man of genius who had foiled a base conspiracy against his honour. In 1892 there were two parties, and Parnell before his death had set fire to all

[1] " From 1891 to 1896 land purchase operations were almost at a standstill." Pomfret, *op. cit.*, p. 271.

the feuds and hatreds that lurk beneath the surface of Irish society. His desperate violence had been defeated, but by whom? By a Church, the dread of whose power was one of the main motives of opposition to Home Rule. By a curious irony the dangers of clericalism were illustrated in the most lurid manner at the expense of a man who was at once anti-Parnellite and anti-Church. When Parnell was drawing up the constitution of his party in 1885, he insisted on giving the parish priest an ex-officio seat on the Conventions for choosing candidates. Davitt, a Catholic but anti-clerical, strongly opposed this, but Parnell, a Protestant, told him that he counted on the Church for defeating his extreme proposals. When the Church denounced Parnell, the Bishops and priests did not spare their language, and Davitt in vain protested against their violent manifestos. He was himself unseated for clerical intimidation when it was proved that a priest in his constituency had told a man that he would turn him into a goat if he voted for Parnell. Revelations of clerical intolerance were hardly likely to disarm the Englishman's fears of the power of the Church in Ireland. Thus an Englishman looking at Irish problems saw a Unionist Government taking in hand great constructive reforms, and looking at Irish politics saw Ireland torn between two factions, with the Church using its worst weapon since " priests first traded with the name of God."

At home too the Government had an admirable record. The reforms which the Liberals had meant to undertake in 1882 were now on the Statute Book, for County Councils had at last been set up in 1888. In addition free education had been granted; a Factory Bill had been passed. And the head of the Government had steadily acquired a reputation as Foreign Minister which spread confidence far outside the ranks of his own party. Salisbury, like Palmerston, sowed wild oats long after he had passed his youth, but, unlike Palmerston, he sowed his wild oats at home. Abroad he showed himself a man of calm, clear, steady, and independent judgment, taking his own line, making his own plans, and preserving his equanimity and his large prudence under the most difficult conditions. Few students of the diplomatic history of that time will doubt that in this, his most successful term of office, he proved himself a Foreign Minister of the temper and quality of Castlereagh. The details on which such a judgment must be based were of course not known to the public at the time, but there was a general and widespread confidence in his wisdom, his skill, his integrity, and his strength. Gladstone acknowledged his great success. In these circumstances it was surely a remarkable achievement for Gladstone to persuade half of the British electorate to put an end to the Government and to make him Prime Minister in order to give Ireland Home Rule.

A Government whose majority was forty, if you counted among its supporters not only the seventy-two Nationalists, but also the nine Parnellites, could hardly expect a long life or an active career. Yet this Government lasted three years, and it was a more capable Government than the Government that took office with such brilliant hopes, after the great triumph of 1880. It was indeed one of the best Governments of the nineteenth century. The explanation is to be found in the broad contrast between this Government and the Government of 1880. Gladstone was now able to use, whereas in the earlier Government he wasted, partly by his own mistakes, largely from the circumstances, the new forces and the new spirit in the Liberal party. Asquith proved in this House of Commons a better debater than Chamberlain had proved in the other, and Fowler than Dilke. For in this Government new men had their chance, whereas in the other the new men had been stifled by the Whig predominance, combined with Gladstone's conservatism.

Alike in debate, in administration and in legislation, the last of Gladstone's Governments covered itself with honour. Before Gladstone resigned on March 3, 1894, it had passed some admirable reforms, giving England district and parish councils, raising the school age, limiting the hours of railway servants, and this although the Home Rule Bill had taken almost all its time and energy from April to

September of 1893. It initiated a new spirit in the treatment of Labour questions. Campbell-Bannerman introduced the eight-hour day into the Ordnance factories, and Spencer into the dockyards.[1] Mundella created the Labour Department in the Board of Trade. At the Home Office, Asquith put great vigour into factory administration, appointing women inspectors for the first time, and changed the atmosphere of the Department; at the Education Office Acland made great improvements, abolishing the bad system of payment by results. In the great coal dispute of 1893, the Government intervened with striking success, Rosebery, the Foreign Secretary, acting as chairman of the conference which brought that long struggle to an end by establishing a new and revolutionary principle to the advantage of the Trade Unions.

Ireland, under Morley and Lord Houghton (afterwards Lord Crewe), was administered with sympathy and success. A Commission was appointed to examine the problem of the Evicted Tenants and, after Gladstone's resignation, a Bill was carried through the Commons giving effect to its recommendations. The House of Lords with its Bourbon obstinacy threw the Bill out, and had in consequence to swallow a stiffer Bill some years later. After Gladstone left, Rosebery's Government passed a Factory Act, and an Equalization of Rates Act for London, together with Harcourt's important reform of the Death Duties. In his conduct of this measure through the House of Commons Harcourt displayed all the debating power for which he was famous and a good temper that astonished the House of Commons as much as his colleagues. When it is remembered that the Government was embarrassed by the bitter hostility of the House of Lords, which made trouble over the Parish Councils Bill, mutilated Asquith's Employers Liability Bill in the Government's first year of office, and so compelled the Government to drop it, this is an astonishing record. Until the last few months of its life,

---

[1] This was announced after Gladstone's retirement, but it had received his sanction. One of the last letters, as Prime Minister, he wrote was a letter to C.B. on the subject.

2 Y

the Government did better than any other Government at its bye-elections. Unfortunately when the General Election came, conditions were very unfavourable, for Rosebery and Harcourt were not on speaking terms, and Harcourt had fallen into the fatal illusion that the British people were eager for local prohibition of the liquor traffic, the sort of illusion that is specially fatal when its victim is a man of the world. Thus, though the record of this Government was remarkably good, the general impression that it could not make much head against the House of Lords which had rejected the Home Rule Bill and destroyed the Employers Liability Bill, gave it at the end a look of weakness, and its unhappy licensing adventure was unpopular enough to have destroyed a more powerful party.

The chief business of the Government was of course the second Home Rule Bill. The Bill was introduced on February 13 : its second reading was carried on April 21 by 347 to 304. The third reading on September 1 by 301 to 267. On September 8 it was rejected in the House of Lords on second reading by 419 to 41 after four days' debate. The House of Commons had given 82 days to the Bill in its different stages. The Bill was prepared by a Committee consisting of Gladstone, Spencer, Morley, Herschell, Campbell-Bannerman, and Bryce. The Irish Legislature was to consist of two Houses, (1) a Legislative Council containing 48 Councillors, elected for eight years for single member constituencies, by voters who were owners or occupiers of land to the rateable value of £20; (2) a Legislative Assembly containing 103 members elected by present constituencies (with the exception of Dublin University). In case of disagreement between the two Houses the Bill in dispute after a dissolution or the lapse of two years was to be voted on by the two Houses sitting together and passed or rejected by the majority. In respect of powers the Bill followed the lines of the Bill of 1886, but in this Bill the Irish members were retained. In the Bill as introduced there were to be eighty Irish members who were not to vote on any matter purely British, but the difficulties of this arrangement were found to be so serious that Gladstone amended the Bill in Committee, carrying an amendment by 327 to 300 which retained the Irish members for all purposes.

The chief improvement in the new arrangement, as compared with the old, was due to Barry O'Brien, the friend and biographer of Parnell. In July, 1893, Algernon West, Gladstone's secretary, and Welby, met O'Brien at Armitstead's, and O'Brien proposed the setting up of a Commission to study the financial relations of Great Britain and Ireland from the time of the Union.[1] Gladstone now accepted the proposal, and gave an answer accordingly to Redmond when he asked a question in the House of Commons, July 18, 1893. The financial arrangements of the Bill were unsatisfactory to the Irish members but, as it was provided that they could be revised at the end of six years, by which time the Commission would have reported, Redmond did not on that account oppose the third reading of the Bill. It was unfortunate that Gladstone had not thought of this method in 1886.

Gladstone's conduct of this Bill was in some respects the most remarkable achievement of his life. He was eighty-four; he had against him Chamberlain and Balfour, Hicks Beach and Henry James. He had a majority so small that the life of his Government was in danger from day to day. His Bill was intricate, difficult, exposing a large surface to the ingenuity of malice in a House where some of the sharpest minds ever given to debate were set on his defeat. Worst of all he was working under the shadow of death. No triumph of argument however brilliant, or of oratory however magnificent, could avert the certain destruction of his Bill in the Lords. The whole of those proceedings were, it was well known, the prelude to prompt

[1] The Commission, which held its first meeting on July 5, 1894, was a very strong body. Childers was chairman; English official experience and views were represented by Welby and Farrer, formerly heads respectively of the Treasury and the Board of Trade; the Nationalists by Redmond, Sexton and Blake; other members were the O'Connor Don, Sir David Barbour and Sir Thomas Sutherland. There were fourteen members. When the Commission reported Gladstone admitted that he had made a mistake when extending the income tax to Ireland in 1853 of going back not to the Union, but to the union of the exchequers in 1817. Morley, *Gladstone*, Vol. I, p. 647. *Private Diaries of Sir Algernon West*, edited by Hutchinson, p. 173.

and contemptuous rejection. Such knowledge of the fate of a Bill has two effects. It takes the heart out of its supporters and it removes any vestige of scruple from its opponents. Gladstone's task was thus as difficult as it was hopeless. Yet he gave to the Bill as much ardour, as much patience, as much power, as if its fate depended on his success in the House of Commons and on that success alone. In debate the Government held its own.

The Home Rule Bill was rejected by the House of Lords on September 8, 1893. The debate lasted four days and the voting was 419 to 41. In February, 1894, the House of Lords drastically amended the Employers Liability Bill and the Parish Councils Bill. If Gladstone had had his way the Government would have gone to the country in 1894 after these events. Later in February, 1897, he drew up a memorandum giving his views of the right tactics for the time and the difficulties in adopting them.

Crisis of 1894 as to the Lords and Dissolution.

The process of working up to the Election of 1892 lasted for six, or I might say for seven years. Before that Election I was sometimes asked what majority I expected that we should gain. This was I think after the Parnell scandals which I conceive had an operation not less wide and mischievous than subtle. My answer was, I do not know what majority we shall have: but I know what majority will content me: nothing less than three figures. Apart from the deplorable case of Parnell, I think we should probably have had them. The forty, to which we were reduced, were quite sufficient for the purpose of holding office; but quite insufficient for the purpose of forcing the House of Lords, as we had done with the Irish Church and Land. Every opportunity of that kind would have been utterly lost, had the Lords been wise enough to keep to that single issue. But they most rashly multiplied the issues: so that, at the moment when they had inflicted a deadly mutilation on the Parish Councils Bill, they (having also refused our measure on Employers' Liability) had placed themselves in sharp conflict with public opinion on great subjects both in England and Ireland. Scotland could be thoroughly depended upon for general reasons. But

here also the Lords had refused a Bill in which the public felt a
real interest though it only related to Salmon Fisheries. It was
therefore not too much to say that they had destroyed the year's
work which had cost the House of Commons two hundred nights
of labour. I was at Biarritz when this happened in January
(or February) of 1894. I suggested Dissolution to my colleagues
in London where half or more than half the Cabinet were found
at the moment. I received by Telegraph a hopelessly adverse
reply. In normal circumstances it would have been my duty
to come home at once and urge the adoption of my views. But
not only was I aware that I had lost all influence in the Cabinet;
I was also fatally as well as directly at variance with my colleagues
upon the Naval Estimates for 1894–5; besides which it was plain
that dissolution at that moment would have required some
exceptional arrangements in order to provide time for the
regular course of financial business; this was however a secondary
matter. But, fatally crippled as I was, I was compelled to
let the matter drop. There was another difficulty also secondary
though not unimportant: we were totally unprovided with
arrangements and with Candidates. Thus there was let slip
an opportunity in my opinion nothing less than splendid for
raising decisively an issue of vital importance to popular government: an opportunity which if rightly used would have given the
Liberal party a decisive preponderance for the full term of one or
probably two Parliaments, quite apart from the vast public
advantages within reach. The great controversy between Lords
and Commons, terrible in 1831–2, formidable in 1860–1, happily
averted with the Queen's wise aid in 1884, but commonly at
work with serious though not always perceived consequences,
would have reached a practical settlement: and the yet graver
controversy (as involving character) of 700 years with Ireland
would have come nearly to a complete settlement by a measure
of Home Rule, that was promised even by the administration
of Lord Fitzwilliam.

(F.13.97.)

The Government did not dissolve, but Gladstone resigned.
The Lords drew back from their quarrel over the Parish
Councils and dropped their serious amendments. On
March 1, 1894, Gladstone made his last speech in the
Commons and on March 3 he resigned. He resigned
because he was at variance with the whole of his Cabinet

except Shaw Lefevre on the question of an increase of three millions in the naval estimates. He objected to the increase, partly as an economist, but mainly as a European. In a letter to Mundella of February 5, 1894, he described his difficulty.

" . . . I am told that the Govt. cannot go on without me. I have not adopted that opinion. But if others adopt it, I will, for argument's sake, suppose it to be true. The meaning is that the country has a confidence in the party with me at the head, which it will not have if I am not at the head. *If* this be so, some essential part of that confidence is confidence in me. If it is confidence in me, it is founded on my life and my actions. Now in them has been embedded for 60 years a constant effort to do all I could for economy and for peace; not the peace of this country only but of the world. I do not put the two, peace and economy, quite on the same footing; and it is not now economy but peace which supplies the key note of the situation; and which together with honour also supplies the highest standard of duty for a public man. Because then, I have (so it is supposed) acquired confidence by my life and acts, I am now asked to depart from their essential law, and to use all such authority as they have acquired for me, in order to become (as I shd. be) the main recommender of a policy which in my view directly contradicts them. I ask you how can I do this? If the thing is to be done at all let it be done by those who think it *right*."

In an earlier letter, January 5, 1894, to Morley he put his own position even more emphatically.

" A very great difficulty for me in this matter is that circumstances have imposed on me an absolute isolation. It was in process of time determined for, not by, me, that a large portion of my political character and action should be lodged outside this country. I feel keenly for my colleagues that this is hard upon them, that they should have to act under or with a man who has been moulded, and that by pretty strong hands, under influences to which they are wholly strangers."

Thus Gladstone recognized that he was leaving public life because he was asked as an Englishman to do something that he could not sanction as a European. He believed that the increase in the naval estimates was bad policy for England, but he believed still more strongly that it would lead Europe further along the evil course into which Bismarck had led her in 1870.

Gladstone resigned his office on March 3, 1894, at the age of eighty-five, and he died on May 19, 1898, at the age of eighty-nine. The last years of his life were busily occupied with tasks that embraced his dominating interests. He finished his edition of Butler and published it in 1896. In the same year he addressed an appeal to Pope Leo XIII for Christian unity.

" I would most earnestly venture to urge that, inspired by the example of one of the greatest of your predecessors, that of Gregory the Great, a name associated with some of the greatest glories of the Roman Church, and intimately connected with the history of Christianity in this country, Your Holiness should make use of the thirteenth hundred anniversary of the mission of St. Augustine to England, which will be celebrated next year by a meeting of all the bishops of the Anglican Communion at Lambeth, as an opportunity for a new message of peace and goodwill, by asking the Bishops and Archbishops there assembled to take part in such Conference upon the disputed points which now divide Christendom . . . were it not for my advanced age, which makes the fatigues of the journey at the present time impossible, I should have wished to put this letter personally in the hands of your Holiness."

" The Vatican replied," says Morley, " in such language as might have been expected by anybody with less than Mr. Gladstone's inextinguishable faith in the virtues of argumentative persuasion."[1]

In the same year he wrote in the *Nineteenth Century* on Sheridan. A book on Sheridan published by Rae had fallen rather flat. Gladstone, whose Irish ideas had drawn him both to Fox and to Sheridan, but more especially to Sheridan for his active resistance to the Union, wrote to Rae praising his book. Dufferin, whose friendship had survived the Home Rule split, hearing of this, urged Gladstone to publish something on the subject. " You are the only living person," he wrote, " in whose recollection still survive the traditions of the men of that time, and my poor

[1] *Gladstone*, III, 521.

ancestor has been so ill-used and maligned that a few short sentences from your pen would, indeed, be a charity to his memory. I remember Lord Russell always spoke of Sheridan with great respect." Gladstone responded to this appeal, with a most interesting discussion of the treatment of Sheridan by the Whigs, which is all the more interesting to the modern reader because it inevitably suggests a comparison, which would not have occurred to the writer, with Gladstone's treatment of Chamberlain. In this article Gladstone put Grey, Wilberforce, Dundas, and North in one category as men who would make competent Ministers, and Pitt, Fox, Burke, and Sheridan in another as men of outstanding genius. He made out a strong case for Sheridan pointing not only to his courage and his passion for freedom but to his patient work on the dull and unrewarding subject of burgh reform in Scotland. Sheridan's claims to gratitude and fame are indeed stronger than Gladstone knew, for it is only recent research that had brought out his enlightened services to the working classes in the fight over the Combination Laws and the hardships of the calico printers. Dufferin was delighted with the article. " Thank you a thousand times for having lent your great authority to the vindication of Sheridan's fame and character."

Gladstone's last public speech was made at Hengler's circus, Liverpool, on September 24, 1896, on the Armenian question. His speech was one of the causes of the retirement in the following month of his successor in the leadership of the party. " I find myself," Rosebery said in his letter to Ellis the chief Liberal Whip, " in apparent difference with a considerable mass of the Liberal party, on the Eastern question, and in some conflict of opinion with Mr. Gladstone, who must necessarily always exercise a matchless authority in the party."[1] Gladstone had spoken in favour of breaking off relations with Turkey and doing what we could directly to repress outrages. Rosebery was anxious to preserve the

---

[1] Crewe, *Rosebery*, Vol. II, p. 523. Gladstone never gave much consideration to the difficulties he might create for others. In the height of the controversy over Local Veto he came out with a strong eulogy of the Gothenburg system. Harcourt was incensed with some reason. See his letter to Morley, September 24, 1897, Gardiner, II, 307.

principle of " concerted action of the Powers." Rosebery told Gladstone in a letter of October 7, " I will not disguise that you have, by again coming forward and advocating a policy which I cannot support, innocently and unconsciously dealt the *coup de grâce*"[1] Gladstone replied with a most characteristic letter, saying that he had believed Rosebery to be " not warm but concurrent or acquiescent in his policy." How often and with what consequences had Gladstone fallen under such illusions. To the end of his life he never learnt to distinguish between out-talking a man and convincing him.

The Eastern tragedy was not the only sign of the ruin that was overtaking all Gladstone's plans and hopes for civilization. Everywhere the passion for empire was overwhelming the passion for liberty. Of his own country this was for the moment painfully true. He lived to see the Jameson raid, but he was spared its sequel, the Boer War. The struggle over Home Rule was bound to leave England either more generous or more selfish, to fill her imagination with the dream of justice or with the dream of power. In the temper that it spread, the expansion and consolidation of empire seemed to most educated Englishmen the only duty their country owed to civilization. Gladstone, whose whole life had been spent stemming this spirit, had lost almost all the prizes that had fallen to the rich beauty with which heaven had crowned his words. One alone remained. As he passed through the crowded streets of Liverpool to give his last message, he beheld again the wonder of the common people gazing upon him as upon a god.[2]

[1] Crewe, *Rosebery*, II, 526.
[2] *Odyssey*, 8, 174.

CHAPTER XXXIV

GLADSTONE AND DEMOCRACY

It is easy to understand how Shaftesbury gained a great place in the affection and respect of the poor. He gave up his life to crusades for the rescue of the weak. It is easy to understand how Chamberlain set on fire the enthusiasm of the working classes. He preached a class war; the wrongs of the dispossessed were his weapons; his phrases were battle cries; his speeches were blows against power. Shaftesbury and Chamberlain had little sympathy for each other. To Chamberlain, Shaftesbury symbolized condescending patronage; to Shaftesbury, Chamberlain symbolized an unscrupulous Jacobinism. But with neither is there any mystery about his popularity or his place in the emotions of the age.

Gladstone at first regarded Shaftesbury's crusades with something of Peel's scepticism, doubting whether the State could supply the wisdom that Shaftesbury's reforms demanded of it.[1] He regarded Chamberlain's rhetoric with a good deal of Salisbury's distaste, thinking his judgments of the rich crude and unjust. Yet he held in the affections of the mass of the working-classes a place deeper and higher than either Shaftesbury or Chamberlain. It is safe to say that for one portrait of anybody else in working-class houses in the 'eighties of last century there were ten of Gladstone.

[1] The Gladstone papers reveal the interesting fact that Gladstone differed from Peel on the Factory question in 1844. He was a very young Cabinet Minister and immersed in his own Department, so that he could hardly expect to carry great weight or be expected to resign on it. He was out of Parliament in January, 1847, when the Ten Hours Bill was carried. It is clear from his note that he would have voted with Russell and not with Peel. The Peel Government had fallen in 1846, and Gladstone would have been free to vote as he pleased. See Hammond, *Shaftesbury*, Fourth Edition, p. 283.

To an age more and more alive to the importance of social questions that Gladstone neglected, more and more sensible of truths that he missed, this is a mystery so strange that superficial critics call Gladstone an impostor; a man who, by the use or abuse of his immense power as an orator, gained an ascendancy that he did not deserve. But if the view that has been taken in these pages of the development of his Irish policy is correct, the explanation of that development gives the key to his conquest of the esteem and affection of the English workman. Both alike were the result of ideas that distinguished him from other public men. This will become clear if we analyse those ideas and see how important they were to him. They reflect ultimately the influence on his mind of Homer and Dante.

It is often a help in studying Gladstone's mind to see where he agrees with, and where he differs from Newman to whom Leslie Stephen found so close a resemblance. Perhaps we can best describe that relationship with the help of a saying by a French bishop in the eighteenth century. " Le chrétien est tout à la fois cosmopolite et patriote. Ces deux qualités ne sont pas incompatibles. La monde est à la vérité une patrie commune, ou, pour parler plus chrétiennement, un exil commun."[1] Both Newman and Gladstone had this feeling for the unity of mankind, but it might be said of Gladstone that his sense of the world as a common country was stronger than his sense of the world as a common exile, whereas in Newman the sense of the world as a common exile was stronger than the sense of the world as a common country. Whence did they derive the idea of the world as a common exile? The bishop speaks of it as the more Christian way of looking at the world. He was thinking, of course, of the sense of the Christian life as a pilgrimage that had dominated the medieval mind. Caird pointed out that this conception enabled the Church to keep the revolutionary teaching of Christianity and yet acquiesce in the status quo in the world:

" The kingdoms of this world were allowed to subsist, nay, their

[1] *Instruction pastorale de Le Franc de Pompignan, évêque du Puy*, 1763, quoted by Julien Benda, *La·Trahison des clercs*, p. 107.

authority was consecrated by a Church which repudiated all their principles of life and government; and the doctrine that this life is merely a preparation for another enabled Christianity to be used as an anodyne to reconcile men to the injustices under which they were suffering, rather than as a call to change the institutions which caused such evils. On the other hand, the Church, at least in its dedicated orders, in its priests, monks and nuns, sought to realize within itself that higher life which it refrained from demanding from the world."[1]

Newman's famous outburst about the state of the world which seemed to him so clearly discarded by God, and his argument that Paul laboured not to civilize the world but for the sake of the elect were significant of this spirit.[2]

Dante said of the *Commedia* that its subject is the state of souls after death but that if the work be taken allegorically its subject is man as, by the good or the ill use of his freedom, he becomes worthy of reward or punishment. Caird quoted this letter to illustrate his view that Dante was at once the first of modern and the last of medieval writers. He kept, that is, the medieval representation of life as a preparation for another world, but he " escaped the medieval dualism by exhibiting the other world as simply the clear revelation of ideal forces which are hidden from us amid the confused phenomena of our earthly existence." Dante was one of Gladstone's chief teachers. Gladstone said in a letter to an Italian correspondent in 1883: " In the school of Dante I have learned a great part of that mental provision (however insignificant it may be) which has served me to make the journey of human life up to the term of nearly seventy-three years."[3] In the *Paradiso*, his favourite poem, he could dwell on his ideal of the unity of the religious mind, with heaven the home of the human soul. Thus Gladstone, as a disciple of Dante, the spokesman, in Carlyle's phrase, of ten silent centuries, could think of the world as a common exile. He had in his nature something of the divine melancholy of Newman.

But great as was Gladstone's debt to Dante, it was,

---

[1] Edward Caird, *Essays on Literature and Philosophy*, Vol. I, p. 21.
[2] *Difficulties felt by Anglicans*, Vol. I, p. 305.
[3] Morley, *Gladstone*, Vol. I, p. 203.

MR. GLADSTONE READING THE LESSONS

[*From Lathbury's Gladstone's Letters on Religion. John Murray.*]

perhaps, not greater than his debt to Homer. Now Homer's men and women are not pilgrims, dreaming wistfully of another world, waiting and suffering on the threshold of a vast and solemn future. Homer paints a world of action, with men and women absorbed in its cares and its fortunes, its dangers and its duties. Gladstone was fascinated by that picture and he found it full of sparkling truth. For it was not a poet's fantasy but a poet's portrait, and a portrait in which, as we have seen, God was teaching man lessons of great significance.

" We may, as I am disposed to think, even if we should disbelieve the existence of Helen, of Agamemnon, or of Troy, yet hold, in all that is most essential, by the historical character of Homer. For myself, I ask to be allowed to believe in these, and in much besides these; yet I also plead that the main question is not whether he has correctly recorded a certain set of transactions, but whether he has truly and faithfully represented manners and characters, feelings and tastes, races and countries, principles and institutions. Here lies the pith of history; these it has for its soul, and fact for its body."[1]

Gladstone was intensely interested in this society and its men and women, and in the mind whose beauty gave their world its splendid mirror. He examines their character, their actions, their speeches with the devotion and care that Newman gave to the lives of the Saints. He studies Achilles and Odysseus, Priam and Hector, Menelaos and Helen, as Newman studied Chrysostom or Benedict.[2] Of Homer's sensibility to the beauty of colour and sound, of his feeling for nature, wild or gentle, for the life of man, now filled with gay pride now haunted by undertones of sorrow and destiny, he speaks with the emotion with which Newman speaks of the life of silent piety behind sacred windows. What man was making of his life as a scene of action seemed to Gladstone at such moment not less im-

---

[1] *Homer and the Homeric Age*, Vol. I, p. 35.

[2] If he gives the Greeks the ascendancy in " the strong mind and the strong hand," he justifies the medieval preference for Hector because " no one of the Homeric heroes exhibits a combination of qualities supplying so appropriate a basis for the character of a Christian hero; a tone so sensibly approximating to that of the Gospel." Vol. III, 568.

portant than what man was making of his life as a school of patience. Thus the Greek in him who thought of the world as a common country was as vivid and real as the schoolman who thought of it as a common exile. Gladstone then combined with the solemn sense of his life as a preparation for another which he derived from medieval Christianity, this strong respect for the life of a self-governing society as something in itself important and noble that he derived from the Greeks. A phrase used by Professor Powicke describes exactly what it was that moved Gladstone in the spectacle of public life. " Human intelligence and will, fierce with freedom "[1] Thus if Gladstone had the divine melancholy of Newman, deep in the Middle Ages, he had also the noble buoyancy of Fox, bred like himself on Homer and the Greeks. He brought to public life the strength of two powerful impulses not often found together. Politics, however ignoble their evil hours, belonged, as he believed, to man's spiritual nature, and summoned to their duties man's spiritual power. He reached this conclusion by a path of his own; he held it with a passion of his own; he lived by it with a conviction of his own. This we shall see if we consider a little more closely the studies that fed and inspired his mind.

For Gladstone, as we have seen, had his own view of the source of the belief that politics was the noblest field for the mind and the energy of man. He pointed out that though the world had taken Rome as its great teacher in the mere business of law and political organization, this large truth had been taught by the Greek philosophers. Where he differed from most men was in his belief that this Greek idea belongs not to the maturity but to the infancy of Greek society; not to fifth-century Athens but to the Greece of the Homeric age. His strongly romantic temperament, which made him think Scott the greatest man Scotland had ever produced, drew his sympathies to that age and he found in it both the qualities that his conservative Christian spirit had always admired and the qualities that his growing sense for liberty was teaching him to admire. In the three great

[1] *History, Freedom and Religion*, p. 42.

volumes on Homer that he published in 1858, he treats the Greeks of the Homeric age as the pioneers of great politics in respect both of order and liberty. He says that they laid the great corner stones of society, γάμος, ὅρκος, θέμις, θεός. Conservative Christians would have agreed that these were the basis of social life, though they would not have traced their history to this source; early in his career Gladstone was attacked by Shaftesbury for suggesting in the House of Commons that Roman religion had served a civilizing purpose on the ground that any such reading of history disparaged the special glory of the Christian revelation. But Gladstone went on to describe other qualities of Homeric society about which such Christians would have been less cordial.

" Amid undeveloped ideas, rude methods, imperfect organization, and liability to the frequent intrusion of the strong hand, there lies in them the essence of a popular principle of government." " That which is beyond everything distinctive, not of Greece only, but of Homeric Greece, is, that along with an outline of sovereignty and public institutions highly patriarchal, we find the full, constant and effective use of two great instruments of government, since and still so extensively in abeyance, namely publicity and discussion."

It is unnecessary here to discuss Gladstone's arguments for his thesis; his criticisms of the views of Grote; his analysis of the proceedings in the Homeric debates; his examination of the βουλή and ἀγορή ; his minute scrutiny of the great characters and great speeches in the *Iliad* and *Odyssey*. We are concerned with this searching discussion not for the light it throws on Homer but for the light it throws on Gladstone. For this purpose it is only necessary to note that what he likes in this society is that it is a patriarchal society in which rulers have a strong sense of obligation, where mutual respect may sometimes be invaded by the violence to which primitive societies are liable but is not destroyed by the steady and habitual contempt that comes with the worship of wealth and power, where force is the weapon for defence and persuasion the instrument of government at home. The public life of the age expresses not what a tyrant wants but what a society feels; it is the field of its virtues, the theatre of its ideas, the ultimate expression of its dignity and its spirit. Gladstone contrasts this simplicity with the injustices and corruptions that followed the great disturbance of the Trojan War. " A Shield of Achilles, manufactured after the fashion of the Hesiodic age, would not have given us, for the pattern of a king, one who stood smiling in his fields, behind the reapers as they felled the corn."

The clearest insight into the source and the power of Gladstone's feeling for a self-governing society is given in the elaborate contrast that he draws between Homer's live world and Virgil's dead world. Critics to-day would be astonished by Gladstone's failure to do justice to the ideas and purposes served by the *Aeneid*.[1] The modern view of Virgil's importance is based on his share in the moral recovery of Roman civilization after the Civil Wars. A group of powerful writers, following Cicero's example, sought to create a new spirit of reverence for law and self-restraint in place of the passion for plunder and power that had so nearly put out the light in the ancient world. Under this influence the great pirate State became the great law-giver and peacemaker. This moral crusade set up, as we see in Livy, a fable or legend of the old Roman character giving to it not only the hardy simplicity of the early Romans but other qualities that were less Roman than Greek. Professor Henry has shown how Roman writers took the philosophy of Greek teachers like Panaetius and ascribed to the old Roman farmers not only the virtues they had possessed but the virtues of sympathy, tolerance and modera-tion that came from the larger view of human life which those Greek teachers had brought to Rome. The *Aeneid* served to give a background of history and folklore to this great effort to put the Roman Empire on a basis of justice, duty and civilized conduct.

Gladstone saw nothing of this in Virgil's poem. For him

---

[1] It is interesting to note that Gladstone's Socialist contemporary, Proudhon, praised the *Aeneid*, as a book of social ethics which would have transformed the world if Virgil had lived to complete it as he designed it. Virgil, he believed, ordered it to be burnt because he could not finish it and make its full meaning clear. Faguet: *Politicians and moralists of the nineteenth century*, p. 117.

it was an epic for a court and a corrupt court, in which Virgil had to keep his eyes closely on the " cold unheroic character of Augustus " in drawing the portrait of Aeneas and describing the exploits of his hero. Even Virgil's vast power as an artist could hardly have gained for his poem the place it has held in the affections of mankind if its theme had been merely the theme of a court poet. But if we want to understand how Gladstone came to nurse so deep a respect for a free society as a spiritual force, to give to the idea of a nation that is moral and in the wide sense Christian by its exercise of freedom, the reverence that at first he gave to the idea of a nation moral and Christian by imposed discipline, his contrast between Homer and Virgil is full of significance. For this purpose his blindness to the larger purposes of the great Latin literary crusade is irrelevant. For it is true that as between the society he finds in Homer and the society of the age of Augustus there is the difference between a society with a vigorous spirit of freedom and a society without it. And as Homer represented to Gladstone the youth of the world, in its native freshness and simplicity, all that he finds in Homer and misses in Virgil can be described in his conclusion that " from Virgil back to Homer is a greater distance than from Homer back to life."

" His genuine touches of nature," he says of Virgil, " are rare. Such of them as occur have been carefully noted and applauded for he is always studious to set them off by choice and melodious diction. For my own part I find scarcely any among them so true as the simile of the mother labouring with her maidens at night which he owes to Homer.

> castum ut servare cubile
> Conjugis et possit parvos educere natos."[1]

Gladstone doubted whether Virgil could have written the *Iliad* if he had changed places with Homer, but he was sure

---

[1] This passage is an interesting illustration of the debater's temperament· Even Virgil's skill as a poet is made to look sinister and his debt to Homer is overstated, as anybody will see who compares the simile in the *Aeneid* (viii, 407–413) with that in the *Iliad* (xii, 433).

that Homer could not have written it if he had changed places with Virgil. For religion had been corrupted and liberty was dead. " Homer saw before him both a religion and a polity young, fresh and vigorous; for Virgil both were practically dead; and whatever this world has of true greatness is so closely dependent upon them that it was not his fault if his poem felt and bears cogent witness to the loss."

This view of the life of a society as the spiritual expression of its character and ideas, explains why Gladstone became more and more obnoxious and mysterious to the rich and more and more attractive and intelligible to the poor. To most men of his class the idea that the sense of taking part in the public life of his society was of importance to the happiness of a poor man was a sentimental illusion. Shaftesbury thought that the poor wanted to vote because they wanted to take the property of the rich. He devoted his whole life to saving them from ill usage but to the end of his career he kept this conviction, believing that England had taken a fatal step in 1832. Chamberlain thought that the poor man wanted to vote in order to protect himself from the rapacity of the rich and to serve the neglected interests of his class. Gladstone became the greatest popular leader of his age, though he never mastered or seriously studied great social problems on which their comfort largely depended, because he offered the working classes something that satisfied their self-respect. It has often been remarked about his Midlothian campaign that none of his speeches were addressed to the self-interest or the self-pride of his audiences. The secret of their power was not merely that they were eloquent and persuasive; it was that they made the most obscure man in the hall feel that he was contributing to the moral judgment of the world on great events. This sensation frees the listener, as nothing else can, from all the burdens that vex and check his freedom. He stands or sits in a vast audience, not a miner or a boilermaker brooding over the hardships of his life, but a classless man whose mind is playing freely, able to give a disinterested study to a great issue. To make a man in this sense a God is an object of all great art and Gladstone never lost this power.

A man might be successful in inducing this condition with his audience before him without gaining the permanent confidence that Gladstone enjoyed; the triumph of the occasion might be entertainment, entertainment doubtless of a noble quality, but still entertainment. All great oratory in itself creates a special relationship between orator and audience. For oratory, as Professor Alexander has shown, is an art in which the orator and the audience affect and animate each other; in which the artist creates, receives and recreates truths, ideas, fancies, that are moving in the atmosphere, forming and reforming, flashing from mind to mind, in a highly sensitive medium of emotions and intuitions. What distinguished Gladstone as an orator from most politicians was that his oratory was not so much creating a bond for a few hours, between himself and the simple men and women in his audience, as creating a permanent bond and giving to it the charm and power of poetry and imagination. The bond was based on mutual respect and moral affinities. For that " wonderful power of speech " of which Jowett spoke, brought home to the working classes who listened to him the truth that Gladstone was passionately in earnest, sincere not only in his opinions but in his treatment of their right to be asked their opinion. His sensibility for the self-respect of others which might seem pompous and portentous to men of his own class, where a certain touch of cynicism goes to the making of an easy-going and adaptable temperament, gained for him their intuitive sympathy.

Gladstone's passion for addressing meetings, which shocked both the Queen and Shaftesbury as wanting in dignity, was largely due to this mutual attraction. He could have said with truth:

> " Ever have I longed to slake
> My thirst for the world's praises "[1]

But what was it he wanted in the world's praises? He wanted the sympathy and understanding he often missed in his relations with public men. No statesman ever lived

[1] *Endymion*, l. 769.

in greater solitude, for on all his politics there was the stamp of an individual mind, pursuing ideas that were not shared with his colleagues, fascinated by lights and colours in which they found no truth or charm, guided by hopes and fears that were faint and distant to his age.[1] Jowett wrote to Lady Oxford about his last effort in 1893, on behalf of a principle which he had defended in the Balkans, in Italy, and in South Africa, " It is very pathetic to think of this aged man, making his last great display almost in opposition to the convictions of his whole life."[2] If Jowett had been as little able to understand Plato as he was to understand Gladstone, he would never have been Master of Balliol. But if Gladstone was a puzzle to educated men, his colleagues were just as much a puzzle to him. He said, as we have seen, that of all the men who had been his Cabinet colleagues in his long public life, and there were seventy of them, Aberdeen was the only one whom he ever understood. How many of his mistakes were due to misreading of the minds and wishes of the men with whom he worked. Herbert Paul put it aptly when he said that Gladstone had little tact when dealing with individuals and a great deal of tact when dealing with assemblies.

This was partly due to the special character and special source of his political judgment and partly due to the temperament of the orator. That temperament impedes success in some of the arts of public life as Gladstone himself recognized.[3] It is significant that almost all the great orators in English life mismanaged their relations with other men. This is true of orators who differed as widely in character among themselves as Chatham and Burke, Fox and Canning, Gladstone and Churchill. Fox, like Gladstone, was a man of almost irresistible charm and power, but no man blundered so often or so badly in his treatment of personal questions. Even a man who liked and admired Gladstone as much as Dufferin, said that he rarely left him

[1] See his letter to Morley, p. 694.

[2] *Autobiography of Lady Oxford*, l. 127.

[3] See his very interesting discussion of the characters of the two orators he most admired in Homer, Odysseus and Achilles, with special reference to their control of temper. *Homer and Homeric Age*, II, 454.

without a feeling of irritation. Selborne, describing him as a colleague, complained of his vehemence in discussion, and said that he was impatient of the dry light of facts when they told against him. Selborne wrote after their bitter quarrel over Home Rule, but he remembered enough of the old atmosphere to say of Gladstone what Burke said in sad reminiscence of Fox " I know how impossible it is not to admire, and how very easy to love him."[1]

Gladstone then found in his mass meetings the kind of moral strength that Antaeus found when he was thrown to the ground. It is curious to reflect that a public man, whose democratic ideas came ultimately from his study of ancient literature, should have been brought into a closer relationship than any of his contemporaries to great numbers of men, to whom that world was a closed book. Salisbury, Hartington or Goschen would not have felt their self-esteem increased by the applause of random crowds at a railway station, glad though they would have been on political grounds of any sign of popular support. It is clear from his diaries that Gladstone sat back in his carriage with a confidence and a spirit immensely strengthened and encouraged by the friendship of a thousand unknown faces; a man to whom Greek was God's light, upheld by the admiration of men to whom Greek was Greek. The Queen and Shaftesbury were not alone in finding fault with his enjoyment of such scenes, but it was, in fact, a mark of the noble simplicity that belonged to his subtle and complicated character. His study of Greek had convinced him that the spirit of justice lurked somewhere in masses of men still " fierce with freedom " and not yet corrupted by power.

Most men of his own class so little understood his feeling that they thought it a pose. There is an excellent illustration of this view in Mr. Bernard Holland's Life of Hartington. Mr. Holland quoted a letter Gladstone wrote to Clemenceau in the winter of 1882:

" What I hope for and desire, what I labour for and have at heart, is to decentralize authority in Ireland. We have disestablished the Church, we have relieved the tenant class of

[1] Selborne *Memorials*, II, 360.

many grievances, and we are now going to produce a state of things which will make the humblest Irishman realize that he is a governing agency and that the government is to be carried on by him and for him."

On this Mr. Holland notes: " Lord Salisbury, who was averse to any cant, said that he did not much like the idea of the humblest Irishman as a governing agency."[1] What his contemporaries took for cant was the most important quality of Gladstone's moral and intellectual liberalism: his feeling for the life of a society as the expression of its spirit and character. And this feeling for the spiritual aspect of a free society made him, as it happens, a better judge of popular opinion than his contemporaries. In 1886 Chamberlain used, and not unfairly, the argument that all social reform in England was being sacrificed to the Irish, in trying to persuade the working men to follow him rather than Gladstone. But when the Liberal party split it voted by more than four to one for the leader whose democracy was best symbolized in his passionate question: " Are they not our flesh and blood? " and not for the leader whose democracy was best symbolized by the famous phrase about ransom.

To us to-day (except to those who see the English mind thrown on the defensive by the rise and the claims of the totalitarian States) Gladstone's religious feeling for the value and importance of public discussion, as a school of virtue, is difficult to understand. Living in an age of universal suffrage and unlimited debate, we are concerned not so much with the methods of public life as with the results; Gladstone was so much interested in the methods that he seemed almost indifferent to the results. We have an excellent illustration of his spirit in a speech he made in Dublin on November 8, 1877, when receiving the freedom of the city. In this speech he singled out Birmingham for special praise:

" There is one very remarkable case of energy in England. I might mention others such as Glasgow and Manchester but there is one in particular that I would mention, the town of Bir-

[1] Vol. I, p. 383.

mingham. No one I think can visit that town without being struck by the extraordinary energy that pervades the whole of the institutions and the whole of the public life of the place. The consequence is that men have their own peculiar opinions and entertain them freely; but with regard to one another they do not attempt to coerce one another. They resent and have put down all class ascendancy and class interests are not known in the municipal elections. And what is the result? They have in that town the best men to fill their public places."

Thus what impresses Gladstone is this spectacle of self-government; of a spirit that is at once eager and tolerant. He says nothing about the immense reforms that had swept away the slums and made Birmingham the pioneer city in respect of public amenities and the general level of its social life. Six months earlier he had visited Birmingham, where he had spoken to 25,000 people on the Eastern question. Chamberlain was his host and he had thus every opportunity of learning about the destruction of the slums, and the other great reforms that had marked Chamberlain's municipal career.[1] But his diary though enthusiastic about his visit, only makes one reference and that a significant reference to this aspect of Birmingham's recent history. " Then to the fine (qy overfine?) board school where addresses were presented. . . ."[2] Thus Gladstone's warm praise of Birmingham in November, 1877, had little to do with its municipal achievements or with the use it had made of its best men; it was concerned with its active life of discussion and government and its power of attracting its best citizens to its service. These were to him of sovereign value.

The history of Gladstone's second Government illustrates his lack of any warm interest or strong confidence in the concrete benefit to be expected from municipal enterprise. His Government made a notable contribution to the creation of a general system of local administration in England.

[1] The London slums supplied Gladstone with a fine simile for Homer " Like the sun, which furnishes with its light the close courts and alleys of London, while himself unseen by their inhabitants, Homer has supplied with the illumination of his ideas millions of minds that were never brought into direct contact with his work, and even millions more, that have hardly been aware of his existence." *Homer and the Homeric Age*, Vol. III, p. 555.

[2] Morley, *Gladstone*, Vol. II, p. 570.

When it took office England was, as Goschen described it, " a chaos as regards authorities, a chaos as regards rates, and a worse chaos than all as regards areas." Gladstone's Government set out to put an end to this chaos. It began with two ambitious Bills, designed and introduced by Goschen, of which the second set up a complete system of local government for parish and county. These proposals were too sweeping for the public temper; Goschen went to the Admiralty and Stansfeld, who took his place, proceeded to legislate on the more modest lines of the report produced in 1871, by a strong and representative Commission of which C. B. Adderley (afterwards Lord Norton) was the chairman. Stansfeld's first Bill unified the different central authorities under the Local Government Board; his second set up for the first time sanitary authorities for rural districts all over England. He soon found himself involved in a hard struggle with powerful vested interests. The Gladstone Government was by this time unpopular; the coal owners were concentrating their forces in attacking a Coal Mining Bill, introduced by Bruce, the Home Secretary, and all the forces of property were at once angry with the Government and sanguine about the prospect of defeating it. Stansfeld could only save his Bill by dropping half of it, and throwing overboard a great part of his constructive plan. The Bill was thus reduced to a Bill for setting up authorities (in itself, of course, a reform of great moment), and it was left to succeeding Governments to arm them with the powers that Stansfeld had proposed to give them. Even then the fate of his Bill was in doubt and Disraeli had to appeal to his followers to let it pass. A study of the opposition of these interests to the social reforms of the Gladstone Government, of which the *Times* gave a formidable picture, must make the reader appreciate the great courage that Disraeli showed in the next four years in forcing his own ideas on a reluctant party.

The trouble about the Bill was that though it brought landlords and other vested interests into the field against these reforms, there was no driving force behind it. The nation was lukewarm and ignorant, knowing little and caring less about public health. The *Times* gave a description of the House of Commons when the debates began.

" The House of Commons presented an appearance which might have been expected if the subject under discussion had been a Turnpike Bill, instead of a measure involving the health and happiness, the moral and material prosperity of the nation. A mere handful of members were thinly scattered over the Ministerial benches while the opposition side of the House looked still more deserted and forlorn. Dr. Lyon Playfair, in the opening sentence of his speech in favour of the Bill, took occasion to twit the Conservative party with their apparent indifference to the new Tory watchword ' Sanitas sanitatum, omnia sanitas '. It must be allowed, however, that Liberal members showed little more interest than their opponents."

One man in the House of Commons could have destroyed the apathy. If Gladstone had spent two or three hours with the Adderley report and then gone to the House of Commons and spent two or three hours describing its revelations, there would have been little left of this Turnpike Bill atmosphere. The fact that he made no such effort, shows that he took no great interest in the larger scheme and nursed no great expectations of its results.[1]

This curious want of interest and hopefulness about the development of public services belongs to the complications of Gladstone's character. To understand it we must look again at the atmosphere of his education.

Nothing is more striking in the eighteenth century than the contrast between the large views of the best statesmen on foreign questions and their small views on domestic questions. Chatham, Fox, Pitt, Burke and Lansdowne brought to bear on the problems of Europe, of India, and of the new world a wide imagination that was quickened and guided by an education in the mind and the experience of past civilizations. Anybody must admire their strength in this respect who contrasts the spirit displayed by the Governments of Fox and Pitt in handling a powerful interest in India with that displayed by a nineteenth-

[1] It is only fair to Gladstone to state that the Gladstone Papers show that, if his Government had survived, Stansfeld was to have brought in a new Local Government Bill in 1874.

century Government in handling a powerful interest in Africa after the Jameson Raid. Domestic problems on the other hand, where exact knowledge and the mastery of detail were needed, never gained their intelligent attention and never elicited their active public spirit.

The record of statesmen of this class in the history of town government for most of the nineteenth century is indolent and selfish. For the public-school politician still lived half in the atmosphere of the eighteenth century; the atmosphere of a territorial class that had been uninterested in the towns except as pocket boroughs. It is significant that the men who showed initiative and spirit about the squalid condition of the English towns in the nineteenth century, were almost always men brought up outside the public schools and old Universities. Chadwick, Southwood Smith, Joseph Parkes, Joseph Toynbee, doctors like Duncan, Currie, and Playfair, come to the mind when we review that history. Now Gladstone's genius had derived from his education something that none of his contemporaries had derived from it; his large European temper. But except when his imagination was excited, as it had been excited by Homer and Dante, he was conservative, acquiescent, and conventional; and his imagination had never been touched by a sense either of the evils or the opportunities of England's new town life. Disraeli who was outside this class, and in revolt against many of its traditions, had in this respect a freer mind.

There is, perhaps, a second element in Gladstone's scepticism. The Oxford movement, it will be remembered, was, in the first instance, a revolt against the Liberal reformers who wanted to use the power of the State to abolish, among other evils, the scandals of the Established Church in England and Ireland. These reformers stood in the view of men like Newman for what Peacock had called the " steam intellect society "; they believed in substituting reason for custom, in tidying up the confusion of town life, in overtaking the neglect of a generation of conservative fear and inaction. What seemed to Newman their raw confidence, their implicit belief in the efficacy of cocksure strokes at ignorance and mis-government, made their schemes in his eyes a danger to the higher interests of society. When Newman drew up the eighteen propositions of Liberalism that he denounced as a leader of the Oxford Movement, he included among them the proposition that " Virtue is the child of knowledge, and vice of ignorance. Therefore, e.g., education, periodical literature, railroad travelling, ventilation, drainage, and the arts of life, when fully carried out, serve to make a population moral and happy."[1] In the series of sermons he preached in 1850 on the Difficulties felt by Anglicans, he developed his contrast between what he called " mere civilization " and the great secret work of the Church. Some critics had urged that Catholic countries like Italy and Spain were behind Protestant countries in civilization, and he replied that that was not improbable, and he drew out, in some of his most eloquent pages, the difference between what the world admires and what the Church pursues.

" Take a mere beggar woman, lazy, ragged and filthy and not overscrupulous of truth—I do not say she has arrived at per-fection—but if she is chaste, and sober, and cheerful, and goes to her religious duties (and I am supposing a not impossible case) she will, in the eyes of the Church, have a prospect of heaven, which is quite closed and refused to the State's pattern man, the just, the upright, the generous, the honourable, the conscientious, if he be all this not from a supernatural power (I do not determine whether this is likely to be the fact, but I am contrasting views and principles)—not from a supernatural power, but from mere natural virtue."[2]

When Newman was attacking Liberalism for these false ideals, or this false confidence, Chadwick's great report was just beginning to stir the conscience and the fear of the House of Commons. Of the state of the towns we can judge when we remember that even after the first reforms had been made, Newcastle was in such a condition that so easy-going a man as Palmerston said that to read about it made a man shudder.

[1] *Apologia*, p. 296.
[2] *Difficulties felt by Anglicans*, Vol. I, p. 249.

Gladstone, as we have seen, had been as distrustful of the " march of mind " men as Newman himself, and it is difficult not to think that there still hung about his view of municipal action something of this air of misgiving; that he feared that if England counted too much on these plans for " mere civilization," she might forget that, as Newman put it, " good and evil were not lights and shades passing over the surface of society but living powers springing from the depths of the heart."[1] Essentially Greek rather than Roman in spirit he was afraid of putting too much power into the hands of any Government, central or local, and he had a faith as strong as that of any of the philosophers of the industrial revolution in the virtues of individual energy. His caution blinded him to some urgent facts about the town life of his own time, but the dangers of which he was afraid seem less unsubstantial to-day then they would have seemed a few years ago. For he saw on the horizon the shadows of the evils that fill the mind of all liberal Europe to-day; the dangers of an age in which the organized worship of the power of the State threatens to destroy all sense of spiritual values.

If he was excessively cautious, it must be remembered that his own experience gave him a certain bias.

It is here, perhaps, that we come to the most important element in his scepticism. He was the last and the greatest of the men who had driven out of public life one of the chief evils of the eighteenth century: its widespread corruption and family patronage. Burke and Pitt began the work; Hume, Graham, and Peel had all in different ways helped to bring integrity and efficiency into administration; Gladstone had been the most powerful single agent in that great series of reforms. When he left office in 1874 the public interest in honesty and impartiality in the service of the Government was secured by the existence of the Public Accounts Committee, established in 1861, the Exchequer and Audit Department, established in 1866, and the famous Order in Council of June, 1870, throwing open the Civil Service to public competition. Gladstone had played a

---

[1] Newman, *op. cit.*, p. 237.

leading part in this great process. His experience thus, as a man who had held at bay the private interests that threatened the integrity of the State, was as deterrent as Chamberlain's was encouraging in respect of experiments in municipal enterprise. And though his excessive caution was unfortunate, it is unreasonable not to recognize that the regulation of the growth of town life offered opportunities for corruption against which local administration was at the time poorly protected, and that the success of our municipal government is largely due to the stricter atmosphere created by Gladstone's vigilance and firmness in public administration.

The difference between Gladstone and Chamberlain in these respects was that one was chiefly afraid of the abuse of power and the other of the neglect of problems. Shaftesbury, though no more ready than Newman to think that a people could be saved by " mere civilization " was more ready than Gladstone to defy the economists and use the power of the State to relieve distress. He complained bitterly that Gladstone had done little for his causes. Some would say that Gladstone was under the influence of Newman, and Shaftesbury under that of Wilberforce and his crusading tradition. But there is something that goes deeper in their difference. Shaftesbury's life had been governed by his memory of suffering. In his old age he used to dream of his misery and terror as a friendless boy. The strongest force in his character was pity, and pity is strongest among those who are keenly sensible of the power of circumstances over character. Shaftesbury could not bear to see the misery of the slum and think that the victims were left to their fate. The terrible memories of his boyhood flooded his mind and he stood up in the House of Commons to call for help. He was one of those:

> " To whom the miseries of the world
> Are misery, and will not let them rest."[1]

Gladstone, a man of immense and almost arbitrary power, was much less conscious of the dependence of men and

[1] *The Fall of Hyperion*, l. 148.

women on the circumstances of their lives. " Put him in the middle of a moor," said Huxley, " with nothing in the world but his shirt and you could not prevent him from being anything he liked."[1] Gladstone, therefore, had less pity in his nature than Shaftesbury. On the other hand he was stronger than Shaftesbury in sympathy; in the quality that enables a man to enter into the imagination of others. As a man bred on Homer and Dante he lived naturally in men's minds; he believed as Bridges put it, that " human sorrow springeth from man's thought."[2] Shaftesbury could pity the slum dweller and the woman working in the mine and out of his pity he did most noble work for England. But he could not sympathise with the down-trodden agricultural labourer who listened to Arch and wanted to form trade unions, as he could not sympathise with the Irish tenant fighting a battle for liberty and a home. In both these cases his dread of popular movement was stronger than his sensibility to hardship. Gladstone, on the other hand, held that the worst evils are those of which men and women are passionately aware, and that the fact that a man agitates for his release is a reason for considering his wrongs, and not a reason for dismissing them.

In this spirit Gladstone was closer to the fourth of the remarkable group of men who were all born and bred in an Evangelical atmosphere in the early years of the nineteenth century. Shaftesbury and Newman were both born in 1801, Gladstone was born in 1809. Manning in 1808. Manning was as obnoxious to the respectable English Catholics for his social ideas as Gladstone to the respectable English Churchmen for his political ideas. He denounced the Land System; he rejected the fashionable political economy; he was the active champion of the trade unions, and he fought the battles of the dockers and the labourers. " As far as the life of mortals is concerned," said St. Augustine, " which is spent and ended in a few days, what does it matter under whose government a dying man lives if they who govern do not force him to impiety and iniquity?[3]

---

[1] Morley, *Gladstone*, II, 562. [2] *Testament of Beauty*, l. 179.
[3] *De Civitate Dei*, Bk. V.

Manning took a very different view. He told the Pope that if he had been Archbishop of Dublin or Cashel, he would certainly have been in prison. The shock he gave to Catholic opinion was described by the *Times*, no admirer of his crusades. " It was indeed something new for the Roman Catholics of England to see more clearly every day that one of the most eminent Catholic priests in the country, a man of extraordinary refinement and ability, a man of more than commonly aristocratic appearance, was animated by democratic instincts of the most unmistakeable kind and determined to make the poor recognize Roman Catholicism as an instrument of social reform and regeneration." When Manning died the *Figaro* remarked that the mourners at his funeral would include Socialists, Conservatives, Atheists and Catholics, "so truly does real greatness command universal respect." Manning thus combined Ruskin's heresies on political economy "I hold that every man has a right to work or bread," he wrote on November 5, 1890) with Gladstone's heresies on Ireland, and the heresies of the new Socialists on the use of trade unions for the defence of unskilled labour. Well might the poor Irishwoman say of him " He will walk through Purgatory like a King."

Thus these four men, all of them deeply religious, reached different conclusions about public life. Perhaps in each case the impressions of childhood had a lasting effect. Shaftesbury, as is well known, was profoundly moved as a boy at Harrow, by the sight of a pauper's funeral. Manning, as he told Gladstone, was profoundly impressed as a boy by the talk about Peterloo. Gladstone may also have owed something to an episode in his early years as a politician. In 1834 he served on a committee with O'Connell and O'Connell told him that he had come to London from France in 1793 " a violent aristocrat," and that he was converted as he sat listening to the trial of Thomas Hardy for treason, before a London jury, in 1794. What seems to be true of all these reformers is that religion had more effect in giving them courage and devotion than in giving definite shape to their opinions.

Thus Gladstone was the most complete believer in self-government because he believed in it, not for what it did, but for what it was.[1] He had little of the confidence that Bentham had put into his philosophy and Chamberlain into his politics; he did not think that cities were to be swept clean by drastic bye-laws or that the evils of social life could be corrected or abolished by a programme of public works. In this sense he was not a reformer or a man of wide or bold outlook. For many of the evils that politicians expected to cure by politics, he, like Newman, would have looked rather to the remedies of religion and to its influence on the conscience of the rich.[2] But he was a most ardent democrat because he believed that free discussion and self-government were essential to man's dignity and self-respect.

[1] " In the great sphere of politics the process of life is greater than its objectives." Ernest Barker, *Constructive Democracy*, p. 88.

[2] See the interesting account of his view of Carnegie's Gospel of Wealth. Hirst, *Gladstone as Financier and Economist*, pp. 289-294.

CHAPTER XXXV

CONCLUSION

With his strong sense of the value and place of self-respect in the life of a nation, Gladstone saw the whole Irish problem with very different eyes from his contemporaries. For many of them Ireland was just a bad joke, amusing but tiresome. For some, as for the later Disraeli, Ireland was discontented because her life " on a damp island contiguous to the melancholy ocean " was monotonous, and her life was monotonous because her bad habits kept away the British capital which would give her variety and wealth. Hence the fault was not British but Irish.[1] For others, as for Salisbury, she was like Imogen in the eyes of her father Cymbeline—

> "She looks us like
> A thing more made of malice than of duty."

For others she represented a series of hard problems; each of which needed serious and consecutive study. In several respects Gladstone showed less insight into those problems than others. Mill understood the agrarian problem better; Chamberlain the problem of the development of Irish resources; the brothers Balfour the problem of the congested districts. But what distinguished him was that from first to last he thought of the Irish as a people, and he held that the ultimate test of a policy was whether or not it helped this people to satisfy its self-respect and to find its dignity and happiness in its self-governing life.

This large imaginative understanding gave him a confidence in action greater than he would have gained from

[1] Speech at Aylesbury, November 19, 1868, quoted in Moneypenny and Buckle, II, 431.

the mastery of Ireland's individual problems. His land legislation is a good example. When it was proposed to fix rents by the decision of a court, educated men looked on this suggestion much as Pope Innocent I looked on the proposal to revive the old abandoned sacrifices to the Pagan gods in the hope of saving Rome from Alaric at the beginning of the fifth century. Gladstone had little liking for it and accepted it with extreme reluctance. But once he was convinced that it was necessary as a step towards rebuilding a free, stable and self-respecting Ireland, he threw himself into the task with a resolution that could not have been greater if he had been an ardent adherent of the new system on its merits. No smaller faith could have overcome the obstacles he had to face.[1]

There is the same spirit in his use and treatment of coercion. When he made the supreme mistake of putting Parnell in prison he regarded him as a violent man who stood between Ireland and the success of the Land Act, a man that is who for purposes of his own was preventing Ireland from advancing by this means from a false and imperfect social life to a full life of self-government.[2] Here we see the difference between him and most of his contemporaries. So long as Parnell seemed to him to be arresting Ireland's development on a free and orderly basis he treated him as a public enemy. From the moment Parnell dropped this character Gladstone changed his whole tone. Parnell was clearly a strange and dangerous force in politics. He hated England and did not conceal his hatred. Gladstone's contemporaries saw therefore no reason for ceasing to hate and distrust him. But for Gladstone the important thing was that he was no longer what he had seemed at first, a

---

[1] Salisbury, when Colonel Greville in 1868 sketched at dinner a plan of Irish land reform and disestablishment, " listened, attentively, with an ironical smile, and said . . . ' Well you have just sketched out as pretty a scheme of revolution as I have seen for a long time '." *Memoirs of Maccoll*, p. 267. This was a much milder scheme than the Bill Gladstone passed in 1881.

[2] He wrote to Herbert Gladstone then serving with Forster in Dublin on October 15, 1881: " It ought I think to be kept carefully before the public mind, that the arrest of Parnell and Co. is *secondarily* on behalf of order but *primarily* on behalf of liberty." Gladstone made the same mistake of judgment about Arabi in Egypt but there the error was irreparable.

bad Irishman. From the moment that Parnell accepted the Land Act Gladstone regarded him as a man whose policy, whether wise or unwise at the moment, was no longer a deliberate and settled policy of obstruction. Gladstone wanted to see Ireland a free, vigorous society and for that it was necessary to put an end to the spirit and tradition of lawlessness and to set up social and political institutions in which Ireland could develop and employ her self-respect. Any man who was ready to accept that programme was in Gladstone's opinion a man who was able to take his part in solving the largest problem before the British Empire. In his view Parnell went into Kilmainham a wrecker and came out a builder.[1]

There was another respect in which Gladstone's fundamental view of the Irish question caused him to look at coercion in a special light. There were two elements in Irish violence. There was the class hatred caused by evictions and social wrongs; there was the Irish sentiment excited by British misgovernment and British negligence. The ordinary Englishman disliked the first but disliked the second even more. We can see this in the case of Bright. From 1882 onwards Bright was bitterly anti-Irish; with the kind of bitterness that a man feels who finds that he has given much to a cause and earned nothing but ingratitude and disappointment. When Bright wanted to abuse the Irish he called them rebels; a term of abuse that seemed more biting than moonlighter. Gladstone on the other hand found in the Nationalist spirit, in revolt in Ireland, something akin to the spirit that had drawn his sympathy to the Italian movement. He saw that in combating Fenianism an English Government was struggling with crimes prompted by patriotic feeling. He never believed that coercion could or should be used against national

---

[1] "Almost immediately after Parnell came out of Kilmainham, I learned from a person most intimate with him, and one whom I was inclined to believe, that imprisonment had greatly altered the man. Observation confirmed me in this belief. . . . From his return onwards I altogether abstained from denouncing him, or (I believe) from generally denouncing his party beyond special replies in debate on special matters, I determined to throw no obstacle in the way of his doing right." Gladstone to Argyll, May 15, 1886.

demands.[1] In Forster's time he warned his chief secretary against the kind of coercion that would involve a struggle with the Irish people. In all his efforts to soften coercion he made it clear that he disapproved of coercion designed to punish or repress Irish discontent with England and English rule. Indeed he stipulated in the spring of 1885 that the Coercion Bill to be adopted should be a Bill that would be suitable for England and Scotland; a Bill merely making the detection of crime easier. Thus even when his Government was under nightly assault from the Irish benches Gladstone himself never ceased to think of the Irish people as a people with rights that were as sacred as those of England or Scotland. Healy was not the only Irishman who noticed in 1882 that the fiercest storms lost some of their passion when Gladstone rose, just because, after men had been attacking each other with the passions of race, he spoke with a larger historical sense in which passions passed from anger into sorrow; in which the calamities of the Irish people seemed due less to British or to Irish crime than to the hard destiny overruling the life of man about which Achilles made his touching speech to Priam when he gave back the body of Hector.

In this respect Gladstone was the largest-minded man of his age. In this respect, but not in all respects. His debating instinct made him too tenacious of small points, and if he were judged simply by his manners and methods of controversy, he might sometimes seem a man of small nature. He gave the impression of refusing to make any admission on principle and showing ingenuity in defending a bad argument or an inaccurate statement where a generous concession would have been more becoming.[2]

[1] In October, 1881, Gladstone wrote to his son Herbert: "The Land Leaguers seem to be gradually finding out what the Duke of Wellington told George the Fourth in 1828, that a Government possesses no force wherewith to overcome the passive resistance of a nation. Our powers are limited. Its powers are unlimited. True we think and hope it is not the nation which is against us but the fear is of its becoming so."

[2] There are of course exceptions. On April 30, 1885, he wrote to Hartington to say that he was thinking of expressing his regret in the House of Commons that he had allowed himself to be drawn in a recent debate into an irrelevant attack on the Conservative policy of 1878. " It would be an unusual pro-

Nor did he always seem to distinguish clearly between important and unimportant. In his comparisons of Homer and Virgil he condemns Virgil for giving to the river Simois, which Homer treats as a mere stream, more notice than he gave to the river Scamander, which Homer had made a fierce and powerful river, with as much passion as he would have shown in denouncing an historian who had made Croker more important than Peel. So in the House of Commons. There was sometimes something perverse in the way in which he would degrade his superb power to put a plausible face on a trifling mistake which he was too stubborn to admit. For his excitable temper, as he had seen when writing to his brother in 1831, was a dangerous gift. In his great moments he could touch with his spell even the man of mean and shallow mind, making him dream that he was sitting not in the House of Commons with its selfish stratagems but in some sublime senate caring only for lofty justice; at such a moment the bitterest of his opponents could see " the God within him light his face." But there were moments when his temper was not his servant but his master, when his eagle eyes flashed with an anger that had no glory in it, answering not some stern summons to which his conscience had to listen but some taunting challenge to which his pride had best been deaf.[1]

The large problems demanding historical imagination and sympathy always called out Gladstone's greater qualities. His treatment of the Irish problem regarded simply as a display of character is a superb example of magnanimity. In his two first terms of office as Prime Minister he had spent on Ireland strength, health, power, and popularity, as no politician had ever done. He had carried a social revolution against all his natural prejudices and he had given Ireland a popular franchise against all his interests as a Liberal leader. Yet Dilke's picture of Spencer's position in Dublin, even if we allow for exaggeration,

ceeding but perhaps justified by the time and circumstances." Hartington replied that he saw no objection and Gladstone made his apology.

[1] See e.g. Grey's criticism of his speech after the Gordon disaster. Trevelyan, *Grey of Falloden*, p. 29.

exhibits a state of mind and temper in which gratitude seemed overpowered by resentment. The Irish leaders in the House of Commons had voted against Gladstone in the most critical divisions, including the division in which his Government was put out of office. A smaller minded man might well think he had done his duty and that nothing more could be expected from him. Still more might he think this when a new Government took office and, disregarding all its past professions, attracted the warm support of the Irish Party by throwing over coercion. Many Liberals resented bitterly the new departure of the Conservatives who, after blaming the Liberals with unmeasured violence for not going far enough in repressing Irish agitation, were now hand in glove with Irishmen whose sedition went all lengths in their speeches. No Government ever exposed such a surface to attack and no political leader could rival Gladstone in his power of exciting indignation. But Gladstone had only one desire in his heart and that desire ruled his conduct. He longed to see the Irish problem solved by a plan that gave Ireland her self-respect and England security. Everything else he put on one side. He would not say a word that might make it more difficult for the Conservatives to attempt that solution or to embitter the atmosphere in which the new Parliament would face this urgent summons. The forbearance with which he treated the Conservative Government was only equalled by the forbearance with which he treated the violent manifesto that the Irish party launched against him on the eve of the election. If he could always have ruled his combative, sensitive and passionate nature as he ruled it then, his power would have been irresistible. History does not afford a greater example of magnanimity.

Gladstone and Gladstone alone among political leaders treated the Irish question as the supreme problem, because he differed from his contemporaries both in his love and his fear of the self-conscious impulses of national sentiment. He was astonished that most of them seemed to think that the effect of a popular movement for Home Rule in Ireland could be measured by the difference between a party of fifty members and a party of eighty in the House of Commons. Such calculations disregarded all the moral authority of the sense for freedom in a society. As he put it to Spencer in May 1885, with a prescience to be justified thirty years later:

" My opinion is that when once you have in Parliament a large majority of the 103 Members prepared to act in the sense of so-called Nationalism, you will struggle in vain to avoid the inconvenience, be it great or small, of the pretensions of some body or other to speak for Ireland. Will it be a thing beyond expectation if eighty members acting under Parnell assume this office, and meet in London or Dublin from time to time for this purpose? "

He feared, that is, the consequences of a popular movement, but he feared them in a different way from his fellows. What he feared was that England might mismanage this new movement, try to overrule it, put herself in a position morally unjust and in the eyes of the world discreditable, and create a lasting hostility between Ireland and Great Britain.

But he differed from others also in looking to this spirit with hope as well as fear; in seeing an opportunity as well as a danger. From his first contact with Irish politics he had sought to create in Ireland the conditions under which the Irish people could find a field for a self-respecting patriotism. With this in his mind he had removed what seemed a great cause of discord in the Establishment; he had tried to substitute a Royal for a political Viceroy; he had wished to set up Provincial Councils and to make peace between landlord and peasant. All these efforts had failed. Might not the new movement bring success? To Salisbury or Hartington the idea would have been preposterous. They saw nothing in the new movement but ignorance and hatred. But Gladstone had come more and more to put his trust in the popular sense of justice. The *Spectator* said, in an article reviewing his career, that he had made a persistent effort to enforce on England a Christian instead of a pagan conception of her duty to foreign peoples, and that he had converted to his view the people, though not the aristocracy and the educated classes. A political leader,

728 GLADSTONE AND THE IRISH NATION

whose appeals to a large imagination had awakened a
generous response in popular audiences and little but dislike
in his own class, might well think that a popular movement
in Ireland might improve rather than degrade the public
spirit of the country, and raise rather than depress the level
of its politics.

This hope was warmed by his sympathies with the democratic life and spirit of the small communities in Europe.
The little Balkan peoples had fired his imagination
as once it had been fired by the struggles of Garibaldi's
red shirts. As he looked back on their history he
made the interesting discovery that in the great Mussul-
man persecutions in Greece and Bosnia the renegades had
been the upper classes and the masses had remained Christian. In his last months of meditation on the prospect of
Home Rule he made his visit to Norway where he saw with
delight a small people living under the forms and in
the spirit of democracy, its manners unspoilt, its self-respect
uncorrupted by the insolence of wealth, as proud of Norway
as the English of England, her only empire the mysteries of
her mountains and the sagas of her seas. To a man
feeling his way to Home Rule these weeks in Norway
were perhaps not less important than the weeks spent
thirty years earlier in the capital of the Two Sicilies.

Between the old Ireland and the old England there
remained suspicion and evil memories. No concessions had
broken them down or brought the two peoples any closer.
With a new Ireland and a new England there came a new
opportunity of peace and friendship. Gladstone's study of
Irish history had convinced him that Ireland had been
grossly ill-treated by England. His experience in the Eastern
campaign had convinced him that the common people had
a sense of justice which wealth and power had corrupted in
the governing classes.[1] The politicians who laughed at his
indignation over the crimes of the Union, thinking him
wilder than the Irishmen who still resented Cromwell's

---

[1] In some notes he wrote towards the end of his life when he was giving
his mind to Trade Union questions, he says: " on great controverted matters
Labour has judged more truly than Leisure."

savage violence or the more distant wrongs of Shane O'Neill, were the men who had laughed at his indignation over the cruelties of the Turks. Gladstone had little hope of converting them. But of the mass of the people he was convinced that if once they were persuaded that a wrong had been done, they would desire to make reparation.[1]

To his contemporaries Gladstone looked in 1886 like a Catiline, a purely destructive force; but in truth he was trying to do for the British Empire what Augustus, to whose " cold and unheroic character " he had been so severe, had done for the Roman Empire.[2] He was not a wrecker but a builder. What was the character of the Roman Empire that Augustus rebuilt? " In the first centuries of the Christian era Italy was surrounded by a Roman Gaul, a Roman Egypt, a Roman Greece, a Roman Africa, but in these double names each term keeps its own value, and the special character of the people did not disappear under a dull uniform façade."[3] The English people like the Romans had taken a good part of the world into their hands. There was a powerful school that wanted to increase these possessions. Jowett had written in 1877 that we ought to keep Egypt because Africa would fall to us in the next century as India had fallen in the last.[4] Gladstone, like Augustus, dreaded an increase of the Empire. He was anxious to remove a danger that threatened it and to put its foundations on a basis of consent. " Within this vast Empire," he wrote, " there is but one spot where the people are discontented with their relation

[1] Carnarvon's hostility to Gladstone and his Irish schemes which it is difficult to explain or to excuse was partly due to his dislike of Gladstone's appeals to the democratic instinct for justice. Harding, *op. cit.*, III, 221.

[2] The view that Gladstone was dangerous was compatible with great personal admiration for him. Hort, the famous Cambridge scholar, wrote in February, 1886, on the fall of the Salisbury Government: " The shameless opportunism of the Cabinet made it impossible to desire their continuance in office. Gladstone who seems to me each year to soar higher morally above other politicians seems to me also to be discarding convictions for feelings and dragging us into deeper and deeper quagmires." Hort, *Life and Letters*, Vol. II, p. 340.

[3] *Economic Life of the Ancient World*, by Toutain, p. 252.

[4] *Jowett's Letters*, Vol. II, p. 91.

to the central power. That spot is Ireland." " Rightly or wrongly," wrote Salisbury to Carnarvon on March 27, 1890, " I have not the slightest desire to satisfy the national aspirations of Ireland." Gladstone believed that those aspirations had to be satisfied if Ireland was to be kept within the Empire.

Few would doubt to-day that Gladstone read the history of Europe with more wisdom and imagination than his opponents. Salisbury argued in a speech in December, 1887, that Home Rule was running counter to the great processes of history which made for consolidation; that the great States of Europe were made up of small States; had not Germany once had 400, the French any number? Gladstone asked under what conditions had consolidation succeeded? He asked Salisbury to notice

" how an unsatisfied Poland is commonly reputed to be the scandal, the difficulty, perhaps even the danger of Russia; how Turkey lost Bulgaria, Servia and Greece; how Austria lost Lombardy and Venetia and was only saved from losing Hungary by the intervention of the Tsar; how Denmark lost Schleswig and Holland Belgium."

His sympathy with the nationalist movements of the Continent enabled him to divine the strength and the power of this passion in politics, and to know that Great Britain could not expect that there should be one law in history for Europe and another for the British Empire.

It is possible to-day to review Gladstone's Irish policy in the light of half a century of experience, and to see how much truth there was in those large ideas.

He believed that Irish nationalism was not a passing mood but an inextinguishable passion, and that the safety as well as the credit of the British Empire depended on the will and the power of British statesmanship to satisfy it. His opponents held that it could be appeased by material concessions designed to relieve Irish poverty, and at the worst held down by superior force. This policy was tried under the most favourable conditions. Salisbury asked in 1886 for twenty years of resolute government. No man, since democratic government began, ever had a better opportunity of testing his own remedy. During the next twenty years his party was in office for seventeen, and so far as Ireland was concerned it was able to overrule British policy during the three short years that it was in opposition. Salisbury himself was Prime Minister for thirteen years; he was succeeded by his nephew who was Prime Minister for the remaining four. Almost for the whole time during which Salisbury was Prime Minister the office of Chief Secretary was held by one of his nephews. Let us imagine what it would have meant to Gladstone to have held office for seventeen years out of a period of twenty years with his nephews serving at Dublin, with a handsome majority in the House of Commons, and the House of Lords obedient to his will. To complete the picture we must suppose that of the three greatest debaters in the Conservative party, two had crossed the floor and become his most active supporters, bringing with them most of the wealth of their party. This great preponderance of strength at Westminster represented a similar preponderance of strength outside. The *Times* threw itself into this contest with a vigour it rarely showed in the conflicts of party; of the Liberal newspapers some of the most powerful were behind the Conservative Government. These included the chief Scottish papers, the *Daily Telegraph* in London, the *Birmingham Post* and among the weekly reviews the *Economist* and the *Spectator* which had hitherto been the most ardent of all Gladstone's admirers. Thus Salisbury had behind him the House of Lords, a great majority in the House of Commons, a great superiority in debating power,[1] Ministries in which his personal ascendancy was never questioned, some of the ablest minds in politics as his Irish executive Ministers, and the support and confidence of the great mass of the wealth, the press, and the educated opinion, of Great Britain.

So far as political power went, the advocates of the Salisbury policy had advantages of which it is safe to say that if Gladstone had possessed one half of them the history of his 1880 Government would have been, not a history of disaster,

---

[1] Chamberlain, Hartington, Goschen, Argyll, Balfour, Hicks Beach, Churchill.

but a history of triumph. The Compensation for Disturbance Bill would have passed into law; evictions would have been stopped; coercion would have been avoided; the Land Act would have been stronger and better; Parnell would never have been put into prison; Ireland would have had her Provincial Councils. Under these conditions Chamberlain would never have formed his fatal friendship with O'Shea, and Parnell would have treated directly with the Government.

This however does not exhaust Salisbury's good fortune. His political power was unlimited. His circumstances enabled him to make the best use of it. He had at the Irish office not only men personally loyal and devoted, but men of great executive ability. Arthur Balfour was without fear, as he was without compunction, in using the drastic powers that Parliament gave him for repressing and punishing agitation. Land Purchase was pushed ahead, for a Conservative Government was not afraid of treating the landlords with too lavish a generosity. Excellent social measures and local government reforms were introduced, for Home Rule was to be killed by kindness as well as by firmness. Meanwhile in Ireland there sprang up one of those spontaneous movements of self-help for which Gladstone had prayed so ardently. Horace Plunkett was the leader of a great agricultural renaissance bringing to Ireland a new spirit of hope, a new habit of co-operation, a new source of wealth and a new field for self-respecting effort, based on the experience and example of a happy and vigorous little nation, in some respects not unlike the Irish. The old Irish party had been crippled by a shattering catastrophe and these new interests, these new expectations, these new experiences and these new opportunities might well have been expected to draw a great deal of popular support away from a movement that had suffered such eclipse and seemed in comparison little able to help the peasants' immediate need. Everything thus combined to give the Unionist remedy for Irish discontent the most favourable atmosphere; to extinguish whatever in Irish sentiment was not inextinguishable. The result can be described in a single sentence. Does anybody doubt that if the Great War had come, not in 1914 when there was a Home Rule Bill on the Statute Book, but in 1904, Ireland, instead of sending a quarter of a million of Nationalist soldiers to fight for the Allies, would have been from the first day of the war to the last a greater danger to the British Empire than she was for a few weeks in 1796 when Hoche's army was tossing on the seas?

For when the Unionist Government left office in December 1905, Ireland was not less but more self-conscious than she had been in 1885; more self-conscious and more Irish. The Gaelic League was founded in 1895; the Irish Literary Theatre in 1899; Arthur Griffith's *United Irishman* in 1899; Sinn Fein held its first annual Convention in 1905. The sequence is significant. Wherever a stream rises it runs into the same sea. The Gaelic League was non-political and Unionists and Nationalists, Protestant Ulstermen and Catholics from the south worked at first side by side in its ranks. Yet all the new forces that were gathering in Irish life during these twenty years of Unionist experiment were to find their ultimate expression in a new nationalism. For this dominant influence was able to draw into its orbit all the energy that started into life, even when that energy was itself quite unrelated to politics. The great renaissance that rescued an ancient culture which seemed in danger of losing its individual colour and strength—the rich beauty of the art of Yeats and A.E., the rare quality of Synge's drama, the scholarship and learning of Douglas Hyde and John MacNeill, were a few only of its gifts to Ireland—this great renaissance was not primarily or directly a political event, but it fostered the spirit to which Sinn Fein gave unity and direction. In other words, when kindness and firmness had extinguished everything in Irish sentiment that Gladstone had sought to satisfy by Home Rule which was not inextinguishable, there remained a force strong enough not merely to keep nationalism alive but to redouble its power. Parnell made a new party out of the hereditary passions of the peasants; Griffith was making a new party out of Ireland's undeveloped resources of vitality, imagination, self-confidence and historical emotion; resources discovered by these several revivals of the Irish genius.

This new nationalism represented and reflected Irish self-consciousness at a higher level than the old; it had more initiative, more imagination, greater variety of life and mind. But it differed from the old in another respect. It was a more insulating atmosphere.

The two leaders of the great nationalist movement of the 'eighties were Parnell and Davitt. Parnell, though he disliked England, lived more among Englishmen than among Irishmen. His mistress had no Irish blood. He was completely lacking in the strongest impulse in the Griffith movement, for he shocked Gladstone by his indifference and ignorance about Irish history. It is safe to say that if the two men had lived in the early years of the twentieth century it would have been Gladstone and not Parnell who would have been attracted by the Irish literary renaissance.[1] Davitt too had lived a great deal among Englishmen. He had worked in an English mill. He had spent his youth in an English town. He had suffered unspeakable afflictions in an English prison. A man with less of the saint in his character would have learnt in this school to hate England and Englishmen. But Davitt was one of the largest-hearted men of his time and his experiences of life in England had made him feel as keenly for the wrongs of the English poor as for those of the Irish peasant. And he had an enthusiasm that was inspired by a universal doctrine, for he was a follower of Henry George. When he came out of prison he wrote two sentences in an English newspaper that showed that nothing could sour his fine spirit.

" I have suffered by their power and as I believe by their ignorance and prejudice; but there is no bitterness in my heart

---

[1] " I could not describe the tumult almost of thought and emotion that a visit to Ireland brings into the mind. I see from your antiquities, which formerly I knew the existence of only in the abstract, how remarkable was the position Ireland occupied in those days, we may say those centuries, when she had almost a monopoly of learning and piety, when she nearly alone held up the truths of civilisation, of true Christian civilisation, in North and Western Europe. They have made a deep impression on me and they have enabled me the better to understand the intense feeling with which an Irishman loves his country." Gladstone's speech at Dublin. *Times*, November 9, 1877.

towards the English people. The doctrine of the land for the people is a universal gospel and in its triumph is involved the social regeneration of England as clearly as the social regeneration of Ireland."

Thus Davitt, though he differed widely in most respects from Parnell, was, like him, in touch with British habits of mind. This was true also of the party that Parnell led at Westminster. It was not merely a party with experience of the life and atmosphere of the House of Commons. It had mastered the methods of that institution and acquired such skill in using them that Balfour could describe it as the ablest set of parliamentarians of the day.

If then Ireland had entered on her new career in 1886, her first politicians would have been men who had shared experiences with Englishmen. They were among the best speakers in the House of Commons; they served on select committees; they supplied chairmen and vice-chairmen for the sessions when the whole House was in committee. One of the most hopeful of the younger Parnellites had started life as a clerk at the table. The two Parliaments would thus have been composed in part of men who had learnt something from each other in actual co-operation. The new nationalism found its chief leaders in thinkers who had never associated with Englishmen or only known them as enemies.

The difference between the English and the Irish way of looking at politics is so sharp that the loss of this medium has been an important political event. The Irish, sensitive in pride and memory, look carefully at all the implications of a speech or a name where Englishmen apply a rough and ready practical judgment. An excellent example was afforded by the discussion of Dominion status in 1921. The English thought that giving Dominion status was an immense concession, for it meant giving full political power and putting the Free State in the League at Geneva. The Irish, remembering that Ireland had lighted a lamp for Europe in the days when England was a dark and barbarous island, thought it a slur on their dignity to be given a title that was held by the newest and youngest peoples in the world. The English, who rarely ask what is implied in this or that, are neither as bad or as good as they seem, judged by the strict standards of logic, for their brutalities are not as cold blooded or their generosities as deliberate and considered as they look. Irishmen like Sexton and Healy, moving in the House of Commons with men whose minds were so much less sensitive and logical than their own, had some understanding of this truth and it made them less suspicious. Irishmen steeped in Irish history and inexperienced in British politics were apt to think that in every English brain there still lurked the evil spirit of the Penal Laws and the Act of Union.

Gladstone hoped that if the opportunity was taken in 1886 and Ireland received the Parliament she had demanded, she would set out on her new career in a spirit of goodwill, and that her sense of wrong would be merged in the new ambitions and the new tasks on which she was entering. Nobody can tell how this relationship would have developed afterwards, but the conditions would have been more favourable for co-operation than the conditions under which the Free State came to life. The renaissance of Irish culture might have been associated not with political discontent but with political enthusiasm, and the first politicians would have been brought up in a school less self-conscious, suspicious and remote. Of the ultimate value to the human spirit of the forces released or created by those movements it is too early to speak; it may be that they owed something of their power to the sense of wrong that Gladstone wished to remove. But everything that has happened since has vindicated his belief that Great Britain was losing her best opportunity of creating friendship and mutual respect between the two peoples. Ireland in 1886 after Home Rule had become the policy of a British party was less hostile than she had ever been since first her politics had become active and militant.[1] This was true, not only of Ireland in Ireland, but of Ireland in America. Davitt on his first

---

[1] When Bright died in 1889, Parnell, Sexton, Justin McCarthy and T. P. O'Connor joined the General Committee for raising a memorial to him; such a thing would have been unthinkable before Gladstone took up Home Rule.

visit to the United States after Gladstone had adopted
Home Rule was amazed by the change of temper " even
among people formerly irreconcilable foes of England."
Carnegie wrote in a similar strain. Meetings were held
in several American towns at which resolutions of sympathy
with the new English policy to Ireland were passed with
great enthusiasm and the State of New York sent official
messages. Nearly forty years later the concession that
might then have been made to a friendly people and to moral
force was made after a guerrilla war under pressure that
looked to Ireland like political necessity. When in 1921
the long struggle that began with the rise of Parnell reached
its climax, Ireland and England had suffered all the moral
and spiritual damage of a violent conflict in which, under the
flag of the most orderly and experienced people in Europe,
law, justice and politics had been overwhelmed by desperate
passions, crime answered by crime, and murder by murder.

The Irish question was not merely a domestic question;
it belonged also to the politics of Europe and the politics
of the United States. In a world where armed strength was
becoming more and more the undisputed master, a great
statesman was asking one of the leading peoples to make its
undoubted power obey the unarmed voice of justice. It is
difficult to believe that Europe would not have had a
nobler history if there had been a Gladstone in each of the
great States moving so steadily towards war. Nations, as
Bjornson said, acclaiming Gladstone's action, had sometimes acted justly from necessity; but in this case a great
nation was to act justly from choice.[1] This would be Gladstone's last service to Europe; his last and his greatest. We
know how much his mind was troubled by the state of
Europe; with what foreboding he had watched the growing
strength of imperialism as all the calamities he had foreseen

---

[1] The Scandinavian Club in London sent Gladstone a translation of a speech
made by Bjornson at Christiania on his Home Rule Bill. " I will give you the
greatest example of the politics of the heart in the world. I mean the policy
under the leadership of Mr. Gladstone. Many times in the world the weak
have been given their rights but to say, before you are compelled, ' We give
them their rights, because it is right and because to do right is the politics of
the heart and the wisest policy in the world,' that is original."

3 B

followed Bismarck's fatal use of victory. But his conscience was troubled as well as his mind; his conscience as an Englishman and his conscience as a Minister. For he believed that British policy had given an impetus to this movement and that the Cyprus Convention, the acquisitive and self-regarding policy that had inspired it, the intrigues and bargains to which it had led, had helped to create this lawless Europe. And his conscience as a Minister was uneasy, for he knew that his own Government, which had taken office to undo the mischief spread by that spirit, had been defeated by its difficulties and that it had so handled the confusion of Egypt as to add to the dangers of the world. As he brooded over an unhappy chapter in his life, as he recalled how step by step he had been drawn into that false position, he thought perhaps of his Irish policy as reparation not only from England to Ireland but from England to Europe. And as he threw his mind further back to the fatal phrase that Jefferson Davis had made a nation, which had lingered so long in the wounded memory of the North, he could think of his Irish policy as a reparation from England to the United States. In one hour of courage and generosity England could gain strength at home, and shake the violent forces that were mastering the world.

If the view taken in these pages has any truth in it, Gladstone was at once a great politician and a great prophet, a great Englishman and a great European, a great Minister of State and a great minister of justice. Gladstone the politician was trained early to office like Pitt and Fox; moulded in Peel's fine discipline he had a sense of duty alert for every summons; he was the master of figures and facts, however complex; in argument he was invincible. By the 'sixties this Gladstone had learnt that the statesman's conscience must be strong rather than tender;[1] he had composed his early doubts, made as a Peelite his choice of party,

---

[1] See Chapter IX of Sir Henry Taylor's brilliant essay, *The Statesman*. Gladstone was not only a friend of Taylor but a careful student of his work. It is interesting to note that Taylor praised aloofness in statesmen, the quality for which Gladstone was so often blamed.

and given such an impression of power that he was marked out for the succession to Palmerston. When he became Prime Minister he seemed to most educated minds just the man to guide a State through difficult changes; his finance had given it stability; his eloquence and character won general respect. Yet before he died he was widely regarded in the ruling world as a mighty force, but a force for disturbance, the Alaric of his world, not the man to conserve and consolidate a State but the man to destroy it.

For in the last twenty years of Gladstone's life politics took more and more the character of a struggle between the spirit of empire and the spirit of justice. Bulgaria, Afghanistan, Majuba, the Sudan, and Ireland, all stand for that struggle in some aspect; a struggle that perplexed the minds of politicians and disturbed the peace of parties. Here Gladstone the European came into conflict with the firm and fixed ideas of the ruling class. For five years the strain wore him down; those were the five years of his second Government when his duty was often obscure to him, and the struggle itself was, not a pitched battle, but a series of manœuvres within the Cabinet and a series of experiments within his conscience. His mistakes and his misfortunes aged him fast, and doubt and sorrow cast their gloom over his spirit. In 1886 as in 1877, the battle was open, his course was clear, and strength and youth returned to him. It was now a battle between men moving within the circle of an island mind and a man who lived in the wisdom of the ages, among

" The mighty ones who have made eternal day
For Greece and England."[1]

Gladstone the great Englishman sleeps with the great English dead beneath the solemn beauty of the Christian dream that gave his strength its patient power. That Gladstone was the loyal Minister of the Queen, the faithful servant of the nation, the glory of its Parliament. But the other Gladstone belongs to a world older than the world of England's life; that Gladstone was the heir of Europe's centuries of hope and sorrow, her tempests

[1] *Endymion*, II, 243.

in his blood, her burdens on his brow, her ancient wisdom
in his eagle eyes. His place is among the mighty shadows
that people the distant memories of man; the memories of
the twilight towers of Priam's Troy, once sad with Helen's
gaze watching the battle; of the plain, once bright with
swift chariots and the glancing beauty of the horses brought
from Thessaly and Argos in the hollow ships; of Scamander,
once a sea of surging wrath when the son of Peleus tempted
the anger of a god, as he himself had tempted the anger of
an empire. There, perhaps, like

> " Some lone man who in a desert hears
> The music of his home "[1]

the man, in whose stern passion, silent now in the silent
dusk, justice once spoke with thunder to the world, can
sometimes hear the music of the mountain winds driving
the storms of Thrace across the sea.

[1] *Revolt of Islam.*

INDEX

741

INDEX

745

Chamberlain, Joseph

The Times charges him with destructive purposes, 399; and the Irish question, 403 *et seq.*; the interests of, 427; Salisbury's coalition scheme and, 444; his speech at Birmingham (Dec. 1885), 458, 459; and Hartington, 462; the English programme of, 463; resignation of, 472, 483; and the Government's Bills, 472; his conflict with Gladstone, 473 *et seq.*; and the Party, 474; his objections to Home Rule scheme, 483, 568; Gladstone's hostility to, 483; refuses to attend Foreign Office meeting, 490; interview with Barry O'Brien, 493; the Radical past of, 495; characteristics of, 496, 497, 499; on the Boer War, 501; and the Central Board, 502, 511; on Home Rule resolutions, 504; and protective duties, 506; and the Colonial Office, 512; and the fiscal system, 519, 520; *Truth*, on the expectations of, 525; Gladstone's concessions to, 527; and Protection, 557; the working-class and, 558, 698; taunts the Irish party, 560; his speech for Parnell's land policy, 563; and Churchill's resignation, 566; and the Round Table, 567; *The Times* and the Land League speech of, 579; Morley's tributes to, 582; compares Ireland with Poland, 593; as debater, 594; the following of, 601; bitter speech on the Parnell divorce, 631; expectation that Liberals would drop Home Rule, 649; and the Irish landlords, 661, 662; and the poor, 706; on English social reform, 710; Gladstone's host at Birmingham (1877), 711; and the Whigs, 714; and municipal enterprise, 717; relation with O'Shea, 270, 271, 272, 275, 288, 413, 414, 415, 498, 521, 525, 609, 611, 613, 614, 731; mentioned, 597, 625, 630, 650.

Chaplin, Henry, 293, 303.

Chartists, The, 9, 15, 23, 25, 41, 578.

Chatham, Earl of, 708, 713.

Chester Castle, a plot to capture, 654 *n.*

Chesterton, G. K., 214.

Childers, H. C. E., proposed Home Rule speech (1885), 408, 409; letters from Gladstone, 165 *n.*, 185, 186, 329, 473, 691 *n.*

China (and the war in), 35, 62, 63, 70, 163.

Chinese labour, 501.

Church, Dean; quoted, 74.

Church (Irish) Fund, The, 273, 342.

Churchill, Lord Randolph; on Gladstone and Home Rule, 117, 118; friend of Butt, 147; compared to Chamberlain, 145; attacks Compensation for Disturbance Bill, 178; attacks Gladstone on Kilmainham, 287; on the Maamtrasna case, 319, 320, 380, 382; hostility to Northcote, 357, 391; Hartington, 406; on Parnell, 417; *The Spectator* criticizes, 334, 387; supporters inclusion of Ireland in Franchise Bill, 345; praises Gladstone's " magnanimous speech " (June 1885), 379; idea of a coalition, 443; speeches in election of 1885, 458; violent speeches of, 358, 467; and the Bradlaugh case, 539; attacks Gladstone, 555; leader of Commons, 561; resignation of, 566; on Balfour's coercion, 574; speech on the Parnell Commission, 596, 597; mentioned, 421, 429, 433, 522, 599, 708, 731 *n.*

—, Winston; *Life of Lord Randolph Churchill*, 429, 474, 597.

Civil Service, The, 716.

Clanricarde, Lord, 565, 566, 572, 625, 668.

Clapham, J. H., 128.

Clare, County, 609.

—, Lord; quoted, on Union with Ireland, 21 and *n.*; alluded to, 38.

Clarendon, Lord, 30, 80, 93, 112.

Clarke, Sir Edward, 319, 320, 357, 600, 605 and *n.*, 606, 608, 615, 616, 618.

Clerkenwell prison, 47, 294.

Clifford, Dr. John, 626 *n.*, 627, 637.

Clonmacnois, University of, 5 *n.*

Coal; the Coal Mines Act (1872), 132, 712; the strike (1893), 570, 578, 689; Shaftesbury and the mine-owners, 718.

Cobbett, William, 73, 624.

Cobden, Richard, 49, 50; his commercial Treaty with France, 70, 71; Senator Summer, on, 213 *n.*; and Free Trade, 633.

Gladstone, W. E

335, 336; and the Liberal Party, 336, 337; and Irish liabilities, 338; and the Purchase clauses, 339, 340; his reluctance to face Irish questions, 341, 343; his wish to resign, 344; the Franchise Bill, 344, 345; neglects Chamberlain, 348; the Phoenix Park murders and, 351, 352; and the Whigs, 356, 359; and Dilke, 358 and *n.*; on the House of Commons, 360; and Parnell, 360, 361, 365, 410, 411, 674, 675; and the Vatican intervention, 363; Spencer on coercion, and, 366; favours Chamberlain's Central Board scheme, 367-71; letters on his personal position, 369, 370, 371 *n.*; and the Cabinet, 372; his accomplishments for Ireland, 374; a "magnanimous" speech of, 379; on Gordon and Carnarvon, 388, 389; as Party leader (1885), 390 *et seq.*; his address to Midlothian, 394, 395; and discord in the Party, 397, 398; his address to the electors of Midlothian 400-2; and the demand for Home Rule 402 *et seq.*; and Conservative policy, 403; and Hartington, 404-8; his correspondence with Chamberlain, 406-8; correspondence with other colleagues, 408, 409, 411, 412; Duffy, on the obscurity of, 417; and Mrs. O'Shea, on Irish support, 419; Parnell's proposed Constitution for Ireland, 422-5; speaks at Edinburgh, on the Irish question, 425; his overtures to the Conservatives, 428, 436; Conservatives' attitude to, 429; and co-operation with Salisbury, 433, 434; his hopes of Salisbury, 437 and *n.*; his meeting with Parnell, 438; an intrigue to shelve, 439, 440; the Hawarden Kite, 442, 443, 444; inclines to a large policy, 444, 445; Hartington and, 445; pressed to discuss policy, 446; letters to Herbert Gladstone, *app.* 446-9; desires a non-party settlement, 456; anxious to help Government, 458, 459, 462; and coercion, 463, 569, 572; forms a Home

Rule Government, 464, 467; *The Times* and the plans of, 465; and Bismarck, 466; and his Home Rule scheme, 467, 468; the Liberal split, 472 *et seq.*; his Government defeated on Home Rule, 472; his treatment of Chamberlain, 473-81; prepares his Irish Bills, 481-3; his Home Rule scheme, 483; in conflict with Chamberlain, 483, 484, 486, 487, 496-9; a meeting on Irish affairs, 488 and *n.*, 489, 490; the Home Rule debate, 488; Chamberlain's opposition to the Bills, 490-5; the first Home Rule Bill of, 504 *et seq.*; *Truth,* and concessions of, *app.* 525-8; Herbert Gladstone's letters on, *app.* 528-31; Tyndall quoted, on, 532; Leslie Stephen, on, *ib.*; Courtney, on, *ib.*; early intellectual influences of, 533; and Liberalism, 534, 535; and the Church, 537, 538, 542, 543; *The State in its Relation to the Church,* 537; defends the Parliamentary Oath Bill, 539; isolation of, 541, 542; and scientific men, 543, 546; his five main schools of religious thought, 543, 544; Huxley, on, 549; the religion of, 549, 551, 552; a letter on Newman and Butler, *app.* 553, 554; Churchill attacks, 555; Home Rule (1886), defeat of, 555 *et seq.*; the General Election of 1886, 555 *et seq.*; and the Italian problem, 559; and the Round Table, 567, 568, 569; his friendly meetings with Chamberlain, 568; working-class questions, 570; on the "Plan of Campaign," 571; his feeling for Irish sentiment, 578; Salisbury taunts, 583, 594; and the Parnell Commission, 597; his desire for peace with Ireland, 598; his prayers for Ireland, 601; to Döllinger on Home Rule, 602; Parnell visits, 602-5, 676; and the Parnell divorce, 605, 614; and Parnell's offer of the Nationalist vote, 609, 610; notes for his conversation with Parnell, 619-21; his policy restated, 624, 625; Manning's letter to, 628; letter to Acton, 632; advises Morley, 633, 634; and W. T.

764

INDEX

Religion, the Acts of Union with
Scotland and Ireland, and, 2;
Gladstone and, 51–3, 55 *et seq.*;
Mr. Dillwyn's motion, 78; and
Home Rule, 503; Greek Cul-
ture and Christianity, 533;
Christianity, 535–40, 544, 545,
547, 549, 550, 551, 628, 699, 705;
Nonconformists and politics, 626–
9.
Rhodesia, 45.
Ribbon Movement, The, 38, 195,
266, 315.
Richmond, Duke of, the Agriculture
Commission of, 190.
Ripon, Earl of, 245, 418, 473, 604,
667 *n.*
Risorgimento, The, 578.
Ritchie, C. T., 518.
Robbins, Sir Alfred, 614.
Robert Elsmere, 534.
Robertson, C. Grant, *Life of Bis-
marck*, 466 and *n.*
Rockites, The, 8, 15.
Roden, Lord, 35.
Rogers, Dawson, 440.
Rogers, Sir F. (later Lord Blachford),
Gladstone's letters to, on New-
man and Butler, *app.* 553, 554.
—, Guinness, 637.
Rome, 62, 79, 134, 250, 363, 364,
550 *n.*, 635, 702, 704, 721.
Roscommon, 192.
Rosebery, Lord, 2, 428, 439 *n.*, 443,
445, 458, 473, 482, 486, 500, 504,
506, 511, 512, 521, 604, 660,
689; the Government of, 689,
690, 696, 697; *Life of*, quoted,
446, 500, 696.
Rossa, O'Donovan, 112.
Rossendale, 668.
Rossi, 559.
Rossmore, Lord, 349.
Round Table Conference, The, 567,
569, 601, 673.
Ruskin, John, 719.
Russell, Sir Charles (later Lord
Russell of Killowen), 297, 299,
319, 320, 589 *n.*, 590; withdraws
from the Parnell Commission,
591.
—, George, 671.
—, Lord John, 15, 17 and *n.*, 21, 29,
and *n.*, 31, 63, 70, 71, 75, 89;
and Sheridan, 696.
—, G. W. E.; *Memoirs of Maccoll*,
quoted, 501, 502, 599.
—, T. W., 597 *n.*
Russia, 63, 370, 501, 729.

S

Sacred Congregation de Propaganda
Fide, The, 364.
Sadler, Michael, 94.
St. Ambrose, 496.
St. Augustine, 52, 53, 59, 533, 535,
718.
St. Francis, 550.
St. James, Monastery of, 5 *n.*
St. James's Hall (London), 468.
St. Jerome, 59.
St. Thomas More, 42.
Salford, 157, 556.
Salisbury, Marquis of, alluded to, x, 6,
54, 302, 303, 355, 357 and *n.*,
358, 475, 518, 573, 594, 624, 630,
643, 710, 721 *n.*, 727, 730, 731;
on a speech of Gladstone's, 68;
Disestablishment, 89, 90; and
Gladstone's Land Bill, 101; and
the Land Bill of 1881, 216, 220,
224, 257; the Government of,
225, 456, 560–2; and the Irish
trouble, 242 *n.*; on Irish policy,
291; characteristics of, *ib.*; *The
Spectator*, on leadership of, 292 *n.*;
and the Arrears Bill, 304;
Duffy's scheme and, 377; makes
Carnarvon Viceroy, 378; and
Carnarvon's policy, 380–5; and
the Irish problem, 386, 729;
decides against Home Rule, 387;
caustic criticisms of, 387, 388;
his mistake over Carnarvon, 388,
389; as Party leader, 391; on
Chamberlain, 392; and the
Conservatives, 397 and *n.*; the
Central Board scheme and, 412;
the interests of, 427; Carnarvon
and Government of, 427; and
Irish self-government, 428, 429,
434, 437 and *n.*; Gladstone proposes co-operation with, 433,
434, 436, 438; decides against
Home Rule, 442, 443; and
coalition, 444; the Queen's
correspondence with, 457; on
emigration, 467 *n.*; on self-
government, 469; as Foreign
Minister, 470; Gladstone and,
484, 485, 506; arguments used
against, 487; letter to Maccoll,
quoted, 502; and leadership,
520; and dogma, 538; Churchill
to, quoted, 561; and Churchill,
566; and the Land Act of 1887,
579; and the forged Parnell
letter, 583; and Parnell, 588,
618, 625, 627, 673; the caustic